THE SELECTED ESSAYS
OF MONTAIGNE

The Selected Essays of
MONTAIGNE

John Florio's Translation

New York

CARLTON HOUSE

MANUFACTURED IN THE UNITED STATES OF AMERICA

INTRODUCTION

In the late summer of 1570 Michel de Montaigne, thirty-seven years old, came by Tours and Orleans and the woods of Blois to his favourite Paris. The Essays were unwritten and probably unthought of. His journey represented the attempt of an intelligence over-acute for the life of a country gentleman to enter the world of action and to find scope for its energies and ambitions in the field of late Renaissance diplomacy. The moment seemed felicitous. By the death of his father two years before Montaigne had inherited a substantial patrimony, sufficient to support the considerable state in which nobles of the period were wont to conduct the affairs of their princes. In Paris he had powerful friends, and his character and address recommended him to the favour of the great. Most important of all, a recent political settlement, the peace of St. Germain, seemed for a moment likely to end the insensate struggle, already of ten years' duration, between Catholic and Protestant, Guise and Bourbon, and to herald a regime of comparative reasonableness and good sense in France. And it was for the careful debating of life and of affairs that the maturing mind of Montaigne had genius. In England he would have been a useful servant in the national policy of Burghley, and in France he might have followed the moderate chancellor de L'Hospital had de L'Hospital ever held a settled power. But now in Paris Montaigne found the hopes of his journey frustrated. Catharine de Medici still exercised over France an authority gained by Italianate deceit, by ingenious crime and by the encouraging of her own children in disabling frivolity and vice. From her influence the young Charles IX. was making uncertain efforts to free himself; the city was alive with all the fragmentary complottings, now starkly clear, now darkly involved, that beset an unstable and divided monarchy. All round, strained to catch from these confused currents a first presage of storm, waited the armed camps of France. Henri of Anjou and the Catholics stood eager to press home the victories of Jarnac and Moncontour; the Guises, sworn allies of Philip of Spain, were not less ready to strike and strike again for their declining reputation; in Montauban, in Cognac, in La Charité, in La Rochelle the Huguenots kept bright the swords that were to avenge Condé and a thousand martyrs of reform.

It became clear as autumn advanced that the peace of St. Germain, like the treaty of Longjumeau before it, was delusory. After some months of hesitancy and observation (exercises more congenial to him than were the constant decisions of active life) and eighteen months before that so pronounced action, the massacre of St. Bartholomew, Montaigne left Paris. By Saumur and the Loire, through a troubled and dangerous country in which no man rested on his neighbour's or fellow-traveller's faith, he came to his Perigord estates and to his home—to live removed from public negotiation in such tranquillity as might be. The district round Montaigne lay in the heart of the tumult. Every pleasure-excursion might end in armed skirmish and death; and always some neighbouring château—newly built perhaps and without defences, in the prevailing Italian taste—might redden the night sky with its flames. In the oak and chestnut forests of the Limousin, beyond the sweep of the peaceful Lidoire, lurked war and pitched battle with pillage and private outrage enfranchised, but the portals of the Château de Montaigne stood open, with an old porter to do the courtesies of the gate. Amid this adventurous pacificism, in a tower raised above but not removed from men's follies, the Essays came to birth.

Libertati suæ tranquillitatique et otio dicavit. To the temper of this retirement much besides the immediate situation in France had contributed: the flood of disillusionment, of detachment, had gathered from many sources, and the channels into which it was to flow were determined in the early years of his life. From an initial system of reasonable education devised by his father the young Montaigne had been abruptly despatched to the aridities and mechanical severities of the orthodox Collège de Guienne, a change of regimen little successful in deflecting him from his naturally introverted temper, 'heavy, sluggish and dull,' but which may well have traced out the first course of a retraction from society. And on the nature of the retirement thirty years later its effect was definitive. For to these years may be traced Montaigne's estrangement from the pursuit of exact knowledge; with a distaste for the prosaic enthusiasm and learned triviality of the schools he acquired too an aversion from sustained application. Whether involved in or removed from affairs his intelligence was to be free, roving and comprehensive; if he forewent the statesman's or courtier's progress it was not to earn a grammarian's funeral. 'Logical quiddities' and 'sophistical syllogisms' he lumped somewhat light-heartedly together; when Aristotle and Plato wrote on these themes —barren and remote as they were—they must surely have written in jest. Scholastical questions, he had already decided, were a diversion from rather than a grappling with the problems of well living.

Montaigne had turned, or been directed, to the study of law, obviously a subject of moment. For the rule of law, for the enforcement of common order and justice France seemed to cry aloud—and of the significance of established law Montaigne was always to remain aware. But the laws of France as he found them appeared to bear no relation to any integrated conception of the state; they were lax, oppressive, confusedly executed, and the field of rank and tangled corruption. Above all they were beyond belief barbarous and unreasonable: judicial torture was everywhere practised; and when Montaigne was fifteen, disturbance over the municipal status of his native city of Bordeaux had resulted in the hanging of a hundred and fifty of the more substantial citizens out of hand. Here, typically, in the profession to which he was dedicated, Montaigne could find no common ground with his age. A distaste for the tenacity with which it asserted opinions accepted without thought, for the 'tyrant custom' against which he was to make such bold sallies, an impatience with its rationalising rather than with its unreason—these would seem to have been the reactions produced in him by the Parlement of Bordeaux and the France it epitomised. Already his mind, through the medium of books, of report, and by its own inherent imaginative range, must have begun its long task of searching out and out and beyond—'to dwell with all the better world of men.'

But it was another influence, positive and quickening, that had chiefly determined Montaigne's development in these critical years and now brought him to his retirement, already assured of the final verdict of Saint-Beuve as 'the wisest of all Frenchmen.' Etienne de La Boëtie is of the inheritors of unfulfilled renown; he has left us his name —and Montaigne. The friendship formed at Bordeaux in 1558, strange and beautiful in its intensity and tragic brevity, makes the wisdom, it may be said, and the humanity of the Essays; and their Stoical temper clarified itself and deepened with the years as the sense of the severance of 1563 made itself felt through the numbness of immediate loss. All the response to feeling as distinct from intellection that the Essays contain, those finer vibrations that echo from emotional experience, seem to derive from La Boëtie. The intimate and immediate contact of mind with living mind was for Montaigne concentrated in those years, and when his brooding philosophy came to cast all in doubt he remembered them. La Boëtie's life gave Montaigne's a tension which it might otherwise have lacked, and the sense of emptiness and frustration which followed his death was, with its hunger for communication, the genesis of the Essays. And—last and most significant debt to La Boëtie—there runs profoundly, almost privately, through Montaigne's book a resolute and never-satisfied sense of the necessity of some system of affirmations, of that by which his intellect might find an order of life positive and worthy, as his friendship with La Boëtie had been positive and worthy.

This moral sense (as it may be called) is the tempering of Montaigne's inordinate scepticism, that inherent and pervasive intellectual quality, divorced from his studied moderation in conduct, which, in one aspect a finely-edged critical weapon, was in another a form of spiritual impotence delivering him alike from enthusiasms and affections—the 'melancholic humour' in his character. For from the philosophers of China to the savages of Peru he surveyed mankind and found his opinions vain, divers and wavering; he ranged the centuries for confusion and, like an artist in search of his material, sometimes found it at his own door or within himself. The great self-portrait which he composed is also a great problem-picture—its title *What can I tell?* 'What truth is that,' he cries, 'which these Mountains bound, and is a lie in the world beyond them?' And we feel that the question carries us far—but not far enough. It is not that Montaigne declines the responsibility of judgment; it is that he deliberately neglects the technique of discovery and resolution. As Sir Thomas Browne a hundred years later, gravely citing Androvandi or Albertus Magnus on the anatomy of badgers, ignored experimental method, so Montaigne in the realm of ethics and metaphysic would press to no text between the 'sophistical' syllogism and the true. He loved the doubt—and the doubt of the doubt—of itself.

That 'reason lends apparence to divers effects'—all the mere contention of Montaigne lies in this great pseudo-statement, and in this aspect the book that grew amid the stir of battle became itself a battle-ground of centuries. But it may be that the main interest of the Essays is no longer polemic, and lies in the observation of the tact and integrity with which Montaigne, not venturing in opinion beyond the famous *Que sçais-je?* dealt with life from day to day. It is his perfect good sense, his caution, his anxious observance of the golden mean, that aids him here—a profound reasonableness rather than a profound reasoning. But these qualities again, often adversely criticised in him as little heroic, are not his total measure. Amid the retreating thunder of a later Revolution a Wordsworth, a Shelley, with the stage-scenery of the temple of perfectibility about his ears, suddenly faced by the stars, is a figure heroic enough, and Montaigne, standing, two hundred years before, so firm amid the waste of his own exhausting demolitions, has some tincture of that quality. The troubled road from the halls of Paris and the secret counsels of kings led to a small book-lined room peaceful enough in seeming, but the scene of single-handed combats without number, of severances and renunciations and problems pressing and unsystematised. It is here that Walter Pater's gentle summation, the 'Suspended Judgment' of *Gaston de Latour,* may seem inadequate, inapprehensive from amid the familiar affirmations of Oxford of the stresses of uncharted speculation. And yet so justly does Montaigne's balanced humanism poise itself amid these stresses that we are indeed little aware of them in the final impression. Debating the struggle but briefly, we accept the fruits of victory, and having the Essays in our hand cry gratefully—if too lightly—with Madame de Sévigné: *Ah, Charming man! What good company he is!*

J.I.M. Stewart.

CONTENTS

The First Booke of Essayes

CONTENTS

CONTENTS

The Second Booke of Essayes

CHRONOLOGICAL TABLE

1477 Ramon Eyquem, merchant of Bordeaux and great-grandfather of Montaigne, bought the property of Montaigne in Perigord.

1495 Pierre Eyquem, Montaigne's father, born. He followed François I in the Marignano campaign of 1515: on his journey back to France he met and married Antoinette de Louppe, a girl of Jewish family and a convert to Protestantism.

1525 Martin Luther encouraged the merciless suppression of the Peasant Revolt in Germany.

1533 Michel de Montaigne, third son of Pierre, born at Montaigne on the 28th February.

1536 The Inca Atahualpa murdered by Pizarro. Erasmus died. Calvin at Geneva.

1539 Montaigne, hitherto reared and educated according to the system devised by his father, was sent to the Collège de Guienne at Bordeaux. Among his teachers were George Buchanan and Mark-Antoine Muret.

1546 Luther died. Étienne Dolet was burnt at Paris.

1548 Montaigne began to study law. The insurrection against the *gabelle* in Bordeaux was suppressed by extensive civil execution.

1553 Michel Servet was burnt at Geneva. Rabelais died. Mary succeeded to the throne of England.
John Florio born about this time of Italian parents, refugees in England.

1556 Cranmer burnt. Abdication of Charles V. Ignatius of Loyola died.

1557 Montaigne became a Councillor of the Parlement of Bordeaux.

1557–8 Montaigne met Étienne de La Boëtie. Elizabeth came to the throne of England.

1559 Amyot's French translation of Plutarch's *Lives* published. Peace of Le Cateau. Accession of François II. Montaigne visited Paris and accompanied the king to Bar-le-Duc.

1560 Accession of Charles IX.

1561–2 Montaigne again visited Paris and followed the Court to Rouen, meeting the savages on whose information he was to base his essay on Cannibals.

1561–92 The struggle for religious unity in France became the pretext for thirty years' almost unintermitted civil warfare.

1563 Étienne de La Boëtie died.

1564 Shakespeare and Galileo born.

1565 Montaigne married Françoise de la Chassaigne, an accomplished housekeeper and of some fortune. Of five daughters one only, Léonore, survived.

1568 Pierre Eyquem died. Michel, the eldest surviving son, succeeded to the estates.

1568–73 Alva and the Council of Blood in the Netherlands. Alva boasted the execution of 18,000 heretics and rebels: 60,000 emigrated to England.

1569 Montaigne published the translation, made by him at his father's request, of the *Theologia Moralis* of Raymond Sebon.

1570 Signature of the peace of Saint-Germain. The prospect of a liberal

xiii

settlement drew Montaigne to Paris, probably in the hope of an active political career.

1571 Montaigne returned to a retired life at home and began the composition of the *Essais*.

1572 The Massacre of Saint Bartholomew.
The capture of Brill by the Sea Beggars assured the revolt of the Netherlands.

1574 Accession of Henri III.

1576 Formation of the Catholic League.
The Spanish Fury in Antwerp.

1577 Montaigne, already a Gentleman of the Chamber of Henri III, received a like title at the Court of Henri of Navarre.

1580 Publication of the first two Books of the *Essais*.

1580–81 Montaigne travelled in Switzerland, Germany and Italy. At Rome he was requested by the Sacred College to remove certain passages from the *Essais*: these appeared in the later editions somewhat augmented. On hearing of his election as Mayor of Bordeaux, Montaigne returned to France and held the office, exceptionally, for two successive terms.

1584 Henri of Navarre, now heir to the French crown, visited Montaigne at his château.
Assassination of William the Silent.

1585 Ronsard died.

1587 Execution of Mary Stuart.

1588 Montaigne went to Paris and published the fourth known edition of the *Essais*, containing for the first time the third Book. He met Mlle. de Gournay, whom he came to name his adopted daughter.
The Spanish Armada.

1589 Henri III assassinated. Henri of Navarre became king of France.

1592 Michel de Montaigne died at the Château de Montaigne on the 13th September at the age of fifty-nine.

1595 Mlle. de Gournay and Pierre de Brach published the authorised posthumous edition of the *Essais*.

1597 Bacon's Essayes.

1600 Florio's translation entered on the Stationers' Rolls. Publication of Essays by Sir William Cornwallis.

1603 Publication of Florio's translation.

1605 Sir Thomas Browne born.

1611 Authorized Version of the English Bible.

1613 Florio published the second edition of his translation.

1616 Shakespeare died.

1625 Florio died.

1632 Publication of the third and twice-revised folio of Florio's translation.

PREFACE

["The Epistle Dedicatorie"] TO THE RIGHT HO-norable my best-best Benefactors, and most-most honored Ladies, *Lucie, Countesse of Bedford;* and hir best-most loved-loving Mother, *Ladie Anne Harrington.*

Strange it may seeme to some, whose seeming is mis-seeming, in one worthlesse patronage to joyne two so severallie all-worthy Ladies. But to any in the right, it would be judged wrong, to disjoyne them in ought, who never were neerer in kinde, then ever in kindnesse. None dearer (dearest Ladies) I have seene, and all may say, to your Honorable husbands then you, to you then your Honorable husbands; and then to other, then eyther is to th' other. So as were I to name but the one, I should surely intend the other: but intending this Dedication to two, I could not but name both. To my last Birth, which I held masculine, (as are all mens conceipts that are their owne, though but by their collecting; and this was to *Montaigne* like *Bacchus,* closed in, or loosed from his great *Iupiters* thigh) I the indulgent father invited two right Honorable Godfathers, with the ONE of your Noble Lady-shippes to witnesse. So to this defective edition (since all translations are reputed femalls, delivered at second hand; and I in this serve but as *Vulcan,* to hatchet this *Minerva* from that *Iupiters* bigge braine) I yet at least a fondling foster-father, having transported it from *France* to *England;* put it in English clothes; taught it to talke our tongue (though many-times with a jerke of the French *Iargon*) would set it forth to the best service I might; and to better I might not, then You that deserve the best. Yet hath it this above your other servants: it may not onely serve you two, to repeate in true English what you reade in fine French, but many thousands more, to tell them in their owne, what they would be taught in an other language. How nobly it is descended, let the father in the ninth Chapter of his third booke by letters testimoniall of the Romane Senate and Citty beare record: How rightly it is his, and his beloved, let him by his discourse in the eight'th of his second, written to the Lady of *Estissac* (as if it were to you concerning your sweete heire, most motherly-affected Lady *Harrington*) and by his acknowledgement in this first to all Readers give evidence, first that it is *de bonne foy,* then more than that, *c'est moy:* How worthily qualified, embellished, furnished it is, let his faire-spoken, and fine-witted Daughter by alliance passe her verdict, which shee need not recant. Heere-hence to offer it into your service, let me for him but do and say, as he did for his other-selfe, his peerlesse paire *Steven de Boetie,* in the 28. of this first, and thinke hee speakes to you my praise-surmounting Countesse of *Bedford,* what hee there speakes to the Lady of *Grammont,* Countesse of *Guissen:* Since as his Maister-Poet saide,

>———*mutato nomine, de te*
>*Fabula narratur:*—Hor. ser. lib. i. *Sat.* i. 69.

>Do you but change the name,
>Of you is saide the same:

So do hir attributes accord to your demerites; whereof to runne a long-breathed careere, both so faire and large a field might envite mee, and my in-burning spirits would encite mee, if I were not held-in by your sweete reining hand (*who have ever helde this desire, sooner to exceede what you are thought, then be thought what you are not*) or should I not prejudice by premonstration your assured advantage, *When your value shall come to the weighing.* And yet what are you not that may excell? What weight would you not elevate in truest ballance of best judgements? More to be followed by glorie, since you fly-it; which yet many good follow: Most to be praised, for refusing all praises; which yet will presse on vertue; will she, nill she. In which matter of fame (and that exceeding good) wel may you (I doubt not) use the word, which my Authour heere (I feare) usurpeth:

>———*Virésque acquirit eundo.*—Virg. *Æn.* i. 4, 175.

>The further that she goeth,
>The more in strength she groweth:

Since (as in the originall) if of his vertue or glory, more of yours, his Arch-Poet might verifie.

>*Ingrediturque solo, & caput inter nubila condit:*—177.

>She (great and good) on earth doth move,
>Yet veiles hir head in heaven above:

But being by your limit-lesse moderation lockt in limits (who *more desire, nothing may be said, than too much*) though I can never say too much; as he of *Carthage,* so I of your praise-worthinesse, were better to say nothing, then too little. For this in hand (if it may be so honored to kisse your Honors gracious hand) if any grace or good be either afforded to it, or deserved by it, all that by the father, foster-father, and all that are of kinne or kinde unto it, must be to your Honor, grace, and goodnesse imputed and ascribed. For (that I may discharge me of all this, and charge you with your owne; pardon Madame my plainenesse) when I with one Chapter found my selfe over-charged, whereto the charge or choise of an Honorable person, and by me not-to-be-denied Benefactor (Noble and vertuous Sir

Edward Wotton) had engaged me, (which I finished in your owne
house) your Honor having dayned to read it, without pitty of my
failing, my fainting, my labouring, my languishing, my gasping for
some breath (O could so Honorable, be so pitty-lesse? Madame, now
doe I flatter you?) Yet commaunded me on: (and let me die outright,
ere I doe not that commaund.) I say not you tooke pleasure at shore
(as those in this Author) to see me sea-tosst, wether-beaten, shippe-
wrackt, almost drowned (*Mon. lib.* iii. *c.* 1). Nor say I like this mans
Indian King, you checkt with a sower-sterne countenance the yerne-
ful complaint of your drooping, neere-dying subject (*Lib.* iii, *c.* 6).
Nor say I (as he alleadgeth out of others) like an ironically modest
Virgin, you enduced, yea commaunded, yea delighted to see mee strive
for life, yet fall out of breath (*Lib.* ii. *c.* 23). Unmercifull you were,
but not so cruell. (Madame, now do I flatter you?) Yet this I may
and must say, like in this French-mans report, our third in name, but
first and chiefe in fame, K. *Edward,* you would not succour your
blacke, not sonne, but servaunt, but bade him fight and conquere, or
die (*Lib.* i. *c.* 41): Like the Spartane imperirious Mother, a shield
indeede you gave mee, but with this Word. *Aut cum hoc; aut in hoc*
(*Giou. Imp. Mar Pes.*). I must needes say while this was in dooing,
to put and keepe mee in hart like a captived Canniball fattend against
my death, you often cryed *Coraggio,* and called *çà çà,* and applauded
as I passt, and if not fet mee in, yet set mee on, even with a Syrens
ô tresloüable Ulisse (*Mont.* li. ii. *c.* 16). O Madame who then spake
faire? As for mee, I onely say, as this mans embossed Hart out of hart
(*Lib.* ii. *c.* 11), I sweat, I wept, and I went-on, til now I stand at bay:
howsoever, I hope that may yet save me, which from others strangles
others, I meane the coller you have put about my neck with your
inscription, *Noli me cædere, nam sum Dianæ.* Yet nor can you denie,
nor I dissemble, how at first I pleaded this Authors tedious difficultie,
my selfe-knowne insufficiencie, and others more leisurefull abilitie.
But no excuse would serve him, that must serve without excuse. Little
power had I to performe, but lesse to refuse what you impos'de: for
his length you gave time: for his hardnesse you advised help: my
weaknesse you might bidde doe it's best: others strength you
would not seeke-for-further. Yet did your honoured name r'ally to my
succour the forces of two deare friends, both devoted to your service,
both obliged to your vertues: The one Maister *Theodoro Diodati,* as
in name, so indeede Gods-gift to me, my *bonus genius,* and sent me as
the good Angel to *Raimond* in *Tasso* (*Tas. Gior. can.* 7) for my assistant to combat this great *Argante:* Who as he is happy in you, and
you in him, that like *Aristotle* to *Alexander,* he may in all good learning,
and doeth with all industrious attention, instruct, direct, adorne that
noble, hopefull, and much-promising spirit of your beloved brother
and house-heire Maister *Iohn Harrington:* So was he to me in this
inextricable laberinth like *Ariadnaes* threed; in this rockie-rough

Ocean, a guide-fish to the Whale; in these darke-uncouth wayes, a cleare relucent light. Had not he beene, I had not bin able to wade through: and had not he dissolved these knottes, none had, few could. The other (my onelie dearest and in love-sympathising friend, Maister Doctor *Guinne*, of whome I may justly say what my Authour saieth of his second-selfe *Steven de la Boetie* (*Lib.* i. *c.* 27; *Lib.* iii. *c.* 9): for, he could not better pourtray him for him selfe, then hee hath lively delineated him for me) willing to doe me ease, and as willing to doe your Honour service, as you know him a scholler (and pitty is it the World knowes not his worth better; for as the Prince of Italian Poets saide of *Valerius Corvinus*, *Non so se miglior Duce o Cavalliero* (*Pet. triu. fam. cap.* i. *ver.* 99), so may I truely say of him. *Non so se meglior Oratore e Poeta, o Philosopho e Medico*). So Scholler-like did he undertake what Latine prose; Greeke, Latine, Italian or French Poesie should crosse my way (which as Bugge-beares affrighted my unacquaintance with them) to ridde them all afore mee, and for the most part drawne them from their dennes: Wherein what indefatigable paines he hath undergone, and how successfully overgone, I referre to your Honor, I remit to the learned; for, who but he could have quoted so divers Authors, and noted so severall places? So was hee to mee in this bundle of riddles an understanding *Oedipus*, in this perilous-crook't passage a monster-quelling *Theseus* or *Hercules:* With these two supporters of knowledge and friendship, if I upheld and armed have passt the pikes, the honor be all yours, since all by yours was done for your Honor. That all this is thus, the reply of that friend upon my answer to your Ho: invitation in a sonet of the like, (but not same) terminations may signifie and testifie to all the world. Then let none say I flatter, when I forbeare not to tell all. Yet more I must needs say, if Poets be inspired by their muse, if souldiers take corage by the eie or memory of their mistrisses (as both have made some long believe) having already said, as *Petrark* to his mistris,

In questo stato son Donna per vui,—PETR. p. i, son. 107.

By you, or for you, Madame thus am I.

I now rather averre as the Lyricke to his *Melpomene*.

Quod spiro, & placeo, si placeo, tuum est.

That I doe breath and please, if please I doe,
It is your grace, such grace proceed's from you.

For, besides your owne inexplicable bounty first-mover of my good, *La quale ritogli me peregrino errante, e fra gli scoglii e l'onde agitato, al furor di Fortuna, e benignamente guidi in porto di salute e pace* (*Tasso. Gior. can.* i. *st.* 4), Your noblest Earles beneficence, fore-running all as farre in curtesie as pedegree, and bearing not onely in his heart or hand, but even in aspect and due respect the native magnanimity of *Bedford,* and magnificent francke-Nature of the RVSSELS, hath so kindly bedewed my earth when it was sunburnt, so gently thawed it when it was frost-bound, as (were there anie good in me) I were more sencelesse then earth, if I returned not some fruite in good measure. This may be thought too much for no better a deserver than I am: Yet more must I acknowledge joyned to this: for as to all, that professe any learning, & do you (but small) steade therein, you and your husbands hand (most bounteous Ladie *Harrington*) have beene still open, & your hospitable house, my retreate in storms, my reliefe in neede, Yea, your hearts ever enlarged: so for an instance, in doing wel by me (the meanest) as if honorable father and mother with their noblest sonne and daughter should contend in that onely praise-worthy emulation of well doing, you seemed even to strive, who should excel ech other, who should best entertaine, cherish and foster mee: And as if this river of benignitie did runne in a blood, your worthie Sonne in-law, and vertuous Daughter *Chichester* with like-sweete liquor have supplied my drie cesterns. So as to the name and house of *Bedford* and *Harrington,* without prophanenesse, let me vow but one worde of the Pastorall, ILLIVS ARAM, and with that word my selfe Your Honorable Ladiships in humble hartie service, IOHN FLORIO.

TO THE RIGHT HO-norable, *Lucie* Countesse of Bedford.

Relucent lustre of our English Dames,
   In one comprising all most priz'de of all,
   Whom Vertue hirs, and bounty hirs doth call,
   Whose vertue honor, beauty love enflames,
Whose value wonder writes, silence proclaimes,
   Though, as your owne, you know th' originall
   Of this, whose grace must by translation fall;
   Yet since this, as your owne, your Honor claimes,
Yours be the honour; and if any good
   Be done by it, we give all thanks and praise
   For it to you: but who enough can give?
Aye-honor'd be your Honorable Blood;
   Rise may your Honor, which your merites raise:
   Live may you long, your Honor you out-live.
                     Il Candido.

[Matthew Gwinne, M.D. (1558?-1627), was probably the author of some of the verses signed Il Candido.]

To the noble-minded Ladie, *Anne Harrington.*

If Mothers love exceeding others love,
   If Honours heart excelling all mens hearts,
   If bounties hand with all her beauteous parts,
   Poets, or Painters would to pourtray prove,
Should they seeke earth below, or heav'n above,

Home, Court or Countrie, forraine moulds or marts,
For Maister-point, or modell of their artes,
For life, then here, they neede no further move:
For Honour, Bountie, Love, when all is done,
(Detract they not) what should they adde, or faine,
But onely write, Lady *ANNE HARRINGTON*.
Her picture lost, would Nature second her,
She could not, or she must make her againe.
So vowes he, that himselfe doth hers averre.

Il Candido.

To the curteous Reader.

Shall I apologize translation? Why but some holde (as for their free-hold) that such conversion is the subversion of Universities. God holde with them, and withholde them from impeach or empaire. It were an ill turne, the turning of Bookes should be the overturning of Libraries. Yea but my olde fellow Nolano *tolde me, and taught publikely, that from translation all Science had it's of-spring. Likely, since even Philosophie, Grammar, Rhethorike, Logike, Arithmetike, Geometrie, Astronomy, Musike, and all the Mathematikes yet holde their name of the Greekes: and the Greekes drew their baptizing water from the conduit-pipes of the Egiptians, and they from the wellsprings of the Hebrews or Chaldees. And can the wel-springs be so sweete and deepe; and will the well-drawne water be so sower and smell? And were their Countries so ennobled, advantaged, and embellished by such deriving; and doth it drive our noblest Colonies upon the rockes of ruine? And did they well? and prooved they well? and must we proove ill that doe so? Why but Learning would not be made common. Yea but Learning cannot be too common, and the commoner the better. Why but who is not jealous, his Mistresse should be so prostitute? Yea but this Mistresse is like ayre, fire, water, the more breathed the clearer; the more extended the warmer; the more drawne the sweeter. It were inhumanitie to coope her up, and worthy forfeiture close to conceale her. Why but Schollers should have some privilege of preheminence. So have they: they onely are worthy Translators. Why but the vulgar should not knowe at all. No, they can not for all this; nor even Schollers for much more: I would, both could and knew much more than either doth or can. Why but all would not be knowne of all. No nor can: much more we know not than we know: all know something, none know all: would all know all? they must breake ere they be so bigge. God only; men farre from God. Why but pearles should not be cast to swine: yet are rings put in their noses; and a swine should know his stie, and will know his meate and his medicine, and as much beside, as any swine doth suppose it to be Marjoram. Why, but it is not wel Divinitie should be a childes or olde wives, a coblers, or clothiers tale or table-talke. There is use, and abuse: use*

*none too much: abuse none too little. Why but let Learning be wrapt
in a learned mantle. Yea but to be unwrapt by a learned nurse: yea,
to be lapt up againe. Yea, and unlapt againe.* Else, hold we ignorance
*the mother of devotion; praying and preaching in an unknowne
tongue: as sory a mother, as a seely daughter: a good minde perhaps,
but surely an ill manner. If the best be meete for us, why should the
best be barrd? Why but the best wrote best in a tongue more unknowne: Nay in a tongue more knowne to them that wrote, and not
unknowne of them to whom they wrote. Why but more honour to him
that speakes more learned. Yea such perhaps, as* Quintilians *Orator;
a learned man I warrant him, for I understand him never a word. Why
but let men write for the most honour of the Writer. Nay, for most
profit of the Reader: and so haply, most honour. If to write obscurely
be perplexedly offensive, as* Augustus *well judged: for our owne not
to write in our owne but unintelligible, is haply to fewer and more criti-
call, but surely without honor, without profit, if he goe not, or send
not an interpreter; who else what is he but a Translator? Obscure be
he that loves obscuritie. And therefore willingly I take his worde,
though wittingly I doe mistake it,* Translata proficit. *Why but who
ever did well in it? Nay, who did ever well without it? If nothing can
be now sayd, but hath beene saide before (as hee sayde well) if there
be no new thing under the Sunne. What is that that hath beene? That
that shall be: (as he sayde that was wisest) What doe the best then,
but gleane after others harvest? borrow their colours, inherite their
possessions? What doe they but translate? perhaps, usurpe? at least,
collect? if with acknowledgement, it is well; if by stealth, it is too bad:
in this, our conscience is our accuser; posteritie our judge: in that our
studie is our advocate, and you Readers our jurie. Why but whom can
I name, that bare a great name for it? Nay who great else, but either
in parte of* Plato *and* Aristotle *out of many;* Tullie, Plutarch, Plinie
out of Plato, Aristotle *and many; or of purpose, as all that since have
made most know the Greeke, and almost the Latine, even translated
their whole treatises? Why* Cardan *maintaineth, neither* Homers *verse
can be well exprest in Latine, nor* Virgils *in Greeke, nor* Petrarch *in
either. Suppose* Homer *tooke nothing out of any, for we heare of none
good before him, and there must be a first; yet* Homer *by* Virgil *is
often so translated as* Scaliger *conceives there is the armour of* Hercules
most puissant put on the backe of Bacchus *most delicate: and* Petrarch,
*if well tracked, would be found in their footesteps, whose verie garbage
lesse Poets are noted to have gathered. Why but that* Scaliger *thinkes
that* Ficinus *by his rusticall simplicitie translated* Plato, *as if an Owle
should represent an Eagle, or some tara-rag Player should act the
princely* Telephus *with a voyce, as rag'd as his clothes, a grace as bad
as his voyce. If the famous* Ficinus *were so faulty, who may hope to
scape foot-free? But for him and us all let me confesse, as he heere*

censureth; and let confession make halfe amends, that every language hath it's Genius *and inseparable forme; without* Pythagoras *his* Metempsychosis *it can not rightly be translated. The Tuscan altiloquence, the* Venus *of the French, the sharpe state of the Spanish, the strong significancy of the Dutch cannot from heere be drawne to life. The sense may keepe forme; the sentence is disfigured; the fineness, fitnesse, featenesse diminished: as much as artes nature is short of natures arte, a picture of a body, a shadow of a substance. Why then belike I have done by* Montaigne, *as* Terence *by* Menander, *made of good French no good English. If I have done no worse, and it be no worse taken, it is well. As he, if no Poet, yet am I no theefe, since I say of whom I had it, rather to imitate his and his authors negligence, then any backebiters obscure diligence. His horse I set before you; perhaps without his trappings; and his meate without sause. Indeede in this specially finde I fault with my maister, that as* Crassus *and* Antonius *in* Tullie, *the one seemed to contemne, the other not to know the Greeks, whereas the one so spake Greeke as he seemed to know no other tongue; the other in his travells to* Athens *and* Rhodes *had long conversed with the learnedst Græcians: So he, most writing of himselfe, and the worst rather than the best, disclaimeth all memorie, authorities, or borrowing of the ancient or moderne; whereas in course of his discourse he seemes acquainted not onely with all, but no other but authours; and could out of question like* Cyrus *or* Cæsar *call any of his armie by his name and condition. And I would for us all he had in this whole body done as much, as in most of that of other languages my peerelesse deere-deerest and never sufficiently commended friend hath done for mine and your ease and inteligence. Why then againe, as* Terence, *I have had helpe. Yea, and thanke them for it, and thinke you neede not be displeased by them that may please you in a better matter. Why but Essayes are but mens school-themes pieced together; you might as wel say, several texts. Al is in the choise & handling. Yea mary; but* Montaigne, *had he wit, it was but a French wit ferdillant, legier, and extravagant. Now say you English wits by the staydest censure of as learned a wit as is among you. The counsel of that judicious worthy Counsellor (honorable Sir* Edward Wotton) *would not have embarked me to this discovery, had not his wisedome knowne it worth my paines, and your perusing. And should or would any dogtooth'de Criticke, or adder-tongu'd Satirist scoff or finde fault, that in the course of his discourses, or webbe of his Essayes, or entitling of his chapters, he holdeth a disjoynted, broken and gadding stile; and that many times they answere not his titles, and have no coherence together, to such I will say little, for they deserve but little; but if they lift, else let them chuse, I send them to the ninth chapter of the third books, folio 956,[1] where himselfe preventeth their carping, and fore-*

[1] The Second Booke, Chap. XII, p. 483, present edition.

*seeing their critikisme answereth them for me at full. Yet are there
herein errors. If of matter, the Authours; if of omission, the printers:
him I would not amend, but send him to you as I found him: this I
could not attend; but where I now finde faults, let me pray and entreate you for your owne sake to correct as you reade; to amend as
you list. But some errors are mine, and mine by more then translation.
Are they in Grammar, or Orthographie? as easie for you to right, as me
to be wrong; or in construction, as mis-attributing him, her, or it, to
things alive, or dead, or newter; you may soone know my meaning,
and eftsoones use your mending: or are they in some uncouth termes;
as entraine, conscientious, endeare, tarnish, comporte, efface, facilitate,
ammusing, debauching, regret, effort, emotion, and such like; if you
like them not, take others most commonly set by them to expound
them, since there they were set to make such likely French words
familiar with our English, which well may beare them. If any be capitall in sense mistaking, be I admonished, and they shall be recanted:
Howsoever, the falsenesse of the French prints, the diversities of copies,
editions and volumes (some whereof have more or lesse then others),
and I in* London *having followed some, and in the countrie others;
now those in folio, now those in octavo, yet in this last survay recon-
ciled all; therefore or blame not rashly, or condemne not fondly the
multitude of them set for your further ease in a Table (at the end of
the booke) which ere you beginne to reade, I entreate you to peruse:
this Printers wanting a diligent Corrector, my many employments, and
the distance betweene me, and my friends I should conferre-with, may
extenuate, if not excuse, even more errors. In summe, if any think he
could do better, let him trie; then will he better thinke of what is done.
Seven or eight of great wit and worth have assayed, but found these
Essayes no attempt for French apprentises or Littletonians. If this
doone it may please you, as I wish it may, and I hope it shall, I with
you shall be pleased: though not, yet still I am* the same resolute
IOHN FLORIO.

[Montaigne's Preface, "The Author to the Reader" (see p. xxvii, present edition), follows the above address.]

Al mio amato Istruttore Mr. Giovanni Florio.

Florio, che fai? Vai cosi ardito al Monte?
    Al monte più scoscese che Parnasso,
    Ardente più che Mongibello? Ahi lasso:
    Plinio qui muore prima, che qui monte.
Se'l Pegaso non hai, che cavi'l fonte,
    Ritirati dal periglioso passo.
    L'hai fatto pur', andand' hor' alt' hor basso:
    Ti sò ben dir', tu sei Bellerophonte.

Tre corpi di Chimera di Montagna
    Hai trapassato, scosso, rinversato.
    Del' honorat' impres' anch' io mi glorio.
Premiar' ti potess' io d'or' di Spagna,
    Di più che Bianco-fior' saresti ornato.
    Ma del' honor' ti basti, che sei Florio.
                      Il Candido.

A reply upon Maister Florio's *answere to the Lady of* Bedfords
Invitation to this worke, in a Sonnet of like terminations. Anno. 1599.

Thee to excite from Epileptique fits,
    Whose lethargie like frost benumming bindes
    Obstupefying sence with sencelesse kindes,
    Attend the vertue of *Minervas* writtes;
Colde sides are spurrd, hot mouthes held-in with bittes;
    Say No, and grow more rude, then rudest hindes;
    Say No, and blow more rough, then roughest windes.
    Who never shootes, the marke he never hitt's.
To take such taske, a pleasure is, no paine;
    Vertue and Honor (which immortalize)
    Not stepdame *Iuno* (who would wish thee slaine)
Calls thee to this thrice-honorable prize;
    Montaigne, no cragg'd Mountaine, but faire plaine.
    And who would resty rest, when SHEE bids rise?
                      Il Candido.

[The "Table of the Chapters" follows the above sonnets.]

To my deere friend M, *Iohn* Florio, concerning *his translation of*
Montaigne.

Bookes the amasse of humors, swolne with ease,
The Griefe of peace, the maladie of rest,
So stuffe the world, falne into this disease,
As it receives more then it can digest:
And doe so overcharge, as they confound
The apetite of skill with idle store:
There being no end of words, nor any bound
Set to conceipt, the Ocean *without shore.*
As if man labo'rd with himself to be
As infinite in words, as in intents,
And draws his manifold incertaintie
In ev'ry figure, passion represents;
That these innumerable visages,
And strange shapes of opinions and discourse
Shadowed in leaves, may be the witnesses
Rather of our defects, then of our force.
And this proud frame of our presumption,
This Babel *of our skill, this* Towre *of wit,*

Seemes onely checkt with the confusion
Of our mistakings, that dissolveth it.
And well may make us of our knowledge doubt,
Seeing what uncertainties we build upon,
To be as weake within booke as without;
Or els that truth hath other shapes then one.

But yet although we labor with this store
And with the presse of writings seeme opprest,
And have too many bookes, yet want we more,
Feeling great dearth and scarsenesse of the best;
Which cast in choiser shapes have bin produc'd,
To give the best proportions to the minde
To our confusion, and have introduc'd
The likliest images frailtie can finde.
And wherein most the skill-desiring soule
Takes her delight, the best of all delight,
And where her motions evenest come to rowle
About this doubtful center of the right.

Which to discover this great Potentate,
This Prince Montaigne *(if he be not more)*
Hath more adventur'd of his owne estate
Then ever man did of himselfe before:
And hath made such bolde sallies out upon
Custome, *the mightie tyrant of the earth,*
In whose Seraglio *of subjection*
We all seeme bred-up, from our tender birth;
As I admire his powres, and out of love,
Here at his gate do stand, and glad I stand
So neere to him whom I do so much love,
T' applaude his happie setling in our land:
And safe transpassage by his studious care
Who both of him and us doth merit much,
Having as sumptously, as he is rare
Plac'd him in the best lodging of our speach.
And made him now as free, as if borne here,
And as well ours as theirs, who may be proud
That he is theirs, though he be every where
To have the franchise of his worth allow'd

It be'ing the portion of a happie Pen,
Not to b' invassal'd to one Monarchie,
But dwell with all the better world of men
Whose spirits are all of one communitie.
Whom neither Ocean, Desarts, Rockes nor Sands
Can keepe from th' intertraffique of the minde,
But that it vents her treasure in all lands,
And doth a most secure commercement finde.

Wrap Excellencie *up never so much,*
In Hierogliphicques, Ciphers, Caracters,
And let her speake never so strange a speach,
Her Genius *yet finds apt discipherers:*
And never was she borne to dye obscure,
But guided by the Starres of her owne grace,
Makes her owne fortune, and is ever sure
In mans best hold, to hold the strongest place.
And let the Critic *say the worst he can,*
He cannot say but that Montaigne *yet,*
Yeeldes most rich pieces and extracts of man;
Though in a troubled frame confus'dly set.
Which yet h'is blest that he hath ever seene,
And therefore as a guest in gratefulnesse,
For the great good the house yeelds him within
Might spare to taxe th' unapt convayances.
But this breath hurts not, for both worke and frame,
Whilst England English *speakes, is of that store*
And that choyse stuffe, as that without the same
The richest librarie can be but poore.
And they unblest who letters do professe
And have him not: whose owne fate beates their want
With more sound blowes, then Alcibiades
Did his Pedante that did Homer *want.*

SAM : DANYEL.

THE AUTHOR TO

THE READER

READER, loe here a well-meaning Booke. It doth at the first entrance forewarne thee, that in contriving the same, I have proposed unto my selfe no other than a familiar and private end: I have no respect or consideration at all, either to thy service, or to my glory: my forces are not capable of any such desseigne. I have vowed the same to the particular commodity of my kinsfolks and friends: to the end, that losing me (which they are likely to doe ere long) they may therein find some lineaments of my conditions and humours, and by that meanes reserve more whole, and more lively foster the knowledge and acquaintance they have had of me. Had my intention beene to forestal and purchase the worlds opinion and favour, I would surely have adorned my selfe more quaintly, or kept a more grave and solemne march. I desire therein to be delineated in mine owne genuine, simple and ordinarie fashion, without contention, art or study; for it is my selfe I pourtray. My imperfections shall therein be read to the life, and my naturall forme discerned, so farre-forth as publike reverence hath permitted me. For if my fortune had beene to have lived among those nations, which yet are said to live under the sweet liberty of Natures first and uncorrupted lawes, I assure thee, I would most willingly have pourtrayed my selfe fully and naked. Thus gentle Reader my selfe am the groundworke of my booke: It is then no reason thou shouldest employ thy time about so frivolous and vaine a Subject. Therefore farewell. From *Montaigne,* the first of March, 1580.

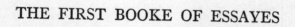

THE FIRST BOOKE OF ESSAYES

THE ESSAYES OF
MICHAEL LORD OF MONTAIGNE
The First Booke
CHAPTER I

BY DIVERS MEANES MEN COME UNTO A LIKE END

THE most usuall way to appease those minds we have offended
(when revenge lies in their hands, and that we stand at their mercy) is,
by submission to move them to commiseration and pitty: Neverthelesse, courage, constancie, and resolution (meanes altogether opposite) have sometimes wrought the same effect. *Edward* the black Prince
of *Wales* (who so long governed our Country of *Guienne*, a man whose
conditions and fortune were accompanied with many notable parts
of worth and magnanimitie) having beene grievously offended by the
Limosins, though he by maine force tooke and entred their Citie,
could by no meanes be appeased, nor by the wailefull out-cries of all
sorts of people (as of men, women, and children) be moved to any
pitty, they prostrating themselves to the common slaughter, crying
for mercy, and humbly submitting themselves at his feet, untill such
time as in triumphant manner passing thorow their Citie, he perceived
three French Gentlemen, who alone, with an incredible and undaunted
boldnesse, gainstood the enraged violence, and made head against the
furie of his victorious armie. The consideration and respect of so
notable a vertue, did first abate the dint of his wrath, and from those
three began to relent, and shew mercy to all the other inhabitants of
the said towne. *Scanderbeg*, Prince of *Epirus*, following one of his souldiers, with purpose to kill him, who by all means of humilitie, and
submisse entreatie, had first assaied to pacifie him, in such an unavoidable extremitie, resolved at last, resolutely to encounter him with his
sword in his hand. This resolution did immediately stay his Captains
fury, who seeing him undertake so honourable an attempt, not only
forgave, but received him into grace and favour. This example may
haply, of such as have not knowne the prodigious force and matchlesse
valour of the said Prince, admit another interpretation. The Emperour
Conradus, third of that name, having besieged *Guelphe*, Duke of
Bavaria, what vile or base satisfaction soever was offered him, would

yeeld to no other milder conditions, but only to suffer such Gentle-women as were with the Duke in the Citie (their honours safe) to issue out of the Towne afoot, with such things as they could carry about them. They with an unrelenting courage advised and resolved themselves (neglecting all other riches or jewels) to carry their husbands, their children, and the Duke himselfe, on their backs: The Emperour perceiving the quaintnesse of their device, tooke so great pleasure at it, that hee wept for joy, and forthwith converted that former inexorable rage, and mortall hatred he bare the Duke, into so milde a relenting and gentle kindnesse, that thence forward he entreated both him and his with all favour and courtesie. Either of these wayes might easily perswade mee: for I am much inclined to mercie, and affected to mildnesse. So it is, that in mine opinion, I should more naturally stoope unto compassion, than bend to estimation. Yet is pitty held a vicious passion among the Stoicks. They would have us aid the afflicted, but not to faint, and co-suffer with them. These examples seeme fittest for mee, forsomuch as these minds are seene to be assaulted and environed by these two meanes, in undauntedly suffering the one, and stooping under the other. It may peradventure be said, that to yeeld ones heart unto commiseration, is an effect of facility, tendernesse, and meeknesse: whence it proceedeth, that the weakest natures, as of women, children, and the vulgar sort are more subject unto it. But (having contemned teares and wailings) to yeeld unto the onely reverence of the sacred Image of vertue, is the effect of a couragious and imployable minde, holding a masculine and constant vigour, in honour and affection. Notwithstanding, amazement and admiration may in lesse generous minds worke the like effect. Witnesse the Thebanes, who having accused and indited their Captaines, as of a capitall crime, forsomuch as they had continued their charge beyond the time prescribed them, absolved and quit *Pelopidas* of all punishment, because he submissively yeelded under the burden of such objections, and to save himselfe, imployed no other meanes, but suing-requests, and demisse intreaties; where on the contrary, *Epaminondas* boldly relating the exploits achieved by him, and with a fierce and arrogant manner upbraiding the people with them, had not the heart so much as to take their lots into his hands, but went his way, and was freely absolved; the assembly much commending the stoutnesse of his courage. *Dionysius* the elder, after long-lingering and extreme difficulties, having taken the Citie of *Reggio,* and in it the Captaine *Phyton,* (a worthy honest man) who had so obstinately defended the same, would needs shew a tragicall example of revenge. First, he told him, how the day before, he had caused his sonne and all his kinsfolkes to be drowned. To whom *Phyton,* stoutly out-staring him, answered nothing, but that they were more happy than himselfe by the space of one day. Afterward he caused him to be stripped, and by his executioners to be taken and dragged thorow the Citie most ignominiously, and

cruelly whipping him, charging him besides with outragious and con-
tumelious speeches. All which notwithstanding, as one no whit dis-
mayed, he ever shewed a constant and resolute heart; and with a
cheerfull and bold countenance went on still, loudly recounting the
honourable and glorious cause of his death, which was, that he would
never consent to yeeld his Country into the hands of a cruell tyrant,
menacing him with an imminent punishment of the Gods. *Dionysius*
plainly reading in his Souldiers lookes, that in lieu of animating them
with braving his conquered enemie, they in contempt of him, and scorne
of his triumph, seemed by the astonishment of so rare a vertue, to be
moved with compassion, and inclined to mutinie, yea, and to free
Phyton from out the hands of his *Sergeants* or *Guard*, caused his
torture to cease, and secretly sent him to be drowned in the sea. Surely,
man is a wonderfull, vaine, divers, and wavering subject: it is very
hard to ground any directly-constant and uniforme judgement upon
him. Behold *Pompey*, who freely pardoned all the Citie of the *Mamer-
tines*, (against which he was grievously enraged) for the love of the
magnanimitie, and consideration of the exceeding vertue of *Zeno*, one
of their fellow-citizens, who tooke the publike fault wholly upon himselfe, and desired no other favour, but alone to beare the punishment
thereof; whereas *Syllaes* host having used the like vertue in the Citie
of *Perugia*, obtained nothing, neither for himselfe, nor for others. And
directly against my first example, the hardiest amongst men, and so
gracious to the vanquished, *Alexander* the great, after many strange
difficulties, forcing the Citie of *Gaza*, encountered by chance with
Betis, that commanded therein, of whose valour (during the siege) he
had felt wonderfull and strange exploits, being then alone, forsaken of
all his followers, his armes all-broken, all-besmeared with bloud and
wounds, fighting amongst a number of Macedonians, who pell-mell laid
still upon him; provoked by so deare a victorie, (for among other mis-
haps he had newly received two hurts in his body) said thus unto him;
*Betis, thou shalt not die as thou wouldest: for make account thou must
indure all the torments may possibly bee devised or inflicted upon a
caitife wretch, as thou art.* But he, for all his enemies threats, without
speaking one word, returned only an assured, sterne, and disdainefull
countenance upon him; which silent obstinacie *Alexander* noting, said
thus unto himselfe: *What? would hee not bend his knee? could he not
utter one suppliant voyce? I will assuredly vanquish his silence, and
if I cannot wrest a word from him, I will at least make him to sob or
groane.* And converting his anger into rage, commanded his heeles to
bee through-pierced, and so all alive with a cord through them, to be
torne, mangled, and dismembred at a carts-taile. May it be, the force
of his courage, was so naturall and peculiar unto him, that because he
would no-whit admire him, he respected him the lesse? or deemed he
it so proper unto himselfe, that in his height, he could not without the
spight of envious passion, endure to see it in an other? or was the

naturall violence of his rage incapable of any opposition? surely, had it received any restraint, it may be supposed, that in the ransacking and desolation of the Citie of *Thebes,* it should have felt the same; in seeing so many Worthies lost, and valiant men put to the sword, as having no meanes of publike defence; for above six thousand were slaine and massacred, of which not one was seene, either to run away, or beg for grace. But on the contrary, some here and there seeking to affront, and endeavouring to check their victorious enemies, urging and provoking them to force them die an honourable death. No one was seene to yeeld, and that to his last gaspe did not attempt to revenge himselfe, and with all weapons of dispaire, with the death of some enemie, comfort and sweeten his owne miserie. Yet could not the affliction of their vertue find any ruth or pitie, nor might one day suffice to glut or asswage his revengefull wrath. This butcherous slaughter continued unto the last drop of any remaining bloud; where none were spared but the unarmed and naked, the aged and impotent, the women and children; that so from amongst them, they might get thirtie thousand slaves.

CHAPTER II

OF SADNESSE OR SORROWE

No man is more free from this passion than I, for I neither love nor regard it: albeit the world hath undertaken, as it were upon covenant, to grace it with a particular favour. Therewith they adorne age, vertue, and conscience. Oh foolish and base ornament! The Italians have more properly with it's name entitled malignitie: for, it is a qualitie ever hurtfull, ever sottish; and as ever base and coward, the Stoikes inhibit their Elders and Sages to be therewith tainted, or have any feeling of it. But the Storie saith; that *Psamneticus* king of *Ægypt,* having been defeated and taken by *Cambises* king of *Persia,* seeing his owne daughter passe before him in base and vile aray, being sent to draw water from a well, his friends weeping and wailing about him (he with his eyes fixed on the ground, could not be moved to utter one word), and shortly after beholding his sonne led to execution, held still the same undaunted countenance: but perceiving a familiar friend of his haled amongst the captives, he began to beat his head, and burst forth into extreame sorrow. This might well be compared to that which one of our Princes was lately seene to doe, who being at *Trent,* and receiving newes of his elder brothers death; but such a brother as on him lay all the burthen and honour of his house; and shortly after tidings of his yonger brothers decease, who was his second hope; and having with an unmatched countenance and exemplar constancie endured these two affronts; it fortuned not long after, that one of his servants dying, he by this latter accident suffered himselfe to be so far transported, that quitting and forgetting his former resolution, he so abandoned himselfe to all manner of sorrow and griefe, that some argued, only this last mischance had toucht him to the quicke: but verily the reason was, that being otherwise full, and over-plunged in sorrow, the least surcharge brake the bounds and barres of patience. The like might (I say) be judged of our storie, were it not it followeth, that *Cambises* inquiring of *Psamneticus*, why he was nothing distempered at the misfortune of his sonne and daughter, he did so impatiently beare the disaster of his friend: *It is*, answered he, *Because this last displeasure may be manifested by weeping, whereas the two former exceed by much, all meanes and compasse to be expressed by teares*. The invention of that ancient Painter might happily fit this purpose, who in the sacrifice of *Iphigenia*, being to represent the griefe of the bystanders, according to the qualitie and interest each one bare for the death of so faire, so young and innocent a Lady, having ransacked the utmost skill and effects of his art, when he came to the Virgins father, as if no countenance were able to represent that degree of sorrow, he drew him with a vaile over his face. And that is the reason why our Poets faine miserable *Niobe*, who first having lost seven sonnes, and immediately as many daughters, as one over-burthened with their losses, to have been transformed into a stone;

Diriguisse malis:—Ovid. *Metam.* vi. 303.

And grew as hard as stone,
By miserie and moane.

Thereby to expresse this mournfull silent stupiditie, which so doth pierce us, when accidents surpassing our strength orewhelme us. Verily the violence of a griefe, being extreme, must needs astonie the mind, and hinder the liberty of her actions. As it hapneth at the sudden alarum of some bad tidings, when we shall feele our selves surprised, benummed, and as it were deprived of all motion, so that the soule bursting afterward forth into teares and complaints, seemeth at more ease and libertie, to loose, to cleare and dilate it selfe.

Et via vix tandem voci laxata dolore est.
Virg. *Æn.* xi. 151.

And scarce at last for speach,
By griefe was made a breach.

In the warres which king *Ferdinando* made against the widow of *John* king of *Hungaria*, about *Buda;* a man at armes was particularly noted of all men, forsomuch as in a certaine skirmish he had shewed exceeding prowesse of his body, and though unknowne, being slaine, was highly commended and much bemoaned of all: but yet of none so greatly as of a Germane Lord, called *Raisciac,* as he that was amased at so rare vertue: his body being covered and had off, this Lord, led by a common curiositie, drew neere unto it, to see who it might be, and having caused him to be disarmed, perceived him to be his owne sonne; which knowne, did greatly augment the compassion of all the camp: he only without framing word, or closing his eyes, but earnestly viewing the dead body of his sonne, stood still upright, till the vehemencie of his sad sorrow, having suppressed and choaked his vitall spirits, fell'd him starke dead to the ground.

Chi puo dir com' egli arde è in picciol fuoco,
PET. *p.* i. *Son.* 140.

He that can say how he doth frie
In pettie-gentle flames doth lie,

say those Lovers that would lively represent an intolerable passion.

misero quod omnes
Eripit sensus mihi; Nam simul te
Lesbia aspexi, nihil est super mî
Quod loquar amens.
Lingua sed torpet, tenuis sub artus
Flamma dimanat, sonitu suopte
Tinniunt aures, gemina teguntur
Lumina nocte.—CATUL. *Epig.* xlviii. 5.

miserably from me
This bereaves all sense: for I can no sooner
Eie thee my sweet heart, but I wot not one word to speake
amazed.
Tongue-tide as in trance, while a sprightly thin flame
Flowes in all my joynts, with a selfe-resounding
Both my eares tingle, with a night redoubled
Both mine eies are veild.

Nor is it in the liveliest, and most ardent heat of the fit, that wee are able to display our plaints and perswasions, the soule being then aggravated with heavie thoughts, and the body suppressed and languishing for love. And thence is sometimes engendered that casuall faintness, which so unseasonably surpriseth passionate Lovers, and that chilnesse, which by the [power of an extreame heate doth seize on them in the verie midst of their joy and enjoying. All passions that may be tasted and digested, are but meane and slight.]

Curæ leves loquuntur, ingentes stupent.
SEN. *Hip.* act ii. sc. 2.

Light cares can freely speake,
Great cares heart rather breake.

The surprize of an unexpected pleasure astonieth us alike.

> *Ut me conspexit venientem, et Troja circum*
> *Arma amens vidit, magnis exterrita monstris,*
> *Diriguit visu in medio, calor ossa relinquit,*
> *Labitur, et longo vix tandem tempore fatur.*
>
> VIRG. Æn. iii. 306.

When she beheld me come, and round about
Senselesse saw Trojan armes, she stood afraid
Stone-still at so strange sights: life heat flew out.
She faints: at last, with long pause thus she said.

Besides the Romane Ladie, that died for joy to see her sonne returne alive from the battell of *Cannæ, Sophocles* and *Dionysius* the Tyrant, who deceased through overgladnes: and *Talva,* who died in *Corsica,* reading the newes of the honours the Roman Senate had conferred upon him: It is reported that in our age, Pope *Leo* the tenth having received advertisement of the taking of the Citie of *Millane,* which he had so exceedingly desired, entred into such excesse of joy, that he fell into an ague, whereof he shortly died. And for a more authenticall testimonie of humane imbecillitie, it is noted by our Ancients, that *Diodorus* the Logician, being surprized with an extreme passion or apprehension of shame, fell downe starke dead, because neither in his Schoole, nor in publique, he had beene able to resolve an argument propounded unto him. I am little subject to these violent passions. I have naturally a hard apprehension, which by discourse I daily harden more and more.

CHAPTER III

OUR AFFECTIONS ARE TRANSPORTED BEYOND OUR SELVES

THOSE which still accuse men for ever gaping after future things, and go about to teach us, to take hold of present fortunes, and settle our selves upon them, as having no hold of that which is to come; yea much lesse than we have of that which is already past, touch and are ever harping upon the commonest humane error, if they dare call that an error, to which Nature her selfe, for the service of the continuation of her worke, doth addresse us, imprinting (as it doth many others) this false imagination in us, as more jealous of our actions, than of our knowledge. We are never in our selves, but beyond. Feare, desire, and hope, draw us ever towards that which is to come, and remove our sense and consideration from that which is, to amuse us on that which shall be, yea when we shall be no more. *Calamitosus est animus futuri anxius* (SEN. *Epi.* 98). *A minde in suspense what is to come, is in a pittifull case.*

This notable precept is often alleaged in *Plato. Follow thy businesse and know thy selfe;* Each of these two members, doth generally imply all our duty; and likewise enfolds his companion. He that should doe his businesse, might perceive that his first lesson is, to know what he is, and what is convenient for him. And he that knoweth himselfe, takes no more anothers matters for his owne, but above all other things, loveth and correcteth himselfe, rejecteth superfluous occupations, idle imaginations, and unprofitable propositions. As if you grant follie what it desireth, it will no-whit be satisfied; so is wisdome content with that which is present, and never displeased with it selfe. *Epicurus* doth dispense with his [s]age touching the foresight and care of what shal insue. Amongst the lawes that regard the deceased, that which ties the actions of Princes to be examined when they are dead, seemes to me verie solid. They are companions, if not masters of the lawes: That which justice could not worke on their heads, it is reason it effect upon their reputation, and goods of their successors: things wee many times preferre before our lives. It is a custome brings many singular commodities unto nations that observe it, and to be desired of all good Princes: who have cause to complaine that the memorie of the wicked is used as theirs. Wee owe a like obedience and subjection to all Kings; for it respects their office: but estimation and affection, we owe it only to their vertue. If they be unworthy, wee are to endure them patiently, to conceale their vices, and to aid their indifferent actions with our commendations, as long as their authoritie hath need of our assistance, and that ought to be ascribed unto politike order. But our commerce with them being ended, there is no reason we should refuse the unfolding of our felt wrongs unto justice and our libertie. And specially to refuse good subjects, the glory to have reverently and faithfully served a master, whose imperfections were so well knowne unto them: exempting posteritie from so profitable an example. And such as for the respect of some private benefit or interest, doe wickedly embrace the memorie of an unworthy Prince, doe particular justice at the charge of publike justice. *Titus Livius* speaketh truly, where he saith, that the speech of men brought up under a royaltie is ever full of vaine ostentations, and false witnesses; every man indifferently extolling the King, to the furthest straine of valour and soveraigne greatnesse. The magnanimitie of those two Souldiers may be reproved, one of which being demanded of *Nero,* why he hated him, answered him to his teeth; I loved thee whilest thou wast worthy of love, but since thou becamest a parricide, a firebrand, a Juglar, a Player, and a Coach-man, I hate thee, as thou deservest. The other being asked, wherefore he sought to kill him, answered, Because I finde no other course to hinder thy uncessant outrages and impious deeds. But can any man, that hath his senses about him, justly reprove the publike and generall testimonies that since his death have beene given, and so shall be for ever, both against him and all such like reprobates, of his tyrannicall and wicked demeanours? I am sorrie that in so sacred a policie as the Lacedemonian was, so fained and fond a ceremonie at the death of their Kings was ever devised and brought in use. All their confederates and neighbours, all the slave-He[l]otes, men and women pell-mell, for a testimonie of their griefe and sorrow, did mangle and gash their foreheads, and in their out-cries and lamentations exclaimed, that their deceased King, howsoever he had lived, was and had beene the best Prince that ever they had, ascribing in order the commendations due unto desert, and to the last and latter ranke, what belongs unto the first merit. *Aristotle* that hath an oare in every water, and medleth with all things, makes a question about *Solons* speech, who saith, that no man can truly be counted happy before his death, Whether he that lived and died according to his wish, may be named happy, whether his renowne be good or ill, and whether his posteritie be miserable or no. Whilest wee stirre and remove, wee transport our selves by preoccupation wheresoever wee list: but no sooner are wee out of being, but wee have no communication at all with that which is. And it were better to tell *Solon,* that never man is happy then, since he never is so, but when he is no more.

> —*Quisquam*
> *Vix radicitus è vita se tollit, et ejicit:*
> *Sed facit esse sui quiddam super inscius ipse,*
> *Nec removet satis à projecto corpore sese, et*
> *Vindicat.*—Lucr. *Rer. nat.* iii. 912.

Scarce any rids himselfe of life so cleere,
But leaves unwitting some part of him heere:
Nor frees or quits himselfe sufficiently
From that his body which forlorne doth lie.

Bertrand of *Gelsquin* died at the siege of the castle of *Rancon,* neere unto *Puy* in *Avergne:* the besieged yeelding afterward, were forced to carry the keies of the Castle, upon the deceased [body] of the Captaine. *Bartholomew* of *Alviano,* Generall of the Venetian forces dying in their service and wars about *Brescia,* and his bodie being to be transported to *Venice,* through the territory of *Verona,* which then was enemie unto them, the greatest part of the army thought it expedient to demand a safe conduct for their passage of those of *Verona,* to which *Theodoro Trivulcio* stoutly opposed himselfe, and chose rather to passe it by maine force, and to hazard the day, saying it was not convenient, that he who in his life time had never apprehended feare of his enemies should now being dead, seeme to feare them. Verily in like matters, by the lawes of *Greece,* hee that required a dead body of his enemies, with intent to bury the same, renounced the victory, and might no more erect any trophy of it: and he who was so required, purchased the title of honour and gaine. So did *Nicias* lose the advantage hee had clearly gained of the Corinthians; and contrariwise, *Agesilaus* assured that, hee doubtfully had gotten of the Bœtians. These actions might bee deemed strange, if in all ages it were not a common-received opinion, not only to extend the care of our selves, beyond this life, but also to beleeve, that heavenly favours doe often accompany us unto our grave, and continue in our posterity. Whereof there are so many examples (leaving our moderne a part) that I need not wade farre into it.

   Edward the first King of *England,* in the long wars he had with *Robert* King of *Scotland,* having by triall found how greatly his presence advantaged the successe of his affaires, and how he was ever victorious in any enterprise he undertooke in his owne person; when hee died, bound his sonne by solemne oath, that being dead he should cause his body to be boyled, untill the flesh fell from the bones, which he should cause to be interred, and carefully keeping the bones, ever carry them about him, whensoever hee should happen to have wars with the Scots: As if destiny had fatally annexed the victory unto his limmes. *John Zisca,* who for the defence of *Wickliffs* opinions so much troubled the state of *Bohemia,* commanded that after his death his body should be flead, and a drum made of his skin, to be carried and sounded in all the wars against his enemies: deeming the sound of it would be a meanes to continue the advantages, which in his former warres hee had obtained of them. Certaine Indians did likewise carry the bones of one of their Captaines in the skirmishes they had with the Spaniards, in regard of the good successe hee had, whilest hee lived, against them: And other nations of that new-found world, doe likewise carry the bodies of such worthy and fortunate men with them, as have died in their battels, to serve them in stead of good fortune and encouragement. The first examples reserve nothing else in their tombes, but the reputation acquired by their former atchievements: but these will also adjoyne unto it the power of working. The act of Captaine *Bayart* is of better composition, who perceiving himselfe deadly wounded by a shot received in his body, being by his men perswaded to come off and retire himselfe from out the throng, answered, he would not now so neere his end, begin to turn his face from his enemie: and having stoutly foughten so long as he could stand, feeling himselfe to faint and stagger from his horse, commanded his steward to lay him against a tree, but in such sort, that he might die with his face toward the enemie; as indeed hee did. I may not omit this other example, as remarkable for this consideration, as any of the precedent. The Emperour *Maximilian,* great grandfather to *Philip* now King of *Spaine,* was a Prince highly endowed with many noble qualities, and amongst others with a well-nigh matchlesse beauty and comeliness of body; but with other customes of his, hee had this one much contrarie to other Princes, who to dispatch their weightiest affaires make often their close stoole,

their regall Throne or Councel-chamber, which was, that hee would
not permit any groome of his chamber (were hee never so neere about
him) to see him in his inner chamber, who if he had occasion but to
make water, would as nicely and as religiously withdraw himselfe as
any maiden, and never suffer so much as a Physitian, much lesse any
other whatsoever, to see those privie parts that all in modestie seek
to keepe secret and unseene. My self, that am so broad-mouthed and
lavish in speeches, am notwithstanding naturally touched with that
bashfulnesse. And unlesse it bee by the motion of necessity or of
voluptuousnesse, I never willingly imparted those actions and parts
(which custome willeth to bee concealed) to the view of any creature.
I endure more compulsion, than I deeme befitting a man, especially
of my profession. But hee grew to such superstition, that by expresse
words in his last will and Testament, hee commanded, that being
dead, hee should have linnen-flops put about them. Hee should by
codicile have annexed unto it, that hee who should put them on,
might have his eies hood-winckt. The instruction which *Cyrus* giveth
his children, that neither they nor any other should either see or
touch his body, after the breath were once out of it; I ascribe it unto
some motive of devotion in him. For both his historian and himselfe,
amongst many other notable qualities they are endued with, have
throughout all the course of their life seemed to have a singular respect
and awfull reverence unto religion. That story displeased mee very
much, which a nobleman told me of a kinsman of mine (a man very
famous and well known both in peace and warre) which is, that dying
very aged in his court, being much tormented with extreme pangs
of the stone, hee with an earnest and unwearied care, employed all
his last houres, to dispose the honour and ceremony of his funerals,
and summoned all the nobilitie that came to visit him, to give him
assured promise to be as assistants, and to convey him to his last
resting place. To the very same Prince, who was with him at his last
gasp, he made very earnest suit, he would command all his houshold
to wait upon him at his interment, inforcing many reasons, and
alleaging divers examples, to prove that it was a thing very convenient.
and fitting a man of his qualitie: which assured promise when he had
obtained, and had at his pleasure marshalled the order how they
should march, he seemed quietly and contentedly to yeeld up the
ghost. I have seldome seene a vanitie continue so long. This other
curiositie meere opposite unto it (which to prove I need not labour
for home-examples) seemeth in my opinion cosen-german to this, that
is, when one is ever ready to breathe his last, carefully and passionately to endevour how to reduce the convoy of his obsequies unto
some particular and unwonted parcimonie, to one servant and to one
lanterne. I heare the humour and appointment of *Marcus Æmilius
Lepidus* commended, who expresly forbade his heires to use those
ceremonies about his interment, which in such cases were formerly

accustomed. Is it temperance and frugalitie, to avoid charge and voluptuousnesse, the use and knowledge of which is imperceptable unto us? Loe here an easie reformation, and of small cost. Were it requisite to appoint any, I would be of opinion, that as well in that, as in all other actions of mans life, every man should referre the rule of it to the qualitie of his fortune. And the Philosopher *Lycon* did wisely appoint his friends to place his body where they should thinke it fittest and for the best: and for his obsequies, they should neither be superfluous and over-costly, nor base and sparing. For my part, I would wholly relie on custome, which should dispose this ceremonie, and would yeeld my selfe to the discretion of the first or next into whose hands I might chance to fall. *Totus hic locus est contemnendus in nobis, non negligendus in nostris: All this matter should be despised of us, but not neglected of ours.* And religiously said a holy man; *Curatio funeris, conditio sepulturæ, pompa exequiarum, magis sunt vivorum solatia, quàm subsidia mortuorum* (Aug. *Civ. Dei.* i. 12, verb. apost. ser. 32). *The procuration of funerals, the maner of buriall, the pomp of obsequies, are rather comforts to the living, than helps to the dead.* Therefore *Socrates* answered *Criton*, who at the houre of his death asked him how he would be buried: *Even as you please*, said he. Were I to meddle further with this subject, I would deeme it more gallant to imitate those who yet living and breathing, undertake to enjoy the order and honour of their sepulchres, and that please themselves to behold their dead countenance in Marble. Happy they that can rejoyce and gratifie their senses with insensibilitie, and live by their death! A little thing would make me conceive an inexpiable hatred against all popular domination; although it seeme most naturall and just unto me; when I call to minde that inhumane injustice of the Athenians, who without further triall or remission, yea without suffering them so much as to reply or answer for themselves, condemned those noble and worthy Captaines, that returned victoriously from the sea-battell, which they (neere the Iles *Argusinæ*) had gained of the Lacedemonians; the most contested, bloodie and greatest fight the Grecians ever obtained by sea with their owne forces: forsomuch as after the victory, they had rather followed those occasions, which the law of warre presented unto them, for their availe, than to their prejudice staid to gather and bury their dead men. And the successe of *Diomedon* makes their ruthlesse execution more hatefull, who being a man of notable and exemplar vertue, both military and politike, and of them so cruelly condemned; after he had heard the bloudy sentence, advancing himselfe forward to speake, having fit opportunitie and plausible audience; he, I say, in stead of excusing himselfe, or endevouring to justifie his cause, or to exasperate the evident iniquity of so cruell a doome, expressed but a care of the Judges preservation, earnestly beseeching the Gods to turne that judgement to their good, praying that for want of not satisfying the

vowes which hee and his companions had vowed in acknowledgement
and thanksgiving for so famous a victory, and honourable fortune,
they might not draw the wrath and revenge of the Gods upon them,
declaring what their vowes were. And without more words, or urging
further reasons, couragiously addressed himselfe to his execution.
But fortune some yeares after punished him alike, and made him
taste of the verie same sauce. For *Chabrias,* Captaine Generall of
their sea-fleet, having afterward obtained a famous victory of *Pollis,*
Admirall of *Sparta,* in the Ile of *Naxos,* lost absolutely the benefit of
it, and onely contented with the day (a matter of great consequence
for their affaires) fearing to incurre the mischiefe of this example,
and to save a few dead carcasses of his friends, that floated up and
downe the sea, gave leasure to an infinite number of his living enemies,
whom he might easily have surprized to saile away in safety, who
afterward made them to purchase their importunate superstition, at
a deere-deere rate.

> *Quæris, quo jaceas, post obitum, loco?*
> *Quo non nata jacent.*—SEN. *Troas. chor.* ii. 30.

Where shall you lie when you are dead?
Where they lye that were never bred:

This other restores the sense of rest unto a body without a soule.

> *Neque sepulchrum, quo recipiat, habeat portum corporis.*
> *Ubi remissa humana vita, corpus requiescat à malis.*
> CIC. *Tusc. Qu.* i. Enni.

To turne in as a hav'n, have he no grave,
Where life left, from all griefe he rest may have.

Even as Nature makes us to see, that many dead things have yet
certaine secret relations unto life. Wine doth alter and change in
sellers, according to the changes and alterations of the seasons of its
vineyard. And the flesh of wilde beasts and venison doth change
qualitie and taste in the powdering-tubs, according to the nature of
living flesh, as some say that have observed it.

CHAPTER IV

HOW THE SOULE DISCHARGETH HER PASSIONS UPON FALSE OBJECTS, WHEN THE TRUE FAILE IT

A GENTLEMAN of ours exceedingly subject to the gowt, being instantly solicited by his Physitions, to leave all manner of salt-meats,
was wont to answer pleasantly, that when the fits or pangs of the
disease tooke him, hee would some body to quarell with; and that

crying and cursing, now against *Bolonie*-sausege, and sometimes by railing against salt neats-tongues, and gammons of bakon, he found some ease. But in good earnest even as the arme being lifted up to strike, if the stroke hit not, but fall void, wee feele some paine in it, and many times strike it out of joynt; and that to yeeld our sight pleasant, it must not be lost and dispiersed in the vast ayre, but ought rather to have a limited bound to sustaine it by a reasonable distance.

> *Ventus ut amittit vires, nisi robore densæ*
> *Occurrant silvæ, spatio diffusus inani.*—LUCAN. iii. 362.

As windes in emptie ayre diffus'd, strength lose,
Unlesse thick-old-growne woods of their strength oppose.

So seemes it that the soule moved and tossed, if she have not some hold to take, loseth it selfe in it selfe, and must ever be stored with some object, on which it may light and worke. *Plutarch* saith fitly of those who affectionate themselves to Monkies and little Dogges, that the loving part which is in us, for want of a lawfull hold, rather than it will be idle, doth forge a false and frivolous hold unto it selfe. And wee see that the soule in her passions doth rather deceive it selfe, by framing a false and fantasticall subject unto it selfe, yea against her owne conceit, than not to worke upon something. So doth their owne rage transport beasts, to set upon the stone or weapon that hath hurt them; yea and sometimes with irefull teeth to revenge themselves against themselves, for the hurt or smart they feele.

> *Pannonis haud aliter post ictum sævior ursa*
> *Cui jaculum parva Lybis amentavit habena,*
> *Se rotat in vulnus, telumque irata receptum*
> *Impedit, et secum fugientem circuit hastam.*—LUCAN. vi. 220.

Even so the wound-enraged Austrian beare,
On whom a Moore hath thirl'd his slinged speare,
Wheeles on her wound, and raging bites the dart,
Circling that flies with her, and cannot part.

What causes doe wee not invent, for the crosses that happen unto us? bee it right, or wrong: what take we not hold of, to have something to strive withall? It is not the golden locks thou tearest, nor the whitenesse of the breast, which thou through vexation so cruelly dost smite, that have by meanes of an unluckie bullet, lost thy deere-beloved brother: on something else shouldest thou wreake thy selfe. *Livius* speaking of the Romane army in *Spaine,* after the losse of two great Captaines that were brethren. *Flere omnes repentè, et offensare capita* (LIV. dec. iii. lib. 5): *They all wept and often beat their heades.* It is an ordinarie custome: And the Philosopher *Byon* was very pleasant with the king, that for griefe tore his haire, when he said, *Doth this man thinke, that baldnesse will asswage his griefe?*

who hath not seene some to chew and swallow cardes, and wel-nigh choake themselves with bales of dice, only to be revenged for the losse of some money? *Xerxes* whipped the Sea, and writ a cartell of defiance to the hill *Athos:* And *Cyrus* for many daies together ammused his whole armie to be revenged of the river *Gyndus,* for the feare he tooke passing over the same: and *Caligula* caused a verie faire house to be defaced, for the pleasure his mother had received in the same. When I was young, my countrimen were wont to say, *That one of our neighbour-Kings, having received a blow at Gods hand, sware to be revenged on him, and ordained, that for ten yeares space no man should pray unto him, nor speak of him, nor (so long as he were in authority,) beleeve in him.* By which report, they doe not so much publish the sottishnesse, as the ambitious glorie, peculiar unto that nation of whom it was spoken. They are vices that ever goe together: But in truth such actions encline rather unto selfe-conceit, than to fondnes. *Augustus Cæsar* having beene beaten by a tempest on the sea, defied the God *Neptune,* and in the celebration of the Circensian games, that so he might be avenged on him, he caused his image to be removed from out the place, where it stood amongst the other Gods; wherein he is also lesse excusable, than the former, and lesse than hee was afterward, when having lost a battell, under *Quintilius Varus* in *Germanie,* all in a rage and desperate, he went up and downe beating his head against the walls, mainly crying out: *Oh! Varus, restore me my Souldiers againe:* For, those exceed all follie, (forsomuch as impietie is joyned unto it) that will wreake themselves against God, or fortune, as if she had eares subject to our batterie: In imitation of the Thracians, who when it lightens or thunders, begin with a Titanian revenge to shoot against heaven, thinking by shooting of arrowes to draw God to some reason. Now, as saith that ancient Poet in *Plutarch,*

> *Point ne se faut corroucer aux affaires,*
> *Il ne leur chaut de toutes noz choleres.*—PLUT.

> We ought not angry be at what God dooth,
> For he cares not who beares an angry tooth.

But we shall never raile enough against the disorder and unrulinesse of our minde.

CHAPTER V

WHETHER THE CAPTAINE OF A PLACE BESIEGED OUGHT TO SALLIE FORTH TO PARLIE

LUCIUS MARCIUS Legate of the Romans, in the warre against *Perseus* King of *Macedon,* desirous to get so much time, as he wanted to prepare his army, gave out some motives of accord, wherewith the King inveagled, yeelded unto a truce for certaine daies: by which meanes he furnished his enemie with opportunitie and leasure to arme himself: wherof proceeded the Kings last ruine and over-throw. Yet is it, that the elders of the Senate, mindfull of their forefathers customes, condemned this practice as an enemie to their ancient proceedings, which was, said they, to fight with vertue, and not with craft, nor by surprises, or stratagems by night, nor by set-flights, and unlookt-for approches, never undertaking a warre, but after it was proclaimed, yea many times after the appointed houre and place of the battell. With this conscience did they send backe to *Pirrhus* his traitorous Physitian, and to the *Phalisci* their disloyall schoolemaster. These were true Romane proceedings, and not Grecian policies, nor Punike wiles, with whom to vanquish by force is lesse glorious than to conquer by treacherie. To deceive may serve for the instant, but hee only is judged to be overcome, that knowes he was not vanquished by craft or deceit, nor by fortune or chance, but by meere valour, betweene troupe and troupe, in an overt and just warre. It appeareth manifestly by the speech of these good men, they had not yet received this sentence.

> ——*Dolus, an virtus, quis in hoste requirat?*
> VIRG. *Æn*. ii. 390.

Deceit, or vertue, either, in foes, it skill's not whether.

The Achaians, saith *Polibius,* detested all manner of deceit in their warres, deeming that no victorie, where their enemies courages were not quelled. *Eam vir sanctus, et sapiens sciat esse victoriam veram, quæ salva fide, et integra dignitate parabitur. A wise and religious man will know that is victorie indeed, which shall be attained with credit unimpeached, and dignitie untainted,* saith another.

> *Vos ne velit, an me regnare hera, quid-ve ferat fors,*
> *Virtute experiamur.*—CIC. *Offic.* i. ex. Enn. de Pyrrh.

If fortune will have you to raigne, or me,
And what chance bring's, let vertues triall be.

In the Kingdome of *Ternates,* among those nations, which wee so full-mouthed, call Barbarous, the custome beareth, that they never undertake a warre, before the same be denounced; thereunto adding an ample declaration of the meanes they have to employ therein, what manner, and how many men, what munition, and what Armes either offensive or defensive: which done, they also establish as a law, that without reproach or imputation, it shall be lawfull for any man, in their warres, to use what advantage soever, may in any sort further or helpe them to vanquish. The ancient *Florentines* were so far from desiring any advantage of their enemies by sudden surprises, that a moneth before they could bring their Armie into the field, they would give them warning, by the continuall sound of their common bell, which they called *Martinella*. As for us, who are lesse superstitious, and deeme him to have the honour of the warre, that hath the profit of it, and according to *Lisander*, say, that *Where the Lions-skinne will not suffice, wee must adde a scantling of the Foxes;* the most ordinarie occasions of surprises are drawne from this practice, and as wee say, there is no time, wherein a Captaine ought to be more warie and circumspect to looke about him, than that of parlies, and treaties of accord: And therefore is it a common rule in the mouth of all our modern men of warre, that the Governour or Commaunder of a besieged place, ought never to sallie forth himselfe to parlie. In the time of our forefathers, the same was cast in the teeth, (as a reproach) unto the Lord of *Montmord* and *Assigni*, who defended *Mouson*, against the Earle of *Nanseaw*. Yet in this case it were excusable in him, that should so sallie out, that the assurance and advantage, might still be on his side. As did the Earle *Guido Rangoni* in the Citie of *Reggio* (if credit may be given to *Bellay;* for *Guicciardin* affirmeth, that it was himselfe) when as the Lord of *Escute*, comming to parlie made his approaches unto it; for he did so little forsake his fort, that whilest they were in parlie, a commotion being raised, the Lord of *Escute* and the troupes which came with him, in that tumult found himselfe to be the weakest, so that *Alexander Trivultio* was there slaine, and hee deeming it the safest way, was forced to follow the Earle, and on his word to yeeld himselfe to the mercie and shelter of blowes, into the Citie. *Eumenes* in the Citie of *Nera*, being urged by *Antigonus*, that besieged him, to sallie forth to parlie, alleaging that there was reason he should come to him, sith he was the better man, and the stronger: after he had made this noble answer, *I will never thinke any man better than my selfe, so long as I can hold or rule my sword;* nor did he ever yeeld untill *Antigonus* had delivered him *Ptolomey*, his owne nephew for a pledge, whom he required. Yet shall wee see some to have prospered well in sallying foorth of their holdes to parlie, upon the word and honor of the assailant; witnes *Henrie* of *Vaulx*, a knight of *Champaigne*, who being beleagred by the Englishmen in the Castle of *Commercie*, and *Bartholomew* of *Bones*, who at that siege commaunded as Chiefe having caused the greatest part of the Castle to be undermined, so that there wanted nothing but the giving of fire, utterly to subvert the same, under the ruines of it, summoned the said *Henrie* to issue out, and for his owne good to parlie with him, which he did, accompanied but with three more, who manifestly seeing the evident ruine, wherein he was undoubtedly like to fall, acknowledged himselfe infinitely beholding to his enemie, unto whose discretion, after he had yeelded together with this troup, and that fire was given to the Mine, the maine props of the Castle failing, it was utterly overthrowne and carried away. I am easily perswaded to yeeld to other mens words and faith, but hardly would

I doe it, when I should give other men cause to imagine, that I had rather done it through despaire and want of courage, than of a free and voluntary choise, and confidence in his honestie and well-meaning.

CHAPTER VI

THAT THE HOURE OF PARLIES IS DANGEROUS

NOTWITHSTANDING I saw lately, that those of *Musidan,* a place not farre from mee, who with others of their partie, were by our forces compelled to dislodge thence, exclaimed, they were betraid, because during the speech of accord, and the treatie yet continuing, they had been surprized and defeated; which thing might haply in other ages have had some apparence of truth; but, as I say, our manner of proceeding in such cases, is altogether differing from these rules, and no man ought to expect performance of promise from an enemie, except the last seale of bond be fully annexed thereunto, wherein notwithstanding is then much care and vigilancie required, and much adoe shall be found. And it was ever a dangerous counsell to trust the performance of word or oath given unto a Citie, that yields unto gentle and favourable composition, and in that furie to give the needie, bloudthirstie, and prey-greedy Souldier free entrance into it, unto the free choise and licence of a victorious armie. *Lucius Æmilius Regillus* a Romane Prætor, having lost his time in attempting by force to take the Citie of the *Phocens* by reason of the singular prowesse, which the inhabitants shewed, in stoutly defending themselves, covenanted to receive them as friends unto the people of *Rome,* and to enter their Citie as a place confederate, removing all feare of hostile-action from them. But to the end hee might appeare more glorious and dreadfull, having caused his armie to enter with him, doe what he might, he could not bridle the rage of his Souldiers; and with his owne eies saw most part of the Citie ransacked and spoiled: the rights of covetousnesse and revenge supplanting those of his authoritie and militarie discipline. (*Cleomenes* was wont to say, that *What hurt soever a man might doe his enemies in time of warre, was beyond justice, and not subject unto it, as well towards the Gods as towards men:* who for seven dayes having made truce with those of *Argos,* the third night, whilest they were all asleepe mistrusting no harme, hee charged and overthrew them, alleaging for his excuse, that in the truce no mention had beene made of nights.) But the Gods left not his perfidious policie unrevenged: For during their enter-parlie and businesse about taking hostages, the Citie of *Casilinum* was by surprise taken from him: which happened in the times of the justest Captaines, and of the most perfect Romane discipline: For it is not said, that time and place serving, wee must not make use and take advantage of our enemies foolish oversight, as we doe of their cowardise. And verily warre hath naturally many reasonable privileges to the prejudice of reason. And here failes the rule; *Neminem id agere, ut ex alterius prædetur inscitia* (Cic. *Offic.* iii.): *That no man should endevour to prey upon another mans ignorance.* But I wonder of the scope that *Xenophon* allowes them, both by his discourse, and by divers exploits of his perfect Emperour: an Author of wonderfull consequence in such things, as a great Captaine and a Philosopher, and one of *Socrates* chiefest Disciples, nor doe I altogether yeeld unto the measure of his dispensation. The Lord of *Aubigny* besieging *Capua,* after he had given it a furious batterie, the Lord *Fabritius Colonna,* Captaine of the towne, having from under a bastion or skonce begunne to parlie, and his men growing negligent and carelesse in their offices and guard, our men did suddenly take the advantage offered them, entered the towne, overranne it, and put all to the sword. But to come to later examples, yea in our memorie, the Lord *Julio Romero* at *Yvoy,* having committed this oversight to issue out of his holde, to parlie with the Constable of *France,* at his returne found the Towne taken, and himselfe jack-out-of-doores. But that wee may not passe unrevenged, the Marques of *Pescara* beleagering *Genova,* where Duke *Octavian Fregoso* commanded under our protection, and an accord between them having so long been treated, and earnestly solicited, that it was held as ratified, and upon the point of conclusion, the Spaniards being entred the Towne, and seeing themselves the stronger, tooke their opportunitie, and used it as a full and compleate victorie: and since at *Lygny* in *Barroe,* where the Earle of *Brienne* commanded, the Emperour having besieged him in person, and *Bartholemy* Lieutenant to the saide Earle being come foorth of his hold to parlie, was no sooner out, whilest they were disputing, but the Towne was surprised, and he excluded, They say,

> *Fu il vincer sempre mai laudabil cosa,*
> *Vincasi per fortuna ò per ingegno.*
>   Arist. cant. xv. stan. 1.

To be victorious, evermore was glorious,
Be we by fortune or by wit victorious.

But the Philosopher *Chrysippus* would not have beene of that opinion; nor I neither, for he was wont to say, *That those who run for the masterie may well employ all their strength to make speed, but it is not lawfull for them to lay hands on their adversaries, to stay him, or to crosse leggs, to make him trip or fall.* And more generously answered *Alexander* the great, at what time *Polypercon* perswaded him to use the benefit of the advantage which the darknesse of the night afforded him, to charge *Darius; No, no,* said hee, *it fits*

not mee to hunt after night-stolne victories: Malo me fortunæ pœni-
teat, quàm victoriæ pudeat (CURT. iv.). *I had rather repent me of*
my fortune, than be ashamed of my victorie.

> *Atque idem fugientem haud est dignatus Orodem*
> *Sternere, nec jacta cæcum dare cuspide vulnus:*
> *Obvius adversoque occurrit, seque viro vir*
> *Contulit, haud furto meliôr, sed fortibus armis.*
>   VIRG. Æn. x. 732. Mezent.

He deign'd not to strike downe Orodes flying,
Or with his throwne-launce blindely-wound him running:
But man to man afront himselfe applying,
Met him, as more esteem'd for strength than cunning.

CHAPTER VII

THAT OUR INTENTION JUDGETH OUR ACTIONS

THE common saying is, that *Death acquits us of all our bonds.*
I know some that have taken it in another sence. *Henry* the seventh,
King of *England*, made a composition with *Philip* son to *Maximilian*
the Emperour or (to give him a more honorable title) father to the
Emperour *Charles* the fifth, that the said *Philip* should deliver into
his hands, the Duke of Suffolke, his mortall enemie, who was fled
out of *England*, and saved him selfe in the Low countries, alwayes
provided the King should attempt nothing against the Dukes life;
which promise notwithstanding, being neere his end, he expresly by
will and testament commanded his succeeding-sonne, that immediately after his decease, he should cause him to be put to death. In
the late tragedie, which the Duke of *Alva* presented us withall at
Brussels, on the Earles of *Horne* and *Egmond*, were many remarkable
things, and worthy to be noted: and amongst others, that the said
Count *Egmond* upon whose faithfull word and assurance, the Earle
of *Horne* was come in and yeelded himselfe to the Duke of *Alva*,
required very instantly to be first put to death, to the end his death
might acquit and free him of the word and bond, which he ought
and was engaged for, to the said Earle of *Horne*. It seemeth that
death hath no whit discharged the former of his word given, and
that the second, without dying, was quit of it. We cannot be tied
beyond our strength and meanes. The reason is, because the effects
and executions are not any way in our power, and except our will,
nothing is truely in our power: on it onely are all the rules of mans
dutie grounded and established by necessitie. And therefore Count
Egmond, deeming his minde and will indebted to his promise, how beit
the power to effect it, lay not in his hands, was no doubt cleerely

absolved of his debt and dutie, although he had survived the Count *Horne*. But the King of *England* failing of his word by his intention, cannot be excused, though hee delaide the execution of his disloyaltie untill after his death. No more than *Herodotus* his Mason who during his naturall life, having faithfully kept the secret of his Master the King of *Egypts* treasure, when he died discovered the same unto his children. I have in my dayes seene many convicted by their owne conscience, for detaining other men's goods, yet by their last will and testament to dispose themselves, after their decease to make satisfaction. This is nothing to the purpose. Neither to take time for a matter so urgent, nor with so small interest or shew of feeling, to goe about to establish an injurie. They are indebted somewhat more. And by how much more they pay incommodiously and chargeably, so much the more just and meritorious is their satisfaction. Penitence ought to charge, yet doe they worse, who reserve the revealing of some heinous conceit or affection towards their neighbour, to their last will and affection, having whilest they lived ever kept it secret. And seeme to have little regard of their owne honour, by provoking the partie offended against their owne memory, and lesse of their conscience, since they could never for the respect of death cancell their ill-grudging affection, and in extending life beyond theirs. Oh wicked and ungodly judges, which referre the judgement of a cause to such time as they have no more knowledge of causes! I will as neere as I can prevent, that my death reveale or utter any thing, my life hath not first publikely spoken.

CHAPTER VIII

OF IDLENESSE

"As we see some idle-fallow grounds, if they be fat and fertile, to bring foorth store and sundrie roots of wilde and unprofitable weeds, and that to keepe them in ure we must subject and imploy them with certaine seeds for our use and service. And as wee see some women, though single and alone, often to bring foorth lumps of shapeless flesh, whereas to produce a perfect and naturall generation, they must be manured with another kinde of seede: So is it of mindes, which except they be busied about some subject, that may bridle and keepe them under, they will here and there wildely scatter themselves through the vaste field of imaginations."

> *Sicut aquæ tremulum labris ubi lumen ahenis*
> *Sole repercussum, aut radiantis imagine Lunæ,*
> *Omnia pervolitat latè loca, jámque sub auras*
> *Erigitur, summique ferit laquearia tecti.*—VIRG. *Æn.* viii. 22.

As trembling light reflected from the Sunne,
Or radiant Moone on water-fild brasse lavers,
Flies over all, in aire upraised soone,
Strikes house-top beames, betwixt both strangely wavers.

And there is no folly, or extravagant raving, they produce not in that agitation.

———veluti ægri somnia, vanæ
Finguntur species.—Hor. *Art. Poet.* vii.

Like sicke mens dreames, that feigne
Imaginations vaine.

The minde that hath no fixed bound, will easily loose it selfe: For, as we say, *To be everie where, is to be no where.*

Quisquis ubique habitat, Maxime, nusquam habitat.
Mart. vii. *Epig.* 72, 6.

Good sir, he that dwels every where,
No where can say, that he dwels there.

It is not long since I retired my selfe unto mine owne house, with full purpose, as much as lay in me, not to trouble my selfe with any businesse, but solitarily and quietly to weare out the remainder of my well-nigh-spent life; where me thought I could doe my spirit no greater favour, than to give him the full scope of idlenesse, and entertaine him as he best pleased, and withall, to settle him-selfe as he best liked: which I hoped he might now, being by time become more setled and ripe, accomplish very easily: but I finde,

Variam semper dant otia mentem.—Lucan. iv. 704.

Evermore idlenesse,
Doth wavering mindes addresse.

That contrariwise playing the skittish and loose-broken jade, he takes a hundred times more cariere and libertie unto himselfe, than hee did for others; and begets in me so many extravagant *Chimeraes,* and fantasticall monsters, so orderlesse, and without any reason, one hudling upon an other, that at leasure to view the foolishnesse and monstrous strangenesse of them, I have begun to keepe a register of them, hoping, if I live, one day to make him ashamed, and blush at himselfe.

CHAPTER IX

OF LYERS

THERE is no man living, whom it may lesse beseeme to speak of memorie, than my selfe, for to say truth, I have none at all: and am fully perswaded that no mans can be so weake and forgetfull as mine. All other parts are in me common and vile, but touching memorie, I thinke to carrie the prise from all other, that have it weakest, nay and to gaine the reputation of it, besides the naturall want I endure (for truely considering the necessitie of it, *Plato* hath reason to name it *A great and mighty Goddesse*). In my countrie, if a man will imply that one hath no sense, he will say, such a one hath no memorie: and when I complaine of mine, they reprove me, and will not beleeve me, as if I accused my selfe to be mad and senselesse. They make no difference between memorie and wit; which is an empairing of my market: But they doe me wrong, for contrariwise it is commonly seene by experience, that excellent memories do rather accompany weake judgements. Moreover they wrong me in this (who can do nothing so well as to be a perfect friend) that the same words which accuse my infirmitie, represent ingratitude. From my affection they take hold of my memorie, and of a naturall defect, they infer a want of judgement or conscience. Some will say, he hath forgotten this entreaty or request, or that promise, he is not mindfull of his old friends, he never remembred to say, or doe, or conceale this or that, for my sake. Verily I may easily forget, but to neglect the charge my friend hath committed to my trust, I never do it. Let them beare with my infirmitie, and not conclude it to be a kind of malice; which is so contrarie an enemie to my humor. Yet am I somewhat comforted. First, because it is an evill, from which I have chieflie drawne the reason to correct a worse mischiefe, that would easily have growen upon me, that is to say, ambition; which defect is intolerable in them that meddle with worldly negotiations. For as divers like examples of natures progresse, say, she hath happily strengthned other faculties in me, according as it hath growne weaker and weaker in me, and I should easily lay downe and wire-draw my minde and judgement, upon other mens traces, without exercising their proper forces, if by the benefit of memorie, forren inventions and strange opinions were present with me. That my speech is thereby shorter: For the Magazin of Memorie is peradventure more stored with matter, than is the store-house of Invention. Had it held out with me, I had ere this wearied all my friends with pratling: the subjects rouzing the meane facultie I have to manage and imploy them, strengthning and wrestling my discourses. It is pitie; I have assayed by the trial of some of my private friends: according as their memory hath ministred them a whole and perfect matter, who recoile their narration so farre-backe, and stuff-it with so many vaine circumstances, that if the story bee good, they smoother the goodnesse of it: if bad, you must needs either curse the good fortune of their memorie, or blame the misfortune of their judgement. And it is no easie matter, being in the midst of the cariere of a discourse, to stop cunningly, to make a sudden period, and to cut it off. And there is nothing whereby the cleane strength of a horse is more knowne, than to make a readie and cleane stop. Among the skilfull I see some, that strive, but cannot stay their race. Whilest they labour to finde the point to stop their course, they stagger and falter, as men that faint through weaknesse. Above all, old men are dangerous, who have onely the memorie of things past left them, and have lost the remembrance of their repetitions. I have heard some very pleasant reports become most irkesome and tedious in the mouth of a certaine Lord, forsomuch as all the by-standers had many times beene cloyed with them. Secondly, (as said an ancient Writer) that, *I doe not so much remember injuries received.* I had need have a prompter as *Darius* had, who not to forget the wrong he had received of the Athenians, whensoever he sate downe at his table, caused a page to sing unto him, *Sir, remember the* Athenians, and that the places or bookes which I read-over, do ever smile upon me, with some new noveltie. It is not without reason, men say, *that he who hath not a good and readie memorie, should never meddle with telling of lies, and feare to become a liar.* I am not ignorant how the Grammarians make a difference betweene speaking untrue and lying; and say that to speake untruly, is to speake that which is false, but was reputed true; and that the definition of the Latin word, *mentiri,* whence the French word, *mentir,* is derived, which in English is to lie, implieth and meaneth to goe against ones conscience: and by consequence it concerneth onely those, who speake contrary to that which they know, of whom I speake. Now, these, either invent, seale, stampe and all, or else they disguise and change a true ground. When they disguise or change, if they be often put to the repetition of one thing, it is hard for them to keepe still in one path, and very strange if they lose not themselves: because the thing, as it is, having first taken up her stand in the memory, and there by the way of knowledge and witting, imprinted it-selfe, it were hard it should not represent it selfe to the imagination, displacing and supplanting falshood, which therein can have no such footing, or setled fastnesse: and that the circumstances of the first learning, still diving into the minde, should not cause it to disperse the remembrance of all false or bastardizing parts gotten together. Where they altogether invent, forsomuch as there is no [contrarie] impression, to front their falshood, they seeme to have so much the lesser feare to mistake or forget themselves, which also notwithstanding being an airie bodie, and without hold-fast, may easily escape the memorie, except it be well assured: whereof I have often (to my no small pleasure) seene the experience, at the cost of those, who professe never to frame their speech, but as best shall fit the affaires they negotiate, and as best shall please the great men they speake unto. For the circumstances to which they will subject their credit and conscience, being subject to many changes, their speech must likewise diversifie and change with them, whence it followeth that of one selfe-same subject they speak diversly, as now yellow, now gray, to one man thus, and thus to another. And if peradventure these kind of men hoard-up their so contrarie instructions, what becomes of this goodly art? Who besides, often most foolishly forget themselves, and run at random: For, what memorie shall suffice them, to remember so many different formes they have framed to one same subject? I have in my dayes seene divers that have envied the reputation of this worthy kind of wisedome, who perceive not, that if there be a reputation, there can be no effect. "Verily, lying is an ill and detestable vice. Nothing makes us men, and no other meanes keeps us bound one to another, but our word; knew we but the horror and waight of it, we would with fire and sword pursue and hate the same, and more justly than any other crime." I see all men generally busied (and that verie improperly) to punish certaine innocent errours in children, which have neither impression nor consequence, and chastice and vex them for rash and fond actions. Onely lying, and stubbornnesse somewhat more, are the faults whose birth and progresse I would have severely punished and cut off; for they grow and increase with them: and if the tongue have once gotten this ill habit, good Lord how hard, nay how impossible it is to make her leave it? whereby it ensueth, that we see many very honest men in other matters, to bee subject and enthralled to that fault. I have a good lad to my tailour, whom I never heard speak a truth; no not when it might stand him in stead of profit. If a lie had no more faces but one, as truth hath, we should be in farre better termes than we are: For, whatsoever a lyer should say, we would take it in a contrarie sense. But the opposite of truth hath many-many shapes, and an undefinite field. The Pythagoreans make good to be certaine and finite, and evill to bee infinite and uncertaine. A thousand by-wayes misse the marke, one onely hits the same. Surely I can never assure my selfe to come to a good end, to warrant an extreme and evident danger, by a shamelesse and solemne lie.

An ancient Father saith, *We are better in the companie of a knowne dogge, than in a mans societie, whose speech is unknowne to us. Ut externus alieno non sit hominis vice* (PLIN. *Nat. Hist.* vii. 1). *A stranger to a stranger is not like a man.* And how much is a false speech lesse sociable than silence? King *Francis* the first, vaunted himselfe to have by this meanes brought *Francis Taverna*, Ambassador to *Francis Sforza*, Duke of *Millane*, to a non-plus; a man very famous for his rare eloquence, and facilitie in speech, who had beene dispatched to excuse his master, toward his Majestie, of a matter of great importance, which was this. The King to keepe ever some intelligence in *Italy*, whence he had lately beene expelled, but especially in the Dukedome of *Millane*, thought it expedient to entertaine a Gentleman of his about the Duke, in effect as his Ambassador, but in appearance as a private man; who should make shew to reside there about his particular affaires, forsomuch as the Duke, who depended much more of the Emperour (chiefely then that he was treating a mariage with his niece, daughter of the King of *Denmarke,* who is at this day Dowager of *Loraine*) could not without great prejudice unto himselfe discover to have any correspondencie and conference with us. For which commission and purpose a Gentleman of *Millane,* named *Merveille,* then serving the King in place of one of the Quiers of his Quierie, was deemed fit. This man being dispatched with secret letters of credence, and instructions of an Ambassador, together with other letters of commendation to the Duke in favour of his particular affaires, as a maske and pretence of his proceedings, continued so long about the Duke, that the Emperour began to have some suspition of him; which as we suppose was cause of what ensued, which was, that under colour of a murther committed, the Duke one night caused the said *Merveille* to be beheaded, having ended his processe in two dayes. Master *Francis* being come to the Court, fraught with a long counterfet deduction of this storie (for the King had addressed himselfe to all the Princes of Christendome, yea and to the Duke himselfe for justice, for such an outrage committed upon his servant) had one morning audience in the Kings councell-chamber: who for the foundation of his cause having established and to that end projected many goodly and colourable apparences of the fact: namely, that the Duke his Master had never taken *Merveille* for other than a private gentleman, and his owne subject, and who was come thither about his private busines, where he had never lived under other name, protesting he had never knowne him to be one of the Kings houshold, nor never heard of him, much lesse taken him for his Majesties Agent. But the King urging him with divers objections and demands, and charging him on every side, prest him so farre with the execution done by night, and as it were by stealth, that the seely man, being much entangled and suddenly surprised, as if he would set an innocent face on the matter, answered, that for the love and respect of his Majestie, the Duke his Master would have beene very loth that such an execution should have beene done by day. Heere every man may guesse whether he were taken short or no, having tripped before so goodly a nose, as was that of our King *Francis* the first. Pope *Julius* the second, having sent an Ambassador to the King of *England* to animate him against our foresaid King: the Ambassador having had audience touching his charge, and the King in his answer urging and insisting upon the difficultie he found and foresaw in levying such convenient forces, as should be required to withstand so mightie, and set upon so puisant a King, and alleaging certaine pertinent reasons: The Ambassador fondly and unfitly replied, that himselfe had long before maturely considered them, and had told the Pope of them. By which answer so farre from his proposition (which was with all speed, and without more circumstances to undertake and undergoe a dangerous warre) the King of *England* tooke hold of the first argument which in effect he afterward found true, which was, that the said Ambassador, in his owne particular intent, was more affected to the French side, whereof advertising his Master, his goods were all confiscate, himselfe disgraced, and he very hardly escaped with life.

CHAPTER X

OF READIE OR SLOW SPEECH

Onc ne furent à tous toutes graces donnes.

All Gods good graces are not gone
To all, or of all any one.

So doe we see that in the gift of eloquence, some have such a facility and promptitude, and that which we call utterance, so easie and at command, that at all assaies, and upon everie occasion, they are ready and provided; and others more slow, never speake any thing except much laboured and premeditated. As Ladies and daintie Dames are taught rules to take recreations and bodily exercises, according to the advantage of what they have fairest about them. If I were to give the like counsel, in those two different advantages of eloquence wherof Preachers and pleading-lawiers of our age seeme to make profession; the slow speaker in mine opinion should be the better preacher, and the other the better lawier. Forsomuch as charge of the first allowes him as much leisure as he pleaseth to prepare himselfe; moreover his cariere continueth still in one kinde without interruption: whereas the Lawyers occasions urging him still upon any accident to be ready to enter the lists: and the unexpected replies and answers of his adverse partie, do often divert him from his purpose, wher he is enforced to take a new course. Yet is it, that at the last enterview which was at *Marseilles* betweene Pope *Clement* the seventh, and *Francis* the first, our King, it hapned cleane contrarie, where Monsieur *Poyet,* a man of chiefe reputation, and all dayes of his life brought up to plead at the bar, whose charge being to make an Oration before the Pope, and having long time before premeditated and con'd the same by roat, yea, and as some report, brought it with him ready penned from *Paris;* the very same day it should have beene pronounced; the Pope suspecting he might haply speake something, might offend the other Princes Ambassadors, that were about him, sent the argument, which he at that time & place thought fittest to be treated of, to the King, but by fortune cleane contrarie to that which *Poyet,* had so much studied for: So that his Oration was altogether frustrate, and he must presently frame another. But he perceiving himselfe unable for it, the Cardinall *Bellay* was faine to supply his place and take that charge upon him. The Lawyers charge is much harder than the Preachers: (yet in mine opinion) shall we find more passable Lawyers than commendable Preachers, at least in *France.* It seemeth to be more proper to the mind, to have her operation ready and sudden, and more incident to the judgement, to have it slow and considerate. But who remaineth mute, if he hath no leisure to prepare himselfe, and he likewise to whom leisure giveth no advantage to say better, are both in one selfe degree of strangenesse. It is reported that *Severus Cassius* spake better extempore, and without premeditation. That he was more beholding to fortune, than to his diligence; that to be interrupted in his speech redounded to his profit: and that his adversaries feared to urge him, lest his sudden anger should redouble his eloquence. I know this condition of nature by experience, which cannot abide a vehement and laborious premeditation: except it hold a free, a voluntarie, and selfe pleasing course, it can never come to a good end. We commonly say of some compositions, that they smell of the oile, and of the lampe, by reason of a certaine harshnesse, and rudenesse, which long plodding labour imprints in them that be much elaborated. But besides the care of well-doing, and the contention of the minde, overstretched to her enterprise, doth breake and impeach the same; even as it hapneth unto water, which being closely pent in, through it's own violence and abundance, can not finde issue at an open gullet. In this condition of nature, whereof I now speake, this also is joyned unto it, that it desireth not to be pricked forward by these strong passions, as the anger of *Cassius* (for that motion would be over-rude) it ought not to be violently shaken, but yeeldingly solicited: it desireth to be rouzed and prickt forward by strange occasions, both present and casuall. If it goe all alone, it doth but languish and loyter behinde: agitation is her life and grace. I cannot well containe my selfe in mine own possession and disposition, chance hath more interest in it than my selfe; occasion, company, yea the change of my voice, drawes more from my minde than I can finde therein, when by my selfe I [sound] and endevor to employ the same. My words likewise are better than my writings, if choice may be had in so worthlesse thing. This also hapneth unto me, that where I seeke my selfe, I finde not my selfe: and I finde my selfe more by chance, than by the search of mine owne judgment. I shall perhaps have cast foorth some suttletie in writing, haply dull and harsh for another, but smooth and curious for my selfe. Let us leave all these complements and quaintnesse. That is spoken by everie man, according to his owne strength. I have so lost it, that I wot not what I would have said, and strangers have sometimes found it before me. Had I alwayes a razor about me, where that hapneth, I should cleane raze my selfe out. Fortune may at some other time make the light thereof appeare brighter unto me, than that of mid-day, and will make mee wonder at mine owne faltring or sticking in the myre.

CHAPTER XI

OF PROGNOSTICATIONS

As touching Oracles it is very certaine, that long before the comming of our Saviour *Jesus Christ,* they had begun to lose their credit: for we see that *Cicero* laboureth to finde the cause of their declination: and these be his words: *Cur isto modo jam oracula Delphis non eduntur non modo nostra œtate, sed jamdiu, ut nihil possit esse contemptius?* (CIC. *Divin.* ii.). *Why in like sort are not Oracles now uttered, not onely in our times, but a good while since, so as now nothing can be more contemptible?* But as for other Prognostikes, that were drawne from the anatomie of beasts in sacrifice, to which *Plato* doth in some sort ascribe the naturall constitution of the internall members of them, of the scraping of chickens, of the flight of birds, *Aves quasdam rerum augurandarum causa natas esse putamus* (ID. *Nat Deor.*). *We are of opinion, certain birds were even bred to prognosticate some things; of thunders, of turnings and backe-recourse of rivers. Multa cernunt aruspices: multa augures provident: multa oraculis declarantur: multa vaticinationibus: multa somniis: multa portentis* (ID. *Ib.* ii.). *Soothsayers see much: bird-prophets foresee as much: much is foretold by Oracles; much by prophecies; much by portentuous signes,* and others, upon which antiquitie grounded most of their enterprises, as well publike as private: our religion hath abolished them. And albeit there remaine yet amongst us some meanes of divination in the starres, in spirits, in shapes of the body, in dreames, and elsewhere a notable example of the mad and fond curiositie of our nature, ammusing it selfe to preoccupate future things, as if it had not enough to doe to digest the present.

> *—cur hanc tibi rector Olympi*
> *Sollicitis visum mortalibus addere curam,*
> *Noscant venturas ut dira per omnia clades?*
> *Sit subitum quodcunque paras, sit cœca futuri*
> *Mens hominum fati, liceat sperare timenti.*—LUCAN. ii. 4.

Why pleas'd it thee, thou ruler of the spheares,
To adde this care to mortals care-clog'd minde,
That they their miserie know, ere it appeares?
Let thy drifts sudden come; let men be blinde
T'wards future fate: oh let him hope that feares.

Ne utile quidem est scire quid futurum sit: Miserum est enim nihil proficientem angi (CIC. *Nat. Deor.* iii.). *It is not so much as profitable for us, to know what is to come, for it is a miserable thing, a man should fret and be vexed, and do no good.* Yet is it of much lesse authoritie, loe here wherefore the example of *Francis Marquis* of *Saluzzo,* hath seemed remarkable unto me: who being Lieutenant General unto *Francis* our King, and over all his forces, which he then had beyond the Mountaines in *Italie*, a man highly favoured in al our court, and otherwise infinitly beholding to the King for that very Marquisate, which his brother had forfeited: and having no occasion to doe it, yea and his minde and affections contradicting the same, suffering himselfe to be frighted and deluded (as it hath since been manifestly prooved) by the fond prognostications, which then throughout all *Europe* were given out to the advantage of the Emperor *Charles* the fifth, and to our prejudice and disadvantage (but specially in *Italie*, where these foolish prædictions had so much possessed the Italians, that in *Rome* were laid great wagers, and much money given out upon the exchange, that we should utterly be overthrowne) that after he had much condoled, yea and complained with his secret friends, the unavoidable miseries which he foresaw prepared by the fates against the Crowne of *France*, and the many friends he had there, he unkindly revolted, and became a turn-cote on the Emperors side, to his intolerable losse and destruction, notwithstanding all the constellations then reigning. But was drawne unto it as a man encompassed and beset by divers passions; for having both strong castles, and all maner of munition and strength in his owne hands, the enemies armie under *Antonio Leva* about three paces from him, and we nothing mistrusting him, it was in his power to do worse than he did. For notwithstanding his treason, we lost neither man nor towne, except *Fossan*, which long after was by us stoutly contested and defended.

> *Prudens futuri temporis exitum*
> *Caliginosâ nocte premit Deus,*
> *Ridétque, si mortalis ultra*
> *Fas trepidat.*—Hor. *iii. Od.* xxix. 29.

Our wise God hides in pitch-darke night
Of future time th' event decreed,
And laughes at man, if man (affright)
Feare more than he to feare hath need.

> *Ille potens sui*
> *Lætusque deget, cui licet in diem*
> *Dixisse, vixi, cras vel atrâ*
> *Nube polum pater occupato,*
> *Vel sole puro.*—41.

He of himselfe lives merily,
Who each day, I have liv'd, can say,
Tomorrow let God charge the skie
With darke clouds, or faire sun-shine-ray.

> *Lætus in præsens animus, quod ultra est,*
> *Oderit curare.*—Ibid. ii. *Od.* xvi. 25.

For present time a mery mind
Hates to respect what is behind.

And those who take this word in a contrary sense are in the wrong. *Ista sic reciprocantur, ut et si divinatio sit, dii sint, et si dii sint, sit divinatio* (CIC. *Div.* i. p.). *This consequence is so reciprocall, as if there be any divination, there are Gods: and if there be Gods, there is divination.* Much more wisely *Pacuvius.*

Nam istis qui linguam avium intelligunt,
Plusque ex alieno jecore sapiunt, quàm ex suo,
Magis audiendum, quàm auscultandum censeo.—Ibid. f. Pas.

Who understand what language birds expresse,
By their owne, than beasts-livers knowing lesse,
They may be heard, not hearkned to, I guesse.

This so famous art of divination of the Tuskanes grew thus. A husband-man digging very deepe into the ground, with his plough-share, saw *Tages,* a demy-God appeare out of it, with an infantine face, yet fraught with an aged-like wisedome. All men ran to see him, and both his words and knowledge were for many ages after remembred, and collected, containing the principles and meanes of this art. An of-spring sutable to her progresse. I would rather direct affaires by the chance of dice, than by such frivolous dreames. And truly in all com-monwealths, men have ever ascribed much authoritie unto lot. *Plato* in the policie which he imagineth by discretion, ascribeth the deciding of many important effects unto it, and amongst other things would have marriages betweene the good to bee contrived by lot. And giveth so large privileges unto this casuall election, that he appoints the chil-dren proceeding from them to bee brought up in the countrie; and those borne of the bad to be banished and sent abroad. Notwithstand-ing if any of those so exiled shall by fortune happen, whilest he is growing, to show some good hope of him-selfe, that he may be re-voked and sent-for backe, and such amongst the first as shall in their youth give small hope of future good to be banished. I see some that studie, plod, and glosse their Almanackes, and in all accidents alleage their authoritie. A man were as good to say, they must needs speake truth and lies. *Quis est enim qui totum diem jaculans, non aliquando conlineet?* (CIC. *Div.* ii.). *For who is he that shooting all day, some-times hits not the white?* I thinke not the better of them, though what they say proove sometimes true. It were more certaine, if there were either a rule or a truth to lie over. Seeing no man recordeth their fables, because they are ordinarie and infinit; and their predictions are made to be of credit, because they are rare, incredible and prodigious. So answered *Diagoras* surnamed the Atheist (being in *Samothrace*) to him, who in shewing him divers vowes and offrings hanging in the Temple, brought thither by such as had escaped shipwracke, said thus

unto him: *You that thinke the Gods to have no care of humane things,*
what say you by so many men saved by their grace and helpe? Thus
is it done, answered he: *Those which were drowned farre exceeding*
their number, are not here set-forth. Cicero saith, *That amongst all*
other Philosophers that have avowed and acknowledged the Gods, onely
Xenophanes the Colophonian hath gone about to root out all maner of
divination. It is so much the lesse to be wondered at, if at any time
we have seene some of our Princes mindes to their great damage, relie
upon such like vanities. I would to *God,* I had with mine owne eyes
seene those two wonders, mentioned in the booke of *Joachin* the Abbat
of *Calabria,* who foretold all the Popes that should ensue, together
with their names and shapes: And that of *Leo* the Emperor, who fore-
spake all the Emperors and Patriarkes of *Greece.* This have I seene
with mine owne eyes, that in publike confusions, men amazed at their
owne fortune, give themselves head-long, as it were to all maner of
superstition, to search in heaven the causes and ancient threats of
their ill-lucke; and in my time are so strangely successfull therein, as
they have perswaded me, that it is an ammusing of sharpe and idle
wits, that such as are inured to this subtletie, by folding and unfolding
them, may in all other writings be capable to finde out what they
seeke-after. But above all, their dark, ambiguous, fantasticall, and
propheticall gibrish, mends the matter much, to which their authors
never give a plaine sense, that posterity may apply what meaning and
construction it shall please unto it. The *Dæmon* of *Socrates* was peradventure a certaine impulsion [of] will, which without the advice of
his discourse presented it selfe unto him. In a mind so well purified,
and by continuall exercise of wisedome and vertue so wel prepared, as
his was, it is likely, his inclinations (though rash and inconsiderate)
were ever of great moment, and worthie to be followed. Every man
feeleth in himselfe some image of such agitations, of a prompt, vehement and casuall opinion. It is in me to give them some authoritie, that
affoord so little to our wisedome. And I have had some, equally weake
in reason, and violent in perswasion and disswasion (which was more
ordinarie to *Socrates*) by which I have so happily and so profitably
suffered my selfe to be transported, as they might perhaps be thought
to containe some matter of divine inspiration.

CHAPTER XII

OF CONSTANCIE

THE law of resolution and constancie implieth not, we should not,
as much as lieth in our power shelter our selves from the mischiefes
and inconveniences that threaten us, nor by consequence feare, they
should surprise us. Contrariwise, all honest meanes for a man to war-

rant himselfe from evils are not onely tolerable, but commendable. And the part of constancie is chiefly acted, in firmely bearing the inconveniences, against which no remedie is to be found. So that, there is no nimblenesse of bodie, nor wealding of hand-weapons, that we will reject, if it may in any sort defend us from the blow, meant at us. Many most warlike nations in their conflicts and fights, used retreating and flight as a principall advantage, and shewed their backs to their enemie much more dangerously than their faces. The Turkes at this day retaine something of that humour. And *Socrates* in *Plato* doth mocke at *Laches*, because he had defined fortitude, to keepe herselfe steadie in her rancke against her enemies; *What*, saith hee, *were it then cowardise to beat them in giving them place?* And alleageth *Homer* against him, who commendeth in *Æneas* his skill in flying and giving ground. And because *Laches* being better advised, avoweth that custome to be amongst the Scithians, and generally amongst all horsemen, he alleageth further unto him the example of the Lacedemonian footmen (a nation above all other used to fight on foot) who in the battell of *Plateæ*, unable to open and to put to rowt the Persian Phalanx, advised themselves to scatter and put themselves backe, that so by the opinion of their flight, they might if they should pursue them, rush in upon them, and put that so combined-masse to rout. By which meanes they gained the victorie. Touching the Scithians, it is reported, that when *Darius* went to subdue them, he sent their King many reprochfull speeches, for so much as hee ever saw him retire and give ground before him, and to avoid the maine battell. To whom *Indathirsez* (for so was his name) answered, that, *They did it not for feare of him, nor any other man living, but that it was the fashion of his nation to march thus: as having neither cities, nor houses, nor manured land to defend, or to feare their enemies should reape any commoditie by them.* But if hee had so great a desire to feed on them, he might draw neerer to view the place of their ancient Sepulchers, and there hee should meet with whom to speake his belly-full. Notwithstanding when a man is once within reach of cannon-shot, and as it were point-blancke before them, as the fortune of warre doth diverse times bring men unto, it ill beseemeth a resolute minde to start-aside, or be daunted at the threat of a shot, because by the violence and suddennesse thereof wee deeme it inevitable: and there are some, who by lifting up of a hand, or stooping their head, have sometimes given their fellowes cause of laughter: yet have we seene, that in the voyage, the Emperour *Charles* the fifth made against us in *Provence*, the Marquis of *Guasto*, being gone out to survey the citie of *Arles*, and shewne himselfe out of a winde-mill, under colour of which he was come somewhat neere the Towne, he was discovered by the Lord of *Bonevall*, and the Seneshall of *Agenois*, who were walking upon the Theatre *Aux arenes* (so called in French because it is full of sand) who shewing him to the Lord of *Villiers*, Commissairie of the Artillerie, hee mounted a culverin so levell, that had not the Marquis perceived the fire, and so started aside, it was constantly affirmed, hee had beene shot through the body. Likewise not many yeeres before, *Lorence* of *Medicis,* Duke of *Urbin,* and father to the Queene-mother of *France,* besieging *Mondolphe,* a place in *Italie,* in the province name *Vicariate,* seeing fire given to a piece that stood upright upon him, stooped his head, and well befell him that he plaide the ducke, for otherwise the bullet, which went right over, and within a little of his head, had doubtlesse shot him through the paunch. But to say truth, I will never thinke these motions were made with discourse, for what judgement can you give of an aime, either high or low in a matter so sudden? It may rather be thought that fortune favoured their feare: and which an other time might as well bee a meane to make them fall into the cannons-mouth, as to avoid the same. I cannot chuse, if the cracke of a musket doe suddenly streeke mine eares, in a place where I least looke for it, but I must needs start at-it: which I have seene happen to men of better sort than my selfe. Nor doe the Stoickes meane, that the Soule of their wisest man in any sort resist the first visions and sudden fantasies, that surprise the same: but rather consent that, as it were unto a naturall subjection, he yeelds and shrinks unto the loud clattering and roare of heaven, or of some violent downefall; for example-sake, unto palenesse, and contraction. So likewise in other passions, alwayes provided, his opinion remaines safe and whole, and the situation of his reason, admit no tainting or alteration whatsoever: and hee no whit consent to his fright and sufferance. Touching the first part; the same hapneth to him, that is not wise, but farre otherwise concerning the second. For the impression of passions doth not remaine superficiall in him: but rather penetrates even into the secret of reason, infecting and corrupting the same. He judgeth according to them, and conformeth himselfe to them. Consider precisely the state of the wise Stoicke:

> *Mens immota manet, lachrymæ volvuntur inanes.*
> VIRG. *Æn.* iv. 449.

His minde doth firme remaine,
Teares are distill'd in vaine.

The wise Peripatetike doth not exempt himselfe from perturbations of the mind, but doth moderate them.

CHAPTER XIII

OF CEREMONIES IN THE ENTERVIEW OF KINGS

THERE is no subject so vaine, that deserveth not a place in this rapsodie. It were a notable discourtesie unto our common rules, both

towards an equall, but more toward a great person, not to meete with
you in your house, if he have once warned you that he will come: And
Margaret Queene of *Navarre,* was wont to say to this purpose, *That it
was a kinde of incivilitie in a gentleman, to depart from his house, as
the fashion is, to meet with him that is comming to him, how worthy
soever he be: and that it more agreeth with civilitie and respect, to stay
for him at home, and there to entertaine him: except it were for feare
the stranger should misse his way: and that it sufficeth to companie
and wait upon him, when he is going away againe.* As for me, I oftentimes forget both these vaine offices; as one that endevoureth to abolish all maner of ceremonies in my house. Some will be offended at it,
what can I doe withall? I had rather offend a stranger once, than my-
self everie day; for it were a continuall subjection. To what end doe
men avoid the servitude of Courts, and entertaine the same in their
owne houses? Moreover it is a common rule in all assemblies, that
hee who is the meaner man, commeth first to the place appointed,
forsomuch as it belongs to the better man to be staid-for, and waited
upon by the other. Neverthelesse we saw that at the enterview, prepared at *Merceilles* betweene Pope *Clement* the seventh, and *Francis*
the first, King of *France,* the King having appointed all necessarie
preparations, went him-selfe out of the Towne, and gave the Pope two
or three dayes leasure, to make his entrie into it, and to refresh himselfe, before he would come to meet him there. Likewise at the meeting
of the said Pope with the Emperour at *Bologna,* the Emperour gave
the Pope advantage and leasure to be first there, and afterward came
himselfe. It is (say they) an ordinarie ceremonie at enterparlies betweene such Princes, that the better man should ever come first to
the place appointed; yea before him in whose countrey the assembly is:
and they take it in this sence, that is, because this complement should
testifie, he is the better man, whom the meaner goeth to seeke, and
that hee sueth unto him. Not onely each countrey, but every Citie, yea
and every vocation hath his owne particular decorum. I have very
carefully beene brought up in mine infancie, and have lived in verie
good company, because I would not bee ignorant of the good maners
of our countrey of *France,* and I am perswaded I might keepe a schoole
of them. I love to follow them, but not so cowardly, as my life remaine
thereby in subjection. They have some painfull formes in them, which
if a man forget by discretion, and not by errour, hee shall no whit bee
disgraced. I have often seene men proove unmanerly by too much
maners, and importunate by over-much courtesie. The knowledge of
entertainment is otherwise a profitable knowledge. It is, as grace and
beautie are, the reconciler of the first accoastings of society and familiarity: and by consequence, it openeth the entrance to instruct us by
the example of others, and to exploit and produce our example, if it
have any instructing or communicable thing in it.

CHAPTER XIV

MEN ARE PUNISHED BY TOO-MUCH OPINIATING THEMSELVES IN A PLACE WITHOUT REASON

VALOUR hath his limits, as other vertues have: which if a man out-go, hee shall find himselfe in the traine of vice: in such sort, that unlesse a man know their right bounds, which in truth are not on a sudden, easily hit upon, he may fall into rashnesse, obstinacie, and folly. For this consideration grew the custome wee hold in warres, to punish, and that with death, those who wilfully opiniate themselves to defend a place, which by the rules of warre, cannot be kept. Otherwise upon hope of impunitie, there should bee no cottage, that might not entertaine an Armie. The Lord Constable *Momorancie* at the siege of *Pavia*, having beene appointed to passe over the river *Tesine*, and to quarter himselfe in the suburbs of Saint *Antonie*, being impeached by a tower, that stood at the end of the bridge, and which obstinately would needs hold out, yea and to be battered, caused all those that were with-in it, to be hanged. The same man afterward, accompanying my Lord the *Dolphin* of *France* in his journey beyond the *Alpes*, having by force taken the Castle of *Villane*, and all those that were within the same, having by the furie of the Souldiers bin put to the sword, except the Captaine, and his Ancient, for the same reason, caused them both to be hanged and strangled: As did also, Captaine *Martin du Bellay*, the Governour of *Turin*, in the same countrey, the Captaine of Saint *Bony*: all the rest of his men having beene massacred at the taking of the place. But for somuch as the judgement of the strength or weaknesse of the place, is taken by the estimate and counterpoise of the forces that assaile it (for som man might justly opiniate himselfe against two culverins, that wold play the madman to expect thirtie cannons) where also the greatnesse of the Prince conquering must be considered, his reputation, and the respect that is due unto him: there is danger a man should somewhat bend the ballance on that side. By which termes it hapneth, that some have so great an opinion of themselves, and their meanes, and deeming it unreasonable, any thing should be worthie to make head against them, that so long as their fortune continueth, they overpasse what hill or difficultie soever they finde to withstand or resist them: As is seene by the formes of sommonings and challenges, that the Princes of the East, and their successors yet remaining have in use, so fierce, so haughtie, and so full of a barbarous kinde of commandement. And in those places where the Portugales abated the pride of the Indians, they found some states observing this universall and inviolable law, that what enemie soever he be, that is overcome by the King in person, or by his Lieutenant, is exempted from all composition of ransome or mercie. So above all, a man who is able should take heed, lest he fall into the hands of an enemie-judge, that is victorious and armed.

CHAPTER XV

OF THE PUNISHMENT OF COWARDISE

I HAVE heretofore heard a Prince, who was a very great Captaine, hold opinion, that a souldier might not for cowardise of heart be condemned to death: who sitting at his table heard report of the Lord of *Vervins* sentence, who for yeelding up of *Bollein,* was doomed to lose his head. Verily there is reason a man should make a difference between faults proceeding from our weaknesse, and those that grow from our malice. For in the latter we are directly bandied against the rules of reason, which nature hath imprinted in us; and in the former it seemeth, we may call the same nature, as a warrant, because it hath left us in such imperfection and defect. So as divers nations have judged, that no man should blame us for any thing we doe against our conscience. And the opinion of those which condemne heretikes and miscreants unto capitall punishments, is partly grounded upon this rule: and the same which establisheth, that a Judge or an advocate may not bee called to account for any matter committed in their charge through oversight or ignorance. But touching cowardise, it is certain, the common fashion is, to punish the same with ignominie and shame. And some hold that this rule was first put in practice by the Law-giver *Charondas,* and that before him the lawes of *Greece* were wont to punish those with death, who for feare did run away from a Battell: where hee onely ordained, that for three dayes together, clad in womens attire, they should be made to sit in the market-place: hoping yet to have some service at their hands, and by meanes of this reproch, they might recover their courage againe. *Suffundere malis hominis sanguinem quám effundere: Rather move a mans bloud to blush in his face, than remove it by bleeding from his body.*

It appeareth also that the Roman lawes did in former times punish such as had run away, by death. For *Ammianus Marcellinus* reporteth, that *Julian* the Emperor condemned ten of his Souldiers, who in a charge against the *Parthians,* had but turned their backs from it; first to be degraded, and then to suffer death, as he saith, according to the ancient lawes, who neverthelesse, condemneth others for a like fault, under the ensigne of bag and baggage, to be kept amongst the common prisoners. The sharp punishment of the Romans against those Souldiers that escaped from *Cannæ:* and in the same warre against those that accompanied *Cn. Fulvius* in his defeat, reached

not unto death, yet may a man feare, such open shame may make
them despaire, and not only prove faint and cold friends, but cruell
and sharpe enemies. In the time of our forefathers, the Lord of
Franget, Whilom Lieutenant of the Marshall of *Chastillions* company, having by the Marshall of *Chabanes* beene placed Governor
of *Fontarabie,* in stead of the Earle of *Lude,* and having yeelded the
same unto the Spaniards, was condemned to be degraded of all Nobilitie, and not onely himselfe, but all his succeeding posteritie declared
villains and clownes, taxable and incapable to beare armes; which
severe sentence was put in execution at *Lyons.* The like punishment
did afterward all the Gentlemen suffer, that were within *Guise,* when
the Earle of *Nansaw* entred the towne: and others since. Neverthelesse if there were so grosse an ignorance, and so apparant cowardize,
as that it should exceed all ordinary, it were reason it should be taken
for a sufficient proofe of inexcusable treacherie, and knavrie, and for
such to be punished.

CHAPTER XVI

A TRICKE OF CERTAINE AMBASSADORS

In all my travels I did ever observe this custome, that is, alwaies
to learne something by the communication of others (which is one
of the best schooles that may be) to reduce those I confer withall,
to speake of that wherein they are most conversant and skilfull.

> *Basti al nochiero ragionar de' venti,*
> *Albifolco de' tori, e le sue piaghe*
> *Conti il guerrier, conti il pastor gl' armenti.*
>
> > Idem PROPERT. ii. *El.* i. 43.

Sailers of windes plow-men of beasts take keepe,
Let Souldiers count their wounds, shepherds their sheepe.

For commonly we see the contrary, that many chuse rather to
discourse of any other trade than their owne; supposing it to be so
much new reputation gotten: witnes the quip *Archidamus* gave *Peri-
ander,* saying that he forsooke the credit of a good Physitian, to
become a paltry Poet. Note but how *Cæsar* displaieth his invention
at large, when he would have us conceive his inventions how to build
bridges, and devices, how to frame other war-like engins; and in
respect of that how close and succinct he writes, when he speaketh
of the offices belonging to his profession, of his valour, and of the
conduct of his war-fare. His exploits prove him a most excellent
Captaine, but he would be known for a skilfull Ingenier, a quality
somewhat strange in him. *Dionysius* the elder was a very great chieftaine and Leader in warre, as a thing best fitting his fortune: but he

greatly laboured by meanes of Poetry, to assume high commendation unto himselfe, howbeit he had but little skill in it. A certaine Lawier was not long since brought to see a study, stored with all manner of bookes, both of his owne, and of all other faculties, wherein he found no occasion to entertaine himselfe withall, but like a fond cunning clarke earnestly busied himselfe to glosse and censure a fence or barricado, placed over the screw of the study, which a hundred Captaines and Souldiers see everie day, without observing or taking offence at them.

Optat ephippia bos piger, optat arare caballus.
Hor. i. *Epist.* xiv. 43.

The Oxe would trappings weare,
The Horse, ploughs-yoake would beare.

By this course you never come to perfection, or bring any thing to good passe. Thus must a man endevour to induce the Architect, the Painter, the Shoomaker to speake of their owne trade, and so of the rest, every man in his vocation. And to this purpose am I wont, in reading of histories (which is the subject of most men) to consider who are the writers: If they be such as professe nothing but bare learning, the chiefe thing I learne in them, is their stile and language: If Physitians, I beleeve them in whatsoever they shall report concerning the temperatenesse of the aire, the health and complexion of Princes, or of hurts and infirmities: If Lawiers, we should observe the controversies of rights, titles, and pretenses of lawes and customes, the establishments of policies, and such like things: If Divines, we may note the affaires of the Church, the Ecclesiasticall censures, dispensations, cases of conscience, and marriages: If Courtiers, manners, complements, ceremonies, and entertainments: If Warriors, what belongs unto their charge, but chiefly the managing and conduct of the atchievements or exploits wherein they have been themselves in person: If Ambassadors, the negotiations, intelligences, practices, policies, and manner how to direct, complot, and conduct them. And therefore what in another Writer I should peradventure have cursorie passed over, I have with some advisednesse considered and marked the same in the historie of the Lord of *Langey,* a man most expert and intelligent in such matters: which is, that after he had exactly set downe and declared those glorious, and farre-fecht remonstrances of the Emperor *Charles* the fifth made in the consistorie of *Rome,* in the presence of the Bishop of *Mascon,* and the Lord of *Velly,* our Ambassadors; wherein he entermixed many bitter and outrageous words against us; and amongst others, that if his Captaines and Souldiers were not of much more faithfulnesse and sufficiencie in the art of warre than our Kings, he would forthwith tie a rope about his necke, and goe aske him mercy: whereof he seemed to beleeve something: for afterward whilest he lived, he chanced twice or thrice to utter the verie same words. Moreover, that he had challenged the King to fight with him, man to man in his shirt, with Rapier and Dagger in a boat. The said Lord of *Langey,* following his storie, addeth that the said Ambassadors making a dispatch of what had passed unto the king, dissembled the chiefest part unto him, yea and concealed the two precedent articles from him. Now me thought it very strange, that it should lie in the power of an Ambassador to dispence with any point, concerning the advertizements he should give unto his Master, namely of such consequence, coming from such a person, and spoken in so great an assembly, whereas me seemed it should have beene the office of a trustie servant, truly and exactly to set downe things as they were, and in what manner they had succeeded: to the end the libertie of disposing, judging and chusing, might wholly lie in the master. For to alter and conceale the truth from him, for feare he should conster and take it otherwise than he ought, and lest that might provoke him to some bad resolution; and in the meane while to suffer him to be ignorant of his owne affaires, mee thought should rather have appertained to him that giveth the law, than to him that receiveth the same; to the Master or over-seer of the schoole, and not to him who should thinke himself inferior, as well in authority, as in wisdome and good counsell. Howsoever it were, I would be loth be so used in mine owne small and particular businesse, we doe so willingly upon every slight occasion and pretence neglect and forgoe commandement, and are so farre from obeying, that we rather usurp a kinde of masterie, and free power: every man doth so naturally aspire unto liberty and authoritie, that no profit ought to be so deare unto a superiour, proceeding from those that serve him as their simple and naturall obedience. Whosoever obeyeth by discretion, and not by subjection, corrupteth and abuseth the office of commanding. And *P. Crassus* he whom the Romans deemed five times happy, when he was Consull in *Asia,* having sent a Græcian Inginer, to bring the greatest of two ship-masts before him, which he had seene in *Athens,* therewith to frame an engine of batterie: This man under colour of his skill, presumed to doe otherwise than he was bidden, and brought the lesser of the two masts which according to his arts reason hee deemed the fittest. *Crassus* having patiently heard his reasons and allegations, caused him to be well whipped; preferring the interest of true discipline, before that of the worke. On the other side a man might also consider, that this so strict obedience belongs but to precise and prefixed commandements. Ambassadors have a more scopefull and free charge, which in many points dependeth chiefly of their disposition. They doe not meerely execute, but frame and direct by their owne advice and counsell, the will of their Master. I have in my dayes seene some persons of commandement, checked and found fault withall, because they had rather obeyed the literall sense, and bare words of the Kings letters, than the occasions of the affaires they had in hand. Men of understanding and experience doe yet at this day condemne the custome of the Kings of *Persia*, which was to mince the instructions given to their Agents, and Lieutenants so small, that in the least accident they might have recourse to their directions and ordinances: This delay, in so farre reaching a scope of domination, having often brought great prejudice, and notable dammage unto their affaires. And *Crassus* writing unto a man of that profession, and advertizing him of the use whereto he purposed the foresaid mast; seemeth he not to enter into conference with him concerning his determination, and wish him to interpose his censure or advice of it.

CHAPTER XVII

OF FEARE

Obstupui, steteruntque comæ, et vox faucibus hæsit.
                                                    Virg. *Æn.* ii. 774.

I stood agast, my haire on end,
My jaw-tide tongue no speech would lend.

I AM no good Naturalist (as they say) and I know not well by what springs feare doth worke in us: but well I wot it is a strange passion: and as Physitians say, there is none doth sooner transport our judgement out of his due seat. Verily I have seene divers become mad and senselesse for feare: yea and in him, who is most settled and best resolved, it is certaine that whilest his fit continueth, it begetteth many strange dazelings, and terrible amazements in him. I omit to speake of the vulgar sort, to whom it sometimes representeth strange apparitions, as their fathers and grandfathers ghosts, risen out of their graves, and in their winding sheets: and to others it sometimes sheweth Larves, Hobgoblins, Robbin-good-fellowes, and such other Bug-beares and *Chimeraes*. But even amongst Souldiers, with whom it ought to have no credit at all, how often hath she changed a flocke of sheep into a troupe of armed men? Bushes and shrubs into men-at-armes and Lanciers? our friends into our enemies? and a red crosse into a white? At what time the Duke of *Bourbon* tooke *Rome*, an Ancient that kept sentinell, in the borough Saint *Peter*, was at the first alarum surprised with such terror, that with his colours in his hand, he suddenly threw himselfe thorow the hole of a breach out of the Citie, and fell just in the midst of his enemies, supposing the way to goe straight in the heart of the Citie: but in the end he no sooner perceived the Duke of *Bourbons* troupes, advancing to withstand him, imagining it to bee some sallie the Citizens made that way, hee better bethinking himselfe, turned head, and the very same way, he came out, he went into the towne againe, which was more than three hundred paces distance towards the fields. The like happened, but not so successfully unto Captaine *Julius* his ensigne-bearer at what time Saint *Paul* was taken from us by the Earle of *Bures*, and the Lord of *Reu*, who was so frighted with feare, that going about to cast himselfe over the towne wals, with his Ancient in his hand, or to creepe thorow a spike-hole, he was cut in peeces by the assailants. At which siege likewise, that horror and feare is very memorable, which so did choake, seize upon, and freeze the heart of a gentleman, that having received no hurt at all, he fell downe starke dead upon the ground before the breach. The like passion [or] rage doth sometimes possesse a whole multitude. In one of the encounters that *Germanicus* had with the Germanes, two mightie troupes were at one instant so frighted with feare, that both betooke themselves to their heeles, and ran away two contrary wayes, the one right to that place whence the other fled. It sometimes addeth wings unto our heeles, as unto the first named, and other times it takes the use of feet from us: as we may reade of *Theophilus* the Emperor, who in a battell hee lost against the Agarens, was so amazed and astonied, that he could not resolve to scape away by flight: *adeò pavor etiam auxilia formidat: Feare is so afraid even of that should help.* Untill such time as *Manuel*, one of the chiefe leaders in his armie, having rouzed and shaken him, as it were out of a dead sleepe, said unto him, *Sir, if you will not presently follow me, I will surely kill you, for better were it you should lose your life, than being taken prisoner, lose your Empire and all.* Then doth she shew the utmost of her power, when for her owne service, she casts us off unto valour, which it hath exacted from our duty and honour. In the first set battell, the Romans lost against *Hanibal*, under the Consul *Sempronius*, a troupe of wel-nigh ten thousand footmen, was so surprised with feare, that seeing no other way to take, nor by what other course to give their basenes free passage, they headlong bent their flight toward the thickest and strongest squadron of their enemies, which with such furie it rowted and brake through, as it disranked, and slew a great number of the Carthaginians: purchasing a reproachfull and disgracefull flight, at the same rate it might have gained a most glorious victorie. It is feare I stand most in feare of. For, in sharpnesse it surmounteth all other accidents. What affection can be more violent and just than that of *Pompeyes* friends, who in his owne ship were spectators of that horrible massacre? yet is it, that the feare of the Ægyptian sailes, which began to approach them, did in such sort daunt and skare them, that some have noted, they only busied themselves to hasten the mariners, to make what speed they could, and by maine strength of oares to save themselves, untill such time, as being arrived at *Tyre*, and that they were free from feare, they had leasure to bethinke themselves of their late losse, and give their plaints and teares free passage, which this other stronger passion had suspended and hindred.

Tum pavor sapientiam omnem mihi ex animo expectorat.
1 CIC. *Tusc. Qu.* iv. ex Enn.; *De Orat.* iii.

Feare then unbreasts all wit,
That in my minde did sit.

Those who in any skirmish or sudden bickering of warre have been throughly skared, sore-hurt, wounded, and gored as they be, are many times the next day after, brought to charge againe. But such as have conceived a true feare of their enemies, it is hard for you to make them looke them in the face againe. Such as are in continuall feare to lose their goods, to be banished, or to be subdued, live in uncessant agonie and languor; and thereby often lose both their drinking, their eating, and their rest. Whereas the poore, the banished, and seely servants, live often as carelesly and as pleasantly as the other. And so many men, who by the impatience and urging of feare, have hanged, drowned, and headlong tumbled downe from some rocke, have plainly taught us, that feare is more importunate and intolerable than death. The Græcians acknowledge another kinde of it, which is beyond the error of our discourse: proceeding, as they say, without any apparent cause, and from an heavenly impulsion. Whole Nations and Armies are often seene surprised with it. Such was that, which brought so wonderfull a desolation to *Carthage,* where nothing was heard but lamentable outcries, and frightfull exclamations: the inhabitants were seene desperately to runne out of their houses, as to a sudden alarum, and furiously to charge, hurt, and enter-kill one another, as if they had beene enemies come to usurpe and possesse their Citie. All things were there in a disordered confusion, and in a confused furie, untill such time as by praiers and sacrifices they had appeased the wrath of their Gods. They call it to this day, the Panike terror (ERAS. *Chil.* ii. cent. x. ad. 19; *Chil.* iii. cet. vii. ad. 3).

CHAPTER XVIII

THAT WE SHOULD NOT JUDGE OF OUR HAPPINESSE, UNTILL AFTER OUR DEATH

—scilicet ultima semper
Expectanda dies homini est, dicique beatus
Ante obitum nemo, supremaque funera debet.
OVID. *Met.* iii. 135.

We must expect of man the latest day,
Nor er'e he die, he's happie, can we say.

THE very children are acquainted with the storie of *Crœsus* to this purpose: who being taken by *Cyrus*, and by him condemned to die, upon the point of his execution, cried out aloud: Oh *Solon, Solon!* which words of his, being reported to *Cyrus*, who inquiring what he meant by them, told him, hee now at his owne cost verified the advertisement *Solon* had before times given him: which was, "that no man, what cheerefull and blandishing countenance soever fortune shewed them, may rightly deeme himselfe happie, till such time as he have passed the last day of his life, by reason of the uncertaintie and vicissitude of humane things, which by a very light motive, and slight occasion, are often changed from one to another cleane contrary state and degree." And therefore *Agesilaus* answered one that counted the King of *Persia* happy, because being very young, he had gotten the garland of so mightie and great a dominion: yea but said he, *Priam* at the same age was not unhappy. Of the Kings of *Macedon,* that succeeded *Alexander* the great, some were afterward seene to become Joyners and Scriveners at *Rome:* and of Tyrants of *Sicilie,* Schoolemasters at *Corinth:* One that had conquered halfe the world, and been Emperour over so many Armies, became an humble, and miserable suter to the raskally officers of a king of *Ægypt:* At so high a rate did that great *Pompey* purchase the irkesome prolonging of his life but for five or six moneths. And in our fathers daies, *Lodowicke Sforze,* tenth Duke of *Millane,* under whom the state of *Italie* had so long beene turmoiled and shaken, was seene to die a wretched prisoner at *Loches* in *France,* but not till he had lived and lingered ten years in thraldome, which was the worst of his bargaine. The fairest Queene, wife to the greatest King of Christendome, was she not lately seene to die by the hands of an executioner? Oh unworthie and barbarous crueltie! And a thousand such examples. For, it seemeth that as the sea-billowes and surging waves, rage and storme against the surly pride and stubborne height of our buildings; So are there above, certaine spirits that envie the rising prosperities and greatnesse heere below.

> *Usque adeò res humanas res abdita quædam*
> *Obterit, et pulchros fasces sœvásque secures*
> *Proculcare, ac ludibrio sibi habere videtur.*—LUCR. V. 1243.

A hidden power so mens states hath out-worne
Faire swords, fierce scepters, signes of honours borne,
It seemes to trample and deride in scorne.

And it seemeth Fortune doth sometimes narrowly watch the last day of our life, thereby to shew her power, and in one moment to overthrow what for many yeares together she had beene erecting, and makes us crie after *Laberius, Nimirum hac die una plus vixi, mihi quam vivendum fuit.* Thus it is, *I have lived longer by this one day, than I should.* So may that good advice of *Solon* be taken with reason.

But forsomuch as hee is a Philosopher, with whom the favours or dis-
favours of fortune, and good or ill lucke have no place, and are not
regarded by him; and puissances and greatnesses, and accidents of
qualitie, are well nigh indifferent: I deeme it very likely he had a
further reach, and meant that the same good fortune of our life, which
dependeth of the tranquillitie and contentment of a welborne minde,
and of the resolution and assurance of a well ordered soule, should
never be ascribed unto man, untill he have beene seene play the last
act of his comedie, and without doubt the hardest. In all the rest there
may be some maske: either these sophisticall discourses of Philosophie
are not in us but by countenance, or accidents that never touch us to
the quick, give us alwaies leasure to keep our countenance setled. But
when that last part of death, and of our selves comes to be acted, then
no dissembling will availe, then is it high time to speake plaine English,
and put off all vizards: then whatsoever the pot containeth must be
shewne, be it good or bad, foule or cleane, wine or water.

Nam veræ voces tum demum pectore ab imo
Eiicuntur, et eripitur persona, manet res.—LUCR. iii. 57.

For then are sent true speeches from the heart,
We are our selves, we leave to play a part.

Loe heere, why at this last cast, all our lives other actions must be
tride and touched. It is the master-day, the day that judgeth all others:
it is the day, saith an auncient Writer, that must judge of all my fore-
passed yeares. To death doe I referre the essay of my studies fruit.
There shall wee see whether my discourse proceed from my heart, or
from my mouth. I have seene divers, by their death, either in good or
evill, give reputation to all their forepassed life. *Scipio*, father in law
to *Pompey*, in well dying, repaired the ill opinion which untill that
houre men had ever held of him. *Epaminondas* being demanded, which
of the three he esteemed most, either *Chabrias*, or *Iphicrates*, or himselfe; *It is necessary*, said he, *that we be seene to die, before your*
question may well be resolved. Verily we should steale much from
him, if he should be weighed without the honour and greatnesse of his
end. God hath willed it, as he pleased: but in my time three of
the most execrable persons, that ever I knew in all abomination of
life, and the most infamous, have beene seen to die very orderly and
quietly, and in every circumstance composed even unto perfection.
There are some brave and fortunate deaths. I have seene her cut the
twine of some mans life, with a progresse of wonderful advancement,
and with so worthie an end, even in the flowre of his growth, and
spring of his youth, that in mine opinion, his ambitious and haughtie
couragious designes, thought nothing so high, as might interrupt them:
who without going to the place where he pretended, arived there more
gloriously and worthily, than either his desire or hope aimed at. And

by his fall fore-went the power and name, whither by his course he aspired. When I judge of other mens lives, I ever respect, how they have behaved themselves in their end; and my chiefest study is, I may well demeane my selfe at my last gaspe, that is to say, quietly, and constantly.

CHAPTER XIX

THAT TO PHILOSOPHIE, IS TO LEARNE HOW TO DIE

Cicero saith, that to *Philosophie is no other thing, than for a man to prepare himselfe to death:* which is the reason, that studie and contemplation doth in some sort withdraw our soule from us, and severally employ it from the body, which is a kind of apprentisage and resemblance of death; or else it is, that all the wisdome and discourse of the world, doth in the end resolve upon this point, to teach us, not to feare to die. Truly either reason mockes us, or it only aimeth at our contentment, and in fine, bends all her travell to make us live well, and as the holy Scripture saith, *at our ease.* All the opinions of the world conclude, that pleasure is our end, howbeit they take divers meanes unto, and for it, else would men reject them at their first comming. For, who would give eare unto him, that for it's end would establish our paine and disturbance? The dissentions of philosophicall sects in this case, are verball: *Transcurramus solertissimas nugas: Let us run over such over-fine fooleries, and subtill trifles.* There is more wilfulnesse and wrangling among them, than pertaines to a sacred profession. But what person a man undertakes to act, he doth ever therewithall personate his owne. Allthough they say, that in vertue it selfe, the last scope of our aime is voluptuousnes. It pleaseth me to importune their eares still with this word, which so much offends their hearing: And if it imply any chiefe pleasure or exceeding contentments, it is rather due to the assistance of vertue, than to any other supply, voluptuousnes being more strong, sinnowie, sturdie, and manly, is but more seriously voluptuous. And we should give it the name of pleasure, more favorable, sweeter, and more naturall; and not terme it vigor, from which it hath his denomination. Should this baser sensuality deserve this faire name, it should be by competencie, and not by privilege. I finde it lesse void of incommodities and crosses, than vertue. And besides that, her taste is more fleeting, momentarie, and fading, she hath her fasts, her eves, and her travels, and both sweat and bloud. Furthermore she hath particularly so many wounding passions, and of so severall sorts, and so filthie and loathsome a s[a]cietie waiting upon her, that shee is equivalent to penitencie. Wee are in the wrong, to thinke her incommodities serve her as a provocation, and seasoning to her sweetnes, as in nature one contrarie is vivified by another contrarie: and to say, when we come to vertue, that like suc-

cesses and difficulties over-whelme it, and yeeld it austere and inaccessible. Whereas much more properly then unto voluptuousnes, they
ennoble, sharpen, animate, and raise that divine and perfect pleasure,
which it [mediates] and procureth us. Truly he is verie unworthie her
acquaintance, that counter-ballanceth her cost to his fruit, and knowes
neither the graces nor use of it. Those who go about to instruct us, how
her pursuit is very hard and laborious, and her jovisance well pleasing
and delightfull: what else tell they us, but that shee is ever unpleasant
and irksome? For, what humane meane did ever attaine unto an
absolute enjoying of it? The perfectest have been content but to aspire
and approach her, without ever possessing her. But they are deceived;
seeing that of all the pleasures we know, the pursute of them is pleasant. The enterprise is perceived by the qualitie of the thing, which it
hath regard unto: for it is a good portion of the effect, and consub-
stantiall. That happines and felicitie, which shineth in vertue, replen-
isheth her approaches and appurtenances, even unto the first entrance
and utmost barre. Now of all the benefits of vertue, the contempt of
death is the chiefest, a meane that furnisheth our life with an ease-full
tranquillitie, and gives us a pure and amiable taste of it: without which
every other voluptuousnes is extinguished. Loe, here the reasons why
all rules encounter and agree with this article. And albeit they all leade
us with a common accord to despise griefe, povertie, and other aciden-
tall crosses, to which mans life is subject, it is not with an equall care:
as well because accidents are not of such a necessitie, for most men
passe their whole life without feeling any want or povertie, and othersome without feeling any griefe or sicknes, as *Xenophilus* the Musitian,
who lived an hundred and six yeares in perfect and continuall health:
as also if the worst happen, death may at all times, and whensoever
it shall please us, cut off all other inconveniences and crosses. But as
for death, it is inevitable.

> *Omnes eodem, cogimur, omnium*
> *Versatur urna, serius, ocyus*
> *Sors exitura, et nos in æter-*
> *num exilium impositura cymbæ.*
> HOR. iii. Od. iii. 25.

> All to one place are driv'n, of all
> Shak't is the lot-pot, where-hence shall
> Sooner or later drawne lots fall,
> And to deaths boat for aye enthrall.

And by consequence, if she make us affeard, it is a continual subject
of torment, and which can no way be eased. There is no starting-hole
will hide us from her, she will finde us wheresoever we are, we may as
in a suspected countrie start and turne here and there: *quæ quasi
saxum Tantalo semper impendet* (CIC. *Fin.* i.): *Which evermore hangs*

like the stone over the head of Tantalus: Our lawes doe often condemne
and send malefactors to be executed in the same place where the crime
was committed: to which whilest they are going, leade them along the
fairest houses, or entertaine them with the best cheere you can,

> *non Siculæ dapes*
> *Dulcem elaborabunt saporem:*
> *Non avium, cithareæque cantus*
> *Somnum reducent.*—Hor. iii. *Od.* i. 18.

> Not all King *Denys* daintie fare,
> Can pleasing taste for them prepare:
> No song of birds, no musikes sound
> Can lullabie to sleepe profound.

Doe you thinke they can take any pleasure in it? or be any thing
delighted? and that the finall intent of their voiage being still before
their eies, hath not altered and altogether distracted their taste from
all these commodities and allurements?

> *Audit iter, numeratque dies, spatioque viarum*
> *Metitur vitam, torquetur peste futura.*
> > Claud. *in Ruff.* ii. 1. 137.

> He heares his journey, counts his daies, so measures he
> His life by his waies length, vext with the ill shall be.

The end of our cariere is death, it is the necessarie object of our
aime: if it affright us, how is it possible we should step one foot further
without an ague? The remedie of the vulgar sort is, not to thinke on
it. But from what brutall stupiditie may so grosse a blindnesse come
upon him? he must be made to bridle his Asse by the taile,

> *Qui capite ipse suo instituit vestigia retro.*

> Who doth a course contrarie runne
> With his head to his course begunne.

It is no marvell if he be so often taken tripping; some doe no sooner
heare the name of death spoken of, but they are afraid, yea the most
part will crosse themselves, as if they heard the Devill named. And
because mention is made of it in mens wils and testaments, I warrant
you there is none will set his hands to them, til the Physitian have
given his last doome, and utterly forsaken him. And God knowes,
being then betweene such paine and feare, with what sound judgement
they endure him. For so much as this syllable sounded so unpleasantly
in their eares, and this voice seemed so ill-boding and unluckie, the
Romans had learned to allay and dilate the same by a Periphrasis. In
liew of saying, he is dead, or he hath ended his daies, they would say,
he hath lived. So it be life, be it past or no, they are comforted: from
whom we have borrowed our phrases *quondam, alias, or late such a*

one. It may haply be, as the common saying is, the time we live, is worth the mony we pay for it. I was borne betweene eleven of the clocke and noone, the last of Februarie 1533, according to our computation, the yeare beginning the first of Januarie. It is but a fortnight since I was 39. yeares old. I want at least as much more. If in the meane time I should trouble my thoughts with a matter so farre from me, it were but folly. But what? we see both young and old to leave their life after one selfe-same condition. No man departs otherwise from it, than if he but now came to it, seeing there is no man so crazed, bedrell, or decrepit, so long as he remembers *Methusalem,* but thinkes he may yet live twentie yeares. Moreover, seely creature as thou art, who hath limited the end of thy daies? Happily thou presumest upon Physitians reports. Rather consider the effect and experience. By the common course of things, long since thou livest by extraordinarie favour. Thou hast alreadie over-past the ordinarie tearmes of common life: And to prove it, remember but thy acquaintances and tell me how many more of them have died before they came to thy age, than have either attained or outgone the same: yea and of those that through renoune have ennobled their life, if thou but register them, I will lay a wager, I will finde more that have died before they came to five and thirty yeares, than after. It is consonant with reason and pietie, to take example by the humanity of *Jesus Christ,* who ended his humane life at three and thirtie yeares. The greatest man that ever was being no more than a man, I meane *Alexander* the great, ended his dayes, and died also of that age. How many severall meanes and waies hath death to surprise us!

> *Quid quisque vitet, nunquam homini satis*
> *Cautum est in horas.*—Hor. ii. *Od.* xiii. 13.

A man can never take good heed,
Hourely what he may shun and speed.

I omit to speake of agues and pleurisies; who would ever have imagined, that a Duke of *Brittanie* should have beene stifled to death in a throng of people, as whilome was a neighbour of mine at *Lyons,* when Pope *Clement* made his entrance there? Hast thou not seene one of our late Kings slaine in the middest of his sports? and one of his ancestors die miserably by the chocke of an hog? *Eschilus* forethreatned by the fall of an house, when he stood most upon his guard, strucken dead by the fall of a Tortoise shell, which fell out of the tallants of an Eagle flying in the aire? and another choaked with the kernell of a grape? And an Emperour die by the scratch of a combe, whilest he was coming his head: And *Æmylius Lepidus* with hitting his foot against a doore-seele? And *Aufidius* with stumbling against the Consull-Chamber doore as he was going in thereat? And *Cornelius Gallus* the Prætor, *Tigillinus* Captaine of the Romane watch, *Lodo-*

wike, sonne of *Guido Gonzaga,* Marquis of *Mantua,* end their daies
betweene womens thighs? And of a farre worse example *Speusippus* the
Platonian Philosopher and one of our Popes? Poore *Bebius* a Judge
whilest he demurreth the sute of a plaintife but for eight daies, behold
his last expired; And *Caius Julius* a Physitian, whilest he was annointing the eies of one of his patients, to have his owne sight closed for
ever by death. And if amongst these examples, I may adde one of a
brother of mine, called Captaine *Saint Martin,* a man of three and
twentie yeares of age, who had alreadie given good testimonie of his
worth and forward valour, playing at tennis, received a blow with a
ball, that hit him a little above the right eare, without apparance of
any contusion, bruse, or hurt, and never sitting or resting upon it,
died within six houres after of an Apoplexie, which the blow of the
ball caused in him. These so frequent and ordinary examples, hapning,
and being still before our eies, how is it possible for man to forgo or
forget the remembrance of death? and why should it not continually
seeme unto us, that shee is still ready at hand to take us by the throat?
What matter is it, will you say unto me, how and in what manner it is,
so long as a man doe not trouble and vex himselfe therewith? I am of
this opinion, that howsoever a man may shrowd or hide himselfe from
her dart, yea were it under an oxe-hide, I am not the man would
shrinke backe: it sufficeth me to live at my ease; and the best recreation I can have, that doe I ever take; in other matters, as little vain-
glorious, and exemplare as you list.

> —*prætulerim delirus inersque videri,*
> *Dum mea delectent mala me, vel denique fallant,*
> *Quam sapere et ringi.*—ID. ii. *Epi.* ii. 126.

A dotard I had rather seeme, and dull,
So me my faults may please make me a gull,
Than to be wise, and beat my vexed scull.

But it is folly to thinke that way to come unto it. They come, they
goe, they trot, they daunce: but no speech of death. All that is good
sport. But if she be once come, and on a sudden and openly surprise,
either them, their wives, their children, or their friends, what torments, what out-cries, what rage, and what despaire doth then over-
whelme them? saw you ever any thing so drooping, so changed, and
so distracted? A man must looke to it, and in better times fore-see it.
And might that brutish carelessenesse lodge in the minde of a man of
understanding (which I find altogether impossible) she sels us her
ware at an over-deere rate: were she an enemie by mans wit to be
avoided, I would advise men to borrow the weapons of cowardlinesse:
but since it may not be, and that be you either a coward or a runaway,
an honest or valiant man, she overtakes you,

Nempe et fugacem persequitur virum,
Nec parcit imbellis juventæ
Poplitibus, timidoque tergo.—ID. iii. *Od.* ii. 14.

Shee persecutes the man that flies,
Shee spares not weake youth to surprise,
But on their hammes and backe turn'd plies.

And that no temper of cuirace may shield or defend you,

Ille licet ferro cautus se condat et ære,
Mors tamen inclusum protrahet inde caput.
PROP[ER]T. iii. *El.* xvii. 25.

Though he with yron and brasse his head empale,
Yet death his head enclosed thence will hale.

Let us learne to stand, and combat her with a resolute minde. And begin to take the greatest advantage she hath upon us from her, let us take a cleane contrary way from the common, let us remove her strangenesse from her, let us converse, frequent, and acquaint our selves with her, let us have nothing so much in minde as death, let us at all times and seasons, and in the ugliest manner that may be, yea with all faces shapen and represent the same unto our imagination. At the stumbling of a horse, at the fall of a stone, at the least prick with a pinne, let us presently ruminate and say with our selves, what if it were death it selfe? and thereupon let us take heart of grace, and call our wits together to confront her. Ammiddest our bankets, feasts, and pleasures, let us ever have this restraint or object before us, that is, the remembrance of our condition, and let not pleasure so much mislead or transport us, that we altogether neglect or forget, how many waies, our joyes, or our feastings, be subject unto death, and by how many hold-fasts shee threatens us and them. So did the Ægyptians, who in the middest of their banquetings, and in the full of their greatest cheere, caused the anatomie of a dead man to be brought before them, as a memorandum and warning to their guests.

Omnem crede diem tibi diluxisse supremum,
Grata superveniet, quæ non sperabitur hora.
HOR. i. *Epi.* iv. 13.

Thinke every day shines on thee as thy last,
Welcome it will come whereof hope was past.

It is uncertaine where death looks for us; let us expect her everie where: the premeditation of death, is a forethinking of libertie. He who hath learned to die, hath unlearned to serve. There is no evill in life, for him that hath well conceived, how the privation of life is no evill. To know how to die, doth free us from all subjection and constraint.

Paulus Æmilius answered one, whom that miserable king of *Macedon* his prisoner sent to entreat him, he would not lead him in triumph, let him make that request unto him selfe. Verily, if Nature afford not some helpe, in all things, it is very hard that art and industrie should goe farre before. Of my selfe, I am not much given to melancholy, but rather to dreaming and sluggishnes. There is nothing wherewith I have ever more entertained my selfe, than with the imaginations of death, yea in the most licentious times of my age.

> *Jucundum, cum œtas florida ver ageret.*
> CATUL. *Eleg.* iv. 16.

> When my age flourishing
> Did spend it's pleasant spring.

Being amongst faire Ladies, and in earnest play, some have thought me busied, or musing with my selfe, how to digest some jealousie, or meditating on the uncertaintie of some conceived hope, when God he knowes, I was entertaining my selfe with the remembrance of some one or other, that but few daies before was taken with a burning fever, and of his sodaine end, comming from such a feast or meeting where I was my selfe, and with his head full of idle conceits, of love, and merry glee; supposing the same, either sicknes or end, to be as neere me as him.

> *Jam fuerit, nec post, unquam revocare licebit.*
> LUCR. iii. 947.

> Now time would be, no more
> You can this time restore.

I did no more trouble my selfe or frowne at such a conceit, than at any other. It is impossible, we should not apprehend or feele some motions or startings at such imaginations at the first, and comming sodainely upon us: but doubtlesse, he that shall manage and meditate upon them with an impartiall eye, they will assuredly, in tract of time, become familiar to him: Otherwise for my part, I should be in continuall feare and agonie; for no man did ever more distrust his life, nor make lesse account of his continuance: Neither can health, which hitherto I have so long enjoied, and which so seldome hath beene crazed, lengthen my hopes, nor any sicknesse shorten them of it. At every minute me thinkes I make an escape. And I uncessantly record unto my selfe, that whatsoever may be done another day, may be effected this day. Truly hazards and dangers doe little or nothing approach us at our end: And if we consider, how many more there remaine, besides this accident, which in number more than millions seeme to threaten us, and hang over us; we shall find, that be we sound or sicke, lustie or weake, at sea or at land, abroad or at home, fighting or at rest, in the middest of a battell or in our beds, she is ever alike

neere unto us. *Nemo altero fragilior est, nemo in crastinum sui certior. No man is weaker then other; non surer of himselfe (to live) till to morrow.* Whatsoever I have to doe before death, all leasure to end the same, seemeth short unto me, yea were it but of one houre. Some body, not long since turning over my writing tables, found by chance a memoriall of something I would have done after my death: I told him (as indeed it was true,) that being but a mile from my house, and in perfect health and lustie, I had made haste to write it, because I could not assure my self I should ever come home in safety; As one that am ever hatching of mine owne thoughts, and place them in my selfe: I am ever prepared about that which I may be: nor can death (come when she please) put me in mind of any new thing. A man should ever, as much as in him lieth, be ready booted to take his journey, and above all things, looke he have then nothing to doe but with himselfe.

> *Quid brevi fortes jaculamur ævo*
> *Multa?*—HOR. ii. *Od.* xvi.

> To aime why are we ever bold,
> At many things in so short hold?

For then we shall have worke sufficient, without any more accrease. Some man complaineth more that death doth hinder him from the assured course of an hoped for victorie, than of death it selfe; another cries out, he should give place to her, before he have married his daughter, or directed the course of his childrens bringing up; another bewaileth he must forgoe his wives company; another moaneth the losse of his children the chiefest commodities of his being. I am now by meanes of the mercy of God in such a taking, that without regret or grieving at any worldly matter, I am prepared to dislodge, when-soever he shall please to call me: I am every where free: my farewell is soone taken of all my friends, except of my selfe. No man did ever prepare himselfe to quit the world more simply and fully, or more generally [shake] of all thoughts of it, than I am fully assured I shall doe. The deadest deaths are the best.

> —*Miser, ô miser (aiunt) omnia ademit.*
> *Una dies infesta mihi tot præmia vitæ.*—LUCR. iii. 942.

> O wretch, O wretch, (friends cry) one day,
> All joyes of life hath tane away:

And the builder,

> —*maneant* (saith he) *opera interrupta, minæque,*
> *Murorum ingentes.*—VIRG. *Æn.* iv. 88.

> The workes unfinisht lie,
> And walls that threatned hie.

A man should designe nothing so long aforehand, or at least with such an intent, as to passionate himselfe to see the end of it; we are all borne to be doing.

> *Cùm moriar, medium solvar et inter opus.*
> OVID. *Am.* ii. El. x. 36.

> When dying I my selfe shall spend,
> Ere half my businesse come to end.

I would have a man to be doing, and to prolong his lives offices, as much as lieth in him, and let death seize upon me, whilst I am setting my cabiges, carelesse of her dart, but more of my unperfect garden. I saw one die, who being at his last gaspe, uncessantly complained against his destinie, and that death should so unkindly cut him off in the middest of an historie which he had in hand, and was now come to the fifteenth or sixteenth of our Kings.

> *Illud in his rebus non addunt, nec tibi earum,*
> *Jam desiderium rerum super insidet una.*—LUCE. iii. 944.

> Friends adde not that in this case, now no more
> Shalt thou desire, or want things wisht before.

A man should rid himselfe of these vulgar and hurtfull humours. Even as Church-yards were first placed adjoyning unto churches, and in the most frequented places of the City, to enure (as *Lycurgus* said) the common people, women and children, not to be skared at the sight of a dead man, and to the end that continuall spectacle of bones, souls, tombes, graves and burials, should forwarne us of our condition, and fatall end.

> *Quin etiam exhilarare viris convivia cæde*
> *Mos olim, et miscere epulis spectacula dira,*
> *Certantum ferro, sæpe et super ipsa cadentum*
> *Pocula, respersis non parco sanguine mensis.*
> SYL. *Ital.* xi. 51.

> Nay more, the manner was to welcome guests,
> And with dire shewes of slaughter to mix feasts.
> Of them that fought at sharpe, and with bords tainted
> Of them with much bloud, who o'er full cups fainted.

And even as the Ægyptians after their feastings and carousings, caused a great image of death to be brought in and shewed to the guests and bystanders, by one that cried aloud, *Drinke and be mery, for such shalt thou be when thou art dead:* So have I learned this custome or lesson, to have alwaies death, not only in my imagination, but continually in my mouth. And there is nothing I desire more to be informed of, than of the death of men: that is to say, what words, what countenance, and what face they shew at their death; and in reading of histories, which I so attentively observe. It appeareth by the shuffling and hudling up of my examples, I affect no subject so particularly as this. Were I a composer of books, I would keepe a register, commented of the divers deaths, which in teaching men to die, should after teach them to live. *Dicearcus* made one of that title, but of another and lesse profitable end. Some man will say to mee, the effect exceeds the thought so farre, that there is no fence so sure, or cunning so certaine, but a man shall either lose or forget, if he come once to that point; let them say what they list: to premediate on it, giveth no doubt a great advantage: and [is it] nothing, at the least to goe so farre without dismay or alteration, or without an ague? There belongs more to it: Nature her selfe lends her hand, and gives us courage. If it be a short and violent death, wee have no leisure to feare it; if otherwise, I perceive that according as I engage my selfe in sicknesse, I doe naturally fall into some disdaine and contempt of life. I finde that I have more adoe to digest this resolution, that I shall die when I am in health, than I have when I am troubled with a fever: forsomuch as I have no more such fast hold on the commodities of life, whereof I begin to lose the use and pleasure, and view death in the face with a lesse undanted looke, which makes me hope, that the further I goe from that, and the nearer I approch to this, so much more easily doe I enter in composition for their exchange. Even as I have tried in many other occurrences, which *Cæsar* affirmed, that often somethings seeme greater, being farre from us, than if they bee neere at hand: I have found that being in perfect health, I have much more beene frighted with sicknesse, than when I have felt it. The jollitie wherein I live, the pleasure and the strength make the other seeme so disproportionable from that, that by imagination I amplifie these commodities by one moitie, and apprehended them much more heavie and burthensome, than I feele them when I have them upon my shoulders. The same I hope will happen to me of death. Consider we by the ordinary mutations, and daily declinations which we suffer, how Nature deprives us of the [sight] of our losse and empairing: what hath an aged man left him of his youths vigor, and of his fore-past life?

> *Heu senibus vitæ portio quanta manet!*
>
> Cor. *Gal.* i. 16.

Alas to men in yeares how small
A part of life is left in all?

Cæsar to a tired and crazed Souldier of his guard, who in the open street came to him, to beg leave, he might cause himselfe to be put to death; viewing his decrepit behaviour, answerd plesantly: *Doest thou thinke to be alive then?* Were man all at once to fall into it, I doe not thinke we should be able to beare such a change, but being faire and gently led on by her hand, in a slow, and as it were unperceived descent, by little and little, and step by step, she roules us into that miserable state, and day by day seekes to acquaint us with it. So that when youth failes in us, we feele, nay we perceive no shaking or trans-change at all in our selves: which in essence and veritie is a harder death, than that of a languishing and irkesome life, or that of age. Forsomuch as the leape from an ill being, unto a not being, is not so dangerous or steepie; as it is from a delightfull and flourishing being, unto a painfull and sorrowfull condition. A weake bending, and faint [stooping] bodie hath lesse strength to beare and undergoe a heavie burden: So hath our soule. She must bee rouzed and raised against the violence and force of this adversarie. For as it is impossible, she should take any rest whilest she feareth: whereof if she be assured (which is a thing exceeding humane condition) she may boast that it is impos-sible, unquietnesse, torment, and feare, much lesse the least dis-pleasure should lodge in her.

> Non vultus instantis tyranni
> Mente quatit solida, neque Auster,
> Dux inquieti turbidus Adriæ,
> Nec fulminantis magna Jovis manus.—Hor. iii. Od. iii.

> No urging tyrants threatning face,
> Where minde is sound can it displace,
> No troublous wind the rough seas Master,
> Nor Joves great hand the thunder-caster.

She is made Mistris of her passions and concupiscence, Lady of indulgence, of shame of povertie, and of all fortunes injuries. Let him that can, attaine to this advantage: Herein consists the true and soveraigne liberty, that affords us meanes wherewith to jeast and make a scorne of force and injustice, and to deride imprisonment, gyves, or fetters.

> —in manicis, et
> Compedibus, sævo te sub custode tenebo.
> Ipse Deus simul atque volam, me solvet: opinor,
> Hoc sentit moriar, mors ultima linea rerum est.
> [Hor.] i. Epi. xvi. 76.

> In gyves and fetters I will hamper thee,
> Under a Jayler that shall cruell be:
> Yet, when I will, God me deliver shall,
> He thinkes, I shall die: death is end of all.

Our religion hath had no surer humane foundation, than the con-tempt of life. Discourse of reason doth not only call and summon us unto it. For why should we feare to lose a thing, which being lost, can-not be moaned? but also, since we are threatened by so many kinds of death, there is no more inconvenience to feare them all, than to endure one: what matter is it when it commeth, since it is unavoidable? Soc-

rates answered one that told him, The thirty Tyrants have condemned thee to death; *And Nature them,* said he. What fondnesse is it to carke and care so much, at that instant and passage from all exemption of paine and care? As our birth brought us the birth of all things, so shall our death the end of all things. Therefore is it as great follie to weepe, we shall not live a hundred yeeres hence, so to waile we lived not a hundred yeeres agoe. *Death is the beginning of another life.* So wept we, and so much did it cost us to enter into this life; and so did we spoile us of our ancient vaile in entring into it. Nothing can be grievous that is but once. Is it reason so long to feare a thing of so short time? Long life or short life is made all one by death. For long or short is not in things that are no more. *Aristotle* saith, there are certaine litle beasts alongst the river *Hyspanis,* that live but one day; she which dies at 8. a clocke in the morning, dies in her youth, and she that dies at 5. in the afternoon, dies in her decrepitude, who of us doth not laugh, when we shall see this short moment of continuance to be had in consideration of good or ill fortune? The most and the least in ours, if we compare it with eternitie, or equall it to the lasting of mountaines, rivers, stars, and trees, or any other living creature, is no lesse ridiculous. But nature compels us to it. *Depart* (saith she,) *out of this world, even as you came into it. The same way you came from death to life, returne without passion or amazement, from life to death: your death is but a peece of the worlds order, and but a parcell of the worlds life.*

—*inter se mortales mutua vivunt,*
Et quasi cursores vitai lampada tradunt.—LUCR. ii. 74, 77.

Mortall men live by mutuall entercourse:
And yeeld their life-torch, as men in a course.

Shal I not change this goodly contexture of things for you? It is the condition of your creation: death is a part of your selves: you flie from your selves. The being you enjoy, is equally shared betweene life and death. The first day of your birth doth as wel addresse you to die, as to live.

Prima quæ vitam dedit, hora, carpsit.
SEN. *Her. Fur.* chor. iii.

The first houre, that to men
Gave life, strait, cropt it then.

Nascentes morimur, finisque ab origine pendet.
MANIL. *Ast.* iv.

As we are borne we die; the end
Doth of th' originall depend.

All the time you live, you steale it from death: it is at her charge. The continuall worke of your life, is to contrive death; you are in death, during the time you continue in life: for, you are after death, when you are no longer living. Or if you had rather have it so, you are dead after life: but during life, you are still dying: and death doth more rudely touch the dying, than the dead, and more lively and essentially. If you have profited by life, you have also beene fed thereby, depart then satisfied.

Cur non ut plenus vitæ conviva recedis?—LUCR. iii. 982.

> Why like a full-fed guest,
> Depart you not to rest?

If you have not knowne how to make use of it: if it were unprofitable to you, what need you care to have lost it? to what end would you enjoy it longer?

> *—cur amplius addere quæris*
> *Rursum quod pereat male, et ingratum occidat omne?*
> LUCR. iii. 985.

> Why seeke you more to gaine, what must againe
> All perish ill, and passe with griefe or paine?

Life in it selfe is neither good nor evill: it is the place of good or evill, according as you prepare it for them. And if you have lived one day, you have seene all: one day is equal to all other daies: There is no other light, there is no other night. This Sunne, this Moone, these Starres, and this disposition, is the very same, which your forefathers enjoyed, and which shall also entertaine your posteritie.

> *Non alium videre patres, aliumve nepotes*
> *Aspicient.*

> No other saw our Sires of old,
> No other shall their sonnes behold.

And if the worst happen, the distribution and varietie of all the acts of my comedie, is performed in one yeare. If you have observed the course of my foure seasons; they containe the infancie, the youth, the virilitie, and the old age of the world. He hath plaied his part: he knowes no other wilinesse belonging to it, but to begin againe, it will ever be the same, and no other.

> *—Versamur ibidem, atque insumus usque.*—LUCR. iii. 123.

> We still in one place turne about,
> Still there we are, now in, now out.

> *Atque in se sua per vestigia volvitur annus.*
> VIRG. *Georg.* ii. 403.

> The yeare into it selfe is cast
> By those same steps, that it hath past.

I am not purposed to devise you other new sports.

Nam tibi præterea quod machiner, inveniamque
Quod placeat, nihil est, eadem sunt omnia semper.

LUCR. ii. 978.

Else nothing, that I can devise or frame,
Can please thee, for all things are still the same.

Make roome for others, as others have done for you. *Equalitie is*
the chiefe ground-worke of equitie, who can complaine to be compre-
hended where all are contained? So may you live long enough, you
shall never diminish any thing from the time you have to die: it is
bootlesse; so long shall you continue in that state, which you feare,
as if you had died being in your swathing-clothes, and when you were
sucking.

—licet, quot vis, vivendo vincere secla,
Mors æterna tamen, nihilominus illa manebit.—Ibid. 1126.

Though yeares you live, as many as you will,
Death is eternall, death remaineth still.

And I will so please you, that you shall have no discontent.

In vera nescis nullum fore morte alium te,
Qui possit vivus tibi te lugere peremptum,
*Stansque jacentem.—*LUCR. iii. 911.

Thou know'st not there shall be not other thou,
When thou art dead indeed, that can tell how
Alive to waile thee dying,
Standing to waile thee lying.

Nor shall you wish for life, which you so much desire.

Nec sibi enim quisquam tum se vitamque requirit,
*Nec desiderium nostri nos afficit ullum.—*963, 966.

For then none for himselfe himselfe or life requires:
Nor are we of our selves affected with desires.

Death is lesse to be feared than nothing, if there were any thing lesse
than nothing.

—multo mortem minus ad nos esse putandum,
*Si minus esse potest quam quod nihil esse videmus.—*970

Death is much lesse to us, we ought esteeme,
If lesse may be, than what doth nothing seeme.

Nor alive, nor dead, it doth concerne you nothing. Alive, because
you are: Dead, because you are no more. Moreover, no man dies
before his houre. The time you leave behinde was no more yours, than
that which was before your birth, and concerneth you no more.

Respice enim quàm nil ad nos anteacta vetustas
Temporis æterni fuerit.—1016.

For marke, how all antiquitie fore-gone
Of all time e're we were, to us was none.

Wheresoever your life endeth, there is it all. The profit of life consists not in the space, but rather in the use. Some man hath lived long, that hath had a short life. Follow it whilest you have time. It consists not in number of yeeres, but in your will, that you have lived long enough. Did you thinke you should never come to the place, where you were still going? There is no way but hath an end. And if company may solace you, doth not the whole world walke the same path?

—Omnia te vita perfuncta sequentur.—1612.

Life past, all things at last
Shall follow thee as thou hast past.

Doe not all things move as you doe, or keepe your course? Is there any thing grows not old together with your selfe? A thousand men, a thousand beasts, and a thousand other creatures die in the very instant that you die.

Nam nox nulla diem, neque noctem aurora sequuta est,
Quæ non audierit mistos vagitibus ægris
Ploratus mortis comites et funeris atri.—ii. 587.

No night ensued day light: no morning followed night,
Which heard not moaning mixt with sick-mens groaning,
With deaths and funerals joyned was that moaning.

To what end recoile you from it, if you cannot goe backe? You have seene many who have found good in death, ending thereby many many miseries. But have you seene any that hath received hurt thereby? Therefore is it mere simplicitie to condemne a thing you never proved, neither by your selfe nor any other. Why doest thou complaine of me and of destinie? Doe we offer thee any wrong? is it for thee to direct us, or for us to governe thee? Although thy age be not come to her period, thy life is. A little man is a whole man as well as a great man. Neither men nor their lives are measured by the Ell. *Chiron* refused immortalitie, being informed of the conditions thereof, even by the God of time and of continuance, *Saturne* his father. Imagine truly how much an ever-during life would be lesse tolerable and more painfull to a man, than is the life which I have given him: Had you not death, you would then uncessantly curse, and cry out against me, that I had deprived you of it. I have of purpose and wittingly blended some bitternesse amongst it, that so seeing the commoditie of it's use, I might hinder you from over-greedily embracing, or indiscreetly calling for it. To continue in this moderation, that is, neither to flie from life, nor to run to death (which I require of you) I have tempered both the one and other betweene sweetnes and sowrenes. I first taught *Thales* the chiefest of your Sages and Wisemen, that to live and die, were indifferent, which made him answer one very wisely, who asked him, wherfore he died not; *Because,* said he, *it is indifferent. The water, the earth, the aire, the fire, and other members of this my universe, are no more the instruments of thy life, than of thy death. Why fearest thou thy last day? He is no more guiltie, and conferreth no more to thy death, than any of the others. It is not the last step that causeth wearinesse: it only declares it. All daies march towards death, only the last comes to it.* Behold heere the good precepts of our universall mother Nature. I have often-times bethought my selfe whence it proceedeth, that in times of warre, the visage of death (whether wee see it in us or in others) seemeth without all comparison much lesse dreadful and terrible unto us, than in our houses, or in our beds, otherwise it should be an armie of Physitians and whiners, and she ever being one, there must needs bee much more assurance amongst countrie-people and of base condition, than in others. I verily beleeve, these fearefull lookes, and astonishing countenances wherewith we encompasse it, are those that more amaze and terrifie us than death: a new forme of life; the out-cries of mothers; the wailing of women and children; the visitation of dismaid and swouning friends: the assistance of a number of pale-looking, distracted, and whining servants; a darke chamber: tapers burning round about; our couch beset round with Physitians and Preachers; and to conclude, nothing but horror and astonishment on every side of us: are wee not alreadie dead and buried? The very children are afraid of their friends, when they see them masked; and so are we: The maske must as well be taken from things, as from men, which being removed, we shall finde nothing hid under it, but the very same death, that a seely varlet, or a simple maid-servant, did lately suffer without amazement or feare. Happie is that death, which takes all leasure from the preparations of such an equipage.

CHAPTER XX

OF THE FORCE OF IMAGINATION

FORTIS *imaginatio generat casum: A strong imagination begetteth chance,* say learned clearks. I am one of those that feele a very great conflict and power of imagination. All men are shockt therewith, and some overthrowne by it. The impression of it pierceth me, and for want of strength to resist her, my endevour is to avoid it. I could live with the only assistance of holy and merry-hearted men. The sight of others anguishes doth sensibly drive me into anguish: and my sense hath often usurped the sense of a third man. If one cough continually, he provokes my lungs and throat. I am more unwilling to visit the

sicke dutie doth engage me unto, than those to whom I am little beholding, and regard least. I apprehend the evill which I studie, and place
it in me. I deeme it not strange that she brings both agues and death
to such as give her scope to worke her wil, and applaude her. *Simon
Thomas* was a great Physitian in his daies. I remember upon a time
comming by chance to visit a rich old man that dwelt in *Tholouse,*
and who was troubled with the cough of the lungs, who discoursing
with the said *Simon Thomas* of the meanes of his recoverie, he told
him, that one of the best was, to give me occasion to be delighted in
his companie, and that fixing his eyes upon the livelines and freshnes
of my face, and setting his thoughts upon the jolitie and vigor, wherewith my youthfull age did then flourish, and filling all his senses with
my florishing estate, his habitude might thereby be amended, and his
health recovered. But he forgot to say, that mine might also be empaired and infected. *Gallus Vibius* did so well enure his minde to comprehend the essence and motions of folly, that he so transported his
judgement from out his seat, as he could never afterward bring it to
his right place againe: and might rightly boast, to have become a foole
through wisdome. Some there are, that through feare anticipate the
hangmans hand; as he did, whose friends having obtained his pardon,
and putting away the cloth wherewith he was hood-winkt, that he
might heare it read, was found starke dead upon the scaffold, wounded
only by the stroke of imagination. We sweat, we shake, we grow pale,
and we blush at the motions of our imaginations; and wallowing in
our beds we feele our bodies agitated and turmoiled at their apprehen-
sions, yea in such manner, as sometimes we are ready to yeeld up the
spirit. And burning youth (although asleepe) is often therewith so
possessed and enfolded, that dreaming it doth satisfie and enjoy her
amorous desires.

> *Ut quasi transactis sœpe omnibu' rebu' profundant
> Fluminis ingentes fluctus, vestemque cruentent.*
> LUCR. iv. 1027.

And if all things were done, they powre foorth streames,
And bloodie their night-garment in their dreames.

And although it be not strange to see some men have hornes growing upon their head in one night, that had none when they went to
bed: notwithstanding the fortune or successe of *Cyppus* King of *Italie*
is memorable, who because the day before he had with earnest affection, assisted and beene attentive at a bul-baiting, and having all night
long dreamed of hornes in his head, by the very force of imagination
brought them forth the next morning in his forehead. An earnest passion gave the son of *Crœsus* his voice, which nature had denied him.
And *Antiochus* got an ague, by the excellent beautie of *Stratonice* so
deeply imprinted in his minde. *Plinie* reporteth to have seene *Lucius
Cossitius* upon his marriage day to have beene transformed from a

woman to a man. *Pontanus* and others recount the like Metamorphosies to have hapned in *Italie* these ages past: And through a vehement desire of him and his mother.

Vota puer solvit, quæ fœmina voverat Iphis.

OVID. *Metam*. ix. 794.

Iphis a boy, the vowes then paid,
Which he vow'd when he was a maid.

My selfe traveling on a time by *Vitry* in *France*, hapned to see a man, whom the Bishop of *Soissons* had in confirmation, named *Germane*, and all the inhabitants thereabout have both knowne and seene to be a woman-childe, untill she was two and twentie yeares of age, called by the name of *Marie*. He was, when I saw him, of good yeares, and had a long beard, and was yet unmarried. He saith, that upon a time leaping, and straining himselfe to overleape another, he wot not how, but where before he was a woman, he suddenly felt the instrument of a man to come out of him; and to this day the maidens of that towne and countrie have a song in use, by which they warne one another, when they are leaping, not to straine themselves overmuch, or open their legs too wide, for feare they should bee turned to boies, as *Marie Germane* was. It is no great wonder, that such accidents doe often happen, for if imagination have power in such things, it is so continually annexed, and so forcibly fastened to this subject, that lest she should so often fall into the relaps of the same thought, and sharpnesse of desire, it is better one time for all, to incorporate this virile part unto wenches. Some will not sticke to ascribe the scarres of King *Dagobert*, or the cicatrices of Saint *Francis* unto the power of Imagination. Othersome will say, that by the force of it, bodies are sometimes removed from their places. And *Celsus* reports of a Priest, whose soule was ravished into such an extasie, that for a long time the body remained void of all respiration and sense. Saint *Augustine* speaketh of another, who if hee but heard any lamentable and wailefull cries, would suddenly fall into a swowne, and bee so forcibly carried from himself, that did any chide and braule never so loud, pinch and thumpe him never so much, he could not be made to stirre, untill hee came to himselfe againe. Then would he say, he had heard sundry strange voyces, comming as it were from a farre, and perceiving his pinches and bruses, wondered at them. And that it was not an obstinate conceit, or wilfull humour in him, or against his feeling sense, it plainly appeared by this, because during his extasie, he seemed to have neither pulse nor breath. It is very likely that the principall credit of visions, of enchantments, and such extraordinary effects, proceedeth from the power of imaginations, working especially in the mindes of the vulgar sort, as the weakest and seeliest, whose conceit and beleefe is so seized upon, that they imagine to see what they see not. I am yet in doubt, these pleasant bonds, wherewith our world is so fettered, and

France so pestered, that nothing else is spoken of, are haply but the impressions of apprehension, and effects of feare. For I know by experience, that some one, for whom I may as well answer as for my selfe, and in whom no manner of suspition either of weaknesse or enchantment might fall, hearing a companion of his make report of an extraordinary faint sowning, wherein he was fallen, at such a time, as he least looked for it, and wrought him no small shame, whereupon the horrour of his report did so strongly strike his imagination, as he ranne the same fortune, and fell into a like drooping: And was thence forward subject to fall into like fits: So did the passionate remembrance of his inconvenience possesse and tyrannize him; but his fond doting was in time remedied by another kinde of raving. For himselfe avowing and publishing aforehand the infirmitie he was subject unto, the contention of his soule was solaced upon this, that bearing his evill as expected, his dutie thereby diminished, and he grieved lesse thereat. And when at his choice, he hath had law and power (his thought being cleered and unmasked, his body finding it selfe in his right due and place) to make the same to be felt, seized upon, and apprehended by others knowledge: he hath fully and perfectly recovered himselfe. If a man have once beene capable, he cannot afterward be incapable, except by a just and absolute weaknesse. Such a mischiefe is not to be feared, but in the enterprises, where our minde is beyond all measure bent with desire and respect; and chiefly where opportunitie comes unexpected, and requires a sudden dispatch. There is no meanes for a man to recover himselfe from this trouble; I know some, who have found to come unto it with their bodies as it were halfe glutted else-where, thereby to stupifie or allay the heat of that furie, and who through age, finde themselves lesse unable, by how much more they be lesse able: And another, who hath also found good, in that a friend of his assured him to bee provided with a counter-battery of forcible enchantments, to preserve him in any such conflict: It is not amisse I relate how it was. An Earle of very good place, with whom I was familiarly acquainted, being married to a very faire Lady, who had long beene solicited for love, by one assisting at the wedding, did greatly trouble his friends; but most of all an old Lady his kins-woman, who was chiefe at the marriage, and in whose house it was solemnized, as she that much feared such sorceries and witchcrafts: which shee gave mee to understand, I comforted her as well as I could, and desired her to relie upon me: I had by chance a peece of golden plate in my trunke, wherein were ingraven certaine celestiall figures, good against the Sunnebeames, and for the head-ach, being fitly laid upon the suture of the head: and that it might the better be kept there, it was sewed to a riband, to be fastened under the chin. A fond doting conceit, and cosin-germane to that wee now speake of. *James Peletier* had whilest he lived in my house, bestowed that singular gift upon mee; I advised my selfe to put it to some use, and told the Earle, he might haply be in danger, and

come to some misfortune as others had done, the rather because some
were present, that would not sticke to procure him some ill lucke, and
which was worse, some spitefull shame; but neverthelesse I willed him
boldly to goe to bed: For I would shew him the part of a true friend,
and in his need, spare not for his good to employ a miracle, which
was in my power; alwaies provided, that on his honour he would
promise me faithfully to keepe it very secret; which was only, that
when about midnight he should have his [caudle] brought him, if he
had had no good successe in his businesse, he should make such and
such a signe to me. It fel out, his mind was so quailed, and his eares so
dulled, that by reason of the bond wherewith the trouble of his imagination had tied him, hee could not run on poste: and at the houre
appointed, made the signe agreed upon betweene us, I came and whis-
pered him in the eare, that under pretence to put us all out of his
chamber, he should rise out of his bed, and in jesting manner take my
nightgowne which I had on, and put it upon himselfe (which he might
well doe, because wee were much of one stature) and keepe it on till
he had performed my appointment, which was, that when we should
be gone out of the Chamber, he should withdraw himselfe to make
water, and using certaine jestures, I had shewed him, speake such words
thrice over. And every time hee spake them he should girt the ribband,
which I put into his hands, and very carefully place the plate thereto
fastned, just upon his kidneyes, and the whole figure, in such a posture. All which when he had accordingly done, and the last time so
fastened the ribband, that it might neither be untide nor stirred from
his place, he should then boldly and confidently returne to his charge,
and not forget to spread my night-gowne upon his bed, but so as it
might cover them both. These fopperies are the chiefe of the effect.
Our thought being unable so to free it selfe, but some strange meanes
will proceed from some abstruse learning: Their inanitie gives them
weight and credit. To conclude, it is most certaine, my Characters
proved more venerian than solare, more in action, than in prohibition.
It was a ready and curious humour drew me to this effect, farre from
my nature. I am an enemie to craftie and fained actions, and hate all
suttletie in my hands, not only recreative, but also profitable. If the
action be not vicious, the course unto it is faultie. *Amasis* King of
Ægypt, tooke to wife *Laodice,* a very beauteous yong virgin of *Greece,*
and he that before had in every other place found and shewed himselfe
a lustie gallant, found himselfe so short, when he came to grapple
with her, that he threatned to kill her, supposing it had beene some
charme or sorcerie. As in all things that consist in the fantasie, she
addrest him to devotion. And having made his vowes and promises to
Venus, he found himselfe divinely freed, even from the first night of
his oblations and sacrifices. Now they wrong us, to receive and admit
us with their wanton, squeamish, quarellous countenances, which setting us a fire, extinguish us.

Pythagoras his neece was wont to say, *That a woman which lies with a man ought, together with her petie-coate, leave off all bashfulnesse, and with her petie-coate, take the same againe.* The minde of the assailant molested with sundry different alarums, is easily dismaid. And he whom imagination hath once made to suffer this shame (and she hath caused the same to be felt but in the first acquaintances; because they are then burning and violent, and in the first acquaintance and comming together, or triall a man gives of himselfe, he is much more afraid and quaint to misse the marke he shoots at) having begun ill he fals into an ague or spite of this accident, which afterward continueth in succeeding occasions. Married men, because time is at their command, and they may go to it when they list, ought never to presse or importune their enterprise, unless they be readie. And it is better undecently to faile in hanseling the nuptiall bed, full of agitation and fits, by waiting for some or other fitter occasion, and more private opportunitie, lest sudden and alarmed, than to fall into a perpetuall miserie, by apprehending an astonishment, and desperation of the first refusall. Before possession taken, a patient ought by sallies, and divers times, lightly assay and offer himselfe without vexing or opiniating himselfe, definitely to convince himselfe. Such as know their members docile and tractable by nature, let them only endevour to countercosin their fantasie. Men have reason to checke the indocile libertie of this member, for so importunately insinuating himselfe when we have no need of him, and so importunately, or as I may say impertinently failing, at what time we have most need of him; and so imperiously contesting by his authority with our will, refusing with such fiercenes and obstinacie our solicitations both mentall and manuall. Neverthelesse if a man inasmuch as he doth gormandize and devour his rebellion, and drawes a triall by his condemnation, would pay me for to plead his cause, I would peradventure make other of our members to be suspected to have (in envy of his importance, and sweetnesse of his use) devised this imposture, and framed this set quarrell against him, and by some malicious complot armed the world against him, enviously charging him alone with a fault common to them all. For I referre it to your thought, whether there be any one particular part of our body, that doth not sometimes refuse her particular operation to our will and wish, and that doth not often exercise and practise against our will. All of them have their proper passions, which without any leave of ours doe either awaken or lull them asleepe. How often doe the forced motions and changes of our faces witnesse the secretest and most lurking thoughts we have, and bewray them to by-standers? The same cause that doth animate this member, doth also, unwitting to us, embolden our heart, our lungs, and our pulses. The sight of a pleasing object, reflecting imperceptibly on us, the flame of a contagious or aguish emotion. Is there nought besides these muscles and veines, that rise and fall without the consent, not only of our will, but also of our thought? We cannot command our haire to stand an end, nor our skinne to startle for desire or feare. Our hands are often carried where we direct them not. Our tongue and voice are sometimes to seeke of their faculties, the one loseth her speech, the other her nimblenesse. Even when we have nothing to feed upon, we would willingly forbid it: the appetites to eat, or list to drinke, doe not leave to move the parts subject to them, even as this other appetite, and so, though it be out of season, forsaketh us, when he thinks good. Those instruments that serve to discharge the belly, have their proper compressions and dilatations, besides our intent, and against our meaning, as these are destined to discharge the kidneis. And that which, the better to authorize our wills power, Saint *Augustin* alleageth, to have seene one, who could at all times command his posterior, to let as many scapes as he would, and which *Vives* endeareth by the example of an other in his daies, who could let tunable and organized ones, following the tune of any voice propounded unto his eares, inferreth the pure obedience of that member: than which, none is commonly more indiscreet and tumultuous. Seeing my selfe know one so skittish and mutinous, that these fortie yeares keepes his master in such awe, that will he, or nill he, he will with a continuall breath, constant and unintermitted costume breake winde at his pleasure, and so brings him to his grave. And would to God I knew it but by Histories, how that many times our belly, being restrained thereof, brings us even to the gates of a pining and languishing death: And that the Emperour, who gave us free leave to vent at all times, and every where, had also given us the power to doe it. But our will, by whose privilege we advance this reproch, how much more likely, and consonant to trueth may we tax it of rebellion, and accuse it of sedition, by reason of its unrulinesse and disobedience? Will shee at all times doe that, which we would have her willingly to doe? Is shee not often willing to effect that, which we forbid her to desire? and that to our manifest prejudice and dammage? Doth she suffer her selfe to be directed by the conclusions of our reason? To conclude, I would urge in defence of my client, that it would please the Judges to consider, that concerning this matter, his cause being inseperably conjoyned to a consort, and indistinctly: yet will not a man addresse himselfe but to him, both by the arguments and charges, which can no way appertaine to his said consort. For, his effect is indeed sometime importunately to invite, but to refuse never: and also to invite silently and quietly. Therefore is the sawcinesse and illegalitie of the accusers seene. Howsoever it be, protesting that Advocates and Judges may wrangle, contend, and give sentence, what, and how they please, Nature will in the meane time follow her course: who, had she endued this member with any particular privilege, yet had she done but right, and shewed but reason. Author of the only immortall worke, of mortall men. Divine worke according to *Socrates;* and love, desire of immortalitie, and immortall *Dœmon* himselfe. Some men peradventure, by the effects of imagination leaveth the pox or Kings evill heere, which his companion carrieth into Spaine againe: loe heere why in such cases men are accustomed to require a prepared minde, wherefore doe Physitians labour and practise before hand the conceit and credence of their patients, with so many false promises of their recoverie and health, unlesse it be that the effect of imagination may supple and prepare the imposture of their decoction? They knew that one of their trades-master hath left written, how some men have been found, in whom the only sight of a potion hath wrought his due operation: All which humor or caprice is now come into my minde, upon the report which an Apothecarie, whilome a servant in my fathers house, was wont to tell me, a man by knowledge simple, and by birth a Switzer; a nation little vaine-glorious, and not much given to lying, which was, that for a long time he had knowne a Merchant in *Tholouse,* sickish, and much troubled with the stone, and who often had need of glisters, who according to the fits and occurrences of his evill, caused them diversly to be prescribed by Physitians. Which being brought him, no accustomed forme to them belonging was omitted, and would often taste whether they were too hot, and view them well, and lying along upon his bed, on his bellie, and all complements performed, only injection excepted, which ceremony ended, the Apothecarie gone, and the patient lying in his bed, even as if he had received a glister indeed, he found and felt the very same effect, which they doe that have effectually taken them. And if the Physitian saw it had not wrought sufficiently, he would accordingly give him two or three more in the same manner. My witnesse protesteth, that the sicke mans wife, to save charges (for he paid for them as if he had received them) having sometimes assaid to make them onely with luke warme water, the effect discovered the craft, and being found not to worke at all, they were forced to returne to the former, and use the Apothecarie. A woman supposing to have swallowed a pinne with her bread, cried and vexed her-selfe, even as if she had felt an intolerable paine in her throat, where she imagined the same to sticke; but because there appeared neither swelling or alteration, a skilfull man deeming it to be but a fantasie conceived, or opinion, apprehended by eating of some gretty peece of bread, which haply might pricke her in the swallow, made her vomit, and unknowne to her, cast a pinne in that which she had vomited. Which the woman perceiving, and imagining she had cast the same, was presently eased of her paine. I have knowne a Gentleman, who having feasted a company of very honest Gentlemen and Gentlewomen, in his owne house, by way of sport, and in jest, boasted two or three daies after (for there was no such thing) that he had made them eat of a baked Cat; whereat [a] Gentlewoman of the companie apprehended such horror, that falling into a violent ague and distemper of her stomacke, she could by no meanes be recovered. Even brute beasts, as well as we, are seene to be subject to the power of imagination; witnesse some Dogs, who for sorrow of their Masters death are seene to die, and whom we ordinarily see to startle and barke in their sleep, and horses to neigh and struggle. But all this may be referred to the narrow suture of the Spirit and the body, enter-communicating their fortunes one unto another. It is another thing, that imagination doth sometimes worke, not only against her owne body, but also against that of others. And even as one body ejecteth a disease to his neighbour, as doth evidently appeare by the plague, pox, or sore eies, that goe from one to another:

> Dum spectant oculi læsos, læduntur et ipsi:
> Multaque corporibus transitione nocent.
>
> OVID. *Am.* ii. 219.

Eies become sore, while they looke on sore eies:
By passage many ills our limmes surprise.

Likewise the imagination moved and tossed by some vehemence, doth cast some darts, that may offend a strange object. Antiquitie hath held, that certaine women of *Scithia*, being provoked and vexed against some men, had the power to kill them, only with their looke. The Tortoises and the Estriges hatch their egges with their looks only, a signe that they have some ejaculative vertue. And concerning witches they are said to have offensive and harme-working eies.

> Nescia quis teneros oculus mihi fascinat agnos.
>
> VIRG. *Buc.* Ecl. iii. 193.

My tender Lambs I cannot see,
By what bad eie, bewitched be.

Magitians are but ill respondents for me. So it is, that by experience wee see women to transferre divers markes of their fantasies, unto children they beare in their wombes: witnes she that brought forth a Blacke-a-more. There was also presented unto *Charles* King of *Bohemia*, an Emperour, a young girle, borne about Pisa, all shagd and hairy over and over, which her mother said, to have beene conceived so, by reason of an image of Saint *John Baptist*, that was so painted, and hung over her bed. That the like is in beasts, is witnessed by *Jacob's* sheepe, and also by partriges and hares, that grow white by the snow upon mountaines. There was lately seene a cat about my owne house, so earnestly eyeing a bird, sitting upon a tree, that he seeing the Cat, they both so wistly fixed their looks one upon another, so long, that at last, the bird fell downe as dead in the Cats pawes, either drunken by his owne strong imagination, or drawne by some attractive power of the Cat. Those that love hawking, have haply heard the Falkner tale, who earnestly fixing his sight upon a Kite in the aire, laid a wager that with the only force of his looke, he would make it come stooping downe to the ground, and as some report did it many times. The Histories I borrow, I referre to the consciences of those I take them from. The discourses are mine, and hold together by the proofe of reason, not of experiences: each man may adde his example to them: and who hath none, considering the number and varietie of accidents, let him not leave to think, there are store of them. If I come not well for my selfe, let another come for me. So in the studie wherein I treat of our manners and motions, the fabulous testimonies, alwaies provided they be likely and possible, may serve to the purpose, as well as the true, whether it hapned or no, be it at *Rome*, or at *Paris*, to *John* or *Peter*, it is alwaies a tricke of humane capacite, of which I am profitably advised by this report. I see it and reape profit by it, as well in shadow as in bodie. And in divers lessons that often histories afford, I commonly make use of that, which is most rare and memorable. Some writers there are, whose end is but to relate the events. Mine, if I could attaine to it, should be to declare, what may come to passe, touching the same. It is justly allowed in schooles, to suppose similitudes, when they have none. Yet doe not I so, and concerning that point, in superstitious religion, I exceed all historicall credit. To the examples I here set downe, of what I have read, heard, done, or seene, I have forbid my selfe so much as to dare to change the least, or alter the idlest circumstances. My conscience doth not falsifie the least jot. I wot not whether my insight doth. Concerning this subject I doe sometimes enter into conceit, that it may well become a Divine, a Philosopher, or rather men of exquisite conscience, and exact wisdome, to write histories. How can they otherwise engage their credit upon a popular reputation? How can they answer for the thoughts of unknowne persons? And make their bare conjectures passe for currant paiment? Of the actions of divers members, acted in their presence, they would refuse to beare witnes of them, if by a judge they were put to their corporall oath. And there is no man so familiarly knowne to them, of whose inward intention they would undertake to answer at full. I hold it lesse hazardous to write of things past, than present; forasmuch as the writer is not bound to give account but of a borrowed trueth. Some perswade mee to write the affaires of my time, imagining I can see them with a sight lesse blinded with passion, than other men, and perhaps neerer, by reason of the accesse which fortune hath given me to the chiefest of divers factions. But they will not say, how for the glory of *Salust*, I would not take the paines; as one that am a vowed enemie to observance, to assiduitie, and to constancie, and that there is nothing so contrarie to my stile, as a continued narration. I doe so often for want of breath breake off and interrupt my selfe. I have neither composition nor explication of any worth. I am as ignorant as a childe of the phrases and vowels belonging to common things. And therefore have I attempted to say what I can, accommodating the matter to my power. Should I take any man for a guide, my measure might differ from his. For, my libertie being so farre, I might haply publish judgments, agreeing with me, and consonant to reason, yet unlawfull and punishable. *Plutarke* would peradventure tell us of that which he hath written, that it is the worke of others, that his examples are in all and everie where true, that they are profitable to posteritie, and presented with a lustre, that lights and directs us unto vertue, and that is his worke. It is not dangerous, as in a medicinable drug, whether in an old tale or report, be it thus or thus, so or so.

CHAPTER XXI

THE PROFIT OF ONE MAN IS THE DAMMAGE OF ANOTHER

DEMADES the Athenian condemned a man of the Citie, whose trade was to sell such necessaries as belonged to burials, under colour, hee asked too much profit for them: and that such profit could not come unto him without the death of many people. This judgement seemeth to be ill taken, because no man profiteth but by the losse of others: by which reason a man should condemne all manner of gaine. The Merchant thrives not but by the licentiousnesse of youth; the Husbandman by dearth of corne; the Architect but by the ruine of houses; the Lawyer by suits and controversies betweene men: Honour it selfe, and practice of religious Ministers, is drawne from our death and vices. *No Physitian delighteth in the health of his owne friend,* saith the ancient Greeke Comike: *nor no Souldier is pleased with the peace of his Citie, and so of the rest.* And which is worse, let every man sound his owne conscience, hee shall finde, that our inward desires are for the most part nourished and bred in us by the losse and hurt of others; which when I considered, I began to thinke, how Nature doth not gainesay herselfe in this, concerning her generall policie: for Physitians hold, that *The birth, increase, and augmentation of every thing, is the alteration and corruption of another.*

> *Nam quodcunque suis mutatum finibus exit,*
> *Continuò hoc mors est illius, quod fuit ante.*
> LUCR. 687, 813; ii. 762; iii. 536.

What ever from it's bounds doth changed passe,
That strait is death of that which erst it was.

CHAPTER XXII

OF CUSTOME, AND HOW A RECEIVED LAW SHOULD NOT EASILY BE CHANGED

My opinion is, that hee conceived aright of the force of custome, that first invented this tale; how a country woman having enured herselfe to cherish and beare a young calfe in her armes, which continuing, shee got such a custome, that when he grew to be a great oxe, shee carried him still in her armes. For truly, *Custome is a violent and deceiving schoole-mistris.* She by little and little, and as it were by stealth, establisheth the foot of her authoritie in us; by which mild and gentle beginning, if once by the aid of time, it have setled and planted the same in us, it will soone discover a furious and tyrannicall countenance unto us, against which we have no more the libertie to lift so much as our eies; wee may plainly see her upon every occasion to force the rules of Nature: *Usus efficacissimus rerum omnium magister* (PLIN. *Epis.* xx.): *Use is the most effectuall master of all things.* I beleeve *Platoes* den mentioned in his common-wealth, and the Physitians that so often quit their arts reason by authoritie; and the same King who by meanes of her, ranged his stomacke to be nourished with poyson; and the mayden that *Albert* mentioneth to have accustomed herselfe to live upon spiders, and now in the new-found world of the *Indians,* there were found divers populous nations, in farre differing climates, that lived upon them; made provision of them, and carefully fed them; as also of grasse-hoppers, pissemires, lizards, and night-bats; and a toad was sold for six crownes in a time that all such meats were scarce amongst them, which they boyle, rost, bake, and dresse with divers kinds of sawces. Others have beene found to whom our usuall flesh and other meats were mortall and venomous. *Consuetudinis magna est vis; Pernoctant venatores in nive, in montibus uri se patiuntur: Pugiles cœstibus contusi, ne ingemiscunt quidem* (CIC. *Tusc. Qu.* ii.). *Great is the force of custome: Huntsmen wil watch all night in snow, and endure to bee scorched on the hils: Fencers brused with sand-bags or cudgels, doe not so much as groane.* These forrein examples are not strange, if wee but consider what we ordinarily finde by travell, and how custome quaileth and weakeneth our customary senses. We need not goe seeke what our neighbours report of the Cataracts of *Nile;* and what Philosophers deeme of the celestiall musicke, which is, that the bodies of it's circles, being solid smooth, and in their rowling motion, touching and rubbing one against another, must of necessitie produce a wonderfull harmonie: by the changes and entercaprings of which, the revolutions, motions, cadences, and carrols of the asters and planets are caused and transported. But that universally the hearing senses of these low worlds creatures, dizzied and lulled asleepe, as those of the Ægyptians are, by the continuation of that sound, how loud and great soever it be, cannot sensibly perceive or distinguish the same. Smiths, Millers, Forgers, Armorers, and such other, could not possibly endure the noise that commonly rings in their eares, if it did pierce them as it doth us. My perfumed Jerkin serveth for my nose to smell into, but after I have worne it three or foure daies together, not I, but others have the benefit of it. This is more strange, that notwithstanding long intermissions, custome may joyne and establish the effect of her impression upon our senses; as they prove that dwell neere to bells or steeples. I have my lodging neere unto a tower, where both evening and morning a very great bell doth chime *Ave marie* and *Cover-few*, which jangling doth even make the tower to shake; at first it troubled me much, but I was soone acquainted with it, so that now I am nothing offended with it, and many times it cannot waken me out of my sleepe. *Plato* did once chide a child for playing with nuts, who answered him, *Thou chidest me for a small matter. Custome* (replied Plato) *is no small matter.* I finde that our greatest vices make their first habit in us, from our infancie, and that our chiefe government and education, lieth in our nurses hands. Some mothers thinke it good sport to see a childe wring off a chickens necke, and strive to beat a dog or cat. And some fathers are so fond-foolish, that they will conster as a good Augur or fore-boding of a martiall minde to see their sonnes misuse a poore peasant, or tug a lackey, that doth not defend himselfe; and impute it to a ready wit, when by some wily disloyaltie, or craftie deceit, they see them cousin and over-reach their fellowes: yet are they the true seeds or roots of cruelty, of tyranny, and of treason. In youth they bud, and afterward grow to strength, and come to perfection by meanes of custome.

And it is a very dangerous institution, to excuse so base and vile inclinations, with the weaknesse of age, and lightnesse of the subject. First, it is nature that speaketh, whose voice is then shriller, purer, and more native, when it is tender, newer, and youngest. Secondly, the deformity of the crime consisteth not in the difference betweene crownes and pinnes; it depends of it selfe. I find it more just to conclude thus: Why should not hee as well deceive one of a crowne, as he doth of a pinne? than as commonly some doe, saying, alas, it is but a pinne; I warrant you, he will not doe so with crownes. A man would carefully teach children to hate vices of their owne genuity, and so distinguish the deformity of them, that they may not only eschew them in their actions, but above all, hate them in their hearts: and what colour soever they beare, the very conceit may seeme odious unto them. I know well, that because in my youth I have ever accustomed my selfe to tread a plaine beaten path, and have ever hated to entermeddle any manner of deceipt of cousoningcraft, even in my childish sports, (for truly it is to be noted, that Childrens playes are not sports, and should be deemed as their most serious actions). There is no pastime so slight, and inwardlie I have not a naturall propension, and serious care, yea extreme contradiction, not to use any deceit. I shuffle and handle the cards, as earnestly for counters, and keepe as strict an accompt, as if they were double duckets, when playing with my wife or children, it is indifferent to mee whether I win or lose, as I doe when I play in good earnest. How and wheresoever it be, mine owne eies will suffice to keepe me in office; none else doe watch mee so narrowly; [nor] that I respect more. It is not long since in mine owne house, I saw a little man, who at *Nantes* was borne without armes, and hath so well fashioned his feet to those services, his hands should have done him, that in truth they have almost forgotten their naturall office. In all his discourses he nameth them his hands, he carveth any meat, he chargeth and shoots off a pistole, he threds a needle, he soweth, he writeth, puts off his cap, combeth his head, plaieth at cards and dice; shuffleth and handleth them with a great dexteritie as any other man that hath the perfect use of his hands: the monie I have sometimes given him, he hath carried away with his feet, as well as any other could doe with his hands. I saw another, being a Childe, that with the bending and winding of his necke (because hee had no hands) would brandish a two-hand-Sword, and mannage a Holbard, as nimbly as any man could doe with his hands: he would cast them in the aire, then receive them againe, he would throw a Dagger, and make a whip to yarke and lash, as cunningly as any Carter in *France*. But her effects are much better discovered in the strange impressions, which it worketh in our mindes where it meetes not so much resistance. What cannot she bring to passe in our judgements, and in our conceits? Is there any opinion, so fantastical, or conceit so extravagant (I omit to speake of the grosse imposture of religions, wherewith so many great nations and so many worthy and sufficient men have beene besotted, and drunken: For, being a thing beyond the compasse of our humane reason, it is more excusable if a man that is not extraordinarily illuminated thereunto by divine favour, doe lose and mis-carrie himselfe therein) or of other opinions, is there any so strange, that custome hath not planted and established by lawes in what regions soever it hath thought good? And this ancient exclamation is most just: *Non pudet physicum, id est speculatorem venatoremque naturæ, ab animis consuetudine imbutis quærere testimonium veritatis?* (CIC. *Nat. De.* i.). *Is it not a shame for a naturall Philosopher, that is the watch-man and huntsman of nature, to seeke the testimonie of truth, from mindes endued and double dide with custome?* I am of opinion, that no fantasie so mad can fall into humane imagination, that meetes not with the example of some publike custome, and by consequence that our reason doth not ground and bring to a stay. There are certaine people, that turne their backs towards those they salute, and never looke him in the face whom they would honour or worship. There are others, who when the King spitteth, the most favoured Ladie in his court stretcheth forth her hand; and in another countrey, where the noblest about him, stoope to the ground to gather his ordure in some fine linnen cloth: Let us here by the way insert a tale. A French Gentleman was ever wont to blow his nose in his hand, (a thing much against our fashion) maintaining his so doing; and who in wittie jesting was very famous. He asked me on a time, what privilege this filthie excrement had, that wee should have a daintie linnen cloth or hand-kercher to receive the same; and which is worse, so carefully folded up, and keepe the same about us, which should be more loathsome to ones stomacke, than to see it cast away, as wee doe all our other excrements and filth. Mee thought he spake not altogether without reason: and custome had taken from me the discerning of this strangenesse, which being reported of an other countrie we deeme so hideous. Miracles are according to the ignorance wherein we are by nature, and not according to natures essence; use brings the sight of our judgement asleepe. The barbarous heathen are nothing strange to us, than we are to them: nor with more occasion, as every man would avow, if after he had travelled through these farre-fetcht examples, hee could stay himselfe upon the discourses, and soundly conferre them. Humane reason is a tincture in like weight and measure, infused into all our opinions and customes, what form soever they be of: infinite in matter: infinite in diversitie. But I will returne to my theme. There are certaine people, where, except his wife and children, no man speaketh to the King, but through a trunke. Another nation, where virgins shew their secret parts openly, and married women diligently hide and cover them. To which custome, this fashion used in other places, hath some relation: where chastitie is nothing regarded but for marriage sake; and maidens may at their pleasure lie with whom they list; and being with childe, they may without feare of accusation, spoyle and cast their children, with certaine medicaments, which they have only for that purpose. And in another country, if a Merchant chance to marrie, all other Merchants that are bidden to the wedding, are bound to lie with the bride before her husband, and the more they are in number, the more honour and commendation is hers, for constancie and capacitie: the like if a gentleman or an officer marrie; and so of all others: except it be a day-labourer, or some other of base condition; for then must the Lord or Prince lie with the bride; amongst whom (notwithstanding this abusive custome) loyaltie in married women is highly regarded, and held in speciall account, during the time they are married. Others there are, where publike brothel-houses of men are kept, and where open mart of marriages are ever to be had:

where women goe to the warres with their husbands, and have place, not onely in fight, but also in command, where they doe not onely weare jewels at their noses, in their lip and cheekes, and in their toes, but also big wedges of gold through their paps and buttocks, where when they eat, they wipe their fingers on their thighs, on the bladder of their genitories, and the soles of their feet, where not children, but brethren and nephewes inherit; and in some places, the nephewes onely, except in the succession of the Prince. Where to order the communitie of goods, which amongst them is religiously observed, certaine Soveraigne Magistrats have the generall charge of husbandry and tilling of the lands, and of the distribution of the fruits, according to every mans need: where they howle and weepe at their childrens deaths, and joy and feast at their old mens decease. Where ten or twelve men lie all in one bed with all their wives, where such women as lose their husbands, by any violent death, may marrie againe, others not: where the condition of women is so detested, that they kill all the maiden children, so soone as they are borne, and to supply their naturall need, they buy women of their neighbours. Where men may at their pleasure, without alleaging any cause, put away their wives, but they (what just reason soever they have) can never put away their husbands. Where husbands may lawfully sell their wives, if they be barren. Where they cause dead bodies first to be boyled and then to be brayed in a mortar, so long till it come to a kind of pap, which afterwards they mingle with their wine, and so drinke it. Where the most desired sepulcher that some wish for, is to bee devoured of dogges, and in some places of birds. Where some thinke, that blessed soules live in all liberty, in certaine pleasant fields stored with al commodities, and that from them proceeds that *Eccho*, which we heare. Where they fight in the water, and shoot exceeding true with their bowes as they are swimming. Where in signe of subjection men must raise their shoulders, and stoope with their heads, and put off their shooes when they enter their Kings houses. Where Eunuchs that have religious women in keeping, because they shall not be loved, have also their noses and lips cut off. And Priests that they may the better acquaint themselves with their *Demons*, and take their Oracles, put out their eyes. Where every man makes himselfe a God of what he pleaseth: the hunter of a Lion or a Fox; the fisher, of a certaine kinde of Fish; and frame themselves Idols of every humane action or passion: the Sunne, the Moone, and the earth are their chiefest Gods: the forme of swearing is, to touch the ground, looking upon the Sunne, and where they eat both flesh and fish raw. Where the greatest oath is to sweare by the name of some deceased man, that hath lived in good reputation in the countrie, touching his grave with the hand. Where the newyeares gifts that Kings send unto Princes their vassals every yeare, is some fire, which when it is brought, all the old fire is cleane put out: of which new fire all the neighbouring people are bound upon paine *læsæ majestatis*, to fetch for their uses. Where, when the King (which often commeth to passe) wholly to give himselfe unto devotion, giveth over his charge, his next successor is bound to doe like, and convayeth the right of the Kingdome unto the third heire. Where they diversifie the forme of policie, according as their affaires seeme to require: and where they depose their Kings, when they thinke good, and appoint them certaine ancient grave men to undertake and weald the Kingdoms government, which sometimes is also committed to the communaltie. Where both men and women are equally circumcised, and alike baptised. Where the Souldier, that in one or divers combats hath presented his King with seven enemies heads, is made noble. Where some live under that so rare and unsociable opinion of the mortalitie of soules. Where women are brought a bed without paine or griefe. Where women on both their legs weare greaves of Copper: and if a louse bite them, they are bound by duty of magnanimitie to bite it againe: and no maid dare marrie, except she have first made offer of her Virginitie to the King. Where they salute one another laying the forefinger on the ground, and then lifting it up toward heaven: where all men beare burthens upon their head, and women on their shoulders. Where women pisse standing, and men cowring. Where in signe of true friendship they send one another some of their owne bloud, and offer incense to men which they intend to honour, as they doe to their Gods: where not onely kindred and consanguinitie in the fourth degree, but in any furthest off, can by no meanes be tolerated in marriages: where children sucke till they be four, and sometimes twelve yeares old, in which place they deeme it a dismall thing to give a childe sucke the first day of his birth. Where fathers have the charge to punish their male-children, and mothers onely maid-children, and whose punishment is to hang them up by the feet and so to smoke them. Where women are circumcised; where they eat all manner of herbes, without other distinction, but to refuse those that have ill favour: where all things are open, and how faire and rich soever their houses be, they have neither doores nor windowes, nor any chests to locke; yet are all theeves much more severely punished there, than any where else; where, as monkies doe, they kill lice with their teeth, and thinke it a horrible matter to see them crusht between their nailes; where men so long as they live never cut their hair, nor paire their nailes: another place where they onely paire the nailes of their right hand, and those of the left are never cut, but very curiously maintained: where they endevour to cherish all the haire growing on the right side, as long as it will grow: and very often shave away that of the left-side: where in some Provinces neere unto us, some women cherish their haire before, and other some that behinde, and shave the contrarie: where fathers lend their children, and husbands their wives to their guests, so that they pay ready mony: where men may lawfully get their mother with childe: where fathers may lie with their daughters, and with their sonnes: where, in solemne assemblies and banquets, without any distinction of bloud or alliance, men will lend one another their children. In some places men feede upon humane flesh, and in others, where it is deemed an office of pietie in children to kill their fathers at a certaine age: in other places fathers appoint what children shall live, and be preserved, and which die and be caste out, whilst they are yet in their mothers wombe: where old husbands lend their wives to yong men, for what use soever they please: In other places, where al women are common without sinne or offence: yea in some places, where for a badge of honour, they weare as many frienged tassels, fastened to the skirt of their garment as they have laine with severall men. Hath not custome also made a severall common-wealth of women? hath it not taught them to manage Armes? to levie Armies, to marshall men, and to deliver battles? And that which strict-searching Philosophie could never perswade the wisest, doth she not of her owne naturall instinct teach it to the grosest headed vulgar? For we know whole nations, where death is not only con[t]emned, but cherished; where children of seven years of age, without changing of countenance, or shewing any signe of dismay, endured to be whipped to death; where riches and worldly pelfe was so despised and holden so contemptible, that the miserablest and neediest wretch of a Citie would have scorned to stoope for a purse full of gold. Have we not heard of divers most fertile regions, plenteously yeelding al maner of necessary victuals, where neverthelesse the most ordinary cates and daintiest dishes, were but bread, water-cresses, and water? Did not custome worke this wonder in *Chios*, that during the space of seven hundred yeres it was never found or heard of, that any woman or maiden had her honor or honestie called in question? And to conclude, there is nothing in mine opinion, that either she doth not, or cannot: and with reason doth *Pindarus*, as I have heard say, *Call her the Queene and Empresse of all the world*. He that was met beating of his father, answered, *It was the custome of his house; that his father had so beaten his grandfather, and he his great-grandfather, and pointing to his sonne, said, this child shall also beat mee, when he shall come to my age*. And the father, whom the sonne haled and dragged through thicke and thinne in the street, commanded him to stay at a certaine doore, for himself had dragged his father no further: which were the bounds of the hereditarie and injurious demeanours the children of that family were wont to shew their fathers. *By custome*, said Aristotle, *as often as by sicknesse, doe we see women tug and tear their haires, bite their nailes, and eat cole and earth: and more by custome than by nature doe men meddle and abuse themselves with men*. The lawes of conscience, which we say to proceed from nature, rise and proceed of custome: every man holding in special regard, and inward veneration the opinions approved, and customes received about him, cannot without remorse leave them, nor without applause applie himselfe unto them; when those of *Creet* would in former ages curse any man, they besought the Gods to engage him in some bad custome. But the chiefest effect of her power is to seize upon us, and so entangle us, that it shall hardly lie in us, to free our selves from her hold-fast, and come into our wits againe, to discourse and reason of her ordinances; verily, because wee sucke them with the milke of our birth, and forasmuch as the worlds visage presents it selfe in that estate unto our first view, it seemeth we are borne with a condition to follow that course. And the common imaginations we finde in credit about us, and by our fathers seed infused in our soule, seeme to be the generall and naturall. Whereupon it followeth, that whatsoever is beyond the compasse of custome, wee deeme likewise to bee beyond the compasse of reason; God knowes how for the most part, unreasonably. If as we, who study our selves, have learned to doe, every man that heareth a just sentence, would presently consider, how it may in any sort belonging unto his private state, each man should finde, that this is not so much a good word, as a good blow to the ordinary sottishnesse of his judgement. But men receive the admonitions of truth and her precepts, as directed to the vulgar, and never to themselves; and in lieu of applying them to their manners, most men most foolishly and unprofitably apply them to their memorie. But let us returne to customes soveraignty: such as are brought up to libertie, and to command themselves, esteeme all other forme of policie, as monstrous and against nature. Those that are enured to Monarchie doe the like. And what facilitie soever fortune affordeth them to change, even when with great difficultie they have shaken off the importunitie of a tutor, they run to plant a new one with semblable difficulties, because they cannot resolve themselves to hate tutorship. It is by the [mediation] of custome, that every man is contented with the place where nature hath setled him: and the savage people of *Scotland* have nought to doe with *Touraine*, nor the Scithians with *Thessalie*. *Darius* demanded of certaine Græcians, *For what they would take upon them the Indians custome, to eat their deceased fathers*. (For such was their maner, thinking they could not possibly give them a more noble and favourable tombe than in their owne bowels) they answered him, *That nothing in the world should ever bring them to embrace so inhumane a custome*. But having also attempted to perswade the Indians to leave their fashion, and take the Græcians, which was to burne their corpes, they were much more astonied thereat. Every man doth so, forsomuch as custome doth so bleare us that we cannot distinguish the true visage of things.

Nil adeo magnum, nec tam mirabile quicquam
Principio, quod non minuant mirarier omnes
Paulatim.—LUCR. ii. 1037.

Nothing at first so wondrous is, so great,
But all, t'admire, by little slake their heat.

Having other times gone about to endeare, and make some one of
our observations to be of force, and which was with resolute auctoritie
received in most parts about us, and not desiring, as most men doe,
onely to establish the same by the force of lawes and examples, but
having ever bin from her beginning, I found the foundation of it so
weak, that my selfe, who was to confirme it in others, had much adoe
to keepe my countenance. This is the receipt by which *Plato* undertaketh to banish the unnaturall and preposterous loves of his time, and
which hee esteemeth Soveraigne and principall: To wit, that publike
opinion may condemne them; that Poets, and all men else may tell
horrible tales of them. A receit by meanes whereof the fairest Daughters winne no more the love of their fathers, nor brethren most excellent
in beautie, the love of their sisters. The very fables of *Thyestes,* of
Oedipus, and of *Macareus,* having with the pleasure of their songs
infused this profitable opinion, in the tender conceit of children. Certes,
chastitie is an excellent vertue, the commoditie whereof is very well
knowne: but to use it, and according to nature to prevaile with it, is
as hard as it is easie, to endeare it and to prevaile with it according to
custome, to lawes and precepts. The first and universall reasons are
of a hard perscrutation. And our Masters passe them over in gleaning,
or in not daring so much as to taste them, at first sight cast themselves
headlong into the libertie or sanctuarie of custome. Those that will not
suffer themselves to be drawne out of his originall source, do also
commit a greater error, and submit themselves to savage opinions:
witnesse *Chrysippus;* who in so many severall places of his compositions, inserted the small accompt he made of conjunctions, how in-
cestuous soever they were. Hee that will free himselfe from this violent
prejudice of custome, shall find divers things received with an undoubted resolution, that have no other anker but the hoarie head and
frowning wrimples of custome, which ever attends them: which maske
being pulled off, and referring all matters to truth and reason, he shall
perceive his judgement, as it were overturned, and placed in a much
surer state. As for example, I wil then aske him, what thing can be
more strange than to see a people bound to follow lawes, he never
understood? Being in all his domesticall affaires, as marriages, donations, testaments, purchases, and sales, necessarily bound to customary
rules, which forsomuch as they were never written nor published in his
owne tongue, he cannot understand, and whereof he must of necessity
purchase the interpretation and use. Not according to the ingenious
opinion of *Isocrates,* who counselleth his King *to make the Trafikes*

and negotiations of his subjects, free, enfranchized and gaineful, and their debates, controversies, and quarrels burthensome, and charged with great subsidies, and impositions: But according to a prodigious opinion, to make open sale, and trafficke of reason it selfe, and to give lawes a course of merchandize, is very strange. I commend fortune, for that (as our Historians report) it was a gentleman of *Gaskonie*, and my Countriman, that first opposed himselfe against *Charles* the great, at what time he went about to establish the Latine and Im-periall lawes amongst us. What is more barbarous than to see a nation, where by lawful custome the charge of judging is sold, and judgements are paid for with readie money; and where justice is lawfully denied him, that hath not wherewithall to pay for it; and that this merchan-dize hath so great credit, that in a politicall government there should be set up a fourth estate of Lawyers, breath-sellers, and pettifoggers, and joyned to the three ancient states, to wit, the Clergie, the Nobility, and the Communaltie; which fourth state having the charge of lawes, and sometimes auctoritie of goods and lives, should make a body, apart, and severall from that of Nobilitie, whence double Lawes must follow; those of honour, and those of justice; in many things very contrarie do those as rigorously condemne à lie pocketed up, as these a lie revenged: by the law and right of armes he that putteth up an injurie shall be degraded of honour and nobilitie; and he that re-vengeth himselfe of it, shall by the civill Law incurre a capitall punish-ment. Hee that shall addresse himselfe to the Lawes to have reason for some offence done unto his honour, dishonoreth himselfe. And who doth not so, is by the Lawes punished and chastised. And of these so differ-ent parts, both neverthelesse having reference to one head; those having peace, these war committed to their charge; those having the gaine, these the honor: those knowledge, these vertue: those reason, these strength: those the word, these action: those justice, these valour: those reason, these force: those a long gowne, and these a short coat, in partage and share. Touching indifferent things, as clothes and gar-ments, whosoever will reduce them to their true end, which is the service and commodity of the bodie, whence dependeth their originall grace and comlines, for the most fantasticall to my humour that may be imagined, amongst others I will give them our square caps; that long hood of plaited velvet, that hangs over our womens heads, with his parti-coloured traile, and that vaine and unprofitable modell of a member, which we may not so much as name with modestie, whereof notwithstanding we make publike shew, and open demonstration. These considerations do neverthelesse never distract a man of under-standing from following the common guise. Rather on the contrary, me seemeth, that all severall, strange, and particular fashions proceed rather of follie, or ambitious affectation, than of true reason: and that a wise man ought inwardly to retire his minde from the common presse, and hold the same liberty and power to judge freely of all things, but for outward matters, he ought absolutely to follow the fashions and forme•customarily received. Publike societie hath nought to do with our thoughts; but for other things, as our actions, our travel, our fortune, and our life, that must be accommodated and left to it's service and common opinions: as that good and great *Socrates,* who refused to save his life by disobeying the magistrate, yea a magistrate most wicked and unjust. For that is the rule of rules, and generall law of lawes, for every man to observe those of the place wherein he liveth.

Νόμοις ἕπεσθαι τοῖσιν ἐγχώροις καλὸν.
                                Gnom. Græc. vii.

Lawes of the native place,
To follow, is a grace.

Loe here some of another kind. There riseth a great doubt, whether any so evident profit may be found in the change of a received law, of what nature soever, as there is hurt in removing the same; forsomuch as a well setled policie may be compared to a frame or building of divers parts joyned together with such a ligament as it is impossible to stirre or displace one, but the whole body must needes be shaken, and shew a feeling of it. The Thurians Law-giver instituted, that, *whosoever would goe about, either to abolish any one of the old Lawes, or attempt to establish a new, should present himself before the people with a roape about his necke, to the end, that if his invention were not approved of all men, he should presently bee strangled.* And he of *Lacedæmon* laboured all his life to get an assured promise of his citizens, that they would never infringe any one of his ordinances. That *Ephore* or *Tribune,* who so rudely cut off the two strings, that *Phrinis* had added unto musicke, respecteth not whether musicke be better or no with them, or whether the accords of it be better filled, he hath sufficient reason to condemne them, because it is an alteration of the old forme. It is that which the old rustie sword of justice of *Marseille* did signifie. I am distasted with noveltie, what countenance soever it shew: and I have reason so to be, for I have seene very hurtfull effects follow the same. That which so many yeares since doth so presse us, hath not yet exploited all. But some may alleage with appearance, that by accident, it hath produced and engendred all, yea both the mischiefes and ruines, that since are committed without and against it: it is that a man should blame and finde fault with.

Heu patior telis vulnera facta meis.
                                OVID. *Epist. Phyl.* 43.

Alas I suffer smart
Procur'd by mine owne dart.

Those which attempt to shake an Estate, are commonly the first overthrowne by the fall of it: he that is first mover of the same, reapeth not alwayes the fruit of such troubles; he beats and troubleth the water for others to fish in. The contexture and combining of this mon-archie, and great building, having bin dismist and disolved by it, namely in her old yeares, giveth as much overture and entrance as a man will to like injuries. Royall Majestie doth more hardly fall from the top to the middle, than it tumbleth downe from the middle to the bottom. But if the inventors are more damageable, the imitators are more vicious, to cast themselves into examples, of which they have both felt and punished the horror and mischiefe. And if there be any degree of honour, even in ill doing, these are indebted to others for the glory of the invention, and courage of the first attempt. All sorts of new licentiousnesse doe haply draw out of this originall and fruitfull source, the images and patterns to trouble our common-wealth. We may reade in our very lawes, made for the remedie of the first evill, the apprentisage and excuse of all sorts of wicked enterprises: And in favour of publike vices, they are named with new and more pleasing words for their excuses, bastardizing and allaying their true titles: yet it is to reforme our consciences and our conceits, *Honesta oratio est* (TEREN. *And.* act. i. sc. 1). *It is an honest speech and well said.* But the best pretence of innovation or noveltie is most dangerous: *Adeo nihil motum ex antiquo probabile est. So nothing moved out of the first place is allowable:* Yet me seemeth (if I may speake boldly) that it argueth a great selfe-love and presumption, for a man to esteeme his opinions so far, that for to establish them, a man must be faine to subvert a publike peace, and introduce so many inevitable mischiefes, and so horrible a corruption of manners, as civill warres, and altera-tions of a state bring with them, in matters of such consequence, and to bring them into his owne countrie. Is it not ill husbanded to advance so many certaine and knowne vices, for to combate contested and debatable errors? Is there any worse kinde of vices, than those which shocke a mans owne conscience and naturall knowledge? The Senate durst give this defeate in payment about the controversies betweene it and the people for the mysterie of their religion: *Ad deos, id magis quàm ad se pertinere: ipsos visuros, ne sacra sua polluantur: That that did rather belong to the Gods than to them, and the Gods should looke at it, that their due rites were not polluted.* Agreeing with that, which the Oracle answered those of *Delphos,* in the *Median* warre, fearing the invasions of the *Persians.* They demanded of that God what they should doe with the treasures consecrated to his Temple, whether hide, or cary them away: who answered them, that they should remove nothing, but take care of themselves, for he was able to provide for all things that were fit for him. Christian religion hath all the markes of extreme justice and profit, but none more apparent than the exact commendation of obedience due unto magistrates, and manutention of policies: what wonderfull example hath divine wisdome left us, which to establish the wel-fare of humane kinde, and to conduct this glorious victorie of hers against death and sinne, would not do it but at the mercy of our politik order, and hath submitted the progresse of it, and the conduct of so high and worthie effect, to the blindnesse and injustice of our observations and customes, suffering the innocent bloud of so many her favored elect to run, and allowing a long losse of yeares for the ripening of this inestimable fruit? There is much difference betweene the cause of him that followeth the formes and lawes of his countrie, and him that undertaketh to governe and change them. The first alleageth for his excuse, simplicitie, obedience, and example; whatsoever he doth cannot be malice, at the most it is but ill lucke. *Quis est enim, quem non moveat clarissimis monumentis testata consignataque antiquitas?* (CIC. *Div.* i.). *For who is he whom antiquitie will not move, being witnessed and signed with former monuments?* Besides that which *Isocrates* saith, that *defect hath more part in moderation, that hath excesse.* The other is in much worse case. For he that medleth with chusing and changing, usurpeth the authoritie of judging: and must resolve himselfe to see the fault of what he hunteth for, and the good of what he bringeth in. This so vulgar consideration hath confirmed me in my state, and restrained my youth, that was more rash, from burthening my shoulders with so filthie a burthen, as to make my selfe respondent of so important a science. And in this to dare, what in sound judgement I durst not in the easiest of those wherein I had beene instructed, and wherein the rashnes of judging is of no prejudice. Seeming most impious to me, to goe about to submit publike constitutions and unmoveable observances, to the instabilitie of a private fantasie (private reason is but a private jurisdiction) and to undertake that on divine-lawes, which no policie would tolerate in civill law. Wherein although mans reason have much more commerce, yet are they soveraignly judges of their judges: and their extreme sufficiencie serveth to expound custome and extend the use, that of them is received, and not to divert and innovate the same. If at any time divine providence hath gone beyond the rules, to which it hath necessary constrained us, it is not to give us a dispensation from them. They are blowes of her divine hand, which we ought not imitate, but admire: as extraordinarie examples, markes of an expresse and particular avowing of the severall kinds of wonders, which for a testimonie of her omnipotencie it offereth us, beyond our orders and forces, which it is follie and impietie to goe about to represent, and which we ought not follow but contemplate with admiration, and meditate with astonishment. Acts of her personage, and not of ours. *Cotta* protesteth very opportunely; *Quum de religione agitur, T. Coruncanum, P. Scipionem, P. Scævolam, Pontifices maximos, non Zenonem, aut Cleanthem, aut Chrysippum, sequor* (CIC. *de Nat.* iii. p.). *When we talke of religion, I follow Titus Coruncanus, Publius Scipio, P. Scævola, and the professors of religion, not Zeno, Cleanthes, or Chrysippus.*

May God know it in our present quarrell, wherein are a hundred articles, yea, great and deepe articles, to be removed and altered, although many there are, who may boast to have exactly survaid the reasons and foundations of one and other faction. It is a number, if it be a number, that should have no great meane to trouble us. But whither goeth all this other throng? Under what colours doth it quarter it selfe? It followeth of theirs, as of other weake and ill applied medicines, the humors, that it would have purged in us, it hath enflamed, exasperated, and sharpned, by her conflict, and still do remaine in our bodies. It could not by reason of her weaknesse purge us, but hath rather weakned us; so that we cannot now void it, and by her operation we reap nothing but long, continuall, and intestine griefes and aches, yet is it, that fortune, ever reserving her authoritie above our discourses, doth somtimes present us the urgent necessitie, that lawes must needs yeeld her some place: And when a man resisteth the increase of an innovation, brought in by violence, to keepe himselfe each-where and altogether in rule and bridle against those that have the keyes of fields, to whom all things are lawfull, that may in any sort advance their desseigne, that have not law, nor order, but to follow their advantage, it is a dangerous obligation, and prejudiciall inequalitie.

Aditum nocendi perfido præstat fides.
> SEN. *Oed*. act. iii. sc. 1.

Trust in th' untrustie, may
To hurt make open way.

For so much as the ordinarie discipline of an estate, that hath his perfect health, doth not provide for these extraordinarie accidents, it presupposeth a bodie holding it selfe in his principall members and offices, and a common consent to observe and obey it. Lawfull proceeding is a cold, dull, heavie and forced proceeding: and is not like to hold out against a licentious and unbridled proceeding. It is yet as all men know, a reproach to those two great personages, *Octavius* and *Cato*, in their civill warres; the one of *Scilla*, the other of *Cæsar*, because they rather suffered their countrie to incur all extremities, than by her lawes to aid her, or to innovate any thing. For truly in these last necessities, where nothing is left to take hold by, it were peradventure better, to shrug the shoulders, stoope the head, and somewhat yeeld to the stroke, than beyond possibilitie to make head and resist, and be nothing the better, and give violence occasion to trample all underfoot: and better were it to force the lawes to desire but what they may, since they may not what they would. So did he that ordained them to sleep foure and twentie houres: And he who for a time removed one day from the Calendar: And another who of the moneth of June made a second May. The Lacedemonians themselves, so strict observers of their countries ordinances, being urged by their Lawes, which precisely forbad and inhibited to chuse one man twice to be their Admirall, and on the other side their affaires necessarily requiring, that *Lysander* should once more take that charge upon him, they created one *Aracus* Admirall, but instituted *Lysander* superintendent of all maritime causes. And with the same sutteltie, one of their Ambassadors being sent to the Athenians for to obtaine the change of some ordinance, *Pericles* alleaging, that *it was expresly forbid to remove the table, wherein a law had once beene set downe,* perswaded him but to turne it, for that was not forbidden. It is that whereof *Plutarke* commendeth *Philopœmen,* who being borne to command, could not onely command according to the lawes, but the lawes themselves, whensoever publike necessitie required it.

CHAPTER XXIII

DIVERS EVENTS FROM ONE SELFE SAME COUNSELL

JAMES AMIOT, great Almoner of *France,* did once tell me this storie, to the honour of one of our Princes, (and so he was indeed by very good tokens, albeit by off-spring he were a stranger) that during our first troubles, at the siege of *Roane,* the said Prince being advertised by the Queene-mother of a conspiracie and enterprise, that should be attempted against his life, and by letters particularly informed him of the partie that should performe it, who was a gentleman of *Anjow,* or *Manse,* and who to that purpose did ordinarily frequent the said Princes court; he never imparted that secret or communicated that warning to any man, but the next morrow walking upon Saint *Catherins* hill, whence our batterie played against the towne (for it was, at what time we laid siege to *Roane*) with the said Lord great Almoner: and another Bishop by his side, he chanced to descrie the said gentleman, whom the Queene-mother had described unto him, and caused him to be called, who being come before his presence, said thus unto him, perceiving him alreadie to wax pale, and tremble at the alarums of his conscience: *Master, such a one, I am fully perswaded you fore-imagine what I will charge you with, and your countenance doth plainly shew it, you can conceale nothing from me: for I am so well instructed of your businesse, that would you goe about to hide it, you should but marre all, you have perfect knowledge of this and this thing,* (which were the chiefest props and devices of the secretest drifts of his com-plot and conspiracie) *faile not therefore as you tender your life, to confesse the truth of all your purpose.* When the silly man saw himselfe so surprized and convicted (for the whole matter had beene discovered unto the Queene by one of the complices) he had no other way, but to lift up his hands, and beg for grace and mercie at the Princes hands, at whose feete he would have prostrated himselfe, but that he would not let him: thus following his discourse; *Come hither my friend,* said he, *Did I ever doe you any displeasure? Have I ever through any particu-*

lar hatred, wronged or offended any friend of yours? It is not yet three weeks since I knew you, what reason might move you to conspire and enterprise my death? The Gentleman with a faint trembling voyce, and selfe-accusing looke, answered him, that no particular occasion had ever moved him to that, but the interest of the generall cause of his faction, and that some of them had perswaded him, that to root out, and in what manner soever, to make away so great an enemy of their religion, would be an execution full of pietie, and a worke of supererogation. Then said the Prince, *I will shew you how much the religion which I professe is more milde, than that whereof you make profession: yours hath perswaded you to kill me, without hearing me, having never been offended by me: and mine, commands me to pardon you, convicted as you are, that you would so treacherously and without cause have killed me. Goe your way, withdraw your selfe, let mee never see you here againe, and if you be wise, hence-forward in your enterprises take honester men for your counsellers, than those of your religion.* The Emperour *Augustus* being in *Gaule*, received certaine advertisement of a conspiracie, that *L. Cinna* complotted against him, whereof he purposed to be avenged, and for that purpose sent to all his friends against the next morrow for advice and counsell, but passed the fore-going night with great anxietie and unrest, considering that following his intent, he should bring a yong Gentleman, well borne, of a noble house, and great *Pompeyes* nephew, to his death: which perplexitie produced divers strange discourses and consideration in him. *What?* said he unto himselfe, *Shall it ever be reported, that I doe live in feare, and suffer mine enemie to walke at his pleasure and libertie? Shall he then goe free, that hath attempted and resolved to deprive me of my life, which both by sea and land I have saved from so many civill warres, and from so many battels? And now that I have established an universall peace in the world, shall he be absolved and goe unpunished, that hath not only determined to murther, but to sacrifice me?* (For, the complot of the conspiricie was to murther him, when he should be at sacrifice.) After that, having taken some rest with himselfe, he with a lowder voice began to exclaime and cry out against himselfe, saying, *Why livest thou, if the lives of so many depend on thy death? Shall thy vengeance and cruelties never have an end? Is thy life of that worth, as it may countervaile the sundry mischiefes that are like to ensue, if it be preserved? Livia* his wife being in bed with him, perceiving his agonie, and hearing his speeches, said thus unto him: *And may not womens counsels be admitted? Doe as Physitians are wont, who when their ordinarie receipts will not worke, have recourse to the contrarie. Hitherto thou couldest never doe any good with severitie:* Lepidus *hath followed* Savidienus, Murena Lepidus, [Scipio] Murena, Egnatius [Scipio] ; *begin now to prove what good lenitie and clemencie will doe thee.* Cinna *is convicted, pardon him: To annoy or hurt thee now, he is not able, and thou shalt thereby increase thy glory.* Augustus seemed very glad to have found an Advocate of his humour, and having thanked his wife, and countermanded his friends, whom he had summoned to the Counsell, commanded *Cinna* to be brought before him alone. Then sending all men out of his chamber, and a chaire prepared for *Cinna* to sit in, he thus bespake him: *First* Cinna, *I require to have gentle audience, and that thou wilt not interrupt my speech, which ended, I will give thee time and leasure to answer me: Thou knowest (oh Cinna) that when I had taken thee prisoner in mine enemies campe, who wast not only become, but borne my foe; I saved thee, then put thee in quiet possession of thy goods, and at last, have so enriched thee, and placed thee in so high a degree, that even the conquerours are become envious over the conquered. The Priests office, which thou beggedst at my hands, I freely bestowed on thee, having first refused the same to others, whose fathers and friends had in many battels shed their bloud for me: After all which benefits, and that I had in dutie tied thee so fast unto me, thou hast notwithstanding undertaken to kill me.* To whom *Cinna* replied, crying alowd, *That he had never so much as conceived so wicked a thought, much lesse entertained the same.* Oh Cinna, *this is not according to thy promise,* answered then *Augustus, which was, that thou wouldest not interrupt me: What I say, is true, thou hast undertaken to murther me, in such a place, on such a day, in such a company, and in such manner:* and seeing him so amazed in heart, and by his evidence strucken dumbe, moved thereunto, not by the condition of his promise, but by the guilt of his selfe-accusing conscience; *why wouldest thou doe it,* replied he, *is it because thou wouldest be Emperour? Truely the commonwealth is but in hard condition, if none but my selfe hinder thee from the Empire. Thou canst not so much as defend thine owne house, and didst but lately lose a processe, only by the favor of a seely libertine. What? hast thou no meane or power in any other matter, but to attempt* Cæsars *life? I quit it, if there be no man but my selfe to impeach thy hopes. Supposest thou that* Paulus, *that* Fabius, *that the Cossenians, or the Servillianes will ever permit thee? And so great a troupe of noble men, noble, not only in name, but such as by their vertues honour their nobilitie, will ever suffer it.* After many other such like discourses (for he talked with him more than 2. houres) he said unto him; *Away, oh* Cinna, *that life which once I gave thee, as to an enemie, I now give thee againe, as to a traitour, and a patricide: let a true friendship from this day forward begin betweene us, let us strive together, which of us two with a better faith shall out-goe the other, and whether I have given thy life, or thou hast received the same with great confidence:* and so left him. Shortly after he gave him the Consulship, blaming him that he durst not aske it of him. And ever after held him as his deere friend, and made him alone, heire and executor of his goods. Now after this accident, which hapned to *Augustus* in the xl. yeare of his age, there was never any conspiracie or enterprise attempted against him; and he

received a just reward for his so great clemency. But the like succeeded
not to our Prince, for his mildnesse and lenitie could not so warrant
him, but that afterward he fell into the snares of the like treason: so
vaine and frivolous a thing is humane wisdome: and contrary to all
projects, devices, counsels, and precautions, fortune doth ever keepe
a full sway and possession of all events. We count those Physitians
happy and successeful, that successefully end a desperate cure, or
come to a good issue: as if there were no other art but theirs, that
could not subsist of it selfe, and whose foundations were too feeble to
stand and relie upon her owne strength: and as if there were none but
it, that stands in need of fortunes helpe-affoording hand, for the effect-
ing of her operations. My conceit of it, is both the worst and the best a
man may imagine: for thankes be to God, there is no commerce betweene us: I am contrary to others; for I ever despise it, and when I
am sick, in stead of entring into league or composition with it, I then
beginne to hate and feare it most: and answer such as urge mee to
take Physicke, that at least they will tarie till such time as I have
recovered my health and strength againe; that then I may the better
be enabled to endure the violence and hazard of their potions. I let
nature worke, and presuppose unto my selfe, that she hath provided her
selfe, both of teeth and clawes, to defend her self from such assaults
as shall beset her, and to maintaine this contexture or frame, whose
dissolution it so much hateth. In lieu of bringing helpe unto her, when
shee most striveth, and is combated by sicknesse, I greatly feare lest I
bring succor unto her adversarie, and surcharge her with new enemies.
Now I conclude, that not onely in Physicke, but likewise in sundry
more certaine arts, fortune hath great share in them. The Poeticall
furies, which ravish and transport their Author beyond himselfe, why
shall we not ascribe them to his good fortune, since himselfe con-
fesseth, that they exceed his strength and sufficiencie, and acknowledgeth to proceed from elsewhere, than from himselfe, and that they are
not in his power, no more than Orators say to have those strange motions and extraordinary agitations, that in their art transport them
beyond their purpose? The like wee see to bee in painting, for sometimes the Painters hand shall draw certaine lines or draughts, so farre
exceeding his conception or skill, that himselfe is forced to enter into
admiration and amazement. But fortune yet doth much more evidently shew, the share shee hath in all their workes, by the graces and
beauties that often are found in them, not onely beyond the intent,
but besides the very knowledge of the workman. A heedy Reader shall
often discover in other mens compositions, perfections farre-differing
from the Authors meaning, and such as haply he never dreamed of, and
illustrateth them with richer senses, and more excellent constructions.
As for military enterprises, no man is so blinde but seeth what share
fortune hath in them: even in our counsels and deliberations, some
chance or good lucke must needs be joyned to them, for whatsoever

our wisdome can effect, is no great matter. The sharper and quicker it is, more weaknesse findes it in it selfe, and so much the more doth it distrust it selfe. I am of *Sillaes* opinion: and when I nearest consider the most glorious exploits of warre, me thinkes I see, that those who have the conduct of them, employ neither counsell nor deliberation about them, but for fashion-sake, and leave the best part of the enter-prise to fortune, and on the confidence they have in her ayd, they still go beyond the limits of all discourse. Casuall rejoycings, and strange furies ensue among their deliberations, which for the most induce them to take the counsell least grounded upon appearance or reason, and which quaile their courage beyond reason; whence it hath succeeded unto divers great Captaines, by giving credit to such rash counsels, and alleaging to their souldiers, that by some divine inspiration, and other signes and prognostications, they were encour-aged to such and such enterprises. Loe here wherefore in this uncer-tainty and perplexitie, which the impuissances and inabilitie doth bring us to see and chuse what is most commodious, for the difficulties which the divers accidents and circumstances of everie thing draw with them: the surest way, if other considerations did not invite us thereto, is, in my conceit, to follow the partie, wherein is most honestie and justice; and since a man doubteth of the nearest way, ever to keepe the right. As in these two examples I have lately mentioned, there is no doubt, but that it was more commendable and generous in him, who had re-ceived the offence, to remit and pardon the same, than to have done otherwise. If the first had but ill successe, his good intent is not to be blamed; and no man knoweth, had he taken the contrary way, whether he should have escaped the end, to which his destinie called him; and then had he lost the glorie and commendations of so seld-seene humani-tie. Sundry men possessed with this feare, are read-of in ancient His-tories; the greatest part of which have followed the way of forerunning the conspiracies, which were complotted against them, by revenge or tortures, but I see very few, that by this remedy have received any good; witnesse so many Romane Emperours. Hee that perceiveth him-selfe to bee in this danger, ought not much to relie upon his power, or hope in his vigilancie. For, how hard a matter is it, for a man to war-rant and safeguard himselfe from an enemie, that masks under the visage of the most officious and heartie-seeming friend we have? And to know the inward thoughts and minde-concealed meanings of such as daily attend, and are continually with us? It will little availe him to have forraine nations to his guard, and ever to be encircled about with troupes of Armed men? whosoever he be that resolveth to con[t]emne his owne life, may at any time become Master of other mens lives.

Moreover that continuall suspition, which makes the Prince to mistrust every body, should be a wonderfull vexation to his minde. And therefore when *Dion* was advertised that *Calippus* watched to kill him, could never finde in his heart to informe himselfe of it:

affirming; *He had rather die once, than ever to live in feare and miserie, and to guard himselfe not onely from his enemies, but from his very friends.* Which thing *Alexander* presented more lively and undantedly by effect, who by a letter of *Parmenio* having received advertisement, that *Philip* his nearest and best regarded Physitian, had with money beene suborned and corrupted by *Darius,* to poison him, who at the very instant that he gave *Philip* the letter to reade, swallowed downe a potion he had given him: was it not to expresse his resolution, that if his friends would kill him, he would not shun them, but consent to their treachery? This Prince is the Soveraigne patterne of hazardous attempts: yet know I not whether in all his life, he shewed an act of more resolute constancie, than this, nor an ornament so many wayes famous. Those which daily preach and buzze in Princes eares, under colour of their safetie, a heedy diffidence and ever-warie distrustfulnesse, doe nought but tell them of their ruine, and further their shame and downefall. No noble act is achieved without danger. I know one by his owne complexion of a right martial courage, and ready for any resolution, whose good and hopefull fortune is dayly corrupted by such verball perswasions; as first to keepe close with his friends; never to listen to any reconciliation with his old enemies: to stand upon his owne guard; never to commit himselfe to any stronger than himselfe, what faire promise soever they make him, or whatsoever apparant profit they seeme to containe. I also know another, who because he did ever follow the contrarie counsell, and would never listen to such schoolereasons, hath beyond all hope raised his fortune above the common reach. That boldnesse wherewith they so greedily gape after glory, is alwayes at hand, when ever need shall be, as gloriously in a doublet as in an armour; in a cabinet as in a campe; the arme held down, as lifted up. A wisdome so tenderly precise, and so precisely circumspect, is a mortall enemie to haughty executions. *Scipio,* to sound the depth of *Siphax* intent, and to discover his minde; leaving his armie, and abandoning the yet unsetled country of *Spaine,* which under his new conquest of it, was likely to be suspected, he I say, could passe into *Affrike* onely with two simple ships or small barkes, to commit himselfe in a strange and foe countrie, to engage his person, under the power of a barbarous King, under an unknowne faith, without either hostage, or letters of credence, yea without any body, but onely upon the assurance of the greatnesse of his courage, of his successefull good fortune, and of the promise of his high-raised hopes. *Habita fides ipsam plerumque fidem obligat. Most commonly trusting obligeth trustinesse.* To an ambitious and fame-aspiring minde, contrariwise, a man must yeeld little, and cary a hard hand against suspitions: Feare and distrust draw on offences and allure them. The most mistrustfull of our Kings established his affaires, and setled his estate, especially because he had voluntarily given over, abandoned and committed his life and libertie, to the hands and mercy of his enemies: Seeming to put his whole confidence in them, that so they might likewise conceive an undoubted affiance in him. *Cæsar* did onely confront his mutinous legions, and oppose his hardly-ruled Armies, with the minde-quelling authoritie of his countenance, and awe-moving fiercenesse of his words: and did so much trust himselfe and his fortune, that he no whit feared to abandon and commit himselfe to a seditious and rebellious Armie.

> —*stetit aggere fulti*
> *Cæspitis, intrepidus vultu, meruitque timeri*
> *Nil metuens.*—LUCAN. V. 296.

He on a rampart stood of turfe uprear'd,
Fearelesse, and fearing none was to be fear'd.

True it is, that this undaunted assurance cannot so fully and lively be represented, but by those in whom the imagination or apprehension of death, and of the worst that may happen, can strike no amazement at all: for, to represent it fearefully-trembling, doubtfull and uncertaine, for the service of an important reconciliation, is to effect no great matter: It is an excellent motive to gaine the heart and good will of others, for a man to go and submit himselfe to them, provided it be done freely, and without constraint of any necessitie, and in such sort, that a man bring a pure and unspotted confidence with him, and at least his countenance void of all scruple. Being yet a childe, I saw a gentleman, who had the command of a great Citie, and by a commotion of a seditiously furious people greatly put to his plunges, who to suppresse the rising fire of this tumult, resolved to sally out from a strongly assured place, where he was safe, and yeeld himselfe to that many-headed monster mutinous rowt; thrived so ill by it, that he was miserably slaine amongst them: yet deeme I not his oversight to have beene so great in issuing out, his memorie being of most men condemned, as because he tooke a way of submission, and remissenesse, and attempted to extinguish that rage and hurly-burly, rather by way of following, than of guiding, and by requiring sute, than by demonstrative resolution: and I deeme, a gratiously milde severitie, with a militarie commandement, full of confidence and securitie, beseeming his ranke, and the dignitie of his charge, had better availed him, had beene more successfull, at least with more honour, and well seeming comlinesse. There is nothing lesse to bee expected or hoped for at the hands of this monstrous faced multitude, thus agitated by furie, than humanitie and gentlenesse; it will much sooner receive reverence, and admit feare. I might also blame him, that having undertaken a resolution (in my judgement, rather brave than rash) to cast himselfe inconsiderately, weake and unarmed, amidst a tempestuous

Ocean of senselesse and mad men, he should have gone through stitch with it, and not leave the person he represented in the briers, whereas after he had perceived the danger at hand, he chanced to bleed at the nose; and then to change that demisse and flattering countenance he had undertaken, into a dismaid and drooping looke, filling both voice and eyes with astonishment and repentance: and seeking to squat himselfe, hee the more enflamed, and called them upon him. It was determined, there should be a generall muster made of divers troupes of armed men (a place fittest for secret revenges, and where they may safest be atchieved) there were most apparant reasons, that the place was very unsure, or at least, to be suspected, by such as were to have the principall and necessary charge to survey them. Divers counsels were proposed, sundry opinions heard, as in a subject of great difficultie, and on which depended so many weightie consequences. My advice was, they should carefully avoid to give any testimonie of suspition, or shew of doubt, and that our troupes should be as full as might be, and the Fyles orderly ranked, and every Souldier shew an undaunted carriage, and undismayed countenance, and in stead of keeping some of our forces back (which thing most opinions aimed at) all Captaines should be put in minde to admonish their Souldiers to make their sallies as orderly and as strong as might be, in honour of the assistance; and spare no powder, which would serve as a gratification toward these suspectfull troupes, which afterward caused a mutuall and profitable confidence. I finde the course that *Julius Cæsar* held to be the best a man may take: First he assayed by clemencie to purchase the love of his very enemies, contenting himselfe in the conspiracies that were discovered unto him, simply to shew they were not unknowen to him, but had perfect notice of them. That done, he tooke a most noble resolution, which was, without dread or dismay, or any caretaking, to attend whatsoever might betide him, wholly abandoning and remitting himselfe into the hands of the Gods and of fortune. For certainely, it is the state wherein he was, when he was murthered in the Senate. A stranger having published every where, that he could teach *Dionysius* the tyrant of *Siracusa* a way to understand and discover the very certaintie of all the practices, his subjects or any else should practise against him, if he would bestow a good summe of money upon him: *Dionysius* being thereof advertised, sent for him, to discover the secret and understand the truth of so necessarie an art for his preservation: the stranger told him, there was no other skill in his art, but that he should deliver him a talent, and then boast hee had learned the use of so invaluable a secret of him. *Dionysius* allowed of his invention, and forthwith caused six hundred crownes to be delivered him. It is not likely that ever he would have given so great a summe of mony to an unknowne man, but in reward of a most profitable instruction; for by way of this reputation he

kept his enemies still in awe. And therefore doe Princes wisely publish such advertisements as they receive of the plots conspired, and
treasons practised against their lives and states, thereby to make men
beleeve, that nothing can be attempted against them, but they shall
have knowledge of it. The Duke of *Athens* committed many fond
oversights in the establishing of his late tyrannie upon the Florentines, but this the chiefest, that having received the first advertisement of the Monopolies and Complots the Florentines contrived
against him, by *Mathew*, surnamed *Morozo*, one of the complices,
thinking to suppresse this warning, and conceale that any in the
Citie were offended at him, or grudged at his rule, caused him immediately to be put to death. I remember to have heretofore read the
storie of a Romane (a man of speciall dignitie) who flying the tyrannie of the *Triumvirate*, had many times by the sutteltie of his
invention, escaped those who pursued him. It fortuned upon a day,
that a troupe of horse-men, who had the charge to apprehend him,
passing alongst a hedge, under which he lay lurking, had wellnigh
discovered him; while he perceiving, and considering the dangers
and difficulties he had so long endured, thinking to save himselfe
from the continuall and daily searches that every where were made
after him, and calling to minde the small pleasure he might hope of
such a life, and how much better it were for him to die once, than
live in such continuall feare and agonie, himselfe called them, and
voluntarily discovered his lurking hole, and that he might rid them
and himselfe from further pursuit and care, did willingly yeeld unto
their crueltie. For a man to call his enemies to aid him, is a counsell
somewhat rash, yet thinke I, it were better to embrace it, than remaine still in the continuall fit of such a fever that hath no remedie.
But since the provisions of man may apply unto it, are full of
unquietnesse and uncertaintie, much better is it with a full assurance
to prepare himselfe patiently to endure whatsoever may happen, and
draw some comfort from that, which a man is never sure shall come
to passe.

CHAPTER XXIV

OF PEDANTISME

I HAVE in my youth oftentimes beene vexed, to see a Pedant
brought in, in most of Italian comedies, for a vice or sport-maker,
and the nicke-name of *Magister* to be of no better signification
amongst us. For, my selfe being committed to their tuition, how
could I chuse but be somewhat jealous of their reputation? In deed I
sought to excuse them by reason of the naturall disproportion that is
betweene the vulgar sort, and rare and excellent men, both in judgement and knowledge: forsomuch as they take a cleane contrarie

course one from another. But when I considered, the choysest men were they, that most contemned them, I was far to seeke, and as it were lost my selfe, witnesse our good *Bellay:*

Mais je hay par sur tout un scavoir pedantesque.

BELLAY.

A pedant knowledge, I
Detest out of all cry.

Yet is this custome very ancient; for *Plutarke* saith, *that Greeke and Scholer, were amongst the Romans, words of reproach and imputation.* And comming afterwards to yeares of more discretion, I have found they had great reason, and that *magis magnos clericos, non sunt magis magnos sapientes: The most great Clerkes are not the most wisest men.* But whence it may proceed, that a minde rich in knowledge, and of so many things, becommeth thereby never livelier nor more quicke-sighted; and a grose-headed and vulgar spirit may without amendement containe the discourse and judgement of the most excellent wits the world ever produced, I still remaine doubt-full. To receive so many, so strange, yea and so great wits, it must needs follow (said once a Lady unto me, yea one of our chiefest Princesses, speaking of some body) *that a mans owne wit, force, droope, and as it were diminish it selfe, to make roome for others.* I might say, that as plants are choked by over-much moisture, and lamps dammed with too much oyle, so are the actions of the mind over-whelmed by over-abundance of matter and studie: which occupied and intangled with so great a diversitie of things, loseth the meane to spread and cleare it selfe; and that surcharge keepeth it low-drooping and faint. But it is otherwise, for our mind stretcheth the more by how much more it is replenished. And in examples of former times, the contrary is seene, of sufficient men in the managing of publike affaires, of great Captaines, and notable Counsellers in matters of estate, to have been therewithall excellently wise. And concerning Philosophers, retired from all publike negotiations, they have indeed sometimes been vilified, by the comike libertie of their times, their opinions and demeanors yeelding them ridiculous. Will you make them Judges of the right of a processe, or of the actions of a man? They are readie for it. They enquire whether there be any life yet remaining, whether any motion. Whether man be any thing but an Oxe, what working or suffering is; what strange beasts law and justice are. Speake they of the Magistrate, or speake they unto him; they do it with an unreverent and uncivill libertie. Heare they a Prince or a King commended? Hee is but a shepherd to them, as idle as a Swaine busied about milking of his cattell, or shearing of his sheepe: but yet more rudely. Esteeme you any man the greater for possessing two hundred acres of land? They scoffe at him, as men

accustomed to embrace all the world, as their possession. Do you
boast of your Nobilitie, because you can blazon your descent of
seven or eight rich Grandfathers? They will but little regard you, as
men that conceive not the universall image of nature, and how many
predecessors every one of us hath had, both rich and poore, Kings
and groomes, Greekes and Barbarians. And were you lineally descended in the fiftieth degree from *Hercules,* they deeme it a vanitie
to vaunt or alleage this gift of fortune. So did the vulgar sort disdaine them as ignorant of the first and common things, and as presumptuous and insolent. But this Platonicall lustre is far from that
which our men stand in need of. They were envied as being beyond
the common sort, as despising publike actions, as having proposed
unto themselves a particular and inimitable life, aiming and directed
at certaine high discourses, and from the common use: these are
disdained as men beyond the ordinary fashion, as incapable of publike charges, as leading an unsociable life, and professing base and
abject customes, after the vulgar kind. *Odi homines ignavos opera,
Philosophos sententia* (PACUVIUS, *Lips.* i. 10). *I hate men that are
fooles in working, and Philosophers in speaking.* As for those Philosophers, I say, that as they were great in knowledge, so were they
greater in all action. And even as they report of that *Syracusan*
Geometrician, who being taken from his bookish contemplation, to
shew some practice of his skill, for the defence of his countrie, reared
sodainly certaine terror-moving engines, and shewed effects farre
exceeding all mens conceit, himselfe notwithstanding disdaining all
this his handie-worke, supposing he had thereby corrupted the dignitie of his art; his engines and manuall works being but the appren-
tiships, and trials of his skill in sport: So they, if at any time they
have been put to the triall of any action, they have been seen to
flie so high a pitch, and with so loftie a flight, that men might
apparantly see their minds and spirits were through the intelligence
of things, become wonderfully rich and great. But some perceiving
the seat of politike government possessed by unworthy and incapable men, have withdrawne themselves from it. And hee who demanded of *Crates,* how long men should Philosophize, received this
answer, Untill such time as they who have the conduct of our
Armies be no longer blockish asses. *Heraclitus* resigned the royaltie
unto his brother. And to the Ephesians, who reproved him for spending his time in playing with children before the temple: hee answered, And is it not better to doe so, than to governe the publike
affaires in your companie? Others having their imagination placed
beyond fortune and the world, found the seat of justice, and the
thrones of Kings, to be but base and vile. And *Empedocles* refused
the royaltie, which the *Agrigentines* offered him. *Thales* sometimes
accusing the carke and care men tooke about good husbandry, and
how to grow rich; some replied unto him, that he did as the Fox,

because he could not attaine unto it himselfe: which hearing, by way of sport he would needs shew by experience how he could at his pleasure become both thriftie and rich; and bending his wits to gaine and profit, erected a traffike, which within one year brought him such riches, as the skilfullest in the trade of thriving, could hardly in all their life devise how to get the like. That which *Aristotle* reporteth of some, who called both him, and *Anaxagoras,* and such like men, wise, and not prudent, because they cared not for things more profit- able: besides, I doe not verie well digest this nice difference of words, that serveth my find-fault people for no excuse: and to see the base and needie fortune, wherewith they are content, we might rather have just cause to pronounce them, neither wise nor prudent. I quit this first reason, and thinke it better to say, that this evill pro- ceedeth from the bad course they take to follow sciences; and that respecting the manner we are instructed in them, it is no wonder if neither Schollers nor Masters, howbeit they prove more learned, become no whit more sufficient. Verily the daily care, and continuall charges of our fathers, aymeth at nothing so much, as to store our heads with knowledge and learning; as for judgement and vertue, that is never spoken of. If a man passe by, crie out to our people; *Oh what a wise man goeth yonder!* And of another: *Oh what a good man is yonder!* He will not faile to caste his eyes and respect toward the former. A third crier were needfull, to say, *Oh what blocke- heads are those!* We are ever readie to aske, *Hath he any skill in the Greeke and Latine tongue? can he write well? doth hee write in prose or verse?* But whether hee be growne better or wiser, which should be the chiefest of his drift, that is never spoken of, we should rather enquire who is better wise, than who is more wise. We labour, and toyle, and plod to fill the memorie, and leave both understand- ing and conscience emptie. Even as birds flutter and skip from field to field to pecke up corne, or any graine, and without tasting the same, carrie it in their bils, therewith to feed their little ones; so doe our pedants gleane and picke learning from bookes, and never lodge it further than their lips, only to degorge and cast it to the wind. It is strange how fitly sottishnesse takes hold of mine example. Is not that which I doe in the greatest part of this composition, all one and selfe same thing? I am ever heere and there picking and culling, from this and that booke, the sentences that please me, not to keepe them (for I have no store-house to reserve them in) but to transport them into this: where, to say truth, they are no more mine, than in their first place: we are (in mine opinion) never wise, but by present learning, not by that which is past, and as little by that which is to come. But which is worse, their Schollers, and their little ones are never a whit the more fed or better nour- ished: but passeth from hand to hand, to this end only, thereby to make a glorious shew, therewith to entertaine others, and with its

helpe to frame some quaint stories, or prettie tales, as of a light and
counterfeit coyne, unprofitable for any use or imployment, but to
reckon and cast accompts. *Apud alios loqui didicerunt, non ipsi
secums. Non est loquendum, sed gubernandum* (SEN. *Epist.* cviii.).
*They have learned to speake with others, not with themselves:
speaking is not so requisite as government.* Nature, to shew that
nothing is savage in whatsoever she produceth, causeth oftentimes,
even in rudest and most unarted nations, productions of spirits to
arise, that confront and wrestle with the most artist productions. As
concerning my discourse, is not the Gaskonie proverbe, drawne from
a bag-pipe, prettie and quaint? *Bouha prou bouha, mas à remuda
lous dits quèm. You may blow long enough, but if once you stirre
your fingers, you may go seeke.* Wee can talke and prate, *Cicero* saith
thus, These are *Platoes* customes, These are the verie words of
Aristotle; but what say we our selves? what doe we? what judge
we? A Peroquet would say as much. This fashion puts me in mind of
that rich Romane, who to his exceeding great charge had beene
verie industrious to finde out the most sufficient men in all sciences,
which he continually kept about him, that if at any time occasion
should bee moved amongst his friends to speake of any matter per-
taining to Schollership, they might supplie his place, and be readie to
assist him: some with discourse, some with a verse of *Homer,* othersome with a sentence, each one according to his skill or profession;
who perswaded himselfe that all such learning was his owne, because
it was contained in his servants minds. As they doe whose sufficiencie is placed in their sumptuous libraries. I know some, whom
if I aske what he knoweth, hee will require a book to demonstrate
the same, and durst not dare to tell me that his posteriors are scabious, except he turne over his *Lexicon* to see what posteriors and
scabious is, wee take the opinions and knowledge of others into our
protection, and that is all: I tell you they must be enfeoffed in us,
and made our owne. Wee may verie well be compared unto him,
who having need of fire, should goe fetch some at his neighbours
chimney, where finding a good fire, should there stay to warme himselfe, forgetting to carrie some home, what availes it us to have our
bellies full of meat, if it be not digested? If it bee not transchanged
in us? except it nourish, augment, and strengthen us? May we
imagine that *Lucullus,* whom learning made and framed so great a
Captaine without experience, would have taken if after our manner?
We relie so much upon other mens armes, that we disanull our owne
strength. Will I arme my selfe against the feare of death? it is at
Senecaes cost: will I draw comfort either for my selfe, or any other?
I borrow the same of *Cicero.* I would have taken-it in my selfe, had
I been exercised unto it: I love not this relative and begd-for suffi-
ciencie. Suppose we may be learned by other mens learning. Sure I
am, we can never be wise, but by our owne wisdome.

Μισῶ σοφιστὴν, ὅστις οὐχ αὑτῷ σοφός.—Proverb. Iamb.

That wise man I cannot abide,
That for himself cannot provide.

Ex quo Ennius: Nequidquam sapere sapientem, qui ipsi sibi prodesse non quiret (ENNIUS). Whereupon saith Ennius: *That wise man is vainly wise, who could not profit himselfe.*

—si cupidus, si
Vanus, et Euganeâ quantumvis vilior agnâ.
                        JUVEN. *Sat.* viii. 14.

If covetous, if vaine (not wise)
Than any lambe more base, more nice.

Non enim paranda nobis solum, sed fruenda sapientia est (CIC. *Finib.* i. p.). *For, wee must not only purchase wisdome, but enjoy and employ the same. Dionysius* scoffeth at those Gramarians, who ploddingly labour to know the miseries of *Ulysses*, and are ignorant of their owne; mocketh those Musitians, that so attentively tune their instruments, and never accord their manners; derideth those Orators, that studie to speake of justice, and never put it in execution. Except our mind be the better, unlesse our judgement be the sounder, I had rather my scholler had imployed his time in playing at Tennis; I am sure his bodie would be the nimbler. See but one of these our universitie men or bookish schollers returne from schole, after he hath there spent ten or twelve yeares under a Pedants charge: who is so unapt for any matter? who so unfit for any companie? who so to seeke if he come into the world? All the advantage you discover in him, is, that his Latine and Greeke have made him more sottish, more stupid, and more presumptuous, then before he went from home. Whereas he should returne with a mind full-fraught, he returnes with a wind-puft conceit: in stead of plum-feeding the same, he hath only spunged it up with vanitie. These Masters, as *Plato* speaketh of Sophisters (their cosin Germanes) of all men, are those that promise to be most profitable unto men, and alone, amongst all, that not only amend not what is committed to their charge, as doth a carpenter or a mason, but empaire and destroy the same, and yet they must full dearely be paied. If the law which *Protagoras* proposed to his disciples, were followed, which was, that either they should pay him according to his word, or sweare in the temple, how much they esteemed the profit they had received by his discipline, and accordingly satisfie him for his paines, my Pedagogues would be aground, especially if they would stand to the oath of my experience. My vulgar Perigordin-speech doth verie pleasantly terme such selfe-conceited wizards, Letter-ferits, as if they would say letter-strucken men, to whom (as the common saying is) letters have given a blow with a mallet. Verily for the most part they seeme to be distracted even from common sense. Note but the plaine husbandman,

or the unwilie shoomaker, and you see them simply and naturally plod
on their course, speaking only of what they know, and no further;
whereas these letter-puft pedants, because they would faine raise
themselves aloft, and with their literall doctrine which floteth up and
downe the superficies of their braine, arme themselves beyond other
men, they uncessantly intricate and entangle themselves: they utter
loftie words, and speake golden sentences, but so that another man
doth place, fit, and applie them. They are acquainted with *Galen,* but
know not the disease. They will stuffe your head with lawes, when
God wot they have not yet conceived the ground of the case. They
know the Theorike of all things, but you must seeke who shall put
it in practice. I have seene a friend of mine, in mine owne house, who
by way of sport talking with one of these pedanticall gulls, counterfeited a kind of fustian tongue, and spake a certain gibrish, without
rime or reason, sans head or foot, a hotch-pot of divers things, but
that he did often enterlace it with inke-pot termes, incident to their
disputations, to ammuse the bookish sot for a whole day long with
debating and contending; ever thinking he answered the Objections
made unto him; yet was he a man of letters and reputation, a gradu-
ate, and wore a goodly formall long gowne.

> *Vos ô patritius sanguis quos vivere par est*
> *Occipiti cæco, posticæ occurrite sannæ.*—PERS. *Sat.* I. 61.

You noble blouds, who with a noddle blind,
Should live, meet with the mocke that's made behind.

Whosoever shall narrowly looke into this kind of people, which far
and wide hath spred it selfe, he shall find (as I have done,) that for
the most part, they neither understand themselves, nor others, and
that their memorie is many times sufficiently full fraught, but their
judgement ever hollow and emptie: except their natural inclination
have of it selfe otherwise fashioned them. As I have seene *Adrianus
Turnebus,* who having never professed any thing but studie and letters,
wherein he was, in mine opinion, the worthiest man that lived these
thousand yeares, and who notwithstanding had no Pedanticall thing
about him, but the wearing of his gowne, and some externall fashions,
that could not well be reduced, and incivilized to the courtiers cut;
things of no consequence. And I naturally hate our people, that will
more hardly endure a long robe uncuriously worne, than a crosse
skittish mind: and that observe what leg, or reverence he makes, note
his garbe or demeanor, view his boots, or his hat, and marke what
manner of man he is. For his inward parts, I deeme him to have been
one of the most unspotted and truly honest minds that ever was. I
have sundry times of purpose urged him to speak of matters furthest
from his study, wherein he was so cleare-sighted, and could with so
quicke an apprehension conceive, and with so sound a judgement distinguish them, that he seemed never to have professed or studied

other facultie than warre, and matters of state. Such spirits, such natures may be termed worthy, goodly, and solid.

—*queis arte benigna*
Et meliore luto finxit præcordia Titan.—JUVEN. *Sat.* xiv. 34.

Whose bowels heavens-bright-Sunne composed
Of better mold, art wel diposed.

That maintaine themselves against any bad institution. Now it sufficeth not that our institution marre us not, it must change us to the better. There are some of our Parliaments and Courts, who when they are to admit of any officers, doe only examine them of their learning; others, that by presenting them the judgement of some law cases, endevour to sound their understanding. Me thinks the latter keep the better stile: And albeit these two parts are necessarie, and both ought to concur in one, yet truly should that of learning be lesse prized than judgement, this may well be without the other, and not the other without this. For as the Greeke verse saith.

'Ὡς οὐδὲν ἡ μάθησις, ἢν μὴ νοῦς παρῇ.
Gnom. Græc. χ. *et* φ. ult.

Learning nought worth doth lie,
Be not discretion by.

Whereto serveth learning, if understanding be not joyned to it? Oh would to God, that for the good of our justice, the societies of Lawyers were as wel stored with judgement, discretion, and conscience, as they are with learning and wit. *Non vitæ, sed scholæ discimus* (SEN. *Epist.* cvi. f.). *We learne not for our life, but for the schoole.* It is not enough to joyne learning and knowledge to the minde, it should be incorporated unto it: it must not be sprinckled, but dyed with it; and if it change not and better her estate (which is imperfect) it were much better to leave it. It is a dangerous Sword, and which hindreth and offendeth her master, if it be in a weake hand, and which hath not the skill to manage the same: *Ut fuerit melius non didicisse: So as it were better that we had not learned.* It is peradventure the cause, that neither we, nor divinitie require not much learning in women; and that *Francis* Duke of *Britannie,* sonne to *John* the fifth, when he was spoken unto for a marriage betweene him and *Isabel,* a daughter of *Scotland;* and some told him she was but meanly brought up, and without any instruction of learning, answered, hee loved her the better for it, and that a woman was wise enough, if she could but make a difference between the shirt and dublet of her husbands. It is also no such wonder (as some say) that our auncesters did never make any great accompt of Letters, and that even at this day (except it be by chaunce) they are not often found in our Kings or Princes chiefest councels and consultations: And if the end to grow rich by them, which now adaies is altogether proposed unto us by the studie of

Law, of Phisicke, of Pedantisme, and of Divinitie; did not keep them in credit, without doubt you should see them as beggarly and needy, and as much vilified as ever they were. And what hurt I pray you, since they neither teach us to think well, nor doe well? *Postquam docti prodierunt, boni desunt* (SEN. *Epist.* xcv.). *Since men became learned, good men failed.* Each other science is prejudiciall unto him, that hath not the science of goodnesse. But may not the reason I whilom sought for, also proceed thence? That our studie in France, having as it were no other aime but profit, but those lesse whom nature hath produced to more generous offices, than lucrative, giving themselves unto learning, or so briefly (before they have apprehended any liking of them, retired unto a profession that hath no communitie with bookes) there are then none left, altogether to engage themselves to studie and Bookes, but the meaner kind of people, and such as are borne to base fortune, and who by learning and letters seek some meane to live, and enrich themselves. The minds of which people being both by naturall inclination, by example, and familiar institution, of the basest stampe, doe falsly reap the fruit of learning. For it is not in her power to give light unto the mind, that hath none, nor to make a blind man to see. The mysterie of it is not to affoord him sight, but to direct it for him, to addresse his goings, alwaies provided he have feet of his owne, and good, strait, and capable legs. Knowledge is an excellent drug, but no drug is sufficiently strong to preserve it selfe without alteration or corruption, according to the fault of the vessell, that containes it. Some man hath a cleare sight, that is not right-sighted; and by consequence seeth what good is, and doth not follow it; and [seeth] knowledge, but makes no use of it. The chiefest ordinance of *Plato* in his common wealth is, to give unto his Citizens their charge, according to their nature. Nature can doe all, and doth all. The crookt backt, or deformed, are unfit for any exercise of the bodie, and crooked and misshapen minds unproper for exercises of the minde. The bastard and vulgar sort are unworthy of Philosophie. When we see a man ill shod, if he chance to be a Shoomaker, wee say it is no wonder, for commonly none goes worse shod than they. Even so it seemes, that experience doth often shew us, a Physitian lesse healthy, a Divine lesse reformed, and most commonly a Wiseman lesse sufficient than another. *Aristo Chius* had heretofore reason to say, that Philosophers did much hurt to their auditors, forasmuch as the greatest number of minds are not apt to profit by such instructions, which, if they take not a good, they will follow a bad course: ἀσώτους ἐκ *Aristippi, acerbos ex Zenonis schola exire* (CIC. *Nat. Deor.* iii.). *They proceed licentious out of the Schoole of Aristippus, but bitter out of the Schoole of* Zeno. In that excellent institution which *Zenophon* giveth the Persians, wee find, that as other Nations teach their children Letters, so they taught theirs vertue. *Plato* said the eldest borne sonne, in their royall succession, was thus taught. "As soone as he was borne,

"he was delivered, not to women, but to such Eunuchs, as by reason
"of their vertue was in chiefest authoritie about the King. Their spesiall
"charge was first to shapen his limmes and bodie, goodly and healthy;
"and at seven yeares of age, they instructed and inured him to sit on
"horsebacke and to ride a hunting: when he came to the age of four-
"teene, they delivered him into the hands of foure men, that is to say,
"the wisest, the justest, the most temperate, and the most valiant of
"all the nation. The first taught him religion; the second, to be ever
"upright and true; the third, to become Master of his owne desires;
"and the fourth, to feare nothing." It is a thing worthy great consideration, that in that excellent, and as I may terme it, matchlesse
policie of *Lycurgus,* and in truth, by reason of her perfection, monstrous, yet notwithstanding, so carefull for the education of children,
as of her principall charge, and even in the Muses bosome and resting-
place, there is so little mention made of learning: as if that generous
youth disdaining all other yokes but of vertue, ought only be furnished,
in lieu of tutors of learning, with masters of valour, of justice, of
wisdome, and of temperance. An example which *Plato* hath imitated
in his Lawes. The manner of their discipline was, to propound questions unto them, teaching the judgement of men and of their actions:
and if by way of reason or discourse, they condemned or praised,
either this man, or that deed, they must be told the truth and best:
by which meanes at once they sharpened their wits, and learned the
right. *Astiages* in *Zenophon* calleth *Cyrus* to an accompt of his last
lesson: It is (saith he) that a great lad in our Schoole, having a little
coat, gave it to one of his fellowes, that was of lesser stature than
himselfe, and tooke his coat from him, which was too big for him: our
Master having made me judge of that difference, I judged that things
must be left in the state they were in, and that both seemed to be
better fitted as they were; whereupon he shewed me, I had done ill;
because I had [not] only considered the comelinesse where I should
chiefly have respected justice, which required, that none should be
forced in any thing which properly belonged to him, and said, he was
whipt for it, as we are in our countrie-townes, when we have forgotten
the first preterperfect tense or *Aoriste* of τύπτω. My Regent might
long enough make me a prolixe and cunning Oration *in genere demon-
strativo, in the oratorie kind of praise or dispraise,* before ever hee
should perswade me his Schoole is worth that. They have gone about
to make the way shorter: and since Sciences (even when they are right
taken) can teach us nothing but wisdome, honestie, integritie, and
resolution; they have at first sight, attempted to put their children
to the proper of effects, and instruct them, not by heare-say, but by
assay of action, lively modelling and framing them, not only by precepts and words, but principally by examples and works, that it might
not be a Science in their mind, but rather his complexion and habitude;
not to purchase, but a naturall inheritance.

To this purpose when *Agesilaus* was demanded, what his opinion was, children should learne: answered, *What they should doe being men*. It is no marvell, if such an institution have produced so admirable effects. Some say, that in other Cities of Greece they went to seeke for Rhetoricians, for Painters, and for Musicians; whereas in *Lacedemon*, they sought for Law-givers, for Magistrates, and Generals of armies: In *Athens* men learn'd to say well, but here, to doe well: there to resolve a sophisticall argument, and to confound the imposture and amphibologie of words, captiously enterlaced together; here to shake off the allurements of voluptuousnesse, and with an undanted courage to contemne the threats of fortune, and reject the menaces of death: those busied and laboured themselves about idle words, these after martiall things: there the tongue was ever in continuall exercise of speaking, here the minde in an uncessant practice of well-doing. And therfore was it not strange, if *Antipater* requiring fiftie of their children for hostages, they answered cleane contrarie to that we would doe, *that they would rather deliver him twice so many men;* so much did they value and esteeme the losse of their countries education. When *Agesilaus* inviteth *Xenophon* to send his children to *Sparta*, there to be brought up; it is not, because they should learne Rhetorike, or Logike, but, as himselfe saith, *to the end they may learne the worthiest and best science that may bee, to wit, the knowledge how to obey, and the skill how to command*. It is a sport to see *Socrates*, after his blunt manner, to mocke *Hippias*, who reporteth unto him, what great summes of money he had gained, especially in certaine little Cities, and small townes of *Sicily*, by keeping schoole, and teaching letters, and that at *Sparta* he could not get a shilling. That they were but Idiots and foolish people, who can neither measure nor esteeme; nor make no accompt of Grammer, or of Rythmes; and who only ammuse themselves to know the succession of Kings, the establishing and declination of estates, and such like trash of flim-flam tales. Which done, *Socrates* forcing him particularly to allow the excellencie of their forme of publike government, the happinesse and vertue of their private life, remits unto him to guesse the conclusion of the unprofitablenesse of his arts. Examples teach us both in this martiall policie, and in all such like, that the studie of sciences doth more weaken and effeminate mens minds, than corroborate and adapt them to warre. The mightiest, yea the best setled estate, that is now in the world, is that of the Turkes, a nation equally instructed to the esteeme of armes, and disesteeme of letters. I find *Rome* to have beene most valiant, when it was least learned. The most warlike nations of our daies, are the rudest and most ignorant. The Scithians, the Parthians, and *Tamburlane*, serve to verifie my saying. When the Gothes overran and ravaged *Greece;* that which saved all their Libraries from the fire, was, that one among them, scattered this opinion, that such trash of bookes and papers must be left untoucht and whole for their enemies, as the only meane, and proper instrument to divert them from all militarie exercises, and ammuse them to idle, secure, and sedentarie occupations. When our King *Charles* the eight, in a manner without unsheathing his sword, saw himselfe absolute Lord of the whole Kingdome of *Naples*, and of a great part of *Thuscanie*, the Princes and Lords of his traine ascribed this sodaine, and unhoped for victorie, and facilitie of so noble and prodigious a conquest, only to this, that most of the Princes and nobilitie of *Italie* ammused themselves rather to become ingenious and wise by learning, than vigorous and warriers by militarie exercises.

CHAPTER XXV

OF THE INSTITUTION AND EDUCATION OF CHILDREN; TO THE LADIE DIANA OF FOIX, COUNTESSE OF GURSON

I NEVER knew father, how crooked and deformed soever his sonne were, that would either altogether cast him off, or not acknowledge him for his owne: and yet (unlesse he be meerely besotted or blinded in his affection) it may not be said, but he plainly perceiveth his defects, and hath a feeling of his imperfections. But so it is, he is his owne. So is it in my selfe. I see better than any man else, that what I have set downe, is nought but the fond imaginations of him, who in his youth hath tasted nothing but the paring, and seen but the superficies of true learning: whereof he hath retained but a generall and shapelesse forme: a smacke of every thing in generall, but nothing to the purpose in particular: After the French manner. To be short, I know there is an art of Phisicke; a course of lawes; foure parts of the Mathematikes; and I am not altogether ignorant, what they tend unto. And perhaps I also know the scope and drift of Sciences in generall, to be for the service of our life. But to wade further, or that ever I tired my selfe with plodding upon *Aristotle* (the Monarch of our moderne doctrine) or obstinately continued in the search of any one science: I confesse I never did it. Nor is there any one art, whereof I am able so much as to draw the first lineaments. And there is no scholler (be he of the lowest forme) that may not repute himselfe wiser than I, who am not able to appose him in his first lesson: and if I be forced to it, I am constrained verie impertinently to draw in matter from some generall discourse, whereby I examine, and give a guesse at his naturall judgement: a lesson as much unknowne to them, as theirs is to me. I have not dealt or had commerce with any excellent booke, except *Plutarke* or *Seneca,* from whom (as the *Danaïdes*) I draw my water, uncessantly filling, and as fast emptying: some thing whereof I fasten to this paper, but to my selfe nothing at all. And touching bookes: Historie is my chiefe studie, Poesie my only delight, to which I am particularly affected: for as *Cleanthes* said, that as the voice being forciblie pent in the narrow gullet of a trumpet, at last issueth forth more strong and shriller, so me seemes, that a sentence cunningly and closely couched in measure-keeping Posie, darts it selfe forth more furiously, and wounds me even to the quicke. And concerning the naturall faculties that are in me, (whereof behold here an essay) I perceive them to faint under their owne burthen; my conceits, and my judgement march but uncertaine, and as it were groping, staggering, and stumbling at every rush: And when I have gone as far as I can, I have no whit pleased my selfe: for the further I saile, the more land I descrie, and that so dimmed with fogges, and overcast with clouds, that my sight is so weakned, I cannot distinguish the same. And then undertaking to speake indifferently of all that presents it selfe unto my fantasie, and having nothing but mine owne naturall meanes to imploy therein, if it be my hap (as commonly it is) among good Authors, to light upon those verie places which I have undertaken to treat off, as even now I did in *Plutarke*, reading his discourse of the power of imagination, wherein in regard of those wise men, I acknowledge my selfe so weake, and so poore, so dull and grose-headed, as I am forced both to pittie and disdaine my selfe, yet am I pleased with this, that my opinions have often the grace to jump with theirs, and that I follow them a loofe-off, and thereby possesse, at least, that which all other men have not; which is, that I know the utmost difference betweene them and my selfe: all which notwithstanding I suffer my inventions to run abroad, as weake and faint, as I have produced them, without bungling and botching the faults, which this comparison hath discovered to me in them. A man had need have a strong backe, to undertake to march foot to foot with these kind of men. The indiscreet writers of our age, amidst their triviall compositions, intermingle and wrest in whole sentences taken from ancient Authors, supposing by such filching-theft to purchase honour and reputation to themselves, doe cleane contrarie. For, this infinite varietie and dissemblance of lustres, makes a face so wan, so il-favored, and so uglie, in respect of theirs, that they lose much more than gaine thereby. These were two contrarie humours: The Philosopher *Chrisippus* was wont to foist-in amongst his bookes, not only whole sentences, and other long-long discourses, but whole bookes of other Authors, as in one, he brought in *Euripides* his *Medea*. And *Apollodorus* was wont to say of him, that if one should draw from out his bookes, what he had stolen from others, his paper would remaine blanke. Where as *Epicurus* cleane contrarie to him in three hundred volumes, he left behind him, had not made use of one allegation. It was my fortune not long since to light upon such a place: I had languishingly traced after some French words, so naked and shallow, and so void either of sence or matter, that at last I found them to be nought but meere French words; and after a tedious and wearisome travell, I chanced to stumble upon an high, rich, and even to the clouds-raised piece, the descent whereof had it been somewhat more pleasant or easie, or the ascent reaching a little further, it had been excusable, and to be borne-withall; but it was such a steepie downe-fall, and by meere strength hewen out of the maine rocke, that by reading of the first six words, me thought I was carried into another world: whereby I perceive the bottome whence I came to be so low and deep, as I durst never more adventure to go through it; for, if I did stuffe any one of my dis-courses with those rich spoiles, it would manifestly cause the sottish-nesse of others to appeare. To reprove mine owne faults in others, seemes to me no more unsufferable, than to reprehend (as I doe often) those of others in my selfe. They ought to be accused every where, and have all places of Sanctuarie taken from them: yet do I know how over-boldly, at all times I adventure to equall my selfe unto my filchings, and to march hand in hand with them; not without a fond-hardie hope, that I may perhaps be able to bleare the eyes of the Judges from discerning them. But it is as much for the benefit of my application, as for the good of mine invention and force. And I doe not furiously front, and bodie to bodie wrestle with those old champions: it is but by sleights, advantages, and false-offers I seek to come within them, and if I can, to give them a fall. I doe not rashly take them about the necke, I doe but touch them, nor doe I go as far as by my bargaine I would seeme to doe; could I but keepe even with them, I should then be an honest man; for I seeke not to venture on them, but where they are strongest. To doe as I have seen some, that is, to shroud them-selves under other armes, not daring so much as to show their fingers ends unarmed, and to botch up all their works (as it is an easie matter in a common subject, namely for the wiser sort) with ancient inven-tions, here and there hudled-up together. And in those who endevoured to hide what they have filched from others, and make it their owne, it is first a manifest note of injustice, than a plaine argument of cow-ardlinesse; who having nothing of any worth in themselves to make show of, will yet under the countenance of others sufficiencie goe about to make a faire offer: Moreover (oh great foolishnesse) to seek by such cosening tricks to forestall the ignorant approbation of the com-mon sort, nothing fearing to discover their ignorance to men of under-standing (whose praise only is of value) who will soone trace out such borrowed ware. As for me, there is nothing I will doe lesse. I never spake of others, but that I may the more speake of my selfe. This con-cerneth not those mingle-mangles of many kinds of stuffe, or as the Grecians call them *Rapsodies,* that for such are published, of which kind I have (since I came to yeares of discretion) seen divers most ingenious and wittie; amongst others, one under the name of *Capilu-pus;* besides many of the ancient stampe. These are wits of such excellence, as both here and elsewhere they will soone be perceived, as our late famous writer *Lipsius,* in his learned and laborious work of the Politikes: yet whatsoever come of it, for so much as they are but follies, my intent is not to smother them, no more than a bald and hoarie picture of mine, where a Painter hath drawne not a perfect visage, but mine owne. For, howsoever, these are but my humors and opinions, and I deliver them but to show what my conceit is, and not what ought to be beleeved. Wherin I ayme at nothing but to display my selfe, who peradventure (if a new prentiship change me) shall be another to morrow. I have no authoritie to purchase beliefe, neither do I desire it; knowing well that I am not sufficiently taught to instruct others. Some having read my precedent Chapter, told me not long since in mine owne house, I should somewhat more have extended my selfe in the discourse concerning the institution of children. Now (Madame) if there were any sufficiencie in me, touching that subject, I could not better employ the same, than to bestow it as a present upon that little lad, which ere long threatneth to make a happie issue from out your honorable wombe: for (Madame) you are too generous to begin with other than a man childe. And having had so great a part in the conduct of your successefull marriage, I may challenge some right and interest in the greatnesse and prosperitie of all that shall proceed from it: moreover, the ancient and rightfull possession, which you from time to time have ever had, and still have over my service, urgeth me with more than ordinarie respects, to wish all honour, wellfare and advantage to whatsoever may in any sort concerne you and yours. And truly, my meaning is, but to shew, that the greatest difficultie, and importing all humane knowledge, seemeth to be in this point, where the nurture and institution of young children is in question. For, as in matters of husbandrie, the labor that must be used before sowing, setting, and planting, yea in planting it selfe, is most certaine and easie. But when that which was sowen, set and planted, commeth to take life; before it come to ripenesse, much adoe, and great varietie of proceeding belongeth to it. So in men, it is no great matter to get them, but being borne, what continuall cares, what diligent attendance, what doubts and feares, doe daily wait on their parents and tutors, before they can be nurtured and brought to any good! The fore-shew of their inclination whilest they are young is so uncertaine, their humours so variable, their promises so changing, their hopes so false, and their proceedings so doubtful, that it is very hard, (yea for the wisest) to ground any certaine judgement, or assured successe upon them. Behold *Cymon*, view *Themistocles*, and a thousand others, how they have differed, and fallen to better from themselves, and deceive the expectation of such as knew them. The young whelps both of Dogges and Beares, at first sight shew their naturall disposition, but men headlong embracing this custome or fashion, following that humour or opinion, admitting this or that passion, allowing of that or this law, are easily changed, and soone disguised; yet is it hard to force the naturall propension or readinesse of the mind, whereby it followeth, that for want of heedie fore-sight in those that could not guide their course well, they often employ much time in vaine, to addresse young children in those matters, whereunto they are not naturally addicted. All which difficulties notwithstanding, mine opinion is, to bring them up in the best and profitablest studies, and that a man should slightly passe over those fond presages, and deceiving prognostikes, which we over precisely gather in their infancie. And (without offence be it said) me thinks, that *Plato* in his commonwealth alloweth them too-too much authoritie.

Madame, Learning joyned with true knowledge is an especiall and gracefull ornament, and an implement of wonderfull use and consequence, namely in persons raised to that degree of fortune, wherein you are. And in good truth, learning hath not her owne true forme, nor can she make shew of her beauteous lineaments, if she fall into the hands of base and vile persons. [For, as famous *Torquato Tasso* saith; "Philosophie being a rich and noble Queene, and knowing her owne "worth, graciously smileth upon, and lovingly embraceth Princes and "noble men, if they become suters to her, admitting them as her "minions, and gently affoording them all the favours she can; whereas "upon the contrarie, if she be wooed, and sued unto by clownes, me- "chanicall fellowes, and such base kind of people, she holds her selfe "disparaged and disgraced, as holding no proportion with them. And "therefore see we by experience, that if a true Gentleman, or noble- "man follow her with any attention, and woo her with importunitie, "he shall learne and know more of her, and prove a better scholler in "one yeare, than an ungentle or base fellow shall in seven, though he "pursue her never so attentively."] She is much more readie and fierce to lend her furtherance and direction in the conduct of a warre, to attempt honorable actions, to command a people, to treat a peace with a prince of forraine nation, than she is to forme an argument in Logick, to devise a Syllogisme, to canvase a case at the barre, or to prescribe a receit of pills. So (noble Ladie) forsomuch as I cannot perswade my selfe, that you will either forget or neglect this point, concerning the institution of yours, especially having tasted the sweetnesse thereof, and being descended of so noble and learned a race. For we yet possesse the learned compositions of the ancient and noble Earles of *Foix*, from out whose heroicke loynes your husband and you take your of-spring. And *Francis* Lord of *Candale* your worthie uncle, doth daily bring forth such fruits thereof, as the knowledge of the matchlesse qualitie of your house shall hereafter extend it selfe to many ages; I will therefore make you acquainted with one conceit of mine, which contrarie to the common use I hold, and that is all I am able to affoord you, concerning that matter. The charge of the Tutor, which you shall appoint your sonne, in the choice of whom consisteth the whole substance of his education and bringing-up; on which are many branches depending, which (forasmuch as I can adde nothing of any moment to it) I will not touch at all. And for that point, wherein I presume to advise him, he may so far forth give credit unto it, as he shall see just cause. To a gentleman borne of noble parentage, and heire of a house, that aymeth at true learning, and in it would be disciplined, not so much for gaine or commoditie to himselfe (because so abject an end is far unworthie the grace and favour of the Muses, and besides, hath a regard or dependencie of others) nor for externall shew and ornament, but to adorne and enrich his inward minde, desiring rather to shape and institute an able and sufficient man, than a bare learned man. My desire is therefore, that the parents or overseers of such a gentleman be very circumspect, and carefull in chusing his director, whom I would rather commend for having a well composed and temperate braine, than a full stuft head, yet both will doe well. And I would rather prefer wisdome, judgement, civill customes, and modest behaviour, than bare and meere literall learning; and that in his charge he hold a new course. Some never cease brawling in their schollers eares (as if they were still pouring in a tonell) to follow their booke, yet is their charge nothing else, but to repeat, what hath beene told them before. I would have a tutor to correct this part, and that at first entrance, according to the capacitie of the wit he hath in hand, he should begin to make shew of it, making him to have a smacke of all things, and how to chuse and distinguish them, without helpe of others, sometimes opening him the way, other times leaving him to open it by himselfe. I would not have him to invent and speake alone, but suffer his disciple to speake when his turne commeth. *Socrates,* and after him *Arcesilaus,* made their schollers to speake first, and then would speake themselves. *Obest plerumque iis qui discere volunt, auctoritas eorum qui docent* (Cic. *De Nat.* i.). *Most commonly the authoritie of them that teach, hinders them that would learne.*

It is therefore meet, that he make him first trot-on before him, whereby he may the better judge of his pace, and so guesse how long he will hold out, that accordingly he may fit his strength: for want of which proportion, we often marre all. And to know how to make a good choice, and how far forth one may proceed (still keeping a due measure) is one of the hardest labours I know. It is a signe of a noble, and effect of an undaunted spirit, to know how to second, and how far forth he shall condescend to his childish proceedings, and how to guide them. As for my selfe, I can better and with more strength walke up, than downe a hill. Those which according to our common fashion, undertake with one selfe-same lesson, and like maner of education, to direct many spirits of divers formes and different humours, it is no marvell if among a multitude of children, they scarse meet with two or three, that reap any good fruit by their discipline, or that come to any perfection. I would not only have him to demand an accompt of the words contained in his lesson, but of the sense and substance thereof, and judge of the profit he hath made of it, not by the testimonie of his memorie, but by the witnesse of his life. That what he lately learned, he cause him to set forth and pourtray the same into sundrie shapes, and then to accommodate it to as many different and severall subjects; whereby he shal perceive, whether he have yet apprehended the same, and therein enfeoffed himselfe, at due times taking his instruction from the institution given by *Plato*. It is a signe of cruditie and indigestion for a man to yeeld up his meat, even as he swallowed the same: the stomacke hath not wrought his full operation, unlesse it have changed forme, and altered fashion of that which was given him to boyle and concoct.

[Wee see men gape after no reputation but learning, and when they say, such a one is a learned man, they thinke they have said enough;] Our minde doth move at others pleasure, as tyed and forced to serve the fantasies of others, being brought under by authoritie, and forced to stoope to the lure of their bare lesson; wee have beene so subjected to harpe upon one string, that we have no way left us to descant upon voluntarie: our vigor and libertie is cleane extinct. *Nunquam tutelæ suæ fiunt. They never come to their owne tuition.* It was my hap to bee familiarlie acquainted with an honest man at *Pisa*, but such an *Aristotelian*, as he held this infallible position; that a conformitie to *Aristotles* doctrine was the true touchstone and squire of all solide imaginations, and perfect veritie; for, whatsoever had no coherencie with it, was but fond *Chimeraes*, and idle humours; in asmuch as he had knowne all, seene all, and said all. This proposition of his, being somewhat over amply and injuriously interpreted by some, made him a long time after to be troubled in the inquisition of *Rome*. I would have him make his scholler narrowly to sift all things with discretion, and harbour nothing in his head by meere authoritie, or upon trust. *Aristotles* principles shall be no more axiomes unto him, than the Stoikes or Epicurians. Let this diversitie of judgements be proposed unto him, if he can, he shall be able to distinguish the truth from falsehood, if not, he will remaine doubtfull.

> *Che non men che saper dubbiar m'aggrada.*
>> DANTE, *Inferno*, cant. xii. 48.

No lesse it pleaseth me,
To doubt, than wise to be.

For if by his owne discourse he embrace the opinions of *Xenophon*, or of *Plato*, they shall be no longer theirs, but his. He that meerely followeth another, traceth nothing, and seeketh nothing: *Non sumus sub Rege, sibi quisque se vindicet* (SEN. *Epist.* xxxiii.). *We are not under a Kings command, every one may challenge himselfe, for let him at least know that he knoweth.* It is requisite he endevour as much to feed himselfe with their conceits, as labour to learne their precepts; which, so he know how to applie, let him hardly forget, where, or whence he had them. Truth and reason are common to all, and are no more proper unto him that spake them heretofore, than unto him that shall speake them hereafter. And it is no more according to *Platoes* opinion, than to mine, since both he and I understand and see alike. The Bees doe here and there sucke this, and cull that flower, but afterward they produce the hony, which is peculiarly their owne, then is it no more Thyme or Majoram. So of peeces borrowed of others, he may lawfully alter, transforme, and confound them, to shape out of them a perfect peece of worke, altogether his owne; alwaies provided, his judgement, his travell, studie, and institution tend to nothing, but to frame the same perfect. Let him hardly conceale, where, or whence he hath had any helpe, and make no shew of any thing, but of that which he hath made himselfe. Pirates, filchers, and borrowers, make a shew of their purchaces and buildings, but not of that which they have taken from others: you see not the secret fees or bribes Lawiers take of their Clients, but you shall manifestly discover the alliances they make, the honours they get for their children, and the goodly houses they build. No man makes open shew of his receits, but every one of his gettings. The good that comes of studie (or at least should come) is to prove better, wiser, and honester. It is the understanding power (said *Epicharmus*) that seeth and heareth, it is it, that profiteth all, and disposeth all, that moveth, swayeth, and ruleth all: all things else are but blind, senselesse, and without spirit. And truly in barring him of libertie to doe any thing of himselfe, we make him thereby more servile and more coward. Who would ever enquire of his scholler what he thinketh of Rhetorike, of Grammar, of this, or of that sentence of *Cicero?* Which things throughly fethered (as if they were oracles) are let flie into our memorie; in which both letters and syllables are substantiall parts of the subject. To know by roat is no perfect knowledge, but to keep what one hath committed to his memories charge, is commendable: what a man directly knoweth, that will he dispose-of, without turning still to his booke, or looking to his pattern. A meere bookish sufficiencie is unpleasant. All I expect of it, is an imbellishing of my actions, and not a foundation of them, according to *Platoes* mind, who saith, constancie, faith, and sinceritie, are true Philosophie; as for other Sciences, and tending else-where, they are but garish paintings. I would faine have *Paluel* or *Pompey*, those two excellent dauncers of our time, with all their nimblenesse, teach any man to doe their loftie tricks, and high capers, only with seeing them done, and without stirring out of his place, as some Pedanticall fellowes would instruct our minds without moving or putting it in practice. And glad would I be to find one, that would teach us how to manage a horse, to tosse a pike, to shoot-off a peece, to play upon the lute, or to warble with the voice, without any exercise, as these kind of men would teach us to judge, and how to speake well, without any exercise of speaking or judging. In which kind of life, or as I may terme it, Prentiship, what action or object soever presents it-selfe unto our eies, may serve us in stead of a sufficient booke. A prettie pranke of a boy, a knavish trickle of a page, a foolish part of a lackey, an idle tale or any discourse else, spoken either in jest or earnest, at the table or in companie, are even as new subjects for us to worke-upon: for furtherance whereof, commerce or common societie among men, visiting of forraine countries, and observing of strange fashions, are verie necessary, not only to be able (after the manner of our yong gallants of *France*) to report how many paces the Church of *Santa Rotonda* is in length or breadth, or what rich garments the curtezan *Signora Livia* weareth, and the worth of her hosen; or as some do, nicely to dispute how much longer or broader the face of *Nero* is, which they have seene in some old ruines of *Italie*, than that which is made for him in other old monuments elsewhere. But they should principally observe, and be able to make certaine relation of the humours and fashions of those countries they have seene, that they may the better know how to correct and prepare their wits by those of others. I would therefore have him begin even from his infancie to travell abroad; and first, that at one shoot he may hit two markes, he should see neighbour-countries, namely where languages are most different from ours; for, unlesse a mans tongue be fashioned unto them in his youth, he shall never attaine to the true pronuntiation of them, if he once grow in yeares. Moreover, we see it received as a common opinion of the wiser sort, that it agreeth not with reason, that a childe be alwaies nuzzled, cockered, dandled, and brought up in his parents lap or sight; forsomuch as their naturall kindnesse, or (as I may call it) tender fondnesse, causeth often, even the wisest to prove so idle, over-nice, and so base-minded. For parents are not capable, neither can they find in their hearts to see them checkt, corrected, or chastised, nor indure to see them brought up so meanly, and so far from daintinesse, and many times so dangerously, as they must needs be. And it would grieve them to see their children come home from those exercises, that a Gentleman must necessarily acquaint himselfe with, sometimes all wet and bemyred, other times sweatie, and full of dust, and to drinke being either extreme hot, or exceeding cold; and it would trouble them to see him ride a rough-untamed horse, or with his weapon furiously incounter a skilfull Fencer, or to handle and shoot-off a musket; against which there is no remedy, if he will make him prove a sufficient, compleat, or honest man: he must not be spared in his youth; and it will come to passe, that he shall many times have occasion and be forced to shocke the rules of Physicke.

> *Vitamque sub dio et trepidas agat*
> *In rebus.*—Hor. i. *Od.* ii. 4.

Leade he his life in open aire,
And in affaires full of despaire.

It is not sufficient to make his minde strong, his muskles must also be strengthened: the minde is over-borne if it be not seconded: and it is too much for her alone to discharge two offices. I have a feeling how mine panteth, being joyned to so tender and sensible a bodie, and that lieth so heavie upon it. And in my lecture, I often perceive how my Authors in their writings sometimes commend examples for magnanimitie and force, that rather proceed from a thicke skin and hardnes of the bones. I have knowne men, women, and children borne of so hard a constitution, that a blow with a cudgell would lesse hurt them, than a filip would doe me, and so dull and blockish, that they will neither stir tongue nor eye-browes, beat them never so much. When wrestlers goe about to counterfeit the Philosophers patience, they rather shew the vigor of their sinnewes, than of their heart. For the custome to beare travell, is to tolerate griefe: *Labor callum obducit dolori* (Cɪc. *Tusc. Qu.* ii.): *Labour worketh a hardnesse upon sorrow.* Hee must be enured to suffer the paine and hardnesse of exercises, that so he may be induced to endure the paine of the colicke, of cauterie, of fals, of sprains, and other diseases incident to mans bodie: yea, if need require, patiently to beare imprisonment, and other tortures, by which sufferance he shall come to be had in more esteeme and accompt: for according to time and place, the good as well as the bad man may haply fall into them; we have seen it by experience. Whosoever striveth against the lawes, threats good men with mischiefe and extortion. Moreover, the authoritie of the Tutor (who should be soveraigne over him) is by the cockering and presence of the parents, hindred and interrupted: besides the awe and respect which the household beares him, and the knowledge of the meanes, possibilities, and greatnesse of his house, are in my judgement, no small lets in a young Gentleman. In this schoole of commerce, and societie among men, I have often noted this vice, that in lieu of taking acquaintance of others, we only endevour to make our selves knowne to them: and we are more ready to utter such merchandize as we have, than to ingrosse and purchase new commodities. Silence and modestie are qualities verie convenient to civil conversation. It is also necessary, that a young man be rather taught to be discreetly-sparing, and close-handed, than prodigally-wastfull and lavish in his expences, and moderate in husbanding his wealth when he shall come to possesse it. And not to take pepper in the nose for every foolish tale that shal be spoken in his presence, because it is an uncivil importunity, to contradict, whatsoever is not agreeing to our humour: let him be pleased to correct himselfe. And let him not seeme to blame that in others, which he refuseth to doe himselfe, nor goe about to withstand common fashions. *Licet sapere sine pompa, sine invidia* (Sᴇɴ. *Epist.* ciii. f.). *A man may bee wise without ostentation, without envie,* Let him avoid those imperious images of the world, those uncivil behaviours, and childish ambition, wherewith Gotwot, too-too many are possest: that is, to make a faire shew of that, which is not in him: endevouring to be reputed other than indeed he is; and as if reprehension and new devices were hard to come by, he would by that meane acquire unto himselfe the name of some peculiar vertue. As it pertaineth but to great Poets to use the libertie of arts; so it is tolerable but in noble minds, and great spirits to have a preheminence above ordinarie fashions. *Si quid Socrates et Aristippus contra morem et consuetudinem fecerunt, idem sibi ne arbitretur licere: Magis enim illi et divinis bonis hanc licentiam assequebantur* (Cic. *Off.* i.). *If* Socrates *and* Aristippus *have done ought against custome or good manner, let not a man thinke he may doe the same: for they obtained this licence by their great and excellent good parts:* He shall be taught, not to enter rashly into discourse or contesting, but when he shall encounter with a Champion, worthie his strength; And then would I not have him imploy all the tricks that may fit his turne, but only such as may stand him in most stead. That he be taught to be curious in making choice of his reasons, loving pertinancy, and by consequence brevitie. That above all, he be instructed to yeeld, yea to quit his weapons unto truth, as soone as he shall discerne the same, whether it proceed from his adversarie, or upon better advice from himselfe, for, he shall not be preferred to any place of eminencie above others, for repeating of a prescript part; and he is not engaged to defend any cause, further than he may approove it; nor shall he bee of that trade, where the libertie for a man to repent and readvise himselfe is sold for readie money. *Neque, ut omnia, quæ præscripta et imperata sint, defendat, necessitate ulla cogitur* (Cic. *Acad. Qu.* iv.). *Nor is he inforced by any necessitie to defend and make good all that is prescribed and commanded him.* If his tutor agree with my humour, he shall frame his affection, to be a most loyall and true subject to his Prince, and a most affectionate and couragious Gentleman, in al that may concerne the honor of his Soveraigne, or the good of his countrie. And endevour to suppresse in him all maner of affection to undertake any action otherwise than for a publike good and dutie. Besides many inconveniences, which greatly prejudice our libertie, by reason of these particular bonds; the judgement of a man that is waged and bought, either it is lesse free and honest, or else it is blemisht with oversight and ingratitude. A meere and precise Courtier can neither have law nor will to speake or thinke, otherwise than favourablie of his Master, who among so many thousands of his subjects, hath made choice of him alone, to institute and bring him up with his owne hand. These favours, with the commodities that follow minion Courtiers, corrupt (not without some colour of reason) his libertie, and dazle his judgement. It is therefore commonly seene, that the Courtiers-language differs from other mens, in the same state, and to be of no great credit in such matters. Let therefore his conscience and vertue shine in his speech, and reason be his chiefe direction. Let him be taught to confesse such faults as he shall discover in his owne discourses, albeit none other perceive them but himselfe; for it is an evident shew of judgement, and effect of sinceritie, which are the chiefest qualities he aymeth at. That wilfully to strive, and obstinately to contest in words, are common qualities, most apparent in basest mindes: That to re-advise and correct himselfe, and when one is most earnest, to leave an ill opinion, are rare, noble, and Philosophicall conditions. Being in companie, he shall be put in minde, to cast his eyes round about, and every where: For I note, that the chiefe places are usually seazed upon by the most unworthie, and lesse capable; and that height of fortune is seldome joyned with sufficiencie. I have seene, that whilst they at the upper end of a board were busie entertaining themselves, with talking of the beautie of the hangings about a chamber, or of the taste of some good cup of wine, many good discourses at the lower end, have utterly been lost. He shall weigh the carriage of every man in his calling, a Heardsman, a Mason, a Stranger, or a traveller; all must be imployed; every one according to his worth; for all helps to make up houshold; yea, the follie and the simplicitie of others shall be as instructions to him. By controlling the graces and manners of others, he shall acquire into himselfe envie of the good, and contempt of the bad. Let him hardly be possest with an honest curiositie to search out the nature and causes of all things: let him survay what-soever is rare and singular about him; a building, a fountaine, a man, a place where any battell hath been fought, or the passages of *Cæsar* or *Charlemaine*.

> *Quæ tellus sit lenta gelu, quæ putris ab æstu,*
> *Ventus in Italiam quis bene vela ferat.*—PROP. iv. *El.* iii. 39.

What land is parcht with heat, what clog'd with frost,
What wind drives kindly to th' Italian coast.

He shall endevour to be familiarly acquainted with the customes, with the meanes, with the state, with the dependances and alliances of all Princes; they are things soone and pleasant to be learned, and most profitable to be knowne. In this acquaintance of men, my meaning is, that hee chiefely comprehend them, that live but by the memorie of bookes. He shall, by the help of Histories, informe himselfe of the worthiest minds that were in the best ages. It is a frivolous studie, if a man list, but of unvaluable worth, to such as can make use of it. And as *Plato* saith, the onely studie the Lacedemonians reserved for themselves. What profit shall he not reap, touching this point, reading the lives of our *Plutarke?* Alwayes conditioned, the master bethinke himselfe whereto his charge tendeth, and that he imprint not so much in his schollers mind the date of the ruine of *Carthage,* as the manners of *Hanniball* and *Scipio,* nor so much where *Marcellus* died, as because he was unworthy of his devoire he died there: that he teach him not so much to know Histories, as to judge of them. It is, amongst things that best agree with my humour, the subject to which our spirits doe most diversly applie themselves. I have read in *Titus Livius* a number of things, which peradventure others never read, in whom *Plutarke* haply read a hundred more, than ever I could read, and which perhaps the author himselfe did never intend to set downe. To some kind of men, it is a meere gramaticall studie, but to others a perfect anatomie of Philosophie; but meanes whereof, the secretest part of our nature is searched-into. There are in *Plutarke* many ample discourses most worthy to be knowne: for in my judgement, he is the chiefe work-master of such works, whereof there are a thousand, whereat he hath but slightly glanced; for with his finger he doth but point us out a way to walke in, if we list; and is sometimes pleased to give but a touch at the quickest and maine point of a discourse, from whence they are by diligent studie to be drawne, and so brought into open market. As that saying of his. That the inhabitants of *Asia* served but one alone, be-cause they could not pronounce one onely syllable, which is *Non*, gave perhaps both subject and occasion to my friend *Beotie* to compose his booke of voluntarie servitude. If it were no more but to see *Plutarke* wrest a slight action to mans life; or a word that seemeth to beare no such sence, it will serve for a whole discourse. It is pittie men of under-standing should so much love brevitie, without doubt their reputation is thereby better, but we the worse. *Plutarke* had rather we should commend him for his judgement, than for his knowledge, he loveth better to leave a kind of longing-desire in us of him, than a sacietie. He knew verie well, that even in good things, too much may be said: and that *Alexandridas* did justly reprove him, who spake verie good sentences to the *Ephores*, but they were over tedious. Oh stranger, quoth he, thou speakest what thou oughtest, otherwise then thou shouldest. Those that have leane and thin bodies stuffe them up with bumbasting. And such as have but poore matter, will puffe it up with loftie words. There is a marvelous cleerenesse, or as I may terme it an enlightning of mans judgement drawne from the commerce of men, and by frequenting abroad in the world: we are all so contrived and compact in our selves, that our sight is made shorter by the length of our nose. When *Socrates* was demaunded whence he was, he answered, not of *Athens*, but of the world; for he, who had his imagination more full, and farther stretching, embraced all the world for his native Citie, and extended his acquaintance, his societie, and affections to all man-kind: and not as we do, that looke no further than our feet. If the frost chance to nip the vines about my village, my Priest doth presently argue, that the wrath of God hangs over our head, and threatneth all mankind: and judgeth that the Pippe is alreadie falne upon the Cani-bals.

In viewing these intestine and civill broiles of ours, who doth not exclaime, that this worlds vast-frame is neere unto a dissolution, and that the day of judgement is readie to fall on us? never remembring that many worse revolutions have been seene, and that whilest we are plunged in griefe, and overwhelmed in sorrow, a thousand other parts of the world besides are blessed with all happinesse, and wallow in pleasures, and never thinke on us? whereas, when I behold our lives, our licence, and impunitie, I wonder to see them so milde and easie. He on whose head it haileth, thinks all the Hemispheare besides to be in a storme and tempest. And as that dull-pated *Savoyard* said, that if the seelie King of *France* could cunningly have managed his fortune, he might verie well have made himself chiefe Steward of his Lords household, whose imagination conceived no other greatnesse than his Masters; we are all insensible of this kind of errour: an errour of great consequence and prejudice. But whosoever shall present unto his inward eyes, as it were in a Table, the Idea of the great image of our universall mother Nature, attired in her richest robes, sitting in the throne of her Majestie, and in her visage shall read, so generall, and so constant a varietie; he that therein shall view himselfe, not himselfe alone, but a whole Kingdome, to be in respect of a great circle; but the smallest point that can be imagined, he onely can value things according to their essentiall greatnesse and proportion. This great universe (which some multiplie as *Species* under one *Genus*) is the true looking-glasse wherin we must looke, if we will know whether we be of a good stamp, or in the right byase. To conclude, I would have this worlds-frame to be my Schollers choise-booke: So many strange humours, sundrie sects, varying judgements, diverse opinions, different lawes, and fantasticall customes teach us to judge rightly of ours, and instruct our judgement to acknowledge his imperfections and naturall weaknesse, which is no easie an apprentiship: So many innovations of estates, so may fals of Princes, and changes of publike fortune, may, and ought to teach us, not to make so great accompt of ours: So many names, so many victories, and so many conquests buried in darke oblivion, makes the hope to perpetuate our names, but ridiculous, by the surprising of ten Argo-lettiers, or of a small cottage, which is knowne but by his fall. The pride and fiercenesse of so many strange and gorgeous shewes: the pride-puft majestie of so many courts, and of their greatnesse, ought to confirme and assure our sight, undauntedly to beare the affronts and thunder-claps of ours, without seeling our eyes: So many thousands of men, low-laide in their graves afore us, may encourage us, not to feare, or be dismaied to go meet so good companie in the other world; and so of all things else. Our life (said *Pithagoras*) drawes neare unto the great and populous assemblies of the Olympike games, wherein some, to get the glorie, and to win the goale of the games, exercise their bodies with all industrie; others, for greedinesse of gaine, bring thither marchandise to sell: others there are (and those be not the worst) that seek after no other good, but to marke, how, wherefore, and to what end, all things are done: and to be spectators or observers of other mens lives and actions, that so they may the better judge and direct their owne. Unto examples may all the most profitable Discourses of Philosophie be sorted, which ought to be the touch-stone of humane actions, and a rule to square them by, to whom may be said,

> —*quid fas optare, quid asper*
> *Utile nummus habet, patriæ charisque propinquis*
> *Quantum elargiri deceat, quem te Deus esse*
> *Jussit, et humana qua parte locatus es in re,*
> *Quid sumus, aut quidnam victuri gignimur.*
>
> Pers. Sat. iii. 69, 67.

What thou maiest wish, what profit may come cleare,
From new-stampt coyne, to friends and countrie deare,
What thou ought'st give: whom God would have thee bee,
And in what part mongst men he placed thee.
What we are, and wherefore,
To live heer we were bore.

What it is to know, and not to know (which ought to be the scope of studie) what valour, what temperance, and what justice is: what difference there is betweene ambition and avarice, bondage and free-dome, subjection and libertie, by which markes a man may distinguish true and perfect contentment, and how far-forth one ought to feare or apprehend death, griefe, or shame.

> *Et quo quemque modo fugiátque ferátque laborem.*
>
> VIRG. Æn. viii. 853.

How ev'ry labour he may plie,
And beare, or ev'ry labour flie.

What wards or springs move us, and the causes of so many motions in us: For me seemeth, that the first discourses, wherewith his conceit should be sprinkled, ought to be those, that rule his manners, and direct his sense; which will both teach him to know himselfe, and how to live, and how to die well. Among the liberall Sciences, let us begin with that which makes us free: Indeed, they may all in some sort stead us, as an instruction to our life, and use of it, as all other things else serve the same to some purpose or other. But let us make especiall choice of that, which may directly and pertinently serve the same. If we could re-straine and adapt the appurtenances of our life to their right byase and naturall limits, we should find the best part of the Sciences that now are in use, cleane out of fashion with us: yea, and in those that are most in use, there are certaine by-wayes and deep-flows most profit-able, which we should do well to leave, and according to the institution of *Socrates*, limit the course of our studies in those where profit is wanting.

—sapere aude,
Incipe: vivendi qui rectè prorogat horam,
Rusticus expectat dum defluat amnis, at ille
Labitur, et labetur in omne volubilis œvum.

HOR. i. *Epist.* ii. 40.

Be bold to be wise: to begin, be strong,
He that to live well doth the time prolong,
Clowne-like expects, till downe the streame be run;
That runs, and will run, till the world be done.

It is more simplicitie to teach our children.

Quid moveant Pisces, animosáque signa Leonis,
Lotus et Hesperia quid Capricornus aqua.

PROP. iv. *El.* i. 85.

What *Pisces* move, or hot-breath'd *Leos* beames,
Or *Capricornus* bath'd in westerne streames.

The knowledge of the starres, and the motion of the eighth spheare, before their owne.

Τί Πλειάδεσσι κἀμοί   τί δ' ἠστράσι βοώτεω.

What longs it to the seaven stars, and me,
Or those about *Boôtes* be.

Anaximenes writing to *Pythagoras,* saith, *with what sense can I ammuse my selfe to the secrets of the Starres, having continually death or bondage before mine eyes?* For at that time the Kings of *Persia* were making preparations to war against his Countrie. All men ought to say so. Being beaten with ambition, with avarice, with rashnesse, and with superstition, and having such other enemies unto life within him. Wherefore shall I study and take care about the mobility and variation of the world? When hee is once, taught what is fit to make him better and wiser, he shall be entertained with Logicke, naturall Philosophy, Geometry, and Rhetoricke, then having setled his judgement, looke what science he doth most addict himselfe unto, he shall in short time attaine to the perfection of it. His lecture shall be somtimes by way of talke and somtimes by booke: his tutor may now and then supply him with the same Author, as an end and motive of his institution: sometimes giving him the pith and substance of it ready chewed. And if of himselfe he be not so throughly acquainted with bookes, that hee may readily find so many notable discourses as are in them to effect his purpose, it shall not be amisse, that some learned man being appointed to keepe him company, who at any time of need, may furnish him with such munition, as hee shall stand in need of; that hee may afterward distribute and dispense them to his best use. And that this kind of lesson be more easie and naturall than that of *Gaza,* who will make question? Those are but harsh, thornie, and unpleasant precepts; vaine, idle and immateriall words, on which small hold may be taken; wherein is nothing to quicken the minde. In this, the spirit findeth substance to [bite] and feed upon. A fruit without all comparison much better, and that will soone be ripe. It is a thing worthy consideration, to see what state things are brought unto in this our age; and how Philosophie, even to the wisest, and men of best understanding, is but an idle, vaine and fantasticall name, of small use, and lesse worth, both in opinion and effect. I thinke these Sophistries are the cause of it, which have forestalled the wayes to come unto it: They doe very ill, that goe about to make it seeme as it were inaccessible for children to come unto, setting it foorth with a wrimpled, gastlie, and frowning visage; who hath masked her with so counterfet, pale, and hideous a countenance? There is nothing more beauteous, nothing more delightfull, nothing more gamesome; and as I may say, nothing more fondly wanton: for she presenteth nothing to our eyes, and preacheth nothing to our eares, but sport and pastime. A sad and lowring looke plainly declareth, that that is not her haunt. *Demetrius* the Gramarian, finding a companie of Philosophers sitting close together in the Temple of *Delphos,* said unto them, *Either I am deceived, or by your plausible and pleasant lookes, you are not in any serious and earnest discourse amongst your selves;* to whom one of them named *Heracleon* the Megarian answered, *That belongeth to them, who busie themselves in seeking, whether future tense of the verbe* βάλλω *hath a double* λ, *or that labour to find the derivation of the comparatives,* χείρων, βέλτιων, *and of the superlatives* χείριστον, βέλτιστον, *it is they, that must chafe in intertaining themselves with their science: as for discourses of Philosophie they are wont to glad, rejoyce, and not to vex and molest those that use them.*

> *Deprendas animi tormenta latentis in ægro*
> *Corpore, deprendas et gaudia, sumit utrumque*
> *Inde habitum facies.*—JUVEN. *Sat.* ix. 18.

You may perceive the torments of the mind,
Hid in sicke bodie, you the joyes may find,
The face such habit takes in either kind.

That mind which harboureth Philosophie, ought by reason of her sound health, make that bodie also sound and healthie: it ought to make her contentment to through-shine in all exterior parts: it ought to shapen and modell all outward demeanours to the modell of it: and by consequence arme him that doth possesse it, with a gracious stoutnesse, and lively audacitie, with an active and pleasing gesture, and with a setled and cheerefull countenance. The most evident token, and apparant signe of true wisdome, is a constant, and unconstrained rejoycing, whose estate is like unto all things above the Moone, that is, ever cleare, alwaies bright. It is *Baroco* and *Baralipton*, that makes their followers prove so base and idle, and not Philosophie; they know her not, but by hearesay; what? Is it not shee, that cleereth all stormes of the mind? And teacheth miserie, famine, and sicknesse to laugh? Not by reason of some imaginarie Epicicles, but by naturall and palpable reasons. Shee aymeth at nothing but vertue: it is vertue shee seekes after; which as the schoole saith, is not pitcht on the top of an high, steepie, or inaccessible hill; for they that have come unto her, affirme, that cleane-contrarie, shee keeps her stand, and holds her mansion, in a faire, flourishing, and pleasant plaine, whence as from an high watch tower, she survaieth all things, to be subject unto her, to whom any man may with great facilitie come, if he but know the way or entrance to her palace: for, the pathes that lead unto her, are certaine fresh, and shadie greene allies, sweet and flowrie waies, whose ascent is even, easie, and nothing wearisome, like unto that of heavens-vaults. Forsomuch as they have not frequented this vertue, who gloriously, as in a throne of Majestie sits soveraigne, goodly, triumphant, lovely, equally delicious, and couragious, protesting her selfe to be a professed and irreconciliable enemie to all sharpnesse, austeritie, feare, and compulsion; having nature for her guide, fortune and voluptuousnesse for her companions; they according to their weaknesse have imaginarily fained her, to have a foolish, sad, grim, quarelous, spitefull, threatning, and disdainfull visage, with an horride and unpleasant looke; and have placed her, upon a craggie, sharpe, and unfrequented rocke, amidst desert cliffes, and uncouth crags, as a skar-crow, or bug-beare, to affright the common people with. Now the tutour, which ought to know, that he should rather seek to fill the mind, and store the will of his disciple, as much, or rather more, with love and affection, than with awe, and reverence unto vertue, may shew and tell him, that Poets follow common humours, making him plainly to perceive, and as it were palpably to feele, that the Gods have rather placed labour and sweat at the entrances, which lead to *Venus* chambers, than at the doores, that direct to *Pallas* cabinets.

And when he shall perceive his scholler to have a sensible feeling of himselfe, presenting *Bradamant*, or *Angelica* before him, as a Mistresse to enjoy, embelished with a naturall, active, generous, and unspotted beautie, not uglie, or Giant-like, but blithe and livelie, in respect of a wanton, soft, affected, and artificiall-flaring beautie; the one attired like unto a young man, coyfed with a bright-shining helmet, the other disguised and drest about the head like unto an impudent harlot, with embroyderies, frizelings, and carcanets of pearles: he will no doubt deeme his owne love to be a man and no woman, if in his choice he differ from that effeminate shepherd of *Phrygia*. In this new kind of lesson, he shall declare unto him, that the prize, the glorie, and height of true vertue, consisted in the facilitie, profit, and pleasure of his exercises: so far from difficultie, and incumbrances, that children as well as men, the simple as soone as the wise, may come unto her. Discretion and temperance, not force or waywardnesse are the instruments to bring him unto her. *Socrates* (vertues chiefe favorite) that he might the better walke in the pleasant, naturall, and open path, of her progresses, doth voluntarily and in good earnest, quit all compulsion. Shee is the nurse and foster-mother of all humane pleasures, who in making them just and upright, she also makes them sure and sincere. By moderating them, she keepeth them in ure and breath. In limiting and cutting them off, whom she refuseth; she whets us on toward those she leaveth unto us; and plenteously leaves us them, which Nature pleaseth, and like a kind mother giveth us over unto sacietie, if not unto wearisomnesse, unlesse we will peradventure say, that the rule and bridle, which stayeth the drunkard before drunkennesse, the glutton before surfetting, and the letcher before the losing of his haire, be the enemies of our pleasures. If common fortune faile her, it cleerely scapes her; or she cares not for her, or she frames another unto herselfe, altogether her owne, not so fleeting, nor so rowling. She knoweth the way how to be rich, mightie and wise, and how to lie in sweet-perfumed beds. She loveth life; she delights in beautie, in glorie, and in health. But her proper and particular office is, first to know how to use such goods temperately, and how to lose them constantly. An office much more noble, than severe, without which, all course of life is unnaturall, turbulent, and deformed, to which one may lawfully joyne those rocks, those incumbrances, and those hideous monsters. If so it happen, that his Disciple prove of so different a condition, that he rather love to give eare to an idle fable, than to the report of some noble voiage, or other notable and wise discourse, when he shall heare it; that at the sound of a Drum, or clang of a Trumpet, which are wont to rowze and arme the youthly heat of his companions, turneth to another that calleth him to see a play, tumbling, jugling tricks, or other idle lose-time sports; and who for pleasures sake doth not deeme it more delightsome to returne all sweatie and wearie from a victorious combat, from wrestling, or riding of a horse, than from a Tennis-court, or dancing schoole, with the prize or honour of such exercises; The best remedy I know for such a one, is, to put him prentise to some base occupation, in some good towne or other, yea, were he the sonne of a Duke; according to *Platoes* rule, who saith, *That children must be placed, not according to their fathers conditions, but the faculties of their mind*. Since it is Philosophie that teacheth us to live, and that infancie as well as other ages may plainly read her lessons in the same, why should it not be imparted unto young Schollers?

Udum et molle lutum est, nunc nunc properandus, et acri
Fingendus sine fine rota.—PERS. *Sat*. iii. 23.

He's moist and soft mould, and must by and by
Be cast, made up, while wheele whirl's readily.

We are taught to live, when our life is well-nigh spent. Many schollers have been infected with that loathsome and marrow-wasting disease, before ever they came to read *Aristotles* treatise of Temperance. *Cicero* was wont to say, *That could he out-live the lives of two men, he should never find leasure to study the Lyrike Poets.* And I find these Sophisters both worse and more unprofitable. Our childe is engaged in greater matters; And but the first fifteene or sixteene yeares of his life, are due unto Pedantisme, the rest unto action: let us therefore imploy so short time, as we have to live, in more necessarie instructions. It is an abuse; remove these thornie quiddities of Logike, whereby our life can no whit be amended, and betake our selves to the simple discourses of Philosophy; know how to chuse and fitly to make use of them: they are much more easie to be conceived than one of *Bocace* his tales. A childe comming from nurse is more capable of them, than he is to learne to read or write. Philosophy hath discourses, whereof infancie as well as decaying old-age may make good use. I am of *Plutarkes* mind, which is, that *Aristotle* did not so much ammuse his great Disciple about the arts how to frame Syllogismes, or the principles of Geometrie, as he endevoured to instruct him with good precepts, concerning valour, prowesse, magnanimitie, and temperance, and an undanted assurance not to feare any thing; and with such munition he sent him, being yet verie young, to subdue the Empire of the world, only with 30000. footmen, 4000. horsemen, and 42000. Crownes in monie. As for other arts and sciences; he saith *Alexander* honored them, and commended their excellencie and comlinesse; but for any pleasure he tooke in them, his affection could not easily be drawne to exercise them.

> *—petite hinc juvenesque senesque*
> *Finem animo certum, miserisque viatica canis.—Sat.* v. 64.

> Young men and old, draw hence (in your affaires)
> Your minds set marke, provision for gray haires.

It is that which *Epicurus* said in the beginning of his letter to *Meniceus: Neither let the youngest shun, nor the oldest wearie himselfe in philosophying, for who doth otherwise seemeth to say, that either the season to live happily is not yet come, or is already past.* Yet would I not have this young gentleman pent-up, nor carelesly cast-off to the heedlesse choler, or melancholy humour of the hasty Schoole-master. I would not have his budding spirit corrupted with keeping him fast-tied, and as it were labouring foureteene or fifteene houres a day poaring on his booke, as some doe, as if he were a day-labouring man; neither doe I thinke it fit, if at any time, by reason of some solitarie or melancholy complexion, he should be seene with an over-indiscreet application given to his booke, it should be cherished in him; for, that doth often make him both unapt for civill conversation, and distracts him from better imployments: How many have I seene in my daies, by an over-greedy desire of knowledge, become as it were foolish? *Carneades* was so deeply plunged, and as I may say besotted in it, that he could never have leasure to cut his haire, or pare his nailes: nor would I have his noble manners obscured by the incivilitie and barbarisme of others. The French wisdome hath long since proverbially been spoken of, as verie apt to conceive study in her youth, but most unapt to keepe it long. In good truth, we see at this day, that there is nothing lovelier to behold, than the young children of *France;* but for the most part, they deceive the hope which was fore-apprehended of them: for when they once become men, there is no excellencie at all in them. I have heard men of understanding hold this opinion, that the Colleges to which they are sent (of which there are store) doe thus besot them: whereas to our scholler, a cabinet, a gardin, the table, the bed, a solitarinesse, a companie, morning and evening, and all houres shall be alike unto him, all places shall be a study for him: for Philosophy (as a former of judgements, and modeler of customes) shall be his principall lesson, having the privilege to entermeddle her selfe with all things, and in all places. *Isocrates* the Orator, being once requested at a great banket to speake of his art, when all thought he had reason to answer, said, *It is not now time to doe what I can, and what should now be done, I cannot doe it;* For, to present orations, or to enter into disputation of Rhetorike, before a companie assembled together to be merrie, and make good cheere, would be but a medly of harsh and jarring musicke. The like may be said of all other Sciences. But touching Philosophy, namely in that point where it treateth of man, and of his duties, and offices, it hath been the common judgement of the wisest, that in regard of the pleasantnesse of her conversation, she ought not to be rejected, neither at banquets, nor at sports. And *Plato* having invited her to his solemne feast, we see how kindly she entertaineth the companie with a milde behaviour, fitly suting her selfe to time and place, notwithstanding it be one of his learned'st and profitable discourses.

> *Æquè pauperibus prodest, locupletibus æquè,*
> *Et neglecta æquè pueris senibusque nocebit.*
>
> Hor. i. Ep. i. 25.

Poore men alike, alike rich men it easeth,
Alike it scorned, old and young displeaseth.

So doubtlesse he shall lesse be idle than others; for even as the paces we bestow walking in a gallerie, although they be twice as many more wearie us not so much as those we spend in going a set journey: So our lesson being past over, as it were, by chance, or way of encounter, without strict observance of time or place, being applied to all our actions, shall be digested, and never felt. All sports and exercises shall be a part of his study; running, wrestling, musicke, dancing, hunting, and managing of armes, and horses. I would have the exterior demeanor or decencie, and the disposition of his person to be fashioned together with his mind; for, it is not a mind, it is not a body that we erect, but it is a man, and we must not make two parts of him. And as *Plato* saith, *They must not be erected one without another, but equally be directed, no otherwise than a couple of horses matched to draw in one self-same teeme.* And to heare him, doth he not seem to imploy more time and care in the exercises of his bodie: and to thinke that the mind is together with the same exercised, and not the contrarie? As for other matters, this institution ought to be directed by a sweet-severe mildnesse; Not as some do, who in liew of gently-bidding children to the banquet of letters, present them with nothing but horror and crueltie. Let me have this violence and compulsion removed, there is nothing that, in my seeming, doth more bastardise and dizzie a welborne and gentle nature: If you would have him stand in awe of shame and punishment, doe not so much enure him to it: accustome him patiently to endure sweat and cold, the sharpnesse of the wind, the heat of the sunne, and how to despise all hazards. Remove from him all nicenesse and quaintnesse in clothing, in lying, in eating, and in drinking: fashion him to all things; that he prove not a faire and wanton-puling boy, but a lustie and vigorous boy: When I was a child, being a man, and now am old, I have ever judged and believed the same. But amongst other things, I could never away with this kind of discipline used in most of our Colleges. It had peradventure been lesse hurtfull, if they had somewhat inclined to mildnesse, or gentle intreatie. It is a verie prison of captivated youth, and proves dissolute, in punishing it before it be so. Come upon them when they are going to their lesson, and you heare nothing but whipping and brawling, both of children tormented, and masters besotted with anger and chafing. How wise are they, which go about to allure a childs mind to go to his booke, being yet but tender and fearefull, with a stearne-frowning countenance, and with handsfull of rods? Oh wicked and pernicious manner of teaching! which *Quintillian* hath very wel noted, that this imperious kind of authoritie, namely, this way of punishing of children, drawes many dangerous inconveniences within. How much more decent were it, to see their school-houses and formes strewed with greene boughes and flowers, than with bloudy burchen-twigs? If it lay in me, I would doe as the Philosopher *Speusippus* did, who caused the pictures of Gladnesse and Joy, of *Flora*, and of the Graces, to be set up round about his school-house. Where their profit lieth, there should also be their recreation. Those meats ought to be sugred over, that are healthfull for childrens stomackes, and those made bitter that are hurtfull for them. It is strange to see how carefull *Plato* sheweth himselfe in framing of his lawes about the recreation and pastime of the youth of his Citie, and how far he extends himselfe about their exercises, sports, songs, leaping, and dancing, whereof he saith, that severe antiquitie gave the conduct and patronage unto the Gods themselves, namely, to *Apollo*, to the Muses, and to *Minerva*. Marke but how far-forth he endevoreth to give a thousand precepts to be kept in his places of exercises both of bodie and mind. As for learned Sciences, he stands not much upon them, and seemeth in particular to commend Poesie, but for Musickes sake. All strangenesse and self-particularitie in our manners and conditions, is to be shunned, as an enemie to societie and civill conversation. Who would not be astonished at *Demophons* complexion, chiefe steward of *Alexanders* houshold, who was wont to sweat in the shadow, and quiver for cold in the sunne? I have seene some to startle at the smell of an apple, more than at the shot of a peece; some to be frighted with a mouse, some readie to cast their gorge at the sight of a messe of creame, and others to be scared with seeing a fetherbed shaken: as *Germanicus*, who could not abide to see a cock, or heare his crowing. There may haply be some hidden propertie of nature, which in my judgement might easilie be removed, if it were taken in time. Institution hath gotten this upon me (I must confesse with much adoe) for, except beere, all things else that are mans food agree indifferently with my taste. The bodie being yet souple, ought to be accommodated to all fashions and customes; and (alwaies provided, his appetites and desires be kept under) let a yong man boldly be made fit for al Nations and companies; yea, if need be, for al disorders and surfetings; let him acquaint himselfe with al fashions; That he may be able to do al things, and love to do none but those that are commendable. Some strict Philosophers commend not, but rather blame *Calisthenes*, for losing the good favour of his Master *Alexander*, only because he would not pledge him as much as he had drunke to him. He shall laugh, jest, dally, and debauch himselfe with his Prince. And in his debauching, I would have him out-go al his fellawes in vigor and constancie, and that he omit not to doe evill, neither for want of strength or knowledge, but for lacke of will. *Multum, interest, utrum pecarre quis nolit, aut nesciat: There is a great difference, whether one have no will, or no wit to doe amisse.* I thought to have honoured a gentleman (as great a stranger, and as far from such riotous disorders as any is in *France*) by enquiring of him in verie good companie, how many times in all his life he had bin drunke in *Germanie*, during the time of his abode there, about the necessarie affairs of our King; who tooke it even as I meant it, and answered three times, telling the time and manner how. I know some, who for want of that qualitie, have been much perplexed when they have had occasion to converse with that nation. I have often noted with great admiration, that wonderfull nature of *Alcibiades*, to see how easilie he could sute himselfe to so divers fashions, and different humors, without prejudice unto his health; sometimes exceeding the sumptuousnesse and pompe of the Persians, and now and then surpassing the austeritie and frugalitie of the Lacedemonians, as reformed in *Sparta*, as voluptuous in *Ionia*.

> *Omnis Aristippum decuit color, et status, et res.*
>
> HOR. *Epist.* xvii. 23.

> All colours, states, and things are fit
> For courtly *Aristippus* wit.

Such a one would I frame my Disciple,

> *—quem duplici panno patientia velat,*
> *Mirabor, vitæ via si conversa decebit.*—25.

> Whom patience clothes with sutes of double kind,
> I muse, if he another way will find.

> *Personamque feret non inconcinnus utramque.*—29.

> He not unfitly may,
> Both parts and persons play.

Loe here my lessons, wherein he that acteth them, profiteth more, than he that but knoweth them, whom if you see, you heare, and if you heare him, you see him. God forbid, saith some bodie in *Plato*, that to Philosophize, be to learne many things, and to exercise the arts. *Hanc amplissimam omnium artium bene vivendi disciplinam, vita magis quàm litteris persequuti sunt* (CIC. *Tusc. Qu.* iv.). *This discipline of living well, which is the amplest of all other arts, they followed rather in their lives, than in their learning or writing.* Leo Prince of the Phliasians, enquiring of *Heraclides Ponticus*, what art he professed, he answered, Sir, I professe neither art nor science; but I am a Philosopher. Some reproved *Diogenes*, that being an ignorant man, he did nevertheless meddle with Philosophie, to whom he replied, so much the more reason have I, and to greater purpose doe I meddle with it. *Hegesias* praid him upon a time to reade some booke unto him; *You are a merry man*, said he: As you chuse naturall and not painted right and not counterfeit figges to eat, why doe you not likewise chuse, not the painted and written, but the true and naturall exercises? He shall not so much repeat, as act his lesson. In his actions shall he make repetition of the same. We must observe, "whether there bee wisdome in his enterprises, integritie in his demeanor, modestie in his jestures, justice in his actions, judgement and grace in his speech, courage in his sicknesse, moderation in his sports, temperance in his pleasures, order in the government of his house, and indifferencie in his taste, whether it be flesh, fish, wine, or water, or whatsoever he feedeth upon." *Qui disciplinam suam non ostentationem scientiæ, sed legem vitæ putet: quique obtemperet ipse sibi, et decretis pareat* (CIC. *ibid.* ii). *Who thinks his learning not an ostentation of knowledge, but a law of life, and himselfe obayes himselfe, and doth what is decreed.*

The true mirror of our discourses, is the course of our lives. *Xeuxidamus* answered one that demaunded of him, why the Lacedemonians did not draw into a booke, the ordinances of prowesse, that so their yong men might read them; *it is*, saith he, *because they would rather accustome them to deeds and actions, than to bookes and writings.* Compare at the end of fifteene or sixteene yeares one of these collegiall Latinizers, who hath imployed all that while onely in learning how to speake, to such a one as I meane. The world is nothing but babling and words, and I never saw man, that doth not rather speake more than he ought, than lesse. Notwithstanding halfe our age is consumed that way. We are kept foure or five yeares learning to understand bare words, and to joine them into clauses, then as long in proportioning a great bodie extended into foure or five parts; and five more at least ere we can succinctly know how to mingle, joine, and interlace them handsomely into a subtil fashion, and into one coherent orbe. Let us leave it to those, whose profession is to doe nothing else. Being once on my journey toward *Orleans*, it was my chance to meet upon that plaine that lieth on this side *Clery*, with two Masters of Arts, traveling toward *Burdeaux*, about fiftie paces, one from another, far off behind them, I describe a troupe of horsemen, their Master riding formost, who was the Earle of *Rochefocault*; one of my servants enquiring of the first of those Masters of arts, what Gentleman he was that followed him; supposing my servant had meant his fellow-scholler, for he had not yet seen the Earles traine, answered pleasantly, *He is no gentleman, Sir, but a Gramarian, and I am a Logitian.* Now, we that contrariwise seek not to frame a Gramarian, nor a Logitian, but a compleat gentleman, let us give them leave to mispend their time; we have else-where, and somewhat else of more import to doe. So that our Disciple be well and sufficiently stored with matter; words will follow apace, and if they will not follow gently, he shall hale them on perforce. I heare some excuse themselves, that they cannot expresse their meaning, and make a semblance that their heads are so fullstuft with many goodly things, but for want of eloquence they can neither utter nor make shew of them. It is a meere fopperie. And will you know what, in my seeming, the cause is? They are shadows and *Chimeraes*, proceeding of some formelesse conceptions, which they cannot distinguish or resolve within, and by consequence are not able to produce them, in asmuch as they understand not themselves: And if you but marke their earnestnesse, and how they stammer and labour at the point of their deliverie, you would deeme, that what they go withall, is but a conceiving, and therefore nothing neere downe-lying; and that they doe but licke that imperfect and shapelesse lump of matter. As for me, I am of opinion, and *Socrates* would have it so, that he who hath a cleare and lively imagination in his mind, may easilie produce and utter the same, although it be in *Bergamask,* or *Welsh,* and if he be dumbe, by signes and tokens.

Verbáque prævisam rem non invita sequentur.
HOR. *Art. Poet.* 311.

When matter we fore-know,
Words voluntarie flow.

As one said, as poetically in his prose, *Cùm res animum occu-pavere, verba ambiunt* (SEN. *Controv.* vii. Proæ.). *When matter hath possest their minds, they hunt after words:* and another: *Ipsæ res verba rapiunt. Things themselves will catch and carry words:* He knowes neither Ablative, Conjunctive, Substantive, nor Gramar, no more doth his Lackey, nor any Oyster-wife about the streets, and yet if you have a mind to it, he will intertaine you your fill, and peradventure stumble as little and as seldome against the rules of his tongue, as the best Master of arts in *France.* He hath no skill in Rhetoricke, nor can he with a preface fore-stall and captivate the Gentle Readers good will: nor careth he greatly to know it. In good sooth, all this garish painting is easilie defaced, by the lustre of an in-bred, and simple truth; for these dainties and quaint devices, serve but to ammuse the vulgar sort; unapt and incapable to taste the most solid and firme meat: As *Afer* verie plainly declareth in *Cornelius Tacitus.* The Ambassadours of *Samos* being come to *Cleomenes* King of *Sparta,* prepared with a long prolix Oration, to stir him up to war against the tyrant *Policrates,* after he had listned a good while unto them, his answer was: *Touching your Exordium or beginning I have forgotten it; the middle I remember not; and for your conclusion I will do nothing in it.* A fit, and (to my thinking) a verie good answer; and the Orators were put to such a shift, as they knew not what to replie. And what said another? the *Athenians* from out two of their cunning Architects, were to chuse one to erect a notable great frame: the one of them more affected and selfe-presuming, presented himselfe before them, with a smooth fore-pre-meditated discourse, about the subject of that piece of worke, and thereby drew the judgements of the common people unto his liking; but the other in few words, spake thus: *Lords of Athens, what this man hath said, I will performe.* In the greatest earnestnesse of *Ciceroes* eloquence many were drawn into a kind of admiration; But *Cato* jesting at it, said, *"Have we not a pleasant Consull?* A quicke cunning Argument, and a wittie saying, whether it go before, or come after, it is never out of season. If it have no coherence with that which goeth before, nor with what commeth after; it is good and commendable in it selfe. I am none of those that thinke a good Ryme, to make a good Poeme; let him hardly (if so he please) make a short syllable long, it is no great matter: if the invention be rare and good, and his wit and judgement have cunningly played their part. I will say to such a one; he is a good Poet, but an ill Versifier.

Emunctœ naris, durus componere versus.

Hor. i. *Sat.* iv. 8. Lucil.

A man whose sense could finely pierce,
But harsh and hard to make a verse.

Let a man (saith *Horace*) make his worke loose all seames, measures, and joynts.

*Tempora certa modósque, et quod prius ordine verbum est,
Posterius facias, præponens ultima primis:
Invenias etiam disjecti membra Poetæ.*—58, 62.

Set times and moods, make you the first word last,
The last word first, as if they were new cast:
Yet find th' unjoynted Poets joints stands fast.

He shall for all that, nothing gain-say himselfe, every piece will make a good shew. To this purpose answered *Meander* those that chid him, the day being at hand, in which he had promised a Comedy, and had not begun the same, *Tut-tut,* said he, *it is alreadie finished, there wanteth nothing but to adde the verse unto it:* for, having ranged and cast the plot in his mind, he made small account of feet, of measures, or cadences of verses, which indeed are but of small import in regard of the rest. Since great *Ronzarde* and learned *Bellay,* have raised our French Poesie unto that height of honour, where it now is: I see not one of these petty-balad-makers, or prentise-dogrell rymers, that doth not bumbast his labours with highswelling and heaven-disimbowelling words, and that doth not marshall his cadences verie neere as they doe. *Plus sonat quàm valet* (Sen. *Epist.* xl.). *The sound is more than the weight or worth.* And for the vulgar sort, there were never so many Poets, and so few good: but as it hath been easie for them to represent their rymes, so come they far short in imitating the rich descriptions of the one, and rare inventions of the other. But what shall he doe, if he be urged with sophisticall subtilties about a Sillogisme? A gammon of Bacon makes a man drink, drinking quencheth a mans thirst, *Ergo,* a gammon of bacon quencheth a mans thirst. Let him mock at it, it is more wittie to be mockt at, than to be answered. Let him borrow this pleasant counter-craft of *Aristippus; Why shall I unbind that, which being bound doth so much trouble me?* Some one proposed certaine Logicall quiddities against *Cleanthes,* to whom *Chrisippus* said; use such jugling tricks to play with children, and divert not the serious thoughts of an aged man to such idle matters. If such foolish wiles, *Contorta et aculeata sophismata* (Cic. *Acad. Qu.* iv.),

Intricate and stinged sophismes, must perswade a lie, it is dangerous; but if they proove void of any effect, and move him but to laughter, I see not why he shall beware of them. Some there are so foolish that will go a quarter of a mile out of the way to hunt after a quaint new word, if they once get in chace; *Aut qui non verba rebus aptant, sed res extrinsecus arcessunt, quibus verba conveniant. Or such as fit not words to matter, but fetch matter from abroad, whereto words be fitted.* And another, *Qui alicuius verbi decore placentis, vocentur ad id quod non proposuerunt scribere* (SEN. *Epist.* lix.). *Who are allured by the grace of some pleasing word, to write that they intended not to write.* I doe more willingly winde up a wittie notable sentence, that so I may sew it upon me, than unwinde my thread to go fetch it. Contrariwise, it is for words to serve and wait upon the matter, and not for matter to attend upon words, and if the French tongue cannot reach unto it, let the Gaskonie, or any other. I would have the matters to surmount, and so fill the imagination of him that harkneth, that he have no remembrance at all of the words. It is a naturall, simple, and unaffected speech that I love, so written as it is spoken, and such upon the paper, as it is in the mouth, a pithie, sinnowie, full, strong, compendious and materiall speech, not so delicate and affected, as vehement and piercing.

> *Hæc denum sapiet dictio, quæ feriet.*
> *Epitaph. Lucan.* 6.

> In fine, that word is wisely fit,
> Which strikes the fence, the marke doth hit.

Rather difficult than tedious, void of affection, free, loose and bold, that every member of it seeme to make a bodie; not Pedanticall, nor Frier-like, nor Lawier-like, but rather downe right, Souldier-like. As *Suetonius* calleth that of *Julius Cæsar,* which I see no reason wherefore he calleth it. I have sometimes pleased my selfe in imitating that licenciousnesse or wanton humour of our youths, in wearing of their garments; as carelesly to let their cloaks hang downe over one shoulder; to weare their cloakes scarfe or bawdrikewise, and their stockings loose hanging about their legs. It represents a kind of disdainfull fiercenesse of these forraine embellishings, and neglect carelesnesse of art: But I commend it more being imployed in the course and forme of speech. All manner of affectation, namely in the livelinesse and libertie of *France,* is unseemely in a Courtier. And in a Monarchie every Gentleman ought to addresse himselfe unto a Courtiers carriage. Therefore do we well somewhat to incline to a native and carelesse behaviour. I like not a contexture, where the seames and pieces may be seene: As in a well compact bodie, what need a man distinguish and number all the bones and veines severally? *Quæ veritati operam dat oratio, incomposita sit et simplex.*

Quis accuraté loquitur, nisi qui vult putidè liqui? (SEN. *Epist.* xl. m. lxxv. p.). *The speech that intendeth truth must be plaine and unpollisht: Who speaketh elaborately, but he that meanes to speake unsavouredly?* That eloquence offereth injurie unto things, which altogether drawes us to observe it. As in apparell, it is a signe of pusillanimitie for one to marke himselfe, in some particular and unusuall fashion: so likewise in common speech, for one to hunt after new phrases, and unaccustomed-quaint words, proceedeth of a scholasticall and childish ambition. Let me use none other than are spoken in the hals of *Paris*. *Aristophanes* the Gramarian was somewhat out of the way, when he reproved *Epicurus*, for the simplicitie of his words, and the end of his art oratorie, which was onely perspicuitie in speech. The imitation of speach, by reason of the facilitie of it, followeth presently a whole nation. The imitation of judging and inventing, comes more slow. The greater number of Readers, because they have found one selfe-same kind of gowne, suppose most falsely to holde one like bodie. Outward garments and cloakes may be borrowed, but never the sinews and strength of the bodie. Most of those that converse with me, speake like unto these Essayes; but I know not whether they thinke alike. The Athenians (as *Plato* averreth) have for their part great care to be fluent and eloquent in their speech; The Lacedemonians endevour to be short and compendious; And those of *Crect* labour more to bee plentifull in conceits, than in language. And these are the best. *Zeno* was wont to say, *That he had two sorts of disciples; the one he called* φιλολόγους, *curious to learne things,* and those were his darlings, the other he termed λογοφίλους, who respected nothing more than the language. Yet can no man say, but that to speake well, is most gracious and commendable, but not so excellent as some make it: and I am grieved to see how we employ most part of our time about that onely. I would first know mine owne tongue perfectly, then my neighbours with whom I have most commerce. I must needs acknowledge, that the Greeke and Latine tongues, are great ornaments in a Gentleman, but they are purchased at over-high a rate. Use it who list, I will tell you how they may be gotten better cheape, and much sooner than is ordinarily used, which was tried in my selfe. My late father, having by all the meanes and industrie, that is possible for man, sought amongst the wisest, and men of best understanding, to find a most exquisite and readie way of teaching, being advised of the inconveniences then in use; was given to understand, that the lingring while, and best part of our youth, that we imploy in learning the tongues, which cost them nothing, is the onely cause we can never attaine to that absolute perfection of skill and knowledge, of the Greekes, and Romanes. I doe not beleeve that to be the onely cause. But so it is, the expedient my father found out, was this; that being yet at nurse, and before the first loosing of my tongue, I was delivered to a Germane (who died since, a most excellent Physitian in *France*) he being then altogether ignorant of the French tongue, but exquisitely readie and skilfull in the Latine. This man, whom my Father had sent for of purpose, and to whom he gave verie great entertainment, had me continually in his armes, and was mine onely overseer. There were also joyned unto him two of his countrimen, but not so learned; whose charge was to attend and now and then, to play with me; and all these together did never entertaine me with other than the Latine tongue. As for others of his houshold, it was an inviolable rule, that neither himselfe, nor my mother, nor man, nor maid-servant, were suffered to speake one word in my companie, except such Latine words, as every one had learned to chat and prattle with me. It were strange to tell how every one in the house profited therein. My Father and my Mother learned so much Latine, that for a need they could understand it, when they heard it spoken, even so did all the houshold servants, namely such as were neerest and most about me. To be short, we were all so Latinized, that the townes round about us had their share of it; insomuch as even at this day, many Latine names both of workmen and of their tooles, are yet in use among them. And as for my selfe, I was about six yeares old, and could understand no more French or Perigordine, than Arabike, and that without art, without bookes, rules, or grammer, without whipping or whining. I had gotten as pure a Latine tongue as my Master could speake; the rather because I could neither mingle or confound the same with other tongues. If for an Essay they would give me a theme, whereas the fashion in Colleges is, to give it in French, I had it in bad Latine, to reduce the same into good. And *Nicholas Grucchi,* who hath written, *De comitiis Romanorum, William Guerenti,* who hath commented *Aristotle; George Buchanan,* that famous Scottish Poet, and *Marke-Antonie Muret,* whom (while he lived) both *France* and *Italie* to this day, acknowledge to have been the best Orator: all which have beene my familiar tutors, have often told me, that in mine infancie I had the Latine tongue so readie and so perfect, that themselves feared to take me in hand. And *Buchanan,* who afterward I saw attending on the Marshall of *Brissacke,* told me, he was about to write a treatise of the institution of children, and that he tooke the model and patterne from mine: for, at that time he had the charge and bringing up of the young Earle of *Brissack,* whom since we have seene prove so worthy and so valiant a Captaine. As for the Greeke, wherein I have but small understanding, my father purposed to make me learne it by art; But by new and uncustomed meanes, that is, by way of recreation and exercise. We did tosse our declinations, and conjugations to and fro, as they doe, who by way of a certaine game at tables learne both Arithmetike and Geometrie. For, amongst other things he had especially beene perswaded to make me taste and apprehend the fruits of dutie and science by an unforced kinde of will, and of mine owne choice; and without any compulsion or rigor to bring me up in all mildnesse and libertie: yea with such kinde of superstition, that, whereas some are of opinion, that suddenly to awaken young children, and as it were by violence to startle and fright them out of their dead sleepe in a morning (wherein they are more heavie and deeper plunged than we) doth greatly trouble and distemper their braines, he would every morning cause me to be awakened by the sound of some instrument; and I was never without a servant; Who to that purpose attended upon me. This example may serve to judge of the rest; as also to commend the judgement and tender affection of so carefull and loving a father: who is not to be blamed, though hee reaped not the fruits answerable to his exquisite toyle, and painefull manuring. Two things hindered the same; first the barrennesse and unfit soyle: for howbeit I were of a sound and strong constitution, and of a tractable and yeelding condition, yet was I so heavie, so sluggish, and so dull, that I could not be rouzed (yea were it to goe to play) from out mine idle drowzinesse. What I saw, I saw it perfectly; and under this heavy, and as it were Lethe-complexion did I breed hardie imaginations, and opinions farre above my yeares. My spirit was very slow, and would goe no further than it was led by others; my apprehension blockish, my invention poore; and besides, I had a marvelous defect in my weake memorie: it is therefore no wonder, if my father could never bring me to any perfection. Secondly, as those that in some dangerous sicknesse, moved with a kind of hopefull and greedie desire of perfect health againe, give eare to every Leach or Emperike, and follow all counsels, the good man being exceedingly fearefull to commit any oversight, in a matter he tooke so to heart, suffered himselfe at last to be led away by the common opinion, which like unto the Cranes, followeth ever those that go before, and yeeled to custome: Having those no longer about him, that had given him his first directions, and which they had brought out of *Italie*. Being but six yeares old I was sent to the College of *Guienne*, then most flourishing and reputed the best in *France*, where it is impossible to adde any thing to the great care he had, both to chuse the best and most sufficient Masters, that could be found, to reade unto me, as also for all other circumstances partaining to my education; wherein contrary to usuall customes of Colleges, he observed many particular rules. But so it is, it was ever a College. My Latin tongue was forthwith corrupted, whereof by reason of discontinuance, I afterward lost all manner of use: which new kind of institution, stood me in no other stead, but that at my first admittance, it made me to over-skip some of the lower formes, and to be placed in the highest. For at thirteene yeares of age, that I left the College, I had read over the whole course of Philosophie (as they call it) with so small profit, that I can now make no account of it. The first taste or feeling I had of bookes, was of the pleasure I tooke in reading the fables of *Ovids* Metamorphosies; for, being but seven or eight yeares old, I would steale and sequester my selfe from all other delights, only to reade them: Forsomuch as the tongue wherein they were written was to me naturall; and it was the easiest booke I knew, and by reason of the matter therein contained most agreeing with my young age. For of King *Arthur,* of *Lancelot du Lake,* of *Amadis,* of *Huon* of *Burdeaux,* and such idle time-consuming, and wit-besotting trash of bookes wherein youth doth commonly ammuse it selfe, I was not so much as acquainted with their names, and to this day know not their bodies, nor what they containe: So exact was my discipline. Whereby I became more carelesse to studie my other prescript lessons. And well did it fall out for my purpose, that I had to deale with a very discreet Master, who out of his judgement could with such dexteritie winke at, and second my untowardlinesse, and such other faults that were in me. For by that meanes, I read over *Virgils Æneados, Terence, Plautus,* and other Italian Comedies, allured thereunto by the pleasantnesse of their severall subjects: Had he beene so foolishly-severe, or so severely froward as to crosse this course of mine, I think verily I had never brought any thing from the College, but the hate and contempt of Bookes, as doth the greatest part of our Nobilitie. Such was his discretion, and so warily did he behave himselfe, that he saw and would not see: he would foster and increase my longing: suffering me but by stealth, and by snatches to glut my selfe with those Bookes; holding ever a gentle hand over me, concerning other regular studies. For, the chiefest thing my father required at their hands (unto whose charge he had committed me) was a kinde of well conditioned mildenesse, and facilitie of complexion. And, to say truth, mine had no other fault, but a certaine dull languishing, and heavie slothfulnesse. The danger was not, I should doe ill, but that I should doe nothing.

No man did ever suspect, I would prove a bad, but an unprofitable man: foreseeing in me rather a kind of idlenesse, than a voluntary craftinesse. I am not so selfe-conceited but I perceive what hath followed. The complaints that are daily buzzed in mine eares are these; that I am idle, cold, and negligent in offices of friendship, and dutie to my parents, and kins-folkes; and touching publike offices, that I am over singular and disdainfull. And those that are most injurious cannot aske, wherefore I have taken, and why I have not paied? but may rather demand, why I doe not quit, and wherefore I doe not give? I would take it as a favour, they should wish such effects of supererogation in me. But they are unjust and over partiall, that will goe about to exact that from me, which I owe not, with more rigor than they will exact from themselves that which they owe; wherein if they condemne me, they utterly cancell both the gratifying of the action, and the gratitude, which thereby would be due to me. Whereas the active well doing should be of more consequence, proceeding from my hand, in regard I have no passive at all. Wherefore I may so much the more freely dispose of my fortune, by how much more it is mine, and of my selfe that am most mine owne. Notwithstanding, if I were a great blazoner of mine owne actions, I might peradventure barre such reproches, and justly upbraid some, that they are not so much offended, because I doe not enough, as for that I may, and it lies in my power to doe much more than I do. Yet my minde ceased not at the same time to have peculiar unto it selfe well setled motions, true and open judgements concerning the objects which it knew; which alone, and without any helpe or communication it would digest. And amongst other things I verily beleeve, it would have proved altogether incapable and unfit to yeeld unto force, or stoope unto violence. Shall I account or relate this qualitie of my infancie, which was, a kinde of boldnesse in my lookes, and gentle softnesse in my voice, and affabilitie in my gestures, and a dexteritie in conforming my selfe to the parts I undertooke? for before the age of the

> *Alter ab undecimo tum me vix ceperat annus:*
> VIRG. *Buc. Ecl.* viii. 39.

> Yeares had I (to make even.)
> Scarse two above eleven.

I have under-gone and represented the chiefest parts in the Latin Tragedies of *Buchanan, Guerenti,* and of *Muret;* which in great state were acted and plaid in our College of *Guienne:* wherein *Andreas Goveanus* our Rector principall; who as in all other parts belonging to his charge, was without comparison the chiefest Rector of *France,* and my selfe (without ostentation be it spoken) was reputed, if not a chiefe master, yet a principall Actor in them. It is an exercise I rather commend than disalow in young Gentlemen; and have seene some of our Princes (in imitation of some of former ages) both commendably and honestly, in their proper persons act and play some parts in Tragedies. It hath heretofore been esteemed a lawful exercise, and a tolerable profession in men of honor, namely in *Greece. Aristoni tragico actori rem aperit: huic et genus et fortuna honesta erant: nec ars quia nihil tale apud Græcos pudori est, ea deformabat* (LIV. dec. iii. 4). *He imparts the matter to* Ariston *a Player of tragedies, whose progenie and fortune were both honest; nor did his profession disgrace them, because no such matter is a disparagement amongst the Græcians.*

And I have ever accused them of impertinencie, that condemne and disalow such kindes of recreations, and blamed those of injustice, that refuse good and honest Comedians, or (as we call them) Players, to enter our good townes, and grudge the common people such publike sports. Politike and wel ordered common-wealths endevor rather carefully to unite and assemble their Citizens together; as in serious offices of devotion, so in honest exercises of recreation. Common societie and loving friendship is thereby cherished and increased. And besides, they cannot have more formall and regular pastimes allowed them, than such as are acted and represented in open view of all, and in the presence of the magistrates themselves: And if I might beare sway, I would thinke it reasonable, that Princes should some-times, at their proper charges, gratifie the common people with them, as an argument of a fatherly affection, and loving goodnesse towards them; and that in populous and frequented cities, there should be Theatres and places appointed for such spectacles; as a diverting of worse inconveniences, and secret actions. But to come to my intended purpose, there is no better way than to allure the affection, and to entice the appetite: otherwise a man shall breed but asses laden with Bookes. With jerkes of rods they have their satchels full of learning given them to keepe. Which to doe well, one must not only harbor in himselfe, but wed and mary the same with his minde.

CHAPTER XXVI

IT IS FOLLIE TO REFERRE TRUTH OR FALSHOOD TO OUR SUFFICIENCIE

It is not peradventure without reason, that we ascribe the facilitie of beleeving and easines of perswasion, unto simplicitie and igno-rance: For me seemeth to have learnt heretofore, that beliefe was, as it were an impression conceived in our minde, and according as the same was found either more soft, or of lesse resistance, it was easier to imprint anything therein. *Ut necesse est lancem in libra ponderi-bus impositis deprimi: sic animum perspicuis cedere* (Cic. *Acad. Qu.* iv.). *As it is necessarie a scale must goe down the ballance when weights are put into it, so must a minde yeeld to things that are manifest.* Forasmuch therefore, as the minde being most emptie and without counterpoize, so much the more easily doth it yeeld under the burthen of the first perswasion. And that's the reason why chil-dren, those of the common sort, women, and sicke-folke, are so subject to be mis-led, and so easie to swallow gudgeons. Yet on the other side it is a sottish presumption to disdaine and condemne that for false, which unto us seemeth to beare no shew of likelihood or truth: which is an ordinarie fault in those who perswade themselves to be of more sufficiency than the vulgar sort. So was I sometimes wont to doe, and if I heard any body speake, either of ghosts walking, of foretelling future things, of enchantments, of witchcrafts, or any other thing reported, which I could not well ceonceive, or that was beyond my reach.

Somnia, terrores magicos, miracula, sagas,
Nocturnos lemures, portentaque Thessali.

HOR. ii. Ep. ii. 208.

Dreames, magike terrors, witches, uncouth-wonders,
Night-walking sprites, Thessalian conjur'd-thunders.

I could not but feele a kinde of compassion to see the poore and seely people abused with such follies. And now I perceive, that I was as much to be moaned myselfe: Not that experience hath since made me to dicerne any thing beyond my former opinions: yet was not my curiositie the cause of it, but reason hath taught me, that so resolutely to condemne a thing for false, and impossible, is to assume unto himselfe the advantage, to have the bounds and limits of God's will, and of the power of our common mother Nature tied to his sleeve: And that there is no greater folly in the world, than to reduce them to the measure of our capacitie, and bounds of our sufficiencie. If we terme those things monsters or miracles to which our reason cannot attaine, how many such doe daily present themselves unto our sight? Let us consider through what clouds, and how blinde-fold we are led to the knowledge of most things, that passe our hands: verily we shall finde, it is rather custome, than science that removeth the strangenesse of them from us:

—jam nemo fessus saturusque vivendi,
Suspicere in cæli dignatur lucida templa.—LUCR. ii.

Now no man tir'd with glut of contemplation,
Deignes to have heavn's bright Church in admiration.

And that those things, were they newly presented unto us, wee should doubtlesse deeme them, as much, or more unlikely, and in-credible, than any other.

—si nunc primùm mortalibus adsint
Ex improviso, ceu sint objecta, repentè,
Nil magis his rebus poterat mirabile dici,
Aut minus antè quod auderent fore credere gentes.—1042.

If now first on a sudden they were here
Mongst mortall men, object to eie or eare,
Nothing, than these things, would more wondrous bee,
Or that, men durst lesse thinke, ever to see.

He who had never seene a river before, the first he saw, he thought it to be the Ocean: and things that are the greatest in our knowledge, we judge them to be the extremest that nature worketh in that kinde.

Scilicet et fluvius qui non est maximum, ei est
Qui non antè aliquem majorem vidit, et ingens
Arbor homoque videtur, et omnia de genere omni
Maxima quæ vidit quisque, hæc ingentia fingit.—vi. 671.

A streame none of the greatest, may so seeme
To him, that never saw a greater streame.
Trees, men, seeme huge, and all things of all sorts,
The greatest one hath seene, he huge reports.

Consuetudine oculorum assuescunt animi, neque admirantur,
neque requirunt rationes earum rerum, quas semper vident (CIC. *Nat.*
De. ii.). *Mindes are acquainted by custome of their eies, nor do they*
admire, or enquire the reason of those things which they continually
behold. The novelty of things doth more incite us to search out the
causes, than their greatnesse: we must judge of this infinit power of
nature, with more reverence, and with more acknowledgement of
our owne ignorance and weaknesse. How many things of small
likelihood are there, witnessed by men, worthie of credit, whereof
if we cannot be perswaded, we should at least leave them in sus-
pence? For, to deeme them impossible, is by rash presumption to
presume and know how farre possibilitie reacheth. If a man did well
understand, what difference there is betweene impossibilitie, and that
which is unwonted, and betweene that which is against the course of
nature, and the common opinion of men, in not beleeving rashly, and
in not disbeleeving easily; the rule of *Nothing too-much*, commanded
by *Chilon*, should be observed. When we finde in *Froysard*, that the
Earl of *Foix*, (being in *Bearne*) had knowledge of the defeature at
Inberoth, of King *John* of *Castile*, the morrow next it hapned, and the
meanes he alleageth for it, a man may well laugh at it: And of that
which our Annales report, that Pope *Honorius*, the very same day
that King *Philip Augustus* died at *Mantes*, caused his publike funerals
to be solemnized, and commanded them to be celebrated throughout
all *Italie*. For, the authoritie of the witnesses hath peradventure no
sufficient warrant to restraine us. But what if *Plutarke*, besides divers
examples which he alleageth of antiquitie, saith to have certainly
knowne, that in *Domitians time, the newes of the battle lost by*
Antonius in Germany many daies journeies thence, was published
at Rome, and divulged through the world, the very same day it
succeeded: And if *Cæsar* holds, that it hath many times happened,
that report hath foregone the accident: Shall we not say, that those
simple people have suffered themselves to be cousened and seduced
by the vulgar sort, because they were not as cleare-sighted as we?
Is there any thing more daintie, more unspotted, and more lively
than *Plinies* judgement, whensoever it pleaseth him to make shew
of it? Is there any farther from vanitie? I omit the excellencie of
his learning and knowledge, whereof I make but small reckoning: in

which of those two parts doe we exceed him? Yet there is no
scholler so meanely learned, but will convince him of lying, and read
a lecture of contradiction against him upon the progresse of natures
works. When wee read in *Bouchet* the myracles wrought by the
reliques of Saint *Hillarie*, his credit is not sufficient to barre us the
libertie of contradicting him: yet at randon to condemne all such
like histories, seemeth to me a notable impudencie. That famous
man Saint *Augustine* witnesseth to have seene a blinde childe to
recover his sight, over the reliques of Saint *Gervase* and *Protaise* at
Milane: and a woman at *Carthage,* to have been cured of a canker,
by the signe of the holy Crosse, which a woman newly baptized made
unto her: and *Hesperius* a familiar friend of his, to have expelled
certaine spirits, that molested his house, with a little of the earth of
our Saviours sepulcher; which earth being afterwards transported
into a Church, a Paralitike man was immediately therewith cured:
and a woman going in procession, having as she past by with a nose-
gaie toucht the case wherein Saint *Stevens* bones were, and with the
same afterward rubbed her eies, she recovered her sight, which long
before she had utterly lost: and divers other examples, where he
affirmeth to have beene an assistant himselfe. What shal we accuse
him of, and two other holy Bishops, *Aurelius* and *Maximinus,* whom
he calleth for his witnesses? Shal it be of ignorance, of simplicity, of
malice, of facility, or of imposture? Is any man living so impudent,
that thinks he may be compared to them, whether it be in vertue
or piety, in knowledge or judgement, in wisdome or sufficiency?
Qui ut rationem nullam afferrent, ipsa authoritate me frangerent
(Cic. *Div.* i.): *Who though they alleaged no reason, yet might
subdue me with their very authoritie.* It is a dangerous fond hardinesse,
and of consequence, besides the absurd temerity it drawes with it, to
despise what we conceive not. For, after that according to your best
understanding, you have established the limits of truth, and bounds
of falshood, and that it is found, you must necessarily beleeve things,
wherein is more strangenesse, than in those you deny; you have alreadie bound your selfe to abandon them. Now that which me thinkes
brings as much disorder in our consciences, namely in these troubles
of religion wherein we are, is the dispensation Catholikes make of
their beliefe. They suppose to shew themselves very moderate and
skilfull, when they yeeld their adversaries any of those articles now
in question. But besides that, they perceive not what an advantage
it is for him that chargeth you, if you but once begin to yeeld and
give them ground; and how much that encorageth him to pursue his
point: those articles which they chuse for the lightest, are oftentimes
most important. Either a man must wholy submit himselfe to the
authoritie of our Ecclesiasticall policie, or altogether dispence himselfe from it: It is not for us to determine what part of obedience
we owe unto it. And moreover, I may say it, because I have made

triall of it, having sometimes used this libertie of my choice, and particular election, not regarding certaine points of the observance of our Church, which seeme to beare a face, either more vaine, or more strange; comming to communicate them with wise men, I have found that those things have a most solid and steadie foundation, and that it is but foolishnesse and ignorance, makes us receive them with lesse respect and reverence than the rest. Why remember we not, what, and how many contradictions we finde and feele even in our owne judgement? How many things served us but yesterday as articles of faith, which to day we deeme but fables? Glory and curiositie are the scourges of our soules. The latter induceth us to have an oare in every ship, and the former forbids us to leave any thing unresolved or decided.

CHAPTER XXVII

OF FRIENDSHIP

CONSIDERING the proceeding of a Painters worke I have; a desire hath possessed mee to imitate him: He maketh choice of the most convenient place and middle of everie wall, there to place a picture, laboured with all his skill and sufficiencie; and all void places about it he filleth up with antike Boscage or Crotesko works; which are fantasticall pictures, having no grace, but in the variety and strangenesse of them. And what are these my compositions in truth, other than antike workes, and monstrous bodies, patched and hudled up together of divers members, without any certaine or well ordered figure, having neither order, dependencie, or proportion, but casuall and framed by chance?

> *Desinit in piscem mulier formosa supernè.*
> HOR. *Art. Poe.* 4.

A woman faire for parts superior,
Ends in a fish for parts inferior.

Touching this second point I goe as farre as my Painter, but for the other and better part I am farre behinde: for my sufficiency reacheth not so farre, as that I dare undertake, a rich, a polished, and according to true skill, and artlike table. I have advised my selfe to borrow one of *Steven de la Boetie*, who with this kinde of worke shall honour all the world. It is a discourse he entitled, *Voluntary Servitude*, but those who have not knowne him, have since very properly rebaptized the same, *The against one.* In his first youth he writ, by way of Essaie, in honour of libertie against Tyrants. It hath long since beene dispersed amongst men of understanding, not without great and well deserved commendations: for it is full of wit, and containeth as much learning as may be: yet doth it differ much from the best he can do.

And if in the age I knew him in, he would have undergone my dessigne, to set his fantasies downe in writing, we should doubtlesse see many rare things, and which would very neerely approch the honour of antiquity: for especially touching that part of natures gifts, I know none may be compared to him. But it was not long of him, that ever this Treatise came to mans view, and I beleeve he never saw it since it first escaped his hands: with certaine other notes concerning the edict of Januarie, famous by reason of our intestine warre, which haply may in other places finde their deserved praise. It is all I could ever recover of his reliques (whom when death seized, he by his last will and testament, left with so kinde remembrance, heire and executor of his librarie and writings) besides the little booke, I since caused to be published: To which his pamphlet I am particularly most bounden, forsomuch as it was the instrumentall meane of our first acquaintance. For it was shewed me long time before I saw him; and gave me the first knowledge of his name, addressing, and thus nourishing that unspotted friendship, which we (so long as it pleased God) have so sincerely, so entire and inviolably maintained betweene us, that truly a man shall not commonly heare of the like; and amongst our moderne men no signe of any such is seene. So many parts are required to the erecting of such a one, that it may be counted a wonder, if fortune once in three ages contract the like. There is nothing to which Nature hath more addressed us than to societie. And *Aristotle* saith, *that perfect Law-givers have had more regardfull care of friendship than of justice.* And the utmost drift of its perfection is this. For generally, all those amities which are forged and nourished by voluptuousnesse or profit, publike or private need, are thereby so much the lesse faire and generous, and so much the lesse true amities, in that they inter-meddle other causes, scope, and fruit with friendship, than it selfe alone: Nor doe those foure ancient kindes of friendships, *Naturall, sociall, hospitable,* and *venerian,* either particularly or conjointly be-seeme the same. That from children to parents may rather be termed respect: Friendship is nourished by communication, which by reason of the over-great disparitie cannot bee found in them, and would happly offend the duties of nature: for neither all the secret thoughts of parents can be communicated unto children, lest it might engender an unbeseeming familiaritie betweene them, nor the admonitions and corrections (which are the chiefest offices of friendship) could be exercised from children to parents. There have nations beene found, where, by custome, children killed their parents, and others, where parents slew their children, thereby to avoid the hindrance of enter-bearing one another in aftertimes: for naturally one dependeth from the ruine of another. There have Philosophers beene found disdaining this naturall conjunction, witnesse *Aristippus,* who being urged with the affection he ought his children, as proceeding from his loynes, began to spit, saying, *That also that excrement proceeded from him, and that also we*

engendred wormes and lice. And that other man, whom *Plutarke* would
have perswaded to agree with his brother, answered, *I care not a straw
the more for him, though he came out of the same wombe I did.* Verily
the name of Brother is a glorious name, and full of loving kindnesse,
and therefore did he and I terme one another sworne brother: but
this commixture, dividence, and sharing of goods, this joyning wealth
to wealth, and that the riches of one shall be the povertie of another,
doth exceedingly distemper and distract all brotherly alliance, and
lovely conjunction: If brothers should conduct the progresse of their
advancement and thrift in one same path and course, they must necessarily oftentimes hinder and crosse one another. Moreover, the correspondencie and relation that begetteth these true and mutually
perfect amities, why shall it be found in these? The father and the
sonne may very well be of a farre differing complexion, and so [may]
brothers: He is my sonne, he is my kinsman; but he may be a foole,
a bad, or a peevish-minded man. And then according as they are friendships, which the law and dutie of nature doth command us, so much
the lesse of our owne voluntarie choice and libertie is there required
unto it: And our genuine libertie hath no production more properly her
owne, than that of affection and amitie. Sure I am, that concerning the
same I have assaied all that might be, having had the best and most
indulgent father that ever was, even to his extremest age, and who
from father to sonne was descended of a famous house, and touching
this rare-seene vertue of brotherly concord very exemplare:

>   *Notus in fratres animi paterni.*—HOR. ii. *Od*. ii. 6.
>   *—et ipse*

>   To his brothers knowne so kinde,
>   As to beare a fathers minde.

To compare the affection toward women unto it, although it proceed
from our owne free choise, a man cannot, nor may it be placed in this
ranke: Her fire, I confesse it

>   (—*neque enim est dea nescia nostri
>   Quæ dulcem curis miscet amaritiem.*)

>   (Nor is that Goddesse ignorant of me,
>   Whose bitter-sweets with my cares mixed be,)

to be more active, more fervent, and more sharpe. But it is a rash and
wavering fire, waving and divers: the fire of an ague subject to fits
and stints, and that hath but slender hold-fast of us. In true friendship, it is a generall and universall heat, and equally tempered, a constant and setled heat, all pleasure and smoothnes, that hath no pricking
or stinging in it, which the more it is in lustfull love, the more is it but
a ranging and mad desire in following that which flies us,

Come segue la lepre il cacciatore
Al freddo, al caldo, alla montagna, ad lito,
Ne piu l'estima poi che presa vede,
E sol dietro a chi fugge affretta il piede.

ARIOS. can. x. st. 7.

Ev'n as the huntsman doth the hare pursue,
In cold, in heat, on mountaines, on the shore,
But cares no more, when he her tan'e espies,
Speeding his pace, only at that which flies.

As soone as it creepeth into the termes of friendship, that is to say,
in the agreement of wils, it languisheth and vanisheth away: enjoying
doth lose it, as having a corporall end, and subject to sacietie. On the
other side, friendship is enjoyed according as it is desired, it is neither
bred, nor nourished, nor increaseth but in jovissance, as being spirituall,
and the minde being refined by use and custome. Under this chiefe
amitie, these fading affections have sometimes found place in me, lest
I should speake of him, who in his verses speakes but too much of it.
So are these two passions entred into me in knowledge one of another,
but in comparison never: the first flying a high, and keeping a proud
pitch, disdainfully beholding the other to passe her points farre under
it. Concerning marriage, besides that it is a covenant which hath
nothing free but the entrance, the continuance being forced and constrained, depending else-where than from our will, and a match ordinarily concluded to other ends: A thousand strange knots are therein
commonly to be unknit, able to break the web, and trouble the whole
course of a lively affection; whereas in friendship, there is no commerce or busines depending on the same, but it selfe. Seeing (to speake
truly) that the ordinary sufficiency of women, cannot answer this conference and communication, the nurse of this sacred bond: nor seeme
their mindes strong enough to endure the pulling of a knot so hard, so
fast, and durable. And truly, if without that, such a genuine and
voluntarie acquaintance might be contracted, where not only mindes
had this entire jovissance, but also bodies, a share of the alliance, and
where a man might wholy be engaged: It is certaine, that friendship
would thereby be more compleat and full: But this sex could never
yet by any example attaine unto it, and is by ancient schooles rejected
thence. And this other Greeke licence is justly abhorred by our customes, which notwithstanding, because according to use it had so
necessarie a disparitie of ages, and difference of offices between lovers,
did no more sufficiently answer the perfect union and agreement, which
here we require: *Quis est enim iste amor amicitiæ? cur neque defor-
mem adolescentem quisquam amat, neque formosum senem?* (CIC.
Tusc. Que. iv.). *For, what love is this of friendship? why doth no man
love either a deformed young man, or a beautifull old man?* For even
the picture the *Academie* makes of it, will not (as I suppose) disavowe

mee, to say thus in her behalfe: That the first furie, enspired by the
son of *Venus* in the lovers hart, upon the object of tender youths-flower,
to which they allow all insolent and passionate violences, an immoderate heat may produce, was simply grounded upon an externall beauty;
a false image of corporall generation: for in the spirit it had no power,
the sight whereof was yet concealed, which was but in his infancie, and
before the age of budding. For, if this furie did seize upon a base
minded courage, the meanes of its pursuit, [were] riches, gifts, favour
to the advancement of dignities, and such like vile merchandice, which
they reprove. If it fell into a most generous minde, the interpositions
were likewise generous: Philosophicall instructions, documents to
reverence religion, to obey the lawes, to die for the good of his countrie:
examples of valor, wisdome and justice. The lover endevoring and
studying to make himselfe acceptable by the good grace and beauty of
his minde (that of his body being long since decayed) hoping by this
mentall societie to establish a more firme and permanent bargaine.
When this pursuit attained the effect in due season, (for by not
requiring in a lover, he should bring leasure and discretion in his
enterprise, they require it exactly in the beloved; forasmuch as he was
to judge of an internall beauty, of a difficile knowledge, and abstruse
discovery) [then] by the interposition of a spiritual beauty was the
desire of a spirituall conception engendred in the beloved. The latter
was here chiefest; the corporall, accidentall and second, altogether contrarie to the lover. And therefore doe they preferre the beloved, and
verifie that the gods likewise preferre the same: and greatly blame the
Poet *Æschylus,* who in the love betweene *Achilles* and *Patroclus* ascribeth the lovers part unto *Achilles,* who was in the first and beardlesse
youth of his adolescency, and the fairest of the Græcians. After this
generall communitie, the mistris and worthiest part of it, predominant
and exercising her offices (they say the most availefull commodity did
thereby redound both to the private and publike) That it was the force
of countries received the use of it, and the principall defence of equitie
and libertie: witnesse the comfortable loves of *Hermodius* and *Aris-
togiton.* Therefore name they it sacred and divine, and it concerns not
them whether the violence of tyrants, or the demisnesse of the people
be against them: To conclude, all can be alleaged in favour of the
Academy, is to say, that it was a love ending in friendship, a thing
which hath no bad reference unto the Stoical definition of love:
Amorem conatum esse amicitiæ faciendæ ex pulchritudinis specie (Cɪc.
ibid.). *That love is an endevour of making friendship, by the shew of
beautie.* I returne to my description in a more equitable and equall
manner. *Omnino amicitiæ corroboratis jam confirmatisque ingeniis et
ætatibus judicandæ sunt* (Cɪc. *Amic.*). *Clearely friendships are to be
judged by wits, and ages already strengthened and confirmed.* As for
the rest, those we ordinarily call friendes and amities, are but acquaintances and familiarities, tied together by some occasion or commodities,

by meanes whereof our mindes are entertained. In the amitie I speake of, they entermixe and confound themselves one in the other, with so universall a commixture, that they weare out, and can no more finde the seame that hath conjoyned them together. If a man urge me to tell wherefore I loved him, I feele it cannot be expressed, but by answering; Because it was he, because it was my selfe. There is beyond all my discourse, and besides what I can particularly report of it, I know not what inexplicable and fatall power, a meane and Mediatrix of this indissoluble union. Wee sought one another, before we had seene one another, and by the reports we heard one of another; which wrought a greater violence in us, than the reason of reports may well beare: I thinke by some secret ordinance of the heavens, we embraced one another by our names. And at our first meeting, which was by chance at a great feast, and solemne meeting of a whole towneship, we found our selves so surprized, so knowne, so acquainted, and so combinedly bound together, that from thence forward, nothing was so neere unto us, as one unto another. He writ an excellent Latyne Satyre; since published; by which he excuseth and expoundeth the precipitation of our acquaintance, so suddenly come to her perfection; Sithence it must continue so short a time, and begun so late (for we were both growne men, and he some yeares older than my selfe) there was no time to be lost. And it was not to bee modelled or directed by the paterne of regular and remisse friendship, wherein so many precautions of a long and preallable conversation are required. This hath no other *Idea* than of it selfe, and can have no reference but to it selfe. It is not one especiall consideration, nor two, nor three, nor foure, nor a thousand: It is I wot not what kinde of quintessence, of all this commixture, which having seized all my will, induced the same to plunge and lose it selfe in his, which likewise having seized all his will, brought it to lose and plunge it selfe in mine, with a mutuall greedinesse, and with a semblable concurrance. I may truly say, lose, reserving nothing unto us, that might properly be called our owne, nor that was either his, or mine. When *Lelius* in the presence of the Romane Consuls, who after the condemnation of *Tiberius Gracchus,* pursued all those that had beene of his acquaintance, came to enquire of *Caius Blosius* (who was one of his chiefest friends) what he would have done for him, and that he answered, *All things. What? All things?* replied he: *And what if he had willed thee to burne our Temples? Blosius* answered, *He would never have commanded such a thing. But what if he had done it?* replied *Lelius:* The other answered, *I would have obeyed him:* If hee were so perfect a friend to *Gracchus,* as Histories report, he needed not offend the Consuls with this last and bold confession, and should not have departed from the assurance hee had of *Gracchus* his minde. But yet those, who accuse this answer as seditious, understand not well this mysterie: and doe not presuppose in what termes he stood, and that he held *Gracchus* his will in his sleeve, both by power and knowledge.

They were rather friends than Citizens, rather friends than enemies of their countrey, or friends of ambition and trouble. Having absolutely committed themselves one to another, they perfectly held the reines of one anothers inclination: and let this yoke be guided by vertue and conduct of reason (because without them it is altogether impossible to combine and proportion the same). The answer of *Blosius* was such as it should be. If their affections miscarried, according to my meaning, they were neither friends one to other, nor friends to themselves. As for the rest, this answer sounds no more than mine would doe, to him that would in such sort enquire of me; if your will should command you to kill your daughter, would you doe it? and that I should consent unto it: for, that beareth no witnesse of consent to doe it: because I am not in doubt of my will, and as little of such a friends will. It is not in the power of the worlds discourse to remove me from the certaintie I have of his intentions and judgements of mine: no one of its actions might be presented unto me, under what shape soever, but I would presently finde the spring and motion of it. Our mindes have jumped so unitedly together, they have with so fervent an affection considered of each other, and with like affection so discovered and sounded, even to the very bottome of each others heart and entrails, that I did not only know his, as well as mine owne, but I would (verily) rather have trusted him concerning any matter of mine, than my selfe. Let no man compare any of the other common friendships to this. I have as much knowledge of them as another, yea of the perfectest of their kinde: yet wil I not perswade any man to confound their rules, for so a man might be deceived. In these other strict friendships a man must march with the bridle of wisdome and precaution in his hand; the bond is not so strictly tied, but a man may in some sort distrust the same. *Love him* (said *Chilon*) *as if you should one day hate him againe. Hate him as if you should love him againe.* This precept, so abhominable in this soveraigne and mistris Amitie, is necessarie and wholesome in the use of vulgar and customarie friendships: toward which a man must employ the saying *Aristotle* was wont so often to repeat, *Oh you my friends, there is no perfect friend.*

In this noble commerce, offices and benefits (nurses of other amities) deserve not so much as to bee accounted of: this confusion so full of our wils is cause of it: for even as the friendship I beare unto my selfe, admits no accrease, by any succour I give my selfe in any time of need, whatsoever the Stoickes alleage; and as I acknowledge no thanks unto my selfe for any service I doe unto my selfe, so the union of such friends, being truly perfect, makes them lose the feeling of such duties, and hate, and expell from one another these words of division, and difference; benefit, good deed, dutie, obligation, acknowledgement, prayer, thanks, and such their like. All things being by effect common betweene them; wils, thoughts, judgements, goods, wives, children, honour, and life; and their mutuall agreement, being no other than one soule in two bodies, according to the fit definition of *Aristotle,* they can neither lend or give ought to each other. See here the reason why Lawmakers, to honour marriage with some imaginary resemblance of this divine bond, inhibite donations betweene husband and wife; meaning thereby to inferre, that all things should peculiarly bee proper to each of them, and that they have nothing to divide and share together. If in the friendship whereof I speake, one might give unto another, the receiver of the benefit should binde his fellow. For, each seeking more than any other thing, to doe each other good, he who yeelds both matter and occasion, is the man sheweth himselfe liberall, giving his friend that contentment, to effect towards him what he desireth most. When the Philosopher *Diogenes* wanted money, he was wont to say; *That he re-demanded the same of his friends, and not that he demanded it:* And to shew how that is practised by effect, I will relate an ancient singular example. *Eudamidas* the Corinthian had two friends. *Charixenus* a Sycionian, and *Aretheus* a Corinthian; being upon his deathbed, and very poore, and his two friends very rich, thus made his last will and testament. *To* Aretheus, *I bequeath the keeping of my mother, and to maintaine her when she shall be old: To* Charixenus *the marrying of my daughter, and to give her as great a dowry as he may: and in case one of them shall chance to die before, I appoint the surviver to substitute his charge, and supply his place.* Those that first saw this testament, laughed and mocked at the same; but his heires being advertised thereof, were very well pleased, and received it with singular contentment. And *Charixenus* one of them, dying five daies after *Eudamidas,* the substitution being declared in favour of *Aretheus,* he carefully, and very kindly kept and maintained his mother, and of five talents that he was worth, he gave two and a halfe in mariage to one only daughter he had, and the other two and a halfe to the daughter of *Eudamidas,* whom he married both in one day. This example is very ample, if one thing were not, which is the multitude of friends: For, this perfect amity I speake of, is indivisible; each man doth so wholy give himselfe unto his friend, that he hath nothing left him to divide else-where: moreover he is grieved that he is [not] double, triple, or quadruple, and hath not many soules, or sundry wils, that he might conferre them all upon this subject. Common friendship may bee divided; a man may love beauty in one, facility of behaviour in another, liberality in one, and wisdome in another, paternity in this, fraternity in that man, and so forth: but this amitie which possesseth the soule, and swaies it in all soveraigntie, it is impossible it should be double. If two at one instant should require helpe, to which would you run? Should they crave contrary offices of you, what order would you follow? Should one commit a matter to your silence, which if the other knew would greatly profit him, what course would you take? Or how would you discharge your selfe? A singular and principall friendship dissolveth all other duties, and freeth all other obligations. The secret I have sworne not to reveale to another, I may without perjurie impart it unto him, who is no other but my selfe. It is a great and strange wonder for a man to double himself; and those that talke of tripling, know not, nor cannot reach unto the height of it. *Nothing is extreme, that hath his like.* And he who shal presuppose, that of two I love the one as wel as the other, and that they enter-love one another, and love me as much as I love them: he multiplieth in brother-hood, a thing most singular, and alonely one, and than which one alone is also the rarest to be found in the world. The remainder of this history agreeth very wel with what I said; for, *Eudamidas* giveth as a grace and favor to his friends to employ them in his need: he leaveth them as his heires of his liberality, which consisteth in putting the meanes into their hands, to doe him good. And doubtlesse, the force of friend-ship is much more richly shewen in his deed, than in *Aretheus*. To conclude, they are [inimaginable] effects, to him that hath not tasted them; and which makes me wonderfully to honor the answer of that young souldier to *Cyrus*, who enquiring of him, what he would take for a horse, with which he had lately gained the prize of a race, and whether he would change him for a Kingdome? *No surely my Liege* (said he) *yet would I willingly forgoe him to gaine a true friend, could I but finde a man worthy of so precious an alliance.* He said not ill, in saying, *could I but finde.* For, a man shall easily finde men fit for a superficiall acquaintance; but in this, wherein men negotiate from the very centre of their harts, and make no spare of any thing, it is most requisite, all the wards and springs be sincerely wrought, and per-fectly true. In confederacies, which hold but by one end, men have nothing to provide for, but for the imperfections, which particularly doe interest and concerne that end and respect. It is no great matter what religion my Physitian and Lawier is of: this consideration hath nothing common with the offices of that friendship they owe mee. So doe I in the familiar acquaintances, that those who serve me contract with me. I am nothing inquisitive whether a Lackey be chaste or no, but whether he be diligent: I feare not a gaming Muletier, so much as if he be weake; nor a hot swearing Cooke, as one that is ignorant and unskilfull; I never meddle with saying what a man should doe in the world; there are over many others that doe it; but what my selfe doe in the world.

> *Mihi sic usus est: Tibi, ut opus est facto, face.*
> TER. *Heau.* act. i. sc. i. 28.

So is it requisite for me;
Doe thou as needfull is for thee.

Concerning familiar table-talke, I rather acquaint my selfe with, and follow a merry conceited humour, than a wise man: And in bed I rather prefer beauty, than goodnesse; and in society or conversation of familiar discourse, I respect rather sufficiency, though without

Preud'hommie, and so of all things else. Even as he that was found riding upon an hobby-horse, playing with his children, besought him, who thus surprized him, not to speake of it, untill he were a father himselfe, supposing the tender fondnesse, and fatherly passion, which then would possesse his minde, should make him an impartiall judge of such an action. So would I wish to speake to such as had tried what I speake of: but knowing how far such an amitie is from the common use, and how seld seene and rarely found, I looke not to firde a competent judge. For, even the discourses, which stern antiquitie hath left us concerning this subject, seeme to me but faint and forcelesse in respect of the feeling I have of it: And in that point the effects exceed the very precepts of Philosophie.

> *Nil ego contulerim jucundo sanus amico.*
>
> HOR. i. *Sat.* v. 44.

> For me, be I well in my wit,
> Nought, as a merry friend, so fit.

Ancient *Menander* accounted him happy, that had but met the shadow of a true friend: verily he had reason to say so, especially if he had tasted of any: for truly, if I compare all the rest of my fore-passed life, which although I have by the meere mercy of God, past at rest and ease, and except the losse of so deare a friend, free from all grievous affliction, with an ever-quietnesse of minde, as one that have taken my naturall and originall commodities in good payment, without searching any others: if, as I say, I compare it all unto the foure yeares, I so happily enjoied the sweet company, and deare-deare society of that worthy man, it is nought but a vapour, nought but a darke and yrkesome [night]. Since the time I lost him,

> *quem semper acerbum,*
> *Semper honoratum (sic Dii voluistis) habebo.*
>
> VIRG. *Æn.* v. 49.

> Which I shall ever hold a bitter day,
> Yet ever honor'd (so my God t' obey).

I doe but languish, I doe but sorrow: and even those pleasures, all things present me with, in stead of yeelding me comfort, doe but redouble the griefe of his losse. We were co-partners in all things. All things were with us at halfe; me thinkes I have stolne his part from him.

> —*Nec fas esse ulla me voluptate hîc frui*
> *Decrevi, tantisper dum ille abest mes particeps.*
>
> TER. *Heau.* act. i. sc. i. 97.

> I have set downe, no joy enjoy I may,
> As long as he my partner is away.

I was so accustomed to be ever two, and so enured to be never single, that me thinks I am but halfe my selfe.

> *Illam meæ si partem animæ tulit,*
> *Maturior vis, quid moror altera,*
> *Nec charus æquè nec superstes,*
> *Integer? Ille dies utramque*
> *Duxit ruinam.*—Hor. ii. *Od.* xvii. 5.

Since that part of my soule riper fate reft me,
Why stay I heere the other part he left me?
Nor so deere, nor entire, while heere I rest:
That day hath in one ruine both opprest.

There is no action can betide me, or imagination possesse me, but I heare him saying, as indeed he would have done to me: for even as he did excell me by an infinite distance in all other sufficiencies and vertues, so did he in all offices and duties of friendship.

> *Quis desiderio sit pudor aut modus,*
> *Tam chari capitis?*—i. *Od.* xxiv. 1.

What modesty or measure may I beare,
In want and wish of him that was so deare?

> *O misero frater adempte mihi!*
> *Omnia tecum unà perierunt gaudia nostra,*
> *Quæ tuus in vita dulcis alebat amor.*
> *Tu mea, tu moriens fregisti commoda frater,*
> *Tecum unà tota est nostra sepulta anima,*
> *Cujus ego interitu tota de mente fugavi*
> *Hæc studia, atque omnes delicias animi.*
> *Alloquar? audiero nunquam tua verba loquentem?*
> *Nunquam ego te vita frater amabilior,*
> *Aspiciam posthac? at certè semper amabo.*
> CATUL. *Ele.* iv. 20, 92, 23, 95, 21, 94, 25; *El.* i. 9.

A brother reft from miserable me,
All our delight's are perished with thee,
Which thy sweet love did nourish in my breath.
Thou all my good hast spoiled in thy death:
With thee my soule is all and whole enshrinde,
At whose death I have cast out of minde
All my mindes sweet-meats, studies of this kinde;
Never shall I, heare thee speake, speake with thee?
Thee brother, than life dearer, never see?
Yet shalt thou ever be belov'd of mee,

but let us a little heare this yong man speake, being but sixteene yeares of age.

Because I have found this worke to have since beene published (and to an ill end) by such as seeke to trouble and subvert the state of our common-wealth, nor caring whether they shall reforme it or no; which they have fondly inserted among other writings of their invention, I have revoked my intent, which was to place it here. And lest the Authors memory should any way be interessed with those that could not thoroughly know his opinions and actions, they shall understand, that this subject was by him treated of in his infancie, only by way of exercise, as a subject, common, bare-worne, and wyer-drawne in a thousand bookes. I will never doubt but he beleeved what he writ, and writ as he thought: for hee was so conscientious, that no lie did ever passe his lips, yea were it but in matters of sport or play: and I know, that had it beene in his choyce, he would rather have beene borne at *Venice,* than at *Sarlac;* and good reason why: But he had another maxime deeply imprinted in his minde, which was, carefully to obey, and religiously to submit himselfe to the lawes, under which he was borne. There was never a better Citizen, nor more affected to the welfare and quietnesse of his countrie, nor a sharper enemie of the changes, innovations, new-fangles, and hurly-burlies of his time: He would more willingly have imployed the utmost of his endevours to extinguish and suppresse, than to favour or furthen them: His minde was modelled to the patterne of other best ages. But yet in exchange of his serious treatise, I will here set you downe another, more pithie, materiall, and of more consequence, by him likewise produced in that tender age.

CHAPTER XXVIII

NINE AND TWENTIE SONNETS OF STEVEN DE LA BOETIE, TO THE LADY OF GRAMMONT, COUNTESSE OF GUISSEN

MADAME, I present you with nothing that is mine, either because it is already yours, or because I finde nothing therein worthy of you. But wheresoever these verses shall be seene, for the honour which thereby shall redound to them, by having this glorious *Corisanda* of *Andoins* for their guide, I thought it good to adorne them with your worthy name. I have deemed this present fit for your Ladiship, forsomuch as there are few Ladies in *France,* that either can better judge of Poesie, or fitter apply the use of it, than your worthy selfe: and since in these her drooping daies, none can give it more life, or vigorous spirit, than you, by those rich and high-tuned accords, wherewith amongst a million of other rare beauties, nature hath richly graced you. Madame, these verses deserve to be cherished by you: and I am perswaded you will be of mine opinion, which is, that none have come out of *Gaskonie,* that either had more wit, or better invention, and that witnesse to have proceeded from a richer veine. And let no jealousie possesse you, inasmuch as you have but the remainder of that, which whilome I caused to be printed under the name of my Lord of *Foix,* your worthy, noble and deare kinsman: For truly, these have a kinde of livelinesse, and more piercing Emphasis than any other, and which I cannot well expresse: as hee that made them in his Aprils youth, and when he was enflamed with a noble glorious flame, as I will one day tell your honour in your care. The other were afterward made by him in favour of his wife, at what time he wooed and solicited her for marriage, and began to feele I wot not what [maritall]-chilnesse, and husbandscoldnesse. And I am one of those, whose opinion is, that divine Poesie doth no where fadge so well, and so effectually applaudeth, as in a youthfull, wanton, and unbridled subject. The above mentioned nine and twentie Sonnets of *Boetie,* and that in the former impressions of this booke were here set downe, have since beene printed with his other works.

CHAPTER XXIX

OF MODERATION

As IF our sense of feeling were infected, wee corrupt by our touching, things that in themselves are faire and good. We may so seize on vertue, that if we embrace it with an over-greedy and violent desire, it may become vitious. Those who say, *There is never excesse in vertue, because it is no longer vertue if any excesse be in it,* doe but jest at words.

> *Insani sapiens nomen ferat, œquus iniqui,*
> *Ultra-quàm satis est, virtuem si petat ipsam.*
> HOR. i. *Epi.* vi. 15.

> A wise man mad, just unjust, may I name,
> More than is meet, ev'n vertue if he claime.

Philosophy is a subtile consideration. A man may love vertue too much, and excessively demeane himselfe in a good action. Gods holy word doth apply it selfe to this byase: *Be not wiser than you should, and be soberly wise.* I have seene some great men, blemish the reputation of their religion, by shewing themselves religious beyond the example of men of their qualitie. I love temperate and indifferent natures. Immoderation towards good, if it offend me not, it amazeth, and troubleth me how I should call it. Neither *Pausanias* his mother, who gave the first instruction, and for her sonnes death brought the first stone: Nor *Posthumius* the Dictator, that brought his owne sonne to his end, whom the heat and forwardnesse of youth, had haply before his ranke, made to charge his enemies, seeme so just as strange unto me. And I neither love to perswade or follow so savage and so deare a vertue. The Archer that overshoots his marke, doth no otherwise than he that shooteth short. Mine eies trouble me as much in climbing up toward a great light, as to goe downe in the darke. *Callicles* in *Plato* saith, *The extremitie of Philosophy to bee hurtfull: and perswades no man to wade further into it, than the bounds of profit: And that taken with moderation, it is pleasant and commodius, but in the end it makes a man wilde and vicious, disdainfull of religion and of common lawes: an enemie of civill conversation: a foe to humane sensualitie, and worldly pleasures: incapable of all politike administration; and unfit to assist others or to helpe himself: apt to be without revenge buffeted, and baffled.* He saith true: for in her excesse, she enthralleth our naturall libertie, and by an importunate wile, diverts us from the faire and plaine path, which nature traceth out for us. The love we beare to women, is very lawful; yet doth Divinitie bridle and restraine the same. I remember to have read in Saint *Thomas,* in a place where he condemneth marriages of kinsfolkes in forbidden degrees, this one reason amongst others: that the love a man beareth to such a woman may be immoderate; for, if the wedlocke, or husband-like affection be sound and perfect, as it ought to be, and also surcharged with that a man oweth to alliance and kindred, there is no doubt, but that surcease may easily transport a husband beyond the bounds of reason. Those Sciences that direct the manners of men, as Divinitie and Philosophy, medleth with all things. There is no action so private and secret may be concealed from their knowledge and jurisdiction. Well doe they learne that search and censure their libertie. It is women communicate their parts as much as a man list to wantonize with them: but to phisicke them bashfulnesse forbids them. I will then in their behalfe teach husbands this, if there be any too much flesht upon them: which is, that the verie pleasures they have by the familiaritie of their wives, except moderately used; they are reproved: and not only in that, but in any other unlawfull subjects, a man may trespasse in licentiousnesse, and offend in excesse. Those shamelesse endearings, which the first heat suggests unto us in that sportfull delight, are not only undecently, but hurtfully employed towards our wives. Let them at least learne impudencie from another hand. They are ever broad-waking when wee need them. I have used no meanes but naturall and simple instruction. Marriage is a religious and devout bond: and that is the reason the pleasure a man hath of it, should be a moderate, staied and serious pleasure, and mixed with severitie, it ought to bee a voluptuousnesse somewhat circumspect and conscientious. And because it is the chiefest of generation, there are that make a question, whether it be lawfull to require them of copulation, as well when we have no hope of children, as when they are over-aged, or big with childe. *It is an homicide,* according to *Plato.* Certaine nations (and amongst others, the Mahometane) abhorre Conjunction with women great with childe. Many also with those that have their monethly disease. *Zenobia* received her husband but for one charge; which done, all the time of her conception, she let him goe at randon, and that past, she gave him leave to begin againe; a notable and generous example of marriage.

Plato borroweth the narration (of some needy and hunger-starven Poet) of this sport. That *Jupiter* one day gave his wife so hot a charge, impatient to stay till she came to bed, hee laid her along upon the floore, and by the vehemence of his pleasure forgot the urgent and weighty resolutions lately concluded upon with the other gods of his cælestiall court; boasting he found it as sweet at that time, as he had done, when first he spoiled her of her virginitie, by stealth and unknowne to their parents. The Kings of *Persia*, called for their wives, when they went to any solemne feast, but when much drinking and wine began to heat them in good earnest, they sent them to their chambers, seeing they could no longer refrain, but must needs yeeld to sensualitie, lest they should be partakers of their immoderate lust; and in their stead sent for other women, whom this duty of respect might not concerne. *All pleasures and gratifications are not well placed in all sorts of people. Epaminondas* had caused a dissolute young man to be imprisoned: *Pelopidas* intreated him, that for his sake he would set him at libertie, but he refused him, and yeelded to free him at the request of an harlot of his, which likewise sued for his enlargement; saying, *it was a gratification due unto a Courtizan, and not to a Captaine. Sophocles* being partner with *Pericles* in the Pretorship, seeing by chance a faire boy to passe by: *Oh what a beauteous boy goeth yonder!* said he to *Pericles: That speech were more fitting another than a Pretor*, answered *Pericles, who ought not only to have chaste hands, but also unpolluted eies. Ælius Verus* the Emperour, his wife complaining that he followed the love of other women, answered *he did it for conscience sake, for so much as marriage was a name of honour, and dignity, and not of foolish and lascivious lust*. And our Ecclesiasticall Historie, hath with honour preserved the memorie of that wife, which sued to be devorced from her husband, because she would not second and consent to his over-insolent and lewde embracements. To conclude, there is no voluptuousnesse so just, wherein excesse and intemperance is not reprochfull unto us. But to speake in good sooth, is not a man a miserable creature? He is scarce come to his owne strength by his naturall condition, to taste one only compleate, entire and pure pleasure, but he laboreth by discourse to cut it off: he is not wretched enough, except by art and study he augment his miserie.

Fortunæ miseras auximus arte vias.
PROPERT. iii. *El.* vi. 32.

Fortunes unhappie ill,
We amplifie by skill.

Humane wisdom doth foolishly seeke to be ingenious in exercising her selfe to abate the number, and diminish the pleasure of sensualities, that pertaine to us: as it doth favorably and industriously in employing her devises, to paint and set a luster on evils, before our eies, and therewith to recreate our sense. Had I beene chiefe of a faction, I would have followed a more naturall course, which to say true, is both commodious and sacred, and should peradventure have made my selfe strong enough to limite the same. Although our spirituall and corporall Physitians: as by covenant agreed upon betweene them, finde no way of recoverie, nor remedies for diseases of body and minde, but by torment, griefe and paine, watching, fasting, haire-shirts, farre and solitarie exile, perpetuall prison, roddes and other afflictions, have therefore been invented: But so, that they be truly afflictions, and that there be some stinging sharpenesse in them: And that the successe be not as *Gallios* was, who having been confined to the ile of *Lesbos,* newes came to *Rome,* that there he lived a merry life: and what the Senate had laid upon him for a punishment, redounded to his commodity: whereupon they agreed to revoke him home to his owne house and wife, strictly enjoyning him to keepe the same, thereby to accommodate their punishment to his sense and feeling. For he to whom fasting should procure health and a merrie heart, or he to whom poison should be more healthy than meat, it would be no longer a wholesome receipt, no more than drugs in other medicines, are of no effect to him that takes them with appetite and pleasure. Bitternesse and difficultie are circumstances fitting their operation. That nature which should take Reubarbe as familiar, should no doubt corrupt the use of it; it must be a thing that hurts the stomacke, if it shal cure it: and here the common rule failes, that infirmities are cured by their contraries: for one ill cureth another. This impression hath some reference to this other so ancient, where some thinke they gratifie both heaven and earth by killing and massacring themselves, which was universally embraced in all religions. Even in our fathers age; *Amurath* at the taking of *Isthmus,* sacrificed six hundred young Græcians to his fathers soule: to the end their bloud might serve as a propitiation to expiate the sinnes of the deceased. And in the new countries discovered in our daies yet uncorrupted, and virgins, in regard of ours, it is a custome well nigh received everie where. All their idolles are sprinkled with humane bloud, not without divers examples of horrible crueltie. Some are burnt alive, and halfe roasted drawne from the fire, that so they may pull out their hearts and entrails; othersome, yea women are fleade quicke, and with their yet-bleeding skins, they invest and cover others. And no lesse of examples of constant resolution. For these wretched sacrifiable people, old men, women and children, some daies before, goe themselves begging their almes, for the offering of their sacrifice, and all of full glee, singing, and dancing with the rest, they present themselves to the slaughter. The Ambassadours of the Kings of *Mexico*, in declaring and magnifying the greatnesse of their Master to *Fernando Cortez*, after they had told him, that he had thirtie vassals, whereof each one was able to levie a hundred thousand combatants, and that he had his residence in the fairest and strongest Citie under heaven, added, moreover, that he had fiftie thousand to sacrifice for every yeare: verily some affirme that they maintain continuall warres with certaine mighty neighbouring Nations, not so much for the exercise and training of their youth, as that they may have store of prisoners taken in warre to supply their sacrifices. In another province, to welcome the said *Cortez*, they sacrificed fiftie men at one clap. I will this one storie more: Some of those people having beene beaten by him, sent to know him, and intreat him of friendship. The messengers presented him with three kinds of presents, in this manner: *Lord, if thou be a fierce God, that lovest to feed on flesh and bloud, here are five slaves, eat them, and we will bring thee more: if thou be a gently mild God, here is incense and feathers; but if thou be a man, take these birds and fruits, that here we present and offer unto thee.*

CHAPTER XXX

OF THE CANIBALLES

AT what time King *Pirrhus* came into *Italie*, after he had survaid the marshalling of the Armie, which the Romans sent against him: *I wot not*, said he, *what barbarous men these are* (for so were the Græcians wont to call all strange nations) *but the disposition of this Armie, which I see, is nothing barbarous.* So said the Græcians of that which *Flaminius* sent into their countrie: And *Philip* viewing from a Tower the order and distribution of the Romaine camp, in his kingdome under *Publius Sulpitius Galba.* Loe how a man ought to take heed, lest he over-weeningly follow vulgar opinions, which should be measured by the rule of reason, and not by the common report. I have had long time dwelling with me a man, who for the space of ten or twelve yeares had dwelt in that other world, which in our age was lately discovered in those parts where *Villegaignon* first landed, and surnamed *Antartike France.* This discoverie of so infinit and vast a countrie, seemeth worthy great consideration. I wot not whether I can warrant my selfe, that some other be not discovered hereafter, sithence so many worthy men, and better learned than we are, have so many ages beene deceived in this. I feare me our eies be greater than our bellies, and that we have more curiositie than capacitie. We embrace all, but we fasten

nothing but wind. *Plato* maketh *Solon* to report (Plat. *Timœ.*), that
he had learn't of the Priests of the citie of *Says* in *Ægypt*, that whilom,
and before the generall Deluge, there was a great Iland called
Atlantis, situated at the mouth of the strait of *Gibraltar*, which contained more firme land than *Affrike* and *Asia* together. And that the
Kings of that countrie, who did not only possesse that Iland, but had
so farre entred into the maine land, that of the bredth of *Affrike*, they
held as farre as *Ægypt;* and of *Europes* length, as farre as *Tuscanie:*
and that they undertook to invade *Asia*, and to subdue all the nations
that compasse the Mediterranean Sea, to the gulfe of *Mare-Maggiore*,
and to that end they traversed all *Spaine, France*, and *Italie*, so farre
as *Greece*, where the Athenians made head against them; but that a
while after, both the Athenians themselves, and that great Iland, were
swallowed up by the Deluge. It is verie likely this extreme ruine of
waters wrought strange alterations in the habitations of the earth: as
some hold that the Sea hath divided *Sicilie* from *Italie*,

> *Hæc loca vi quondam, et vasta convulsa ruina*
> *Dissiluisse ferunt, cùm protinus utraque tellus*
> *Una foret.*—Virg. *Æn.* iii. 414, 416.

Men say, sometimes this land by that forsaken,
And that by this, were split, and ruine-shaken,
Whereas till then both lands as one were taken.

Cypres from *Soria*, the Iland of *Negroponte* from the maine land of
Beotia, and in other places joyned lands that were sundred by the
Sea, filling with mud and sand the chanels betweene them.

> *sterilisque diu palus aptaque remis*
> *Vicinas urbes alit, et grave sentit aratrum.*
> Hor. *Art. Poet.* 65.

The fenne long barren, to be row'd in, now
Both feeds the neighbour townes, and feeles the plow.

But there is no great apparence, the said Iland should be the new
world we have lately discovered; for, it well-nigh touched *Spaine*,
and it were an incredible effect of inundation, to have removed the
same more than twelve hundred leagues, as we see it is. Besides, our
moderne Navigations have now almost discovered, that it is not an
Iland, but rather firme land, and a continent, with the East *Indias* on
one side, and the countries lying under the two Poles on the other;
from which if it be divided, it is with so narrow a strait, and intervall,
that it no way deserveth to be named an Iland: For, it seemeth there
are certaine motions in these vast bodies, some naturall, and other
some febricitant, as well as in ours. When I consider the impression
my river of *Dordoigne* worketh in my time, toward the right shoare
of her descent and how much it hath gained in twentie yeares, and

how many foundations of divers houses it hath overwhelmed, and violently caried away; I confesse it to be an extraordinarie agitation: for, should it alwaies keepe one course, or had it ever kept the same, the figure of the world had ere this beene overthrowne: But they are subject to changes and alterations. Sometimes they overflow and spread themselves on one side, sometimes on another; and other times they containe themselves in their naturall beds or chanels. I speak not of sudden inundations, whereof we now treat the causes. In *Medoc* alongst the Sea-coast, my brother the Lord of *Arsacke,* may see a towne of his buried under the sands, which the Sea casteth up before it: The tops of some buildings are yet to be discerned. His Rents and Demaines have beene changed into barren pastures. The inhabitants thereabouts affirme, that some yeares since, the Sea encrocheth so much upon them, that they have lost foure leagues of firme land: These sands are her fore-runners. And we see great hillocks of gravell moving, which march halfe a league before it, and usurpe on the firme land. The other testimonie of antiquitie, to which some will referre this discoverie, is in *Aristotle* (if at least that little booke of unheard of wonders be his) where he reporteth that certaine Carthaginians having sailed athwart the *Atlantike* Sea, without the strait of *Gibraltar,* after long time, they at last discovered a great fertill Iland, all replenished with goodly woods, and watred with great and deepe rivers, farre distant from al land, and that both they and others, allured by the goodness and fertility of the soile, went thither with their wives, children, and houshold, and there began to inhabit and settle themselves. The Lords of *Carthage* seeing their countrie by little and little to be dispeopled, made a law and expresse inhibition, that upon pains of death no more men should goe thither, and banished all that were gone thither to dwell, fearing (as they said) that in successe of time, they would so multiply as they might one day supplant them, and overthrow their owne estate. This narration of *Aristotle* hath no reference unto our new found countries. This servant I had, was a simple and rough-hewen fellow: a condition fit to yeeld a true testimonie. For, subtile people may indeed marke more curiously, and observe things more exactly, but they amplifie and glose them: and the better to perswade, and make their interpretations of more validitie, they cannot chuse but somewhat alter the storie. They never represent things truly, but fashion and maske them according to the visage they saw them in; and to purchase credit to their judgement, and draw you on to beleeve them, they commonly adorne, enlarge, yea, and Hyperbolize the matter. Wherein is required either a most sincere Reporter, or a man so simple, that he may have no invention to build upon, and to give a true likelihood unto false devices, and be not wedded to his owne will. Such a one was my man; who besides his owne report, hath many times shewed me divers Mariners, and Merchants, whom hee had knowne in that voyage. So am I pleased with

his information, that I never enquire what Cosmographers say of it.
We had need of Topographers to make us particular narrations of the
places they have beene in. For some of them, if they have the advantage of us, that they have seene *Palestine,* will challenge a privilege,
to tell us newes of all the world besides. I would have everie man
write what he knowes, and no more: not only in that, but in all other
subjects. For one may have particular knowledge of the nature of one
river, and experience of the qualitie of one fountaine, that in other
things knowes no more than another man: who neverthelesse to publish
this little scantling, will undertake to write of all the Physickes. From
which vice proceed divers great inconveniences. Now (to returne to
my purpose) I finde (as farre as I have beene informed) there is nothing in that nation, that is either barbarous or savage, unlesse men call
that barbarisme which is not common to them. As indeed, we have no
other ayme of truth and reason, than the example and *Idea* of the
opinions and customes of the countrie we live in. There is ever perfect
religion, perfect policie, perfect and compleat use of all things. They
are even savage, as we call those fruits wilde, which nature of her
selfe, and of her ordinarie progresse hath produced: whereas indeed
they are those which our selves have altered by our artificiall devices,
and diverted from their common order, we should rather terme savage.
In those are the true and most profitable vertues, and naturall proper-
ties most lively and vigorous, which in these we have bastardized,
applying them to the pleasure of our corrupted taste. And if notwithstanding, in divers fruits of those countries that were never tilled, we
shall finde, that in respect of ours they are most excellent, and as delicate unto our taste; there is no reason, art should gaine the point of
honour of our great and puissant mother Nature. We have so much by
our inventions surcharged the beauties and riches of her workes, that
we have altogether overchoaked her: yet where ever her puritie shineth, she makes our vaine and frivolous enterprises wonderfully
ashamed.

> *Et veniunt hederæ sponte sua melius,*
> *Surgit et in solis formosior arbutus antris,*
> *Et volucres nulla dulcius arte canunt.*—PROPERT. i. *El.* ii. 10.

Ivies spring better of their owne accord,
Unhanted plots much fairer trees afford.
Birds by no art much sweeter notes record.

All our endevour or wit, cannot so much as reach to represent the
nest of the least birdlet, its contexture, beautie, profit and use, no nor
the web of a seely spider. *All things* (saith *Plato*) *are produced, either
by nature, by fortune, or by art. The greatest and fairest by one or
other of the two first, the least and imperfect by the last.* Those nations
seeme therefore so barbarous unto me, because they have received very
little fashion from humane wit, and are yet neere their originall

naturalitie. The lawes of nature doe yet command them, which are but little bastardized by ours. And that with such puritie, as I am sometimes grieved the knowledge of it came no sooner to light, at what time there were men, that better than we could have judged of it. I am sorie *Lycurgus* and *Plato* had it not: for me seemeth that what in those nations we see by experience, doth not only exceed all the pictures wherewith licentious Poesie hath proudly imbellished the golden age, and all her quaint inventions to faine a happy condition of man, but also the conception and desire of Philosophy. They could not imagine a genuitie so pure and simple, as we see it by experience; nor ever beleeve our societie might be maintained with so little art and humane combination. It is a nation, would I answer *Plato,* that hath no kinde of traffike, no knowledge of Letters, no intelligence of numbers, no name of magistrate, nor of politike superioritie; no use of service, of riches or of povertie; no contracts, no successions, no partitions, no occupation but idle; no respect of kinred, but common, no apparell but naturall, no manuring of lands, no use of wine, corne, or mettle. The very words that import lying, falshood, treason, dissimulations, covetousnes, envie, detraction, and pardon, were never heard of amongst them. How dissonant would hee finde his imaginarie commonwealth from this perfection!

Hos natura modos primùm dedit.

Nature at first uprise,
These manners did devise.

Furthermore, they live in a country of so exceeding pleasant and temperate situation, that as my testimonies have told me, it is verie rare to see a sicke body amongst them; and they have further assured me, they never saw any man there, either shaking with the palsie, toothlesse, with eies dropping, or crooked and stooping through age. They are seated alongst the sea-coast, encompassed toward the land with huge and steepie mountaines, having betweene both, a hundred leagues or thereabout of open and champaine ground. They have great abundance of fish and flesh, that have no resemblance at all with ours, and eat them without any sawces, or skill of Cookerie, but plaine boiled or broiled. The first man that brought a horse thither, although he had in many other voyages conversed with them, bred so great a horror in the land, that before they could take notice of him, they slew him with arrowes. Their buildings are very long, and able to containe two or three hundred soules, covered with barkes of great trees, fastned in the ground at one end, enterlaced and joyned close together by the tops, after the manner of some of our Granges; the covering whereof hangs downe to the ground, and steadeth them as a flancke. They have a kinde of wood so hard, that ryving and cleaving the same, they make blades, swords, and grid-irons to broile their meat with. Their beds are of a kinde of cotton cloth, fastned to the house-roofe, as our ship-cabbanes: everie one hath his severall cowch; for the women lie from their husbands. They rise with the Sunne, and feed for all day, as soone as they are up: and make no more meales after that. They drinke not at meat, as *Suidas* reporteth of some other people of the East, which dranke after meales, but drinke many times a day, and are much given to pledge carowses. Their drinke is made of a certaine root, and of the colour of our Claret wines, which lasteth but two or three daies; they drinke it warme: It hath somewhat a sharpe taste, wholsome for the stomack, nothing heady, but laxative for such as are not used unto it, yet verie pleasing to such as are accustomed unto it. In stead of bread, they use a certaine white com-position, like unto Corianders confected. I have eaten some, the taste whereof is somewhat sweet and wallowish. They spend the whole day in dancing. Their young men goe a hunting after wilde beasts with bowes and arrowes. Their women busie themselves therewhil'st with warming of their drinke, which is their chiefest office. Some of their old men, in the morning before they goe to eating, preach in common to all the houshold, walking from one end of the house to the other, repeating one selfe-same sentence many times, till he have ended his turne (for their buildings are a hundred paces in length) he com-mends but two things unto his auditorie, *First, valour against their enemies, then lovingnesse unto their wives*. They never misse (for their restraint) to put men in minde of this dutie, that it is their wives which keep their drinke luke-warme and well-seasoned. The forme of their beds, cords, swords, blades, and wooddden bracelets, wherewith they cover their hand wrists, when they fight, and great Canes open at one end, by the sound of which they keepe time and cadence in their dancing, are in many places to be seene, and namely in mine owne house. They are shaven all over, much more close and cleaner than wee are, with no other Razors than of wood or stone. They beleeve their soules to be eternall, and those that have deserved well of their Gods, to be placed in that part of heaven where the Sunne riseth, and the cursed toward the West in opposition. They have certaine Prophets and Priests, which commonly abide in the mountaines, and very seldome shew themselves unto the people; but when they come downe, there is a great feast prepared, and a solemne assembly of manie townships together (each Grange as I have de-scribed maketh a village, and they are about a French league one from another). The Prophet speakes to the people in publike, exhorting them to embrace vertue, and follow their dutie. All their morall disci-pline containeth but these two articles; first an undismaied resolution to warre, then an inviolable affection to their wives. Hee doth also Prognosticate of things to come, and what successe they shall hope for in their enterprises: hee either perswadeth or disswadeth them from warre; but if he chance to misse of his divination, and that it succeed otherwise than hee foretold them, if hee be taken, hee is hewen in a thousand peeces, and condemned for a false Prophet. And therefore he that hath once misreckoned himselfe is never seene againe. Divination is the gift of God; the abusing whereof should be a punishable imposture. When the Divines amongst the Scythians had foretold an untruth, they were couched along upon hurdles full of heath or brushwood, drawne by oxen, and so manicled hand and foot, burned to death. Those which manage matters subject to the conduct of mans sufficiencie, are excusable, although they shew the utmost of their skill. But those that gull and conicatch us with the assurance of an extraordinarie facultie, and which is beyond our knowledge, ought to be double punished; first because they performe not the effect of their promise, then for the rashnesse of their imposture and unadvisednesse of their fraud. They warre against the nations, that lie beyond their mountaines, to which they go naked, having no other weapons than bowes, or woodden swords, sharpe at one end, as our broaches are. It is an admirable thing to see the constant resolution of their combats, which never end but by effusion of bloud and murther: for they know not what feare or rowts are. Every Victor brings home the head of the enemie he hath slaine as a Trophey of his victorie, and fastneth the same at the entrance of his dwelling place. After they have long time used and entreated their prisoners well, and with all commodities they can devise, he that is the Master of them; sommoning a great assembly of his acquaintance; tieth a corde to one of the prisoners armes, by the end whereof he holds him fast, with some distance from him, for feare he might offend him, and giveth the other arm, bound in like manner, to the dearest friend he hath, and both in the presence of all the assembly kill him with swords: which done, they roast, and then eat him in common, and send some slices of him to such of their friends as are absent. It is not as some imagine, to nourish themselves with it, (as anciently the Scithians wont to doe), but to represent an extreme, and inexpiable revenge. Which we prove thus; some of them perceiving the Portugales, who had confederated themselves with their adversaries, to use another kinde of death, when they tooke them prisoners; which was, to burie them up to the middle, and against the upper part of the body to shoot arrowes, and then being almost dead, to hang them up; they supposed, that these people of the other world (as they who had sowed the knowledge of many vices amongst their neighbours, and were much more cunning in all kindes of evils and mischiefe than they) undertooke not this manner of revenge without cause, and that consequently it was more smartfull, and cruell than theirs, and thereupon began to leave their old fashion to follow this. I am not sorie we note the barbarous horror of such an action, but grieved, that prying so narrowly into their faults we are so blinded in ours. I thinke there is more barbarisme in eating men alive, than to feed upon them, being dead; to mangle by tortures and torments a body full of lively sense, to roast him in peeces, to make dogges and swine to gnaw and teare him in mammockes (as wee have not only read, but seene very lately, yea and our own memorie, not amongst ancient enemies, but our neighbours and fellow-citizens; and which is worse, under pretence of pietie and religion) than to roast and eat him after he is dead. *Chrysippus* and *Zeno*, arch-pillers of the Stoicke sect, have supposed that it was no hurt at all, in time of need, and to what end soever, to make use of our carrion bodies, and to feed upon them, as did our forefathers, who being besieged by *Cæsar* in the Citie of *Alexia*, resolved to sustaine the famine of the siege, with the bodies of old men, women, and other persons unserviceable and unfit to fight.

> *Vascones (fama est) alimentis talibus usi*
> *Produxere animas.*—JUVEN. *Sat.* xv. 93.

> *Gascoynes* (as fame reports)
> Liv'd with meats of such sorts.

And Physitians feare not, in all kindes of compositions availefull to our health, to make use of it, be it for outward or inward applications: But there was never any opinion found so unnaturall and immodest, that would excuse treason, treacherie, disloyaltie, tyrannie, crueltie, and such like, which are our ordinarie faults. We may then well call them barbarous, in regard of reasons rules, but not in respect of us that exceed them in all kinde of barbarisme. Their warres are noble and generous, and have as much excuse and beautie, as this humane infirmitie may admit: they ayme at nought so much, and have no other foundation amongst them, but the meere jelousie of vertue. They contend not for the gaining of new lands; for to this day they yet enjoy that naturall ubertie and fruitfulnesse, which without labouring toyle, doth in such plenteous abundance furnish them with all necessary things, that they need not enlarge their limits. They are yet in that happy estate, as they desire no more, than what their naturall necessities direct them: whatsoever is beyond it, is to them superfluous. Those that are much about one age, doe generally enter-call one another brethren, and such as are younger, they call children, and the aged are esteemed as fathers to all the rest. These leave this full possession of goods in common, and without division to their heires, without other claime or title, but that which nature doth plainely impart unto all creatures, even as shee brings them into the world. If their neighbours chance to come over the mountaines to assaile or invade them, and that they get the victorie over them, the Victors conquest is glorie, and the advantage to be and remaine superior in valour and vertue: else have they nothing to doe with the goods and spoyles of the vanquished, and so returne into their countrie, where they neither want any necessarie thing, nor lacke this great portion, to know how to enjoy their condition happily, and are contented with what nature affoordeth them. So doe these when their turne commeth. They require no other ransome of their prisoners, but an acknowledgement and confession that they are vanquished. And in a whole age, a man shall not finde one, that doth not rather embrace death, than either by word or countenance remissely to yeeld one jot of an invincible courage. There is none seene that would not rather be slaine and devoured, than sue for life, or shew any feare: They use their prisoners with all libertie, that they may so much the more hold their lives deare and precious, and commonly entertaine them with threats of future death, with the torments they shall endure, with the preparations intended for that purpose, with mangling and slicing of their members, and with the feast that shall be kept at their charge. All which is done, to wrest some remisse, and exact some faint-yeelding speech of submission from them, or to possesse them with a desire to escape or run away; that so they may have the advantage to have danted and made them afraid, and to have forced their constancie. For certainly true victorie consisteth in that only point.

—*Victoria nulla est*
Quàm quæ confessos animo quoque subjugat hostes.
CLAUD. vi. *Cons. Hon. Pan.* 245.

No conquest such, as to suppresse
Foes hearts, the conquest to confesse.

The Hungarians, a most warre-like nation, were whilome wont to pursue their prey no longer than they had forced their enemie to yeeld unto their mercie. For, having wrested this confession from him, they set him at libertie without offence or ransome, except it were to make him sweare, never after to beare armes against them. Wee get many advantages of our enemies, that are but borrowed and not ours: It is the qualitie of porterly-rascall, and not of vertue, to have stronger armes, and sturdier legs: Disposition is a dead and corporall qualitie. It is a tricke of fortune to make our enemie stoope, and to bleare his eies with the Sunnes-light: It is a pranke of skill and knowledge to be cunning in the art of fencing, and which may happen unto a base and worthlesse man. The reputation and worth of a man consisteth in his heart and will: therein consists true honour: Constancie is valour, not of armes and legs, but of minde and courage: it consisteth not in the spirit and courage of our horse, nor of our armes, but in ours. He that obstinately faileth in his courage, *Si succiderit, de genu pugnat, If hee slip or fall, he fights upon his knee.* He that in danger of imminent death, is no whit danted in his assurednesse; he that in yeelding up his ghost beholding his enemie with a scornefull and fierce looke, he is vanquished, not by us, but by fortune: he is slaine, but not conquered. The most valiant, are often the most unfortunate. So are there triumphant losses in envie of victories. Not those foure sister victories, the fairest that ever the Sunne beheld with his all-seeing eie, of *Salamis*, of *Plateœ*, of *Micale*, and of *Sicilia*, durst ever dare to oppose all their glorie together, to the glorie of the King *Leonidas* his discomfiture and of his men, at the passage of *Thermopylœ:* what man did ever run with so glorious an envie, or more ambitious desire to the goale of a combat, than Captaine *Ischolas* to an evident losse and overthrow? who so ingeniously or more politikely did ever assure himselfe of his welfare, than he of his ruine? He was appointed to defend a certaine passage of *Peloponesus* against the Arcadians, which finding himselfe altogether unable to performe, seeing the nature of the place, and inequalitie of the forces, and resolving, that whatsoever should present it selfe unto his enemie, must necessarily be utterly defeated: On the other side, deeming it unworthy both his vertue and magnanimitie, and the Lacedemonian name, to faile or faint in his charge, betweene these two extremities he resolved upon a meane and indifferent course, which was this. The youngest and best disposed of his troupe, he reserved for the service and defence of their countrie, to which hee sent them backe; and with those whose losse was least, and who might best be spared, hee determined to maintaine that passage, and by their death to force the enemie, to purchase the entrance of it as deare as possibly he could; as indeed it followed. For being suddenly environed round by the Arcadians: After a great slaughter made of them, both himselfe and all his were put to the sword. Is any Trophey assigned for conquerors, that is not more duly due unto these conquered? A true conquest respecteth rather an undanted resolution, and honourable end, than a faire escape, and the honour of vertue doth more consist in combating than in beating. But to returne to our historie, these prisoners, howsoever they are dealt withall, are so farre from yeelding, that contrariwise during two or three moneths that they are kept, they ever carry a cheerefull countenance, and urge their keepers to hasten their triall, they outragiously defie, and injure them. They upbraid them with their cowardlinesse, and with the number of battels, they have lost againe theirs. I have a song made by a prisoner, wherein is this clause, Let them boldly come altogether, and flocke in multitudes, to feed on him; for with him they shall feed upon their fathers, and grandfathers, that heretofore have served his body for food and nourishment: These muscles, (saith he) this flesh, and these veines, are your owne; fond men as you are, know you not that the substance of your forefathers limbes is yet tied unto ours? Taste them well, for in them shall you finde the relish of your owne flesh: An invention, that hath no shew of barbarisme. Those that paint them dying, and that represent this action, when they are put to execution, delineate the prisoners spitting in their executioners faces, and making mowes at them. Verily, so long as breath is in their body, they never cease to brave and defie them, both in speech and countenance. Surely, in respect of us these are very savage men: for either they must be so

in good sooth, or we must be so indeed: There is a wondrous distance
betweene their forme and ours. Their men have many wives, and by
how much more they are reputed valiant, so much the greater is their
number. The manner and beautie in their marriages is wondrous
strange and remarkable: For, the same jealousie our wives have to
keepe us from the love and affection of other women, the same have
theirs to procure it. Being more carefull for their husbands honour and
content, than of any thing else: They endevour and apply all their
industrie, to have as many rivals as possibly, they can, forasmuch as it
is a testimonie of their husbands vertue. Our women would count it a
wonder, but it is not so: It is vertue properly Matrimoniall; but of
the highest kinde. And in the Bible, *Lea, Rachell, Sara,* and *Jacobs*
wives, brought their fairest maiden servants unto their husbands beds.
And *Livia* seconded the lustfull appetites of *Augustus* to her great
prejudice. And *Stratonica* the wife of King *Dejotarus* did not only
bring a most beauteous chamber-maide, that served her, to her husbands bed, but very carefully brought up the children he begot on
her, and by all possible meanes aided and furthered them to succeed
in their fathers roialtie. And least a man should thinke, that all this
is done by a simple, and servile, or awefull dutie unto their custome,
and by the impression of their ancient customes authoritie, without
discourse or judgement, and because they are so blockish, and dull
spirited, that they can take no other resolution, it is not amisse, wee
alleage some evidence of their sufficiencie. Besides what I have said
of one of their warlike songs, I have another amorous canzonet, which
beginneth in this sence: *Adder stay, stay good adder, that my sister may
by the patterne of thy partie-coloured coat drawe the fashion and worke
of a rich lace, for me to give unto my love; so may thy beautie, thy
nimblenesse or disposition be ever preferred before all other serpents.*
The first couplet is the burthen of the song. I am so conversant with
Poesie, that I may judge, this invention hath no barbarisme at all in
it, but is altogether Anacreontike. Their language is a kinde of pleasant
speech, and hath a pleasing sound, and some affinitie with the Greeke
terminations. Three of that nation, ignorant how deare the knowledge
of our corruptions will one day cost their repose, securitie, and happinesse, and how their ruine shall proceed from this commerce, which
I imagine is already well advanced, (miserable as they are to have
suffered themselves to be so cosoned by a desire of new-fangled novelties, and to have quit the calmenesse of their climate, to come and
see ours) were at *Roane* in the time of our late King *Charles* the ninth,
who talked with them a great while. They were shewed our fashions,
our pompe, and the forme of a faire Citie; afterward some demanded
their advise, and would needs know of them what things of note and
admirable they had observed amongst us: they answered three things,
the last of which I have forgotten, and am very sorie for it, the other
two I yet remember. They said, *First, they found it very strange, that*

so many tall men with long beards, strong and well armed, as it were about the Kings person (it is very likely they meant the Switzers of his guard) would submit themselves to obey a beardlesse childe, and that we did not rather chuse one amongst them to command the rest. Secondly (they have a manner of phrase whereby they call men but a moytie one of another.) *They had perceived, there were men amongst us full gorged with all sortes of commodities, and others which hunger-starved, and bare with need and povertie, begged at their gates: and found it strange, these moyties so needy could endure such an injustice, and that they tooke not the others by the throte, or set fire on their houses.* I talked a good while with one of them, but I had so bad an interpreter, and who did so ill apprehend my meaning, and who through his foolishnesse was so troubled to conceive my imaginations, that I could draw no great matter from him. Touching that point, wherein I demanded of him, what good he received by the superioritie he had amongst his countriemen (for he was a Captaine and our Marriners called him King) he told me, it was to march formost in any charge of warre: further, I asked him, how many men did follow him, hee shewed me a distance of place, to signifie they were as many as might be contained in so much ground, which I guessed to be about 4. or 5. thousand men: moreover I demanded, if when warres were ended, all his authoritie expired; he answered, that hee had only this left him, which was, that when he went on progresse, and visited the villages depending of him, the inhabitants prepared paths and high-waies athwart the hedges of their woods, for him to pass through at ease. All that is not verie ill; but what of that? They weare no kinde of breeches nor hosen.

CHAPTER XXXI

THAT A MAN OUGHT SOBERLY TO MEDDLE WITH JUDGING OF DIVINE LAWES

THINGS unknowne are the true scope of imposture, and subject of Legerdemaine: forasmuch as strangenesse it selfe doth first give credit unto matters, and not being subject to our ordinarie discourses, they deprive us of meanes to withstand them. To this purpose, said *Plato, it is an easie matter to please, speaking of the nature of the Gods, than of mens:* For the Auditors ignorance lends a faire and large cariere, and free libertie, to the handling of secret hidden matters. Whence it followeth, that nothing is so firmly beleeved, as that which a man knoweth least; nor are there people more assured in their reports, than such as tell us fables, as Alchumists, Prognosticators, Fortune-tellers, Palmesters, Physitians, *id genus omne, and such like.* To which, if I durst, I would joyne a rable of men, that are ordinarie interpreters and controulers of Gods secret desseignes, presuming to finde out the causes of every accident, and to prie into the secrets of Gods divine will, the incomprehensible motives of his works. And howbeit, the continuall varietie and discordance of events drive them from one corner to another, and from East to West, they will not leave to follow their bowle, and with one small pensill drawe both white and blacke. There is this commendable observance in a certaine Indian nation, who if they chance to be discomfited in any skirmish or battle, they publikely beg pardon of the Sunne, who is their God, as for an unjust action, referring their good or ill fortune to divine reason, submitting their judgement and discourses unto it. It suffiseth a Christian to beleeve, that all things come from God, to receive them from his divine and inscrutable wisdome with thanksgiving, and in what manner soever they are sent him, to take them in good part. But I utterly disalow a common custome amongst us, which is to ground and establish our religion upon the prosperitie of our enterprises. Our beleefe hath other sufficient foundations, and need not be authorized by events. For the people accustomed to these plausible arguments, and agreeing with his taste, when events sort contrarie and disadvantageous to their expectation, they are in hazard to waver in their faith: As in the civil warres, wherein we are now for religions sake, those which got the advantage, at the conflict of *Rochelabeille,* making great joy and bonefires for that accident, and using that fortune, as an assured approbation of their faction: when afterward they come to excuse their disasters of *Montcontour* and *Jarnac,* which are scourges and fatherly chastisements: if they have not a people wholy at their mercy, they will easily make him perceive, what it is to take two kinds of corne out of one sacke: and from one and the same mouth to blow both hot and cold. It were better to entertaine it with the true foundations of veritie. It was a notable Sea-battle, which was lately gained against the Turkes, under the conduct of *Don John* of *Austria.* But it hath pleased God to make us at other times both see and feele other such, to our no small losse and detriment. To conclude, it is no easie matter to reduce divine things unto our ballance, so they suffer no impeachment: And he that would yeeld a reason, why *Arrius* and *Leo* his Pope, chiefe Principals, and maine supporters of this heresie, died both at severall times, of so semblable and so strange deaths (for being forced through a violent bellyach to goe from their disputations to their close-stoole, both suddenly yeelded up their ghosts on them) and exaggerate that divine vengeance by the circumstance of the place, might also adde the death of *Heliogabalus* unto it, who likewise was slaine upon a privie. But what? *Ireneus* is found to be engaged in like fortune: Gods intent being to teach us, that the good have some thing else to hope for, and the wicked somewhat else to feare, than the good or bad fortune of this world: He manageth and applieth them according to his secret disposition: and depriveth us of the meanes, thereby

foolishly to make our profit. And those, that according to humane
reason will thereby prevaile, doe but mocke themselves. They never
give one touch of it, that they receive not two for it. S. *Augustine* giveth
a notable triall of it upon his adversaries. It is a conflict, no more
decided by the armes of memorie, than by the weapons of reason. A
man should be satisfied with the light, which it pleaseth the Sunne to
communicate unto us by vertue of his beames; and he that shall lift
up his eies to take a greater within his body, let him not thinke it
strange, if for a reward of his overweening and arrogancie he loseth
his sight. *Quis hominum potest scire consilium Dei? aut quis poterit
cogitare, quid velit dominus?* (Wisd. ix. 13). *Who amongst men can
know Gods counsell, or who can thinke what God will doe?*

CHAPTER XXXII

TO AVOID VOLUPTUOUSNESSE IN REGARD OF LIFE

I HAVE noted the greatest part of ancient opinions to agree in this:
That *when our life affords more evill than good, it is then time to die:
and to preserve our life to our torment and incommoditie, is to spurre
and shocke the very rules of nature:* as say the old rules.

ἤ ζῆν ἀλύπως ἤ θανεῖν εὐδαιμόνως.—*Gnom. Græc. θ.*

Or live without distresse,
Or die with happinesse.

Καλὸν τὸ θνῄσκειν οἷς ὕβριν τὸ ζῆν φέρει.—*Ibid.*

'Tis good for them to die,
Whom life brings infamie.

Κρεῖσσον τὸ μὴ ζῆν ἐστίν, ἤ ζῆν ἀθλίως.

SOPH. STOB. *Ser.* 118.

'Tis better not to live,
Than wretchedly not thrive.

But to drive off the contempt of death to such a degree, as to imploy
it to distract, and remove himselfe from honours, riches, greatnesse,
and other goods and favours, which wee call the goods of fortune: as
if reason had not enough to doe, to perswade us to forgoe and leave
them, without adding this new surcharge unto it, I had neither seene
the same commanded nor practised untill such time as one place of
Seneca came to my hands, wherein counselling *Lucilius* (a man
mightie and in great authoritie about the Emperour) to change this
voluptuous and pompous life, and to withdraw himselfe from this
ambition of the world, to some solitarie, quiet and philosophicall life:
about which *Lucilius* alleaged some difficulties: *My advice is* (saith
he) *that either thou leave and quit that life, or thy life altogether:*

But I perswade thee to follow the gentler way, and rather to untie than breake what thou hast so ill knit: alwaies provided thou breake it, if thou canst not otherwise untie the same. There is no man so base minded, that loveth not rather to fall once, than ever to remaine in feare of falling. I should have deemed this counsell agreeing with the Stoickes rudenes: But it is more strange it should be borrowed of *Epicurus,* who to that purpose writeth this consonant unto *Idomeneus.* Yet thinke I to have noted some such like thing amongst our own people, but with Christian moderation. Saint *Hilarie* Bishop of *Poitiers,* a famous enemie of the *Arrian* heresie, being in *Syria,* was advertised that *Abra* his only daughter whom hee had left at home with her mother, was by the greatest Lords of the countrie solicited and sued unto for marriage, as a damosell very well brought up, faire, rich, and in the prime of her age: he writ unto her (as we see) that she should remove her affections, from all the pleasures and advantages [that] might be presented her: for, in his voyage he had found a greater and worthier match or husband of far higher power and magnificence, who should present her and endow her with roabes and jewels of unvaluable price. His purpose was to make her lose the appetite and use of worldly pleasures, and wholly to wed her unto God. To which, deeming his daughters death, the shortest and most assured way, he never ceased by vowes, prayers, and orisons, humbly to beseech God to take her out of this world, and to call her to his mercie, as it came to pass; for shee deceased soone after his returne: whereof he shewed manifest tokens of singular gladnesse. This man seemeth to endeere himselfe above others, in that at first sight he addresseth himselfe to this meane, which they never embrace but subsidiarily, and sithence it is towards his only daughter. But I will [not] omit the successe of this storie, although it be not to my purpose. Saint *Hilarie's* wife, having understood by him, how her daughters death succeeded with his intent and will, and how much more happy it was for her to be dislodged from out this world, than still to abide therein, conceived so lively an apprehension of the eternall and heavenly blessednesse, that with importunate instancie she solicited her husband, to doe as much for her. And God, at their earnest entreatie, and joynt-common prayers, having soone after taken her unto himselfe: it was a death embraced with singular and mutuale contentment to both.

CHAPTER XXXIII

THAT FORTUNE IS OFTENTIMES MET WITHALL IN PURSUIT OF REASON

THE inconstancie of Fortunes diverse wavering, is the cause shee should present us with all sorts of visages. Is there any action of justice more manifest than this? *Cæsar Borgia,* Duke of *Valentinois,* having resolved to poison *Adrian* Cardinall of *Cornetto,* with whom Pope *Alexander* the sixth, his father and he were to sup that night in *Vaticane,* sent certaine bottles of empoysoned wine before, and gave his Butler great charge to have a speciall care of it. The Pope comming thither before his sonne, and calling for some drinke; the butler supposing the Wine had beene so carefully commended unto him for the goodnesse of it, immediately presented some unto the Pope, who whilest he was drinking, his sonne came in and never imagining his bottles had beene toucht, tooke the cup and pledged his father, so that the Pope died presently; and the sonne, after he had long time beene tormented with sicknesse, recovered to another worse fortune. It sometimes seemeth, that when we least think on her, shee is pleased to sport with us. The Lord of *Estree,* then guidon to the Lord of *Vandosme,* and the Lord of *Liques,* Lieutenant to the Duke of *Ascot,* both servants to the Lord of *Foungueselles* sister, albeit of contrarie factions (as it hapneth among neighbouring bordurers) the Lord of *Liques* got her to wife: But even upon his wedding day, and which is worse, before his going to bed, the bridegroome, desiring to breake a staffe in favour of his new Bride and Mistris, went out to skirmish neere to Saint *Omer,* where the Lord of *Estree* being the stronger tooke him prisoner, and to endeare his advantage, the Lady her selfe was faine,

> *Conjugis ante coacta novi dimittere collum,*
> *Quàm veniens una atque altera rursus hyems*
> *Noctibus in longis avidum saturasset amorem,*
>
> CATUL. *Ele.* iv. 81.

Her new feeres necke for'st was she to forgoe,
Ere winters one and two returning sloe,
In long nights had ful-fil'd
Her love so eager wil'd,

in courtesie, to sue unto him for the deliverie of his prisoner, which he granted; the French Nobilitie never refusing Ladies any kindnesse. Seemeth she not to be a right artist? *Constantine* the sonne of *Helen* founded the Empire of *Constantinople,* and so, many ages after, *Constantine* the sonne of *Helen* ended the same. She is sometimes pleased to envie our miracles: we hold an opinion, that King *Clovis* besieging *Angoulesme,* the wals by a divine favour fell of themselves. And *Bouchet* borroweth of some author, that King *Robert* beleagring a Citie, and having secretly stolne away from the siege to *Orleans,* there to solemnize the feasts of Saint *Aignan,* as he was in his earnest devotion, upon a certaine passage of the Masse, the walles of the towne besieged, without any batterie, fell flat to the ground. She did altogether contrarie in our warres of *Millane:* For, Captaine *Rense,* beleagring the Citie of *Eronna* for us, and having caused a forcible mine to be wrought under a great curtine of the walles, by force whereof, it being violently flowne up from out the ground, did notwithstanding, whole and unbroken, fall so right into his foundation againe, that the besieged found no inconvenience at all by it. She sometimes playeth the Physitian. *Jason Phereus* being utterly forsaken of all Physitians, by reason of an impostume he had in his breast, and desirous to be rid of it, though it were by death, as one of the forlorne hope, rusht into a battel amongst the thickest throng of his enemies, where he was so rightly wounded acrosse the body, that his impostume brake, and he was cured. Did shee not exceed the Painter *Protogenes* in the skill of his trade? who having perfected the image of a wearie and panting dog, and in all parts over-tired, to his content, but being unable, as he desired, lively to represent the drivel or slaver of his mouth, vexed against his own worke, took his spunge, and moist as it was with divers colours, threw it at the picture, with purpose to blot and deface all hee had done: fortune did so fitly and rightly carrie the same toward the dogs chaps, that there it perfectly finished, what his art could never attaine unto. Does she not sometimes addresse and correct our counsels? *Isabell* Queene of *England*, being to repasse from *Zeland* into her Kingdome with an armie, in favour of her sonne against her husband, had utterly beene cast away, had she come unto the Port intended, being there expected by her enemies: But fortune against her will, brought her to another place, where shee safely landed. And that ancient fellow, who hurling a stone at a dog, misst him, and therewithall hit and slew his step-dame, had [he] not reason to pronounce this verse,

Ταυτόαμιον ἥμῶν καλλίω βουλεύεται.

Chance of it selfe, than wee,
Doth better say and see?

Fortune hath better advice than wee. *Icetes* had practised and sub-orned two souldiers to kill *Timoleon*, then residing at *Adrane* in *Sicily*. They appointed a time to doe, as he should be assisting at some sacrifice; and scattering themselves amongst the multitude, as they were winking one upon another, to shew how they had a verie fit opportunitie to doe the deed: Loe here a third man, that with a huge blow of a sword, striketh one of them over the head, and fels him dead to the ground and so runs away. His fellow supposing himselfe discovered and un-done, runs to the altar, suing for sanctuarie, with promise to confesse the truth; Even as he was declaring the conspiracie, behold the third man, who had likewise beene taken, whom as a murtherer the people tugged and haled through the throng toward *Timoleon* and the chiefest of the assembly, where he humbly calleth for mercy, alleaging that he had justly murthered the murtherer of his father, whom his good chance was to finde there, averring by good witnesses, before them all, that in the Citie of the Leontines, his father had been proditoriously slaine by him, on whom he had now revenged himselfe. In meede whereof, because he had beene so fortunate (in seeking to right his fathers untimely death) to save the common father of the Sicilians from so imminent a danger, he had ten Attike mines awarded him. This fortune in her directions exceedeth all the rules of humane wisdome. But to conclude, is not an expresse application of her favour, goodnesse, and singular pietie manifestly discovered in this action? *Ignatius* the Father and the Sonne, both banished by proscription by the Triumvirs of *Rome,* resolved on this generous act, to yeeld their lives one into anothers hands, and thereby frustrate the Tyrants cruelty. They furiously with their keene rapiers drawne, ran one against another: Fortune so directed their points, that each received his mortall stroke; adding to the honour of seld-seene an amity, that they had just so much strength left them, to draw their armed and bloudy hands from out their goared wounds, in that plight, so fast to embrace, and so hard to claspe one another, that the hangmen were forced, at one stroke, and together, to cut off both their heads; leaving their bodies for ever tied in so honourable a knot, and their wounds so joyned, that they lovingly drew and suckt each others bloud, breath, and life.

CHAPTER XXXIV

OF A DEFECT IN OUR POLICIES

My whilome-father, a man who had no helpe but from experience, and his owne nature, yet of an unspotted judgement, hath heretofore told me, that he much desired to bring in this custome, which is, that in all cities there should be a certaine appointed place, to which, whosoever should have need of any thing, might come and cause his businesse to be registred by some officer appointed for that purpose: As for example, if one have pearles to sell, he should say, I seeke to sell some pearls: and another, I seeke to buy some pearls: Such a man would faine have companie to travell to *Paris;* Such a one enquireth for a servant of this or that qualitie; Such a one seeketh for a Master; another a workman; Some this; some that; every man as he needed. And it seemeth that this meanes of enter-warning one another would bring no small commoditie unto common commerce and societie; For there are ever conditions that enter-seeke one another, and because they understand not one another, they leave men in great necessitie. I understand, to the infamous reproach of our age, that even in our sight, two most excellent men in knowledge, have miserably perished for want of food and other necessaries: *Lilus Gregorius Giraldus* in *Italie,* and *Sebastianus Castalio* in *Germanie:* And I verily beleeve there are many thousands, who had they knowne or understood their wants, would either have seent for them, and with large stipends entertained them, or would have convaid them succour, where ever they had beene. The world is not so generally corrupted, but I know some, that would earnestly wish, and with harty affections desire, the goods which their forefathers have left them, might, so long as it shall please fortune they may enjoy them, be emploied for the reliefe of rare, and supply of excellent mens necessitie, and such as for any kind of worth and vertue are remarkable; many of which are daily seene to be pursued by ill fortune even to the utmost extremitie, and that would take such order for them, as had they not their ease and content, it might only be imputed to their want of reason or lacke of discretion. In this Oeconomicke or houshold order my father had this order, which I can commend, but no way follow: which was, that besides the day-booke of houshold affaires, wherein are registred at least expences, paiments, gifts, bargains and sales, that require not a Notaries hand to them, which booke a receiver had the keeping of: he appointed another journall-booke to one of his servants, who was his clerke, wherein he should insert and orderly set downe all accidents worthy the noting, and day by day register the memories of the historie of his house: A thing very pleasant to read, when time began to weare out the remembrance of them, and fit for us to passe the time withall, and to resolve some doubts: when such a worke was begun, when ended, what way or course was taken, what accidents hapned, how long it continued; all our voyages, where, and how long we were from home; our marriages, who died, and when; the receiving of good or bad tidings, who came, who went, changing or removing of houshold officers, taking of new, or discharging of old servants, and such like matters. An ancient custome, and which I would have all men use and bring into fashion againe in their severall homes: and I repent my selfe, I have so foolishily neglected the same.

CHAPTER XXXV

OF THE USE OF APPARELL

WHATSOEVER I ayme at, I must needs force some of customes contradictions, so carefully hath she barred all our entrances. I was devising in this chil-cold season, whether the fashion of these late discovered Nations to go naked, be a custome forced by the hot temperature of the ayre, as we say of the Indians and Moores, or whether it be an originall manner of mankind. Men of understanding, forasmuch as whatsoever is contained under heaven (as saith the holy Writ) is subject to the same lawes, are wont in such like considerations, where naturall lawes are to be distinguished from those invented by man, to have recourse to the generall policie of the world, where nothing that is counterfet can be admitted. Now all things being exactly furnished elsewhence with all necessaries to maintaine this being, it is not to be imagined that we alone should be produced in a defective and indigent estate, yea, and in such a one, as cannot be maintained without forrain helpe. My opinion is, that even as all plants, trees, living creatures, and whatsoever hath life, is naturally seene furnished with sufficient furniture to defend it selfe from the injurie of all wethers:

Proptereáque ferè res omnes, aut corio sunt,
Aut seta, aut conchis, aut callo, aut cortice tectæ.

Lucr. iv. 932.

Therefore all things almost we cover'd marke,
With hide, or haire, or shels, or brawne, or barke.

Even so were we: But as those who by an artificiall light extinguish the brightnesse of the day, we have quenched our proper meanes, by such as wee have borrowed. And wee may easily discerne, that only custome makes that seeme impossible unto us, which is not so: For of those nations that have no knowledge of cloaths, some are found situated under the same heaven, and climate, or paralell, that we are in, and more cold and sharper than ours. Moreover, the tenderest parts of us are ever bare and naked, as our eyes, face, mouth, nose and eares; and our countrie-swaines (as our forefathers wont) most of them at this day goe bare-breasted downe to the navill. Had we beene borne needing petti-coats and breeches, there is no doubt, but nature would have armed that which she hath left to the batterie of seasons, and furie of wethers, with some thicker skin or hide, as shee hath done our finger ends, and the soales of our feet. Why seemes this hard to be believed? Betweene my fashion of apparell, and that of one of my countrie-clownes, I find much more difference betweene him and me, than betweene his fashion, and that of a man who is cloathed but with his bare skin. How many men (especially in *Turkie,*) go ever naked for devotions sake? A certaine man demanded of one of our loytring rogues, whom in the deep of frosty Winter, he saw wandring up and downe with nothing but his shirt about him, and yet as blithe and lusty as another that keepes himself muffled and wrapt in warme furres up to the eares; how he could have patience to go so. *And have not you, good Sir,* (answered he) *your face all bare? Imagine I am all face.* The Italians report (as far as I remember) of the Duke of *Florence* his foole, who when his Lord asked him, how being so ill clad, he could endure the cold, which he hardly was able to doe himselfe; To whom the foole replied; *Master, use but my receipt, and put all the cloaths you have upon you, as I doe all mine; you shall feele no more cold than I doe.* King *Massinissa,* even in his eldest daies, were it never so cold, so frosty, so stormie, or sharpe wether, could never be induced to put some thing on his head, but went alwaies bare-headed. The like is reported of the Emperor *Severus*. In the battels that past between the Ægyptians, and the Persians, *Herodotus* saith, that both himselfe and divers others tooke speciall notice, that of such as lay slaine on the ground, the Ægyptians sculls were without comparison much harder than the Persians: by reason that these go ever with their heads covered with coifs and turbants, and those from their infancie ever shaven and bare-headed. And King *Agesilaus*, even in his decrepit age, was ever wont to weare his cloaths both Winter and Summer alike. *Suetonius* affirmeth, that *Cæsar* did ever march formost before his troupes, and most commonly bare-headed, and on foot, whether the sunne shone, or it rained. The like is reported of *Hanniball*,

> —*tum vertice nudo,*
> *Excipere insanos imbres, cœlique ruinam.*
>
> Syl. Ital. 250.

> Bare-headed then he did endure,
> Heav'ns ruine and mad-raging showre.

A Venetian that hath long dwelt amongst them, and who is but lately returned thence, writeth, that in the Kingdome of *Pegu*, both men and women, having all other parts clad, goe ever bare-footed, yea, and on horse-back also. And *Plato* for the better health and preservation of the body doth earnestly perswade, that no man should ever give the feet and the head other cover, than Nature hath allotted them. He whom the Polonians chuse for their King next to ours, who may worthily be esteemed one of the greatest Princes of our age, doth never weare gloves, nor what wether soever it be, winter or summer, other bonnet abroad than in the warme house. As I cannot endure to goe unbuttoned or untrussed, so the husbandmen neighbouring about me, would be, and feele themselves as fettered or handbound, with going so. *Varro* is of opinion, that when we were appointed to stand bare headed before the Gods, or in the presence of the Magistrates, it was rather done for our health, and to enure and arme us against injuries of the wether, than in respect of reverence. And since we are speaking of cold, and are Frenchmen, accustomed so strangely to array our selves in party-coloured sutes (not I, because I seldome weare any other then blacke or white, in imitation of my father) let us adde this one thing more, which Captaine *Martyn du Bellay* relateth in the voyage of *Luxemburg*, where hee saith to have seene so hard frosts, that their munition-wines were faine to be cut and broken with hatchets and wedges, and shared unto the Souldiers by weight, which they caried away in baskets; and *Ovid*,

> *Nudáque consistunt formam servantia testæ*
> *Vina, nec hausta meri, sed data frusta bibunt.*
>
> Ovid. *Trist.* iii. El. x. 23.

Bare wines, still keeping forme of caske, stand fast,
Not gulps, but gobbets of their wine they taste.

The frosts are so hard and sharpe in the emboguing of the Meotis
fennes, that in the very place where *Mithridates* Lieutenant had
delivered a battel to his enemies, on hard ground, and drie-footed,
and there defeated them; the next summer, he there obtained another
sea-battel against them. The Romanes suffered a great disadvantage
in the fight they had with the Carthaginians neere unto *Placentia*,
for so much as they went to their charge with their bloud congealed,
and limbes benummed, through extreme cold: whereas *Hanniball* had
caused many fires to be made through-out his campe, to warme his
souldiers by, and a quantitie of oile to be distributed amongst them,
that therewith annointing themselves, they might make their sinewes
more supple and nimble, and harden their pores against the bitter
blasts of cold wind, which then blew, and nipping piercing of the
ayre. The Græcians retreat from *Babilon* into their countrie, is re-
nowned, by reason of the many difficulties and encombrances they
encountred withall, and were to surmount: whereof this was one,
that in the mountaines of *Armenia*, being surprised and encircled with
so horrible and great quantitie of snow, that they lost both the
knowledge of the countrie, and the wayes: wherewith they were so
straitly beset, that they continued a day and a night without eating
or drinking; and most of their horses and cattell died: of their men
a great number also deceased; many with the glittering and whitenesse of the snow, were strucken blinde: divers through the extremitie
were lamed, and their limbes shrunken up, many starke stiffe, and
frozen with colde, although their senses were yet whole. *Alexander*
saw a nation, where in winter they burie their fruit-bearing trees
under the ground, to defend them from the frost: a thing also used
amongst some of our neighbours. Touching the subject of apparell:
the King of *Mexico* was wont to change and shift his clothes foure
times a day, and never wore them againe, employing his leavings
and cast-suites for his continuall liberalities and rewards; as also
neither pot nor dish, nor any implement of his kitchin or table were
twice brought before him.

CHAPTER XXXVI

OF CATO THE YOUNGER

I AM not possessed with this common errour, to judge of others
according to what I am my selfe. I am easie to beleeve things differing from my selfe. Though I be engaged to one forme, I doe not tie
the world unto it, as every man doth. And I beleeve and conceive a

thousand manners of life, contrarie to the common sort: I more easily admit and receive difference, than resemblance in us. I discharge as much as a man will, another being of my conditions and principles, and simply consider of it my selfe without relation, framing it upon its owne modell. Though my selfe be not continent, yet doe I sincerely commend and allow the continencie of the Capuchins and Theatines, and highly praise their course of life. I doe by imagination insinuate my selfe into their place: and by how much more they bee other than my selfe, so much the more doe I love and honour them. I would gladly have every man judged apart, and not be drawne my selfe in consequence by others examples. My weaknesse doth no way alter the opinions I should have of the force and vigor of those that deserve it. *Sunt, qui nihil suadent, quàm quod se imitari posse confidunt* (Cic. *Orat. ad Br.*) *There be such as advise to nothing, but what they trust themselves can imitate.* Crawling on the face of the earth, I cease not to marke, even into the clouds, the inimitable height of some heroicke minds. It is much for me to have a formall and prescript judgement, if the effects bee not so, and at least to maintaine the chiefe part exempted from corruption. It is something to have a good minde, when my forces faile me. The age we live in (at least our climate) is so dull and leaden, that not only the execution, but the very imagination of vertue is farre to seeke, and seemes to be no other thing than a College supposition, and a gibrish word.

> *—virtutem verba putant, ut*
> *Lucum ligna:*—Hor. *Ep.* vi. i. 31.

> Vertue seemes words to these,
> As trees are wood, or woods are trees.

Quam vereri deberent, etiam si percipere non possent. Which yet they should reverence, though they could not reach unto. It is an eare-ring or pendent to hang in a cabinet, or at the tongues end, as well as at an eare for an ornament. There are no more vertuous actions knowne; those that beare a shew of vertue, have no essence of it: for profit, glorie, custome, feare, and other like strange causes direct us to produce them. Justice, valour, integritie, which we then exercise, may by others consideration, and by the countenance they publikely beare, be termed so: but with the true workman, it is no vertue at all. There is another end proposed; another efficient cause. Vertue alloweth of nothing, but what is done by her, and for her alone. In that great battell at Potidæa which the Græcians under *Pausanias* gained of *Mardonius* and the Persians, the victors following their custome, comming to share the glorie and prise of the victorie betweene them, ascribed the pre-excellencie of valor in that conflict to the *Spartane* nation. The Spartanes impartiall Judges of vertue, when they came to decide, to what particular man of their countrie, the honour to have done best in that day, should of right belong, they found that *Aristodemus* had most couragiously engaged and hazarded himselfe: Yet gave him not the prise of honour of it, because his vertue had beene therunto incited, by an earnest desire to purge himselfe from the reproch and infamie, which hee had incurred in the action at *Thermopyles,* and from all daring ambition to die couragiously, thereby to warrant his former reputation. Our judgements are yet sicke, and follow the depravations of our customes. I see the greatest part of our spirits to affect wit, and to shew themselves ingenious, by obscuring and detracting from the glorie of famous and generall ancient actions, giving them some base and malicious interpretation, fondly and enviously charging them with vaine causes, and frivolous occasions. A subtill invention no doubt. Let any man present me, with the most excellent and blamelesse action, and I will oppose it with fiftie vicious and bad intentions, all which shall carrie a face of likeli-hood. God knowes (to him that will extend them) what diversitie of images our internal will doth suffer: They doe not so maliciously as grosely and rudely endevor to be ingenious with all their railing and detraction. The same paine a man taketh to detract from these noble and famous names, and the verie same libertie, would I as willingly take to lend them my shoulders to extoll and magnifie them. I would endevour to charge these rare and choise figures, selected by the consent of wise men, for the world's example, as much, and as high, as my invention would give me leave with honour, in a plausible interpretation, and favourable circumstance. And a man must thinke, that the diligent labours of our invention, are farre beyond their merit. It is the part of honest minded men to pourtray vertue, as faire as possible faire may be. A thing which would no whit be mis-seeming or undecent, if passion should transport us to the favour and pursuit of so sacred formes, what these doe contrarie, they either doe it through malice or knaverie, with purpose to reduce and sute their beleefe to their capacitie, whereof I lately spake: or rather as I thinke, because their sight is not of sufficient power or clearnes, nor addressed to conceive or apprehend the farre-shining brightnes of vertue in naturall and genuine puritie: As *Plutarke* saith, that in his time, some imputed the cause of *Cato* the youngers death to the feare he had conceived of *Cesar:* whereat he hath some reason to be moved: by which a man may judge, how much more he would have beene offended with those that have ascribed the same unto ambition. Oh foolish people! Hee would no doubt have performed a faire action, so generous and so just, rather with ignominie, than for glorie. This man was truly a patterne, whom nature chose to shew how farre humane vertue may reach, and mans constancie attaine unto. But my purpose is not here to treat this rich argument: I will only confront together the sayings of five Latin Poets upon *Catoes* commendations, and for the interest of

Cato, and by incidencie for theirs also. Now ought a gentleman well-bred, in respect of others, finde the two former somewhat languishing. The third more vigorous, but suppressed, by the extravagancie of force. He will judge there were yet place for one or two degrees of invention, to reach unto the fourth, in consideration of which he will through admiration joyne hands. For the last (yet first in some degree and space, but which space he will sweare can by no humane spirit be filled up) he will be much amazed, he will be much amated. Loe here are wonders, we have more Poets than judges and interpreters of poesie. It is an easier matter to frame it, than to know it: Being base and humble, it may be judged by the precepts and art of it: But the good and loftie, the supreme and divine, is beyond rules, and above reason. Whosoever discerneth her beautie, with a constant, quicke-seeing, and setled looke, he can no more see and comprehend the same than the splendor of a lightning flash. It hath no communitie with our judgement; but ransacketh and ravisheth the same. The furie which prickes and moves him that can penetrate her, doth also stricke and wound a third man, if he heare it either handled or recited, as the Adamant stone drawes, not only a needle, but infuseth some of her facultie in the same to draw others: And it is more apparently seene in theaters, that the sacred inspiration of the Muses, having first stirred up the Poet with a kinde of agitation unto choler, unto griefe, unto hatred, yea and beyond himselfe, whither and howsoever they please, doth also by the Poet strike and enter into the Actor, and [consecutively] by the Actor, a whole auditorie or multitude. It is the ligament of our senses depending one of another. Even from my infancie, Poesie hath had the vertue to transpierce and transport me. But that lively and feeling-moving that is naturally in me, hath diversly beene handled, by the diversitie of formes, not so much higher or lower (for they were ever the highest in every kind) as different in colour. First a blithe and ingenious fluiditie, then a quaint-wittie, and loftie conceit. To conclude, a ripe and constant force. *Ovid, Lucan,* and *Virgil,* will better declare it. But here our Gallants are in their full cariere.

> *Sit Cato dum vivit sanè vel Cæsare major.*
> MART. *Epig.* xxxii. 5.

> Let *Cato Junior,* while he
> doth live, greater than *Cæsar* be,

Saith one.

> *—et invictum devictâ morte Catonem:*
> MANIL. *Astr.* iv. 87.

> *Cato* unconquered, death being vanquished.

Saith another: And the third speaking of the civill warres betweene *Cæsar* and *Pompey.*

Victrix causa Diis placuit, sed victa Catoni.
LUCAN, *Bel. Civ.* i. 127.

The cause that overcame with Gods was greater;
But the cause overcome pleasd *Cato* better.

And the fourth upon *Cæsars* commendations:

Et cuncta terrarum subacta,
Præter atrocem animum Catonis.—HOR. ii. *Od.* i. 23.

Of all the earth all parts inthralled,
Catoes minde only unappalled.

And the harts-master, after he hath enstalled the names of the greatest Romanes in his picture, endeth thus:

—his dantem jura Cantonem.—VIRG. *Æn.* viii. 670.

Chiefe justice *Cato* doe decree
Lawes that for righteous soules should be.

CHAPTER XXXVII

HOW WE WEEPE AND LAUGH AT ONE SELFE-SAME THING

WHEN we reade in Histories (PLUT. *Vit. Pyrrh.* f.), that *Antigonus* was highly displeased with his sonne, at what time he presented unto him the head of King *Pirrhus* his enemie, slaine but a little before in fight against him; which he no sooner saw, but hee burst foorth a weeping. And that *Renate* Duke of *Lorraine*, wept for the death of *Charles* Duke of *Burgundie*, whom hee had eftsoones discomfited, and was as an assistant mourner at his funeralls: And that in the battel of *Auroy* (which the Earle of *Montfort* had gained against the faction of *Charles de Blois*, for the Dutchy of *Britanie*) the victorious conqueror met with the body of his enemie deceased, mourned very grievously for him; a man must not suddenly exclaime.

E cosie auvien', che l'animo ciascuna
Sua passion, sotto contrario manto
Ricuopre, con la vista hor chiara, hor bruna.

So happens it, the minde covers each passion
Under a cloake of colours opposite,
To sight now cleare, now darke, in divers fashon.

When *Cæsar* was presented with *Pompeis* head, Histories report that he turn'd his looks aside, as from a ghastly and unpleasing spectacle. There hath beene so long a correspondencie and societie in the managing of publike affaires, mutually betweene them, such a communitie of fortunes, so many reciprocall offices and bonds of alliance, that a man cannot thinke his countenance to have beene forced, false, and wily, as this other supposeth.

> *—tutumque putavit*
> *Jam bonus esse socer, lacrymas non sponte cadentes*
> *Effudit gemitusque expressit pectore læto.—*LUCAN. ix. 1040.

Now to be kinde indeed he did not doubt
Father in law, teares, which came hardly out
He shed, and grones exprest
From inward pleased brest.

For certainly, howbeit the greatest number of our actions be but masked and painted over with dissimulation, and that it may sometimes be true,

> *Hæredias fletus sub persona risus est.*
> AUL. GELL. *Noct. Att.* xvii. c. 14.

The weeping of an heire, is laughing under a visard or disguise.

Yet must a man consider by judging of his accidents, how our mindes are often agitated by divers passions; For (as they say) there is a certaine assembly of divers humors in our bodies, whereof she is soveraigne mistris, who most ordinarily, according to our complexions doth command us: so in our minde, although it containe severall motions that agitate the same, yet must one chiefly be predominant. But it is not with so full an advantage, but for the volubilitie and supplenesse of our minde, the weakest may by occasion reobtaine the place againe, and when their turne commeth, make a new charge, whence we see, not only children, who simply and naturally follow nature, often to weepe and laugh at one selfe-same thing; but none of us all can vaunt himselfe, what wished for, or pleasant voyage soever he undertake, but that taking leave of his family and friends, he shall feele a chilling and panting of the heart, and if he shed not teares, at least he puts his foot in the stirrop with a sad and heavie cheere. And what gentle flame soever doth warme the heart of young virgins, yet are they hardly drawne to leave and forgoe their mothers, to betake them to their husbands: whatsoever this good fellow say;

> *Est ne novis nuptis odio Venus, ánne parentum*
> *Frustrantur falsis gaudia lacrymulis,*
> *Ubertim thalami quas intra limina fundunt?*
> *Non, ita me divi, vera gemunt, juverint.*
> CATUL. *Eleg.* ii. 15.

Doe young Birds hate indeed fresh *Venus* toyes,
   Or with false teares delude their parents joyes,
Which in their chambers they powre out amaine?
   So helpe me God, they doe not true complaine.

So is it not strange to mourne for him dead, whom a man by no meanes would have alive againe. When I chide my boy, I doe it with the best heart I have: They are true and not fained imprecations: but that fit past over, let him have need of me, I will gladly doe him all the good I can, and by and by I turne over another leafe. If I chance to call one knave or asse, my purpose is not for ever to enfeoffe him with those nick-names; nor doe I thinke to say, tong thou liest, if immediately after I call him an honest man. No qualitie doth embrace us purely and universally. If it were not the countenance of a foole to speake alone, or to him selfe, there would scarce be day, or houre, wherein some body should not heare me mutter and grumble to my selfe, and against my selfe. A ( ) in the fooles teeth, yet doe not I thinke it to be my defini-tion. He that seeth me sometimes to cast a frowning looke upon my wife, or sometimes a loving countenance, and thinkes, that either of them is but fained, he is a foole. *Nero* taking leave of his mother, whom hee sent to be drowned, felt notwithstanding the emotion of that motherly farewell, and at one instant was strucken with horror and pitie. It is said, that the Sunnes-light is not of one continued piece, but that it so uncessantly, and without intermission doth cast so thicke new raies, one in the necke of another upon us, that wee cannot per-ceive the space betweene them.

Largus enim liquidi fons luminis æthereus sol
Inrigat assiduè cælum candore recenti,
Suppeditátque novo confestim lumine lumen.—LUCR. v. 281.

Heav'ns Sunne the plenteous spring of liquid light
Still heav'n bedewes with splendor fresh and bright,
Still light supplies with light of fresher sight.

So doth our minde cast her points diversly and imperceptibly. *Artab-anus* surprised *Xerxes* his nephew, and chid him for the sudden changing of his countenance. He was to consider the unmeasurable greatnesse of his forces at the passage of *Hellespont*, for the enterprise of *Greece*. First he was suddenly assailed by an excessive joy, to see so many thousands of men at his service, and witnessed the same by the alacritie and cheerefulnes of his countenance: And immediately at the verie moment, his thoughts suggesting, how so many lives were to be consumed, and should come to nothing (at the furthest, within one age) he gan to frowne his browes, and grew so pensive, that he wept. We have with a resolute and inexorable minde pursued the revenge of an injurie, and felt a singular content for the victorie; yet upon better advice doe we weepe: it is not that we weepe for: the thing is as it was, there is nothing changed: But that our minde beholds the thing with another eie, and under an other shape it presents it selfe unto us. For every thing hath divers faces, sundry byases, and severall lustres. Aliance, kinred, old acquaintances, and long friendship seize on our imagination, and at that instant, passionate the same according to their qualitie, but the turne or change of it, is so violent, that it escapes us.

> *Nil adeo fieri celeri ratione videtur,*
> *Quàm si mens fieri proponit et inchoat ipsa.*
> *Ocius erog animus quàm res se perciet ulla,*
> *Ante oculos quarum in promptu natura videtur.*
>
> L. iii. 183.

> Nothing in so quicke sort seemes to be done,
> As minde set on a thing, and once begun,
> The minde that swifter stirres before our eies,
> Than any thing, whose forme we soone comprize.

And therefore, intending to continue one body of all this pursuit, we deceive our selves. When *Timoleon* weepeth the murther he hath perpetrated with so mature and generous a determination, he weepeth not for the libertie restored to his countrie, nor the tyrant, but he weepeth for his brother. One part of his dutie is acted, let us permit him to play the other.

CHAPTER XXXVIII

OF SOLITARINESSE

LET us leave apart this outworne comparison, betweene a solitarie and an active life: And touching that goodly saying under which ambition and avarice shroud themselves; that we are not borne for our particular, but for the publike good: Let us boldly refer our selves to those that are engaged; and let them beat their conscience, if on the contrarie, the states, the charges, and this trash of the world, are not rather sought and sued for to draw a private commoditie from the publike. The bad and indirect meanes where-through in our age men canvase and toyle to attaine the same, doe manifestly declare the end thereof to be of no great consequence. Let us answer ambition, that herselfe gives us the taste of solitarinesse. For what doth she shun so much as company? What seeketh shee more than elbow-roome? There is no place, but there are meanes and waies to doe well or ill. Neverthelesse if the saying of *Bias* be true; *That the worst part is the greatest:* Or that which *Ecclesiastes* saith, *That of a thousand there is not one good.*

> *Rari quippe boni, numero vix sunt totidem, quot*
> *Thebarum portæ, vel divitis ostia Nili:*
>
> JUVEN. *Sat.* xiii. 26.

> Good men are rare, so many scarce (I feare)
> As gates of *Thebes,* mouths of rich *Nilus* were.

Contagion is very dangerous in a throng. A man must imitate the vicious, or hate them: both are dangerous: for to resemble them is perilous, because they are many, and to hate many is hazzardous, because they are dissemblable, and Merchants that travell by sea, have reason to take heed, that those which goe in the same ship, be not dissolute, blasphemers, and wicked, judging such company unfortunate. Therefore *Bias* said pleasantly to those, that together with him passt the danger of a great storme, and called to the Gods for helpe: *Peace my masters, lest they should heare, that you are here with me.* And of a more militarie example, *Albuberque,* Viceroy in *India* for *Emanuel* King of *Portugall,* in an extreme danger of a sea-tempest, tooke a young boy upon his shouldiers, for this only end, that in the common perill his innocencie might be his warrant, and recommending to Gods favour, to set him on shore: yet may a wise man live every where contented, yea and alone, in the throng of a Pallace: but if he may chuse, he will (saith he) *Avoid the sight of it.* If need require, he will endure the first: but if he may have his choice, he will chuse the latter. He thinks he hath not sufficiently rid himselfe from vices, if he must also contest with other mens faults. *Charondas* punished those for wicked, that were convicted to have frequented lewd companies. There is nothing so dis-sociable and sociable as man, the one for his vice, the other for his nature. And I think *Antisthenes* did not satisfie him that upbraided him with his conversation with the wicked, saying, *That Physicians live amongst the sicke.* Who if they stead sick-mens healths, they empaire their owne, by the infection, continuall visiting, touching and frequenting of diseases. Now (as I suppose) the end is both one, thereby to live more at leasure, and better at ease. But man does not alwaies seeke the best way to come unto it, who often supposeth to have quit affaires, when he hath but changed them. There is not much lesse vexation in the government of a private family, than in the managing of an entire state: wheresoever the minde is busied, there it is all. And though domesticall occupations be lesse important, they are as importunate. Moreover, though we have freed our selves from the court, and from the market, we are not free from the principall torments of our life.

> —*ratio et prudentia curas,*
> *Non locus effusi latè maris arbiter aufert.*
>
> HOR. i. *Epist.* xi. 25.

Reason and wisdome may set cares aside,
Not place the Arbiter of seas so wide.

Shift we, or change we places never so often, ambition, avarice, irresolution, feare and concupiscences never leave us.

> *Et post equitem sedet atra cura.*—HOR. iii. *Od.* i. 39.

Care looking grim and blacke, doth sit
Behinde his backe that rides from it.

They often follow us, even into immured cloisters, and into schooles of Philosophy; nor doe hollow rocks, nor wearing of haire-shirts, nor continuall fastings rid us from them.

> *Hæret lateri lethalis arundo.*—Virg. Æn. iv. 73.

> The shaft that death implide
> Sticks by the flying side.

It was told *Socrates*, that one was no whit amended by his travell: *I beleeve it well* (saith he) *for he carried himselfe with him.*

> *Quid terras alio calentes*
> *Sole mutamus? patriâ quis exul*
> *Se quoque fugit?*—Hor. ii. *Od.* xvi. 18.

> Why change we soyles warm'd with another Sunne?
> Who from home banisht hath himselfe out-runne?

If a man doe not first discharge both himselfe and his minde from the burthen that presseth her, removing from place to place will stirre and presse her the more; as in a ship, wares well stowed, and closely piled, take up least roome, you doe a sicke-man more hurt than good, to make him change place, you settle an evill in removing the same; as stakes or poles, the more they are stirred and shaken, the faster they sticke, and sinke deeper into the ground. Therefore is it not enough, for a man to have sequestred himselfe from the concourse of people: it is not sufficient to shift place, a man must also sever himselfe from the popular conditions, that are in us. A man must sequester and recover himselfe from himselfe.

> *—rupi jam vincula, dicas,*
> *Nam luctata canis nodum arripit, attamen illa*
> *Cùm fugit, à collo trahitur pars longa catenæ.*
> Pers. *Sat.* v. 158.

> You will say haply I my bonds have quit,
> Why so the striving dog the knot hath bit;
> Yet when he flies, much chaine doth follow it.

We carry our fetters with us: it is not an absolute libertie; we still cast backe our lookes towards that we have left behinde: our minde doth still run on it; our fansie is full of it.

> *—nisi purgatum est pectus, quæ prælia nobis*
> *Atque pericula tunc ingratis insinuandum?*
> *Quantæ conscindunt hominem cupidinis acres*
> *Sollicitum curæ, quantique perinde timores?*
> *Quidve superbia, spurcitia, ac petulantia, quantas*
> *Efficiunt clades, quid luxus desidiesque?*—Lucr. v. 44.

> Unlesse our breast be purg'd, what warres must wee
> What perils then, though much displeased, see?

How great feares, how great cares of sharpe desire
Doe carefull man distract, torment, enfire?
Uncleannesse, wantonnesse, sloth, riot, pride,
How great calamities have these implide?

Our evill is rooted in our minde: and it cannot scape from it selfe.

In culpa est animus, qui se non effugit unquam.

Hor. i. *Epist*. xiv. 13.

The minde in greatest fault must lie,
Which from it selfe can never flie.

Therefore must it be reduced and brought into it selfe: It is the true solitarinesse, and which may be enjoyed even in the frequencie of peopled Cities, and Kings courts: but it is more commodiously enjoyed apart. Now sithence wee undertake to live solitarie, and without companie, let us cause our contentment to depend of our selves: Let us shake off all bonds that tie us unto others: Gaine we that victorie over us, that in good earnest we may live solitarie, and therein live at our ease. *Stilphon* having escaped the combustion of his Citie, wherein he had lost, both wife, and children, and all his goods; *Demetrius Poliorcetes* seeing him in so great a ruine of his Countrie, with an unaffrighted countenance, demanded of him, whether he had received any losse; *He answered, No: and that (thanks given to God) he had lost nothing of his owne.* It is that, which *Antiisthenes* the Philosopher said very pleasantly, *That man ought to provide himselfe with munitions, that might float upon the water, and by swimming escape the danger of shipwracke with him.* Verily, *a man of understanding hath lost nothing, if he yet have himselfe.* When the Citie of *Nola* was over-run by the Barbarians, *Paulinus* Bishop thereof, having lost all he had there, and being their prisoner, prayed thus unto God: *Oh Lord deliver me from feeling of this losse: for thou knowest as yet they have toucht nothing that is mine.* The riches that made him rich, and the goods which made him good, were yet absolutely whole. Behold what it is to chuse treasures well, that may be freed from injurie; and to hide them in a place, where no man may enter, and which cannot be betraied but by our selves. A man that is able, may have wives, children, goods, and chiefly health, but not so tie himselfe unto them, that his felicitie depend on them. We should reserve a store-house for our selves, what need soever chance; altogether ours, and wholly free, wherein we may hoard up and establish our true libertie, and principall retreit and solitarinesse, wherein we must go alone to our selves, to take our ordinarie entertainment, and so privately, that no acquaintance or communication of any strange thing may therein find place: there to discourse, to meditate and laugh, as, without wife, without children, and goods, without traine, or servants; that if by any occasion they be lost, it seeme not strange to us to passe it over; we have a mind moving and turning in it selfe; it may keep it selfe companie; it hath where-with to offend and defend, wherewith to receive, and wherewith to give. Let us not feare that we shall faint and droop through tedious and mind-trying idlenesse in this solitarinesse.

In solis sis tibi turba locis.

Be thou, when with thee is not any,
As good unto thy selfe as many.

Vertue is contented with it selfe, without discipline, without words, and without effects. In our accustomed actions, of a thousand there is not one found that regards us: he whom thou seest so furiously, and as it were besides himselfe, to clamber or crawle up the citie wals, or breach, as a point-blank to a whole voly of shot, and another all wounded and skarred, crazed and faint, and wel-nie hunger-starven, resolved rather to die, than to open his enemie the gate, and give him entrance; doest thou think he is there for himselfe? No verily, It is peradventure for such a one, whom neither he, nor so many of his fel-lowes ever saw, and who haply takes no care at all for them; but is there-whilst wallowing up to the eares in sensualitie, slouth, and all manner of carnal delights. This man whom about midnight, when others take their rest, thou seest come out of his study meagre-looking, with eyes-trilling, flegmatike, squalide, and spauling, doest thou thinke, that plodding on his books he doth seek how he shall become an hon-ester man; or more wise, or more content? There is no such matter. He wil either die in his pursuit, or teach posteritie the measure of *Plautus* verses, and the true Orthography of a Latine word. Who doth not willingly chop and counter-change his health, his ease, yea, and his life for glorie, and for reputation? The most unprofitable, vaine, and counterfet coine, that is in use with us. Our death is not sufficient to make us afraid, let us also charge our selves with that of our wives, of our children, and of our friends, and people. Our owne affaires doe not sufficiently trouble and vexe us; Let us also drudge, toile, vex, and torment our selves with our neighbours and friends matters.

Vah quemquámne hominem in animum instituere, aut
Parare, quod sit charius, quàm ipse est sibi?
TER. *Adel.* act i. scen. i. 13.

Fie, that a man should cast, that ought, than he
Himselfe of himselfe more belov'd should be.

Solitarinesse mee seemeth hath more apparance and reason in those which have given their most active and flourishing age unto the world, in imitation of *Thales.* We have lived long enough for others, live we the remainder of our life unto our selves: let us bring home our cogita-tions and inventions unto our selves, and unto our ease. It is no easie matter to make a safe retreit: it doth over-much trouble us with [out] joyning other enterprises unto it. Since God gives us leasure to dispose of our dislodging. Let us prepare our selves unto it, packe wee up our baggage. Let us betimes bid our companie farewell. Shake we off these violent hold-fasts, which else-where engage us, and estrange us from our selves. These so strong bonds must be untied, and a man may eft-soones love this or that, but wed nothing but himselfe; That is to say, let the rest be our owne: yet not so combined and glued together, that it may not be sundred, without fleaing us, and there-withall, pull away some peece of our owne. The greatest thing of the world, is for a man to know how to be his owne. It is high time to shake off societie, since we can bring nothing to it. And he that cannot lend, let him take heed of borrowing. Our forces faile us: retire we them, and shut them up into our selves. He that can suppresse and confound in himselfe the offices of so many amities, and of the company, let him doe it. In this fall, which makes us inutile, irkesome, and importunate to others, let him take heed he be not importunate, irkesome, and un-profitable to himselfe. Let him flatter, court, and cherish himself, and above all let him governe himselfe, respecting his reason and fearing his conscience, so that he may not without shame stumble or trip in their presence. *Rarum est enim, ut satis se quisque vereatur. For it is a rare matter, that every man sufficiently should stand in awe and rever-ence of himselfe.* Socrates saith, *That young men ought to be in-structed, and men exercised in well doing; and old men withdraw themselves from all civill and military negotiations, living at their owne discretion, without obligation to any certaine office.* There are some complexions, more proper for these precepts of retreit than others. Those which have a tender and demisse apprehension, a squemish affection, a delicate will, and which cannot easily subject or imploy it selfe (of which both by naturall condition and propense discourse I am one) wil better apply themselves unto this counsell than active minds, and busie spirits; which imbrace all, every where engage, and in all things passionate themselves; that offer, that present, and yeeld themselves to all occasions. A man must make use of all these acci-dentall commodities, and which are without us, so long as they be pleasing to us; but not make them our principall foundation: It is not so, nor reason, nor nature permit it. Why should we against their lawes subject our contentment to the power of others? Moreover, to antici-pate the accidents of fortune; for a man to deprive himselfe of the commodities he hath in possession, as many have done for devotion, and some Philosophers by discourse; to serve themselves, to lie upon the hard ground, to pull out their owne eyes, to cast their riches into the Sea, to seeke for paine and smart (some by tormenting this life, for the happinesse of another; othersome placing themselves on the lowest step, thereby to warrant themselves from a new fall) is the action of an excessive vertue. Let sterner and more vigorous complexions make their lurking glorious and more exemplar.

—tuta et parvula laudo,
Cùm res deficiunt, satis inter vilia fortis:
Verùm ubi quid melius contingit et unctius, idem
Hos sapere, et solos aio bene vivere, quorum
Conspicitur nitidis fundata pecunia villis.

Hor. i. *Epist.* xv. 42.

When riches faile, I praise the safe estate,
Though small; base things doe not high thoughts abate.
But when tis better, finer with me, I
They only live well, and are wise, doe crie,
Whose coine in fair farmes doth well-grounded lie.

There is worke enough for me to doe without going so far. It sufficeth me under fortunes favour, to prepare my selfe for her disfavour; and being at ease, as far as imagination may attaine unto, to represent the evill to come unto my selfe: Even as we enure our selves to Tilts and Tourneyes, and counterfeit warre in time of peace. I esteeme not *Arcesilaus* the Philosopher lesse reformed, because I know him to have used houshold implements of gold and silver, according as the condition of his fortune gave him leave. I rather value him the more, than if he had not done it, forsomuch as he both moderately and liberally made use of them. I know unto what limits naturall necessitie goeth; and I consider the poore almesman begging at my doore, to be often more plumb-cheekt, in better health and liking than I am: Then doe I enter into his estate, and assay to frame and sute my mind unto his byase. And so over-running other examples, albeit I imagine death, povertie, contempt, and sicknesse to be at my heeles, I easily resolve my selfe, not to apprehend any feare of that, which one of lesse worth than my selfe doth tolerate and undergoe with such patience: And I cannot beleeve, that the basenesse or shallownesse of understanding, can doe more than vigor and far-seeing, or that the effects and reason of discretion, cannot reach to the effects of custome and use. And knowing what slender hold-fast these accessorie commodities have, I omit not in full jovyssance of them, humbly to beseech God of his mercie (as a soveraigne request) to make me contented with my selfe, and with the goods proceeding from me. I see some gallantly-disposed young men, who notwithstanding their faire-seeming shew, have many boxes full of pils in their coffers at home, to take when the rhume shall assaile them; which so much the lesse they feare, when they thinke the remedy to be at hand. So must a man doe: as also if he feele himselfe subject to some greater infirmitie, to store himselfe with medicaments that may asswage, supple, and stupifie the part grieved. The occupation a man should chuse for such a life, must neither be painfull nor tedious, otherwise, in vaine should we accompt to have sought our abiding there, which depends from the particular taste of every man.

Mine doth no way accommodate it selfe to husbandrie. Those that love it, must with moderation apply themselves unto it.

> *Conentur sibi res, non se submittere rebus.*
>
> *Epist.* i. 19.

Endevour they things to them to submit,
Not them to things (if they have *Horace* wit).

Husbandrie is otherwise a servile office, as *Salust* termeth it: It hath more excusable parts, as the care of gardening, which *Xenophon* ascribeth to *Cyrus:* A meane or mediocritie may be found, between this base and vile carking care, extended and full of toiling labor, which we see in men that wholly plunge themselves therein, and that profound and extreme retchlesnesse to let all things goe at six and seven, which is seen in others.

> *—Democriti pecus edit agellos*
> *Cultaque, dum peregrè est animus sine corpore velox.*
>
> *Epist.* xii. 12.

Cattle destroyd *Democritus* his sets,
While his mind bodilesse vagaries fets.

But let us heare the counsell, which *Plinie* the younger giveth to his friend *Cornelius Rufus,* touching this point of Solitarinesse: *I perswade thee in this full-gorged and fat retreit, wherein thou art, to remit this base and abject care of husbandrie unto thy servants, and give thy selfe to the study of letters, whence thou maist gather something, that may altogether be thine owne;* He meaneth reputation: like unto *Ciceroes* humor, who saith, *That he will imploy his solitarinesse and residence from publike affaires, to purchase unto himselfe by his writings an immortall life.*

> *—usque adeone*
> *Scire tuum nihil est, nisi te scire hoc sciat alter?*
>
> PERS. *Sat.* i. 27.

Is it then nothing worth that thou doost know,
Unlesse what thou doost know, thou others show?

It seemeth to be reason, when a man speaketh to withdrawe himselfe from the world, that one should looke beyond him. These doe it but by halfes. Indeed they set their match against the time they shall be no more: but pretend to reap the fruit of their dessignes, when they shall be absent from the world, by a ridiculous contradiction. The imagination of those, who through devotion seeke solitarinesse, filling their minds with the certaintie of heavenly promises, in the other life, is much more soundly consorted. They propose God as an object infinit in goodnes, and incomprehensible in power, unto themselves. The soule hath therein, in all free libertie, wherewith to glut her selfe.

Afflictions and sorrowes redound to their profit, being imployed for the purchase and attaining of health, and eternall gladnesse. Death, according to ones wish, is a passage to so perfect an estate. The sharpnesse of their rules, is presently made smooth and easie by custome; and carnall concupiscences, rejected, abated, and lulled asleep by refusing them; for nothing entertaineth them but use and exercise. *This only end of another life, blessedly immortall, doth rightly merit we should abandon the pleasures and commodities of this our life. And he that can enlighten his soule with the flame of a lively faith and hope, really and constantly, in his solitarinesse, doth build unto himselfe a voluptuous and delicious life, far surmounting all other lives.* Therefore doth neither the end nor middle of this counsell please me. We are ever falling into a relaps, from an ague to a burning fever. This plodding occupation of bookes, is as painfull as any other, and as great an enemie unto health, which ought principally to be considered. And a man should not suffer himselfe to be inveagled by the pleasure he takes in them: It is the same pleasure, that loseth the thriving husband-man, the greedy-covetous, the sinning-voluptuous, and the puft-up ambitious. The wisest men teach us sufficiently to beware and shield us from the treasons of our appetites, and to discerne true and perfect pleasures, from delights blended and entermingled with more paine. For, most pleasures (say they) tickle, fawne upon, and embrace us, with purpose to strangle us, as did the theeves whom the Ægyptians termed *Philistas:* And if the head-ach would seize upon us before drunkennesse, we would then beware of too much drinking: but sensualitie the better to entrap us, marcheth before, and hideth her tracke from us. Bookes are delightfull; but if by continuall frequenting them, we in the end lose both health and cheerefulnesse (our best parts) let us leave them. I am one of those who thinke their fruit can no way countervaile this losse. As men that have long time felt themselves enfeebled through some indisposition, doe in the end yeeld to the mercie of Physicke, and by art have certaine rules of life prescribed them, which they will not transgresse: So he that with-drawes himselfe, as distasted and over-tired with the common life, ought likewise to frame and prescribe this unto the rules of reason; direct and range the same by premeditation, and discourse. He must bid all manner of travell farewell, what shew soever it beare; and in generall shun all passions that any way empeach the tranquillitie of mind and body, and follow the course best agreeing with his humour.

> *Unusquisque sua noverit ire via.*
> PROPERT. ii. *El.* xxv. 38.

> His owne way every man
> Tread-out directly can.

A man must give to thriving husbandrie, to laborious study, to toilesome hunting, and to every other exercise, the utmost bounds of pleasure; and beware he engage himselfe no further, if once paine begin to intermeddle it selfe with her; we should reserve businesse and negotiations, only for so much as is behoovefull to keepe us in breath, and to warrant us from the inconveniences which the other extremitie of a base, faint-harted idlenesse drawes after it. There are certaine barren and thornie sciences, which tor the most part are forged for the multitude: they should be left for those, who are for the service of the world. As for my selfe, I love no books, but such as are pleasant, and easie, and which tickle me, or such as comfort and counsell me, to direct my life and death.

> —*tacitum sylvas inter reptare salubres*
> *Curantem quidquid dignum sapiente bonóque est.*
>
> Hor. i. *Epist.* iv. 4.

Silently creeping midst the wholesome wood
With care what's for a wise man and a good.

The wiser sort of men, having a strong and vigorous mind, may frame unto themselves an altogether spirituall life. But mine being common, I must help to uphold my selfe by corporall commodities: And age having eftsoones dispoiled me of those that were most sutable to my fantasie, I instruct and sharpen my appetite to those remaining most sortable this other season. We must tooth and naile retaine the use of this lives pleasures, which our yeares snatch from us, one after another:

> *Carpamus dulcia, nostrum est,*
> *Quòd vivis: cinis et manes et fabula fies.*
>
> Pers. *Sat.* v. 155.

Plucke we sweet pleasures: we thy life give thee.
Thou shalt a tale, a ghost, and ashes be.

Now concerning the end of glorie, which *Plinie,* and *Cicero* propose unto us, it is far from my discourse: The most opposite humour to solitarie retiring, is ambition. *Glorie and rest, are things that cannot squat in one same forme:* as far as I see, these have nought but their armes and legs out of the throng, their mind and intent is further and more engaged in them than ever it was.

> *Tun' vetule auriculis alienis colligis escas?*—Pers. *Sat.* i. 22.

Gatherst thou dotard at these yeares,
Fresh baits, fine food, for others eares?

They have gone backe that they might leap the better, and with a stronger motion make a nimbler offer amidst the multitude. Will you see how they shoot-short by a cornes breadth? let us but counterpoise the advice of two Philosophers, and of two most different sects: The one writing to *Idomeneus,* the other to *Lucilius* their friends, to divert them from the managing of affaires and greatnesse, unto a solitarie kind of life. *You have* (say they) *lived hitherto swimming and floating adrift, come and die in the haven; you have given the past of your life unto light, give the remainder unto darknesse. It is impossible to give over occupations, if you doe not also give over the fruits of them: Therefore cleare your selfe from all care and glorie. There is great danger, lest the glittering of your fore-passed actions should over-much dazle you, yea, and follow you even to your den. Together with other concupiscences, shake off that which commeth from the approbation of others. And touching your knowledge and sufficiencie, take you no care of them, they will lose no whit of their effect; if your selfe be any thing the better for them. Remember but him, who being demanded, to what purpose he toyled so much about an Art, which could by no meanes come to the knowledge of many.* Few are enow for me; one will suffice, yea, lesse than one will content me, answered he. He said true: you and another are a sufficient theatre one for another; or you to your selfe alone. Let the people be one unto you, and one be all the people to you: It is a base ambition to goe about to draw glorie from ones idlenesse, and from ones lurking hole. A man must doe as some wilde beasts, which at the entrance of their caves, will have no manner of footing seene. You must no longer seeke, what the world saith of you, but how you must speake unto your selfe: withdraw your selfe into your selfe; but first prepare your selfe to receive your selfe: it were folly to trust to your selfe, if you cannot governe your selfe. A man may as well faile in solitarinesse, as in companie, there are waies for it, untill such time as you have framed your selfe such, that you dare not halt before your selfe, and that you shall be ashamed of, and beare a kind of respect unto your selfe, *Obversentur species honestæ animo* (Cic. *Tusc. Qu.* ii.): *Let honest* Ideaes *still represent themselves before your mind:* Ever present *Cato, Phocion,* and *Aristides* (Senec. *Epist.* xi.) unto your imagination, in whose presence even fooles would hide their faults, and establish them as controulers of all your intentions. If they be disordered and untuned, their reverence will order and tune them againe: they will containe you in a way, to be contented with your selfe; to borrow nothing but from your selfe, to settle and stay your mind in assured and limited cogitations, wherein it may best please it selfe, and having gotten knowledge of true felicities, which according to the measure a man understands them, he shall accordingly injoy, and with them rest satisfied, without wishing a further continuance, either of life or name. Loe heere the counsell of truly-pure, and purely-true philosophie, not of a vaine-glorious, boasting, and prating philosophie, as is that of the two first.

CHAPTER XXXIX

A CONSIDERATION UPON CICERO

ONE word more in comparison of these two. There are gathered out of *Ciceroes* writings and from *Plinies*, (in mine opinion little agreeing with his unckle) infinite testimonies of a nature beyond measure ambitious. Amongst others, that they openly solicit the Historians of their times, not to forget them in their writings: and fortune, as it were in spight, hath made the vanitie of their request to continue even to our daies, and long since the histories were lost. But this exceedeth all hearts-basenesse in persons of that stampe, to have gone about to draw some principall glorie from prating and speaking, even to imploy their private Epistles written to their friends; in such sort, as some missing the opportunitie to be sent, they notwithstanding cause them to be published, with this worthy excuse, that they would not lose their travell and lucubrations. Is it not a seemly thing in two *Romane Consuls*, chiefe magistrates of the common-wealth, Empresse of the world, to spend their time in wittily devising, and closely hudling up of a quaint missive or wittie epistle, thereby to attaine the reputation, that they perfectly understand their mother tongue? What could a seely Schoolmaster, who gets his living by such trash, doe worse? If the acts of *Xenophon*, or of *Cæsar*, had not by much exceeded their eloquence, I cannot beleeve, they would ever have written them. They have endevored to recommend unto posterity, not their sayings, but their doings. And if the perfection of well-speaking might bring any glorie sutable unto a great personage, *Scipio* and *Lelius* would never have resigned the honour of their Comedies, and the elegancies, and smooth-sportfull conceits of the Latine tongue, unto an Affrican servant: For, to prove this labour to be theirs, the exquisit eloquence, and excellent invention thereof doth sufficiently declare it: and *Terence* himselfe doth avouch it: And I could hardly be removed from this opinion. It is a kind of mockerie and injurie, to raise a man to worth, by qualities mis-seeming his place, and unfitting his calling, although for some other respects praise-worthy; and also by qualities that ought not to be his principall object. As he that would commend a King to be a cunning Painter, or a skilfull Architect, or an excellent Harquibuzier, or a never missing runner at the Ring. These commendations acquire a man no honour, if they be not presented altogether with those that are proper and convenient unto him, that is to say, justice, and the skill to governe, and knowledge to direct his people both in peace and warre. In this sort doth Agriculture honour *Cyrus*, and Eloquence *Charlemaine*, together with his knowledge in good letters. I have in my time seen some, who by writing did earnestly get both their titles and living, to disavow their aprentissage, mar their pen, and affect the ignorance of so vulgar a qualitie; and which our people holds, to be seldome found amongst wise men, endevouring to be commended for better qualities. *Demosthenes* his companions in their ambassage to *Philip, praised their Prince to be faire, eloquent, and a good quaffer. Demosthenes* said, *they were commendations rather fitting a woman, an advocate, and a spunge, than a King.*

> *Imperet bellante prior, jacentem*
> *Lenis in hostem.*—Hor. Car. Secul. 51.

Better he rule, who mercifull will rue
His foe subdued, than he that can subdue.

It is not his profession to know, either how to hunt cunningly, or to dance nimbly.

> *Orabunt causas alii, cœlique meatus*
> *Describent radio, et fulgentia sidera dicent;*
> *Hic regere imperio populos sciat.*—Virg. Æn. vi. 850.

Others shall causes plead, describe the skies
Motion by instrument, say how stars rise:
But let him know to rule (just, valiant, wise).

Plutarke saith moreover, *That to appeare so absolutely excellent in these lesse-necessarie parts, is to produce a witnesse against himselfe, to have ill spent his houres, and fondly bestowed his study, which might better have beene imployed to more behoovefull and profitable use.* So that *Philip* King of *Macedon*, having heard great *Alexander* his sonne sing at a feast and vie with the best Musitians: *Art thou not ashamed* (said he unto him) *to sing so well?* And to the same *Philip*, said a Musitian, gainst whom he contended about his Art, *God forbid, my Soveraigne, that ever so much hurt should befall you, that you should understand these things better than my selfe.* A King ought to be able to answer, as *Ipicrates* did the Orator who in his invective urged him in this manner: *And what art thou thou shouldst so brave it? Art thou a man at Armes? Art thou an Archer? Art thou a Pike-man? I am none of all those, but I am he who command all those.* And *Antisthenes* made it as an argument of little valour in *Ismenias*, when some commended him to be an excellent Flutist. Well I wot, that when I heare some give themselves to imitate the phrase of my Essayes, I would rather have them hold their peace: They doe not so much raise the words, as depresse the sense; so much the more sharply, by how much more obliquely. Yet am I deceived if some others take not more hold on the matter; and how well or ill soever if any writer hath scattered the same, either more materiall, or at least thicker on his paper: That I may collect the more, I doe but hudle up the arguments or chiefe heads. Let me but adde what followes them, I shall daily increase this volume. And how many stories have I glanced at therein, that speake not a word, which whosoever shal unfold, may from them draw infinite Essayes? Nor they, nor my allegations doe ever serve simply for examples, authoritie, or ornament. I doe not only respect them for the use I draw from them. They often (beyond my purpose) produce the seed of a richer subject, and bolder matter, and often collaterally, a more harmonious tune, both for me, that will expresse no more in this place, and for them that shall hit upon my tune.

But returning to vertue, *I find no great choice, betweene him that can speake nothing but evill, and one that can talke nothing but to talke well. Non est ornamentum virile concinnitas* (SEN. *Epist.* cxv. p.). *Finenesse is no great grace for a man. Wise men say, that in respect of knowledge, there is nothing but Philosophy and in regard of effects, but Vertue;* which is generally fit for all degrees, and for all orders. Something there is alike in these two other Philosophers; for they also promise eternitie to the Epistles, they write to their friends. But after another fashion, and to a good purpose, accommodating themselves to others vanitie; For they send them word, that if care to make themselves knowen unto future ages, and respect of renowne, doth yet retaine them in the managing of affaires, and makes them feare solitarinesse, and a retired life, to which they would call them, that they take no more paines for it: forasmuch as they have sufficient credit with posteritie, by answering them; and were it but by the Epistles they write unto them, they will make their name as famous, and as farre knowen, as all their publike actions might doe. Besides this difference, they are not frivolous, idle, and triviall Epistles, and only compact and held together with exquisit choise words, hudled-up and ranged to a just smoothe cadence, but stufft and full of notable sayings, and wise sentences; by which a man doth not only become more eloquent, but more wise, and that teach us, not to say well, but to doe well. Fie on that eloquence, which leaves us with a desire of it, and not of things: unlesse a man will say, that *Ciceroes* being so exceedingly perfect, doth frame it selfe a body of perfection. I will further alleage a storie, which to this purpose we reade of him, to make us palpably feele his naturall condition. He was to make an Oration in publike, and being urged betimes to prepare himselfe for it, *Eros* one of his servants came to tel him, the Auditorie was deferred till the morrow next; he was so glad of it, that for so good newes he gave him his libertie. Touching this subject of Epistles, thus much I will say: It is a worke wherein my friends are of opinion I can doe something: And should more willingly have undertaken to publish my gifts, had I had who to speake unto. It had been requisite (as I have had other times) to have had a certaine commerce to draw me on, to encourage me, and to uphold me. For, to goe about to catch the winde in a net, as others doe, I cannot; and it is but a dreame. I am a sworne enemie to all falsifications. I should have beene more attentive, and more assured, having a friendly and strong direction, than to behold the divers images of a whole multitude: and I am deceived, if it had not better succeeded with me. I have naturally a comical and familiar stile: But after a maner peculiar unto my selfe, inept to all publike Negotiations, answering my speech, which is altogether close, broken, and particular: I have no skill in ceremonious letters, which have no other substance, but a faire contexture of complemental phrases and curteous words. I have no taste nor faculty of these tedious offers of service and affection. I believe not so much as is said, and am nothing pleased to say more than I believe. It is farre from that which is used now adaies: For, there was never so abject and servile a prostitution of presentations; life, soule, devotion, adoration, servant, slave; all these words are so generally used, that when they would expresse a more emphaticall intent and respective will, they have no meanes left them to expresse it. I dearly hate to heare a flatterer: which is the cause I naturally affect a pithy, sinnowie, drie, round, and harsh kind of speech; which, of such as have no further acquaintance with me, is judged to encline to disdaine. I honor them most, whom I seeme to regard least: And where my mind marcheth most cheerefully, I often forget the steps of gravitie: And I offer my selfe but faintly and rudely to those whose I am indeed, and present my selfe least, to such as I have most given my selfe. Me thinkes they should read it in my heart, and that the expression of my words, wrongeth my conception. To welcome, to take leave, to bid farewell, to give thanks, to salute, to present my service, and such verball complements of the ceremoniall lawes of our civilitie, I know no man so sottishly-barren of speech, as my selfe. And I was never imployed to indite Letters of favour or commendatorie, but he for whom they were, judged them drie, barren, and faint. The Italians are great Printers of Epistles, whereof I thinke I have a hundred severall Volumes. I deeme those of *Hanniball Caro* to be the best. If all the paper I have heretofore scribled for Ladies were extant, at what time my hand was truly transported by my passion, a man should haply find some page worthy to be communicated unto idle and fond-doting youth, embabuinized with this furie. I ever write my letters in post-hast, and so rashly-head long, that howbeit I write intolerably ill, I had rather write with mine owne hand, than imploy another: for I find none that can follow me, and I never copy them over againe. I have accustomed those great persons that know me, to endure blots, blurs, dashes, and botches, in my letters, and a sheete without folding or margine. Those that cost me, either most labour or studie, are they that are least worth. When I once begin to traile them, it is a signe my mind is not upon them. I commonly begin without project: the first word begets the second. Our moderne letters are more fraught with borders, and prefaces, than with matter, as I had rather write two, than fold and make up one, which charge I commonly resigne to others: So likewise when the matter is ended, I would willingly give another the charge, to adde these long orations, offers, praiers, and imprecations, which we place at the end of them, and wish hartily, some new fashion would discharge us of them. As also to superscribe them with a legend of qualities, titles, and callings, wherein, lest I might have tripped, I have often times omitted writing, especially to men of Justice, Lawiers, and Financiers. So many innovations of offices, so difficult a dispensation and ordinance of divers names and titles of honour, which being so dearely bought, can neither be exchanged or forgotten without offence. I likewise find it gracelesse and idly-fond, to charge the front and inscription of the many bookes and pamphlets, which we daily cause to be imprinted with them.

CHAPTER XL

THAT THE TASTE OF GOODS OR EVILS DOTH GREATLY DEPEND ON THE OPINION WE HAVE OF THEM

MEN (saith an ancient Greeke sentence) *are tormented by the opinions they have of things, and not by things themselves.* It were a great conquest for the ease of our miserable humane condition, if any man could establish every where this true proposition. For if evils have no entrance into us, but by our judgement, it seemeth that it lieth in our power, either to contemne or turne them to our good. If things yeeld themselves unto our mercie, why should we not have the fruition of them, or apply them to our advantage? If that which we call evill and torment, be neither torment, nor evill, but that our fancie only gives it that qualitie, it is in us to change it: and having the choice of it, if none compell us, we are very fooles, to bandy for that partie, which is irkesome unto us: and to give infirmities, indigence, and contempt, a sharpe and ill taste, if we may give them a good: And if fortune simply affoord us the matter, it lieth in us to give it the forme. Now that [that] which we terme evill, is not so of it selfe, or at least, such as it is, that it depends of us to give it another taste, and another countenance (for all comes to one) let us see whether it can be maintained. If the originall being of those things we feare, had the credit of its owne authoritie to lodge it selfe in us, alike and semblable would it lodge in all: For men be all of one kind, and except the most or least, they are furnished with like meanes to judge, and instruments to conceive. But the diversitie of opinions, which we have of those things, doth evidently shew, that but by composition they never enter into us. Some one peradventure doth lodge them in him-selfe, as they are in essence, but a thousand others give them a new being, and a contrarie. We accompt of death, of povertie, and of sorrow, as of our chiefest parts. Now death, which some of all horrible things call the most horrible, who knowes not, how others call it, the only haven of this lives-torments? the soveraigne good of nature? the only staie of our libertie? and the ready and common receit of our evils? And as some doe fearefully-trembling, and senslesly-affrighted, expect her comming, others endure it more easily than life: And one complaineth of her facilitie:

Mors utinam pavidos vitæ subducere nolles,
Sed virtus te sola daret!—LUCAN. iv. 580.

O death! I would thou would'st let cowards live,
That resolv'd valour might thee only give!

But let us leave these glorious minds: *Theodorus* answered *Lysimachus*, who threatned to kill him: *Thou shalt doe a great exploit to come to the strength of a Cantharides*. The greatest number of Philosophers are found to have either by designe prevented, or hastned and furthered their deaths. How many popular persons are seen brought unto death, and not to a simple death, but entermixt with shame, and sometimes with grievous torments, to embrace it with such an undaunted assurance; some through stubborne wilfulnesse, other some through a naturall simplicitie, in whom is nothing seene changed from their ordinarie condition; setling their domesticall affaires, recommending themselves unto their friends, preaching, singing, and entertaining the people: yea, and sometimes uttering words of jesting and laughter, and drinking to their acquaintance, as well as *Socrates?* One who was led to the gallowes, desired it might not be thorow such a street, for feare a Merchant should set a Serjant on his backe, for an old debt. Another wished the hang-man not to touch his throat, lest hee should make him swowne with laughing, because he was so ticklish. Another answered his confessor, who promised him he should sup that night with our Saviour in heaven, Goe thither your selfe to supper, for I use to fast a nights. Another upon the Gibbet calling for drinke, and the hang-man drinking first, said, hee would not drinke after him, for feare hee should take the pox of him. Everie man hath heard the tale of the Piccard, who being upon the ladder ready to be throwen downe, there was a wench presented unto him, with this offer (as in some cases our law doth sometimes tolerate) that if hee would marrie her, his life should be saved, who after he had a while beheld her, and perceiving that she halted, said hastily, *Away, away, good hang-man, make an end of thy busines, she limps.* The like is reported of a man in Denmarke, who being adjudged to have his head cut off, and being upon the scaffold, had the like condition offered him, but refused it, because the wench offered him was jaw-falne, long cheekt, and sharpe-nosed. A young lad at *Tholous*, being accused of heresie, in all points touching his beleefe, referred himselfe wholly to his Masters faith, (a young scholar that was in prison with him) and rather chose to die, than hee would be perswaded his Master could erre. We reade of those of the Towne of *Arras,* at what time King *Lewis* the eleventh tooke it, that amongst the common people many were found, who rather than they would say, *God save the King,* suffered themselves to be hanged. And of those base-minded jesters or buffons, some have beene seene, that even at the point of death, would never leave their jesting and scoffing. He whom the heads-man threw off from the Gallowes, cried out, Row the Gally, which was his ordinarie by-word. Another, who being at his last gaspe, his friends had laid him upon a pallet alongst the fire-side, there to breathe his last, the Physitian demanding where his griefe pained him? answered, betweene the bench and the fire: And the Priest to give him the last unction, seeking for his feet, which by reason of his sicknesse were shrunken up, he told him, My good friend you shal finde them at my legges ends, if you looke well. To another that exhorted him to recommend himselfe to God, he asked, who is going to him? And the fellow answering, your selfe shortly: If it be his good pleasure, I would to God it might be to morrow night, replied he: Recommend but yourselfe to him, said the other, and you shall quickly be there: It is best then, answered he, that my selfe carry mine owne commendations to him. In the kingdome of *Narsinga,* even at this day their Priests wives are buried alive with the bodies of their dead husbands. All other wives are burnt at their husbands funerals, not only constantly, but cheerfully. When the king dieth, his wives, his concubines, his minions, together with al his officers and servants, which make a whole people, present themselves so merrily unto the fire, wherein his body is burned, that they manifestly seeme to esteeme it as a great honour, to accompanie their deceased master to his ashes. During our last warres of *Millaine,* and so many takings, losses, miseries, and calamities of that Citie, the people impatient of so many changes of fortune, tooke such a resolution unto death, that I have heard my father say, he kept accompt of five and twentie chiefe housholders, that in one weeke made them-selves away: An accident which hath some affinitie with that of the Xanthians, who being besieged by *Brutus,* did pell-mell-headlong, men, women, and children, precipitate them-selves into so furious a desire of death, that nothing can be performed to avoid death, which these did not accomplish to avoid life: So that *Brutus* had much adoe, to save a verie small number of them. Every opinion is of sufficient power to take hold of a man in respect of life. The first Article of that couragious oath, which the Countrie of *Greece* did sweare, and keepe, in the Median warre, was, that every particular man should rather change his life unto death, than the Persian lawes for theirs. What a world of people are daily seene in the Turkish warres, and the Græcians, more willing to embrace a sharpe, a bitter, and violent death, than to be uncircumsized and baptized? An example whereof no religion is incapable. The Kings of *Castile* having banished the Jewes out of their Countrie, King *John* of *Portugall* for eight crownes a man, sold them a retreit in his dominion, for a certaine time, upon condition (the time expired) they should avoid, and he find them ships to transport them into Affrike. The day of their departure come, which past, it was expressed, that such as had not obeyed, should for ever remaine bond-slaves; ships were provided them, but very scarce and sparingly: And those which were imbarked, were so rudely, churlishly, and villainously used, by the passengers and marriners; who besides infinite other indignites, loitred so long on the seas, now forward, now backward, that in the end, they had consumed all their victuals, and were forced, if they would keepe themselves alive, to purchase some of them, at so excessive a rate, and so long, that they were never set a shore, till they had brought them so bare, that they had nothing left them but their shirts. The newes of this barbarous inhumanitie being reported to those that were yet on land, most of them resolved to yeeld and continue bond-slaves: whereof some made a semblance to change their religion. *Emanuel* that immediately succeeded John, being come to the Crowne, first set them at libertie, then changing his minde, commanded them to depart out of his dominions, and for their passages assigned them three ports. He hoped, as Bishop *Osorius* reporteth, (a Latine Historian of our ages, not to be despised) that the favor of the libertie, to which he had restored them, having failed to convert them unto Christianitie, the difficultie to commit themselves unto marriners and pyrates robberies, to leave a Countrie where they were setled with great riches, for to goe seeke unknowen and strange regions, would bring them into *Portugall* againe. But seeing all his hopes frustrate, and that they purposed to passe away, he cut off two of the three ports he had promised them, that so the tedious distance and incommoditie of the passage might retaine some, or rather that he might have the meane to assemble them all together in one place, for a fitter opportunitie of the execution he intended, which was this. Hee appointed that all their children under fourteene yeares of age, should be taken from out the hands of their parents, and removed from their sight and conversation, to some place where they might be brought up, and instructed in our religion. He saith that this effect caused an horrible spectacle: The naturall affection betweene the fathers and the children; moreover the zeale unto their ancient faith, striving against this violent ordinance. Divers fathers and mothers were ordinarily seene to kill themselves, and with a more cruell example through compassion and love, to throw their young children into pitts and wells, thereby to shun the Law. The terme which he had prefixed them being expired, for want of other meanes, they yeelded unto thraldome. Some became Christians, from whose faith and race, even at this day (for it is an hundred yeares since) few Portugalls assure themselves; although custome, and length of time be much more forcible counsellors unto such mutations, than any other compulsion. In the Towne of *Castelnaw Darry*, more than fifty *Albigeois*, all heretikes, at one time, with a determined courage, suffred themselves to be burned alive, all in one same fire, before they would recant and disavow their opinions. *Quoties non modò ductores nostri, sed universi etiam exercitus, ad non dubiam mortem concurrerunt?* (Cic. *Tusc. Qu.* i.). *How often have, not only our Leader* (saith *Tully*) *but also our whole armies run roundly together to an undoubted death?* I have seene one of my familiar friends runne furiously on death, with such, and so deeply in his heart rooted affection, by divers visages of discourse, which I could never suppresse in him, and to the first that offered it selfe masked with a lustre of honour, without apprehending any sharpe or violent end, therein to precipitate himselfe. We have many examples in our daies, yea in very children, of such as for feare of some slight incommoditie have yeelded unto death. And to this purpose saith an ancient Writer, what shall we not feare, if we feare that, which cowardise it selfe hath chosen for her retrait? Heere to huddle up a long bead-rowle of those of all sexes, conditions, sects, in most happy ages, which either have expected death most constantly, or sought for it voluntarily, and not only sought to avoid the evils of this life, but some, only to shun the societie of living any longer: and some, for the hope of a better condition elsewhere, I should never have done. The number is so infinite, that verily it would be an easier matter for me to reckon up those that have feared the same. Only this more. *Pirro* the Philosopher, finding himselfe upon a very tempestuous day in a boat, shewed them whom he perceived to be most affrighted through feare, and encouraged them by the example of an hog, that was amongst them, and seemed to take no care at all for the storme: Shall wee then dare to say, that the advantage of reason, whereat we seeme so much to rejoyce, and for whose respect we account our selves Lords and Emperours of all other creatures, hath beene infused into us for our torment? *What availeth the knowledge of things, if through them we become more demisse?* If thereby wee lost the rest and tranquillitie wherein we should be without them? and if it makes us of worse condition than was *Pirrhos* hog? Shall we employ the intelligence, heaven hath bestowed upon us for our greatest good, to our ruine? repugning natures desseigne and the universall order and vicissitude of things, which implieth that every man should use his instruments and meanes for his owne commoditie? Wel (will some tell me) let your rule fit you against death; but what will you say of indigence and necessitie? what will you also say of minde-grieving sorrow, which *Aristippus*, *Hieronymus*, and most of the wisest have judged the last evil? and those which denied the same in words, confessed the same in effect? *Possidonius* being extremely tormented with a sharpe and painfull sicknesse, *Pompey* came to see him, and excused himselfe he had chosen so unfit an houre to heare him discourse of Philosophy: *God forbid* (answered *Possidonius*) *that ever paine should so farre usurpe upon me, as to hinder me from discoursing of so worthy a subject.* And thereupon began to speake of the contempt of paine. But there whilst she laied her part, and uncessantly pinched and urged him; gainst whom hee exclaimed: *Paine, doe what thou list, I shall never be drawne to say, that thou art an evill.* That saying, which they would make of such consequence, what doth it inferre against the contempt of paine? it contends but for the word. And if the pangs thereof move him not there-whilst, why breakes he off his discourse for it? Why thinks he to worke a great exploit, not to call it an evill? All doth not consist in imagination. Heere we judge of the rest. It is assured learning that here doth play her part, our owne senses are Judges of it.

> *Qui nisi sunt veri; ratio quoque falsa sit omnis.*
> LUCR. iv. 487.

Which senses if they be not true,
All reason's false, it must ensue.

Shall we make our skin beleeve, the stripes of a whip doe tickle it? and perswade our taste, that Aloes be wine of Graves? *Pirrhos* hog is here in our predicament. He is nothing danted at death, but if you beat him, he will grunt, crie and torment himselfe. Shall wee force the generall law of nature, which in all living creatures under heaven is seene to tremble at paine? The very trees seeme to groane at offences. Death is but felt by discourse, because it is the motion of an instant.

> *Aut fuit, aut veniet, nihil est præsentis in illa.*

Death hath come, or it will not misse;
But in nothing present is.

> *Morsque minus pœnæ, quàm mora mortis habet.*
> OVID. *Epis. Ariad.* 82.

Deaths pain 's lesse, roundly acted,
Than when death is protracted.

A thousand beasts, a thousand men, are sooner dead than threatned. Besides, what wee principally call feare in death, it is paine, her customarie fore-runner. Neverthelesse if we must give credit to an ancient father, *Malam mortem non facit, nisi quod sequitur mortem. Nothing, but what follows death, makes death to be evill.* And I might more truly say, that neither that which goeth before, nor that which commeth after, is no appurtenance of death, we falsely excuse our selves. And I find by experience, that it is rathei the impatience of the imagination of death, that makes us impatient of the paine, and that we feele it two-fold grievous, forasmuch as it threats us to die. But reason accusing our weaknesse, to feare so sudden a thing, so unavoidable, so insensible; we take this other more excusable pretence. All evils that have no other danger, but of the evill, we count them dangerlesse. The toothach, the paine of the gowt, how grievous soever, because they kill not, who reckoneth them in the number of maladies? Well, suppose that in death wee especially regard the paine: As also povertie hath nothing to be feared for, but what she casteth upon us through famine, thirst, cold, heat, and other miseries, it makes us feele and endure. So have we nothing to doe but with paine. I will willingly grant them, that it is the worst accident of our being. For, I am the man that hate and shun it as much as possible may be; because hitherto (thanks be unto God) I have no commerce or dealing with her: But it is in our power, if not to dissanull, at least to diminish the same, through patience: And though the body should be moved thereat, yet to keepe the minde and reason in good temper. And if it were not so, who then hath brought vertue, valour, force, magnanimitie, and reso-lution into credit? Where shall they play their part, if there be no more paine defied? *Avidad est periculi virtus* (SEN. *Quar. Von.* cap. iv.), *Vertue is desirous of danger.* If a man must not lie on the hard ground, armed at all assaies, to endure the heat of the scorch-ing Sunne, to feed hungrily upon a horse, or an asse, to see himselfe mangled and cut in peeces, to have a bullet pluckt out of his bones, to suffer incisions, his flesh to be stitcht up, cauterized, and searched, all incident to a martiall man; how shall we purchase the advantage and preheminence, which we so greedily seek after, over the vulgar sort? It is far from avoiding the evill and paines of it, as wise men say, that of actions equally good, one should most be wished to be done, wherein is most paine and griefe. *Non enim hilaritate nec lasci-via nec risu aut joco comite levitatis, sed sæpe etiam tristes firmitate et constantia sunt beati* (CIC. *De Fin.* ii.). *For men are not happy by mirthfulnesse, or wantonnesse, or laughing, or jesting, which is the companion of lightnesse; but often, even those that are sorrow-full, through their strong heart and constancie.* And therefore was it impossible to perswade our fathers, that conquests atchieved by maine-force, in the hazard of warre, were not more available and advantageous, than those obtained in all securitie by practices and stratagems.

Lætius est, quoties magno sibi constat honestum.

LUCA. ix. 404.

Honesty makes chiefest cheare,
When it doth cost it selfe most deare.

Moreover, this ought to comfort us, that naturally, if paine be violent, it is also short; if long, it is easie: *Si gravis, brevis; si longus, levis* (CIC. *De Fin.* ii. Epic.). *If it be grievous, it is short; if it be long, it is light.* Thou shalt not feele it over long; if thou feele it over much, it will either end it selfe, or end thee: All comes to one: If thou beare not it, it will beare thee away. *Memineris maximos morte finiri, parvos multa habere intervalla requietis; mediocrium nos esse dominos: ut si tolerabiles sint, feramus: sin minus, è vita, quum ea non placeat, tanquàm è theatro exeamus* (i.). *Remember the greatest are ended with death, the lesser have many pauses of rest; we are masters of the meane ones: so as if they be tolerable, we may beare them; if not, we may make an Exit from our life which doth not please, as from a stage.* That which makes us endure paine with such impatience, is, that we are not accustomed to take our chiefe contentment in the soule, and that we doe not sufficiently rely on her; who is the only, and soveraigne mistris of our condition. The body hath (except the least or most) but one course, and one byase. The soule is variable in all manner of formes, and rangeth to her selfe, and to her estate, whatsoever it be, the senses of the body, and all other accidents. Therefore must she be studied, enquired, and sought-after: and her powerfull springs and wards should be rowzed up. There is neither reason, nor prescription, nor force can availe against her inclination and choise. Of so infinit byases, that she hath in her disposition, let us allow her one sutable and fit to our rest and preservation: Then shall we not only be sheltered from all offence, but if it please her, also gratified and flattered of all grievances and evils. She indifferently makes profit of all; even errours and dreames, doe profitably bestead her, as a loyall matter, to bring us unto safetie and contentment. It may easily be seen, that the point of our spirit, is that which sharpneth both paine and pleasure in us. Beasts wanting the same, leave their free and naturall senses unto their bodies: and by consequence, single well-nigh in every kind, as they shew by the semblable application of their movings. If in our members we did not trouble the jurisdiction, which in that belongs unto them; it may be thought, we should be the better for it, and that nature hath given them a just and moderate temperature toward pleasure and toward paine. And it cannot chuse but be good and just, being equall and common. But since we have freed and alienated our selves from her rules, to abandon our selves unto the vagabond libertie of our fantasies: let us at least help to bend them to the most agreeing side. *Plato* feareth our sharp engaging unto paine and voluptuousnesse, forsomuch as he overstrictly tieth and bindeth the soule unto the body: I am rather opposit unto him, because it is sundred and loosed from it. Even as an enemie becommeth more furious when we flie from him, so doth paine grow more proud if it see us tremble under it. It will stoope and yeeld upon better compositions to him that shall make head against it. A man must oppose and bandy against it. In recoyling and giving ground, we call and draw on, the ruine threatning us. Even as the body is more steady and strong to a charge, if it stand stiffely to it, so is the soule. But let us come to examples properly belonging unto weakbackt men, as I am, where we shall find, that it is with paine, as with stones, which take either a higher or deeper colour, according to the foyle that is laid under them, and holdeth no other place in us than we give it. *Tantum doluerunt, quantum doloribus se inseruerunt* (AUGUST.). *So much they grieved, as they interessed themselves in griefes.* We feele a dash of a chirurgions razor more than ten blows with a sword in the heat of fight. The painfull throwes of childbearing, deemed both by Physitians, and by the word of God to be verie great, and which our women passe with so many ceremonies, there are whole Nations that make no reckoning of them. I omit to speake of the *Lacedemonian* women; but come we to the *Swizzers* of our Infanterie, what change doe you perceive in them? But that trudging and trotting after their husbands, to day you see them carrie the child about their necke, which but yesterday they bare in their wombe. And those counterfeit roguing Gyptians, whereof so many are daily seene amongst us, doe they not wash their children so soone as they are borne? and in the next River that comes to hand? Besides so many harlots, which daily steale their children in the delivery as in the conception. The beauteous and noble Lady of *Sabinus,* a Roman Patritian, for the interest of others, did alone, without any bodies helpe or assistance, and without noise or groning endure the bearing and deliverie of two twins. A simple lad of *Lacedemon,* having stolne a Fox (for they more feared the shame of their foolishnesse in stealing, than we feare the paine or punishment of mis-deeds) and hiding the same under his cloake, endured rather to have his guts gnawne out by her, than to discover himselfe. Another who offering incense at a sacrifice, suffered his flesh to burne to the bone by a coale falne into his sleeve, rather than he would trouble that sacred mysterie. And a great number have beene seene, for the only essay of vertue, following their institution, that at the age of seven yeares, without so much as changing their countenance, have indured to be whipped to death. And *Cicero* hath seene whole troops, to beat one another so long with their fists, with their feet, and with their teeth, till they have fainted and fallen downe halfe dead, before ever they would confesse to be overcome. *Nunquam naturam mos vinceret, est enim ea semper invicta, sed nos umbris, delitiis, otio, languore, desidia, animum infecimus: opinionibus maloque more delinitum mollivimus* (CIC. *Tusc. Quest.* v.). *Custome should never overcome nature, for she is still invincible: but we have infected our minde with shadowes, daintinesse, idlenesse, faint-heartednesse, slothfulnesse, and have effeminated it, inveagled with opinions and evill custome.* Every man knows the story of *Scevola,* who being entred the enemies campe, with a full resolution to kill their Chieftaine, and having missed of his purpose, to checke his effect with a stranger invention, and to cleare his country, confessed unto *Prosenna*, (who was the King he intended to kill) not only his dessigne, but added moreover, that in his campe there were a great many Romanes, who had undertaken and sworne the verie same enterprise, and were confederates with him. And to make shew of his dread-lesse magnanimitie, having caused a pan of burning coales to be brought, he saw and suffred his right arme (in penance that it had not effected his project) to be parched and wel-nigh rosted-off: untill such time as his enemie himselfe, feeling a kind of remorce-full horror, commanded the fire to be caried away. What shall we say of him, that would not vouchsafe to leave, or so much as to interrupt the reading of his booke, whil'st he had an incision made into him? And of him who resolved to skoffe and laugh, even in spight and contempt of the tortures which were inflicted upon him, so that the raging crueltie of the hangmen, that held him, and all the inventions of torments that could be devised, being redoubled upon him, one in the necke of another, gave him over? But he was a Philosopher. What? of one of *Cæsars* gladiators, who with a cheerefull and smiling countenance endured his wounds to be slit and sounded? *Quis mediocris gladiator ingemuit? Quis vultum mutavit unquam? Quis non modò stetit, verùm etiam decubuit turpiter? Quis cùm decubuisset, ferrum recipere jussus, collum contraxit?* (Cic. *Tusc. Quest.* ii.). *What meane Fencer hath once groned? Which of them hath once changed his countenance? Which of them not only hath stood up, but even falne with shame? Which of them when he was downe, and was willed to take his death, did once shrinke in his necke?* But let us joyne some women unto them. Who hath not heard of her at *Paris*, which only to get a fresher hew of a new skin, endured to have her face flead all over? There are some, who being sound, and in perfit health, have had some teeth puld-out, thereby to frame a daintier and more pleasing voyce, or to set them in better order. How many examples of contempt of paine or smart have we of that kind and sex? What can they not doe? What will they not doe? What feare they to doe? So they may but hope for some amendment of their beautie?

> *Vellere queis cura est albos à stirpe capillos,*
> *Et faciem dempta pelle referre novam.*
>
> TIBUL. i. *El.* viii. 43.

Who take great care to root out their gray haire.
And skin flead-off a new face to repaire.

I have seene some swallow gravell, ashes, coales, dust, tallow, candles, and for the-nonce, labour and toyle themselves to spoile their stomacke, only to get a pale-bleake colour. To become slender in wast, and to have a straight spagnolized body, what pinching, what girding, what cingling will they not indure; Yea sometimes with yron-plates, with whale-bones, and other such trash, that their very skin, and quicke flesh is eaten in and consumed to the bones; Whereby they sometimes worke their owne death. It is common to divers nations of our times, to hurt and gash themselves in good earnest, to give credit to their words. And our King reporteth sundrie examples, of what himselfe saw in *Polonia*, and towards himselfe. But besides what I know to have by some beene imitated in *France;* when I came from the famous Parliament of *Blois;* I had a little before seene a wench in *Picardie* to witnes the vehemencie of her promises, and also her constancie, with the bodkin she wore in her haire, to give her selfe foure or five thrusts in her arme, which made her skin to crack and gush out bloud. The *Turkes* are wont to wound and scarre themselves for their Ladies sakes, and that the marke may the better appeare, and continue the longer, they will presently lay fire upon the cuttes; and to stanch the bloud, and better to forme the cicatrice, they wil keepe it on, an incredible while. Honest men that have seene it, have written the same, and sworne it unto me. And for ten Aspers you shall daily finde some amongst them, that will give themselves a deepe gash with a Scimitarie, either in their armes or thighes. I am very glad witnesses are so ready at hand, where we have most need of them: For, Christendome affordeth many. and after the example of our holy guide, there have beene divers, who for devotion would needs beare the crosse. We learne by a worthy testimonie of religion, that Saint *Lewes* the King wore a haire-shirt, untill such time as he was so aged, that his confessor gave him a dispensation for it; and that every friday he caused his priests to beat his shoulders with five little yron-chaines, which to that purpose were ever caried with his nightgeare. *William* our last Duke of *Guienne,* father to that *Eleanore,* who transferred that Dutchy unto the houses of *France* and *England,* the last ten or twelve yeares of his life, for penance-sake wore continually a corselet, under a religious habit. *Foulkes* Earle of Anjou went to Jerusalem, there with a rope about his necke, to be whipped by two of his servants, before our Saviours sepulchre. Doe we not upon every good-friday, in sundrie places, see a great number of men and women, scourge and beat themselves so long, till they bruse and teare their flesh, even to the bones? I have often seene it my selfe, and that without enchantment; And some say (for they are masked) there were some amongst them, who for monie would undertake thereby to warrant other mens religion, by a contempt of smart-full paine, so much the greater, by how much the stings of devotion are of more force, than those of covetousnes. *Q. Maximus* buried his son who had beene Consull: *Marcus Cato* his, being elected Pretor; and *L. Paulus* both his, within few daies, with so cheerefull and setled a countenance, and without any shew of sorrow. I have sometimes by way of jesting told one, that he had confronted divine justice: For, the violent death of three tall children of his, comming unto his eares all upon one day, and sent him, as it may be imagined, as a great scourge: he was so farre from mourning, that he rather tooke it as a favour and singular gratification at Gods hand. I doe not follow these monstrous humors. Yet have I lost two or three my selfe, whilst they were young and at nurce, if not without apprehension of sorrow; yet without continuance of griefe. And *there is no accident woundeth men deeper, or goeth so neere the heart, as the losse of children.* I see divers other common occasions of affliction, which were I assailed by them, I should scarcely feele. And I have contemned and neglected some, when it hath pleased God to visit me with them, on which the world setteth so ugly and balefull a countenance, that I hardly dare boast of them without blushing. *Ex quo intelligitur, non in natura, sed in opinione esse ægretudinem* (Cic. *ib.* iii.). *Whereby it is understood, that griefe consisteth not in nature, but opinion.* Opinion is a power-full, bould, and unmeasurable party. Who doth ever so greedily search after rest-full ease and quietnes, as *Alexander* and *Cæsar* have done after difficulties and unquietnesse? *Terez*, the father of *Sitalcez*, was wont to say, *that when he had no warres, hee thought there was no difference betweene him and his horse-keeper.* *Cato* the Consull, to assure himselfe of certaine townes in *Spaine*, having only interdicted some of their inhabitants to weare armes, many of them killed themselves: *Ferox gens nullam vitam rati sine armis esse. A fierce kinde of people, that thought there was no life without armes.* How many know wee who have abandoned and forsaken the pleasure of an ease-full and quiet life in their houses, and to live with their friends and acquaintance; to follow the toyling-horror of unfrequented deserts, and that yeelded and cast themselves unto the abjectnesse, contempt and vilifying of the world, wherwith they have so pleased themselves, as nothing more; Cardinall *Boromeus,* who died lately at *Milane,* in the midst of the pleasures and debawches to which his Nobilitie, and the great riches he possessed, enticed him, and the ayre of *Italie* afforded him, and his youth allured him, did ever keep himselfe in so an austere forme of life, that the same gowne which served him in Summer he wore in winter. He never lay but upon straw; the houres which he might conveniently spare from his charge; he bestowed in continual study, ever kneeling, and having a smal quantitie of bread and water by his bookes side, which was all the provision for his repast, and time he employed in study. I know some who wittingly have drawne both profit and preferment from cuckoldrie, the only name whereof is so yrkesome and bail-ful to so many men. If sight be not the most necessarie of our senses, at least is it the most pleasing: the most plausible and profitable of our members, seeme those that serve to beget us: notwithstanding divers have mortally hated them, only because they were over much amiable, and for their worths-sake have rejected them. So thought he of his eies, that voluntarily put them out. The most common and soundest part of men, holdeth multitude of children to be a signe of great happinesse and comfort; So do I, and many others, the want of them. And when *Thales* was demanded *Wherfore he did not marrie*, he answered, *because he would leave no issue or line of himselfe behinde him*. That our opinion endeareth and increaseth the price of things, it is seene in a great number of them, which we do not regard to esteeme them; but for our use. And we neither consider their qualities nor utilities, but only our cost to recover and attaine them; as if it were a part of their substance; and we call that worth in them, not what they bring us, but what we bring to them. According as it weigheth, and is of consequence, so it serveth. Wherupon I perceive, we are thriftie husbands of what we lay out. Our opinion never suffers it to run a false gallop. *The price giveth a Diamond his title, difficultie to vertue, paine unto devotion, and sharpnesse unto Physicke.* Such a one to come unto povertie, cast those fewe crownes he had into the same sea, wherin so many others, with such carke, danger, and care, on all parts seeke to fish for riches. *Epicurus* saith, *that to be rich is no ease, but a charge of affaires*. Verily, it is not want, but rather plentie that causeth avarice. I will speake of mine owne experience, concerning this subject. I have lived in three kinds of condition, since I came out of my infancie. The first time, which continued well-nigh twentie yeares, I have past it over, as one who had no other means but casual, and depending from the direction and helpe of others; without any certaine maintenance, or regular prescription. My expences were so much the more carelessely layed out, and lavishly employed, by how much more they wholy depended on fortunes rashnesse and exhibition. I never lived so well at ease: my fortune was never to finde my friends purse shut: besides which, I was to frame my selfe to all necessities: the care I tooke to pay every man at his prefixed day, which a thousand times they have prolonged, seeing the care I tooke to satisfie them. So that I had gotten unto myselfe the credit of a thriftie kind of good husbandrie, though it were something shifting and deceitful. I do naturally feele a kind of pleasing contentment in paying of my debts, as if I rid my selfe of a burthenous weight, and free my selfe from the yoake of bondage and ingratitude. Besides, me thinks I feele a kinde of delight, that tickleth me to the quick, in performing a lawfully just action, and contenting of others. I except payments that require delayes, covenants, and after reckonings: for, if I finde any body that will undertake them, I blushingly and injuriously deferre them as long as I can, for feare of that altercation or wrangling, to which my humor and manner of speech is altogether incompatible. There is nothing I hate more than driving of bargaines: It is a meere commerce of dodging and impudencie. After an houres debating and paltring, both parties will goe from their words and oaths for the getting or saving of a shilling: yet did I borrow with great disadvantage. For, having no heart to borrow before others, or by word of mouth, I would adventure it upon a peece of paper, which with some hath no great power to move or force to perswade, and which greatly helps to refuse, I was wont to commit the successe of my wants more freely and more carelessely unto fortune, that I have done since unto my wit and providence. Most good husbands thinke it strange and horrible to live on such uncertainties, but they remember not, that most men in the world live so. How many good and well-borne men have heretofore, and are daily seene to neglect and leave at six and seven, their patrimonies and certaine goods, to follow and seeke after court-holy water, and wavering-favours of Princes and of fortune; *Cæsar* engaged and endebted himselfe above a million of gold, more than he was worth, to become *Cæsar*. And how many merchants and poore beginners, set up and begin their traffike by the sale of their farmes or cottages which they venter to the *Indias*?

Tot per impotentia freta.—CATUL. *Epig.* iv. 18.

In so great scarcitie of devotion, we have thousands of Colleges, which passe the time very conveniently, daily gaping and expecting from the liberalitie of the heavens, what they must dine withall to morrow. Secondly; they consider not, that this certaintie on which they ground themselves, is not much lesse uncertaine and hazardous, than hazard it selfe. I see miserie as neere beyond two thousand crownes rent, as if it were hard at hand. For, besides that fortune hath many-many meanes to open a hundred gaps for povertie to enter at, even through the thickest of our riches, and that often there is no meane betweene the highest and lowest fortune.

Fortuna vitrea est: tum, quum splendet, frangitur.
PROV. SENEC. f.

Fortune is glasse-like, brittle as t'is bright:
Light-gon, Light-broken, when it lends best light.

And to turne all our defences, and raisings of high walles topsie-turvie: I find that want and necessitie is by diverse or different causes, as ordinarily seene to accompanie and follow those that are rich in goods, as those that have none at all: and that peradventure it is somewhat lesse incommodious, when it is alone, than when it meeteth with riches: They rather come from order, than from receit: *Feber est suæ quisque fortunæ* (ERAS. *Chil.* ii. cent. iv. eid. 63). *Every man is the forger of his owne fortune.* And me thinkes that a rich man, who is needy, full of businesse, carke and toyle, and troubled in minde, is more miserable, than he that is simply poore. *In divitiis inopes, quod genus egestatis gravissimum est* (SEN. *Epist.* lxxiv. p.). *In their abundance indigent, which is the most grievous kinde of indigence.* The richest and greatest princes are ordinarily urged by povertie and need unto extreme necessities. For, can any be more extreme, than thereby to become Tyrants, and unjust usurpers of their subjects goods, My second manner of life hath beene to have monie; which when I had once fingred, according to my condition I sought to hoord up some against a rainie day; esteeming that it was no having, unlesse a man had ever somewhat besides his ordinarie expences in possession: and that a man should not trust that good, which he must live in hope to receive; and that, be his hope never so likely, hee may many wayes be prevented. For, I would say unto my selfe; what if I should be surprised by this chance, or that accident? What should I doe then? And in pursuit of these vaine and vicious imaginations, I endevoured by hooke or crooke, and by wile or wit to provide by this superfluous sparing for all inconveniences that might happen: And I could answer him, that would alleage the number of inconveniences to be over infinit; which if they followed not all men, they accompanied some, and haply the greatest number. An apprehension which I did not passe without some painfull care. I kept the matter secret, and I (that dare say so much of my selfe) would never speake of my money but falsly; as others doe, who being rich, would seeme to be poore, or being poore would appeare rich: and dispence with their conscience, never to witnesse sincerely what they are worth. Oh ridiculous and shamefull prudence. Did I travell any where? me thought I was never sufficiently provided; and the more I had laden my selfe with coine, the more I had also burthened my selfe with feare: sometimes of my wayes-safetie, othertimes of their trust that had the charge of my sumpters and baggage, whereof as some others that I know, me thought I was never throughly assured, except it were still in my sight. Left I my keyes or my purse behind me? how many suspitions and thornie imaginations, and which is worse, incommunicable, did uncessantly haunt me? My minde was ever on my halfepenney; my thoughts ever that way. *The summe being right cast, there is ever more paine in keeping, than in getting of monie.* If I did not altogether so much as I say, I at the least endevoured to doe it. Of commoditie I had little or nothing. To have more meanes of expences, is ever to have increase of sorrow. For (as said *Bion*) *The hairie man doth grieve as much as the bald, if he have his haire pulled out.* And after you are once accustomed, and have fixed your thoughts upon a heape of monie, it is no longer at your service; you dare not diminish it; it is a building, which if you touch or take any part from it, you will thinke it will all fall. Necessitie must first pinch you by the throat, and touch you neere, before you will lay hands on it. And I should sooner pawne my clothes, or sell my horse, with lesse care and compulsion, than make a breach into that beloved purse, which I kept in store. But the danger was, that a man can hardly prefix any certaine limits unto his desire (they are hard to be found in things a man deemeth good) and continue at one stay in sparing: A man shall ever encrease this heape, and augment it from one number to another; yea so long, till he basely and niggardly deprive himselfe of the enjoying of his owne goods, and wholy fix it on the safe-keeping of them, and never use them. According to this kind of usage, those are the richest people of the world, that have the charge of keeping the gates and walles of a rich Citie. Every monied man is covetous, according to mine opinion. *Plato* marshalleth [thus] humane or corporall goods; *health, beautie, strength, riches: And riches,* (saith he), *are not blind, but cleere-seeing, if they be illuminated by wisdome.* Dionysius the younger, plaid a notable part; who being advertised, that one of his *Siracusans,* had hidden a certain treasure, under the ground, commanded him to bring it unto him, which he did, reserving secretly one part of it unto himselfe, with which hee removed his dwelling into another Citie, where having lost the humor of hoarding up of treasure, began to live a spending and riotous kinde of life: which *Dionysius* hearing, commanded the remainder of his treasure, and which he had taken from him, to be restored unto him; saying, *That sithence he had learned how to make use of it, hee did most willingly redeliver the same unto him.* I was some yeares of the same humour: I wot not what good *Demon* did most profitably remove me from it, like to the *Siracusan,* and made me to neglect my sparing. The pleasure I apprehended of a farre and chargeable journey, having overthrowne this foolish imagination in me; From which I am falne into a third kinde of life (I speake what I thinke of it) assuredly much more pleasing and formall: which is, that I measure my garment according to my cloth, and let my expences goe together with my comming in; sometimes the one, other-whilst the other exceeds: But they are never farre a sunder. I live from hand to mouth, from day to day, and have I but to supply my present and ordinarie needs, I am satisfied: As for extraordinarie wants, all the provisions of the world will not suffice them. And it is folly to expect that fortune will ever sufficiently arme us against her selfe. It is with our owne weapons that we must combat her. Casuall armes will betray us, when we shall have most need of them. If I lay up anything, it is for the hope of some imployment at hand, and not to purchase lands, whereof I have no need, but pleasure and delight. *Non esse cupidam, pecunia est: non esse emacem, vectigal est* (Cic. *Parad. ult.*). *It is current coine, not to be covetous: it is a thriftie income, not to be still buying.* I am neither possessed with feare, that my goods shall faile me, nor with desire they should encrease and multiply. *Divitiarum fructus est in copia: Copiam declarat satietas* (*Ibid.*). *The fruit of riches is in plentie: sacietie content with enough, approves that plentie.* And I singularly gratifie my selfe this correction came upon me in an age naturally enclined to covetousnesse, and that I am free from that folly so common and peculiar to old men, and the most ridiculous of all humane follies. *Feraulez* who had passed through both fortunes, and found, that encrease of goods, was no accrease of appetite, to drinke, to eat, to sleepe, or to embrace his wife; and who on the other side felt heavily on his shoulders, the importunitie of ordering and directing his Oeconomicall affaires, as it doth on mine, determine with himselfe to content a poore young man, his faithfull friend, greedily gaping after riches, and frankly made him a present donation of all his great and excessive riches; as also of those, he was likely everie day to get by the liberalitie and bountie of his good master *Cyrus*, and by warre: always provided, hee should undertake to entertaine and finde him honestly, and in good sort, as his guest and friend. In which estate they lived afterward most happily, and mutually content with the change of their condition.

Loe heare a part, I could willingly find in my heart to imitate. And I much commend the fortune of an old prelate, whom I see, to have so clearely given over his purse, his receits, and his expences, now to one of his chosen servants, and now to another, that he hath lived many yeares as ignorant of his houshold affaires, as any stranger. The confidence in others honesty, is no light testimonie of ones owne integritie: therefore doth God willingly favour it. And for his regard, I see no houshold order, neither more worthily directed, nor more constantly managed than his. Happy is that man, that hath so proportionably directed his estate, as his riches may discharge and supply the same, without care or encombrance to himselfe; and that neither their consultation or meetings may in any sort interrupt other affaires, or disturbe other occupations, which he followeth, more convenient, more quiet, and better agreeing with his heart. Therefore doth ease and indigencie depend from every mans owne opinion; and wealth and riches no more than glorie or health, have either more preheminence or pleasure, than he who possesseth them, lendeth them. Every man is either well or ill, according as he findes himselfe. Not he whom another thinkes content, but he is content indeed, that thinkes he is so himselfe: And only in that, opinion giveth it selfe essence and veritie. Fortune doth us neither good nor ill: She only offereth us the seed and matter of it, which our minde, more powerfull than she, turneth and applieth as best it pleaseth: as the efficient cause and mistris of condition, whether happy or unhappy. Externall accessions take both savour and colour from the internall constitution: As garments doe not warme us by their heat, but by ours, which they are fit to cover and nourish: he that with clothes should cover a cold body, should draw the very same service from them by cold. So is snow and yce kept in summer. Verily as unto an idle and lazie body, study is but a torment; abstinence from wine to a drunkard, is a vexation; frugalitie is a harts sorrow to the luxurious; and exercise molesteth an effeminate body: so is it of all things else. Things are not of themselves so irksome, nor so hard, but our basenes, and weaknesse maketh them such. To judge of high and great matters, a high and great minde is required; otherwise we attribute that vice unto them, which indeed is ours. A straight oare being under water seemeth to be crooked. It is no matter to see a thing, but the matter is how a man doth see the same. Well, of so many discourses, which diversly perswade men to contemne death, and patiently to endure paine, why shall we not finde some one to make for our purpose; And of so severall and many kinds of imagina-

tions, that have perswaded the same unto others why doth not every
man apply one unto himselfe, that is most agreeing with his humor;
If he cannot digest a strong and abstersive drug, for to remove his
evil, let him at least take a lenitive pill to ease the same. *Opinio est
quædam effœminata ac levis: nec in dolore magis, quam eadem in
voluptate: quâ, quum liquescimus fluimusque mollitia, apis aculem
sine clamore ferre non possumus. Totum in eo est, ut tibi imperes*
(Cɪc. *Tusc. Quest. ii.*). *There is a certaine effeminate and light opinion,
and that no more in sorrow, than it is in pleasure, whereby when we
melt and run over in daintie tendernes, we cannot abide to be stung
of a Bee, but most rore and crie out. This is the totall summe of all,
that you be master of your selfe.* Moreover, a man doth not escape
from Philosophy, by making the sharpnes of paines, and humane
weaknesse to prevaile so far beyond measur: for, she is compelled to
cast her selfe over againe unto these invincible replications, If it be
bad to live in necessitie, at least there is no necessitie, to live in
necessitie. No man is long time ill, but by his owne fault. He that
hath not the heart to endure neither life nor death, and that will
neither resist nor run away, what shall a man doe to him?

CHAPTER XLI

THAT A MAN SHOULD NOT COMMUNICATE HIS GLORIE

Oғ all the follies of the world, the most universall, and of most
men received, is the care of reputation, and studie of glorie, to which
we are so wedded, that we neglect, and cast-off riches, friends, repose,
life and health (goods effectuall and substantiall) to follow that vaine
image, and idlie-simple voice, which hath neither body, nor hold-
fast.

> *La fama, ch'inuaghisce à un dolce suono
> Gli superbi mortali, et par si bella,
> E un echo, un sogno, anzi d'un sogno un ombra,
> Ch'ad ogni vento dilegua e sgombra.*—Tᴀss. *Gior. can.* 14.

Fame that enveagl's high aspiring men
With her harmonious sound, and seemes so faire,
An Eccho is, a dreame, dreames shadow rather,
Which flies and fleets as any winde doth gather.

And of mens unreasonable humors, it seemeth, that the best
philosophers doe most slowly, and more unwillingly cleare themselves
of this, than of another: it is the most peevish, the most forward, and
the most opinative. *Quia etiam bene proficientes animos tentare non
cessat* (Cɪc. *Pro Arc. Po.*). *Because it ceaseth not to tempt even
those Mindes that profit best.* There are not many whereof reason

doth so evidently condemne vanitie, but it is so deeply rooted in us, as I wot not whether any man could ever clearely discharge himselfe of it. When you have alleaged all the reasons you can, and beleeved all to disavow and reject her, she produceth contrarie to your discourses, so intestine inclination, that you have small hold against her. For (as *Cicero* saith,) *Even those that oppugne her, will neverthelesse have the bookes they write against her, to beare their names upon the fronts, endeavoring to make themselves glorious by despising of glorie.* All other things fall within the compasse of commerce: we lend our goods, we employ our lives, if our friends stand in need of us: But seldome shall we see a man communicate his honour, share his reputation, and impart his glorie unto others. *Catulus Luctatius* in the warres against the Cymbres, having done the utmost of his endevours to stay his souldiers that fled before their enemies, put himselfe amongst the run-awaies, and dissembled to bee a coward, that so they might rather seeme to follow their Captaine, than flie from the enemie: This was a neglecting and leaving off his reputation, to conceale the shame and reproach of other. When *Charles* the fifth passed into *Provence,* the yeare a thousand five hundred thirtie seven, some are of opinion, that *Anthony de Leva,* seeing the Emperor his master resolutely obstinate to undertake that voyage, and deeming it wonderfully glorious, maintained neverthelesse the contrarie, and discounselled him from it, to the end all the honour and glorie of this counsell might be attributed unto his Master; and that it might be said, his good advice and fore-sight to have beene such, that contrarie to all mens opinions, he had atchieved so glorious an enterprise: Which was, to honour and magnifie him at his owne charges. The Thracian Ambassadors comforting *Achileonida* the Mother of *Brasidas,* for the death of her son, and highly extolling and commending him, said, he had not left his equall behind him. She refused this private commendation, and particular praise, assigning it to the publike state. *Doe not tell me that* (quoth she,) *For I knowe the Cittie of* Sparta *hath many greater, and more valiant Citizens than he was.* At the battell of *Crecy, Edward,* the blacke Prince of *Wales,* being yet very young, had the leading of the vant-gard: The greatest and chiefe violence of the fight, was in his quarter: The Lords and Captaines that accompanied him, perceiving the great danger, sent unto King *Edward* the Princes father, to come and help them: which when he heard, he enquired what plight his sonne was in, and how he did, and hearing that he was living, and on horse-backe; *I should* (quoth he) *offer him great wrong to goe now, and deprive him of the honour of this combats victorie, which he already hath so long sustained; what danger soever there be in it, it shall wholy be his:* and would neither goe nor send unto him: knowing, that if he had gone, or sent, it would have beene said, that without his ayd all had beene lost, and that the advantage of this exploit would have been ascribed unto him. *Semper enim quod post-*

*remum adjectum est, id rem totam videtur traxisse. For, evermore
that which was last added, seemes to have drawne on the whole matter.*
In *Rome* many thought, and it was commonly spoken, that the chiefest glorious deeds of *Scipio*, were partly due unto *Lælius*, who notwithstanding did ever advance the greatnesse, further the glorie, and
second the renowne of *Scipio*, without any respect of his owne. And
Theopompus King of *Sparta*, to one who told him that the common-
wealth should subsist and continue still, forsomuch as he could command so well: *No*, said he, *it is rather, because the people know so
well how to obey.* As the women that succeeded in the Peeredomes of
France, had (notwithstanding their sex) right to assist, and privilege
to plead in cases appertaining to the jurisdiction of Peeres: So the
Ecclesiasticall Peeres, notwithstanding their profession and function,
were bound to assist our Kings in their warres, not only with their
friends, servants, and tenants, but in their owne person. The Bishop of
Beauvais, being with *Philip Augustus* in the battell of *Bovines*, did
very couragiously take part with him in the effect; but thought hee
should not be partaker of the fruit and glorie of that bloudy and
violent exercise. He overcame, and forced that day many of the enemies to yeeld whom he delivered unto the first gentleman hee met
withall, to rifle, to take them prisoners, or at their pleasure to dispose
of them. Which he also did with *William* Earle of *Salisbury*, whom he
delivered unto the Lord *John* of *Nesle*. With a semblable subtletie of
conscience, unto this other. He desired to fell and strike downe a man,
but not to wound or hurt him: and therefore never fought but with
a great club. A man in my time being accused to the King, to have
laid violent hands upon a Priest, denied it very stoutly, forsomuch as
he had only thumped and trampled him with his feet.

CHAPTER XLII

OF THE INEQUALITIE THAT IS BETWEENE US

PLUTARKE saith in some place, *That he findes no such great difference
betweene beast and beast, as he findeth diversitie betweene man and
man.* He speaketh of the sufficiencie of the minde, and of internall
qualities. Verily I finde *Epaminondas* so farre (taking him as I suppose
him) from some that I know (I meane capable of common sense) as
I could finde in my heart to endeare upon *Plutarke;* and say there is
more difference betweene such and such a man, than there is diversitie betweene such a man, and such a beast.

> *Hem vir viro quid præstat!*—TER. *Phor.* act. v. sc. 3.

> O Sir, how much hath one,
> Another man out-gone?

And that there be so many degrees of spirits, as there are steps betweene heaven and earth, and as innumerable. But concerning the estimation of men, it is marvell, that except our selves, no one thing is esteemed but for its proper qualities. We commend a horse, because he is strong and nimble.

> —*volucrem*
> *Sic laudamus equum, facili cui plurima palma*
> *Fervet, et exultat rauco victoria circo.*—JUVEN. *Sat.* viii. **57.**

We praise the horse, that beares most bells with flying,
And triumphs most in races, hoarse with crying,

and not for his furniture: a grey-hound for his swiftnesse, not for his coller: a hawke for her wing, not for her cranes or bells. Why do we not likewise esteeme a man for that which is his owne? He hath a goodly traine of men following him, a stately pallace to dwell in, so great credit amongst men; and so much rent comming in: Alas, all that is about him, and not in him. No man will buy a pig in a poke. If you cheapen a horse, you will take his saddle and clothes from him, you will see him bare and abroad: or if he be covered as in old times they wont to present them unto Princes to be sold, it is only his least necessarie parts, lest you should ammuse your selfe to consider his colour, or breadth of his crupper; but chiefly to view his legs, his head, his eyes, and his foot, which are the most remarkable parts, and above all to be considered and required in him,

> *Regibus hic mos est, ubi equos mercantur, apertos*
> *Inspiciunt, ne si facies, ut sæpe, decora*
> *Molli fulta pede est, emptorem inducat hiantem,*
> *Quod pulchræ clunes, breve quod caput, ardua cervix.*
> HOR. i. *Sat.* ii. 86.

This is Kings manner, when they horses buy,
They see them bare, lest if, as oft we try,
Faire faces have soft hoofes, gull'd the buyer be,
They buttockes round, short head, high crest may see.

When you will esteeme a man, why should you survey him all wrapt, and envelloped? He then but sheweth us those parts which are no whit his owne: and hideth those from us, by which alone his worth is to be judged. It is the goodnesse of the sword you seeke after, and not the worth of the scabbard; for which peradventure you would not give a farthing, if it want his lyning. A man should be judged by himselfe, and not by his complements. And as an Ancient saith very pleasantly: Doe you know wherefore you esteeme him tall? You account the height of his pattens: The Base is no part of his stature: Measure him without his stilts. Let him lay aside his riches and externall honours, and shew himselfe in his shirt. Hath he a body proper to his functions, sound and cheerefull? What minde hath he? Is it faire, capable and unpolluted, and happily provided with all her necessarie parts? Is shee rich of her owne, or of others goods? Hath fortune nothing of hers to survay therein? If broad-waking she wil looke upon a naked sword: If shee care not which way her life goeth from her, whether by the mouth, or by the throat; whether it be setled, equable, and contented: It is that a man must see and consider, and thereby judge the extreme differences that are between us: Is he

> *—sapiens, sibique imperiosus,*
> *Quem neque pauperies, neque mors, neque vincula terrent,*
> *Responsare cupidinibus, contemnere honores*
> *Fortis, et in se ipso totus teres atque rotundus,*
> *Externi ne quid valeat per læve morari,*
> *In quem manca ruit semper fortuna?*—ii. *Sat.* vii. 83.

A wise man, of himselfe commander high,
Whom want, nor death, nor bands can terrifie,
Resol'd t' affront desires, honors to scorne,
All in himselfe, close, round, and neatly-borne,
As nothing outward on his smooth can stay,
Gainst whom still fortune makes a lame assay.

Such a man is five hundred degrees beyond kingdomes and principalities: Himselfe is a kingdome unto himselfe.

> *Sapiens pol ipse fingit fortunam sibi.*—PLAU. *Trin.* act ii. sc. 2.

Trust me, who beares a wise mans name,
His fortune to himselfe may frame.

What is there else for him to wish for?

> *—nònne videmus*
> *Nil aliud sibi naturam latrare, nisi ut quoi*
> *Corpore sejunctus dolor absit, mente fruatur,*
> *Jucundo sensu cura semotus metuque?*—LUCR. ii. 16.

See we not nature nothing else doth barke
Unto her-selfe, but he, whose bodies barke
Is free from paines-touch, should his minde enjoy,
Remo'd from care and feare, with sense of joy?

Compare the vulgar troupes of our men unto him, stupide, base, servile, wavering, and continually floting on the tempestuous Ocean of divers passions, which tosse and retosse the same, wholy depending of others: There is more difference, than is betweene heaven and earth, and yet such is the blindnesse of our custome, that we make little or no account of it. Whereas, if we consider a Cottager and a King, a noble and a handy-crafts man, a magistrate and a private man, a rich man and a poore; an extreme disparitie doth immediately present it selfe

unto our eies, which, as a man may say, differ in nothing, but in their
clothes. In *Thrace,* the King was after a pleasant manner distinguished
from his people, and which was much endeared: He had a religion
apart: a God severall unto himselfe, whom his subjects might no waies
adore: It was *Mercurie:* And he disdained their gods, which were
Mars, Bacchus, and *Diana;* yet are they but pictures, which make no
essential dissemblance. For, as enterlude-plaiers, you shal now see
them on the stage, play a King, an Emperor, or a Duke, but they are
no sooner off the stage, but they are base rascals, vagabond abjects,
and porterly hirelings, which is their naturall and originall condition: Even so the Emperor, whose glorious pomp doth so dazle you
in publike;

> *Scilicet et grandes viridi cum luce smaragdi*
> *Auro includuntur, teriturque Thalassina vestis*
> *Assidue, et Veneris sudorem exercita potat.*—LUCR. iv. 1137.

Great emerald's with their grasse-greene-light in gold
Are clos'd, nor long can marriage linnen hold,
But worne with use and heat
    of Venerie drink's the sweat.

View him behinde the curtaine, and you see but an ordinarie man,
and peradventure more vile, and more seely, than the least of his subjects. *Ille beatus introrsum est; istius bracteata fœlicitas est* (SEN.
Epist. cxv.). *One is inwardly happy; anothers felicitie is plated and
guilt-over.* Cowardise, irresolution, ambition, spight, anger, and envie,
move and worke in him as in another:

> *Non enim gazæ, neque consularis*
> *Summovet lictor, miseros tumultus*
> *Mentis et curas laqueata circum*
>   *—Tecta [volantes]:*—HOR. ii. *Od.* xvi. 9.

Nor treasures, nor Maires officers remove
The miserable tumults of the minde,
Or cares that lie about, or flie above
Their high-roof't houses with huge beames combinde,

And feare, and care, and suspect, haunt and follow him, even in the
middest of his armed troupes.

> *Re veraque metus hominum, curæque sequaces,*
> *Nec metuunt sonitus armorum, nec fera tela,*
> *Audacterque inter reges, rerumque potentes*
> *Versantur, neque fulgorem reverentur ab auro.*—LUCR. ii. 46.

Indeed mens still-attending cares and feare,
Nor armor's clashing, nor fierce weapons feare,
With Kings converse they boldly, and Kings peeres,
Fearing no lightning that from gold appeares.

Doth the ague, the megrim, or the gout spare him more than us?
When age shall once seize on his shoulders, can then the tall yemen
of his guard discharge him of it? When the terror of ruthles-balefull
death shall assaile him, can he be comforted by the assistance of the
gentlemen of his chamber? If he chance to be jealous or capricious, will
our lowting-curtzies, or putting-off of hats, bring him in tune againe?
His bedstead enchased all with gold and pearles hath no vertue to
allay the pinching pangues of the cholicke.

> *Nec calidæ citius decedunt corpore febres,*
> *Textilibus si in picturis ostroque rubenti*
> *Jacteris, quàm si plebeia in veste cubandum est.*—ID. *ib.* 34.

Feavers no sooner from thy body flie
If thou on arras or red scarlet lie
Tossing, than if thou rest
On coverlets home-drest.

The flatterers of *Alexander* the great, made him beleeve, that he was
the sonne of *Jupiter;* but being one day sore-hurt, and seeing the bloud
gush out of his wounds: *And what thinke you of this?* (saith he unto
them) *Is not this bloud of a lively red hew, and meerly humane?* Me
thinkes, it is not of that temper, which *Homer* faineth to trill from
the Gods wounds. *Hermodorus* the Poet made certaine verses in
honour of *Antigonus,* in which he called him the sonne of *Phœbus;* to
whom he replied; *My friend, He that emptieth my close-stoole know-*
eth well, there is no such matter. He is but a man at all assaies: And
if of himselfe he be a man ill borne, the Empire of the whole world
cannot restore him.

> *—puellæ*
> *Hunc rapiant, quicquid calcaverit, hic rosa fiat.*
> PERS. *Sat.* ii. 37.

Wenches must ravish him, what ever he
Shall tread upon, eftsoones a rose must be.

What of that? If he be of a grose, stupide, and senseles minde:
voluptuousnesse and good fortune it selfe, are not perceived without
vigor, wit, and livelinesse.

> *Hæc perinde sunt, ut illius animus qui ea possidet,*
> *Qui uti scit, ei bona, illi qui non utitur rectè, mala.*
> TER. *Heaut.* act. i. SC. ii. 21.

These things are such, as the possessors minde,
Good, if well us'd; if ill, them ill we finde.

Whatsoever the goods of fortune are, a man must have a proper sense
to savour them: It is the enjoying, and not the possessing of them,
that makes us happy.

Non domus et fundus, non œris acervus et auri,
Ægroto domini deduxit corpore febres,
Non animo curas, valeat possessor oportet,
Qui comportatis rebus benè cogitat uti.
Qui cupit, aut metuit, juvat illum sic domus aut res,
Ut lippum pictœ tabulœ, fomenta podagram.

HOR. i. Ep. ii. 47.

Not house and land, and heapes of coine and gold
Rid agues, which their sicke Lords body hold,
Or cares from minde: th' owner must be in health,
That well doth thinke to use his hoarded wealth.
Him that desires or feares, house, goods, delight,
As foments doe the gout, pictures sore-sight.

He is a foole, his taste is wallowish and distracted, he enjoyeth it [no] more, than one that hath a great cold doth the sweetnesse of Greeke wine, or a horse the riches of a costly-faire furniture, where-with he is trapped. Even as *Plato* saith, *That health, beautie, strength, riches, and all things else he calleth good, are equally as ill to the unjust, as good to the just; and the evill contrariwise.* And then, where the body and the soule are in ill plight, what need these externall commodities? Seeing the least pricke of a needle, and passion of the mind is able to deprive us of the pleasure of the worlds Monarchy. The first fit of an ague, or the first gird that the gout gives him, what availes his goodly titles of Majesty?

Totus et argento conflatus, totus et auro.
TIBUL. i. El. vii. 71.

All made of silver fine,
All gold pure from the mine.

doth he not forthwith lose the remembrance of his pallaces and states? If he be angrie or vexed, can his principalitie keepe him from blushing, from growing pale, from gnashing his teeth like a Bedlam? Now if it be a man of worth, and well borne, his royaltie, and his glorious titles will adde but little unto his good fortune.

Si ventri bene, si lateri est pedibusque tuis, nil
Divitiœ poterunt regales addere majus.—HOR. i. *Ep.* xii. 5.

If it be well with belly, feet, and sides,
A Kings estate no greater good provides.

He seeth they are but illusions, and vaine deceits. He may haply be of King *Seleucus* his advice: *That he who fore-knew the weight of a scepter, should he finde it lying on the ground, he would not daigne to take it up.* This he said, by reason of the weightie, irksome and painefull charges, that are incident unto a good King. Truely, it is no small matter to governe others, since so many crosses and difficulties

offer themselves, if we will governe our selves well. Touching commanding of others, which in shew seemeth to be so sweet, considering
the imbecillitie of mans judgement, and the difficultie of choice in
new and doubtful things. I am confidently of this opinion, that it is
much more easie and plausible to follow, than to guide: and that it
is a great setling of the minde, to be tied but to one beaten-path, and
to answer but for himselfe.

> Ut satiùs multo jam sit, parere quietum,
> Quàm regere imperio res velle.—LUCR. v. 1137.

Much better 'tis, in quiet to obey,
Than to desire with King's-power all to sway.

Seeing *Cyrus* said, *That it belongs not to a man to command, that
is not of more worth, than those whom he commandeth.* But King
Hieron in *Xenophon* addeth moreover, *That in truely-enjoying of
carnall sensualities, they are of much worse condition, than private
men; forasmuch as ease and facilitie, depriveth them of that sowre-
sweet tickling, which we finde in them.*

> Pinguis amor nimiumque potens, in tœdia nobis
> Vertitur, et stomacho dulcis us esca nocet.
>   OVID. *Am.* ii. *El.* xix. 25.

Fat over-powerfull love doth loathsome grow,
As fulsome sweet-meats stomackes overthrow.

Thinke wee, that high-minded men take great pleasure in musicke?
The satietie thereof makes it rather tedious unto them. Feasts, banquets, revels, dancings, masks and turneys, rejoyce them that but
seldome see them, and that have much desired to see them: the taste
of which becommeth cloysome and unpleasing to those that daily see,
and ordinarily have them: Nor doe Ladies tickle those, that at pleasure
and without suspect may be glutted with them. He that cannot stay
till he be thirsty, can take no pleasure in drinking. Enterludes and
commedies rejoyce and make us merry, but to players they are tedious
and tastelesse. Which to prove, we see, it is a delight for Princes, and
a recreation for them, sometimes to disguise themselves, and to take
upon them a base and popular kinde of life.

> Plerumque que gratæ principibus vices.
> Mundæque parvo sub lare pauperum
> Cœnæ sine aulæis ostro,
> Solicitam explicuere frontem.—HOR. iii. *Od.* xxix. 13.

Princes doe commonly like enterchange,
And cleanly meales where poore-men poorely house,
Without all tapistrie or carpets strange,
Unwrinkled have their care-knit, thought-bent browes.

Nothing doth sooner breed a distaste or satietie, than plentie. What longing lust would not bee alaid, to see three hundred women at his dispose and pleasure, as hath the Grand *Turke* in his Seraille? And what a desire and shew of hawking had he reserved to himselfe from his ancestors, that never went aboard without seven thousand falkners at least? Besides which, I thinke, the luster of greatness, brings no small incommodities to the enjoying of sweeter pleasures: they lie too open, and are too much in sight. And I wot not why a man should longer desire them to conceale or hide their fault: for, what in us is indiscretion, the people judgeth to be tyrannie, contempt, and disdaine of the lawes in them: And [be] sides the ready inclination unto vice, it seemeth they also adde unto it the pleasure of gourmandizing, and to prostrate publike observances under their feet. Verily *Plato* in his Gorgias, *defineth him to be a tyrant, that in a Citie hath leave and power to doe what ever he list.* And therefore often, the shew and publication of their vice hurteth more than the sinne it selfe. Every man feareth to be spied and controlled; which they are even in their countenances and thoughts: All the people esteeming to have right and interest to judge of them. And we see that blemishes grow either lesser or bigger, according to the eminence, and light of the place, where they are set, and that a mole or a wart in ones forehead is more apparently perceived, than a scarre in another place. And that is the reason why Poets faine *Jupiters* loves to have beene affected under other countenances, than his owne; And of so many amorous-shifts, and love practises, they impute to him, there is but one (as farre as I remember) where he is to be seene in his greatnesse and majestie. But returne we to *Hieron:* he also relateth, how many incommodities he findeth in his royaltie, being so barred, that he cannot at his libertie travell to goe whether he pleaseth, being as it were a prisoner within the limits of his country; and that in all his actions he is encircled and hemd-in with an importunate and tedious multitude. Truely, to see our Princes all alone, sitting at their meat, beleagred round with so many talkers, whisperers, and gazing beholders, unknowne what they are or whence they come, I have often rather pittied than envied them. King *Alphonsus* was wont to say, *that burthen-bearing asses were in that, in farre better condition than Kings; for, their masters suffer them to feed at their ease, whereas Kings cannot obtaine that privilege of their servants.* And it could never fall into my minde, that it might be any speciall commoditie to the life, of a man of understanding, to have a score of find-faults, picke-thanks, and controlers about his close-stoole, nor that the service of a man, that hath a thousand pound rent a yeare, or that hath taken *Casal,* or defended *Sienna,* is more commodious or acceptable to him, than that of a sufficient, and well-experienced groome. Princelike advantages, are in a manner but imaginarie preheminences. Every degree of fortune, hath some image of Principalitie. *Cæsar* termeth all the Lords, which in his time had justice in *France,* to be Kinglets, or pettie Kings. And truly, except the name of *Sire*, we goe very farre with our Kings. Looke but in the Provinces remote and farre from the court: As for example, in *Britanie*, the attending traine, the flocking subjects, the number of officers, the many affaires, the diligent service, the obsequious ceremonies of a Lord, that liveth retired, and in his owne house, brought up amongst his owne servants, tenants, and followers: And note also the high pitch of his imaginations, and humours, there is no greater royaltie can be seene: He heareth no more talke of his master, than of the *Persian* King, and haply but once a yeare: And knowes but some farre-fetcht, and old kindred or pedigree, which his Secretarie findes or keepes upon some ancient record or evidence. Verily our lawes are very free, and the burthen of soveraigntie, doth scarsly concerne a gentleman of *France* twice in his whole life. Essentiall and effectuall subjection amongst us doth not respect any, but such as allure themselves unto it, and that affect to honour, and love to enrich themselves by such service: For he that can shrowd and retire himselfe in his owne home, and can manage and direct his house without sutes in law, or quarrell with his neighbours, or domesticall encombrances, is as free as the Duke of *Venice*. *Paucos servitus, plures servitutem tenent* (SEN. *Epist.* 22). *Service holds few, but many hold service.* But above all things *Hieron* seemeth to complaine, that he perceiveth himselfe deprived of all mutuall friendship, reciprocall societie, and familiar conversation, wherein consisteth the most perfect and sweetest fruit of humane life. For, what undoubted testimonie of affection and good will, can I expect or exact from him, that will he, or nill he, oweth me all he hath, all he can? Can I make account of his humble speech, of his low-lowting curtzie, or of his curteous offers, since it lieth not in his power to refuse them me? The honour we receive of those which feare and stand in awe of us, is no true honour. Such respects are rather due to royaltie, to majesty, than to me.

> *—maximum hoc regni bonum est,*
> *Quod facta domini cogitur populus sui*
> *Quàm ferre, tam laudare.*—SEN. *Thyest.* act. ii. sc. 1.

This is chiefe good of Princes domination,
Subjects are forc't their sov'raignes actes and fashions
To beare with patience, passe with commendations.

Doe I not see, that both the bad and the good King are served alike? That hee who is hated, and he that is beloved are both courted alike? And the one as much fawned upon as the other? My predecessor was served with the same apparances, and waited upon with the like ceremonies, and so shall my successor be. If my subjects offend me not, it is no testimonie of any good affection. Wherfore shall I take it in that sense, sithence they cannot, if they would? No man followeth me for any friendship that is betweene him and me: inasmuch as no firme friendship can be contracted, where is so small relation, so slender correspondencie, and such disparitie. My high degree hath excluded me from the commerce of men. There is too great an inequalitie, and distant disproportion. They follow for countenance, and of custome, or rather my fortune than my selfe: hoping thereby to encrease theirs. Whatsoever they say, all they doe unto me, is but a glosse, and but dissimulation, their libertie being every where brideled, and checked by the great power I have over them. I see nothing about me, but inscrutable hearts, hollow mindes, fained lookes, dissembled speeches, and counterfeit actions. His Courtiers one day commended *Julian* the Emperour for ministering of right, and doing of justice; *I should easily grow proud* (saith he) *for these praises, if they came from such as durst either accuse or discommend my contrary actions, should I commit any.* All the true commodities that Princes have, are common unto them with men of meane fortune. It is for Gods to mount winged horses, and to feed on Ambrosia. They have no other sleepe, nor no other appetite than ours. Their steele is of no better temper, than that wherewith we arme our selves. Their crowne, their diadem can neither hide them from the Sun, or shelter them from the raine. *Dioclesian* that wore one, so much reverenced, and so fortunate, did voluntarily resigne the same, to withdraw himselfe unto the pleasure of a private life; but a while after, the urgent necessitie of publike affaires requiring his presence, and that he should returne to re-assume his charge againe, he answered those that solicited him unto it; you would never undertake to perswade me to that, had you but seene the goodly rankes of trees, which my selfe have planted in mine Orchard, or the faire muske-melons, I have set in my garden. According to *Anacharsis* his opinion, *The happiest estate of a well ordered common-wealth should be, where all other things being equally common, precedencie should be measured, and preferments suted according to vertue and desert, and the contrarie according to vice.* At what time King *Pirrhus* undertooke to passe into *Italie, Cyneas* his wise and trustie counsellor, going about to make him perceive the vanitie of his ambition, one day bespake him thus. *My good Sir,* (said he) *To what end doe you prepare for so great an enterprise?* He answered suddenly, *To make my selfe Lord of Italie. That done, what will you doe then?* (replied *Cyneas*). *I will then passe* (said *Pirrhus*) *into* Gaule, *and then into* Spaine: *And what afterwards? I will then invade Affrike, and subdue the same, and at last, when I shall have brought all the world under my subjection, I will then take my rest, and live contented at mine ease. Now, for Gods sake Sir,* (replied *Cyneas*) *Tell me, what hinders you, that you be not now, if so you please, in that estate? Wherefore doe you not now place your selfe, where you meane to aspire, and save so much danger, so many hazards, and so great troubles as you enterpose betweene both?*

Nimirum quia non bene norat quæ esset habendi
Finis, et omnino quoad crescat vera voluptas.—LUCR. V. 1443.

The cause forsooth, he knew not what should be the end
Of having, nor how far true pleasure should extend.

I will conclude and shut up this treatise with an ancient verse, which
I singularly applaud, and deeme fit to this purpose.

Mores cuique sui fingunt fortunam.—CIC. *Parad.* V. COR. NEP.

Ev'ry mans manners and his mind,
His fortune to him frame and find.

CHAPTER XLIII

OF SUMPTUARIE LAWES, OR LAWES FOR MODERATING OF EXPENCES

THE manner wherewith our Lawes assay to moderate the foolish and
vaine expences of table-cheare and apparell, seemeth contrarie to its
end. The best course were to beget in men a contempt of gold and silk-
waring, as of vaine and unprofitable things, whereas we encrease their
credit and price: A most indirect course to withdraw men from them.
As for example, to let none but Princes eat dainties, or weare velvets,
and clothes of Tissew, and interdict the people to doe it, what is it but
to give reputation unto those things, and to encrease their longing to use
them? Let Kings boldly quit those badges of honour; They have many
other besides: Such excesse is more excusable in other men, than in
Princes. We may, by the examples of divers Nations, learne sundrie
better fashions to distinguish our selves and our degrees (which truly I
esteeme requisit in an estate,) without nourishing to that purpose, this
so manifest corruption and apparent inconvenience. It is strange how
custome in these indifferent things doth easily encroch and suddenly
establish the footing of her authoritie. We had scarce worne cloth one
whole yeare at the Court, what time we mourned for our King *Henrie*
the second, but certainly in every mans opinion, all manner of silks
were already become so vile and abject, that was any man seene to
weare them, he was presently judged to be some countrie fellow, or
mechanicall man. They were left only for Chyrurgians and Physitians.
And albeit most men were apparreled alike, yet were there other sufficient apparant distinctions of mens qualities. How soone doe plaine
chamoy-jerkins, and greasie canvase doublets creepe into fashion and
credit amongst our souldiers, if they lie in the field? And the garish-
nesse, neatnesse, and riches of silken garments grow in contempt and
scorne? Let Kings first begin to leave these superfluous expences, we
shall all follow, and within a moneth, without edicts, ordinances, procla-
mations, and acts of Parliament, it will be observed as a law. The

statutes should speake contrarie, as thus. That no man or woman, of what qualitie soever, shall, upon paine of great forfeitures. weare any maner of silke, of skarlet, or any gold-smiths worke, except only Enterlude-players, Harlots, and Curtizans. With such an invention did *Zeleucus* whilome correct the corrupted manners of the *Locrines*. His ordinances were such. Be it enacted, that no woman of free condition, shall have any more than one maid-servant to follow her when she goeth abroad, except when she shall be drunken; And further, that she may not goe out of the Citie by night, nor weare any jewels of gold, or precious stones about her, nor any gowne beset with gold-smiths worke, or imbroiderie, except she be a publike-professed whore: and moreover, that except panders and bawds, it shall not be lawful for any man to weare any gold-rings on his fingers, nor any rich garments, as are such of cloth made in the Citie of *Miletum*. So did he by these reprochfull exceptions ingeniously drive his Citizens from vaine superfluities, and pernicious dainties. It was a most profitable course, by honour and am-bition to allure men unto their dutie and obedience. Our Kings have the power to addresse all these externall reformations. Their inclination serveth them as a law. *Quicqaid Principes faciunt, praecipere videntur. Whatsoever Princes doe, that, they seeme to command.* The rest of *France* takes the modell of the court, as a rule unto it selfe to follow. Let Courtiers first begin to leave off and loath these filthy and apish breeches, that so openly shew our secret parts: the bumbasting of long pease-cod-bellied doublets, which makes us seeme so far from what we are, and which are so combersome to arme: These long, effeminate, and dangling locks: That fond custome to kisse what we present to others, and *Beso las manos* in saluting of our friends: (a ceremonie heretofore only due unto Princes;) And for a gentleman to come to any place of respect, without his rapier by his side, all unbraced, all untrust, as if he came from his close-stoole: And that, against our forefathers manner, and the particular libertie of our *French* nobilitie, we should stand bare-headed, aloofe-off from them, wheresoever they be, and as about them, about many others: So many petty-kings, and petty-petty-king-lets have we now adayes: And so of others like new-fangled and vicious introductions: They shall soone be seene to vanish and be left. Although but superficiall faults, yet are they of evill presages. And we are warned, that the foundation or maine summers of our houses faile and shrinke, when we see the quarters bend, or wals to breake. *Plato* in his Lawes, thinkes there is no worse plague, or more pernicious in his Citie, than to suffer youth, to have the reines of libertie in their owne hand, to change in their attires, in their gestures, dances, exercises, and songs, from one forme to another: And to remove their judgement, now to this, now to that place; following new-fangled devices, and regarding their in-ventors: By which, old customes are corrupted, and ancient institutions despised. In all things, except the wicked, mutation is to be feared; yea, even the alteration of seasons, of winds, of livings, and of humours. And no lawes are in perfect credit, but those to which God hath given some ancient continuance: So that no man know their of-spring, nor that ever they were other than they are.

CHAPTER XLIV

OF SLEEPING

REASON doth appoint us ever to walke in one path, but not alwaies to keepe one [pace]: And that a wise man should not permit humane passions to stray from the right carrier; he may (without prejudice unto his dutie) also leave it unto them either to hasten or to slow his pace, and not place himselfe as an immoveable and impassible *Colossus*. Were vertue herselfe corporeall and incarnate, I thinke her pulse would beat and worke stronger, marching to an assault, than going to dinner: For, it is necessarie that she heat and move herselfe. I have therefore mark't it as a rare thing, to see great personages sometimes, even in their weightiest enterprises, and most important affaires, hold themselves so resolutely-assured in their state, that they doe not so much as breake their sleepe for them. *Alexander* the great, on the day appointed for that furious-bloudy battel against *Darius*, slept so soundly and so long that morning, that *Parmenion* was faine to enter his chamber, and approaching neere unto his bed, twice or thrice to call him by his name, to awaken him, the houre of the battle being at hand, and urging him. *Otho* the Emperour having determined to kill himselfe; the very same night, after he had given order for his domestical affaires, shared his monie among his servants, and whetted the edge of a sword, wherewith he intended to wound himselfe, expecting no other thing, but to know whether all his friends were gone to rest, fell into so sound a sleepe, that the groomes of his chamber heard him snort in another roome. This Emperours death hath many parts semblable unto that of great *Cato*, and namely this: For, *Cato* being prepared to defeat himselfe, whilest he expected to heare newes, whether the Senators, whom he caused to retire, were lanched out from the haven of *Utica*, fell so fast asleep, that he was heard to snort into the next chamber: And he whom he had sent toward the port, having awaked him, to tell him, the storme was so rough, that the Senators could not conveniently put out to sea, he sent another, and lying downe a new, fell asleep againe, untill the last messenger assured him they were gone. We may also compare him unto *Alexander*, in that great and dangerous storme, which threatned him, by the sedition of *Metellus* the Tribune, who laboured to publish the decree of *Pompeys* re-appeall into the Citie, together with his army, at what time the commotion of *Catiline* was on foot: against which decree only *Cato* did insist, and to that purpose had *Metellus* and he had many injurious speeches, and menaced one another in the Senate-house: And it was the next day, they were like to come to the execution in the market-place, where *Metellus,* besides the favour of the common people, and of *Cæsar,* then conspiring and complotting for the advancement of Pompey, should come, accompanied with a multitude of strange and forraine slaves and fencers, to doe their utmost: And *Cato* strengthened with his only constancie, and with an unmated resolve: So that his kinsmen, his familiars, and many honest men tooke great care, and were in heavy anxietie and pensivenesse for him: of which many never left him all night, but sate up together, without rest, eating, or drinking, by reason of the danger they saw prepared for him; yea, his wife and sisters did nought but weep and waile, and for his sake torment themselves in their house, whereas contrariwise he alone comforted every body, and blamed them, for their demissenesse: And after he had supped, (as he was wont) he went quietly to his bed, and slept very soundly untill the next morning, that one of his copartners in the Tribuneship, came to call him, to goe to the skirmish. The knowledge we have of this mans unmated-haughty heart, by the rest of his life; may make us judge with all securitie, that it only proceeded from a spirit, so far elevated above such accidents, that he dained not so much as to trouble his minde with them, no more than with ordinarie chances. In the sea-fight, which *Augustus* gained against *Sextus Pompeius* in *Sicilie,* even at the instant he should goe to fight, was surprised with so heavy a sleep, that his friends were compelled to awaken him, to give the signall of the battell; which afterward gave occasion unto *Marcus Antonius,* to charge him with this imputation, that he had not dared with open eyes to survey the marshalling of his army, and that his heart would not suffice him, to present himselfe unto his souldiers, untill such time that *Agrippa* brought him newes of the victorie he had obtained of his enemies. But concerning young *Marius,* who committed a greater errour (for on the day of his last battell against *Sylla,* after he had marshalled his army, and given the word or signall of the battell) he lay downe in the shadow under a tree, a while to rest himselfe, and fell so fast asleep, that he could hardly be awaked with the rout and flight of his men, having seene no part of the fight, they say, it was because he was so exceedingly aggravated with travell, and over-tired with wearinesse, and want of sleep, that nature was overcome, and could no longer endure. And touching this point, Physitians may consider; whether sleep be so necessarie, that our life must needs depend of it: For we finde that *Perseus* King of *Macedon,* prisoner at *Rome,* being kept from sleep, was made to die; but *Plinie* aleageth, that some have lived a long time without any sleep at all. And *Herodotus* reporteth, *There are Nations, where men sleep and wake by halfe yeares.* And those that write the life of *Epimenides* the wise, affirme, *that he slept the continuall space of seven and fifty yeares.*

CHAPTER XLV

OF THE BATTELL OF DREUX

THERE hapned divers rare accidents, and remarkable chances in our battell of *Dreux:* but those who doe not greatly favour the reputation of the Duke of *Guise,* doe boldly aleage, that he cannot be excused, to have made a stand, and temporised with the forces he commanded, whilst the Lord Constable of *France,* Generall of the Armie, was engaged and suppressed with the enemies Artillerie, and that it had beene better for him, to hazard himselfe, to charge the enemie flankwise, than by expecting any advantage, to have him come behind him, to suffer so reprochfull an overthrow, and so shameful a losse. But omitting what the event thereof witnessed, he that shall without passion debate the matter, shall easily (in my conceit) confesse, that the ayme and drift, not onely of a Captaine, but of every particular Souldier, ought chiefly to respect a victory in great: And that no particular occurrences, of what consequence soever, or what interest may depend on them, should never divert him from that point. *Philopœmen* in an encounter with *Machanidas,* having sent before, a strong troupe of Archers, and good marke men, to begin the skirmish: and the enemie, after he had put them to rout and disranked them, ammusing himselfe in mainly pursuing them, and following the victory alongst the maine battell, where *Philopœmen* was, although his souldiers were much moved and offended to see their fellowes put to the worst, he could not be induced to bouge from his place, nor make head against his enemie, to succour his men; but rather, having suffered them to be defeated, and cut in peeces before his face, began then to charge his enemies in the battalion of their Infanterie, when he perceived them forsaken of their horsemen: And albeit they were Lacedemonians, forasmuch as he charged them, at what time (supposing to have gained the day) they began to disorder themselves, he easily overcame them; which done, he pursued *Machanidas.* This case, is cousin-german unto that of the Duke of *Guise.* In that sharpe-bloody battell of *Agesilaus* against the Bœotians which *Xenophon* (who was there present) said, *To have beene the hottest and rudest, that ever he had seene: Agesilaus* refused the advantage, which fortune presented him, to let the battalion of the Bœotians passe, and to charge them behind, what certaine victorie soever he saw likely to follow the same, esteeming that it were rather skill than valour, and to shew his prowesse, and matchlesse-haughty courage, chose rather to charge them in the front of their forces: But what followed? He was well beaten, and himselfe sore-hurt, and in the end compelled to leave his enterprise, and embrace the resolution, which in the beginning he had refused, causing his men to open themselves, to give passage unto that torrent of the Bœotians; who when they were past through, perceiving them to march in disaray, as they who perswaded themselves to be out of all danger, he pursued them, and charged them flank-wise. All which notwithstanding, he could never put to rout, or force them run-away, for they, orderly, and faire and softly made their retreit, ever shewing their face, untill such time as they got safely into their holds and trenches.

CHAPTER XLVI

OF NAMES

WHAT diversitie soever there be in herbs, all are shuffled up together under the name of a sallade. Even so, upon the consideration of names, I will here huddle up a gallymafry of diverse articles. Every several nation hath some names, which, I wot not how are sometimes taken in ill part, as with us *Jacke, Hodge, Tom, Will, Bat, Benet* and so forth. Item, it seemeth that in the genealogies of Princes, there are certaine names fatally affected; as *Ptolemeus* with the *Ægyptians, Henries* in *England, Charles* in *France, Baldwins* in *Flanders,* and *Williams* in our ancient *Aquitanie,* whence some say came the name of *Guienne;* which is but a cold invention: As if in *Plato* himselfe there were not some as harsh and ill-sounding. Item, it is an idle matter, yet neverthelesse, by reason of the strangenesse, worthy the memorie, and recorded by an ocular witnesse, that *Henrie* Duke of *Normandie,* sonne to *Henrie* the second King of *England,* making a great feast in *France,* the assembly of the Nobilitie was so great, that for pastimes sake, being, by the resemblance of their names, divided into severall companies: in the first were found a hundred and ten Knights sitting at one table, and all called *Williams;* besides private Gentlemen and servants. It is as pleasant to distribute the tables by the names of the assistants, as it was unto *Geta* the Emperor, who would have all his messes or dishes served in at his table orderly according to the first letters of their names; As for example, those that began with P. as pig, pie, pike, puddings, pouts, porke, pan-cakes, etc. were all served in together; and so of all the rest. Item, it is a common saying, *That it is good to have a good name:* As much to say, good credit, or good reputation. Yet verely it is very commodious to have a well-sounding and smooth name, and which is easie to be pro-nounced, and facile to be remembred: For Kings, Princes, Lords, and Magistrates know and remember us the better by them, and will not so soone forget us. Marke but of those that serve and follow us, whether we doe not more ordinarily command, and sooner employ such, whose names come readier to our tongue, or memorie. I have seene our King *Henrie* the second, who could never hit on the right name of a Gentle-man of *Gascoigne;* and did ever call a Lady waiting on the Queene, by the generall surname of her house, because that of her father was so harsh, and hard to be remembred. And *Socrates* saith, *It ought to be a fathers speciall care, to give his children good and easie-sounding names*. Item, it is reported, that the foundation of our Lady the great at *Poitiers* had this beginning; A licentious young man having his dwelling-house where the Church now standeth, had one night gotten a wench to lie with him, who so soone as she came to bed, he demanded her name, who answered, *Marie:* The young man hearing that name, was suddenly so strucken with a motive of religion, and an awefull respect unto that sacred name, of the virgin *Marie,* the blessed mother of our Saviour and Redeemer, that he did not onely presently put her away from him, but reformed all the remainder of his succeeding life: And that in consideration of this miracle, there was first erected a Chappell in the place where this young mans house stood, consecrated unto that holy name, and afterward the faire great Church, which yet continueth. This vocal and auricular correction, and so full of devotion, strucke right unto his soule. This other following, of the same kind, insinuated it selfe by the corporall sences. *Pythagoras* being in companie with two young men, whom he heard complot and consult (being somewhat heated with feasting and drinking) to go and ravish a chasthouse, commanded immediately the minstrels to change their tune; and so by a solemne, grave, severe, and spondaicall kinde of musicke, did sweetly inchaunt, allay, and in-trance their rash, violent, and law-lesse lust. Item, shall not succeeding posteritie say, that our moderne reformation hath beene exact and delicate, to have not only oppugned and resisted errors and vices, and filled the world with devotion, humilitie, obedience, peace, and every other kinde of vertue, but even to have combated their ancient names of baptisme, *Charles, Lewis, Francis,* to people the world with *Methusalem, Ezechiel, Malachie,* much better feeling of a lively faith? A Gentleman my neighbour, esteeming the commodities of ancient times in regard of our daies, forgot not to aledge the fiercenesse and magnificence of the names of the Nobilitie of those times, as Don *Grumedan, Quedragan,* and *Agesilan:* And that, but to heare them sounded, a man might easily perceive, they had beene other manner of men, than *Peter, Guillot,* or *Michell.* Item, I commend, and am much beholding to *James Amiot,* in the course of a French oration of his to have still kept the full ancient Latine names, without disguising or changing them, to give them a new French cadence. At the first they seemed somewhat harsh unto the Reader; but now, by reason of the credit, which his *Plutarke* hath deservedly gotten amongst us, custome hath removed all strangenesse from us. I have often wished that those who write histories in Latine, would leave us our names whole, and such as they are: For, altering *Vaudemont,* to *Vallemontanus,* and metamorphosing them, by suting them to the Græcian or Latin tongue, we know not what to make of them, and are often at a non-plus. To conclude my discourse; It is an ill custome, and of exceeding bad consequence in our countrie of *France,* to call every man by the name of his Towne, Mannor, Hamlet, or Lordship, as the thing that doth most confound houses, and bring sur-names out of knowledge. A cadet or yonger-brother of a good house, having had for his appanage a Lordship, by whose name he hath beene knowne and honoured, cannot well forsake and leave the same ten yeares after his death; His Lordship commeth unto a stranger, who doth the like: Ghesse then where we are, and how we shall doe to come to the perfect knowledge of these men. Wee need not goe far for other examples, but looke into our Royall house, where so many partages, so many sur-names, and so many severall titles have so encumbred us, that the originall of the stocke is utterly lost. There is so much libertie in these mutations, that even in my time, I have seene no man nor woman advanced by fortune unto some extraordinarie preferment, that hath not immediately had adjoyned unto him or her Genealogicall titles, new and unknowne to their fathers, and that hath not beene engraffed into some noble stocke or family. And as good lucke serveth, the basest upstart, and most obscure houses are most apt unto adulteration, and falsification. How many privat Gentlemen have we in *France*, which according to their accompt, and blazoning of their gentrie, are of the royall bloud or race? I beleeve more than others. Was it not pretily said, and with a good grace, by one of my friends? There was a great companie bandied together about a quarell which a Gentleman had with another, who in very truth had some prerogative of titles, honours, and alliances above the common sort of Nobilitie; upon which word of his prerogative, every one seeking to equall himselfe unto him, alleaged, some one offspring, some another, some the resemblance of his name, some of his armes, other-some an old far-fecht pedigree, and the meanest of them to be the great grand-child of some King beyond the Seas. When they came all to dinner, this man whom hitherto they had all followed, in lieu of taking his wonted place, making low-lowting reverences, went to the lowest end of the board, entreating the companie to hold him excused, that through rash-unadvisednesse he had hitherto lived with them companion-like, but now being lately enformed of their right qualities, he began to know them according to their ancient degrees, and that it did not duly belong unto him to sit above so many Princes. And after he had acted his play, he began to raile upon them with a thousand injuries; saying thus unto them. For the love of God content your selves, with what your forefathers have beene contented, and with the state whereto God hath called us: we have sufficient if we can maintaine it well, let us not disparage the fortune and condition of our predecessors; and reject we these fond imaginations, which cannot faile any man, whatsoever he be, that is so impudent as to alleage them. Crests, Armes. and Coats have no more certaintie than surnames. I beare Azure seme of trefoiles, a Lions Paw in fæce, Or, armed Gules. What privilege hath this Coat, that it should for ever continue particularly to my house? A sonne in law will transferre the same into another family: Some silly-upstart purchaser of Armes, will make it his chiefe

Coat. There is nothing wherein meet so many alterations, and so much confusion.

But this consideration draweth me perforce unto another field. Let us somewhat narrowly search-into, and for Gods sake consider, on what foundation we ground this glorie and reputation, for which the world is turned topsie-turvie. On what doe we establish this transitorie renowne, which with so great mind-possessing toyle, and industrie we seeke and gape-after? In fine, it is *Peter* or *William,* that beareth the same (marke it well Reader) and to whom it belongeth. Is not hope a couragious facultie, which in a mortall subject, and in a moment, seeks to usurp infinit[i]e, and immensitie, and to replenish his Masters indigence with the possession of all things he can imagine or desire, before it would? Nature hath given us a pleasant joy to play withall in that. Is it *Peter* or *William?* And what is that but a word for al mouths? or three or foure dashes of a pen, first, so easie to be varied, as I would willingly aske those, whom the honor of so many victories concerneth, or whether *Guesquin,* or *Glesquin,* or *Gueaquin?* yet were there more apparence [here], than in *Lucian* that Σ. did sue T. For,

> *—non levia aut ludicra petuntur*
> *Præmia:* VIRG. *Æn.* xii. 764.

> No light prize, no reward in jest
> Is hunted after as the best.

The wager goeth deepe: The question is, which letter must be paid with so many sieges, battels, hurts, emprisonments, and services done unto the Crowne of *France* by her ever renowmed Constable. *Nicholas Denisot* hath had no care but of the letters of his name, and hath changed all the contexture of them, there out to frame the Earle of *Alsinois,* whom he hath honored and presented with the glorie of his Poisie and Painting. And *Suetonius* the Historian hath loved but the sense of his owne, and having taken away *Lenis,* which was his fathers surname, hath left *Tranquillus* successor of his compositions reputation. Who would beleeve, Captaine *Bayard* hath no honor, but that which he hath borrowed from the acts of *Peter Terraill?* And that *Antonio Escalin* (even before his eies) suffered Captaine *Poulin,* and the Baron of La *Garde,* to steal so many Navigations, voyages, and attemps, both by sea and land from him? Secondarily, they are dashes, and trickes of the pen, common unto a thousand men. How many are there in all races or families both of one name and surname? And how many in divers families, races, ages, and countries? Historie hath knowne three *Socrates,* five *Platoes,* eight *Aristotles,* seven *Xenophons,* twenty *Demetrius,* twenty *Theodores:* besides which, imagine how many came not to her knowledge. Who letteth my horse boy to call himselfe *Pompey* the great? But after all, what meanes, what devices, are there that annex unto my horsekeeper deceased, or to that other who had his head cut off in *Ægypt*, or that joyne unto them this glorified and far-renowned word, and these pen-dashes so much honoured that they may thereby advantage themselves?

> *Id cinerem et manes credis curare sepultos?*—iv. 34.

> Thinke you, ghosts buried, ashes dead,
> Care much how we alive are sped?

What feeling motion of revenge have the two companions in chiefe valor amongst men; *Epaminondas* of that glorious verse, which so many ages since is so common in our mouthes for him?

> *Consiliis nostris laus est attrita Laconum.*—CIC. *Tusc. Qu.* v.

> By our complots the haught renowne,
> Of Spartan Gallants was brought downe.

And *Africanus* of that other:

> *A sole exoriente, supra Mœotis paludes*
> *Nemo est, qui factis me œquiparare queat?*—*Ibid.*

> From Sun rise to the Scythian-lake, of fame
> None in exploits can equalize my name.

Those that survive are tickled with the pleasure of these words, and by them solicited with jealousie and desire, doe presently without consideration transmit by fantasie this their proper motion of revenge unto the deceased; and with a fond-deceiving hope perswade themselves, when their turne commeth to be capable of it. God he knowes it, neverthelesse:

> —*ad hœc se*
> *Romanus Graiusque et Barbarus Induperator*
> *Erexit, causas discriminis atque laboris*
> *Inde habuit, tanto major famœ sitis est, quàm*
> *Virtutis.* JUVEN. *Sat.* x. 137

> Heerto himselfe the Romane Generall,
> The Græcian, the Barbarian, rouz'd and rais'd;
> Heere hence drew cause of perils, travells all:
> So more, than to be good, thirst to be prais'd.

CHAPTER XLVII

OF THE UNCERTAINTIE OF OUR JUDGEMENT

IT is even as, that verse saith,

> Ἐπέων δὲ πολὺς νομὸς ἔνθα καὶ ἔνθα.

Of words on either side,
A large doale they divide.

There is law sufficient to speake every where, both *pro* and *contra;* As for example:

Vince Hannibal, et non seppe usar' poi
Ben la vittoriosa sua ventura.—PET, PAR. i. son. lxxxvi. 1.

Hanniball conquer'd, but he knew not after
To use well his victorious good fortune.

He that shall take this part, and with our men go about, to make that over-sight prevaile, that we did not lately pursue our fortune at *Mont-contour:* Or he that shall accuse the King of *Spaine,* who could not use the advantage he had against us at Saint *Quintin,* may say this fault to have proceeded from a minde drunken with his good fortune, and from a courage fulgorged with the beginning of good lucke; loseth the taste how to encrease it, being already hindred from digesting what he hath conceived of it: He hath his hands full, and cannot take hold any more: Unworthy that ever fortune should cast so great a good into his lap: For, what profit hath he of it, if notwithstanding, he give his enemie leasure and meanes to recover himselfe? What hope may one have, that he will once more adventure to charge these re-enforced and re-united forces, and new armed with despite and vengeance, that durst not, or knew not how to pursue them being dismaied and put to rout?

Dum fortuna calet, dum cōnjicū omnia terror.
LUCAN. vii. 734.

While fortune is at height in heat,
And terror worketh all by great.

But to conclude, what can he expect better, than what he hath lately lost? It is not, as at Fence, where the number of venies given, gets the victorie: So long as the enemie is on foot, a man is newly to begin. It is no victorie, except it end the warre. In that conflict where *Cæsar* had the worse, neere the Citie of *Oricum,* he reprochfully said unto *Pompeis* Souldiers, *That he had utterly beene overthrowne, had their Captaine knowne how to conquer: and paid him home after another fashion when it came to his turne.* But why may not a man also hold the contrarie? That it is the effect of an insatiate and rash-headlong minde, not to know how to limit or period his covetousnesse: That it is an abusing of Gods favours, to goe about to make them lose the measure he hath prescribed them, and that a new to cast himselfe into danger after the victorie, is once more to remit the same unto the mercie of fortune: That one of the chiefest policies in militarie profession, is, not to drive his enemie unto despaire. *Silla* and *Marius* in the sociall warre, having discomfited the Marsians, seeing one squadron of them yet on foot, which through despaire, like furious beasts were desperately comming upon them, could not be induced to stay or make head against them. If the fervor of Monsieur de *Foix* had not drewne him over rashly and moodily to pursue the straglers of the victorie at *Ravenna,* he had not blemished the same with his untimely death; yet did the fresh-bleeding memorie of his example serve to preserve the Lord of *Anguien* from the like inconvenience, at *Serisoles.* It is dangerous to assaile a man, whom you have bereaved of all other meanes to escape or shift for himselfe, but by his weapons: for, necessitie is a violent school-mistris, and which teacheth strange lessons: *Gravissimi sunt morsus irritatæ necessitatis. No biting so grievous, as that of necessitie provoked and enraged.*

> *Vincitur haud gratis jugulo qui provocat hostem.*
> LUCAN. iv. 278.

> For nought you over-come him not,
> Who bids his foe come cut his throat.

And that is the reason, why *Pharax* empeached the King of *Lacedæmon,* who came from gaining of a victorie against the Mantinæans, from going to charge a thousand Argians, that were escaped whole from the discomfiture; but rather to let them passe with all libertie, lest he should come to make triall of provoked and despited vertue, through and by ill fortune. *Clodomire* King of *Aquitaine,* after his victorie, pursuing *Gondemar* King of *Burgundie,* vanquished and running away, forced him to make a stand, and make head againe: but his unadvised wilfulnesse deprived him of the fruit of the victorie, for he dyed in the action. Likewise he that should chuse, whether it were best to keepe his souldiers richly and sumptuously armed, or only for necessitie, should seeme to yeeld in favour of the first, whereof was *Sertorius, Philopæmen, Brutus, Cæsar,* and others, urging that it is ever a spur to honour and glorie, for a souldier to see himselfe gorgiously attired, and richly armed, and an occasion to yeeld himselfe more obstinate to fight, having the care to save his armes, as his goods and inheritance. A reason (saith *Xenophon*) why the *Asiatikes* carried with them, when they went to warres their wives and Concubines, with all their jewels and chiefest wealth. And might also encline to the other side, which is, that a man should rather remove from his souldier, all care to preserve himselfe, than to encrease it unto him: for, by that meanes he shall doubly feare to hazard or engage himselfe, seeing these rich spoiles do rather encrease an earnest desire of victorie in the enemie: and it hath beene observed, that the said respect hath sometimes wonderfully encouraged the Romans against the Samnites. *Antiochus* shewing the Armie, he prepared against them, gorgeously accoutred with all pompe and statelinesse, unto *Hanniball,* and demanding of him, whether the Romanes would be contented with it: yea verily, answered the other, they will be very well pleased with it: They must needs be so, were they never so covetous. *Licurgus* forbad his Souldiers, not onely all manner of sumptuousnesse, in their equipage, but also to uncase or strip their enemies, when they overcame them, willing, as he said, that frugalitie and povertie should shine with the rest of the battell. Both at sieges, and elsewhere, where occasion brings us neere the enemie, we freely give our souldiers libertie, to brave, to disdaine, and injurie him with all manner of reproaches: And not without apparance of reason; for, it is no small matter, to take from them all hope of grace and composition, in presenting unto them, that there is no way left to expect it, from him, whom they have so egregiously outraged, and that there is no remedy left but from victorie. Yet had *Vitellius* but bad successe in that; for, having to deale with *Otho,* weaker in his Souldiers valour, and of long disaccustomed from warre, and effeminated through the delights and pleasures of the Citie, himselfe in the end set them so on fire with his reproachfull and injurious words, upbrayding them with their pusilanimitie and faint hartednesse, and with the regret of their Ladies, banquetings and sensualities, which they had left at *Rome,* that he put them into heart againe, which no perswasions or other means could do before; and thereby drew them, whom nought could have driven, to fight, and fall upon him. And verily, when they are injuries that touch a man to the quicke, they shall easily urge him, who was very backward to fight for his Kings quarrel, to be very forward in his owne cause or interest. If a man but consider of what consequence the preservation, and importance, the safetie of a generall is in an Armie, and how the enemies chiefest ayme, is at the fairest marke, which is the head, from which all other depend, it seemeth that that counsell cannot be doubted of, which by sundrie great Chieftaines we have seene put in practice, which is, in the beginning of the fight, or in the fury of the battell, to disguise themselves. Notwithstanding the inconvenience a man may by this meanes incurre, is no lesse than that mischiefe, which a man seeketh to avoid: For the Captaine being unseene and unknowne of his Souldiers, the courage they take by his example, and the heart they keep by his presence, is therewithall empaired and diminished; and losing the knowne and ensignes, and accustomed markes of their Leader, they either deeme him dead, or dispairing of any good successe, to be fled. And touching experience, we sometimes see it to favour the one, and sometimes the other partie. The accident of *Pirrhus* in the battell he had against the Consull *Levinus* in *Italie,* serveth us for both uses: For, by concealing himselfe under the armes of *Demogacles,* and arming him with his owne, indeed he saved his life, but was in great danger to fall into the other mischiefe, and lose the day. *Alexander, Cæsar, Lucullus,* loved (at what time they were to enter fight) to arme and attire themselves with the richest armies, and garish clothes they had, and of particular bright-shining colours. *Agis, Agesilaus,* and that great *Gilippus,* contrarie, would ever goe to warres meanly accoutred, and without any imperiall ornament. Among other reproaches, that *Pompey* is charged withall in the battell of *Pharsalia,* this is one speciall, that he idlely lingred with his Armie, expecting what his enemie would attempt; forasmuch as that (I will heare borrow the very words of *Plutarke,* which are of more consequence than mine) weakneth the violence, that running giveth the first blowes, and therewithall removeth the charging of the Combattans one against another, which more, than any other thing is wont to fill them with fury and impetuosity, when with vehemence they come to enter-shocke one another, augmenting their courage by the crie and running; and in a manner alayeth and quaileth the heat of the Souldiers: Loehere what he saith concerning this. But had *Cæsar* lost, who might not also have said, that contrariwise the strongest and firmest situation, is that, wherein a man keeps his stand without budging, and that who is settled in his march, closing, and against any time of need, sparing his strength in himselfe, hath a great advantage against him, that is in motion and disordered, and that running hath already consumed part of his breath? Moreover, that an armie being a body composed of so many severall parts, it is impossible it should in such furie advance it selfe with so just a march, and proportioned a motion, and not breake and disranke, or at least alter her ordinance, and that the nimblest be not grapling before his fellowes may helpe him. In that drearie battell of the two Persian brethren, *Clearchus* the Lacedemonian, who commanded the Græcians that followed *Cyrus* his faction, led them faire and gently without any hast-making to their charges; but when he came within fifty paces of his enemies, he bad them with all speed to run into it; hoping by the shortnesse of the distance to manage their order, and direct their breath; in the meane time giving them the advantage of the impetuositie, both for their bodies, and for their shooting-armies. Others have ordered this doubt in their army after this manner: If your enemies head-long run upon you, stay for them and bouge not: If they without stirring stay for you, run with furie upon them.

In the passage which the Emperour *Charles* the fifth made into *Provence,* our King *Francis* the first, stood a good while upon this choice; whether it were best, by way of prevention, to go and meet with him in *Italie,* or to stay his comming into *France:* and albeit he considered what an advantage it is, for one to preserve his house from the troubles and mischiefes that warre brings with it, to the end that possessing her whole strength, it may continually in all times of need, store him with money, and supply him with all other helps; and considering how the necessitie of direfull warre, doth daily enforce a Generall to make spoile of goods, and waste the Countrie, which cannot well be done in our owne goods and countrie: and if the countriman doth not as patiently indure this ravage at his friends hands, as at his enemies, so as seditions may ensue amongst our owne factions, and troubles among our friends: That licence to rob and spoile, which in his Countrie may not be tolerated, is a great furtherance in a Souldier, and makes him the more willing, to endure the miseries and toylings that follow warre: And what a hard matter it is to keep the Souldier in office and heart, who hath no other hope of profit, but his bare pay, and is so neere his wife, his children, his friends, and his home: *That he who layeth the cloth, is ever put to the greatest charges: That there is more pleasure in assailing than in defending:* And that the apprehension of a battel lost in our owne home and entrailes, is so violent, that it may easily shake the whole frame, and distemper the whole body. Seeing there is no passion so contagious, as that of feare, nor so easie apprehended and takes a-trust, or doth more furiously possesse all parts of man. And that the Cities or Townes, which have either heard the bustling noise of the Tempest, or seene the sparkles of this all-consuming fire at their gates, or have perhaps received their Captaines wounded, their Citizens pursued, and their Souldiers spoiled, and all out of breath, if they be not more than obstinately constant, it is a thousand to one, if in that brunt of furie, they doe not headlong cast themselves into some desperate resolution: yet did he conclude and chose this resolve for the best. First to revoke his forces, he had beyond the Mountaines in *Italie,* and to stay his enemies approches. For, he might on the contrarie part imagine, that being in his owne Countrie, and amidst good friends, he had the better leasure to reenforce his decayed forces, and more opportunity, to strengthen Townes, to munite Castles, to store Rivers with all necessaries they wanted, and to keepe all passages at his devotion, which done, all the wayes should be open for him, and might by them have all manner of victuals, money, and other habilements of warre brought him, in safety, and without convoy: that he should have his subjects so much the more affectionate unto him, by how much nearer they should see the danger: That having so many Cities, Townes, Holds, Castles, and Barres for his securitie, he might at all times, according to opportunitie and advantage, appoint and give Law unto the fight: And if he were pleased to temporize, whilest he tooke his ease, kept his forces whole, and maintained himself in safety, he might see his enemy consume and waste himself, by the difficulties which daily must necessarily assault, environ and combat him, as he who should be engaged in an enemie-countrie and foe-land; Where he should have nothing, nor meet with any thing, either before, or behind him, or of any side; that did not offer him continuall warre: no way nor meanes to refresh, to ease or give his armie elbow-roome, if any sicknesse or contagion should come amongst his men; nor shelter to lodge his hurt and maymed Souldiers: where neither monie, munition, nor victuals might come unto him, but at the swords point; where he should never have leasure to take any rest, or breath; where he should have no knowledge of places, passages, woods, foords, rivers, or countrie, that might defend him from ambuscados, or surprises: And if he should unfortunately chance to lose a battell, no hope to save, or meanes to re-unite the reliques of his forces. And there want not examples to strengthen both sides. *Scipio* found it better for him to invade his enemies countrie of *Africa*, than to defend his owne, and fight with him in *Italie*, where he was, wherein he had good successe. But contrariwise, *Hanniball*, in the same warre wrought his owne overthrow, by leaving the conquest of a forraine countrie, for to goe and defend his owne. The Athenians having left the enemie in their owne land, for to passe into *Sicilie*, had very ill successe, and were much contraried by fortune: whereas *Agathocles* King of *Siracusa* prospered and was favoured by her, what time he passed into *Africa*, and left the warre on foot in his owne countrie. And we are accustomed to say with some shew of reason, that especially in matters of warre, the events depend (for the greatest part) on fortune; which seldome will yeeld, or never subject her selfe unto our discourse or wisdome, as say these ensuing verses.

> *Et malè consultis pretium est, prudentia fallax,*
> *Nec fortuna probat causas sequiturque merentes:*
> *Sed vaga per cuntos nullo discrimine fertur:*
> *Scilicet est aliud quod nos cogatque regatque*
> *Majus, et in proprias ducat mortalia leges.*
>
> MANIL. Astr. iv. 95.

'Tis best for ill advis'd, wisdome may faile,
Fortune proves not the cause that should prevaile,
But here and there without respect doth saile,
A higher power forsooth us over-drawes,
And mortall states guides with immortall lawes.

But if it be well taken, it seemeth that our counsels and deliberations, doe as much depend of her; and that fortune doth also engage our discourses and consultations in her trouble and uncertaintie. *We reason rashly, and discourse at random*, saith *Timeus* in *Plato: For, even as we, so have our discourses great participation with the temeritie of hazard.*

CHAPTER XLVIII

OF STEEDS, CALLED IN FRENCH DESTRIERS

BEHOLD, I am now become a Gramarian, I, who never learn't tongue but by way of roat, and that yet know not what either Adjective, Conjunctive, or Ablative meaneth. As far as I remember, I have sometimes heard say, that the Romanes had certaine horses, which they called *Funales*, or *Dextrarios*, which on the right hand were led by, as spare horses, to take them fresh at any time of need: And thence it commeth, that we call horses of service *Destriers*, And our ancient Romanes doe ordinarily say, to *Adexter*, in steed of, to accompanie. They also called *Desultorios equos*, certaine horses that were so taught, that mainly-running with all the speed they had, joyning sides to one another, without either bridle or saddle, the Roman gentlemen armed at all assayes, in the middest of their running-race, would cast and recast themselves from one to another horse. The Numidian men at armes, were wont to have a second spare-horse led by hand, that in the greatest furie of the battell, they might shift and change horse: *Quibus, desultorum in modum, binos trahentibus equos, inter acerrimam sæpe pugnam in recentem equum ex fesso armatis transultare, mos erat. Tanta velocitas ipsis, tamque docile equorum genus* (LIV. *Bel. Pun.* dec. iii. 3). *Whose manner was, as if they had beene vaulters, leading two horses with them in armour to leap from their tired horse to the fresh-one, even in the hottest of the fight. So great agilitie was in themselves, and so apt to be taught was the race of their horses.* There are many horses found, that are taught to helpe their master, to run upon any man shall offer to draw a naked sword upon them; furiously to leap upon any man, both with feet to strike, and with teeth to bite, that shall affront them; but that for the most part they rather hurt their friends than their enemies. Considering also, that if they once be grapled, you cannot easily take them off, and you must needs stand to the mercie of their combat. *Artibius,* Generall of the Persian armie had very ill lucke to be mounted upon a horse fashioned in this schoole, at what time he fought man to man against *Onesilus* King of *Salamis;* for, he was the cause of his death, by reason the shield-bearer or squire of *Onesilus* cut him with a faulchon betweene the two shoulders, even as he was leaping upon his master. And if that, which the Italians report be true, that in the battell of *Fornovo,* King *Charles,* his horse with kicking, winching, and flying, rid both his master and himselfe from the enemies that encompast him, to dismount or kill him, and without that, he had beene lost: He committed himselfe to a great hazard, and scap't a narrow scowring. The Mammalukes boast, that they have the nimblest and readiest horses of any men at armes in the world. That both by nature they are instructed to discerne, and by custome taught to distinguish their enemie, on whom they must leap and wince with feet, and bite with teeth, according to the voice their master speaketh, or rider giveth them. And are likewise taught to take up from the ground, lances, darts, or any other weapons with their mouths, and as he commandeth to present them to their rider. It is said of *Cæsar,* and of *Pompey* the Great, that amongst their many other excellent qualities, they were also most cunning and perfect horsemen; and namely of *Cæsar,* that in his youth being mounted upon a horse, and without any bridle, he made him run a full cariere, make a sodaine stop, and with his hands behind his backe performe what ever can be expected of an excellent ready horse. And even as nature was pleased to make both him and *Alexander* two matchlesse miracles in militarie profession, so would you say, she hath also endevoured, yea, enforced herselfe to arme them extraordinarily; For, all men know, that *Alexanders* horse called *Bucephalus,* had a head shaped like unto that of a bull; that he suffered no man to get-on and sit him, but his master; that none could weald and manage him but he; what honours were done him after his death, all know, for he had a Citie erected in his name. *Cæsar* likewise had another, who had his fore-feet like unto a mans, with hoofes cloven in forme of fingers, who could never be handled, drest, or mounted but by *Cæsar,* who when he died, dedicated his image to the Goddesse *Venus.* If I be once on horse-backe, I alight very unwillingly; for, it is the seat I like best, whether I be sound or sicke. Plato *commendeth it to be availefull for health:* And Plinie *affirmeth the same to be health-full for the stomacke, and for the joynts.* And sithence we be falne into this subject, let us a little follow it I pray you. We read of a law in *Xenophon,* by which all men that either had or were able to keepe a horse, were expresly forbidden to travell and goe a foot. *Trogus* and *Justinus* report, that the Parthians were not only accustomed to warre on horse-backe, but also to dispatch all their businesse, and negotiate their affaires both publike and privat; as to bargaine, to buy, to sell, to parly, to meet, to entertaine one another, and to converse and walke together; and that the chiefest difference betweene free men and ser-vants amongst them, is that the first ever ride, and the other goe alwais on foot. An institution first devised by King *Cyrus.* There are many ex-amples in the Romane histories (and *Suetonius* doth more particularly note it in *Cæsar*) of Captaines that commanded their horsemen to alight, whensoever, by occasion, they should be urged unto it, thereby to remove all manner of hope from their Souldiers to save themselves by flight, and for the advantage they hoped for in this manner of fight: *Quo haud dubiè superat Romanus* (Liv. dec. i. 3 & 7). *Wherein un-dauntedly the Romanes is superiour to all,* saith *Titus Livius.* yet shall we see, that the first provision, and chiefe meanes they used to bridle rebellion amongst their new conquered nations, was to deprive them of all armes and horses. Therefore finde we so often in *Cæsar; Arma proferri, jumenta produci, obsides dari jubet* (Cæs. *Comment.* vii.): *He commands all their armour should be brought forth, all their cattell should be driven out, and hostages should be delivered.* The great Turke doth not permit at this day any Christian or Jew, to have or keepe any horse for himselfe, throughout all his large Empire. Our ancestors, and especially at what time we had warres with the English, in all solemne combats, or set battels, would (for the most part) alight from their horses, and fight on foot, because they would not adventure to hazard so precious a thing as their honour and life, but on the trust of their owne proper strength, and vigour of their undaunted courage, and con-fidence of their limbs. Let *Chrisanthes* in *Xenophon* say what he pleas-eth: whosoever fighteth on horsebacke, engageth his valour, and haz-ardeth his fortune on that of his horse; his hurts, his stumbling, his death, drawes your life and fortune into consequence, if he chance to startle or be afraid, then are you induced to doubt or feare: if to leape forward, then to become rash and fond-hardy: if he want a good mouth or a timely spurre, your honour is bound to answer for it. And therefore doe not I finde it strange, that those combats were more firme and furious, than those which now we see foughten on horse-backe.

> —*cedebant pariter, pariterque ruebant*
> *Victores, victique, neque his fuga nota, neque illis.*
> 　　　　　　　　　　　　　　　VIRG. *Æn.* x. 756.

The victors and the vanquisht both together
Gave backe, came on: the flight was knowne in neither.

Their battels are seene much better compact and contrived: They are now but bickerings and routs: *primus clamor atque impetus rem decernit. The first shout and shocke makes an end of the matter.* And the thing we call to helpe us, and keepe us company in so great and hazardous an adventure, ought as much as possible may be, lie still in our disposition and absolute power. As I would counsell a gentleman to chuse the shortest weapons, and such as he may best assure himselfe of. It is most apparant, that a man may better assure himselfe of a sword he holdeth in his hand, than of a bullet shot out of a pistoll, to which belong so many severall parts, as powder, stone, locke, snaphanse, barrell, stocke, scowring-peece, and many others, whereof if the least faile, or chance to breake, and be distempered, it is able to overthrow, to hazard, or miscarry your fortune. Seldome doth that blow come or light on the marke it is aymed at, which the ayre doth carry.

> *Et quò ferre velint permittere vulnera ventis,*
> *Ensis habet vires, et gens quæcunque virorum est,*
> *Bella gerit gladii.*—LUCAN. viii. 384.

Giving windes leave to give wounds as they list,
But swords have strength, and right men never mist
With sword t' assalt, and with sword to resist.

But concerning that weapon, I shall more amply speake of it, where I will make a comparison between ancient and moderne armies: And except the astonishment and frighting of the eare, which nowadaies is growne so familiar amongst men, that none doth greatly feare it; I thinke it to be a weapon of small effect, and hope to see the use of it abolished. That wherewith the Italians were wont to throw, with fire in it, was more frightfull and terrour-moving. They were accustomed to name a kinde of javelin, *Phalarica,* armed at one end with an yron pike of three foot long, that it might pierce an armed man through, which lying in the field they used to lanch or hurle with the hand, and sometimes to shoot out of certain engines, for to defend besieged places: the staffe whereof being wreath'd about with hemp or flax, all pitched and oiled over, flying in the ayre, would soone be set afire, and lighting upon any body or target, deprived the partie hit therewith, of all use of weapons or limbes: Me thinkes neverthelesse, that comming to grapple, it might as well hinder the assailant, as trouble the assailed, and that the ground strewed with such burning truncheons, might in a pell-mell-confusion produce a common incommoditie.

—*magnum stridens contorta phalarica venit*
Fulminis acta modo.—VIRG. Æn. ix. 705.

With monstrous buzzing came a fire-dart thirled,
As if a thunder-bolt had there beene whirled.

They had also other meanes, to the use of which custome enured them, and that by reason of inexperience seeme incredible to us; wherewith they supplied the defect of our powder and bullets. They with such fury darted their *Piles*, and with such force hurled their javelins, that they often pierced two targets and two armed men through, as it were with a spit. They hit as sure and as farre with their slings, as with any other shot: *Saxis globosis funda, mare apertum incessentes: coronas modici circuli magno ex intervallo loci assueti trajicere: non capita modò hostium vulnerabant, sed quem locum destinassent* (LIV. dec. iv. 8). *While they were boyes, with round stones in a sling, making ducks and drakes upon the sea, they accustomed to cast through round marks of small compasse a great distance off: whereby they not only hit and hurt the heads of their enemies, but would strike any place they aymed at.* Their battering or murthering peeces represented, as well the effect, as the clattering and thundering noise of ours: *ad ictus mœnium cum terribili sonitu editos, pavor et trepidatio cœpit. At the batterie of the walles made with a terrible noise, feare and trembling began to attach them within.* The Gaules, our ancient forefathers in *Asia*, hated mortally such treacherous and flying weapons, as they that were taught to fight hand to hand, and with more courage. *Non tam patentibus plagis moventur, ubi latior quàm altior plaga est, etiam gloriosius se pugnare putant; iidem quum aculeus sagittæ, aut glandis abditæ introrsus tenui vulnere in speciem urit: tum in rabiem et pudorem tam parvæ perimentis pestis versi, prosternunt corpora humi* (LIV. dec. iv. 8). *They are not so much moved with wide gashes, where the wound is more broad than it is deepe, there they thinke, that they fight with more bravery; but when the sting of an arrow or a bullet, with a small wound to shew, gals them inwardly, then falling into rage and shame that so slight a hurt should kill them, they cast their bodies on the ground.*

A model or picture very neere unto an harquebusada. The ten thousand Græcians in their long-lingring, and farre-famous retreat, encountered with a certaine nation, that exceedingly much endomaged them with stiffe, strong and great [bowes], and so long arrowes, that taking them up, they might throw them after the manner of a dart, and with them pierce a target and an armed man thorow and thorow.

The engines which *Dionysius* invented in *Siracusa,* to shoot and cast mightie big arrowes, or rather timber-peeces, and huge-great stones, so farre and with such force, did greatly represent, and come very neere our moderne inventions. We may not also forget, the pleasant seat, which one named master *Peter Pol,* doctor in divinitie used to sit upon his mule, who as *Monstrelet* reporteth, was wont to ride up and downe the streets of *Paris,* ever sitting sideling, as women use. He also saith in another place, that the Gascoines had certaine horses, so fierce and terrible, taught to turne and stop suddenly in running, whereat the French, the Piccards, the Flemmings, and Brabantins (as they who were never accustomed to see the like) were greatly amazed, and thought it a wonder: I use his very words. *Cæsar* speaking of those of *Swethen,* saith, In any skirmish or fight on horse-backe, they often alight to combat on foot, having so trayned and taught their horses, that so long as the fight lasteth, they never bouge from their masters side, that if need require, they may suddenly mount up againe: and according to their naturall custome, there is nothing accounted more base or vile, than to use saddles or bardels, and they greatly contemne and scorne such as use them: So that a few of them feare not to en-counter with a troupe farre exceeding them in number. That which I have other times wondered at, to see a horse fashioned and taught, that a man having but a wand in his hand, and his bridle loose hanging over his eares, might at his pleasure manage, and make him turne, stop, run, cariere, trot, gallop, and what ever else may be expected of an excellent ready horse, was common amongst the Massilians, who never used either bridle or sadle.

Et gens quæ nudo residens Massilia dorso,
Ora levi flectit, frænorum nescia virga.—LUCAN. iv. 681.

Massilian horsemen on bare horse-backe-sit
Manage with light rod, without reynes or bit.

Et Numidæ infræni cingunt.—VIRG. *Æn.* iv. 41.

Numidians who their horses ride
Without bit, round about us bide.

Equi sine frænis, deformis ipse cursus, rigida cervice et extento capite currentium: The horses being without bridles, their course is ill fa-voured, they running with a stiffe necke, and outstrech't head (*like a roasted Pigge:*) *Alphonsus* King of *Spaine,* that first established the order of Knights, called the order of the Bend or skarfe, amongst other rules devised this one, that none of them, upon paine to forfeit a marke of silver, for every time offending, should ever ride either mule or mulet; as I lately read in *Guevaras* epistles, of which whosoever called them his golden epistles, gave a judgement farre different from mine. The *Courtier* saith, *That before his time, it was counted a great shame in a gentleman to be seene riding upon a mule:* Whereas the

Abyssines are of a contrarie opinion, who accordingly as they are advanced, to places of honour, or dignitie, about their Prince, called *Prester-John,* so doe they more and more affect in signe of pompe and state, to ride upon large-great mules. *Xenophon* reporteth, that the *Assirians* were ever wont to keepe their horses fast-tied in fetters or gyves, and ever in the stable, they were so wilde and furious. And for that they required so much time to unshackle, and to harnish them, (lest protracting of so long time, might, if they should chance at unawares, and being unready, to be surprised by their enemies, endomage them) they never tooke up their quarter in any place, except it were well dyked and intrenched: His *Cirus,* whom he maketh so cunning in horsemanship, did alwaies keepe his horses at a certaine stint, and would never suffer them to have any meat before they had deserved the same by the sweat of some exercise. If the Scithians in time of warre chanced to be brought to any necessitie of victuals, the readiest remedy they had, was to let their horses bloud, and therewith all quenched their thirst, and nourished themselves.

Venit et epoto Sarmata pastus equo.—Mart. *Spect.* iii. 4.

The Scithian also came, who strangely feedes
On drinking out his horse (or that hee bleedes).

Those of *Crotta* being hardly besieged by *Metellus,* were reduced to so hard a pinch, and strait necessitie of all manner of other beverage, that they were forced to drinke the stale or urine of their horses. To verifie how much better cheape the Turkes doe both levie, conduct, and maintaine their armies, than we Christians doe; They report, that besides their souldiers never drinke any thing but water, and feed on nothing but rice, and drie-salt flesh, which they reduce into a kinde of powder (whereof every private man doth commonly cary so much about him, as will serve for a moneths provision) and for a shift, will live a long time with the bloud of their horses; wherein they use to put a certaine quantitie of salt, as the Tartars and Moskovites doe. These new discovered people of the Indies, when the Spaniards came first amongst them, esteemed that aswell men as horses, were either gods, or creatures far beyond, and excelling their nature in nobilitie. Some of which, after they were vanquished by them, comming to sue for peace and beg pardon at their hands, to whom they brought presents of gold, and such viands as their countrie yeelded; omitted not to bring the same, and as much unto their horses, and with as solemne Oration as they had made unto men, taking their neighings, as a language of truce and composition. In the [h]ether Indies, the chiefe and royallest honour was anciently wont to be, to ride upon an Elephant; the second to goe in Coaches drawne with foure horses; the third, to ride upon a Camell; the last and basest, was to be carried or drawne by one horse alone. Some of our moderne Writers report, to have seene some Countries in that climate, where the people ride oxen, with packe-saddles, stirrops, and bridles, by which they were carried very easily. *Quintus Fabius Maximus Rutilianus,* warring against the Samnites, and seeing that his horsemen, in three or foure charges they gave, had missed to breake and run through his enemies battalion, at last resolved thus, that they should all unbridle their horses, and with maine force of sharpe spurres pricke and broach them; which done, the horses as enraged, tooke such a running, thorow, and athwart the enemies campe, armes and men, that nought was able to resist them; and with such a furie, that by opening, shouldring, and overthrowing, the battallion, they made way for his Infanterie, which there committed a most bloudie slaughter, and obtained a notable victorie. The like was commanded and effected by *Quintus Fulvius Flaccus* against the Celtiberians: *Id cum majore vi equorum facietis, si effrœnatos in hostes equos, immittitis; quod sœpe Romanos equites cum laude fecisse memoriœ proditum est. Detractisque frœnis bis ultrò citroque cum magna strage hostium, infractis omnibus hastis, transcurrerunt* (LIV. dec. iv. 10). *That shall you doe with more violence of horse, if you force your horse unbridled on the enemie; which it is recorded, the Roman horsemen have often performed with great proofe and praise. So pulling off the bridles, they twice ran through forward, and backe againe with great slaughter of the enemie, all their launces broken.*

The duke of *Moscovie* did anciently owe this reverence unto the Tartars, at what time soever they sent any Ambassadors to him, that he must goe meet them on foot, and present them with a goblet full of mares-milke (a drinke counted very delicious amongst them) which whilst they were drinking, if any drop chaunced to be spilt upon their horses haires, he was, by dutie, bound to licke the same up with his tongue. The armie which the Emperor *Bajazeth* had sent into *Russia*, was overwhelmed by so horrible a tempest of snow, that to find some shelter, and to save themselves from the extremitie of the cold, many advised to kill and unpanch their horses, and enter into their panches, to enjoy and find some ease by that vitall heat. *Bajazeth* after that bloudy and tragicall conflict wherein he was overthrowne by the Scithian *Tamburlane,* in seeking to escape, had no doubt saved himselfe, by the swiftnesse of an Arabian mare, on which he was mounted that day, if unluckily he had not been forced to let her drinke her fill in passing over a river, which made her so faint and foundred, that he was easily overtaken and apprehended by those that pursued him. The common saying is, that to let a horse stale after a full cariere, doth take downe his speed, but I would never have thought that drinking had done it, but rather strengthened and heartned him.

Crœsus passing along the citie of *Sardis,* found certaine thickets, wherein were great store of snakes and serpents, on which his horses fed verie hungerly, which thing, as *Herodotus* saith, was an ill-boding-prodigy into his affaires. We call him an entire horse, that hath his full mane, and whole eares, and which in shew, or at a muster, doth not exceed others. The Lacedemonians having defeated the Athenians in *Sicilie*, returning in great pompe and glory from the victory, into the City of *Siracusa*, among other Bravadoes of theirs, caused such horses as they had taken from their enemies to be shorne all over, and so led in triumph. *Alexander* fought with a nation called *Dahas*, where they went to warre two and two, all armed upon one horse, but when they came to combat, one must alight, and so successively one fought on foot, and the other on horse backe, each in his turne one after another. I am perswaded that in respect of sufficiencie, of comlinesse, and of grace on horseback, no Nation goeth beyond us. A good horse-man, (speaking according to our phrase) seemeth rather to respect an undismayed courage, than an affected cleane seat. The man most skilfull, best and surest-sitting, comeliest-graced, and nimblest-handed, to sit, to ride, and mannage a horse cunningly, that ever I knew, and that best pleased my humour, was Monsieur de *Carnavalet*, who was Master of the horse unto our King *Henry the second*. I have seene a man take his full cariere, standing boult-upright on both his feet in the saddle, leap downe to the ground from it, and turning backe, take off the saddle, and presently set it on againe as fast as ever it was, and then leap into it againe, and al this did he whilst his horse was running as fast as might be with his bridle on his necke. I have also seene him ride over a bonnet or cap, and being gone a good distance from it, with his bow shooting backward, to sticke many arrows in the same; then sitting still in the saddle, to take up any thing from the ground, to set one foot to the ground, and keepe the other in the stirrop, and continually running doe a thousand such tumbling and apish tricks, wherewith he got his living. There have in my time two men beene seene in *Constantinople*, both at once upon one horse, and who in his speediest running, would by turnes, first one, and then another, leape downe to the ground, and then into the saddle againe, the one still taking the others place. And another, who only with teeth, and without the helpe of any hand, would bridle, curry, rub, dresse, saddle, girt, and harnish his horse. Another, that betweene two horses, and bothe saddled, standing upright, with one foot in the one, and the second in the other, did beare another man on his armes, standing upright, run a full speedy course, and the uppermost to shoot and hit any marke with his arrowes. Divers have been seene, who standing on their heads, and with their legs out-stretched aloft, having many sharp-pointed cimitaries fastned round about the saddle, to gallop a full speed. While I was a young lad, I saw the Prince of *Sulmona* at *Naples*, manage a young, a rough and fierce horse, and shew all manner of horsemanship; To hold testons, or reals under his knees and toes, so fast, as if they had been nayled there, and all to shew his sure, steady and unmove-able sitting.

CHAPTER XLIX

OF ANCIENT CUSTOMES

I WOULD willingly excuse our people for having no other patterne or rule of perfection, but his owne customes, his owne fashions: For, it is a common vice, not only in the vulgar sort, but as it were in all men, to bend their ayme, and frame their thoughts unto the fashions, wherein they were borne. I am pleased when he shall see *Fabricius* or *Lælius*, who because they are neither attired, nor fashioned according to our manner, that he condemne their countenance to be strange, and their cariage barbarous. But I bewaile his particular indiscretion, in that he suffereth himselfe to be so blinded, and deceived by the authoritie of present custome, and that if custome pleaseth, he is ready to change opinion, and varie advice, every moneth, nay every day, and judgeth so diversly of himselfe. When he wore short-wasted doublets, and but little lower then his breast, he would maintaine by militant reasons, that the waste was in his right place: but when not long after he came to weare them so longwasted, yea almost so low as his privities, then began he to condemne the former fashion, as fond, intolerable and deformed; and to commend the latter, as comely, handsome, and commendable. A new fashion of apparell creepeth no sooner into use, but presently he blameth, and dispraiseth the old, and that with so earnest a resolution, and universall a consent, that you would say, it is some kind of madnesse, or selfe fond humor, that giddieth his understanding.

And forasmuch as our changing or altering of fashions, is so sudden and new-fangled, that the inventions, and new devices of all the tailors in the world, cannot so fast invent novelties, it must necessarily follow, that neglected and stale rejected fashions doe often come into credit and use againe: And the latest and newest, within a while after come to be outcast and despised, and that one self-same judgement within the space of fifteene or twentie yeares admitteth, not only two or three different, but also cleane contrarie opinions, with so light and incredible inconstancie, that any man would wonder at it. There is no man so suttle-crafty amongst us, that suffreth not himselfe to be enveigled and over-reached by this contradiction, and that is not insensibly dazeled, both with his inward and externall eies. I will heere huddleup some few ancient fashions that I remember: Some of them like unto ours, other-some farre differing from them: To the end, that having ever this continuall variation of humane things in our minde, we may the better enlighten and confirme our transported judgement. That manner of fight which we use now adaies with rapier and cloke, was also used among the Romans, as saith *Cæsar. Sinistris sagos involvunt, gladiosque distringunt* (CÆS. *Bel. Civ.* i.): *They wrap their left armes in their clokes, and draw their swords.* We may to this day observe this vice to be amongst us, and which we have taken from them, that is, to stay such passengers as we meet by the way, and force them to tell us, who they are, whence they come, whither they goe, and to count it as an injurie, and cause of quarrell, if they refuse to answer our demand. In Baths, which our forefathers used daily before meales, as ordinarily as we use water to wash our hands, when first they came into them, they washed but their armes and legges, but afterward (which custome lasted many after-ages; and to this day continueth amongst divers nations of the world) their whole body over, with compounded and perfumed waters, in such sort as they held it as a great testimonie of simplicitie, to wash themselves in pure and uncompounded water: Such as were most delicate, and effeminate, were wont to perfume their whole bodies over and over, three or foure times every day; And often (as our French women have lately taken up) to picke and snip out the haires of their forehead, so they of all their body.

Quod pectus, quod crura tibi, quod brachia vellis.
MART. ii. *Epig.* lxii. 1.

That you from breast, legges, armes, the haire
Neately pull off (to make them faire).

Although they had choice of ointments fit for that purpose.

Psilotro nitet, aut arida latet abdita creta.
Lib. vi. *Epi.* xciii. 9.

She shines with ointments that make haire to fall,
Or with dry chalke she over-covers all.

They loved to lie soft, and on fine downe-beds, alleaging lying on hard matresses as a signe of patience. They fed lying on their beds, neere after the manner of the Turkes nowadaies.

Inde thoro pater Æneas sic orsus ab alto.—VIRG. *Æn.* ii. 2.

Father *Æneas* thus gan say,
From stately couch where then he lay.

And it is reported of *Cato Junior,* that after the battell of *Pharsalia,* and that he began to mourne and bewaile the miserable state of the common-wealth, and ill condition of publike affaires, he ever eat sitting on the ground, folowing an austere, and observing a strict kinde of life. The *Beso las manos* was used as a signe of honour and humilitie, only toward great persons. If friends met, after friendly salutations, they used to kisse one another, as the Venetians doe at this day.

Gratatusque darem cum dulcibus oscula verbis.
OVID. *Pont.* iv. *El.* ix. 13.

Give her I would with greetings graced,
Kisses with sweet words enterlaced.

And in saluting or suing to any great man, they touched his knees. *Pasicles* the Philosopher, brother unto *Crates*, comming to salute one, wheras he should have carried his hand to his knee, carried the same unto his genitories: The partie saluted, having rudely push't him away; *What?* quoth he, *is not that part yours as well as the other?* Their manner of feeding was as ours, their fruit last. They were wont to wipe their tailes (this vaine superstition of words must be left unto women) with a sponge, and that's the reason why *Spongia* in Latine is counted an obscene word: which sponge was ever tied to the end of a staffe, as witnesseth the storie of him, that was carried to be devoured of the wild beasts before the people, who desiring leave to goe to a privie before his death, and having no other meanes to kill himselfe, thrust downe the sponge and staffe, hee found in the privie, into his throte, wherewith he choked himselfe. Having ended the delights of nature, they were wont to wipe their privities with perfumed wooll.

> *At tibi nil faciam, sed lotâ mentula lanâ.*
> MART. xi. *Epig.* li. 11.

To thee no such thing will I bring,
But with wash't wooll another thing.

In every street of *Rome* were placed tubs, and such vessels for passengers to make water in.

> *Pusi sœpe lacum propter, se ac dolia curta*
> *Somno dejuncti credunt extollere vestem.*—LUCR. iv. 1018.

Children asleepe oft thinke they take up all
Neere to some pissing tub, some lake, some wall.

They used to breake their fast, and nonchion betweene meales, and all summer time, had men that sold snowe up and downe the streets, wherewith they refreshed their wines; of whom some were so daintie, that all winter long they used to put snow into their wine, not deeming it cold enough. Principall, and noble men had their cup-bearers, tasters, carvers and buffons to make them merrie. In Winter their viandes were brought and set on the boord upon arches, as we use chafing dishes; and had portable kitchins (of which I have seene some) wherein might be drawne, wheresoever one list, a whole service and messe of meat.

> *Has vobis epulas habete lauti,*
> *Nos offendimur ambulante cœna.*—MART. vii. *Epig.* xlvii. 5.

Take you daintie-mouth'd such stirring feasts;
With walking meales we are offended guests.

And in summer they often caused cold water (being carried through pipes) to drill upon them as they sate in their dining-chambers, or lowe parlers, where in cesterns, they kept store of fish alive, which the by-standers might at their pleasure, chuse and take with their hands, and have it drest every man according to his fantasie. Fish hath ever had this privilege, as at this day it hath; that chiefe Gentlemen, are pleased, and have skill to dress-it best: And to say truth, the taste of fish is much more delicat and exquisit, than that of flesh, at least in mine. But in all manner of magnificence, delitiousnes, riotous gluttonie, inventions of voluptuousnes, wantonnes, and sumptuositie, we truly endevour, as much as may be, to equall and come neere them: For, our will and taste is as much corrupted as theirs, but our skill, and sufficiencie is farre short of them: Our wit is no more capable, and our strength no more able to approach and match them in these vitious and blame-worthy parts, than in vertuous and commendable actions: For, both proceede from a vigor of spirit, and farre-reaching wit; which, without comparison, was much greater in them, than now in us. And mindes, by how much more strong, and excellent they are, so much lesse facultie and meanes have they, to doe, either excellently well, or notoriously ill. The chiefest aime amongst them, was a meane or mediocrity. The *Foremost* or *Last,* in writing or speaking, had no signification of preheminence or greatnes, as may evidently appeare by their writings. They would as familiarly and as soone say, *Oppius* and *Cæsar,* as *Cæsar* and *Oppius;* and as indifferently, I and thou, as thou and I. And that's the reason why I have heretofore noted in the life of *Flaminius,* in our French *Plutarke,* a place, where it seemeth that the Author, speaking of the jealousie of glorie, that was betweene the Ætolians and the Romans, for the gaine of a battell, which they had obtained in common, maketh for the purpose, that in Greeke songs the Ætolians were named before the Romans, except there bee some Amphibology in the French words: for, in that toung I reade it. When Ladies came unto stoves or hot-houses, they made it not daintie to admit men into their companie, and to be washed, rubbed, chafed and annointed by the hands of their groomes and pages.

Inguina succinctus nigrà tibi servus alutâ
—Statt, quoties calidis nuda foveris æquis.—Epig. xxxiv. i.

Your man, whose loynes blacke-lether gird's, stand's-by,
Whilst in warme water you starke-naked lie.

They also used to sprinkle themselves all over with certaine powders, thereby to alay and represse all manner of filth or sweat. The ancient *Gaules* (saith *Sidonius Apollinaris*) wore their haire long before, and all the hinder part of their head shaven, a fashion that our wanton youths and effeminate gallants, have lately renued, and in this newfangled and fond-doting age, brought up againe, with wearing of long-dangling locks before. The ancient Romans, paid the watermen their fare or due so soone as they came into the boat, whereas we pay it when they set us on shore.

—dum as exigitur, dum mula ligatur,
Tota abit hora.—HOR. i. *Sat.* v. 13.

While they call for their fare, tie drawe-mule to,
There runs away, a full houre, if not two.

Women were wont to lie on the utmost side of the bed, and therefore
was *Cæsar* called *Sponda Regis Nicomedis* (SUET. *Jul. Cæs.* c. 49):
King Nicomedes his beds side: They tooke breathe while they were
drinking, and used to baptise, or put water in their wines.

—quis puer ocius
Restinguet ardentis falerni
Pocula prætereunte limphâ?—HOR. ii. *Od.* xi. 18.

What boy of mine or thine
Shall coole our cup of wine
With running water fine?

Those cousening and minde-deceiving countenances of lakeis were also
amongst them.

O Jane, à tergo quem nulla ciconia pinsit
Nec manus auriculas imitata est mobilis albas,
Nec linguæ quantum sitiet canis Apula tantum.
PERS. *Sat.* i. 58.

O *Janus,* whom behinde no Storks-bill doth deride,
Nor nimble hand resembling mak's eares white and wide,
Nor so much tongue lil'd out as dogges with thirst ore-dride.

The Argian and Romane Ladies, mourned in white, as our dames
wont to doe; and if I might be credited, and beare-sway amongst them,
they should continue it still. But because there are many bookes, that
treat of this argument, I will say no more of it.

CHAPTER L

OF DEMOCRITUS AND HERACLITUS

JUDGEMENT is an instrument for all subjects, and medleth every
where, And therefore in the Essayes I make of it, there is no maner of
occasion, I seeke not to employ therein. If it be a subject I understand
not my selfe, therein I make triall of it, sounding afarre off the depth
of the ford, and finding the same over deepe for my reach, I keepe my
selfe on the shoare. And to acknowledge not to be able to wade through,
is a part of its effect, yea of such, whereof he vanteth most. If I light
upon a vaine and idle subject, I assay to trie, and endevour to see,
whether I may find a good ground to worke upon, and matter to frame
a body, and wherewith to build and under-lay it. Sometimes I ad-

dresse my judgement and contrive it to a noble and out-worne subject, wherein is nothing found subsisting of it selfe, the high way to it, being so bare-trodden, that it cannot march, but in other steps. There he pleaseth himselfe in chusing the course he thinkes best, and a thousand paths sometimes he saith, this or that was best chosen. I take my first Argument of fortune: All are alike unto me: And I never purpose to handle them throughly: For, there is nothing wherein I can perceive the full perfection: Which they doe not that promise to shew it us. Of a hundred parts and visages that every thing hath, I take one, which sometimes I slightly runne over, and other times but cursorily glance at. And yet other whilst I pinch it to the quicke. And give it a *Stockado*, not the widest, but the deepest I can. And for the most part I love to seize upon them by some unwonted lustre. I would adventure to treat and discourse of some matter to the depth; knew I my selfe lesse, or were I deceived in mine owne impuissance; Scattering here one and there another word: Scantlings taken from their maine ground-work, disorderly dispersed, without any well-grounded designe and promise. I am not bound to make it good, nor without varying to keepe my selfe close-tied unto it; whensoever it shall please me to yeeld my selfe to doubt, to uncertaintie, and to my Mistris forme, which is ignorance. Each motion sheweth and discovereth what we are. The very same minde of *Cæsar*, we see in directing, marshalling, and setting the battel of *Pharsalia*, is likewise seene to order, dispose, and contrive, idle, trifling and amorous devices. We judge of a horse, not only by seeing him ridden, and cunningly managed, but also by seeing him trot, or pace; yea, if we but looke upon him as he stands in the stable. Amongst the functions of the soule, some are but meane and base. He that seeth her no further, can never know her thorowly. And he that seeth her march her naturall and simple pace, doth peradventure observe her best. The winds of passions take her most in her highest pitch, seeing she entirely coucheth herselfe upon very matter, and wholy therein exerciseth herselfe: and handleth but one at once; not according to it, but according to herselfe. Things severall in themselves have peradventure, weight, measure, and condition: But inwardly, in us, she cuts it out for them, as she understandeth the same herselfe. Death is fearefull and ugly into *Cicero;* wished for and desired of *Cato:* and indifferent unto *Socrates*. Health, well-fare, conscience, authoritie, riches, glorie, beautie, and their contraries are dispoyled at the entrance, and receive a new vesture at the soules hand. Yea, and what colour she pleaseth; browne, bright, greene, sad, or any hew else: sharpe or sweete, deepe or superficiall, and what each of them pleaseth. For none of them did ever verifie their stiles, their rules, or formes in common; each one severally is a Queene in her owne estate. Therefore let us take no more excuses from externall qualities of things. To us it belongeth to give our selves accoumpt of it. Our good, and our evill hath no dependancy, but from our selves. Let us offer our vowes and offerings unto it; and not to fortune. She hath no power over our manners. Why shall I not judge of *Alexander*, as I am sitting and drinking at Table, and talking in good company? Or if hee were playing at Chesse, what string of his wit doth not touch or harpe on this fond-childish, and time-consuming play? I lothe and shun it, only because there is not sport enough in it, and that in his recreation, he is over serious with us, being ashamed I must apply that attention therunto, as might be imployed on some good subject. He was no more busied in levying his forces and preparing for his glorious passage into *India;* nor this other in disentangling and discovering of a passage, whence dependeth the well-fare and safety of mankind. See how much our mind troubleth this ridiculous ammuzing, if all her sinnewes bandy not. How amply she giveth every one Law in that, to know and directly to judge of himselfe. I doe not more universally view and feele my selfe in any other posture. What passion does not exercise us thereunto? Choller, spight, hatred, impatience, and vehement ambition to overcome, in a matter wherein it were haply more excusable to be ambitious for to be vanquished. For, a rare pre-excellencie, and beyond the common reach, in so frivolous a thing, is much mis-seeming a man of honour. What I say of this example, may be spoken of all others. Every parcell, every occupation of a man, accuseth, and sheweth him equall unto another. *Democritus* and *Heraclitus* were two Philosophers, the first of which, finding and deeming humane condition to be vaine and ridiculous, did never walke abroad, but with a laughing, scorneful and mocking countenance: Whereas *Heraclitus* taking pitie and compassion of the very same condition of ours, was continually seene with a sad, mournfull, and heavie cheere, and with teares trickling downe his blubbered eyes.

—Alter

Ridebat quoties à limine moverat unum
Protuleràtque pedem, flebat contrarius alter.
                                        JUVEN. *Sat.* x. 28.

One from his doore, his foot no sooner past,
But straight he laught; the other wept as fast.

I like the first humor best, not because it is more pleasing to laugh, than to weepe; but for it is more disdainfull, and doth more condemne us than the other. And me thinkes we can never bee sufficiently despised, according to our merit. Bewailing and commiseration, are commixed with some estimation of the thing moaned and wailed. Things scorned and contemned, are thought to be of no worth. I cannot be perswaded, there can be so much ill lucke in us, as there is apparant vanitie, nor so much malice, as sottishnesse. We are not so full of evill, as of voydnesse and inanitie. We are not so miserable, as base and abject. Even so *Diogenes*, who did nothing but trifle, toy, and dally with himselfe, in rumbling and rowling of his tub, and flurting at *Alexander*, accompting us but flies, and bladders puft with winde, was a more sharp, a more bitter, and a more stinging judge, and by consequence, more just and fitting my humor, than *Timon*, surnamed the hater of all mankinde. For looke what a man hateth, the same thing he takes to hart. *Timon* wisht all evill might light on us; He was passionate in desiring our ruine. He shunned and loathed our conversation, as dangerous and wicked, and of a depraved nature: Whereas the other so little regarded us, that wee could neither trouble nor alter him by our contagion; forsooke our company, not for feare, but for disdaine of our commerce: He never thought us capable or sufficient to doe either good or evill. Of the same stampe was the answer of *Statilius* to whom *Brutus* spake to win him to take part, and adhere to the conspiracie against *Cæsar:* He allowed the enterprize to be very just, but disalowed of the men that should performe the same, as unworthy that any man should put himself in any adventure for them: Conformable to the discipline of *Hegesias,* who said, *That a wise man ought never to doe any thing, but for himselfe;* forasmuch as he alone is worthy to have any action performed for him: and to that of *Theodorus, who thought it an injustice, that a wise man should in any case hazard himselfe for the good and benefit of his countrie, or to indanger his wisdome for fooles.* Our owne condition is as ridiculous, as risible; as much to be laught at, as able to laugh.

CHAPTER LI

OF THE VANITIE OF WORDS

A RETHORICIAN of ancient times, said, that his trade was, to make small things appeare and seeme great. It is a shooemaker, that can make great shooes for a little foot. Had hee lived in *Sparta*, he had doubtlesse beene well whipped, for professing a false, a couzening and deceitfull art. And I thinke, *Archidamus* King of that Citie did not without astonishment listen unto the answer of *Thucydides,* of whom he demanded, whether he, or *Pericles,* was the strongest and nimblest wrestler; whose answer was this, *Your question Sir, is very hard to be decided; for if in wrestling with him, I give him a fall, with his faire words he perswadeth those that saw him on the ground, that he never fell, and so gets the victorie.* Those that maske and paint women, commit not so foule a fault; for it is no great losse, though a man see them not, as they were naturally borne and unpainted: Whereas these professe to deceive and beguile, not our eies, but our judgement; and to bastardize and corrupt the essence of things. Those common-wealths, that have maintained themselves in a regular, formal, and well governed estate, as that of *Creete* and *Lacedemon,* did never make any great esteeme of Orators. *Ariston* did wisely define Rhetorike *to be a Science, to perswade the vulgar people: Socrates* and *Plato, to be an*

Art to deceive and flatter. And those which denie it in the generall description, doe every where in their precepts verifie the same. The Mahometans, by reason of it's inutilitie, forbid the teaching of it to their children. And the Athenians, perceiving how pernicious the profession and use thereof was, and of what credit in their Citie, ordained, that their principall part, which is to move affections, should be dismissed and taken away, together with all *exordiums* and *perorations*. It is an instrument devised, to busie, to manage, and to agitate a vulgar and disordered multitude; and is an implement imployed, but about distempered and sicke mindes, as Physicke is about crazed bodies. And those where either the vulgar, the ignorant, or the generalitie have had all power, as that of *Rhodes,* those of *Athens,* and that of *Rome,* and where things have ever beene in continuall disturbance and uproare, thither have Orators and the professors of that Art flocked. And verily, if it be well looked into, you shall finde very few men in those common-wealths, that without helpe of eloquence have attained to any worthy estimation and credit: *Pompey, Cæsar, Crassus, Lucullus, Lentulus, Metellus,* have thence taken their greatest stay and furtherance, whereby they have ascended unto that height and greatnesse of authoritie, whereunto they at last attained, and against the opinion of better times have more prevailed with words than with armes. For, *L. Volumnius* speaking publikely in favour of the election, which some had made of *Quintus Fabius,* and *Publius Decius,* to be Consuls; saith thus; *They are men borne unto warre, of high spirits, of great performance, and able to effect any thing, but rude, simple, and unarted in the combat of talking; minds truly consulare. They only are good Pretors, to do justice in the Citie* (saith he) *that are subtile, cautelous, well-spoken, wily and lip-wise.* Eloquence hath chiefly flourished in *Rome* when the common-wealths affaires have beene in worst estate, and that the devouring Tempest of civill broyles, and intestine warres did most agitate and turmoyle them. Even as a rancke, free and untamed soyle, beareth the rankest and strongest weeds, whereby it seemeth that those common-weales, which depend of an absolute Monarch, have lesse need of it than others: For, that foolishnesse and facilitie, which is found in the common multitude, and which doth subject the same, to be managed, perswaded, and led by the eares, by the sweet alluring and sense-entrancing sound of this harmonie, without duely weighing, knowing, or considering the trueth of things by the force of reason: This facilitie and easie yeelding, I say, is not so easily found in one only ruler, and it is more easie to warrant him from the impression of this poyson, by good institution and sound counsell. There was never seene any notable or farre-renowned Orator to come out of *Macedon* or *Persia.* What I have spoken of it, hath beene upon the subject of an Italian, whom I have lately entertained into my service. Who during the life of the whilom cardinal *Caraffa* served him in the place of steward of his house. Enquiring of his charge, and particular qualitie, he told me, a long, formall, and eloquent discourse of the science or skill of epicurisme and gluttonie, with such an Ora-torie-gravitie, and Magistrale countenance, as if he had discoursed of some high mysterious point of divinitie, wherein he hath very methodi-cally decifred and distinguished sundrie differences of appetites: First of that which a man hath fasting, then of that men have after the first, the second, and third service. The severall means how sometimes to please it simply, and other times to sharpen and provoke the same; the policie and rare invention of his sawces: First, in general terms, then particularizing the qualities and severall operations of the in-gredients, and their effects: The differences of salades according to their distinct seasons, which must be served in warme, and which cold: The manner how to dresse, how to adorne, and embellish them, to make them more pleasing to the sight. After that, he entred into a large and farre-fetcht narration, touching the true order, and due method of service, full of goodly and important considerations.

> —*Nec minimo sanè discrimine refert,*
> *Quo gestu lepores, et quo gallina secetur.—Sat.* v. 127.

What grace we use it, it makes small diff'rence, when
We carve a Hare, or else breake up a Hen.

And all that, filled up and stuffed with rich magnificent words, well couched phrases, oratorie figures, and patheticall metaphors; yea such as learned men use and imploy in speaking of the Government of an Empire, which made me remember my man.

> *Hoc salsum est, hoc adustum est, hoc lautum est parum,*
> *Illud rectè, iterum sic memento, sedulò,*
> *Moneo quæ possum pro mea sapientia.*
> *Postremò tanquam in speculum, in patinas, Demea,*
> *Inspicere jubeo, et moneo quid facto usus sit.*
> TER. *Adel.* act. iii. sc. iv. 62.

This dish is salt, this burnt, this not so fine,
That is well done, doe so againe; Thus I
As my best wisdome serves, all things assigne.
Lastly Sir, I command, they neatly prie,
On dishes, as a glasse,
And shew what needfull was.

Yet did those strict Græcians commend the order and disposition, which *Paulus Æmilius* observed in the banquet he made them at his returne from *Macedon:* But here I speake not of the effects, but of the words. I know not whether they worke that in others, which they doe in mee. But when I heare our Architects mouth-out those big, and ratling words of *Pilasters, Architraves, Cornixes, Frontispieces, Corin-thian,* and *Dorike* works, and such like fustian-termes of theirs, I cannot let my wandering imagination from a sodaine apprehension of *Apollidonius* his pallace, and I find by effect, that they are the seely, and decayed peeces of my kitchin-doore. Doe but heare one pronounce *Metonymia, Metaphore, Allegory, Etimologie,* and other such trash-names of Grammer, would you not thinke, they meant some forme of a rare and strange language; They are titles and words that concerne your chamber-maids tittle-tattle. It is a fopperie and cheating tricke, cousin-Germane unto this, to call the offices of our estate by the proud titles of the ancient Romans, though they have no resemblance at all of charge, and lesse of authoritie and power. And this likewise, which in mine opinion will one day remaine as a reproch unto our age, un-worthily, and undeservedly to bestow on whom we list, the most glorious Surnames and loftiest titles, wherewith antiquitie in many long-continued ages honoured but one or two persons. *Plato* hath by such an universal consent borne-away the surname of Divine, that no man did ever attempt to envie him for it. And the Italians, which vaunt (and indeed with some reason) to have generally more lively, and farre reaching wits, and their discourse more sound and sinnowy, than other nations of their times, have lately therewith embellished *Peter Aretine;* in whom except it be an high-raised, proudly-pufft, mind-moving, and heart-danting manner of speech, yet in good sooth more than ordinarie, wittie and ingenious; But so new fangled, so extravagant, so fantasticall, so deep-laboured; and to conclud, besides the eloquence, which be it as it may be, I cannot perceive any thing in it, beyond or exceeding that of many other writers of his age, much lesse that it in any sort approacheth that ancient divinitie. And the surname Great, we attribute and fasten the same on Princes, that have nothing in them exceeding popular greatnesse.

CHAPTER LII

OF THE PARCIMONIE OF OUR FOREFATHERS

ATTILIUS REGULUS, Generall of the Romans armie in *Affrike,* in the middest of his glorie and victorie against the Carthaginians, writ unto the common-wealth, that a hyne or plough-boy, whom he had left alone to oversee and husband his land (which in all was but seven acres of ground) was run away from his charge, and had stolne from him all his implements and tools, belonging to his husbandrie, craving leave to be discharged, and that he might come home to looke to his businesse, for feare his wife and children should therby be endomaged: the Senate tooke order for him, and appointed another man to looke to his land and businesse, and made that good unto him, which the other had stolne from him, and appointed his wife and children to be maintained at the common-wealths charge. *Cato* the elder returning

Consul from *Spaine,* sold his horse of service, to save the monie he should have spent for his transport by sea into *Italie:* And being chiefe governor in *Sardinia,* went all his visitations a foot, having no other traine, but one officer of the common-wealth, who carried his gowne, and a vessell to do sacrifice in, and for the most part carried his male himselfe. He boasted that he never woare gowne, that cost him more than ten crowns, nor sent more than one shilling sterling to the market for one whole daies provision, and had no Countrie house rough-cast or painted over. *Scipio Æmilianus,* after he had triumphed twice, and twice been Consull, went on a solemne Legation, accompanied and attended on only with seven servants. It is reported that *Homer* had never any more than one servant. *Plato* three, and *Zeno* chiefe of the Stoikes sect, none at all. *Tiberius Gracchus,* being then one of the principal men amongst the Romanes, and sent in commission about weightie matters of the common-wealth, was allotted but six-pence halfe-penie a day for his charges.

CHAPTER LIII

OF A SAYING OF CÆSAR

IF we shall sometimes ammuse our selves and consider our estate, and the time we spend in controling others, and to know the things that are without us; would we but emploie the same in sounding our selves throughly, we should easily perceive how all this our contexture is built of weake and decaying peeces. Is it not an especiall testimonie of imperfection, that we cannot settle our contentment on any one thing, and that even of our owne desire and imagination, it is beyond our power to chuse what we stand in need of? Whereof the disputation that hath ever beene amongst Philosophers beareth sufficient witnes, to finde out the chiefe felicitie or *summum bonum* of man, and which yet doth, and shall eternally last without resolution or agreement.

> —*dum abest quod avemus, id exuperare videtur*
> *Cætera, post aliud cùm contigit illud avemus,*
> *Et sitis æqua tenet.*—LUCR. iii. 25.

While that is absent which we wish, the rest
That seemes to passe, when ought else is addrest,
That we desire, with equal thirst opprest.

Whatsoever it be that falleth into our knowledge and jovissance, we finde, it doth not satisfie us, and we still follow and gape after future, uncertaine, and unknowne things, because the present and knowne please us not, and doe not satisfie us. Not (as I thinke) because they have not sufficiently wherewith to satiate and please us, but the reason is, that we apprehend and seize on them with an unruly, disordered, and diseased taste and hold-fast.

> *Nam cùm vidit hic ad usum quæ flagitat usus,*
> *Omnia jam fermè mortalibus esse parata,*
> *Divitiis homines et honore et laude potentes*
> *Affluere, atque bonâ natorum excellere famâ,*
> *Nec minus esse domi, cuiquam tamen anxia corda,*
> *Atque animum infestis cogi servire querelis:*
> *Intellexit ibi vitium vas facere ipsum,*
> *Omniaque illius vitio corrumpier intus*
> *Quæ collata foris et commoda quæ que venirent.*
>
> LUCR. ix.

For when the wiseman saw, that all almost,
That use requires, for men prepared was,
That men enriches, honors, praises boast,
In good report of children others passe,
Yet none at home did beare lesse pensive heart,
But that the minde was forst to serve complaint,
He knew, that fault the vessell did empart,
That all was marr'd within by vessels taint,
What ever good was wrought by any art.

Our appetite is irresolute, and uncertaine; it can neither hold nor enjoy any thing handsomly and after a good fashion. Man supposing it is the vice and fault of things he possesseth, feedeth and filleth himselfe with other things, which he neither knoweth, nor hath understanding of, whereto he applyeth both his desires and hopes, and taketh them as an honour and reverence to himselfe; as saith *Cæsar, Communi fit vitio naturæ, ut invisis, latitantibus atque incognitis rebus magis confidamus, vehementiusque exterreamur* (CÆS. *Bel. Civ.* ii.). *It hapneth by the common fault of nature, that both wee are more confident, and more terrified by things unseene, things hidden, and unknowne.*

CHAPTER LIV

OF VAINE SUBTILTIES, OR SUBTILL DEVICES

THERE are certaine frivolous and vaine inventions, or as some call them, subtilties of wit, by meanes of which, some men doe often endevour to get credit and reputation: as divers Poets, that frame whole volumes with verses beginning with one letter: we see Egges, Wings, Hatchets, Crosses, Globes, Columnes, and divers other such like figures anciently fashioned by the Græcians, with the measure and proportion of their verses, spreading, lengthning, and shortning them, in such sort as they justly represent such and such a figure. Such was the science and profession of him, who long time busied himselfe, to number how many severall waies the letters of the Alphabet might be ranged, and found out that incredible number mentioned by *Plutarke*. I allow of his opinion, who having one brought before him, that was taught with such industrie, and so curiously to cast a graine of Millet with his hand, that without ever missing, he would every time make it goe through a needles-eye; and being entreated to bestow some thing upon him, (as a regard for so rare a skill), verie pleasantly and worthily, commanded that this cunning workman should have two or three peckes of Millet delivered him, to the end his rare art and wittie labour might not remaine without daily exercise. It is a wonderfull testimonie of our judgments imbecilitie, that it should commend and allow of things, either for their rarenesse or noveltie, or for their difficultie, though neither goodnesse or profit be joyned unto them. We come but now from my house, where we have a while recreated our selves, with devising who could find out most things, that held by both extreme ends; As for example, *Sir,* is in our tongue a title only given to the most eminent person of our state, which is the King, and yet is commonly given to some of the vulgar sort, as unto Merchants and Pedlers, and nothing concerneth those of the middle sort, and that are betweene both. Women of chiefest calling and qualitie are called *Dames,* the meane sort *Damoisels,* and those of the basest ranke, are also entitled *Dames.* The clothes of estate, which we see set over tables and chaires, are only allowed in Princes houses, yet we see them used in Tavernes. *Democritus* was wont to say, *That Gods and beasts, had quicker senses and sharper wits than men, who are of the middle ranke.* The Romanes used to wear one selfe same garment on mourning and on festivall daies. It is most certaine, that both an extreme feare, and an exceeding heat of courage, doe equally trouble and distemper the belly. The nickname of *Tremblant,* wherewith *Zanchio* the twelfth King of *Navarre* was surnamed, teacheth, that boldnesse, aswel as feare, engender a startling and shaking of the limbs. Those which armed, either him, or any other of like nature, whose skin would quiver, assaied to reassure him, by diminishing the danger wherein he was like to fall; you have no perfect knowledge of me (said he,) for if my flesh knew how far my courage will ere-long carrie it, it would presently fall into a flat swoune. That chilnesse, or as I may terme it, faintnesse, which we feele after the exercises of *Venus,* the same doth also proceed of an over vehement appetite and disordered heat. Excessive heat and extreme cold doe both boile and rost. *Aristotle* saith, *That leaden vessels doe as well melt and consume away by an excessive cold and rigor of winter, as by a vehement heat.* Both desire and satietie fill the seats with sorrow, both above and under voluptuousnesse. Folly and wisdome meet in one point of feeling and resolution, about the suffering of humane accidents. The wiser sort doth gourmondise and command

evill, and others know it not. The latter, (as a man would say) short
of accidents, the other, beyond. Who after they have well weighed and
considered their qualities, and duly measured, and rightly judged what
they are, over-leap them by the power of a vigorous courage. They
disdaine and tread them under foot, as having a strong and solide mind,
against which, if fortunes [darts] chance to light, they must of necessitie be blunted and abated, meeting with so resisting a body, as they
cannot pierce, or make any impression therein. The ordinarie and
meane condition of men abideth betweene these two extremities; which
are those that perceive and have a feeling of mischiefes, but cannot
endure them. Both infancie and decrepitude meet with weaknesse of
the braine. Covetise and profusion in a like desire to acquire and
hoard up. It may with likelyhood be spoken, that there is a kind of
Abecedarie ignorance, preceding science: another doctorall, following
science: an ignorance, which science doth beget: even as it spoileth
the first. Of simple, lesse-curious, and least-instructed spirits are
made good Christians, who simply beleeve through reverence and
obedience, and are kept in awe of the lawes. In the meane vigor
of spirits, and slender capacitie is engendred the error of opinions: They follow the apparance of the first sense; and have some
title to interpret it foolishnesse and sottishnesse, that we are confirmed
in ancient waies, respecting us, that are nothing therein instructed by
study. The best, most-setled, and clearest-seeing spirits, make another
sort of well-beleevers, who by long and religious investigation, penetrate a more profound, and find out a more abstruse light in scriptures;
and discover the mysterious and divine secrets of our ecclesiasticall
policie. And therefore see we some of them, that have reached unto
this last ranke, by the second, with wonderfull fruit and confirmation;
as unto the furthest bounds of Christian intelligence: and injoy their
victorie with comfort, thanks-giving, reformation of manners, and
great modesty. In which ranke, my purpose is not to place these others,
who to purge themselves from the suspicion of their fore-passed errors,
and the better to assure us of them, become extreme, indiscreet, and
unjust in the conduct of our cause, and tax and taint the same with
infinit reproches of violence. The simple peasants are honest men; so
are Philosophers, (or as our time nameth them, strong and cleare
natures) enriched with a large instruction of profitable sciences. The
mongrell sort of husband-men, who have disdained the first forme of
ignorance of letters, and could never reach unto the other (as they
that sit betweene two stooles, of which besides so many others I am
one) are dangerous, peevish, foolish, and importunate, and they which
trouble the world most. Therefore doe I (as much as lieth in me) withdraw my selfe into the first and naturall seat, whence I never assaied
to depart. Popular and meerely naturall Poesie hath certaine graces,
and in-bred livelinesse, whereby it concurreth and compareth it selfe
unto the principall beautie of perfect and artificiall Poesie, as may

plainly be seene in the *Villannelles,* homely gigs, and countrie songs of *Gasconie,* which are brought unto us from Nations that have no knowledge at all, either of any learning, or so much as of writing. Meane and indifferent Poesie, and that consisteth betweene both, is scorned, and contemned, and passeth without honour or esteeme. But forasmuch as since the passage hath beene opened unto the spirit, I have found (as it commonly hapneth) that we had apprehended that which is neither so nor so for a difficult exercise, and of a rare subject; And that since our invention hath beene set on fire, it discovereth an infinit number of like examples; I will onely adde this one: That if these Essayes were worthy to be judged of, it might in mine opinion happen, that they would not greatly please the common and vulgar spirits, and as little the singular and excellent. The first will understand but little of them, the latter over much; they might perhaps live and rub out in the middle region.

CHAPTER LV

OF SMELS AND ODORS

IT is reported of some, namely of *Alexander,* that their sweat, through some rare and extraordinary complexion, yeelded a sweet smelling savour; whereof *Plutarke* and others seeke to finde out the cause. But the common sort of bodies are cleane contrarie, and the best qualitie they have, is to be cleare of any smell at all. The sweetnesse of the purest breaths hath nothing more perfect in them, than to bee without savour, that may offend us: as are those of healthy sound children. And therefore saith *Plautus:*

Mulier tum benè, olet, ubi nihil olet.
PLAU. *Mostel* act. i. sc. 3.

Then smel's a woman purely well,
When she of nothing else doth smell.

The most exquisit and sweetest savour of a woman, it is to smell of nothing; and sweet, well-smelling, strange savours, may rightly be held suspicious in such as use them; and a man may lawfully thinke, that who useth them, doth it to cover some naturall defect: whence proceed these ancient Poeticall sayings. *To smell sweet, is to stinke,*

Rides nos Coracine nil olentes,
Malo quam benè olere, nil olere.—MART. vi. *Epig.* lv. 4.

You laugh at us that we of nothing savour,
Rather smell so, than sweeter (by your favour).

And else where.

Posthume non benè olet, qui benè semper olet.

ii. *Epig.* xii. 4.

Good sir, he smels not ever sweet,
Who smels still sweeter than is meet.

Yet love I greatly to be entertained with sweet smels, and hate exceedingly all manner of sowre and ill savours, which I shall sooner smell, than any other.

—Namque sagacius unus odoror,
Polypus, an gravis hirsutis cubet hircus in alis,
Quàm canis acer ubi lateat sus.—Hor. *Epod.* xii. 4.

Sooner smell I, whether a cancred nose,
Or ranke gote-smell in hairie arme-pits lie,
Than sharpest hounds, where rowting bores repose.

The simplest and meerely-naturall smels are most pleasing unto me; which care ought chiefly to concerne women. In the verie heart of *Barbarie,* the Scithian women, after they had washed themselves, did sprinkle, dawbe, and powder all their bodies and faces over, with a certaine odoriferous drug, that groweth in their Countrie: which dust and dawbing being taken away, when they come neere men, or their husbands, they remaine verie cleane, and with a verie sweet savouring perfume. What odor soever it be, it is strange to see, what hold it will take on me, and how apt my skin is to receive it. He that complaineth against nature, that she hath not created man with a fit instrument, to carrie sweet smels fast-tied to his nose, is much to blame: for, they carrie themselves. As for me in particular, my mostachoes, which are verie thicke, serve me for that purpose. Let me but approach my gloves or my hand-kercher to them, their smell will sticke upon them a whole day. They manifest the place I come from. The close-smacking, sweetnesse-moving, love-alluring, and greedi-smirking kisses of youth, were heretofore wont to sticke on them many houres after; yet am I little subject to those popular diseases, that are taken by conversation, and bred by the contagion of the ayre: And I have escaped those of my time, of which there hath beene many and severall kinds, both in the Townes about me, and in our Armie. We read of *Socrates,* that during the time of many plagues and relapses of the pestilence, which so often infested the Citie of *Athens,* he never forsooke or went out of the Towne: yet was he the only man, that was never infected, or that felt any sicknesse. Physitians might (in mine opinion) draw more use and good from odours, than they doe. For, my selfe have often perceived, that according unto their strength and qualitie, they change and alter, and move my spirits, and worke strange effects in me: which makes me approve the common saying, that the invention of incense and perfumes in Churches, so ancient and so far-dispersed throughout all nations and religions, had an especiall regard to rejoyce, to comfort, to quicken, to rowze, and to purifie our senses, that so we might be the apter and readier unto contemplation. And the better to judge of it, I would I had my part of the skill, which some Cookes have, who can so curiously season and temper strange odors with the savour and rellish of their meats. As it was especially observed in the service of the King of *Tunes,* who in our dayes landed at *Naples,* to meet and enter-parly with the Emperour *Charles* the fifth. His viands were so exquisitely farced, and so sumptuously seasoned with sweet odoriferous drugs, and aromaticall spices, that it was found upon his booke of accompt, the dressing of one peacocke, and two fesants amounted to one hundred duckets; which was their ordinarie manner of cooking his meats. And when they were carved up, not only the dining chambers, but all the roomes of his pallace, and the streets round about it were replenished with an exceeding odoriferous and aromaticall vapour, which continued a long time after. The principall care I take, wheresoever I am lodged, is to avoid, and be far from all manner of filthy, foggy, ill-savouring, and unwholsome aires. These goodly Cities of strangely-seated *Venice,* and huge-built *Paris,* by reason of the muddy, sharp, and offending savors, which they yeeld; the one by her fennie and marish situation, the other by her durtie uncleannesse, and continuall mire, do greatly alter and diminish the favour which I beare them.

CHAPTER LVI

OF PRAIERS AND ORISONS

I PROPOSE certaine formelesse and irresolute fantasies, as do those schollers, who in schooles publish doubtfull and sophisticall questions to be disputed and canvased: not to establish the truth, but to find it out: which I submit to their judgements, to whom the ordering and directing, not only of my actions and compositions, but also of my thoughts, belongeth. The condemnation, as well as the approbation of them, will be equally acceptable and profitable unto me, deeming it absurd and impious, if any thing be, either ignorantly, or unadvisedly set downe in this rapsody, contrarie unto the sacred resolutions, and repugnant to the holy prescriptions of the Catholike, Apostolike, and Romane Church, wherein I was borne, and out of which I purpose not to die. And therefore alwaies referring my selfe unto their censures that have all power over me, doe I meddle so rashly, to write of all manner of purposes and discourses, as I doe here. I wot not whether I be deceived, but sithence, by an especiall and singular favour of Gods divine bountie, a certaine forme of Praier, hath by the very mouth of God, word by word been prescribed and directed unto us, I have ever thought the use of it, should be more ordinarie with us, than it is. And might I be believed, both rising and going to bed, sitting downe and rising from boord, and going about any particular action or businesse, I would have all good Christians, to say the *Pater noster*, and if no other praier, at least not to omit that. The Church may extend, amplifie, and diversifie praiers according to the need of our instruction: For, I know it is alwaies the same substance, and the same thing. But that one should ever have this privilege, that all manner of people, should at all times, and upon every occasion have it in their mouth: For, it is most certaine, that only it containeth whatsoever we want, and is most fit, and effectuall in all events. It is the onely praier I use in every place, at all times, and upon every accident; and in stead of changing, I use often repetition of it: whence it commeth to passe, that I remember none so well as that one. I was even now considering, whence this generall errour cometh, that in all our desseignes and enterprises, of what nature soever, we immediatly have recourse unto God, and every necessitie, we call upon his holy name: And at what time soever we stand in need of any help, and that our weaknesse wanteth assistance, we only invoke him, without considering whether the occasion be just or unjust; and what estate or action we be in, or goe about, be it never so vicious or unlawfull, we call upon his name and power. Indeed, he is our only protector, and of power to affoord us all manner of help and comfort; but although he vouchsafe to honour us with this joy-bringing fatherly adoption, yet is he as just as he is good; and as good and just, as he is mightie: But oftner useth his justice than his might, and favoureth us according to the reason of the same, and not according to our requests. *Plato* in his lawes maketh three sorts of injurious beliefe in the Gods: First, that there is none at all; Secondly, that they meddle not with our affaires; Thirdly, that they never refuse any thing unto our vowes, offerings, and sacrifices. The first errour, according to his opinion, did never continue immutable in man, even from his first infancie unto his latter age. The two succeeding may admit some constancie. His justice and power are inseparable. It is but in vaine to implore his power in a bad cause. Man must have an unpolluted soule when he praieth (at least in that moment he addresseth himselfe to pray) and absolutely free from all vicious passions; otherwise we our selves present him the rods to scourge us withall. In lieu of redressing our fault, we redouble the same, by presenting him with an affection fraught with irreverence, sinne, and hatred, to whom only we should sue for grace and forgivenesse. Loe here, why I doe not willingly commend those Pharisaicall humours, whom I so often behold, and more than ordinarie, to pray unto God, except their actions immediately preceding or succeeding their praiers witnesse some shew of reformation or hope of amendment.

—Si nocturnus adulter
Tempora sanctonico velas adoptera cucullo.
JUVEN. *Sat.* viii. 144.

If in a cape-cloake-hood befrenchifide
Thou a night-whore-munger thy head dost hide.

And the state of a man that commixeth devotion unto an execrable life, seemeth in some sort to be more condemnable, than that of one, that is conformable unto himselfe, and every way dissolute. Therefore doth our Church continually refuse, the favour of her enterance and societie, unto customes and manners, wilfully-obstinate on some egregious villanie. We only pray by custome and use, and for fashion sake, or to say better, we but reade and pronounce our prayers: To conclude, it is nothing but a shew of formalitie, and a formall shew. And it greeveth me to see many men, who at grace before and after meat, will with great shew of devotion, crosse themselves three or four times, (and it vexeth me so much the more, when I call to mind, that it is a signe I greatly reverence, and have in continual use, yea, if I be but gaping) and there whilst, shall you see them bestow all other houres of the day in all maner of hatred, malice, covetousnesse, and injustice. Many houres spend they about vice, but one to God, and that as it were by way of recompence and composition. It is wonderous to see, so far different and divers actions, continue with so even a tenor, that no interruption or alteration at all can be perceived, either about their confines, or passage from one unto another. What prodigious conscience can be at any harts-ease, fostring, and feeding with so mutuall, quiet, and agreeing society in one selfe same mansion, both crime and judge? A man whose *Paillardize* and luxurie, doth uncessantly sway and rule the head, and who judgeth the same abhominable and most hatefull in the sight of God; what saith he unto his all-seeing Majesty, when he openeth his lips, either of mouth or hart, to speake to him of it? He reclaimeth himselfe, but falleth sodainly againe. *If the object of his divine justice, and his presence should strike,* (as he saith) *and chastise his soule, how short-soever the penitence were; feare it self would so often cast his thought on it, that he would presently perceive himselfe master of those vices, which are habituated, inbred, setled, and enfleshed in him.* But what of those, which ground a whole life upon the fruit and benefit of that sinne, they know to be mortall? How many trades, professions, occupations, and vocations, have we daily and continually used, frequented, and allowed amongst us, whose essence is vicious and most pernicious? And he that would needs confesse himselfe unto me, and of his owne accord told me, that for feare of losing his credit, and to keepe the honour of his offices; he had for a whole age, made shew and profession, and acted the effects of a religion, which in his owne selfe-accusing conscience, he judged damnable, and cleane contrarie unto that he had in his hart: How could he admit and foster so contradictorie and impious a discourse in his hart? With what language entertaine they divine justice concerning this subject? Their repentance, consisting in visible amends, and manageable reparation; they lose both towards God and us, the meanes to alleage the same. Are they so malapart and fond-hardy as to crave pardon without satisfaction, and sans repentance? I thinke it goeth with the first, as with these last: But obstinacie is not herein so easie to be vanquished. This so suddaine contrarietie, and violent volubilitie of opinion, which they faine unto us, seemeth to me a miracle. They present us with the state of an indigestible agonie. How fantasticall seemed their imagination unto me who these latter yeares had taken up a fashion, to checke and reprove all men, that professed the Catholike Religion, in whom shined any extraordinarie brightnesse of spirit, saying, that it was but fained: and to doe him honour, held, that whatsoever he said in apparance, he could not inwardly chuse but have his beliefe reformed according to their byase. It is a peevish infirmitie, for a man to thinke himselfe so firmely grounded, as to perswade himselfe, that the contrarie may not be believed: And more peevish also, to be perswaded by such a spirit, that preferreth I wot not what disparitie of fortune, before the hopes and threats of eternall life. They may beleeve me: If any thing could have [tempted] my youth, the ambition of the hazard, and difficultie, which followed this late-moderne enterprize, should have had good part therein. It is not without great reason, in my poore judgement, that the Church forbiddeth the confused, rash and indiscreet use of the sacred and divine songs, which the holy spirit hath indited unto *David*. God ought not to be commixed in our actions, but with awful reverence, and an attention full of honour and respect. The word or voice is too divine, having no other use but to exercise our lungs, and to please our eares. It is from the conscience and not from the tongue that it must proceed. It is not consonant unto reason, that a prentise or shop-keeping boy, amiddest his idle, vaine, and frivolous conceits, should be suffered to entertaine himselfe, and play therewith. Nor is it seemely, or tolerable, to see the sacred booke of our beliefes-Mysteries, tossed up and downe and plaid withall, in a shop, or a hall, or a kitchin. They have heretofore beene accompted mysteries, but through the abuse of times, they are now held as sports and recreations. So serious, and venerable a study should not, by way of pastime, and tumultuarie be handled. It ought to be a fixed, a purposed, and setled action, to which this preface of our office *sursum corda* should ever be adjoyned; and the very exterior parts of the body, should with such a countenance, be referred unto it, that to all mens eyes it may witnesse a particular attention and duteous respect. It is not a study fitting all men, but only such as have vowed themselves unto it, and whom God hath, of his infinit mercie, called thereto. The wicked, the ungodly, and the ignorant are thereby empaired. It is no historie to be fabulously reported, but a historie to be dutifully reverenced, awfully feared, and religiously adored. Are they not pleasantly conceited, who because they have reduced the same into the vulgar tongues, and that all men may understand it, perswade themselves, that the people shall the better conceive and digest the same? Consisteth it but in the words, that they understand not all they find written? Shall I say more? By approaching thus little unto it, they goe backe from it. Meere ignorance, and wholy relying on others, was verily more profitable and wiser, than is this verball, and vaine knowledge, the nurse of presumption, and sourse of temeritie. Moreover, I am of opinion, that the uncontrouled libertie, that all men have to wrest, dissipate, and wyre-draw a word so religious, and important, to so many severall idiomes, hath much more danger than profit following it. The Jewes, the Mahometans, and well-nigh all other nations, are wedded unto, and reverence the language, wherein their mysteries and religion had originally beene conceived; and any change or translation hath not without apparance of reason beene directly forbidden. Know we whether there be Judges enow in *Basque* and in *Brittanie* to establish this translation made in their tongue? The universall Church hath no more difficult and solemne judgement to make. Both in speaking and preaching the interpretation is wandring, free, and mutable, and of one parcell; so is it not alike. One of our Græcian Historians doth justly accuse his age, forasmuch as the secrets of Christian religion were dispersed in all publike places, and even amongst the basest artificers; and that every man might, at his pleasure, dispute of it, and at random speake his mind of the same. And it should be a great shame for us, who by the unspeakable grace of God injoy the pure and sacred mysteries of piety, to suffer the same to be profaned in the mouthes of ignorant and popular people, seeing the very Gentiles interdicted *Socrates* and *Plato,* and the wisest, to meddle, enquire or speake of things committed unto the Priestes of *Delphos*. Saying moreover, *That the factions of Princes, touching the subject of Divinitie, are armed, not with zeale, but with anger. That zeale dependeth of divine reason and justice, holding an orderly and moderate course, but that it changeth into hatred and envie, and in stead of corne and grape, it produceth nettles and darnell, if it be directed by humane passion.* And justly saith this other, who counselling the Emperour *Theodosius,* affirmed *that disputations did not so much appease and lull asleepe the schismes of the Church, as stir up and cause heresies.* And therefore it behooveth, to avoid all contentions, controversies, and logicall arguings, and wholy and sincerely refer himselfe unto the prescriptions and orders of faith, established by our forefathers. And *Andronicus* the Emperour, finding by chance in his pallace, certaine principall men very earnestly disputing against *Lapodius,* about one of our points of great importance, taunted and rated them very bitterly, and threatned if they gave not over, he would cause them to be cast into the river. Children and women doe now adaies governe and sway the oldest and most experienced men concerning Ecclesisaticall Lawes: whereas the first that *Plato* made, forbiddeth them to enquire after the reason of civill Lawes, and which ought to stand in place of divine ordinances. Allowing aged men to communicate the same amongst themselves, and with the Magistrate, adding more-over, alwaies provided it be not in the presence of young men, and before profane persons. A notable Bishop hath left written, that in the other end of the world, there is an Iland called of our predecessours *Dioscorida,* very commodious, and fertile of all sorts of fruits and trees, and of a pure and wholesome ayre; whose people are Christians, and have Churches and Altars; adorned with nothing else but crosses, without other images; great observers of fastings and holy daies; exact paiers of their priests tithes; and so chaste, that none of them may lawfully all his life long know any more than one wife. And in all other matters so well pleased with their fortune, that being seated in the middest of the sea, they have and know no use of ships: and so simple, that of their religion, which they so diligently and awfully observe, they know not, nor understand so much as one only word. A thing incredible, to him that knew not how the Pagans, who are so devout and zealous idolaters, know nothing of their Gods, but only their bare names and statues. The ancient beginning of *Menalippe,* a tragedie of *Euripides,* importeth thus.

> *O Jupiter, car de toy rien sinon,*
> *Je ne cognois seulement que le nom.*—EURIP.

> O *Jupiter,* for unto me,
> Only the name is knowne of thee.

I have also in my time heard certaine writings complained of, for-so much as they are meerly humane and Philosophicall, without medling with divinitie. He that should say to the contrarie (which a man might doe with reason) that heavenly doctrine, as a Queene and governesse doth better keepe her ranke apart; that she ought to be chiefe ruler and principall head evere where, and not suffragant and subsidiarie. And that peradventure examples in Grammar, Rethorike, and Logike, might more fitly and sortably be taken from elsewhere, than from so sacred and holy a subject, as also the arguments of theatres, plots of plaies, and grounds of publike spectacles. That mysteriously divine reasons are more venerably and reverently considered alone, and in their native stile, than joyned and compared to humane discourse. That this fault is oftner seene, which is, that Divines write too humanely, than this other, that humanists write not Theologically enough. *Philosophy,* saith S. *Chrysostome, is long since banished from sacred schools, as an unprofitable servant, and deemed unworthy to behold, but in passing by the entrie, or the vestrie of the sacred treasures of heavenly doctrine.* That the formes of humane speech, are more base, and ought by no meanes to make any use of the dignitie, majestie and preheminence of divine speech. As for my part, I give it leave to say, *Verbis indisciplinatis, with undiscipled words,* Fortune, destinie, chance, accident, fate, good lucke, ill lucke, the Gods, and other phrases, as best it pleaseth. I propose humane fantasies and mine owne, simply as humane conceits, and severally considered; not as setled, concluded, and directed by celestiall ordinance, incapable of any doubt or alteration. A matter of opinion, and not of faith. What I discourse according to my selfe, not what I beleeve according unto God, with a laicall fashion, and not a clericall manner; yet ever most religious. As children propose their essayes, instructable, not instructing. And might not a man also say without apparance, that the institution, which willeth, no man shall dare to write of Religion, but sparingly, and reservedly, except such as make expresse profession of it, would not want some shew of profit and justice; and happily to me to be silent. It hath beene told me, that even those which are not of our consent, doe flatly inhibite amongst themselves the use of the sacred name of God in all their vulgar and familiar discourses. They would have no man use it as an interjection, or exclamation, nor to be alleaged as a witnesse, or comparison; wherein I find they have reason. And howsoever it be, that we call God to our commerce and societie, it should be zealously, seriously, and religiously. There is (as far as I remember) such a like discourse in *Xenophon,* wherein he declareth, *That we should more rarely pray unto God: forasmuch as it is not easie, we should so often settle our minds in so regular, so reformed, and so devout a seat, where indeed it ought to be, to pray aright and effectually:* otherwise our praiers are, not only vaine and unprofitable, but vicious. *Forgive us* (say we) *our offences, as we forgive them that trespasse against us.* What else inferre we by that petition, but that we offer him our soule void of all revenge and free from all rancour? We neverthelesse invoke God and call on his aid, even in the complot of our grievousest faults, and desire his assistance in all manner of injustice and iniquitie.

Quæ nisi seductis nequeas committere divis.

PERS. Sat. ii. 4.

Which you to Saints not drawne aside,
Would thinke unfit to be applide.

The covetous man sueth and praieth unto him for the vaine increase and superfluous preservation of his wrong-gotten treasure. The ambitious, he importuneth God for the conduct of his fortune, and that he may have the victorie of all his desseignes. The theefe, the pirate, the murtherer, yea and the traitor, all call upon him, all implore his aid, and all solicite him, to give them courage in their attempts, constancie in their resolutions, to remove all lets and difficulties, that in any sort may withstand their wicked executions, and impious actions; or give him thanks, if they have had good successe; the one if he have met with a good bootie, the other if he returne home rich, the third if no man have seen him kill his enemie, and the last, though he have caused any execrable mischiefe. The Souldier, if he but goe to besiege a cottage, to scale a Castle, to rob a Church, to pettard a gate, to force a religious house, or any villanous act, before he attempt it, praieth to God for his assistance, though his intents and hopes be full-fraught with crueltie, murther, covetise, luxurie, sacri-lege, and all iniquitie.

> *Hoc ipsum quo tu Jovis aurem impellere tentas,*
> *Dic agedum, Staio, proh Jupiter, ô bone, clamet,*
> *Jupiter, at sese non clamet Jupiter ipse.—21.*

Go-to then, say the same to some bad fellow
Which thou prepar'st for Gods eares: let him bellow,
O God, good God; so God,
On himselfe would not plod.

Margaret Queene of *Navarre,* maketh mention of a young Prince (whom although she name not expresly, yet his greatnesse hath made him sufficiently knowne) who going about an amorous assignation, and to lie with an Advocates wife of *Paris,* his way lying alongst a Church, he did never passe by so holy a place, whether it were in going or comming from his lecherie, and cukolding-labour, but would make his praiers unto God, to be his help and furtherance. I would faine have any impartiall man tell me, to what purpose this Prince invoked and called on God for his divine favour, having his mind only bent to sinne, and his thoughts set on luxurie: Yet doth she alleage him for a speciall testimonie of singular devotion. But it is not only by this example, a man might verifie, that women are not very fit to manage to treat matters of Religion and Divinitie. A true and hartie praier, and an unfained religious reconciliation from us unto God, cannot likely fall into a wicked and impure soule, especially when Sathan swaieth the same. He that calleth upon God for his assistance, whilst he is en-gulphed and wallowing in filthy sinne, doth as the cut-purse, that should call for justice unto his ayd, or those that produce God in witnesse of a lie.

> *—tacito mala vota susurro*
> *Concipimus.*—LUCAN. v. 94.

With silent whispering we,
For ill things suppliants be.

There are few men, that would dare to publish the secret requests they make to God.

> *Haud cuivis promptum est, murmur que humilesque susurros*
> *Tollere de Templis, et aperto vivere voto.*—PERS. *Sat.* ii. 6.

From Church low-whispering murmurs to expell,
'Tis not for all, or with knowne vowes live well.

And that's the reason, why the Pythagorians would have them publike, that all might heare them, that no man should abusively call on
God, and require any undecent or unjust thing of him, as that man;

—clarè cùm dixit, Apollo,
Labra movet metuens audiri: pulchra Laverna
Da mihi fallere, da justum sanctumque videri.
Noctem peccatis, et fraudibus objice nubem.

HOR. i. *Epist.* xvi. 59.

When he alowd hath said, *Apollo* heare,
Loth to be heard, Goddesse of theeves, said he,
Grant me to cousen, and yet just appeare,
My faults in night, my frauds in clouds let be.

The Gods did grievously punish the impious vowes of *Oedipus*, by
granting them unto him. His praier was, that his children might betweene themselves decide in armes the succession of his estate; he was
so miserable, as to be taken at his word. A man should nct request that
all things follow our will, but that it may follow wisdome. Verily, it
seemeth, that we make no other use of our praiers, than of a companie
of gibrish phrases: And as those who employ holy and sacred words
about witchcraft and magicall effects; and that we imagine their effect
dependeth of the contexture, or sound, or succession of words, or from
our countenance. For, our soule, being full-fraught with concupiscence,
and all manner of ungodly thoughts, nothing touched with repentance,
nor moved with new reconciliation towards God, we headlong present
unto him those heedlesse words, which memorie affoordeth our tongue,
by which we hope to obtaine an expiation and remission of our offences.
There is nothing so easie, so sweet, so comfortable and favourable, as
the law of God; she (of his infinit mercie) calleth us unto him, how
faultie and detestable soever we be; she gently stretcheth forth her
armes unto us, and mildly receiveth us into her lap, how guiltie, polluted, and sinfull soever we are, and may be in after-times. But in
recompence of so boundlesse and unspeakable a favour, she must be
thankfully accepted, and cheerfully regarded: and so gracious a pardon
must be received with a gratitude of the soule, and at least, in that
instant, that we addresse our selves unto her presence; to have our
soul grieved for her faults, penitent of her sinnes, hating those passions
and affections, that have caused or provoked us to transgresse his laws,
to offend his Majestie, and to breake his commandements. *Plato* saith,
That neither the Gods, nor honest men will ever accept the offering of
a wicked man.

Immunis aram si tetigit manus,
Non sumptuosa blandior hostia
Mollivit aversos Penates,
Farre pio et saliente mica.—iii. *Od.* xxiii. 17.

If guiltlesse hand the Altar tuch,
No offring, cost it ne're so much,
Shall better please our God offended,
Than corne with crackling-corne-salt blended.

CHAPTER LVII

OF AGE

I CANNOT receive that manner, whereby we establish the continuance of our life. I see that some of the wiser sort doe greatly shorten the same, in respect of the common opinion. What said *Cato Junior,* to those who sought to hinder him from killing himselfe? *Doe I now live the age, wherein I may justly be reproved to leave my life too soone?* Yet was he but eight and fortie yeares old. He thought that age very ripe, yea, and well advanced, considering how few men come unto it. And such as entertaine themselves with, I wot not what kind of course, which they call naturall, promiseth some few yeares beyond, might do it, had they a privilege that could exempt them from so great a number of accidents, unto which each one of us stands subject by a naturall subjection, and which may interrupt the said course, they propose unto themselves. What fondnesse is it, for a man to thinke he shall die, for, and through, a failing and defect of strength, which extreme age draweth with it, and to propose that terme unto our life, seeing it is the rarest kind of all deaths, and least in use? We only call it naturall, as if it were against nature to see a man breake his necke with a fall; to be drowned by shipwracke; to be surprised with a pestilence, or pleurisie, and as if our ordinarie condition did not present these inconveniences unto us all. Let us not flatter our selves with these fond-goodly words; a man may peradventure rather call that naturall, which is generall, common and universall. To die of age, is a rare, singular, and extraordinarie death, and so much lesse naturall than others: It is the last and extremest kind of dying: The further it is from us, so much the lesse is it to be hoped for: Indeed it is the limit, beyond which we shal not passe, and which the law of nature hath prescribed unto us, as that which should not be outgone by any; but it is a rare privilege peculiar unto her selfe, to make us continue unto it. It is an exemption, which through some particular favour she bestoweth on some one man, in the space of two or three ages, discharging him from the crosses, troubles, and difficulties, she hath enterposed betweene both, in this long cariere and pilgrimage. Therefore my opinion is, to consider, that the age unto which we are come, is an age whereto few arive: since men come not unto it by any ordinarie course, it is a signe we are verie forward. And since we have past the accustomed bounds, which is the true measure of our life, we must not hope, that we shall goe much further. Having escaped so many occasions of death, wherein we see the world to fall, we must acknowledge that such an extraordinarie fortune, as that is, which maintaineth us, and is beyond the common use, is not likely to continue long. It is a fault of the verie lawes, to have this false imagination: They allow not a man to be capable and of discretion, to manage and dispose of his owne goods, untill he be five and twentie yeares old, yet shall he hardly preserve the state of his life so long. *Augustus* abridged five years of the ancient Romane Lawes, and declared, that for any man that should take upon him the charge of judgement, it sufficed to be thirtie yeares old. *Servius Tullius* dispensed with the Knights, who were seven and fortie yeares of age, from all voluntarie services of warre. *Augustus* brought them to fortie and five. To send men to their place of sojourning before they be five and fiftie or three score yeares of age, me seemeth, carrieth no great apparance with it. My advice would be, that our vacation, and employment should be extended, as far as might be for the publike commoditie; but I blame some, and condemne most, that we begin not soone enough to employ our selves. The same *Augustus* had been universall and supreme judge of the world, when he was but nineteene yeares old, and would have another to be thirtie, before he shall bee made a competent judge of a cottage or farme. As for my part, I thinke our minds are as full growne and perfectly joynted at twentie yeares, as they should be, and promise as much as they can. A mind which at that age hath not given some evident token or earnest of her sufficiencie, shall hardly give it afterward; put her to what triall you list. Naturall qualities and vertues, if they have any vigorous or beauteous thing in them, will produce and shew the same within that time, or never. They say in Daulphiné,

> *Si l'espine nou picque quand nai,*
> *A peine que picque jamai.*—French prov.

A thorne, unlesse at first it pricke,
Will hardly ever pearce to th' quicke.

Of all humane honourable and glorious actions, that ever came unto my knowledge, of what nature soever they be, I am perswaded, I should have a harder taske, to number those, which both in ancient times, and in ours, have beene produced and atchieved before the age of thirtie yeares, than such as were performed after: yea, often in the life of the same men. May not I boldly speak it of those of *Hanniball*, and *Scipio* his great adversarie? They lived the better part of their life with the glorie which they had gotten in their youth: And though afterward they were great men, in respect of all others, yet were they but meane in regard of themselves. As for my particular, I am verily perswaded, that since that age, both my spirit and my body, have more decreased than encreased, more recoyled than advanced. It may be, that knowledge and experience shall encrease in them, together with life, that bestow their time well: but vivacitie, promptitude, constancie, and other parts much more our owne, more important and more essentiall, they droope, they languish, and they faint.

—ubi jam validis quassatum est viribus ævi
Corpus, et obtusis ceciderunt viribus artus,
Claudicat ingenium, delirat linguaquè mensque.—LUCR. iii. 457.

When once the body by shrewd strength of yeares
Is shak't, and limmes drawne downe from strength that weares,
Wit halts, both tongue and mind
Doe daily doat, we find.

It is the body, which sometimes yeeldeth first unto age; and other times the mind: and I have seene many, that have had their braines weakned before their stomacke or legges. And forasmuch, as it is a disease, little or nothing sensible unto him that endureth it, and maketh no great shew, it is so much the more dangerous. Here I exclaime against our Lawes, not because they leave us so long, and late in working and employment, but that they set us a worke no sooner, and it is so late before we be employed. Me thinkes that considering the weaknesse of our life, and seeing the infinit number of ordinarie rockes, and naturall dangers it is subject unto, we should not so soone as we come into the world, alot so great a share thereof unto unprofitable wantonnesse in youth, il-breeding idlenesse, and slow-learning prentissage.

The end of the first Booke

THE SECOND BOOKE OF ESSAYES

PREFACE

'The Epistle'

TO THE RIGHT HO-norable and all-praise-worthie Ladies, *Elizabeth* Countesse of Rutland, and Ladie Penelope Riche.

Give me leave (peerlesse, and in all good gifts unparagonized Ladies) though I make my fault double to aske leave for a fault, which I might leave; yet thus to paire you without dislike, who like (I imagine) each other above other, and to whom a like paire long may I seeke, but be long ere I finde. Such pairing is no empairing, no disparaging, nor yet comparing, unless in that good comparison of excellence. This is the number appropriate, at least reciprocall, of true love (Mont. l. i. c. 27): as the two Tables comprised in two commandements of due love. And such is Gods proceeding, when Mercie and Truth meete together, Righteousnesse and Peace have kissed each other. Even as body and soule, braine and heart, memory and understanding; so are you two with your two honorablest Lordes made, as you should be, even: two Doves, two Loves: double kinde, double kindnesse. Both like the two Cherubins on the toppes and sides of the propitiatorie, respective mutually; like the two starres of the North, which our Mariners call, the Guardes, directive of our course; like your owne eyes, their owne onely matches; yet as much pleasing others with their sight, as your themselves (Paul. Gio. Imp.). And hereby, as your Cognisance (noblest Countesse of RUTLAND) beares the body or chiefe part of an Imprese made for a worthy Dutchesse of Florence: so (hope we) you ere long shall adde the soule and life of her word, Cum pudore læta fæcunditas: to reape as much joy by Iuno, as labour by Lucina, and honor by them both: which being so well graffed shall be (as the Italian spake in Dutch) Wan Got will (Ibid.): whereof yet a faire patterne you have here (be it auspicious) associated to you: I meane you (truely-richest Ladie RICH) in riches of Fortune not deficient, but of body incomparably richer, of minde most rich: who yet, like Cornelia, were you out-vied, or by rich shewes envited to shew your richest jewelles, would stay till your sweet Images (your deeresweete children) came from schoole. And if you may so joy in those your yong Schollers, of such hope, of such spirit, so nobly borne, so worthily proceeding: how then may I boast of both your Ladiships, of such proofe, of such merite, my not onely proficient, but perfect Schollers? Yea, as of love, so of language, peerlesse Ladies? who like that great and good Cornelia, *not onely with bountie entertaine, but of benignitie invite learned and vertuous strangers, not so much to employ, as rather to releeve, yea oblige, yea ammuse, yea drive them to admiration or veneration of your singular sufficiencies, surmounting magnanimitie, and inestimable value, even from forraine Princes that come to see this happy-happiest Iland to receive gratulations, and merit commendations. Who also, like another of the same name, to your great and good* Pompeys *brought an invaluable dowrie, not onely of Nobilitie, Learning, Language, Musicke, but withall, an uncurious gravitie, and all-accomplish't vertue. So as into this familie of these* Corneliaes, *as many ciences into one stocke, the Orator may well conclude the wisedome and vertue of many engraffed and collected. And though this* Montaigne-Lord, *not so knightly as uncivilly, in this your part acknowledgeth no dozens of good women at any time in one place* (Mont. l. ii. c. 35) (in France *it may be, or of his knowledge) but onely a bare trinity, and those Italians, and that about their husbandes death to die with or afore them; forgetting he had instanced but a little before, out of* Propertius *and others* (Ibid. lib. ii. c. 29), *in many Indians; who, did they ordinarily as much for their husbands, would out of doubt affectionately doe more for them yet living: yet as even those* Corneliaes, *and in that very poynt, both in* Plutarke (Plut. vit. Grac. & Pomp.), *both (as God would have it) surviving their husbands, the one prevented by her husbands wise kindnesse, the other with all sympathy attending his extreame fortune; both while they lived, preserved the dead in Honorable memorie: as also in his kinde three other in* Plutarke *went as farre; namely* Empona, Camma *and* Damocrita: *or this mans* Theoxena, Sextilia, Praxea, Pelagia, Sophronia, Fulvia, *and many more* (Mont. lib. ii. c. 27 & c. 3); *since in the Romane proscriptions, as one of their Historians doth testifie, many wives were found exceeding faithfull, but few men-servants, fewer friends, and fewest sonnes. So neyther is one vertue fit for all, not all fit for one vertue: nor is that one so excellent, but by more it might be mended: not deeme I his three so good, but many have bin, and some be much better: Yea, as a Christian, I must deny them good, who cast backe Gods good gift before he call for it; leave their faire corps-de-guarde ere their Generall discharge them; hope to be deified for being their owne murtherers, who should be damned if they were so to others; more savage to their owne soules, than any beast would be to their owne flesh; not of force, but for feare, or for fame at the best: though even in that (as* Plinie *thinkes of two of the same persons) the same fact is diversly extolled or abased, as the person that doth it, is divers, high or base. Nor would a wiser* Pætus *than his, yea a better man than his* Seneca *permitte as good an* Arria *as his her daughter to die as shee did; though as willingly she would, but charged her to live after for him and his. Better yet (but not much) like I that seely one, which this Author approveth by his wise Duke of* Bretaigne *in choice of* Isabell *of* Scotland (*Ibid. lib.* i. *c.* 24). *But since himselfe likes it better to be well used in life then at death, and better usage proceeds from better vertues (for better vertues make you love as well as be beloved: and loyall love from you makes up his mouth, with sweeter sawce than death) without that extreame triall, I can tell him we have, and by good hap, my dedications name unto him, halfe a dozen, better, because more vertuous, and therefore more loved, and as loving. Or, will hee admitte but three, if not paires, yet their* Peeres, *I must say of three as* Ariosto *saide of one,* Credi ogn' una d' esser quella Fenice (*Orl. fu. can.* 27): *Or as my fellow* Nolano *in his heroycall furies wrote (noble Countesse) to your most heroicke father, and in a Sonnet to you Ladies of* England, You are not women, but in their likenesse Nymphs, Goddesses, and of Celestiall substance (*Gior. Bru. hero. fur. arg.*).

Et siete in terra quel' ch' in ciel' le stelle,

And above all, that onely divine *Diana,*

Qual' è tra voi quel che tra gl' astri il sole.

And cleane contrarie to this Censor, the Nobler *and the* Richer *you are, the more vertuous and worthie we esteeme you by reason and experience. But while I follow my guide, I have forsaken my selfe, and while I would winne him friends he workes (I feare) foes both to him and me of my best friends; while he findes but three good, and that, when they did so, as I pray God keepe mine both from cause and effect, intention and execution: wherein I follow, if not his* Paris Preacher, *at least his douçeur Françoise (Mon. lib. ii. c. 3). But is hee then so capriccious, so opiniative, so paradoxall? I graunt, sometimes extravagant, often od-chocheted, and ever selfe-conceited to write of himselfe out of himselfe. Why wrote he then? for him and his. But why doe I translate him? For your Ladiships and yours. What? to displease? Nay, neither doth such extraordinarinesse ever displease, nor is hee ever in his humour: for, in the judgement (beside others, yea even of the precise* Genevians *he hath so bin judged,* and amongest them allowed to be printed) of your most learned wise and honourable kinsman, sir* Edward Wotton (*who encouraged and set me first upon this Worke) there are in it so pleasing passages, so judicious discourses, so delightsome varieties, so perswasive conclusions, such learning of all sortes, and above all, so elegant a French stile, as (I thinke) for* ESSAYES, *I may say of him, as hee, in this Booke, did of* Homer (*Ibid. lib.* ii. *c.* 36); *Heere shines in him the greatest wit without example, without exception, deserving for his composition to be entituled,* Sole Maister of Essayes: *whose maister-poynt is this, none was before him, whom he might imitate; none hath come after him who could well imitate; or at most equall him: and a wonder it is, he therein should be perfectest, whereof he is first Authour. And for French eloquence, I may adde that of him, which the same Historian doth of* Tullie, *It* *brake-out in full streames, full beames, under this Prince thereof, Lord of* Montaigne; *so as before him you may be delighted with few, but wonder at none, that hath not either seene him, or bin seene of him. His worth then being so eminent, his wit so excelent, his inventions so rare, his elocutions so ravishing; nor are my pains mis-spent in translating, nor will your Honours pleasure and leasure be mis-placed or mis-employed in perusing him. I know, nor this, nor any I have seen, or can conceive, in this or other language, can in aught be compared to that perfect-unperfect* Arcadia, *which all our world yet weepes with you, that your all praise-exceeding father (his praise-succeeding Countesse) your worthy friend (friend worthiest Lady) lived not to mend or end-it: since this end wee see of it, though at first above all, now is not answerable to the precedents: and though it were much easier to mend out of an originall and well corrected copie, than to make-up so much out of a most corrupt, yet see we more marring that was well, then mending what was amisse. And if not any principall invention, much lesse may any translation at second hand come neere it: yet as that* Worthie *did divinely even in French translating some part of that excellent* du Plessis, *and (as I have seene) the first septmaine of that Arch-Poet* du Bartas *(which good Ladies, be so good to all, as all this age may see, and after-ages honor) so though we much more meanely doe in meaner workes (for still I say none can anneare him) yet where our Protonotaries doe holde the chaire, let us poore Secondaries not be thrust out of doores. Of this your Honourable goodnesse dooth assure me, and for this, and much more, I must and ever shall avow my selfe* To your Honours obliged and devoted in all service, IOHN FLORIO.

TO THE RIGHT HO-norable, *Elizabeth* Countesse *of* Rutland.

Thrise-happy Countesse, your thrise-honor'd Sire,
    An other Nature, *Maro*-like, sur-named,
    As he in Arte divinest Poems framed,
    In love did to a love divine aspire,
In both wrought wonders of *Prometheus* fire;
    So got in kind an of-spring no lesse famed,
    His fame's enheritrix to be proclaimed;
    That got, he got himselfe one of Heav'ns quire
As then his, and your Mothers match you are
    In parents, match, and shall (we hope) in breeding,
    England to steade with antient MANORS race:
So be you (when we you in praise compare)
    As kinde, in kindenesse them as kinde succeeding,
    Great good-wils gift not great, t' accept with grace.
                        Il Candido.

¶ To the Honorably-vertuous Ladie, La: Penelope Riche.

Madame, to write of you, and doe you right,
    What meane we, or what meanes to ayde meane might?

Since HE, who admirably did endite,
Entiteling you Perfections heire, loyes light,
Loves life, Lifes gemme, Vertues court, Heav'ns delight,
Natures chiefe worke, Fair'st booke, his Muses spright,
Heav'n on Earth, peerelesse Phœnix, *Phœbe* bright,
Yet said, he was to seeke, of you to write.
Unlesse your selfe be of your selfe devising;
Or that an other such you can inspire.
Inspire you can; but ô none such can be:
Your selfe as bright as your mid-day, as rising.
Yet, though we but repeate who would flie higher,
And though we but translate, take both in gree.

Il Candido.

THE ESSAYES OF

MICHAEL LORD OF MONTAIGNE

The Second Booke

CHAPTER I

OF THE INCONSTANCIE OF OUR ACTIONS

THOSE which exercise themselves in controuling humane actions, finde no such let in any one part, as to peece them together, and bring them to one same lustre: For, they commonly contradict one another so strangely, as it seemeth impossible they should be parcels of one Warehouse. Young *Marius* is sometimes found to be the sonne of *Mars,* and other times the childe of *Venus.* Pope *Boniface* the Eight, is reported to have entred into his charge, as a Fox; to have carried himselfe therein, as a Lion; and to have died like a dog. And who would thinke it was *Nero,* that lively image of cruelty, who being required to signe (as the custome was) the sentence of a criminall offendor, that had beene condemned to die, that ever he should answer? Oh would to God I could never have written! So neare was his heart grieved to doome a man to death. The world is so full of such examples, that every man may store himselfe; and I wonder to see men of understanding trouble themselves with sorting these parcels: Sithence (me seemeth) irresolution is the most apparant and common vice of our nature; as witnesseth that famous verse of *Publius* the Comœdian:

> *Malum consilium est, quod mutari non potest.—Pub. Mim.*

> The counsell is but bad,
> Whose change may not be had.

There is some apparance to judge a man by the most common conditions of his life, but seeing the naturall instability of our customes and opinions; I have often thought, that even good Authors, doe ill, and take a wrong course, wilfully to opinionate themselves about framing a constant and solide contexture of us. They chuse an universall ayre, and following that image, range and interpret all a mans actions; which if they cannot wrest sufficiently, they remit them into dissimulation. *Augustus* hath escaped their hands; for there is so apparant, so sudden and continuall a variety of actions found in him, through the course of his life, that even the boldest Judges and strictest censurers, have beene faine to give him over, and leave him undecided. *There is nothing I so hardly beleeve to be in man, as constancie, and nothing so easie to be found in him, as inconstancy.* He that should distinctly and part by part, judge of him, should often jumpe to speake truth. View all antiquity over, and you shall finde it a hard matter, to chuse out a dozen of men, that have directed their life unto one certaine, setled, and assured course; which is the surest drift of wisdome. For, to comprehend all in one word, saith an ancient Writer, and to embrace all the rules of our life into one, it is at all times to will, and not to will one same thing. I would not vouchsafe, (saith he) to adde any thing; alwayes provided the will be just: for, if it be unjust, it is impossible it should ever continue one. Verily, I have heretofore learned, that vice is nothing but a disorder, and want of measure, and by consequence, it is impossible to fasten constancy unto it. It is a saying of *Demosthenes,* (as some report,) *That consultation and deliberation, is the beginning of all vertue; and constancie, the end and perfection.* If by reason or discourse we should take a certaine way, we should then take the fairest: but no man hath thought on it.

> *Quod petit, spernit, repetit quod nuper omisit,*
> *Astuat, et vitœ disconvenit ordine toto.*—HOR. i. *Epist.* i. 98.

He scorns that which he sought, seek's that he scorned of late,
He flowes, ebbes, disagrees in his lifes whole estate.

Our ordinary manner is to follow the inclination of our appetite, this way and that way; on the left, and on the right hand; upward and downe-ward, according as the winde of occasions doth transport us: we never thinke on what we would have, but at the instant we would have it: and change as that beast that takes the colour of the place wherein it is laid. What we even now purposed, we alter by and by, and presently returne to our former biase: all is but changing, motion, and inconstancy:

> *Ducimur ut nervis alienis mobile lignum.*
> HOR. ii. *Sat.* vii. 82.

So are we drawne, as wood is shoved,
By others sinnewes each way moved.

We goe not, but we are carried: as things that flote, now gliding gently, now hulling violently; according as the water is, either stormy or calme.

> *—nónne videmus*
> *Quid sibi quisque velit nescire et quœrere semper,*
> *Commutare locum quasi onus deponere possit?*
> LUCR. iii. 1100.

See we not, every man in his thoughts height
Knowes not what he would have, yet seekes he streight
To change place, as he could lay downe his weight?

Every day new toyes, each houre new fantasies, and our humours
move and fleet with the fleetings and movings of time.

Tales sunt hominum mentes, quali Pater ipse
Jupiter auctifero lustravit lumine terras.—Cɪᴄ. *Fragm.*

Such are mens mindes, as that great God of might
Surveies the earth with encrease bearing light.

We float and waver betweene divers opinions: we will nothing freely,
nothing absolutely, nothing constantly. Had any man prescribed certaine Lawes, or established assured policies in his owne head; in his
life should we daily see, to shine an equality of customes, an assured
order, and an infallible relation from one thing to another (*Empedocles*
noted this deformity to be amongst the Agrigentines, that they gave
themselves so over unto delights, as if they should die to morrow next,
and built as if they should never die) the discourse thereof were easie
to be made. As is seene in young *Cato:* He that toucht but one step
of it, hath touched all. It is an harmony of well according tunes and
which cannot contradict it selfe. With us it is cleane contrary, so
many actions, so many particular judgements are there requir'd. The
surest way (in mine opinion) were to refer them unto the next circumstances, without entering into further search, and without concluding any other consequence of them. During the late tumultuous broiles
of our mangled estate, it was told me, that a young woman, not farre
from mee, had head-long cast her selfe out of a high window, with
intent to kill herselfe, only to avoid the ravishment of a rascaly-base
Souldier, that lay in her house, who offered to force her: and perceiving
that with the fall she had not killed herselfe, to make an end of her
enterprize, she would have cut her owne throat with a knife, but that
she was hindered by some that came in to her: Neverthelesse having
sore wounded herselfe, she voluntarily confessed, that the Souldier had
yet but urged her with importunate requests, suing-solicitations, and
golden bribes, but she feared he would in the end have obtained his
purpose by compulsion: by whose earnest speeches, resolute countenance, and gored bloud (a true testimony of her chaste vertue) she
might appeare to be the lively patterne of another *Lucrece,* yet know
I certainly, that both before that time, and afterward, she had beene
enjoyed of others upon easier composition. And as the common saying
is; Faire and soft, as squemish-honest as she seems, although you
misse of your intent, conclude not rashly an inviolable chastitie to
be in your Mistresse; For, a groome or a horse-keeper may find an
houre to thrive in; and a dog hath a day. *Antigonus* having taken upon
him to favour a Souldier of his, by reason of his vertue and valour,

commanded his Physitians to have great care of him, and see whether they could recover him of a lingring and inward disease, which had long tormented him, who being perfectly cured, he afterward perceiving him to be nothing so earnest and diligent in his affaires, demanded of him, how he was so changed from himselfe, and become so [cowardish]: your selfe good Sir (answered he) have made me so, by ridding me of those infirmities, which so did grieve me, that I made no accompt of my life. A Souldier of *Lucullus*, having by his enemies beene robbed of all he had, to revenge himselfe undertooke a notable and desperat atempt upon them; and having recovered his losses, *Lucullus* conceived a very good opinion of him, and with the greatest shewes of assured trust and loving kindnesse he could bethinke himselfe, made especiall accompt of him, and in any dangerous enterprize seemed to trust and employ him only:

> *Verbis quæ timido quoque possent addere mentem:*
> Hor. ii. *Epist.* ii. 34.

With words, which to a coward might
Adde courage, had he any spright.

Imploy (said he unto him) some wretch-stripped and robbed Souldier

> —(*quantumvis rusticus ibit,*
> *Ibit eò, quo vis, qui zonam perditit, inquit.*)—39.

(None is, saith he, so clownish, but will-on,
Where you will have him, if his purse be gone)

and absolutely refused to obey him. When we reade that *Mahomet*, having outragiously rated *Chasan*, chiefe leader of his Janizers, because he saw his troup wel-nigh defeated by the Hungarians, and hee to behave himselfe but faintly in the fight, *Chasan* without making other reply, alone as he was, and without more adoe, with his weapon in his hand rushed furiously in the thickest throng of his enemies that he first met withall, of whom hee was instantly slaine: This may haply be deemed, rather a rash conceit, than a justification; and a new spight, than a naturall prowess. He whom you saw yesterday so boldly-venturous, wonder not if you see him a dastardly meacocke to morrow next: for either anger or necessitie, company or wine, a sudden fury or the clang of a trumpet, might rowze-up his heart, and stir up his courage. It is no heart nor courage so framed by discourse or deliberation: These circumstances have setled the same in him: Therefore it is no marvell if by other contrary circumstance he become a craven and change coppy. This supple variation, and easie yeelding contradiction, which is seene in us, hath made some to imagine, that wee had two soules, and others, two faculties; whereof every one as best she pleaseth, accompanieth and doth agitate us; the one towards good, the other towards evill. Forsomuch as such a rough diversitie cannot wel sort and agree in one simple subject. The blast of accidents doth not only remove me according to his inclination; for besides, I remove and trouble my selfe by the instability of my posture, and whosoever looketh narrowly about himselfe, shall hardly see himselfe twise in one same state. Sometimes I give my soule one visage, and sometimes another, according unto the posture or side I lay her in. If I speake diversly of my selfe, it is because I looke diversly upon my selfe. All contrarieties are found in her, according to some turne or removing; and in some fashion or other. Shamefast, bashfull, insolent, chaste, luxurious, peevish, pratling, silent, fond, doting, laborious, nice, delicate, ingenious, slow, dull, froward, humorous, debonaire, wise, ignorant, false in words, true-speaking, both liberall, covetous, and prodigall. All these I perceive in some measure or other to bee in mee, according as I stirre or turne my selfe; And whosoever shall heedfully survay and consider himselfe, shall finde this volubility and discordance to be in himselfe, yea and in his very judgement. I have nothing to say entirely, simply, and with soliditie of my selfe, without confusion, disorder, blending, mingling; and in one word, *Distinguo* is the most universall part of my logike. Although I ever purpose to speake good of good, and rather to enterpret those things, that will beare it, unto a good sense; yet is it that, the strangenesse of our condition admitteth that we are often urged to do well by vice it selfe, if well doing were not judged by the intention only. Therefore may not a couragious act conclude a man to be valiant. He that is so, when just occasion serveth, shall ever be so, and upon all occasions. If it were an habitude of vertue, and not a sudden humour, it would make a man equally resolute at all assayes, in all accidents: Such alone, as in company; such in a single combat, as in a set battel; For, whatsoever some say, valour is all alike, and not one in the street or towne, and another in the campe or field. As couragiously should a man beare a sicknesse in his bed, as a hurt in the field and feare death no more at home in his house, than abroad in an assault. We should not then see one same man enter the breach, or charge his enemie with an assured and undouted fiercenesse, and afterward having escaped that, to vexe, to grieve and torment himselfe like unto a seely woman, or fainthearted milke-sop for the losse of a sute, or death of a childe. If one chance to be carelesly base-minded in his infancie, and constantly-resolute in povertie; if he be timorously-fearefull at sight of a Barbers razor, and afterward stowtly-undismayed against his enemies swords: The action is commendable, but not the man. Divers Græcians (saith *Cicero*) cannot endure to looke their enemy in the face, yet are they most constant in their sickenesses; whereas the *Cimbrians*, and *Celtiberians*, are meere contrary. *Nihil enim potest esse æquabile, quod non à certa ratione profiscatur* (CIC. *Tusc. Qu.* ii. f.): *For nothing can beare it selfe even, which proceedeth not from resolved reason.* There is no valor more extreme in his kinde, than that of *Alexander;* yet it is but in *species*, nor every where sufficiently full and universall. As incomparable as it is, it hath his blemishes, which is the reason that in the idleest suspitions, he apprehendeth at the conspiracies of his followers against his life, we see him so earnestly to vex, and so desperately to trouble himselfe: In search and pursuit whereof he demeaneth himselfe with so vehement and indiscreet an injustice, and with such a demisse feare, that even his naturall reason is thereby subverted. Also the superstition, wherewith he is so thoroughly tainted, beareth some shew of pusilanimitie. And the unlimited excesse of the repentance he shewed for the murther of *Clitus*, is also a witnesse of the inequalitie of his courage. Our matters are but parcels hudled up, and peeces patched together, and we endevour to acquire honour by false meanes, and untrue tokens. *Vertue will not bee followed, but by her selfe:* And if at any time wee borrow her maske, upon some other occasion, she will as soone pull it from our face. It is a lively hew, and strong dye, if the soule be once dyed with the same perfectly, and which will never fade or be gone, except it carry the skin away with it. Therefore to judge a man, we must a long time follow, and very curiously marke his steps; whether constancie doe wholy subsist and continue upon her owne foundation in him, *Cui vivendi via considerata atque provisa est* (Cic. *Parad.* v.): *Who hath forecast and considered the way of life;* whether the variety of occurrences make him change his pace (I meane his way, for his pace may either be hastened or slowed) let him run-on: such a one (as sayeth the imprease of our good Talbot) goeth before the wind. It is no marvell (saith an old writer) that hazard hath such power over us, since wee live by hazard. It is impossible for him to dispose of his particular actions, that hath not in grose directed his life unto one certaine end. It is impossible for him to range all peeces in order, that hath not a plot or forme of the totall frame in his head. What avayleth the provision of all sorts of colours unto one that knowes not what he is to draw? No man makes any certaine designe of his life, and we deliberate of it but by parcels. A skilfull archer ought first to knowe the marke he aimeth at, and then apply his hand, his bow, his string, his arrow and his motion accordingly. Our counsels goe a stray, because they are not rightly addressed, and have no fixed end. *No winde makes for him, that hath no intended port to saile unto.* As for me, I allow not greatly of that judgement, which some made of *Sophocles*, and to have concluded him sufficient in the managing of domesticall matters, against the accusation of his owne Sonne, only by the sight of one of his tragedies. Nor doe I commend the conjecture of the *Parians*, sent to reforme the *Milesians*, as sufficient to the consequence they drew thence. In visiting and surveying the Ile, they marked the Landes that were best husbanded, and observed the country houses that were best governed. And having registred the names of their owners; and afterward made an assembly of the Townes-men of the Citie, they named and instituted those owners as new Governours and

Magistrates, judging and concluding, that being good husbands and carefull of their household affaires, they must consequently be so of publike matters. We are all framed of flaps and patches and of so shapelesse and diverse a contexture, that every peece and every moment playeth his part. And there is as much difference found betweene us and our selves, as there is between our selves and other. *Magnam rem puta, unum hominem agere. Esteeme it a great matter, to play but one man.*

Since ambition may teach men both valour, temperance, liberality, yea and justice: Sith covetousnesse may settle in the minde of a Shopprentise-boy, brought up in ease and idlenesse, a dreadlesse assurance to leave his homebred ease, and forgoe his place of education, and in a small barke to yeeld himselfe unto the mercy of blustring waves, mercilesse windes and wrathful *Neptune;* and that it also teacheth discretion and wisdome; And that *Venus* her selfe ministreth resolution and hardenesse unto tender youth as yet subject to the discipline of the rod, and teacheth the ruthlesse Souldier, the soft and tenderly effeminate heart of women in their mothers laps.

> *Hac duce custodes furtim transgressa jacentes,*
> —*Ad juvenem tenebris sola puella venit.*—TIB. ii. *El.* i. 75.

The wench by stealeth her lodg'd guards having stript,
By this guide, sole, i' th darke, to' th yonker skipt.

It is no part of a well grounded judgement, simply to judge our selves by our exteriour actions: A man must thorowly sound himselfe, and dive into his heart, and there see by what wards or springs the motions stirre. But forasmuch as it is a hazardous and high enterprise, I would not have so many to meddle with it as doe.

CHAPTER II

OF DRUNKENNESSE

The world is nothing but variety, and dissemblance. Vices are all alike, inasmuch as they are all vices: And so doe haply the Stoikes meane it. But though they are equally vices, they are not equall vices; And that hee who hath started a hundred steps beyond the limits

> *Quos ultra citraque nequit consistere rectum,*
> HOR. i. *Sat.* i. 107.

On this side, or beyond the which
No man can hold a right true pitch,

is not of worse condition, than he that is ten steps short of it, is no whit credible: and that sacriledge is not worse than the steaiing of a Colewort out of a Garden.

Nec vincet ratio, tantundem ut peccet idemque
Qui teneros caules alieni fregerit horti,
Et qui nocturnus divum sacra legerit.—Sat. iii. 115.

No reason can evict, as great or same sinne taints
Him that breakes in anothers Garden tender plants,
And him that steales by night things consecrate to Saints.

There is as much diversity in that as in any other thing. The confusion of order and measure of crimes, is dangerous: Murtherers, Traitors and Tyrants, have too much gaine by it: it is no reason their conscience should be eased, in that some is either idle or lascivious, or lesse assiduous unto devotion. Every man poiseth upon his fellowes sinne, and elevates his owne. Even teachers doe often range it ill in my conceit. As *Socrates* said, that the chiefest office of wisdome, was to distinguish goods and evils. We others, to whom the best is ever in vice, should say the like of knowledge, to distinguish vices. Without which, and that very exact, both vertuous and wicked men remaine confounded and unknowen. Now drunkennesse amongst others, appeareth to mee a grose and brutish vice. The minde hath more part else where; and some vices there are, which (if it may lawfully be spoken) have a kinde of I wot not what generosity in them. Some there are, that have learning, diligence, valour, prudence, wit, cunning, dexterity, and subtlety joyned with them; whereas this is meerely corporall, and terrestriall. And the grosest and rudest nation, that liveth amongst us at this day, is only that which keepeth it in credit. Other vices but alter and distract the understanding, whereas this utterly subverteth the same, and astonieth the body.

—cùm vini vis penetravit,
Consequitur gravitas membrorum, præpediuntur
Crura vacillanti, tardescit lingua, madet mens,
Nant oculi, clamor, singultus, jurgia gliscunt.
LUCR. iii. 479.

When once the force of wine hath inly pierst,
Limbes-heavinesse is next, legs faine would goe,
But reeling cannot, tongue drawles, mindes disperst,
Eyes swimme, cries, hickups, brables grow.

The worst estate of man, is where he loseth the knowledge and government of himselfe. And amongst other things, it is said, that as must wine boyling and working in a vessell, workes and sends upward what ever it containeth in the bottome, so doth wine cause those that drinke excessively of it, worke up, and breake out their most concealed secrets.

—tu sapientium
Curas, et arcanum jocoso
*Consilium retegis Lyæo.—*HOR. iii. *Od.* xxi. 14.

Thou (wine-cup) doest by wine reveale
The cares, which wise men would conceale,
And close drifts, at a merry meale.

Josephus reporteth, that by making an Ambassador to tipple-square, whom his enemies had sent unto him, he wrested all his secrets out of him. Neverthelesse *Augustus* having trusted *Lucius Piso,* that conquered *Thrace,* with the secretest affaires he had in hand, had never cause to be discontented with him; Nor *Tiberius* with *Cossus,* to whom he imparted all his seriousest counsels, although we know them both to have so given themselves to drinking of wine, that they were often faine to be carried from the Senat, and both were reputed notable drunkards.

—*Hesterno inflatim venas de more Lyæo.*

VIRG. *Buc. Ec.* vi. 15.

Veines pufft up, as is used alway,
By wine which was drunke yesterday.

And as faithfully as the complot and purpose to kill *Cæsar* committed unto *Cimber,* who would daily be drunke with quaffing of wine, as unto *Cassius,* that drunke nothing but water, whereupon he answered very pleasantly, *What? shall I beare a Tyrant, that am not able to beare wine?* We see our carowsing tospot German souldiers, when they are most plunged in their cups, and as drunke as Rats, to have perfect remembrance of their quarter, of the watch word, and of their files.

—*nec facilis victoria de madidis, et*
Blæsis, atque mero titubantibus.—JUVEN. *Sat.* xv. 47.

Nor is the conquest easie of men sow'st,
Lisping and reeling with wine they carow'st.

I would never have beleeved so sound, so deepe and so excessive drunkennesse, had I not read in Histories, that *Attalus* having envited to sup with him (with intent to doe him some notable indignity) the same *Pausanias,* who for the same cause killed afterward *Philip* King of *Macedon,* (a King who by the eminent faire qualities that were in him, bore a testimonie of the education he had learned in the house and company of *Epaminondas*) made him so dead-drunke, that insensibly and without feeling, he might prostitute his beauty as the body of a common hedge-harlot, to Mulettiers, Groomes, and many of the abject servants of his house. And what a Lady (whom I much honour and highly esteeme) told mee, protesting, that neere *Burdeaux,* towards *Castres,* where her house is, a widdow Country-woman, reputed very chaste and honest, suspecting herselfe to be with childe, told her neighbours, that had she a husband, she should verily thinke she were with childe. But the occasion of this suspition encreasing more and

more, and perceiving herselfe so big-bellied, that shee could no longer
conceale it, she resolved to make the Parish-priest acquainted with it,
whom she entreated to publish in the Church, that whosoever hee were,
that was guilty of the fact, and would avow it, shee would freely forgive him, and if hee were so pleased, take him to her husband. A certaine swaine or hyne-boy of hers, emboldned by this proclamation,
declared, how that having one holliday found her well-tippled with
wine, and so sound asleepe by the chimnie side, lying so fit and ready
for him, that without a waking her he had the full use of her body.
Whom she accepted for her husband, and both live together at this
day. It is assured that antiquitie hath not greatly described this vice.
The compositions of diverse Philosophers speake but sparingly of it.
Yea, and some of the Stoikes deeme it not amisse for man sometimes
to take his liquor roundly, and drinke drunke thereby to recreate his
spirits.

> *Hoc quoque virtutum quondam certamine magnum*
> *Socratem palmam promeruisse jerunt.*—COR. *Gal.* El. i.

> They say, in this too, *Socrates the wise,*
> And great in vertues combats, bare the prize.

Cato that strict censurer, and severe corrector of others, hath beene
reproved for much drinking,

> *Narratur et prisci Catonis*
> *Sæpe mero caluisse virtus.*—HOR. iii. *Od.* xxi. 11.

> 'Tis said, by use of wine repeated,
> Old *Catoes* vertue oft was heated.

Cyrus that so far-renowned King, amongst his other commendations,
meaning to preferre himselfe before his brother *Artaxerxes,* and get the
start of him, aleageth, that he could drinke better, and tipple more than
he. And amongst the best policed and formalest nations, the custome
of drinking, and pledging of healths was much in use. I have heard
Silvius, that excellent Phisitian of *Paris* affirme that to preserve the
vigor of our stomake from empairing, it is not amisse once a moneth to
rowze up the same by this excesse of drinking; and lest it should grow
dull and stupid therby to stirre it up. And it is written, that the *Persians,* after they had well tippled, were wont to consult of their chiefest
affaires. My taste, my rellish and my complexion, are sharper enemies
unto this vice, than my discourse: For, besides that I captivate more
easily my conceits under the auctoritie of ancient opinions, indeed I
finde it to be a fond, a stupid and a base kinde of vice, but lesse malicious and hurtfull than others; all which shocke, and with a sharper
edge wound publike societie. And if we cannot give our selves any
pleasure, except (as they say) it cost us something; I finde this vice to
be lesse chargeable unto our conscience than others; besides, it is not

hard to be prepared, difficult to be found; a consideration not to be despised. A man well advanced in yeares and dignitie, amongst three principall commodities he told me to have remaining in life, counted this: and where shall a man more rightly finde-it, than amongst the naturall? But he tooke it ill, delicatenesse, and the choice of wines is therein to be avoided. If you prepare your voluptuousnes to drinke it with pleasure and daintily neat, you tie your selfe unto an inconvenience to drinke it other than is alwayes to be had. A man must have a milder, a loose and freer taste. To be a true drinker, a man should not have so tender and squeamish a palat. The Germans doe in a manner drinke equally of all sorts of wine with like pleasure. Their end is rather to gulpe it downe freely, than to tast it kindly. And to say truth they have it better cheape. Their voluptuousnesse is more plenteous and fuller. Secondarily, to drinke after the French manner, as two draughts and moderatly, is over much to restraine the favours of that God. There is more time and constancie required thereunto. Our forefathers were wont to spend whole nights in that exercise, yea often times they joyned whole long dayes unto them. And a man must proportion his ordinarie more large and firme. I have in my dayes seene a principall Lord; and man of great employment and enterprises, and famous for good successe, who without straining himselfe, and eating but an ordinary meales-meat, was wont to drinke little lesse than five pottles of wine, yet at his rising seemed to be nothing distempered, but rather as we have found to our no small cost in managing of our affaires, over-wise and considerate. The pleasure of that, whereof we would make account in the course of our life ought to be employed longer space. It were necessary, as shop-boyes or labouring people, that we should refuse no occasion to drinke and continually to have this desire in our minde. It seemeth that wee daily shorten the use of this: and that in our houses, (as I have seene in mine infancie) breakfasts, nunchions, and beavers should be more frequent and often used, than now adayes they are. And should wee thereby in any sort proceed towards amendment? No verily. But it may be, that we have much more given our selves over unto paillardise and all manner of luxurie than our fathers were. They are two occupations, that enter-hinder one another, in their vigor. On the one side, it hath empaired and weakned our stomacke, and on the other, sobrietie serveth to make us more jolly-quaint, lusty, and wanton for the exercise of love matters. It is a wonder to thinke on the strange tales I have heard my father report, of the chastitie of his times. He might well speake of it, as he that was both by art and nature proper for the use and solace of Ladies. He spake little and well, few words, but to the purpose, and was ever wont to entermixe some ornament taken from vulgar bookes, and above all, Spanish, amongst his common speeches: And of all Spanish Authors, none was more familiar unto him than *Marcus Aurelius*. His demeanour and carriage was ever milde, meeke, gentle, and very modest, and above all, grave and stately.

There is nothing he seemed to be more carefull of, than of his honesty, and observe a kinde of decencie of his person, and orderly decorum in his habits, were it on foot or on horsebacke. He was exceeding nice in performing his word or promise; And so strictly conscientious and obsequous in religion, that generally he seemed rather to encline toward superstition, than the contrary. Though he were but a little man, his courage and vigor was great: he was of an upright, and well proportioned stature, of a pleasing, cheerefull-looking countenance, of a swarthy hue, nimbly addicted, and exquisitely nimble unto all noble and gentleman-like exercises. I have seene some hollow staves of his filled with lead, which hee wont to use and exercise his armes withall, the better to enable himselfe to pitch the barre, to throw the sledge, to cast the pole and to play at fence: and shooes with leaden soles, which he wore to enure himselfe, to leape, to vault and to run. I may without blushing say, that in memory of himselfe, he hath left certain petie miracles amongst us. I have seene him when hee was past three-score yeares of age mocke at all our sports, and outcountenance our youthfull pastimes, with a heavy furr'd Gowne about him to leap into his saddle; to make the pommada round about a Table upon his thumb; and seldome to ascend any staires without skipping three or foure steps at once. And concerning my discourse, hee was wont to say, that in a whole Province there was scarse any woman of qualitie, that had an ill name. Hee would often report strange familiarities, namely of his owne, with very honest women, without any suspicion at all. And protested very religiously, that when he was married, he was yet a pure Virgine; yet had he long time followed warres beyond the Mountaines, and therein served long, whereof hee hath left a Journall-Booke of his owne collecting, wherein hee hath particularly noted, whatsoever happened day by day worthy the observation, so long as he served, both for the publike and his particular use. And he was well strucken in yeares, when he tooke a wife. For returning out of *Italie*, in the yeare of our Lord, one thousand five hundred eight and twenty, and being full three and thirty yeares old, by the way hee chose himselfe a wife. But come we to our drinking againe. The incommodities of age, which need some helpe and refreshing, might with some reason beget in me a desire or longing of this faculty: for, it is in a man the last pleasure, which the course of our years stealeth upon us. Good fellowes say, that naturall heat is first taken in our feet: That properly belongeth to infancie. From thence it ascendeth unto the middle region, where it is setled and continueth a long time: and in mine opinion, there produceth the only true, and moving pleasures of this corporall life. Other delight and sensualities in respect of that, doe but sleepe. In the end, like unto a vapour, which by little and little exhaleth, and mounteth aloft, it comes unto the throat, and there makes her last bode. Yet could I never conceive, how any man may either encrease or prolong the pleasure of drinking beyond thirst, and in his imagination frame an artificiall appe-

tite, and against nature. My stomacke could not well reach so farre:
it is very much troubled to come to an end of that which it takes for his
need. My constitution is, to make an accompt of drinking, but to
succeed meat, and therefore doe I ever make my last draught the
greatest. And forasmuch as in age, we have the roofe of our mouthes
commonly furred with rhume, or distempered, distasted and altered
through some other evill constitution, wine seemeth better unto us and
of a quicker relish, according as our pores be either more or lesse open
and washed. At least I seldome relish the same very well, except it be
the first draught I take. *Anacharsis* wondered to see the Græcians
drinke in greater glasses at the end of their meales, than in the beginning. It was (as I imagine) for the very same reason, that the Germans
doe it, who never begin to carouse, but when they have well fed. *Plato*
forbiddeth children to drinke any wine, before they be eighteene yeeres
of age, and to be drunke before they come to forty. But to such as have
once attained the age of fortie, he is content to pardon them, if they
chance to delight themselves with it, and alloweth them somwhat
largely to blend the influence of *Dionysius* in their banquets, that good
God, who bestoweth cheerfulnesse upon men, and youth unto aged
men, who layeth and aswageth the passions of the minde, even as yron
is made flexible by the fire: and in his profitable lawes drinking-
meetings or quaffing companies as necessary and commendable (alwaies
provided there be a chiefe leader amongst them to containe and order
them) drunkennesse being a good and certaine tryall of everie mans
nature; and therewithall proper to give aged men the courage to make
merry in dancing and in musicke; things alowable and profitable, and
such as they dare not undertake being sober and setled. That wine is
capable to supply the mind with temperance, and the bodie with health.
Notwithstanding, these restrictions, partly borrowed of the Carthaginians, please him well. Let those forbeare it that are going about any
expedition of warre. Let every magistrate, and all judges abstain from
it at what time they are to execute their charge, and to consult of
publike affaires. Let none bestow the day in drinking, as the time that
is due unto more serious negotiations, nor the nights wherein a man
intendeth to get children. It is reported, that *Stilpo* the Philosopher,
finding himselfe surcharged with age, did purposely hasten his end, by
drinking of pure wine. The like cause (though not wittingly) did also
suffocate the vital forces, crazed through old age of the Philosopher
Arcesilaus. But it is an old and pleasant question, whether a wisemans
mind were like to yeeld unto the force of wine.

> *Si munitæ adhibet vim sapientiæ.—Od.* xxviii. 4.

If unresisted force it bends,
Gainst wisdome which it selfe defends.

Unto what vanity doth the good opinion we have of our selves provoke us? The most temperate and perfectest minde of the world, findes

it too great a taske to keep herselfe upright, lest she fall by her owne
weaknesse. Of a thousand there is not one perfectly righteous and setled
but one instant of her life, and question might be made, whether
according to her naturall condition she might at any time be so. But to
joyne constancie unto it [is] her last perfection: I meane if nothing
should shocke her: which a thousand accidents may doe. *Lucretius* that
famous Poet, may Philosophie and bandie at his pleasure: Loe where
he lieth senselesse of an amorous potion. Thinkes any man, that an
Apoplexie cannot as soone astonish *Socrates,* as a poore labouring man?
Some of them have by the force of a sicknesse forgot their owne names,
and a slight hurt have overthrowne the judgement of others. Let him
be as wise as he can, in the end he is but a man; what is more fraile,
more miserable, or more vaine? Wisdome forceth not our naturall conditions.

> *Sudores itaque, et pallorem existere toto*
> *Corpore, et infringi linguam vocemque aboriri*
> *Caligare oculos, sonere aures, succidere artus,*
> *Denique concidere ex animi terrore videmus.*
>
> LUCR. iii. 155.

We see therefore, palenesse and sweats ore-grow,
Our bodies, tongues doe falter, voyce doth breake,
Eyes dazle, eares buzze, joints doe shrinke below,
Lastly we swoune by hart-fright, terrours weake.

He must [s]eele his eyes against the blow that threatneth him, being
neere the brimme of a percipise, he must cry out like a child. Nature
having purposed to reserve these light markes of her aucthoritie unto
herselfe, inexpugnable unto our reason, and to the Stoicke vertue: to
teach him his mortalitie, and our insipidite. He waxeth pale for feare,
he blusheth for shame, he groaneth feeling the cholike, if not with a
desperate and lowd-roaring voyce, yet with a low, smothered and
hoarse-sounding noyse.

> *Humani à se nihil alienum putat.*
> TER. *Heaut.* act. i. sc. i. 25.

He thinkes, that nothing strange be can,
To him, that longs to any man.

Giddie-headed Poets, that faine what they list, dare not so much as
discharge their *Heroes* from teares.

> *Sic fatur lachrymans, classique immitit habenas.*
> VIRG. *Æn.* vi. 1.

So said he weeping, and so saide,
Himselfe hand to the sterage laide.

Let it suffice him to bridle his affections, and moderate his inclinations; for, it is not in him to beare them away. *Plutarke* himselfe, who

is so perfect and excellent a judge of humane actions, seeing *Brutus* and *Torquatus* to kill their owne children, remaineth doubtfull, whether vertue could reach so farre, and whether such men were not rather moved by some other passion. *All actions beyond the ordinarie limits, are subject to some sinister interpretation:* Forasmuch as our taste doth no more come unto that which is above it, than to that which is under it. Let us omit that other sect, which maketh open profession of fiercenes. But when in the very same sect, which is esteemed the most demisse, we heare the bragges of *Metrodorus: Occupavite, Fortuna, atque cepi: omnesque aditus tuos interclusi ut ad me aspirare non posses* (Metr. Cic. *Tusc. Quest.* 5). *Fortune, I have prevented, caught, and overtaken thee: I have mured and ramd up all thy passagis, whereby thou mightest attaine unto mee.* When *Anaxarcus,* by the appointment of *Nicocreon,* the tyrant of *Cipres,* being laid along in a trough of stone, and smoten with yron sledges, ceaseth not to crie out, streeke, smite, and breake; it is not *Anaxarcus,* it is but his vaile you martyr so. When we heare our martyrs, in the middest of a flame crie aloude unto the Tyrant, this side is rosted enough, chop it, eat it, it is full rosted, now begin on the other. When in *Josephus* wee heare a childe all to rent with biting snippers, and pierced with the breath of *Antiochus,* to defie him to death, crie with a lowde-assured and undismaid voyce; Tyrant thou losest time, loe I am still at mine ease; where is that smarting paine, where are those torments, wherewith whilom thou didst so threaten me? My constancie doth more trouble thee, than I have feeling of thy crueltie: Oh faint hearted varlet, doest thou yeeld when I gather strength? Make mee to faint or shrinke, cause me to moane or lament, force me to yeeld and sue for grace if thou canst; encourage thy satellities, harten thy executioners; loe how they droope and have no more power; arme them, strengthen them, flesh them. Verely wee must needs confesse there is some alteration, and some furie (how holy soever) in those mindes. When we come unto these Stoick evasions; I had rather be furious than voluptuous: the saying of *Antisthenes. Μανείην μᾶλλον ἢ ἡσθείην* (Antist. Diogen. Laert. vi. c. 1), *Rather would I be mad, than merry.* When *Sextius* telleth us, he had rather be surprised with paine, than sensuality; when *Epicurus* undertakes to have the goute, to wantonize and faune upon him, and refusing ease and health, with a hearty cheerefulnesse defie all evils, and scornefully despising lesse sharpe griefes, disdayning to grapple with them, he blithely desireth and calleth for sharper, more forcible, and worthy of him:

Spumantemque dari pecora inter inertia votis
Optat aprum aut fulvum descendere monte leonem:
　　　　　　　　　　　Virg. *Æn.* iv. 158.

He wisht, mongst hartlesse beasts some foming Bore,
Or mountaine-Lyon would come downe and rore.

Who would not judge them to be prankes of a courage removed from his wonted seate? Our minde cannot out of her place attaine so high. She must quit it and raise her selfe aloft, and taking the bridle in her teeth, carry and transport her man so farre, that afterward hee wonder at himselfe, and rest amazed at his actions. As in exploits of warre, the heat and earnestnesse of the fight doth often provoke the noble minded souldiers, to adventure on so dangerous passages, that afterward being better advised, they are the first to wonder at it. As also Poets, are often surprised and rapt with admiration at their owne labours, and forget the trace, by which they past so happy a career. It is that, which some terme a fury or madnesse in them. And as *Plato* saith, that a setled and reposed man, doth in vaine knocke at Poesies gate. *Aristotle* likewise saith, that no excellent minde is freely exempted from some or other entermixture of folly. And he hath reason, to call any starting or extraordinarie conceit (how commendable soever) and which exceedeth our judgement and discourse, folly. Forsomuch as *wisdome, is an orderly and regular managing of the minde, and which she addresseth with measure, and conducteth with proportion;* and take her owne word for it. *Plato* disputeth thus; that the facultie of prophesying and divination is far above us, and that when wee treat it, we must be besides our selves: our wisdome must be darkened and over shadowed by sleepe, by sickenesse, or by drowzinesse; or by some celestiall fury, ravished from her owne seat.

CHAPTER III

A CUSTOME OF THE ILE OF CEA

IF, as some say, to philosophate be to doubt; with much more reason, to rave and fantastiquize, as I doe, must necessarily be to doubt: For, to enquire and debate, belongeth to a scholler, and to resolve appertaines to a cathedrall master. But know, my cathedrall, it is the authoritie of Gods divine will, that without any contradiction doth sway us, and hath her ranke beyond these humane and vaine contestations. Philip being with an armed hand entred the Countrie of *Peloponnesus,* some one told *Damidas,* the Lacedemonians were like to endure much, if they sought not to reobtaine his lost favour. Oh varlet as thou art (answered he.) And what can they suffer, who have no feare at all of death? *Agis* being demanded, how a man might do to live free, answered; *Despising and contemning to die.* These and a thousand like propositions, which concurre in this purpose, do evidently inferre some thing beyond the patient expecting of death it selfe, to be suffered in this life; witnesse the Lacedemonian child, taken by *Antigonus,* and sold for a slave, who urged by his master, to performe some abject service; Thou shalt see (said he) whom thou hast bought; for, it were a shame for me to serve, having libertie so neere at hand, and there-withall threw himselfe headlong downe from the top of the house. *Antipater*, sharply threatning the Lacedemonians, to make them yeeld to a certaine request of his; they answered, shouldest thou menace us worse than death, we will rather die. And to *Philip*, who having written unto them, that he would hinder all their enterprises; What? (say they) wilt thou also hinder us from dying? That is the reason, why some say, that the wiseman liveth as long as he ought, and not so long as he can. And that the favourablest gift, nature hath bequeathed us, and which removeth all meanes from us to complaine of our condition, is, that she hath left us the key of the fields. She hath appointed but one entrance unto life, but many a thousand wayes out of it: *Well may we want ground to live upon, but never ground to die in.* As *Boiocatus* answered the Romanes. Why dost thou complaine against this world? It doth not containe thee: If thou livest in paine and sorrow, thy base courage is the cause of it, To die there wanteth but will.

> *Ubique mors est: optimè hoc cavit Deus,*
> *Eripere vitam nemo non homini potest:*
> *At nemo mortem: mille ad hanc aditus patent.*
> SEN. *Theb.* act. i. sc. i.

Each where death is: God did this well purvay,
No man but can from man life take away,
But none barr's death, to it lies many 'a way.

And it is not a receipt to one malady alone; *Death is a remedy against all evils:* It is a most assured haven, never to be feared, and often to be sought: All comes to one period, whether man make an end of himselfe, or whether he endure it; whether he run before his day, or whether he expect it: whence soever it come, it is ever his owne, where ever the threed be broken, it is all there, it's the end of the web. The voluntariest death, is the fairest. *Life dependeth on the will of others, death on ours.* In nothing should we so much accommodate our selves to our humours, as in that. Reputation doth nothing concerne such an enterprise, it is folly to have any respect unto it. *To live is to serve, if the libertie to dye be wanting.* The common course of curing any infirmitie, is ever directed at the charge of life: we have incisions made into us, we are cauterized, we have limbes cut and mangled, we are let bloud, we are dieted. Goe we but one step further, we need no more physicke, we are perfectly whole. Why is not our jugular or throat-veine as much at our command as the mediane? To extreme sicknesses, extreme remedies. *Servius* the Grammarian being troubled with the gowt, found no better meanes to be rid of it, than to apply poison to mortify his legs. He cared not whether they were *Podagrees* or no, so they were insensible. God giveth us sufficient privilege, when he placeth us in such an estate, as life is worse than death unto us. *It is weaknesse to yeeld to evils, but folly to foster them.* The Stoikes say, it is a convenient naturall life, for a wise man, to forgoe life, although he abound in all happinesse; if he doe it opportunely: And for a foole to prolong his life, albeit he be most miserable, provided he be in most part of things, which they say to be according unto nature. As I offend not the lawes made against theeves, when I cut mine owne purse, and carry away mine owne goods; nor of destroyers when I burne mine owne wood: so am I nothing tied unto lawes made against murtherers, if I deprive my selfe of mine owne life. *Hegesias* was wont to say, that even as the condition of life, so should the qualitie of death depend on our election. And *Diogenes* meeting with the Philosopher, *Speusippus,* long time afflicted with the dropsie, and therefore carried in a litter, who cried out unto him; All haile *Diogenes:* And to thee no health at all, (replied *Diogenes*) that endurest to live in so wretched an estate. True it is, that a while after, *Speusippus* as overtired with so languishing a condition of life, compassed his owne death. But this goeth not without some contradiction: For, many are of opinion, that without the expresse commandement of him, that hath placed us in this world, we may by no meanes forsake the garrison of it, and that it is in the hands of God only, who therein hath placed us, not for our selves alone, but for his glory, and others service, when ever it shall please him to discharge us hence, and not for us to take leave: *That we are not borne for our selves, but for our Countrie:* The Lawes for their owne interest require an accompt at our hands for our selves, and have a just action of murther against us. Else as forsakers of our owne charge, we are punished in the other world.

> *Proxima deinde tenent mœsti loca, qui sibi lethum*
> *Insontes peperere manu, lucémque perosi*
> *Projecere animas.*—Virg. Æn. vi. 434.

Next place they lamentable hold in hell,
Whose hand their death caus'd causelesse, (but not well)
And hating life did thence their soules expell.

There is more constancie in using the chaine that holds us, than in breaking the same; and more triall of stedfastnesse in *Regulus,* than in *Cato*. It is indiscretion and impatience that hastneth our way. *No accidents can force a man to turne his backe from lively vertue:* She seeketh out evils and sorrowes as her nourishment. The threats of fell tyrants, tortures and torments; executioners and torturers, doe animate and quicken her.

> *Duris ut ilex tonsa bipennibus*
> *Nigræ feraci frondis in Algido*
> *Per damna, per cædes, ab ipso*
> *Ducit opes animumque ferro.*—Hor. iv. *Od*. iv. 57.

As holme-tree doth with hard axe lopt
On hils with many holme-trees topt,
From losse, from cuttings it doth feele,
Courage and store rise ev'n from steele.

And as the other saith.

> *Non est ut putas virtus, pater,*
> *Timere vitam, sed magis ingentibus*
> *Obstare, nec se vertere ac retro dare.*
> > SEN. *Theb.* act. i. SC. I.

Sir, 'tis not vertue, as you understand,
To feare life, but grosse mischiefe to withstand,
Not to retire, turne backe, at any hand.

> *Rebus in adversis facilè est contemnere mortem.*
> *Fortius ille facit, qui miser esse potest.*
> > MART. xi. *Ep.* lvii. 15.

'Tis easie in crosse chance death to despise:
He that can wretched be, doth stronger rise.

It is the part of cowardlinesse, and not of vertue, to seek to squat it selfe in some hollow-lurking hole, or to hide her selfe under some massie tombe, thereby to shun the strokes of fortune. She never forsakes her course, nor leaves her way, what stormie weather soever crosse her.

> *Si fractus illabatur orbis,*
> *Impavidam ferient ruinæ.*—HOR. iii. *Od.* iii. 7.

If the world broken should upon her fall,
The ruines may her strike, but not appall.

The avoyding of other inconveniences doth most commonly drive us into this, yea, sometimes the shunning of death, makes us to run into it.

> *Hic, rogo, non furor est, ne moriare, mori?*
> > MART. ii. *Epig.* lxxx. 2.

Madnesse is't not, say I,
To dye, lest you should dye?

As those who for feare of a break-necke downe-fall, doe headlong cast themselves into it.

> *—multos in summa pericula misit*
> *Venturi timor ipse mali: fortissimus ille est,*
> *Qui promptus metuenda pati, si cominus instent,*
> *Et differre potest.*—LUCAN. vii. 104.

The very feare of ils to come, hath sent
Many to mighty dangers: strongest they,
Who fearfull things t'endure are ready bent,
If they confront them, yet can them delay.

—usque adeo mortis formidine, vitæ
Percipit humanos odium, lucisque videndæ,
Ut sibi consciscant mœrenti pectore lethum,
Obliti fontem curarum hunc esse timorem.
                                    LUCR. iii. 79.

So far by feare of death, the hate of life,
And seeing-light, doth men as men possesse,
They grieving kill themselves to end the strife,
Forgetting, feare is spring of their distresse.

Plato in his lawes, alots him that hath deprived his neerest and deerest friend of life (that is to say, himselfe) and abridged him of the destinies course, not constrained by any publike judgement, nor by any lewd and inevitable accident of fortune, nor by any intolerable shame or infamy, but through basenesse of minde, and weaknesse of a faint-fearfull courage, to have a most ignominious, and ever-re-proachfull buriall. And the opinion which disdaineth our life, is ridiculous: For, in fine it is our being. It is our all in all. Things that have a nobler and richer being, may accuse ours: But it is against nature, we should despise, and carelesly set our selves at naught: It is a particular infirmitie, and which is not seene in any other creature, to hate and disdaine himselfe. It is of like vanitie, that we desire to be other, than we are. The fruit of such a desire doth not concerne us, forasmuch as it contradicteth and hindereth it selfe in it selfe. He that desireth to be made of a man an Angell, doth nothing for him-selfe: He should be nothing the better by it: And being no more, who shall rejoyce or conceive any gladnesse of this change or amendment for him?

Debet enim miserè cui forte ægreque futurum est,
Ipse quoque esse in eo tum tempore, cum male possit
Accidere.—Ibid. 905.

For he, who shall perchance prove miserable,
And speed but ill, should then himselfe be able
To be himselfe, when ils may chance unstable.

The security, indolencie, impassibility, and privation of this lives evils, which we purchase at the price of death, bring us no com-moditie at all. *In vaine doth he avoid warre, that cannot injoy peace; and bootlesse doth he shun paine, that hath no meanes to feele rest.* Amongst those of the first opinion, great questioning hath beene, to know what occasions are sufficiently just and lawfull to make a man undertake the killing of himselfe, they call that εὔλογον ἐξαγωγήν (ALEX. APHROD.), *a reasonable orderly out-let.* For, although they say, a man must often dye for slight causes, since these that keepe us alive, are not very strong; yet is some measure required in them. There are certaine fantasticall and braine-sicke humours, which have not only provoked particular men, but whole Nations to defeat themselves. I have heretofore aleaged some examples of them: And moreover we read of certaine Milesian virgins, who upon a furious conspiracie hanged themselves one after another, untill such time as the Magistrate provided for it, appointing that such as should be found so hanged, should with their owne halters be dragged naked thorow the streets of the Citie. When *Threicion* perswadeth *Cleomenes* to kill himselfe, by reason of the bad and desperate estate his affaires stood in, and having escaped a more honourable death in the battell which he had lately lost, moveth him to accept of this other, which is second to him in honour, and give the Conqueror no leisure to make him endure, either another death, or else a shamefull life. *Cleomenes* with a Lacedemonian and Stoike courage, refuseth this counsell as base and effeminate: It is a receipt, (saith he) which can never faile me, and whereof a man should make no use, so long as there remaineth but one inch of hope: That to live, is sometimes constancie and valour; That he will have his very death serve his Countrie, and by it, shew an act of honour and of vertue. *Threicion* then beleeved, and killed himselfe. *Cleomenes* did afterwards as much, but not before he had tried and assayed the utmost power of fortune. All inconveniences are not so much worth, that a man should dye to eschue them. Moreover, there being so many sudden changes, and violent alterations in humane things, it is hard to judge in what state or point we are justly at the end of our hope:

> *Sperat et in sæva victus gladiator arena,*
> *—Sit licet infesto pollice turba minax.*

The Fencer hopes, though downe in lists he lye,
And people with turn'd hand threat's he must dye.

All things, saith an ancient Proverb, may a man hope for, so long as he liveth: yea, but answereth *Seneca,* wherefore shall I rather have that in minde; that fortune can do all things for him that is living, than this; that fortune hath no power at all over him, who knoweth how to dye? *Joseph* is seene engaged in so an apparent-approaching danger, with a whole nation against him, that according to humane reason, there was no way for him to escape; notwithstanding being (as he saith) counselled by a friend of his, at that instant, to kill himselfe, it fell out well for him to opinionate himselfe yet in hope: for fortune, beyond all mans discourse, did so turne and change that accident, that without any inconvenience at all, he saw himselfe delivered: whereas on the contrarie *Brutus* and *Cassius*, by reason of the downfall and rashnesse, wherewith before due time and occasion, they killed themselves; did utterly lose the reliques of the Roman libertie, whereof they were protectors. The Lord of *Anguien* in the battell of *Serisolles*, as one desperate of the combats successe, which on his side went to wracke, attempted twice to run himselfe thorow the throat with his rapier, and thought by precipitation to bereave himselfe of the enjoying of so notable a victorie. I have seene a hundred Hares save themselves even in the Greyhounds jawes: *Aliquis carnifici suo superstes fuit* (SEN. *Epist.* xiii.). *Some man hath out-lived his Hangman.*

> *Multa dies variusque labor mutabilis ævi*
> *Rettulit in melius, multos alterna revisens*
> *Lusit, et in solido rursus fortuna locavit.*
> VIRG. *Æn.* xi. 426.

Time, and of turning age the divers straine,
Hath much to better brought, fortunes turn'd traine,
Hath many mock't, and set them fast againe.

Plinie saith, there are but three sorts of sicknesses, which to avoid, a man may have some colour of reason to kill himselfe. The sharpest of all is the stone in the bladder, when the urine is there stopped. *Seneca,* those onely, which for long time disturbe and distract the offices of the minde. To avoid a worse death, some are of opinion, a man should take it at his owne pleasure. *Democritus* chiefe of the Ætolians, being led captive to *Rome,* found meanes to escape by night: but being pursued by his keepers, rather than he would be taken againe, ran himselfe thorow with his Sword. *Antinoüs* and *Theodotus,* their Citie of *Epirus* being by the Romans reduced unto great extremitie, concluded, and perswaded all the people to kill themselves. But the counsell, rather to yeeld, having prevailed: they went to seeke their owne death, and rushed amidst the thickest of their enemies, with an intention, rather to strike, than to ward themselves. The Iland of *Gosa,* being some yeares since surprised and over-run by the Turkes, a certaine Sicilian therein dwelling, having two faire daughters ready to be married, killed them both with his owne hands, together with their mother, that came in to help them. That done, running out into the streets, with a crosse-bow in one hand, and a caliver in the other, at two shoots, slew the two first Turks that came next to his gates, then resolutely drawing his Sword, ran furiously among them; by whom he was suddenly hewen in peeces: Thus did he save himselfe from slavish bondage, having first delivered his owne from it. The Jewish women, after they had caused their children to be circumcized, to avoid the crueltie of *Antiochus,* did headlong precipitate themselves and them unto death. I have heard it credibly reported, that a Gentleman of good qualitie, being prisoner in one of our Gaoles, and his parents advertized that he should assuredly be condemned, to avoid the infamie of so reproachfull a death, appointed a Priest to tell him, that the best remedy for his deliverie, was to recommend himselfe to such a Saint, with such and such a vow, and to continue eight dayes without taking any sustenance, what faintnesse or weaknesse soever he should feele in himselfe. He beleeved them, and so without thinking on it, was delivered both of life and danger. *Scribonia* perswading *Libo* his nephew to kill himselfe, rather than to expect the stroke of justice, told him, that for a man to preserve his owne life, to put it into the hands of such as three or foure dayes after should come and seek it, was even to dispatch another mans businesse, and that it was no other, than for one to serve his enemies, to preserve his bloud, therewith to make food. We read in the Bible, that *Nicanor* the persecutor of Gods Law, having sent his Satellites to apprehend the good old man *Rasias*, for the honour of his vertue, surnamed the father of the *Jewes;* when that good man saw no other meanes left him, his gate being burned, and his enemies ready to lay hold on him, chose, rather than to fall into the hands of such villaines, and be so basely abused, against the honour of his place, to dye nobly, and so smote himselfe with his owne sword; but by reason of his haste, having not thoroughly slaine himselfe, he ran to throw himselfe downe from an high wall, amongst the throng of people, which making him roome, he fell right upon his head. All which notwithstanding, perceiving life to remaine in him, he tooke heart againe; and getting up on his feet, all goared with bloud, and loaden with strokes, making way through the prease, came to a craggy and downe-steepy rocke, where unable to go any further, by one of his wounds, with both his hands he pulled out his guts, and tearing and breaking them, cast them amongst such as pursued him, calling and attesting the vengeance of God to light upon them. Of all violences committed against conscience, the most in mine opinion to be avoided, is that which is offered against the chastitie of women, forasmuch as there is naturally some corporall pleasure commixt with it: And therefore the dissent cannot fully enough be joyned thereunto: And it seemeth, that force is in some sort, intermixed with some will. The ecclesiasticall Storie hath in especiall reverence, sundry such examples of devout persons, who called for death to warrant them from the out-rages which some tyrants prepared against their religion and consciences. *Pelagia* and *Sophronia,* both canonized; the first, together with her mother and sisters, to escape the outragious rapes of some souldiers, threw her selfe into a river; the other, to shun the force of *Maxentius* the Emperour, slew her selfe. It shall peradventure redound to our honour in future ages, that a wise Author of these dayes, and namely a Parisian, doth labour to perswade the Ladies of our times, rather to hazard upon any resolution, than to embrace so horrible a counsell of such desperation. I am sorie, that to put amongst his discourses, he knew not the good saying I learnt of a woman at *Tholouse,* who had passed through the hands of some souldiers: God be praised (said she) that once in my life, I have had my belly-full without sinne. Verily these cruelties are not worthy of the French curtesie. And God be thanked, since this good advertisement; our ayre is infinitely purged of them. Let it suffice, that in doing it, they say, *No, and take it,* following the rule of *Marot.* The historie is very full of such, who a thousand wayes have changed a lingering-toylsome life with death. *Lucius Aruntius* killed himselfe (as he said) to avoid what was past, and eschue what was to come. *Granius Sylvanus,* and *Statius Proximus,* after they had beene pardoned by *Nero,* killed themselves, either because they scorned to live by the favour of so wicked a man, or because they would not another time be in danger of a second pardon, seeing his so easie-yeelding unto suspicions and accusations against honest men. *Spargapises* sonne unto Queene *Tomiris,* prisoner by the law of warre unto *Cyrus,* employed the first favour that *Cyrus* did him, by setting him free, to kill himselfe, as he who never pretended to reap other fruit by his liberty, than to revenge the infamie of his taking upon himselfe. *Boges* a Governour for King *Xerxes* in the country of *Ionia,* being besieged by the *Athenians* army under the conduct of *Cymon,* refused the composition, to returne safely, together with his goods and treasure into *Asia,* as one impatient to survive the losse of what his Master had given him in charge; and after he had stoutly and even to the last extremity, defended the Towne, having no manner of victuals left him; first he cast all the gold, and treasure, with whatsoever he imagined the enemy might reap any commoditie by, into the river *Strimon;* Then having caused a great pile of wood to be set on fire, and made all women, children, concubines and servants to be stripped and throwne into the flames, afterwards ran-in himselfe, where all were burned. *Ninachetuen* a Lord in the East *Indies,* having had an inkling of the King of *Portugales* Viceroyes deliberation to dispossesse him, without any apparant cause, of the charge he had in *Malaca,* for to give it unto the King of *Campar;* of himselfe resolved upon this resolution: First, he caused an high scaffold to be set up, somewhat longer than broad, underpropped with pillars, all gorgeously hanged with rich tapestrie, strewed with flowers, and adorned with pretious perfumes: Then having put-on a sumptuous long roabe of cloth of gold, richly beset with store of pretious stones of inestimable worth, he came out of the palace into the street, and by certaine steps ascended the scaffold, in one of the corners whereof, was a pile of aromaticall wood set afire. All the people of the Citie were flocked together, to see what the meaning of such unaccustomed preparation might tend unto. *Ninachetuen* with an undanted-bold, yet seeming-discontented countenance, declared the manifold obligations, which the *Portugal* Nation was endebted unto him for; expostulated how faithfully and truly he had dealt in his charge; that having so often witnessed, armed at all assayes for others; that his honour was much dearer unto him than life, he was not to forsake the care of it for himselfe; that fortune refusing him all meanes to oppose himselfe against the injurie intended against him, his courage, at the least willed him to remove the feeling thereof, and not become a laughing stocke unto the people, and a triumph to men of lesse worth than himselfe: which words as he was speaking, he cast himselfe into the fire. *Sextilia* the wife of *Scaurus* and *Praxea* wife unto *Labeo,* to encourage their husbands, to avoid the dangers, which pressed them, wherein they had no share (but in regard of the interest of their conjugal affection) voluntarily engaged their life, in this extreme necessitie, to serve them, as an example to imitate, and company to regard. What they performed for their husbands; *Cocceius Nerva* acted for his countrie, and though lesse profitable, yet equall in true love. That famous Interpreter of the lawes, abounding in riches, in reputation, in credit, and flourishing in health about the Emperour, had no other cause to rid himselfe of life, but the compassion of the miserable estate, wherein he saw the Romane common-wealth. There is nothing can be added unto the daintinesse of *Fulvius* wives death, who was so inward with *Augustus. Augustus* perceiving he had blabbed a certaine secret of importance, which he on trust had revealed unto him; one morning comming to visit him, he seemed to frowne upon him for it; whereupon as guilty, he returneth home, as one full of despaire, and in piteous sort told his wife, that sithence he was falne into such a mischiefe, he was resolved to kill himselfe; shee as one no whit dismaied, replied unto him; Thou shalt doe but right, since having so often experienced the incontinence of my tongue, thou hast not learnt to beware of it, yet give me leave to kill my selfe first, and without more adoe, ran her selfe thorow with a sword. *Vibius Virius* dispairing of his Cities safetie, besieged by the Romans, and mistrusting their mercie; in their Senates last consultation, after many remonstrances employed to that end, concluded, that the best and fairest way, was to escape fortune by their owne hands. The very enemies should have them in more honour, and *Hanniball* might perceive what faithfull friends he had forsaken: Enviting those that should allow of his advice, to come, and take a good supper, which was prepared in his house, where after great cheere, they should drinke together whatsoever should be presented unto him: a drinke that shall deliver our bodies from torments, free our mindes from injuries, and release our eyes and eares from seeing and hearing so many horrible mischiefes, which the conquered must endure at the hands of most cruell and offended conquerors: I have (quoth he) taken order, that men fit for that purpose shall be ready, when we shall be expired, to cast us into a great burning pile of wood. Diverse approved of his high resolution, but few did imitate the same. Seven and twentie Sena-

tors followed him; who after they had attempted to stifle so irkesome,
and suppresse so terror-moving a thought, with quaffing and swilling
of wine, they ended their repast by this deadly messe: and entre-
embracing one another, after they had in ccmmon deplored and bewailed their countries mis-fortunes; some went home to their owne
houses, othersome stayed there, to be entombed with *Vibius* in his
owne fire; whose death was so long and lingring, forsomuch as the
vapor of the wine having possessed their veines, and slowed the effect
and operation of the poyson, that some lived an houre after they had
seene their enemies enter *Capua,* which they caried the next day after,
and incurred the miseries, and saw the calamities, which at so high a
rate they had sought to eschue. *Taurea Jubellius,* another citizen there,
the Consull *Fulvius* returning from that shameful slaughter, which he
had committed of 225. Senators, called him churlishly by his name,
and having arrested him; Command (quoth he) unto him, that I also
be massacred after so many others, that so thou maist brag to have
murthered a much more valiant man than ever thou wast. *Fulvius,*
as one enraged, disdaining him; forasmuch as he had newly received
letters from *Rome* contrarie to the inhumanitie of his execution, which
inhibited him to proceed any further; *Jubellius* continuing his speech,
said; sithence my Countrie is taken, my friends butchered, and having
with mine owne hands slaine my wife and children, as the onely meane
to free them from the desolation of this ruine; I may not dye the
death of my fellow-citizens, let us borrow the vengeance of this hatefull life from vertue: And drawing a blade, he had hidden under his
garments, therewith ran himselfe thorow, and falling on his face,
died at the Consuls feet. *Alexander* besieged a Citie in *India,* the
inhabitants whereof, perceiving themselves brought to a very narrow
pinch, resolved obstinately to deprive him of the pleasure he might get
of his victorie, and together with their Citie, in despite of his humani-
tie, set both the Towne and themselves on a light fire, and so were all
consumed. A new kinde of warring, where the enemies did all they
could, and sought to save them, they to loose themselves, and to be
assured of their death, did all a man can possible effect, to warrant his
life. *Astapa* a Citie in *Spaine,* being very weake of wals, and other
defences, to withstand the Romanes that besieged the same; the
inhabitants drew all their riches, and wealth into the market-place,
whereof having made a heap, and on the top of it placed their wives
and children, and encompassed and covered the same with drie brush
wood, that it might burne the easier, and having appointed fifty lusty
young men of theirs for the performance of their resolution, made a
sally, where following their determined vow, seeing they could not
vanquish, suffered themselves to be slaine every mothers childe. The
fifty, after they had massacred every living soule remaining in the
Citie, and set fire to the heap, joyfully leaped there-into, ending their
generous liberty in a state rather insensible, than dolorous and re-

prochfull; shewing their enemies, that if fortune had beene so pleased, they should aswell have had the courage to bereave them of the victory, as they had to yeeld it them both vaine and hideous, yea, and mortall to those, who allured by the glittering of the gold, that moulten ran from out the flame, thicke and threefold approching greedily unto it, were therein smothered and burned, the formost being unable to give bake, by reason of the throng that followed them. The *Abideans* pressed by *Philip*, resolved upon the very same, but being prevented, the King whose heart yerned and abhorred to see the fond-rash precipitation of such an execution (having first seized-upon and saved the treasure, and moveables, which they had diversly condemned to the flames and utter spoyle) retiring all the Souldiers, granting them the full space of three dayes to make themselves away, that so they might doe it with more order and leasure; which three dayes they replenished with bloud and murther beyond all hostile cruelty: And which is strange, there was no one person saved, that had power upon himselfe. There are infinite examples of such-like popular conclusions, which seeme more violent, by how much more the effect of them is more universall. They are lesse than severall, what discourse would not doe in every one, it doth in all: The vehemence of societie, ravishing particular judgements. Such as were condemned to dye in the time of *Tiberius*, and delaid their execution any while, lost their goods, and could not be buried; but such as prevented the same, in killing themselves, were solemnly enterred, and might at their pleasure, bequeath such goods as they had to whom they list. But a man doth also sometimes desire death, in hope of a greater good. I desire (saith Saint *Paul*) to be out of this world, that I may be with *Jesus Christ:* and who shal release me out of these bonds? *Cleombrotus Ambraciota* having read *Platoes Phæton*, was so possessed with a desire and longing for an after-life, that without other occasion or more adoe, he went and headlong cast himselfe into the sea. Whereby it appeareth how improperly we call this voluntarie dissolution, despaire; unto which the violence of hope doth often transport us, and as often a peacefull and setled inclination of judgement. *Jaques du Castell* Bishop of *Soissons*, in the voyage which Saint *Lewes* undertooke beyond the Seas, seeing the King and all his Army ready to returne into *France*, and leave the affaires of Religion imperfect, resolved with himselfe rather to goe to heaven; And having bidden his friends farewell, in the open view of all men, rushed alone into the enemies troops of whom he was forthwith hewen in peeces. In a certaine kingdome of these late-discovered *Indies*, upon the day of a solemne procession, in which the Idols they adore, are publikely carried up and downe, upon a chariot of exceeding greatnesse: besides that, there are many seene to cut and slice great mammocks of their quicke flesh, to offer the said Idols; there are numbers of others seene, who prostrating themselves alongst upon the ground, endure very patiently to be mouldred and crushed to death, under the Chariots wheeles, thinking thereby to purchase after their death, a veneration of holinesse, of which they are not defrauded. The death of this Bishop, armed as we have said, argueth more generositie, and lesse sence: the heat of the combat ammusing one part of it. Some common-wealths there are, that have gone about to sway the justice, and direct the opportunitie of voluntarie deaths. In our Citie of *Marseille*, they were wont in former ages, ever to keepe some poison in store, prepared and compounded with hemlocke, at the Cities charge, for such as would upon any occasion shorten their daies, having first approved the reasons of their enterprise unto the six hundred Elders of the Towne, which was their Senate: For, otherwise it was unlawfull for any body, except by the Magistrates permission, and for very law-fully-urgent occasions, to lay violent hands upon himselfe. The very same law was likewise used in other places. *Sextus Pompeius* going into *Asia*, passed thorow the Iland of *Cea*, belonging to *Negropont;* it fortuned whilst he abode there, (as one reporteth that was in his companie) that a woman of great authority, having first yeelded an accompt unto her Citizens, and shewed good reasons why she was resolved to end her life, earnestly entreated *Pompey* to be an assistant at her death, that so it might be esteemed more honourable, which he assented unto; and having long time in vaine sought, by vertue of his eloquence (wherein he was exceeding ready) and force of perswasion, to alter her intent, and remove her from her purpose, in the end yeelded to her request. She had lived foure score and ten years in a most happy estate of minde and body, but then lying on her bed, better adorned than before she was accustomed to have it, and leaning on her elbow, thus she bespake: The Gods, Oh *Sextus Pompeius,* and rather those I forgoe, than those I goe unto, reward and appay thee, for that thou hast vouchsafed to be both a counsellor of my life, and a witnesse of my death. As for my part, having hitherto ever tasted the favourable visage of fortune, for feare the desire of living overlong should make me taste of her frownes, with an happy and successefull end, I will now depart, and licence the remainder of my soule, leaving behind me two daughters of mine, with a legion of grand-children and nephewes. That done, having preached unto, and exhorted all her people and kinsfolks to an unitie and peace, and divided her goods amongst them, and recommended her houshold Gods unto her eldest daughter, with an assuredly-staide hand she tooke the cup, wherein the poyson was, and having made her vowes unto *Mercurie,* and prayers, to conduct her unto some happy place in the other world, roundly swallowed that mortall potion; which done, she intertained the company with the progresse of her behaviour, and as the parts of her body were one after another possessed with the cold operation of that venom; untill such time as shee said, shee felt-it worke at the heart and in her entrals, shee called her daughter to doe her the last office, and close her eyes. *Plinie* reporteth of a certaine *Hiperborean* nation, wherein, by reason of the milde temperature of the aire, the inhabitants thereof, commonly never dye, but when they please to make themselves away, and that being weary and tired with living, they are accustomed at the end of a long-long age; having first made merry and good cheare with their friends, from the top of an high-steepy rocke, appointed for that purpose, to cast themselves headlong into the Sea. Grieving-smart, and a worse death seeme to me the most excusable incitations.

CHAPTER IV

TO MORROW IS A NEW DAY

I DO with some reason, as me seemeth, give pricke and praise unto *Jaques Amiot* above all our French writers, not only for his natural purity, and pure elegancie of the tongue, wherein he excelleth all others, nor for his indefatigable constancie of so long and toyle-some a labour, nor for the unsearchable depth of his knowledge, having so successefully-happy been able to explaine an Author so close and thorny, and unfold a writer so mysterious and entangled (for, let any man tell me what he list; I have no skill of the Greeke, but I see thorowout al his translation a sense so closely-joynted, and so pithily-continued, that either he hath assuredly understood and inned the very imagination, and the true conceit of the Author, or having through a long and continuall [conversation], lively planted in his minde a generall Idea of that of *Plutarke*, he hath at least lent him nothing that doth belye him, or mis-seeme him) but above all, I kon him thanks that he hath had the hap to chuse, and knowledge to cull-out so worthy a worke, and a booke so fit to the purpose, therewith to make so unvaluable a present unto his Countrie. We that are in the number of the ignorant had beene utterly confounded, had not his booke raised us from out the dust of ignorance: God-a-mercy his endevours we dare [now] both speake and write: Even Ladies are therewith able to con-front Masters of arts: It is our breviarie. If so good a man chance to live, I bequeath *Xenophon* unto him, to doe as much. It is an easier peece of worke, and so much the more agreeing with his age. More-over, I wot not how me seemeth, although he roundly and clearly dis-intangle himselfe from hard passages, that notwithstanding his stile is more close and neerer it selfe, when it is not laboured and wrested, and that it glideth smoothly at his pleasure. I was even now reading of that place, where *Plutarke* speaketh of himselfe, that *Rusticus* being present at a declamation of his in Rome, received a packet from the Emperour, which he temporized to open untill he had made an end: wherein (saith he) all the assistants did singularly commend the gravitie of the man. Verily, being on the instance of curiositie, and

on the greedy and insatiate passion of newes, which with such indiscreet impatience, and impatient indiscretion, induceth us to neglect
all things, for to entertaine a new-come guest, and forget al respect and
countenance, whersoever we be, suddenly to break up such letters as
are brought us; he had reason to commend the gravitie of *Rusticus:*
to which he might also have added the commendation of his civilitie
and curtesie, for that he would not interrupt the course of his declamation; But I make a question, whether he might be commended for
his wisdome: for, receiving unexpected letters, and especially from
an Emperour, it might very well have fortuned, that his deferring to
read them, might have caused some notable inconvenience. *Recklesnes
is the vice contrarie unto curiositie;* towards which I am naturally
enclined, and wherein I have seen many men so extremely plunged,
that three or four dayes after the receiving of letters, which hath beene
sent them, they have beene found in their pockets yet unopened. I
never opened any, not only of such as had beene committed to my
keeping, but of such as by any fortune came to my hands. And I make
a conscience, standing neare some great person, if mine eyes chance
at unwares, to steale some knowledge of any letters of importance
that he readeth. Never was man lesse inquisitive, or pryed lesse into
other mens affaires, than I. In our fathers time; the Lord of *Boutieres*
was like to have lost *Turwin,* forsomuch as being one night at supper
in very good company, he deferred the reading of an advertisement,
which was delivered him of the treasons that were practised and complotted against that Citie, where he commanded. And *Plutarke* himself hath taught me, that *Julius Cæsar* had escaped death, if going to
the Senate-house, that day wherein he was murthered by the Con-
spirators, he had read a memorial which was presented unto him. Who
likewise reporteth the storie of *Archias,* the Tyrant of *Thebes,* how
the night fore-going the execution of the enterprise that *Pelopidas* had
complotted to kill him, thereby to set his Countrie at libertie: another
Archias of *Athens* writ him a letter, wherein he particularly related
unto him all that was conspired and complotted against him; which
letter being delivered him whilst he sate at supper, he deferred the
opening of it, pronouncing this by-word: *To morrow is a new day,*
which afterward was turned to a Proverb in *Greece.* A wise man may,
in mine opinion, for the interest of others, as not unmannerly to
breake companie, like unto *Rusticus,* or not to discontinue some other
affaire of importance, remit and defer to understand such newes as are
brought him: but for his owne private interest or particular pleasure,
namely, if he be a man having publike charge, if he regard his dinner
so much, that he will not break it off, or his sleepe, that he will not interrupt it: to doe it, is inexcusable. And in former ages was the Con-
sulare-place in *Rome,* which they named the most honourable at the
table, because it was more free and more accessible for such as might
casually come in, to entertaine him that should be there placed. Wit-

nesse, that though they were sitting at the board, they neither omitted nor gave over the managing of other affaires, and following of other accidents. But when all is said, it is very hard, chiefely in humane actions, to prescribe so exact rules by discourse of reason, that fortune doe not sway, and keepe her right in them.

CHAPTER V

OF CONSCIENCE

My brother the Lord of *Brouze* and my selfe, during the time of our civill warres, travelling one day together, we fortuned to meet upon the way with a Gentleman, in outward semblance, of good demeanour: He was of our contrarie faction, but forasmuch as he counterfeited himselfe otherwise; I knew it not. And the worst of these tumultuous intestine broyles, is, that the cards are so shuffled (your enemie being neither by language nor by fashion, nor by any other apparent marke distinguished from you; nay, which is more, brought up under the same lawes and customes, and breathing the same ayre) that it is a very hard matter to avoid confusion and shun disorder. Which consideration, made me not a little fearefull to meet with our troopes, especially where I was not knowne, lest I should be urged to tell my name, and haply doe worse. As other times before it had befalne me; for, by such a chance, or rather mistaking, I fortuned once to lose all my men and horses, and hardly escaped my selfe: and amongst other my losses, and servants that were slaine, the thing that most grieved me, was the untimely and miserable death of a young Italian Gentleman, whom I kept as my Page, and very carefully brought up, with whom dyed, as forward, as budding and as hopefull a youth as ever I saw. But this man seemed so fearfully-dismaid, and at every encounter of horsemen, and passage, by, or thorow any Towne that held for the King, I observed him to be so strangely distracted, that in the end I perceived, and ghessed they were but guilty alarums that his conscience gave him. It seemed unto this seely man, that all might apparently, both through his blushing selfe-accusing countenance, and by the crosses he wore upon his upper garments, read the secret intentions of his faint heart. Of such marvailousworking power is the sting of conscience: which often induceth us to bewray, to accuse, and to combat our selves; and for want of other evidences shee produceth our selves against our selves.

> *Occultum quatiente animo tortore flagellum.*
>
> JUVEN. *Sat.* xiii. 195.

Their minde, the tormentor of sinne,
Shaking an unseene whip within.

The storie of *Bessus* the Pœnian is so common, that even children have it in their mouths, who being found fault withall, that in mirth he had beaten downe a nest of young Sparrowes, and then killed them, answered, he had great reason to doe it; forsomuch as those young birds ceased not falsly to accuse him to have murthered his father, which parricide was never suspected to have beene committed by him; and untill that day had layen secret; but the revengefull furies of the conscience, made the same partie to reveale it, that by all right was to doe penance for so hatefull and unnaturall a murther. *Hesiodus* correcteth the saying of *Plato*, That punishment doth commonly succeed the guilt, and follow sinne at hand: for, he affirmeth, that it rather is borne at the instant, and together with sinne it selfe, and they are as twinnes borne at one birth together. *Whosoever expects punishment, suffereth the same, and whosoever deserveth it, he doth expect it. Impietie doth invent, and iniquitie doth frame torments against it selfe.*

> *Malum consilium consultori pessimum.*
> Eras. *Chil.* i. cent. ii. ad. 14.

Bad counsell is worst for the counseller that gives the counsell.

Even as the Waspe stingeth and offendeth others, but her selfe much more; for, in hurting others, she loseth her force and sting for ever.

> *—itasque in ulnere ponunt.*—Virg. *Georg.* iv. 238.

> They, while they others sting,
> Death to themselves doe bring.

The *Cantharides* have some part in them, which by a contrarietie of nature serveth as an anidot or counterpoison against their poison: so likewise, as one taketh pleasure in vice, there is a certaine contrarie displeasure engendred in the conscience, which by sundry irksome and painfull imaginations, perplexeth and tormenteth us, both waking and asleepe.

> *Quippe ubi se multi per somnia sæpe loquentes,*
> *Aut morbo delirantes procraxe ferantur,*
> *Et celata diu in medium peccata dedisse.*—Lucr. v. 1168.

> Many in dreames oft speaking, or unhealed,
> In sicknesse raving have themselves revealed,
> And brought to light their sinnes long time concealed.

Apollodorus dreamed he saw himselfe first flead by the Scythians, and then boyled in a pot, and that his owne heart murmured, saying; I only have caused this mischiefe to light upon thee. *Epicurus* was wont to say, that no lurking hole can shroud the wicked; for, they can never assure themselves to be sufficiently hidden, sithence conscience is ever ready to disclose them to themselves.

—prima est hæc ultio, quòd se
Judice nemo nocens absolvitur.—JUVEN. *Sat.* xiii. 2.

This is the first revenge, no guilty mind
Is quitted, though it selfe be judge assign'd.

Which as it doth fill us with feare and doubt, so doth it store us
with assurance and trust. And I may boldly say, that I have waded
thorow many dangerous hazards, with a more untired pace, only in
consideration of the secret knowledge I had of mine owne will, and
innocence of my desseignes.

Conscia mens ut cuique sua est, ita concipit intra
Pectora pro facto spemque metumque suo.
OVID. *Fast.* i. 485.

As each mans minde is guiltie, so doth he
Inlie breed hope and feare, as his deeds be.

Of examples, there are thousands; It shall suffice us to alleage three
only, and all of one man. *Scipio* being one day accused before the
Romane people, of an urgent and capitall accusation; in stead of
excusing himselfe, or flattering the Judges; turning to them, he said.
It will well beseeme you to undertake to judge of his head, by whose
meanes you have authoritie to judge of all the world. The same man,
another time, being vehemently urged by a *Tribune* of the people,
who charged him with sundry imputations, in liew of pleading or
excusing his cause, gave him this sudden and short answer. Let us goe
(quoth he) my good Citizens; let us forthwith goe (I say) to give
hartie thankes unto the Gods for the victorie, which even upon such a
day as this is, they gave me against the Carthaginians. And therewith
advancing himselfe to march before the people, all the assembly, and
even his accuser himselfe did undelayedly follow him towards the
Temple. After that, *Petilius* having beene animated and stirred up
by *Cato* to solicite and demand a strict accompt of him, of the money
he had managed, and which was committed to his trust, whilst he was
in the Province of *Antioch; Scipio* being come into the Senate-house,
of purpose to answer for himselfe, pulling out the booke of his accompts from under his gowne, told them all, that that booke contained
truly, both the receipt and laying out thereof; and being required to
deliver the same unto a Clarke to register it, he refused to doe it,
saying he would not doe himselfe that wrong or indignitie; and thereupon with his owne hands, in presence of all the Senate, tore the
booke in peeces. I cannot apprehend or beleeve, that a guiltie-
cauterized conscience could possibly dissemble or counterfet such an
undismayed assurance: His heart was naturally too great, and enured
to overhigh fortune (saith *Titus Livius*) to know how to be a criminall
offender, and stoopingly to yeeld himselfe to the basenesse, to defend
his innocencie. Torture and racking are dangerous inventions, and

seeme rather to be trials of patience than Essayes of truth. And both
he that can, and he that cannot endure them, conceale the truth. For
wherefore shall paine or smart, rather compell me to confesse that,
which is so indeed, than force me to tell that which is not? And contrariwise, if he who hath not done that whereof he is accused, is sufficiently patient to endure those torments; why shall not he be able
to tolerate them, who hath done it, and is guilty indeed; so deare and
worthy a reward as life being proposed unto him? I am of opinion, that
the ground of his invention, proceedeth from the consideration of the
power and facultie of the conscience. For, to the guilty, it seemeth to
give a kinde of furtherance to the torture, to make him confesse his
fault, and weakneth and dismayeth him: and on the other part, it
encourageth and strengthneth the innocent against torture. To say
truth, it is a meane full of uncertainty and danger. What would not
a man say; nay, what not doe, to avoid so grievous paines, and shun
such torments?

Etiam innocentes cogit mentiri dolor.—SEN. *Prover.*

Torment to lye sometimes will drive,
Ev'n the most innocent alive.

Whence it followeth, that he whom the Judge hath tortured, because
he shall not dye an innocent, he shall bring him to his death, both
innocent and tortured. Many thousands have thereby charged their
heads with false confessions. Amongst which I may well place *Phylotas*,
considering the circumstances of the endictment that *Alexander* framed
against him, and the progresse of his torture. But so it is, that (as
men say) it is the least evill humane weaknesse could invent: though,
in my conceit, very inhumanely, and therewithall most unprofitably.
Many Nations lesse barbarous in that, than the Græcian, or the
Romane, who terme them so, judge it a horrible and cruell thing, to
racke and torment a man for a fault whereof you are yet in doubt. Is
your ignorance long of him? What can he doe withall? Are not you
unjust, who because you will not put him to death without some cause,
you doe worse than kill him? And that it is so, consider but how often
he rather chuseth to dye guiltlesse, than passe by this information,
much more painfull, than the punishment or torment; and who many
times, by reason of the sharpnesse of it, preventeth, furthereth, yea,
and executeth the punishment. I wot not whence I heard this story,
but it exactly hath reference unto the conscience of our Justice. A
countrie woman accused a souldier before his Generall, being a most
severe Justicer, that he, with violence, had snatched from out her
poore childrens hands, the small remainder of some pap or water-
gruell, which shee had onely left to sustaine them, forsomuch as the
Army had ravaged and wasted all. The poore woman had neither
witnesse nor proofe of it; It was but her yea, and his no; which the
Generall perceiving, after he had summoned her to be well advised

what shee spake, and that shee should not accuse him wrongfully; for, if shee spake an untruth, shee should then be culpable of his accusation: But shee constantly persisting to charge him, he forthwith, to discover the truth, and to be thoroughly resolved, caused the accused Souldiers belly to be ripped, who was found faulty, and the poore woman to have said true; whereupon shee was discharged. A condemnation instructive to others.

CHAPTER VI

OF EXERCISE OR PRACTICE

It is a hard matter (although our conceit doe willingly apply it selfe unto it) that Discourse and Instruction, should sufficiently be powerful, to direct us to action, and addresse us to performance, if over and besides that, we doe not by experience exercise and frame our minde, to the traine whereunto we will range it: otherwise, when we shall be on the point of the effects, it will doubtlesse finde it selfe much engaged and empeached. And that is the reason why amongst Philosophers, those that have willed to attaine to some greater excellence, have not beene content, at home, and at rest to expect the rigors of fortune, for feare she should surprise them unexperienced and finde them novices, if she should chance to enter fight with them; but have rather gone to meet and front her before, and witting-earnestly cast themselves to the triall of the hardest difficulties. Some have thereby voluntarily forsaken great riches, onely to practise a voluntarie povertie: others have willingly found out labour, and an austeritie of a toylesome life, thereby to harden and enure themselves to evill, and travell: othersome have frankly deprived themselves of the dearest and best parts of their body, as of their eyes, and members of generation, lest their over-pleasing, and too-too wanton service, might in any sort mollifie and distract the constant resolution of their minde. But to dye, which is the greatest worke we have to doe, exercise can nothing availe us thereunto. A man may, by custome and experience, fortifie himselfe against griefe, sorrow, shame, want, and such like accidents: But concerning death, we can but once feele and trie the same. We are all novices, and new to learne when we come unto it. There have, in former times, beene found men so good husbands and thrifty of time, that even in death they have assayed to taste and [savour] it; and bent their minde to observe and see, what manner of thing that passage of death was; but none did ever yet come backe againe to tell us tidings of it.

> —*nemo expergitus extat*
> *Frigida quem semel est vitai pausa sequuta.*
> LUCR. iii. 973.

No man doth ever-after wake,
Whom once his lifes cold rest doth take.

Canius Julius, a noble Romane, a man of singular vertue and constancie, having beene condemned to death by that lewdly-mischievous
monster of men, *Caligula:* besides many marvelous evident assurances
he gave of his matchlesse resolution, when he was even in the nicke to
endure the last stroke of the executioner; a Philosopher, being his
friend, interrupted him with this question, saying: *Canius,* in what
state is your soule now; what doth she; what thoughts possesse you
now? I thought (answered he) to keepe me ready and prepared with
all my force, to see whether in this instant of death, so short and so
neere at hand, I might perceive some dislodging or distraction of the
soule, and whether it will shew some feeling of her sudden departure;
that (if I apprehend or learne any thing of her) I may afterward, if I
can, returne, and give advertisement thereof unto my friends. Loe-here
a Philosopher, not only untill death, but even in death it selfe: what
assurance was it, and what fiercenes of courage, to will that his owne
death should serve him as a lesson, and have leasure to thinke else
where in a matter of such consequence;

—jus hoc animi morientis habebat.—LUCAN. viii. 636.

This power of minde had he,
When it from him did flee.

Me seemeth neverthelesse, that in some sort there is a meane to
familiarize our selves with it, and to assay it. We may have some experience of it, if not whole and perfect, at least such as may not altogether be unprofitable, and which may yeelde us better fortified and
more assured. If we cannot attaine unto it, we may at least approch
it, and discerne the same: And if we cannot enter her fort, yet shal we
see and frequent the approches unto it. It is not without reason we
are taught to take notice of our sleepe, for the resemblance it hath
with death. How easily we passe from waking to sleeping; with how
little interest we lose the knowledge of light, and of our selves. The
facultie of sleepe might haply seeme unprofitable, and against nature,
sithence it depriveth us of all actions, and barreth us of all sense, were
it not that nature doth thereby instruct us, that she hath equally made
us, as well to live, as to die; and by life presenteth the eternal state
unto us, which she after the same reserveth for us, so to accustome us
thereunto, and remove the feare of it from us. But such as by some
violent accident are falne into a faintnes of heart, and have lost all
senses, they, in mine opinion, have well-nigh beene, where they might
behold her true and naturall visage: For, touching the instant or moment of the passage, it is not to be feared, it should bring any travell or
displeasure with it, forasmuch as we can have, nor sense, nor feeling
without leasure. Our sufferances have need of time, which is so short,

and plunged in death, that necessarily it must be insensible. It is the approches that lead unto it we should feare; and those may fall within the compasse of mans experience. Many things seeme greater by imagination, than by effect. I have passed over a good part of my age in sound and perfect health. I say, not only sound, but blithe and wantonly-lustfull. That state full of lust, of prime and mirth, made me deeme the consideration of sicknesses so yrkesome and horrible, that when I came to the experience of them, I have found their fits but weake, and their assaults but faint, in respect of my apprehended feare. Lo here what I daily prove. Let me be under a roofe, in a good chamber, warme-clad, and well at ease in some tempestuous and stormy night. I am exceedingly perplexed, and much grieved for such as are abroad, and have no shelter: But let me be in the storme my selfe, I doe not so much as desire to be elsewhere. Only to be continually pent up in a chamber, seemed intolerable to me. I have now enured my selfe to live a whole weeke, yea a moneth in my chamber full of care, trouble, alteration and weaknesse; and have found, that in the time of my best health I moaned such as were sicke, much more than I can well moane my selfe when I am ill at ease: and that the power of my apprehension did well-nigh halfe endeare the essence and truth of the thing it selfe. I am in good hope the like will happen to me of death: and that it is not worth the labour I take for so many preparations as I prepare against her: and so many helpes as I call to sustaine, and assemble to endure the shocke and violence of it. But hab or nab we can never take too much advantage of it. During our second or third troubles (I doe not well remember which) I fortuned one day, for recreation sake, to goe forth and take the ayre, about a league from my house, who am seated even in the bowels of all troubles of our civill warres of *France,* supposing to be most safe, so neere mine owne home and [r]etreite, that I had no need of better attendance or equipage. I was mounted upon a very easie-going nag, but not very sure. At my returning home againe, a sudden occasion being offered me, to make use of this nag in a peece of service, whereto he was neither trained nor accustomed, one of my men (a strong sturdy fellow) mounted upon a young strongheaded horse, and that had a desperate hard mouth, fresh, lusty and in breath; to shew his courage, and to out-goe his fellowes, fortuned with might and maine to set spurres unto him, and giving him the bridle, to come right into the path where I was, and as a *Colossus* with his weight riding over me and my nag, that were both very little, he overthrew us both, and made us fall with our heeles upward: so that the nag lay along astonied in one place, and I in a trance groveling on the ground ten or twelfe paces wide of him; my face all torne and brused, my sword which I had in my hand a good way from me, my girdle broken, with no more motion or sense in me than a stocke. It is the only swowning that ever I felt yet. Those that were with me, after they had assayed all possible meanes to bring me to my selfe againe, supposing me dead, tooke me in their armes, and with much adoe were carying me home to my house, which was about halfe a French league thence: upon the way, and after I had for two houres space, by all, beene supposed dead and past all recoverie, I began to stir and breathe: for, so great aboundance of bloud was falne into my stomake, that to discharge it, nature was forced to rowze up her spirits. I was immediately set upon my feet, and bending forward, I presently cast up, in quantitie as much clottie pure bloud, as a bucket will hold, and by the way was constrained to doe the like divers times before I could get home, whereby I began to recover a little life, but it was by little and little, and so long adoing, that my chiefe senses were much more enclining to death than to life.

> *Perche dubbiosa ancor del suo ritorno*
> *Non s'assicura attonita la mente.*

> For yet the minde doubtfull its returne
> Is not assured, but astonished.

The remembrance whereof (which yet I beare deeply imprinted in my minde) representing me her visage and *Idea* so lively and so naturally, doth in some sort reconcile me unto her. And when I began to see, it was with so dim, so weake and so troubled a sight, that I could not discerne anything of the light.

> *—come quel c'hor' apre, hor chiude*
> *Gli occhii, mezzo tral sonno el esser desto.*

> As he that sometimes opens, sometimes shuts
> His eyes, betweene sleepe and awake.

Touching the function of the soule, they started up and came in the same progresse as those of the body. I perceived my selfe all bloudy; for my doublet was all sullied with the bloud I had cast. The first conceit I apprehended, was, that I had received some shot in my head; and in truth, at the same instant, there were divers that shot round about us. Me thought, my selfe had no other hold of me, but of my lips-ends. I closed mine eyes, to helpe (as me seemed) to send it forth, and tooke a kinde of pleasure to linger and languishingly to let my selfe goe from my selfe. It was an imagination swimming superficially in my minde, as weake and as tender as all the rest: but in truth, not only exempted from displeasure, but rather commixt with that pleasant sweetnesse, which they feele that suffer themselves to fall into a soft-slumbring and sense-entrancing sleepe. I beleeve it is the same state, they find themselves in, whom in the agony of death we see to droop and faint thorow weaknesse: and am of opinion, we plaine and moane them without cause, esteeming that either they are agitated with grievous pangs, or that their soule is pressed with painfull cogitations.

It was ever my conceit, against the opinion of many, yea and against that of *Stephanus la Boetie*, that those whom we see, so overwhelmed, and faintly-drooping at the approches of their end, or utterly cast downe with the lingring tediousnesse of their deseases, or by accident of some apoplexie, or falling-evill,

> —(*vi morbi sæpe coactus*
> *Ante oculos aliquis nostros ut fulminis ictu,*
> *Concidit, et spumas agit, ingemit, et fremit artus,*
> *Desipit, extentat nervos, torquetur, anhelat,*
> *Inconstanter et in jactando membra fatigat*)
>
> > Lucr. iii. 490.

> (Some man by force of sicknesse driv'n doth fall,
> As if by thunder stroke, before our eyes;
> He fomes, he grones, he trembles over all,
> He raves, he stretches, he's vext, panting lyes,
> He tyr's his limmes by tossing,
> Now this now that way crossing.)

or hurt in the head, whom we heare throb and rattle, and send forth grones and gaspes, although we gather some tokens from them, whereby it seemeth, they have yet some knowledge left and certaine motions we see them make with their body: I say, I have ever thought, they had their soule and body buried and asleepe.

> *Vivat et est vitæ nescius ipse suæ.*
> > Ovid. *Trist*. i. *El*. iii. 12.

> He lives yet knowes not he,
> That he alive should be.

And I could not beleeve, that at so great an astonishment of members, and deffailance of senses, the soule could maintaine any force within, to know herselfe; and therefore had no manner of discourse tormenting them, which might make them judge and feele the misery of their condition, and that consequently they were not greatly to be moaned. As for my selfe, I imagine no state so intolerable nor condition so horrible, as to have a feelingly-afflicted soule, void of meanes to disburthen and declare her selfe: As I would say of those we send to execution, having first caused their tongue to be cut out were it not that in this manner of death, the most dumbe seemes unto me the fittest, namely, if it be accompanied with a resolute and grave countenance. And as those miserable prisoners which light in the hands of those hard-harted and villenous Souldiers of these times, of whom they are tormented with all maner of cruell entreatie, by compulsion to drawe them unto some excessive and unpossible ransome, keeping them al that while in so hard a condition and place, that they have no way left them to utter their thoughts and expresse their miserie. The Poets have fained, there were some Gods, that favoured the release of such as sufferd so languishing deaths.

> —*hunc ego Diti*
> *Sacrum jussa fero, teque isto corpore solvo.*
> VIRG. *Æn*. iv. 703, Iris.

> This to death sacred, I, as was my charge,
> Doe beare, and from this body thee enlarge.

And the faltering speeches and uncertaine answers, that by continuall ringing in their eares and incessant urging them, are somtimes by force wrested from them or by the motions which seeme to have some simpathy with that whereof they are examined, is notwithstanding no witnes that they live at least a perfect sound life. We do also in yawning, before sleep fully seize upon us, apprehend as it were in a slumber, what is done about us, and with a troubled and uncertaine hearing, follow the voyces, which seeme to sound but on the outward limits of our soule; and frame answers according to the last words we heard, which taste more of chance than of sense: which thing now I have proved by experience, I make no doubt, but hitherto, I have well judged of it. For, first lying as in a trance, I laboured even with my nailes to open my doublet (for I was unarmed) and well I wot, that in my imagination I felt nothing did hurt me. For, there are severall motions in us, which proceed not of our free wil.

> *Semianimesque micant digiti, ferrumque retractant.*—x. 396.

> The halfe-dead fingers stirre, and feele,
> (Though it they cannot stirre) for steele.

Those that fall, doe commonly by a naturall impulsion cast their armes abroad before their falling, which sheweth, that our members have certaine offices, which they lend one to another, and possesse certaine agitations, apart from our discourse:

> *Falciferos memorant currus abscindere membra,*
> *Ut tremere in terra videatur ab artubus, id quod*
> *Decidit abscissum, cùm mens tamen atque hominis vis*
> *Mobilitate mali non quit sentire dolorem.*—LUCR. iii. 648.

> They say, sith-bearing chariots limbes bereave,
> So as on earth, that which cut-off they leave,
> Doth seeme to quake; when yet mans force and minde
> Doth not the paine, through so quick motion, finde.

My stomacke was surcharged with clotted bloud, my hands of themselves were still running to it, as often they are wont (yea against the knowledge of our will) where we feele it to itch. There are many creatures, yea and some men, in whom after they are dead, we may

see their muskles to close and stirre. All men know by experience, there
be some parts of our bodies, which often without any consent of ours
doe stirre, stand and lye downe againe. Now these passions, which but
exteriourly touch us, cannot properly be termed ours; For, to make
them ours, a man must wholy be engaged unto them: And the paines
that our feet or hands feele whilst we sleepe, are not ours. When I
came neere my house, where the tidings of my fall was already come,
and those of my houshold met me, with such outcries as are used in
like times, I did not only answer some words, to what I was demanded,
but some tell me, I had the memory to command my men to give my
wife a horse, whom I perceived to be over-tired, and labouring in the
way, which is very hilly, foule, and rugged. It seemeth this consideration proceeded from a vigilant soule: yet was I cleane distracted from
it, they were but vaine conceits, and as in a cloud, only moved by the
sense of the eyes and eares: They came not from my selfe. All which
notwithstanding, I knew neither whence I came, nor whither I went,
nor could I understand or consider what was spoken unto me. They
were but light effects, that my senses produced of themselves, as it
were of custome. Whatsoever the soule did assist it with, was but a
dreame, being lightly touched, and only sprinkled by the soft impression of the senses. In the meane time my state was verily most pleasant
and easefull. I felt no manner of care or affliction, neither for my selfe
nor others. It was a slumbering, languishing and extreme weaknesse,
without any paine at all. I saw mine owne house and knew it not;
when I was laid in my bed, I felt great ease in my rest, For I had beene
vilely hurred and haled by those poore men, which had taken the paines
to carry me upon their armes a long and wearysome way, and to say
truth, they had all beene wearied twice or thrice over, and were faine
to shift severall times. Many remedies were presently offered me, but
I tooke none, supposing verily I had beene deadly hurt in the head.
To say truth, it had beene a very happy death: For, the weaknesse of
my discourse hinderd me from judging of it, and the feeblenesse of
my body from feeling the same. Me thought I was yeelding up the
ghost so gently, and after so easie and indolent a manner, that I feele
no other action lesse burthensome than that was. But when I began
to come to life againe and recover my former strength,

> *Ut tandem sensus convaluere mei.*
> OVID. *Trist*. i. *El*. iii. 14.

> At last when all the sprites I beare,
> Recall'd and recollected were,

which was within two or three houres after, I presently felt my selfe
full of aches and paines all my body over; for, each part thereof was
with the violence of the fall much brused and tainted; and for two or
three nights after I found my self so ill, that I verily supposed I shold

have had another fit of death: But that a more lively, and sensible one: (and to speak plaine) I feele my bruses yet, and feare me shall do while I live: I will not forget to tell you, that the last thing I could rightly fall into againe, was the remembrance of this accident, and I made my men many times to repeat me over and over againe, whither I was going, whence I came, and at what houre that chance befell me, before I could throughly conceive it. Concerning the manner of my falling, they in favour of him who had beene the cause of it, concealed the truth from me, and told me other flim flam tales. But a while after, and the morrow next when my memorie began to come to it selfe againe, and represent the state unto me, wherein I was at the instant, when I perceived the horse riding over me (for being at my heeles, I chanced to espy him, and helde my selfe for dead; yet was the conceit so sudden, that feare had no leasure to enter my thoughts) me seemed it was a flashing or lightning, that smote my soule with shaking, and that I came from another world. This discourse of so slight an accident, is but vaine and frivolous, were not the instructions I have drawne from thence for my use: For truly, for a man to acquaint himselfe with death, I finde no better way than to approch unto it. Now as *Plinie* saith, every man is a good discipline unto himselfe, alwayes provided he be able to prie into himselfe. This is not my doctrine, it is but my study; And not another mans lesson, but mine owne; Yet ought no man to blame me if I impart the same. What serves my turne, may haply serve another mans; otherwise I marre nothing; what I make use of, is mine owne; And if I play the foole, it is at mine owne cost, and without any other bodies interest. For it is but a kind of folly, that dyes in me, and hath no traine. We have notice but of two or three former ancients, that have trodden this path; yet can we not say, whether altogether like unto this of mine, for we know but their names. No man since hath followed their steps: it is a thorny and crabbed enterprise, and more than it makes shew of, to follow so strange and vagabond a path, as that of our spirit: to penetrate the shady, and enter the thicke-covered depths of these internall winding crankes; To chuse so many, and settle so severall aires of his agitations: And tis a new extraordinary ammusing, that distracts us from the common occupation of the world, yea and from the most recommended: Many yeares are past since I have no other aime, whereto my thoughts bend, but my selfe, and that I controule and study nothing but my selfe. And if I study any thing else, it is immediately to place it upon, or to say better, in my selfe. And me thinkes I erre not, as commonly men doe in other sciences, without all comparison lesse profitable. I impart what I have learn't by this, although I greatly content not my selfe with the progresse I have made therein. *There is no description so hard, nor so profitable, as is the description of a mans owne life;* Yet must a man handsomely trimme-up, yea and dispose and range himself to appeare on the Theatre of this world. Now I continually tricke up my selfe; for I uncessantly describe my selfe. Custome hath made a mans speech of himself vicious. And obstinately forbids it in hatred of boasting, which ever seemeth closely to follow ones selfe witnesses, whereas a man should wipe a childes nose, that is now called to un-nose himselfe.

In vicium ducit culpæ fuga.—HOR. *Art. Poet.* 31.

Some shunning of some sinne,
Doe draw some further in.

I finde more evill than good by this remedy: But suppose it were true, that for a man to entertaine the company with talking of him-selfe, were necessarily presumption: I ought not following my generall intent, to refuse an action that publisheth this crazed quality, since I have it in my selfe: and I should not conceale this fault, which I have not only in use, but in profession. Nevertheless to speake my opinion of it, this custome to condemne wine is much to blame, because many are therewith made drunke. Only good things may be abused. And I beleeve this rule hath only regard to popular defects: They are snaffles wherewith neither Saints, nor Philosophers, nor Divines, whom we heare so gloriously to speake of themselves, will in any sort be bridled. No more doe I, though I be no more the one than other. If they write purposely or directly of it, yet when occasion doth con-veniently leade them unto it, faine they not, headlong to cast them-selves into the lists? Whereof doth *Socrates* treat more at large, than of himselfe? To what doth he more often direct his Disciples discourses, than to speake of themselves, not for their bookes lesson, but of the essence and moving of their soule? We religiously shrive our selves to God and our Confessor, as our neighbours to all the people. But will some answer me, we report but accusation; wee then report all: For, even our vertue it selfe is faulty and repentable; My art and profession, is to live. Who forbids me to speake of it, according to my sense, ex-perience, and custome; Let him appoint the Architect to speake of buildings, not according to himself, but his neighbours, according to anothers skill, and not his owne. If it be a glory, for a man to publish his owne worth himselfe, why doth not *Cicero* prefer the eloquence of *Hortensius,* and *Hortensius* that of *Cicero?* Some may peradventure suppose that by deeds and effects, and not simply by words, I witnesse of my selfe. I principally set forth my cogitations; a shapelesse subject, and which cannot fall within the compasse of a worke-manlike pro-duction; with much adoe can I set it downe in this ayrie body of the voice. Wiser men, and more learned and devout, have lived avoiding all apparent effects. Effects would speake more of fortune, than of me. They witnesse their part, and not mine; unlesse it be conjecturally and uncertainly: Parcels of a particular shew: I wholy set forth and expose my selfe: It is a *Sceletos;* where at first sight appeare all the vaines, muskles, gristles, sinnewes, and tendons, each severall part in his due place. The effect of the cough produceth one part, that of pale-nesse or panting of the heart another, and that doubtfully. I write not my gests, but my selfe and my essence. I am of opinion that a man must be very wise to esteeme himselfe, and equally consciencious to give testimony of it: be it low, be it high indifferently. If I did abso-lutely seeme good and wise unto my selfe, I would boldly declare it. To speake lesse of himselfe than he possesseth, is folly and not modesty. To pay himselfe for less than he is worth, is basenesse and pusilanimity, saith *Aristotle*. No vertue aids it selfe with false-hood; and truth is never a matter of errour. And yet for a man to say more of him selfe, than he can well prove, is not ever presumption, though often sottish-nesse. For a man to over-weene, and please himselfe exceedingly with what he is, and fall into indiscreet love with himselfe, is in my conceit, the substance of this vice. The best remedy to cure him, is to doe cleane contrary to that which those appoint, who in forbidding men to speake of themselves, doe consequently also inhibit more to thinke of them-selves. *Pride consisteth in conceit:* The tongue can have no great share in it. For one to ammuse on himselfe, is in their imagination to please himselfe: And for a man to ferquent and practise himselfe, is at an over-deare rate to please himselfe. But this excesse doth only breed in them, that but superficially feele and search themselves, that are seene to follow their affaires, which call idlenesse and fondnesse, for a man to entertaine, to applaud and to endeare himselfe, and frame Chimeraes, or build Castles in the ayre; deeming themselves as a third person and strangers to themselves. If any be besotted with his owne knowledge, looking upon himselfe, let him cast his eyes towards former ages, his pride shall be abated, his ambition shall be quailed; for there shall he finde many thousands of spirits, that will cleane suppresse and tread him under. If he fortune to enter into any selfe-presumption of his owne worth, let him but call to remembrance the lives of *Scipio* and *Epaminondas;* so many armies, and so many Nations, which leave him so far behind them. No particular quality shall make him proud, that therewith shall reckon so many imperfect and weake qualities that are in him, and at last the nullity of humane condition. Forsomuch as *Socrates* had truly only nibled on the precept of his God, to know himselfe, and by that study had learned to contemne himselfe, he alone was esteemed worthy of the name of Wise. Whosoever shall so know himselfe, let him boldly make himselfe knowne by his owne mouth.

CHAPTER VII

OF THE RECOMPENCES OR REWARDS OF HONOUR

THOSE which write the life of *Augustus Cæsar*, note this in his military discipline, that he was exceeding liberall and lavish in his

gifts to such as were of any desert; but as sparing and strait-handed
in meere recompences of honour. Yet is it that himselfe had beene
liberally gratified by his Unkle with militarie rewards, before ever he
went to warres. It hath beene a witty invention, and received in most
parts of the worlds Common-wealths, to establish and ordaine certaine
vaine and worthles markes, therewith to honor and recompence vertue:
As are the wreathes of Lawrell, the Chaplets of Oake, and the Gar-
lands of Myrtle, the forme of a certaine peculiar garment; the privilege to ride in Coach thorow the City; or by night to have a Torch
carried before one: Some particular place to sit-in in common assemblies; the prerogatives of certaine surnames and titles, and proper
additions in armes, and such like things; the use whereof hath beene
diversly received according to the opinions of Nations, which continueth to this day. We have for our part, together with divers of our
neighbour-Nation, the orders of Knight-hood, which only were established to this purpose. Verily it is a most laudable use, and profitable
custome, to finde meanes to reward the worth, and acknowledge the
valour of rare and excellent men, to satisfie and content them with
such payments, as in no sort charge the common-wealth, and put the
Prince to no cost at all. And that which was ever knowne by ancient
experience, and at other times we have plainely perceived amongst
our selves, that men of qualitie, were ever more jealous of such recompences, than of others, wherein was both gaine and profit: which was
not without reason and great apparence. If to the prize, which ought
simply to be of honour, there be other commodities and riches joyned,
this kinde of commixing, in stead of encreasing the estimation thereof,
doth empaire, dissipate, and abridge it. The order of the Knights of
Saint *Michael* in *France*, which of so long continuance hath beene in
credit amongst us, had no greater commoditie than that it had no
manner of communication with any other advantage or profit, which
hath heretofore beene the cause, that there was no charge or state of
what quality soever, whereto the nobilitie pretended with so much
desire, or aspired with more affection, as it did to obtaine that order;
nor calling, that was followed with more respect or greatnesse. Vertue
embracing with more ambition, and more willingly aspiring after a
recompence, that is meerly and simply her owne, and which is rather
glorious, than profitable. For, to say truth, other gifts have no use so
worthy; inasmuch, as they are imployed to all manner of occasions.
With riches a man doth reward the service of a groome, the diligence
of a messenger, the hopping of a dancer, the tricks of a vaulter, the
breath of a Lawier, and the basest offices a man may receive; yea,
with the same paultry pelfe mony, vice is payed and sinne requited, as
flatterey, murther, treason, *Maquorelage*, and what not? It is then no
marvell, if vertue doth lesse willingly desire this kinde of common
trash, mony, than that which is onely proper and peculiar to her selfe,
and is altogether noble and generous. *Augustus* had therefore reason,

to be much more niggardly and sparing of this last, than of the former, forasmuch as honour is a privilege which drawes his principal essence from rarenesse: And so doth vertue itselfe.

Cui malus est nemo, quis bonus esse potest?

MART. xii. *Epig.* lxxxii. 2.

To him who good can seeme,
Who doth none bad esteeme?

We shall not see a man highly regarded, or extraordinarily commended, that is curiously carefull to have his children well nurtured, because it is a common action, how just and worthy praise soever it be: no more than one great tree, where the forrest is full of such. I doe not thinke that any Spartane Citizen did boastingly glorifie himselfe for his valor, because it was a popular vertue in that Nation: And as little for his fidelity, and contempt of riches. There is no recompence fals unto vertue, how great soever it be, if it once have past into custome: And I wot not whether we might call it great, being common. Since then the rewards of honour, have no other prize and estimation than that few enjoy it, there is no way to disannull them, but to make a largesse of them. Were there now more men found deserving the same than in former ages, yet should not the reputation of it be corrupted. And it may easily happen that more deserve it: For, there is no vertue, doth so easily spread it selfe as military valiancie. There is another, true, perfect, and Philosophicall, whereof I speake not (I use this word according to our custome) farre greater and more full than this, which is a force and assurance of the soule, equally contemning all manner of contrarie accidents, upright, uniforme, and constant, whereof ours is but an easie and glimmering raie. Custome, institution, example and fashion, may effect what ever they list in the establishing of that I speake of, and easily make it vulgare, as may plainly bee seene by the experience our civill warres give us of it. And whosoever could now joyne us together, and eagerly flesh all our people to a common enterprise, we should make our ancient military name and chivalrous credit to flourish againe. It is most certaine that the recompence of our order did not in former times only concerne prowis, and respect valour; it had a further aime. It was never the reward or payment of a valiant souldier; but of a famous Captaine. The skill to obey could not deserve so honourable an hire: for, cast we backe our eyes to antiquity, we shall perceive, that for the worthy obtaining thereof, there was required more universall warrelike expertnesse, and which might embrace the greatest part, and most parts of a military man; *Neque enim eadem militares et imperatoriæ artes sunt; For the same arts and parts belong not to a generall and common Souldier;* and who besides that, should also bee of a fit and accommodable condition for such a dignitie. But I say, that if more men should now adayes be found worthy of it, than have been heretofore, yet should not our Princes be more liberall of it: and it had beene much better, not to bestow it upon all of them to whom it was due, than for ever to lose, (as of late we have done) the use of so profitable an invention. *No man of courage vouchsafeth to advantage himselfe of that which is common unto many.* And those which in our dayes, have least merited that honourable recompence, seeme, in all apparance, most to disdaine it, by that meanes to place themselves in the ranke of those to whom the wrong is offered by unworthy bestowing and vilifying of that badge, which particularly was due unto them. Now by defacing and abolishing this to suppose, suddenly to be able to bring into credit, and renue a semblable custome, is no convenient enterprise, in so licentious, so corrupted, and so declining an age, as is this wherein we now live. And it will come to passe that the last shall even from her birth incur the incommodities, which have lately ruined and overthrowne the other. The rules of this new orders-dispensation had need to be otherwise wrested and constrained, for to give it authority: and this tumultuous season is not capable of a short and ordered bridle. Besides, before a man is able to give credit unto it, it is requisite a man lose the memory of the first, and of the contempt whereinto it is fallen. This place might admit some discourse upon the consideration of valour, and difference betweene this vertue and others: But *Plutarke* having often spoken of this matter, it were in vaine here for mee to repeat what he sayes of it. This is worthy to be considered, that our nation giveth the chiefe preheminence of all vertue unto valiancie, as the Etymology of the word sheweth, which commeth of valour, or worth: and that according to our received custome, when after the phrase of our court and nobility we speake of a worthy man, or of an honest man, we thereby inferre no other thing than a valiant man; after the usuall Roman fashion. For, the generall denomination of vertue doth amongst them take her Etymology, of force or might. The only proper and essentiall forme of our nobility in *France,* is military vocation. It is very likely, that the first vertue that ever appeared amongst men, and which to some hath given preheminence over others, hath beene this by which the strongest and more couragious have become masters over the weakest, and purchased a particular ranke and reputation to themselves: Whereby this honour and dignity of speech is left unto it: or else these nations being very warlike, have given the price unto that of vertues, which was the worthiest and more familiar unto them. Even as our passion, and this heart-panting, and mind-vexing carefull diligence, and diligent carefulnesse, which we continually apprehend about womens chastity, causeth; also that a good woman, an honest woman, a woman of honour and vertue, doth in effect and substance, signifie no other thing unto us, than a chaste wife or woman; as if to bind them to this duty, we did neglect all others, and gave them free liberty to commit any other fault, to covenant with them, never to quit or forsake this one.

CHAPTER VIII

OF THE AFFECTION OF FATHERS TO THEIR CHILDREN
TO THE LADY OF ESTISSAC

MADAME, if strangenesse doe not save, or novelty shield mee, which are wont to give things reputation, I shall never, with honesty, quit my selfe of this enterprise; yet is it so fantasticall, and beares a shew so different from common custome, that that may haply purchase it free passage. It is a melancholy humour, and consequently a hatefull enemy to my naturall complexion, bred by the anxietie, and produced by the anguish of carking care, whereinto some yeares since I cast my selfe, that first put this humorous conceipt of writing into my head. And finding my selfe afterward wholy unprovided of subject, and void of other matter; I have presented my selfe unto my selfe for a subject to write, and argument to descant upon. It is the only booke in the world of this kinde, and of a wilde extravagant designe. Moreover, there is nothing in it worthy the marking but this fantasticalnesse. For, to so vaine a ground and base a subject, the worlds best workman, could never have given a fashion deserving to be accompted of. Now (worthy Lady) sithence I must pourtray my selfe to the life, I should have forgotten a part of importance, if therewithall I had not represented the honour I have ever yeelded to your deserts, which I have especially beene willing to declare in the forefront of this Chapter; Forasmuch as amongst your other good parts, and commendable qualities, that of loving amity, which you have shewen to your children, holdeth one of the first rankes. Whosoever shall understand and know the age, wherein your late husband the Lord of *Estissac* left you a Widdow, the great and honorable matches have beene offered you (as worthy and as many as to any other Lady in *France* of your condition) the constant resolution, and resolute constancie, wherewith so many yeares you have sustained, and even in spight, or athwart so manifold thorny difficulties; the charge and conduct of their affaires, which have tossed, turmoyled and removed you in all corners of *France,* and still hold you besieged; the happy and successefull forwardnes you, which only through your wisdome or good fortune, have given them, he will easily say with mee, that in our age we have no patterne of motherly affection more exemplare, than yours. I praise God (Madam) it hath beene so well employed: For, the good hopes, which the young Lord of *Estissac,* your sonne giveth of himself, fore-shew an undoubted assurance, that when he shall come to yeares of discretion, you shall reape the obedience of a noble, and finde the acknowledgement of a good childe. But because, by reason of his child-hood, he could not take notice of the exceeding kindnesse and many-fold offices he hath received from you, my meaning is, that if ever these my compositions shall haply one day come into his hands (when peradventure I shall neither have mouth nor speech to declare it unto him) he receive this testimonie in all veritie from me; which shall also more lively be testified unto him by the good effects, (whereof, if so it please God, he shall have a sensible feeling) that there is no Gentleman in *France*, more endebted to his mother, than he; and that hereafter he cannot yeeld a more certaine proofe of his goodnes, and testimonie of his vertue, than in acknowledging and confessing you for such. If there be any truly-naturall law, that is to say, any instinct, universally and perpetually imprinted, both in beasts and us, (which is not without controversie) I may, according to mine opinion, say, that next to the care, which each living creature hath to his preservation, and to flie what doth hurt him; the affection which the engenderer beareth his offspring, holds the second place in this ranke. And forasmuch as nature seemeth to have recommended the same unto us, ayming to extend, encrease, and advance, the successive parts or parcels of this her frame. It is no wonder if back-againe, it is not so great from children unto fathers. This other Aristotelian consideration remembred: *That hee who doth benefit another, loveth him better than hee is beloved of him againe:* And hee to whom a debt is owing, loveth better, than hee that oweth: And every workman loveth his worke better, than hee should bee beloved of it againe, if it had sense or feeling. Forasmuch as we love to be; and being consisteth in moving and action. Therefore is every man, in some sort or other in his owne workmanship. *Whosoever doth a good deed, exerciseth a faire and honest action: Whosoever receiveth, exerciseth only a profitable action.* And profit is nothing so much to be esteemed or loved as honesty. Honesty is firme and permanent, affording him that did it, a constant gratification. Profit is very slipperie, and easily lost, nor is the memorie of it so sweet, or so fresh. Such things are dearest unto us, that have cost us most: And to give, is of more cost than to take. Since it hath pleased God to endow us with some capacitie of discourse, that as beasts we should not servily be subjected to common lawes, but rather with judgement and voluntary liberty apply our selves unto them; we ought somewhat to yeeld unto the simple auctoritie of Nature: but not suffer her tyrannically to carry us away: only reason ought to have the conduct of our inclinations. As for me, my tast is strangely distasted to its propensions, which in us are produced without the ordinance and direction of our judgement. As upon this subject I speak of, I cannot receive this passion, wherewith some embrace children scarsly borne, having neither motion in the soule, nor forme well to be distinguished in the body, whereby they might make themselves lovely or amiable. And I could never well endure to have them brought up or nursed neere about me.

A true and well ordred affection ought to be borne and augmented, with the knowledge they give us of themselves; and then, if they deserve it (naturall inclination marching hand in hand with reason) to cherish and make much of them, with a perfect fatherly love and loving friendship, and conformably to judge of them if they be otherwise, alwayes yeelding our selves unto reason, notwithstanding natural power. For the most part, it goeth cleane contrary, and commonly we feele our selves more moved with the sports, idlenesse, wantonnesse, and infant-trifles of our children, than afterward we do with all their actions, when they bee men: As if we had loved them for our pastimes, as we do apes, monkies, or perokitoes, and not as man. And some that liberally furnish them with sporting bables while they be children, will miserably pinch it in the least expence for necessaries when they grow men. Nay, it seemeth that the jelousie we have to see them appeare into, and injoy the world, when we are ready to leave them, makes us more sparing and close-handed toward them. It vexeth and grieveth us when we see them following us at our heeles, supposing they solicite us to be gone hence: And if we were to feare that since the order of things beareth, that they cannot indeed, neither be, nor live, but by our being and life, we should not meddle to be fathers. As for mee, I deeme it a kind of cruelty and injustice, not to receive them into the share and society of our goods, and to admit them as Partners in the understanding of our domestical affaires (if they be once capable of it) and not to cut off and shut-up our commodities to provide for theirs, since we have engendred them to that purpose. It is meere injustice to see an old, crazed, sinnow-shronken, and nigh dead father sitting alone in a Chimny-corner, to enjoy so many goods as would suffice for the preferment and entertainment of many children, and in the meane while, for want of meanes, to suffer them to lose their best dayes and yeares, without thrusting them into publike service and knowledge of men; whereby they are often cast into dispaire, to seeke, by some way how unlawfull soever to provide for their necessaries. And in my dayes, I have seene divers yong-men of good houses so given to stealing and filching, that no correction could divert them from it. I know one very well alied, to whom, at the instance of a brother of his (a most honest, gallant, and vertuous Gentleman) I spake to that purpose, who boldly answered and confessed unto me, that only by the rigor and covetise of his father he had beene forced and driven to fall into such lewdnesse and wickednesse. And even at that time he came from stealing certaine jewels from a Lady, in whose bed-chamber he fortuned to come with certaine other Gentlemen when she was rising, and had almost beene taken. He made me remember a tale I had heard of another Gentleman, from his youth so fashioned and inclined to this goodly trade of pilfering, that comming afterward to be heire and Lord of his owne goods, resolved to give over that manner of life, could notwithstanding (if he chanced to come neere a shop, where he saw any thing he stood in need of) not chuse but steale the same, though afterward he would ever send mony and pay for it. And I have seene diverse so inured to that vice, that amongst their companions, they would ordinarily steale such things, as they would restore againe. I am a Gascoine, and there is no vice wherein I have lesse skill: I hate it somewhat more by complexion, than I accuse it by discourse. I doe not so much as desire another mans goods.

And although my Countrey-men be indeed somewhat more taxed with this fault, than other Provinces of *France*, yet have we seene of late dayes, and that sundry times, men well borne and of good parentage in other parts of *France*, in the hands of justice, and lawfully convicted of many most horrible robberies. I am of opinion that in regard of these debauches and lewd actions, fathers may, in some sort, be blamed, and that it is only long of them. And if any shall answer mee, as did once a Gentleman of good worth and understanding, that he thriftily endevoured to hoard up riches, to no other purpose, nor to have any use and commodity of them, than to be honoured, respected and suingly sought unto by his friends and kinsfolkes, and that age having bereaved him of all other forces, it was the onely remedy he had left to maintaine himselfe in authority with his houshold, and keepe him from falling into contempt and disdaine of all the world. And truly according to *Aristotle*, not only old-age, but each imbecillity, is the promoter, and motive of covetousnesse. That is something, but it is a remedy for an evill, whereof the birth should have beene hindered, and breeding avoyded. That father may truly be said miserable, that holdeth the affection of his children tied unto him by no other meanes than by the need they have of his helpe, or want of his assistance, if that may be termed affection: *A man should yeeld himselfe respectable by vertue and sufficiency, and amiable by his goodnesse, and gentlenesse of manners*. The very cinders of so rich a matter, have their value: so have the bones and reliques of honourable men whom we hold in respect and reverence. No age can be so crazed and drooping in a man that hath lived honourably, but must needs prove venerable, and especially unto his children, whose mindes ought so to be directed by the parents, that reason and wisdome, not necessity and need, nor rudenesse and compulsion, may make them know and performe their dutie.

> —*et errat longe, mea quidem sententia,*
> *Qui imperium credat esse gravius aut stabilius,*
> *Vi quod fit, quam illud quod amicitia adjungitur.*
>
> <div align="right">TER. <i>Adelph.</i> act. i. sc. i. 39.</div>

In mine opinion he doth much mistake,
Who, that command more grave, more firme doth take,
Which force doth get, than that which friendships make.

I utterly condemne all manner of violence in the education of a yong spirit, brought up to honour and liberty. There is a kind of slavishnesse in churlish-rigor, and servility in compulsion; and I hold, that *that which cannot be compassed by reason, wisdome and discretion, can never be attained by force and constraint.* So was I brought up: they tell mee, that in all my youth, I never felt rod but twice, and that very lightly. And what education I have had my selfe, the same have I given my children. But such is my ill hap, that they dye all very yong: yet hath *Leonora* my only daughter escaped this misfortune, and attained to the age of six yeares, and somewhat more: for the conduct of whose youth, and punishment of her childish faults (the indulgence of her mother applying it selfe very mildely unto it) was never other meanes used but gentle words. And were my desire frustrate, there are diverse other causes to take hold of, without reproving my discipline, which I know to be just and naturall. I would also have beene much more religious in that towards male-children, not borne to serve as women, and of a freer condition. I should have loved to have stored their minde with ingenuity and liberty. I have seene no other effects in rods, but to make childrens mindes more remisse, or more maliciously head-strong. Desire we to be loved of our children? Will we remove all occasions from them to wish our death? (although no occasion of so horrible and unnaturall wishes, can either be just or excusable) *nullum scelus rationem habet,* no ill deed hath a good reason.

Let us reasonably accommodate their life, with such things as are in our power. And therefore should not we marry so young, that our age do in a manner confound it selfe with theirs. For, this inconvenience doth unavoidably cast us into many difficulties, and encombrances. This I speake, chiefly unto nobility, which is of an idle disposition, or loitering condition, and which (as we say) liveth only by her lands or rents: for else, where life standeth upon gaine; plurality and company of children is an easefull furtherance of husbandry. They are as many new implements to thrive, and instruments to grow rich. I was married at thirty yeares of age, and commend the opinion of thirty-five, which is said to be *Aristotles. Plato* would have no man married before thirty, and hath good reason to scoffe at them that will defer it till after fifty-five, and then marry; and condemneth their breed as unworthy of life and sustenance. *Thales* appointed the best limits, who by his mother being instantly urged to marry whilest he was young, answered that it was not yet time; and when he came to be old, he said, it was no more time. A man must refuse opportunity to every importunate action. The ancient *Gaules* deemed it a shamefull reproach, to have the acquaintance of a woman before the age of twenty yeares; and did especially recommend unto men that sought to be trained up in warres, the carefull preservation of their maiden-head, untill they were of good yeares, forsomuch as by losing it in youth, courages are therby much weakned and greatly empaired, and by copulation with women, diverted from all vertuous action.

> *Ma hor cogiunto à giovinetta sposa,*
> *Lieto homai de' figli' era invilito*
> *Ne gli affetti di padre et di marito.*

> But now conjoyn'd to a fresh-springing spouse,
> Joy'd in his children, he was thought-abased,
> In passions twixt a Sire, and husband placed.

Muleasses King of *Thunes,* he whom the Emperour *Charles* the fifth restored unto his owne state againe, was wont to upbraid his fathers memorie, for so dissolutely-frequenting of women, terming him a sloven, effeminate, and a lustfull engenderer of children. The Greeke story doth note *Iecus* the *Tarentine, Chryso, Astylus, Diopomus* and others, who to keep their bodies tough and strong for the service of the Olympicke courses, wrestlings and such bodily exercises, they did, as long as they were possessed with that care, heedefully abstaine from all venerian acts, and touching of women. In a certaine country of the Spanish *Indies,* no man was suffered to take a wife, before he were fortie yeares old, and women might marry at ten yeares of age. There is no reason, neither is it convenient, that a Gentleman of five and thirtie yeares, should give place to his sonne, that is but twenty: For then is the father as seemely, and may as well appeare, and set himselfe forward, in all manner of voyages of warres, as well by land as sea, and doe his Prince as good service, in court, or elsewhere, as his sonne: He hath need of all his parts, and ought truly to impart them, but so, that he forget not himselfe for others: And to such may justly that answer serve, which fathers have commonly in their mouthes: *I will not put off my clothes before I be ready to goe to bed.* But a father over-burthend with yeares, and crazed through sicknesse, and by reason of weaknesse and want of health, barred from the common societie of men, doth both wrong himselfe, injure his, idely and to no use to hoord up, and keepe close a great heape of riches, and deale of pelfe. He is in state good enough, if he be wise to have a desire to put off his clothes to goe to bed. I will not say to his shirt, but to a good warme night-gowne: As for other pompe and trash whereof hee hath no longer use or need; hee ought willingly to distribute and bestow them amongst those, to whom by naturall decree they ought to belong. It is reason he should have the use, and bequeath the fruition of them, since nature doth also deprive him of them, otherwise without doubt there is both envy and malice stirring. The worthiest action, that ever the Emperour *Charles* the fifth performed was this, in imitation of some ancients of his quality, that he had the discretion to know, that reason commanded us, to strip or shift our selves when our cloathes trouble and are too heavy for us, and that it is high time to goe to bed, when our legs faile us.

He resigned his meanes, his greatnesse and Kingdome to his Sonne, at what time he found his former undanted resolution to decay, and force to conduct his affaires, to droope in himselfe, together with the glory he had thereby acquired.

Solve senescentem mature sanus equum, ne
Peccet ad extremum ridendus, et ilia ducat.

HOR. i. *Ep.* i. 8.

If you be wise, the horse growne-old betimes cast-off,
Lest he at last fall lame, foulter, and breed a skoffe.

This fault, for a man not to be able to know himselfe betimes, and not to feele the impuissance and extreme alteration, that age doth naturally bring, both to the body and the minde (which in mine opinion is equall, if the minde have but one halfe) hath lost the reputation of the most part of the greatest men in the world. I have in my dayes both seene and familiarly knowen some men of great authority, whom a man might easily discerne, to be strangely fallen from that ancient sufficiency, which I know by the reputation they had thereby attained unto in their best yeares. I could willingly for their honors sake have wisht them at home about their owne businesse, discharged from all negotiations of the commonwealth and employments of war, that were no longer fit for them. I have sometimes beene familiar in a Gentlemans house, who was both an old man and a widdower, yet lusty of his age. This man had many daughters marriageable, and a sonne growne to mans state, and ready to appeare in the world; a thinge that drew-on, and was the cause of great charges, and many visitations, wherein he tooke but little pleasure, not only for the continuall care hee had to save, but more by reason of his age, hee had betaken himselfe to a manner of life farre different from ours. I chanced one day to tell him somewhat boldly (as my custome is) that it would better beseeme him to give us place, and resigne his chiefe house to his sonne (for he had no other mannor-house conveniently well furnished) and quietly retire himselfe to some farme of his, where no man might trouble him, or disturbe his rest, since he could not otherwise avoid our importunitie, seeing the condition of his children; who afterward followed my counsell, and found great ease by it. It is not to be said, that they have any thing given them by such a way of obligation, which a man may not recall againe: I, that am ready to play such a part, would give over unto them the full possession of my house, and enjoying of my goods, but with such libertie and limited condition, as if they should give me occasion, I might repent my selfe of my gift, and revoke my deed. I would leave the use and fruition of all unto them, the rather because it were no longer fit for me to weald the same. And touching the disposing of all matters in grosse, I would reserve what I pleased unto my selfe. Having ever judged, that it must be a great contentment to an aged

father, himselfe to direct his children in the government of his houshold affaires, and to be able whilst himselfe liveth, to checke and controule the demeanors, storing them with instruction and advised
counsell, according to the experience he hath had of them, and himselfe
to addresse the ancient honour and order of his house in the hands of
his successours, and that way warrant himselfe of the hopes hee may
conceive of their future conduct and after successe. And to this effect,
I would not shun their company. I would not be far from them, but as
much as the condition of my age would permit, enjoy and be a partner
of their sports, mirths, and feasts. If I did not continually live amongst
them (as I could not wel without offending their meetings and hinder-
ing their recreation, by reason of the peevish frowardnesse of my age,
and the trouble of my infirmities, and also without forcing their rules,
and resisting the forme of life I should then follow) I would at least live
neere them, in some corner of my house, not the best and fairest in
shew, but the most easefull and commodious. And not as some yeares
since, I saw a Deane of S. *Hillarie* of Poictiers, reduced by reason and
the incommoditie of his melancholy to such a continuall solitarinesse,
that when I entered into his chamber he had never removed one step
out of it in two and twenty yeares before: yet had all his faculties free
and easie, onely a rheume excepted that fell into his stomacke. Scarse
once a weeke would he suffer any body to come and see him. Hee would
ever be shut up in his chamber all alone, where no man should come,
except a boy, who once a day brought him meat, and who might not
tarry there, but as soone as he was in, must goe out againe. All his
exercise was sometimes to walke up and downe his chamber, and now
and then reade on some booke (for he had some understanding of
letters) but obstinately resolved to live and dye in that course, as he
did shortly after. I would endevour by a kinde of civill demeanour and
milde conversation, to breede and settle in my children a true-harty-
loving friendship, and unfained good will towards me. A thing easily
obtained amongst well-borne mindes; For, if they prove, or be such
surly-furious beasts, or given to churlish disobedience, as our age bringeth forth thousands, they must as beasts be hated, as churls neglected,
and as degenerate avoided. I hate this custome, to forbid children to
call their fathers father, and to teach them another strange name, as of
more reverence: As if nature had not sufficiently provided for our
authoritie. We call God-almighty by the name of father, and disdaine
our children should call us so. I have reformed this fault in mine owne
houshold. It is also folly and injustice to deprive children, especially
being of competent age, of their fathers familiaritie, and ever to shew
them a surly, austere, grim, and disdainefull countenance, hoping
thereby to keepe them in awfull feare and duteous obedience. For, it
is a very unprofitable proceeding, and which maketh fathers yrkesome
unto children; and which is worse, ridiculous. They have youth and
strength in their hands, and consequently, the breath and favour of the

world; and doe with mockerie and contempt receive these churlish fierce, and tyrannicall countenances, from a man that hath no lusty bloud left him, neither in his heart, nor in his vaines; meere bug-beares, and scar-crowes, to scare birdes with all. If it lay in my power to make my selfe feared, I had rather make my selfe beloved. There are so many sorts of defects in age, and so much impuissance: It is so subject to contempt, that the best purchase it can make, is the good will, love and affection of hers. Commandement and feare are no longer her weapons. I have knowen one whose youth had beene very imperious and rough, but when he came to mans age, although hee live in as good plight and health as may be, yet he chafeth, he scoldeth, he brawleth, he fighteth, he sweareth, and biteth, as the most boistrous and tempestuous master of *France*, he frets and consumes himselfe with carke and care and vigilancy (al which is but a jugling and ground for his [familie] to play upon, and cozen him the more as for his goods, his garners, his cellers, his coffers, yea his purse, whilst himselfe keepes the keyes of them close in his bosome, and under his boulster, as charily as he doth his eyes, other enjoy and command the better part of them; whilst he pleaseth and flattereth himselfe, with the niggardly sparing of his table, all goth to wracke, and is lavishly wasted in divers corners of his house, in play, in riotous spending, and in soothingly entertaining the accompts or tales of his vaine chafing, foresight and providing. Every man watcheth and keepeth sentinell against him, if any silly or heedlesse servant doe by fortune apply himselfe unto it, he is presently made to suspect him: A quality on which age doth immediately bite of it selfe. How many times hath he vaunted and applauding himselfe told me of the strict orders of his house, of his good husbandry, of the awe he kept his houshold in, and of the exact obedience, and regardfull reverence he received of all his family, and how cleare-sighted he was in his owne businesse:

Ille solus nescit omnia.—Ter. *Adel.* act. iv. sc. ii. 9.

Of all things none but he,
Most ignorant must be.

I know no man that could produce more parts, both naturall and artificiall, fit to preserve his masterie, and to maintaine his absolutenesse, than he doth; yet is hee cleane falne from them like a childe. Therefore have I made choice of him, amongst many such conditions that I know, as most exemplare. It were a matter beseeming a scholasticall question, whether it be better so, or otherwise. In his presence all things give place unto him. This vaine course is ever left unto his authority, that he is never gaine-said. He is had in awe, he is feared, he is beleeved, he is respected his belly-full. Doth he discharge any boy or servant? he presently trusseth up his packe, then is he gone; but whither? onely out of his sight, not out of his house. The steps of age are so slow, the senses so troubled, the minde so distracted, that he shall live and doe his office, a whole yeare in one same house, and never be perceived. And when fit time or occasion serveth, Letters are produced from farre places, humbly suing, and pittifully complayning, with promises to doe better, and to amend, by which he is brought into favour and office againe. Doth the master make any bargaine, or dispatch that pleaseth not? it is immediately smothered and suppressed, soone after forging causes, and devising colourable excuses, to excuse the want of execution or answer. No forraine Letters being first presented unto him, he seeth but such as are fit for his knowledge. If peradventure they come unto his hands, as he that trusteth some one of his men to reade them unto him, he will presently devise what he thinketh good, whereby they often invent, that such a one seemeth to aske him forgivenesse, that wrongeth him by his Letter. To conclude, he never lookes into his owne businesse, but by a disposed, designed and as much as may be pleasing image, so contrived by such as are about him, because they will not stirre up his choler, move his impatience, and exasperate his frowardnesse. I have seene under different formes, many long and constant, and of like effect œconomies. It is ever proper unto women, to be readily bent to contradict and crosse their husbands. They will with might and maine hand over head, take hold of any colour to thwart and withstand them: the first excuse they meet with, serves them as a plenary justification. I have seene some, that would in grosse steale from their husbands, to the end (as they told their Confessors) they might give the greater almes. Trust you to such religious dispensations. They thinke no liberty to have, or managing to possesse sufficient authority, if it come from their husbands consent: They must necessarily usurpe it, either by wily craft or maine force, and ever injuriously, thereby to give it more grace and authoritie. As in my Discourse, when it is against a poore old man, and for children, then take they hold of this Title, and therewith gloriously serve their turne and passion, and as in a common servitude, easily usurpe and monopolize against his government and domination. If they be men-children, tall, of good spirit and forward, then they presently suborne, either by threats, force or favour, both Steward, Bailiffe, Clarke, Receiver, and all the Fathers Officers, and Servant. Such as have neither wife nor children, doe more hardly fall into this mischiefe: but yet more cruelly and unworthily. Old *Cato* was wont to say, *So many servants, so many enemies*. Note whether according to the distance, that was betweene the purity of his age, and the corruption of our times, he did not fore-warne us, that *Wives, Children, and Servants are to us so many enemies*. Well fits it decrepitude to store us with the sweet benefit of ignorance and unperceiving facility wherewith we are deceived.

If we did yeeld unto it, what would become of us? Doe we not see that even then, if we have any suits in law, or matters to be decided before Judges, both Lawiers and Judges, will commonly take part

with, and favour our childrens causes against us, as men interessed in
the same? And if I chance not to spy, or plainely perceive how I am
cheated, cozoned and beguiled, I must of necessitie discover in the end,
how I am subject and maybe cheated, beguiled, and cozoned. And shall
the tongue of man ever bee able to expresse the unvaluable worth of a
friend, in comparison of these civill bonds? The lively image and Idea
whereof, I perceive to be amongst beasts so unspotted. Oh with what
religion doe I respect and observe the same! If others deceive me, yet
do I not deceive my selfe, to esteeme my selfe capable, and of power to
looke unto my selfe, nor to trouble my braines to yeeld my selfe unto it.
I doe beware and keepe my selfe from such treasons, and cunny-catch-
ing in mine owne bosome, not by an unquiet, and tumultuary curiosity,
but rather by a diversion and resolution. When I heare the state of
any one reported or discoursed of, I ammuse not my selfe on him, but
presently cast mine eyes on my selfe, and all my wits together, to see
in what state I am, and how it goeth with me. Whatsoever concerneth
him, the same hath relation to me. His fortunes forewarne me, and
summon up my spirits that way. *There is no day nor houre, but we
speake that of others, we might properly speake of our selves, could we
as well enfold, as we can unfold our consideration.* And many Authours
doe in this manner wound the protection of their cause, by over-rashly
running against that which they take hold-of, thirling such darts at
their enemies, that might with much more advantage be cast at them.
The Lord of *Monluc,* late one of the Lord Marshals of *France,* having
lost his sonne, who died in the Iland of *Madera* a worthy, forward and
gallant young gentleman, and truely of good hope; amongst other his
griefes and regrets, did greatly move me to condole, the infinite displeasure and hearts-sorrow that he felt, inasmuch as he had never
communicated and opened himselfe unto him; for, with his austere
humour and continuall endevoring to hold a grimme-stern-fatherly
gravity over him, he had lost the meanes, perfectly to finde and
throughly to know his sonne, and so to manifest unto him the extreme
affection he bare him, and the worthy judgement he made of his vertue. Alas (was he wont to say) the poore lad saw never any thing in
me, but a severe-surly-countenance, full of disdaine, and haply was
possessed with this conceit, that I could neither love nor esteeme him
according to his merits. Ay-me, to whom did I reserve, to discover that
singular and loving affection, which in my soule I bare unto him? Was
it not he that should have had all the pleasure and acknowledgement
thereof? I have forced and tormented my selfe to maintaine this vaine
maske, and have utterly lost the pleasure of his conversation, and
therwithal his good will, which surely was but faintly cold towards me,
forsomuch as he never received but rude entertainment of mee, and
never felt but a tyrannicall proceeding in me towards him. I am of
opinion, his complaint was reasonable and well grounded. For, as I
know by certaine experience, there is no comfort so sweet in the losse

of friends, as that our owne knowledge or conscience tels us, we never omitted to tell them everything, and expostulate all matters unto them, and to have had a perfect and free communication with them. Tell me my good friend, am I the better or the worse by having a taste of it? Surely I am much the better. His griefe doth both comfort and honour mee. Is it not a religious and pleasing office of my life, for ever to make the obsequies thereof? Can there be any pleasure worth this privation? I doe unfold and open my self as much as I can to mine owne people, and willingly declare the state of my will and judgment toward them, as commonly I doe towards all men: I make haste to produce and present my selfe, for I would have no man mistake me, in what part soever. Amongst other particular customes, which our ancient Gaules had, (as *Cæsar* affirmeth) this was one, that children never came before their fathers, nor were in any publike assembly seene in their company, but when they began to beare armes; as if they would infer, that then was the time, fathers should admit them to their acquaintance and familiarity. I have also observed another kinde of indiscretion in some fathers of our times, who during their owne life, would never be induced to acquaint or impart unto their children, that share or portion, which by the Law of Nature, they were to have in their fortunes: Nay, some there are, who after their death bequeath and commit the same auctoritie, over them and their goods, unto their wives, with full power and law to dispose of them at their pleasure. And my selfe have knowen a Gentleman, a chiefe officer of our crowne, that by right and hope of succession (had he lived unto it) was to inherit above fifty thousand crownes a yeere good land, who at the age of more than fifty yeeres fell into such necessity and want, and was run so farre in debt, that he had nothing left him, and as it is supposed died for very need; whilest his mother in her extreme decrepitude, enjoyed all his lands and possessed all his goods, by vertue of his fathers will and testament, who had lived very neere foure-score years. A thing (in my conceit) no way to be commended, but rather blamed. Therefore doe I thinke, that a man but little advantaged or bettered in estate, who is able to live of himselfe, and is out of debt, especially if he have children, and goeth about to marry a wife, that must have a great joynter out of his lands, assuredly there is no other debt, that brings more ruine unto houses then that. My predecessors have commonly followed this counsell, and so have I, and all have found good by it. But those that disswade us from marrying of rich wives, lest they might proove over disdainefull and peevish, or lesse tractable and loving, are also deceived to make us neglect and for-goe a reall commoditie, for so frivolous a conjecture. To an unreasonable woman, it is all one cost to her, whether they passe under one reason, or under another. *They love to be where they are most wronged.* Injustice doth allure them; as the honour of their vertuous actions enticeth the good. And by how much richer they are, so much more milde and gentle are they: as more

willingly and gloriously chaste, by how much fairer they are. Some colour of reason there is, men should leave the administration of their goods and affaires unto mothers, whilest their children are not of competent age, or fit according to the lawes to manage the charge of them: And ill hath their father brought them up, if he cannot hope, these comming to yeares of discretion, they shal have no more wit, reason, and sufficiencie, than his wife, considering the weaknesse of their sexe. Yet truly were it as much against nature, so to order things, that mothers must wholy depend of their childrens discretion. They ought largely and competently to be provided, wherewith to maintaine their estate, according to the quality of their house and age: because *need and want is much more unseemely and hard to be indured in women, than in men:* And children rather than mothers ought to be charged therewith. In generall, my opinion is, that the best distribution of goods, is when we dye, to distribute them according to the custome of the Country. The Lawes have better thought upon them than we: And better it is to let them erre in their election, than for us rashly to hazard to faile in ours. They are not properly our owne, since without us, and by a civil prescription, they are appointed to certaine suc-cessours. And albeit we have some further liberty, I thinke it should be a great and most apparant cause to induce us to take from one, and barre him from that, which Fortune hath allotted him, and the common Lawes and Justice hath called him unto: And that against reason wee abuse this liberty, by suting the same unto our private humours and frivolous fantasies. My fortune hath beene good, inasmuch as yet it never presented mee with any occasions, that might tempt or divert my affections from the common and lawful ordinance. I see some, towards whom it is but labour lost, carefully to endevour to doe any good offices. *A word ill taken defaceth the merit of ten yeeres.* Happy he, that at this last passage is ready to sooth and applaud their will. The next action transporteth him; not the best and most frequent offices, but the freshest and present worke the deed. They are people that play with their wils and testaments, as with apples and rods, to gratifie or chastize every action of those who pretend any interest there-unto. It is a matter of over-long pursute, and of exceeding conse-quence, at every instance to be thus dilated, and wherein the wiser sort establish themselves once for all, chiefely respecting reason, and publike observance. We somewhat over much take these masculine substitutions to hart, and propose a ridiculous eternity unto our names. We also over-weight such vaine future conjectures, which infant-spirits give-us. It might peradventure have beene deemed injustice, to dis-place me from out my rancke, because I was the dullest, the slowest, the unwillingest, and most leaden-pated to learne my lesson or any good, that ever was, not onely of all my brethren, but of all the children in my Countrie; were the lesson concerning any exercise of the minde or body. It is follie to trie anie extraordinarie conclusions upon the trust of their divinations, wherein we are so often deceived. If this rule may be contradicted, and the destinies corrected, in the choice they have made of our heires, with so much more apparence, may it be done in consideration of some remarkable and enormous corporall deformitie; a constant and incorrigible vice; and according to us great esteemers of beautie; a matter of important prejudice. The pleasant dialogue of *Plato* the law-giver, with his citizens, will much honour this passage. Why then (say they) perceiving their end to approch, shall we not dispose of that which is our owne, to whom and according as we please? Oh Gods what cruelty is this? That it shall not be lawfull for us, to give or bequeath more or lesse according to our fantasies, to such as have served us, and taken paines with us in our sicknesses, in our age, and in our busines? To whom the Law-giver answereth in this manner; My friends (saith he) who doubtlesse shall shortly die, it is a hard matter for you, both to know your selves, and what is yours, according to the *Delphike* inscription: As for me, who am the maker of your lawes, I am of opinion that neither your selves are your owne, nor that which you enjoy. And both you and your goods, past and to come, belong to your familie; and moreover both your families and your goods are the common wealths: Wherfore, lest any flatterer, either in your age, or in time of sicknes, or any other passion, should un-advisedly induce you to make any unlawfull convayance or unjust will and testament, I will looke to you and keepe you from it. But having an especiall respect both to the universall interest of your Citie, and particular state of your houses, I will establish lawes, and by reason make you perceive and confesse that a *particular commoditie ought to yeeld to a publike benefit.* Follow that course meerely, whereto humane necessitie doth call you. To me it belongeth, who have no more regard to one thing, than to another, and who as much as I can, take care for the general, to have a regardfull respect of that which you leave behind you. But to returne to my former discourse, me thinkes, we seldome see that woman borne, to whom the superioritie or majestie over men is due, except the motherly and naturall; unlesse it be for the chastisement of such, as by some fond-febricitant humor have voluntarily submitted themselves unto them; But that doth nothing concerne old women, of whom we speake here. It is the apparance of this consideration, hath made us to frame, and willingly to establish this law (never seene else-where) that barreth women from the succession of this crowne, and there are few principalities in the world, where it is not alleaged, aswel as here, by a likely and apparant reason, which authoriseth the same. But fortune hath given more credit unto it in some places, than in other some. It is dangerous to leave the dispensation of our succession unto their judgement, according to the choyse they shall make of their chil-dren, which is most commonly unjust and fantasticall. For, the same unrulie appetite, and distasted relish, or strange longings, which they have when they are great with child, the same have they at al times in their minds. They are commonly seene to affect the weakest, the simplest and most abject, or such (if they have any) that had more need to sucke. For, wanting reasonable discourse to chuse, and embrace what they ought, they rather suffer themselves to be directed, where natures impressions are most single, as other creatures, which take no longer knowledge of their young ones, than they are sucking. Moreover, experience doth manifestly shew unto us, that the same naturall affection, to which we ascribe so much auctoritie, hath but a weake foundation. For a very small gaine, we daily take mothers owne children from them and induce them to take charge of ours; Doe we not often procure them to bequeath their children to some fond, filthie, sluttish, and unhealthie nurce, to whom we would be very loth to commit ours, or to some brutish Goat, not onely forbidding them to nurce and feed their owne children (what danger soever may betide them) but also to have any care of them, to the end they may the more diligently follow, and carefully attend the service of ours? Whereby wee soone see through custome a certain kinde of bastard-affection to be engendred in them, more vehement than the naturall, and to be much more tender and carefull for the welfare and preservation of other mens children, than for their owne. And the reason why I have made mention of Goats, is, because it is an ordinarie thing round about me where I dwell, to see the countrie women, when they have not milke enough to feed their infants with their owne breasts, to call for Goats to helpe them. And my selfe hae now two lackies wayting upon me, who except it were eight daies never suck't other milke than Goats; They are presently to come at call, and give young infants sucke, and become so well acquainted with their voice, that when they heare them crie, they runne forthwith unto them. And if by chance they have any other child put to their teats, than their nurseling, they refuse and reject him, and so doth the childe a strange Goat. My selfe saw that one not long since, from whom the father tooke a Goat, which he had sucked two or three daies, because he had but borrowed it of one of his neighbours, who could never be induced to sucke any other, whereby he shortly died; and as I verily thinke, of meere hunger. *Beasts as well as we doe soone alter, and easily bastardize their naturall affection.* I beleeve, that in that, which *Herodotus* reporteth of a certaine province of *Libia*, there often followeth great error and mistaking. He saith, that men doe indifferently use, and as it were in common frequent women; And that the childe as soone as he is able to goe, comming to any solemne meetings and great assemblies, led by a naturall instinct, findeth out his owne father: where being turned loose in the middest of the multitude, looke what man the childe doth first addresse his steps unto, and then goe to him, the same is ever afterward reputed to be his right father. Now if we shall duly consider this simple occasion of loving our children, because we have begotten them, for which we call them our other selves. It seemes there is another production comming from us, and which is of no lesse recommendation and consequence. For what we engender by the minde, the fruits of our courage, sufficiencie, or spirit, are brought forth by a far more noble part, than the corporall, and are more our owne. We are both father and mother together in this generation: such fruits cost us much dearer, and bring us more honour, and chiefly if they have any good or rare thing in them. For the value of our other children, is much more theirs, than ours. The share we have in them is but little; but of these all the beautie, all the grace, and all the worth is ours. And therefore doe they represent, and resemble us much more lively than others. *Plato* addeth moreover, that these are immortall issues, and immortalize their fathers, yea and deifie them, as *Licurgus*, *Solon*, and *Minos*. All histories being full of examples of this mutuall friendship of fathers toward their children, I have not thought it amisse to set downe some choice one of this kinde. *Heliodorus* that good Bishop of *Tricea*, loved rather to lose the dignity, profit and devotion of so venerable a Prelateship, than to for-goe his daughter, a young woman to this day commended for hir beautie, but haply somewhat more curiously and wantonly pranked-up than be-seemed the daughter of a churchman and a Bishop, and of over-amorous behaviour. There was one *Labienus* in *Rome*, a man of great worth and authority, and amongst other commendable qualities, most excellent in all maner of learning, who (as I thinke) was the sonne of that great *Labienus*, chiefe of all the captaines that followed and were under *Cæsar* in the warres against the Gaules, and who afterward tak-ing great *Pompeys* part, behaved himselfe so valiantly and so con-stantly, that he never forsooke him untill *Cæsar* defeated him in *Spaine*. This *Labienus* of whom I spake, had many that envied his vertues; But above all (as it is likely) courtiers, and such as in his time were favored of the Emperors, who hated his franknesse, his fatherly humours, and distaste he bare still against tyrannie, wherewith it may be supposed he had stuffed his bookes and compositions. His adversaries vehemently pursued him before the Magistrate of *Rome*, and prevailed so far, that many of his works which he had published were condemned to be burned. He was the first on whom this new example of punishment was put in practice, which after continued long in *Rome*, and was executed on divers others, to punish learning, studies, and writings with death and consuming fire. There were neither meanes enough, or matter sufficient of crueltie, unless we had entermingled amongst them things, which nature hath exempted from all sense and sufferance, as reputa-tion, and the inventions of our minde: and except we communicated corporall mischiefes unto disciplines and monuments of the Muses. Which losse *Labienus* could not endure, nor brooke to survive those his deare, and highly-esteemed issues: And therefore caused himselfe to be carried, and shut up alive within his auncestors monument, where, with a dreadlesse resolution, he at once provided, both to kill himselfe and be buried together. It is hard to shew any more vehement fatherly affection, than that. *Cassius Severus,* a most eloquent man, and his familiar friend, seeing his Bookes burnt, exclaimed, that by the same sentence hee should therewithall be condemned to be burned alive, for hee still bare and kept in minde, what they contained in them. A like accident happened to *Geruntius Cordus,* who was accused to have commended *Brutus* and *Cassius* in his Bookes. That base, servile, and corrupted Senate, and worthie of a farre worse master than *Tiberius,* adjudged his writings to be consumed by fire. And he was pleased to accompany them in their death; for, he pined away by abstaining from all manner of meat. That notable man, *Lucane,* being adjudged by that lewd varlet *Nero* to death; at the latter end of his life, when al his bloud was well-nigh spent from out the veines of his arme, which by his Physitian he had caused to be opened, to hasten his death, and that a chilling cold began to seize the uttermost parts of his limbes, and approch his vital spirits, the last thing he had in memory, was some of his owne verses, written in his booke of the *Pharsalian* warres, which with a distinct voice hee repeated, and so yeelded up the ghost, having those last words in his mouth. What was that but a kinde, tender, and fatherly farwell which he tooke of his children? representing the last adiewes, and parting imbracements, which at our death we give unto our dearest issues? And an effect of that naturall inclination, which in that last extremity puts us in minde of those things, which in our lifetime we have held dearest and most precious? Shall we imagine that *Epicurus,* who (as himselfe said) dying tormented with the extreme paine of the chollik, had all his comfort in the beauty of the doctrine which he left behinde him in the world, would have received as much contentment of a number of well-borne, and better-bred children (if he had had any) as he did of the production of his rich compositions? And if it had beene in his choise, to leave behind him, either a counterfeit, deformed, or ill-borne childe, or a foolish, triviall, and idle booke, not onely he, but all men in the world besides of like learning and sufficiencie, would much rather have chosen to incurre the former than the later mischiefe. It might peradventure be deemed impiety, in Saint *Augustine* (for example-sake) if on the one part one should propose unto him, to bury all his bookes, whence our religion receiveth so much good, or to interre his children (if in case he had any) that he would not rather chuse to bury his children, or the issue of his loynes, than the fruits of his minde. And I wot not well, whether my selfe should not much rather desire to beget and produce a perfectly-well-shaped, and excellently-qualited infant, by the acquaintance of the Muses, than by the copulation of my wife. Whatsoever I give to this, let the world allow of it as it please, I give it as purely and irrevocable, as any man can give to his corporal children. That little good which I have done him, is no longer in my disposition. He may know many things, that my selfe know no longer, and hold of me what I could not hold my selfe: and which (if need should require) I must borrow of him as of a stranger. If I be wiser than he, he is richer than I. There are few men given unto Poesie, that would not esteeme it for a greater honour, to be the fathers of *Virgils Æneidos,* than of the goodliest boy in *Rome,* and that would not rather endure the losse of the one than the perishing of the other. For, according to *Aristotle, Of all workemen, the Poet is principally the most amorous of his productions and conceited of his Labours.* It is not easie to be beleeved, that *Epaminondas,* who vanted to leave some daughters behind him, which unto all posterity, should one day highly honour their father (they were the two famous victories, which he had gained of the Lacedemonians) would ever have given his free consent, to change them, with the best-borne, most gorgeous, and goodliest damsels of all *Greece:* or that *Alexander,* and *Cæsar,* did ever wish to be deprived of the greatnesse of their glorious deeds of warre, for the commodity to have children and heires of their owne bodies, how absolutely-perfect, and well-accomplished so ever they might be. Nay, I make a great question, whether *Phidias* or any other excellent Statuary, would as highly esteeme, and dearely love the preservation, and successefull continuance of his naturall children, as he would an exquisite and match-lesse-wrought Image, that with long study, and diligent care he had perfected according unto art. And as concerning those vicious and furious passions, which sometimes have inflamed some fathers to the love of their daughters, or mothers towards their sonnes; the very same, and more partially-earnest is also found in this other kinde of childe-bearing and aliance. Witnesse that which is reported of *Pigmalion,* who having curiously framed a goodly statue, of a most singularly-beauteous woman, was so strange-fondly, and passionately surprised with the lustfull love of his owne workmanship, that the Gods through his raging importunity were faine in favour of him to give it life.

> *Tentatum mollescit ebur, positoque rigore*
> *Subsidit digitis.*—OVID. *Metam.* x. 283.

As he assaid it, th' yvorie softned much,
And (hardnesse left) did yeeld to fingers touch.

CHAPTER IX

OF THE PARTHIANS ARMES

It is a vitious, fond fashion of the Nobility and Gentry of our age, and full of nice-tendernesse, never to betake themselves to armes, except upon some urgent and extreme necessitie; and to quit them as soone as they perceive the least hope or apparance, that the danger is past: Whence ensue many disorders, and inconveniences: For, every

one running and calling for his armes when the alarum is given, some
have not yet buckled their cuirace, when their fellowes are already
defeated. Indeed our forefathers would have their Caske, Lance, Gant-
lets, and Shields carried, but so long as the service lasted, themselves
would never leave-off their other peeces. Our troopes are now all confounded and disordered, by reason of bag and baggage, or carriages,
of lackies, and foot-boies, which because of their masters armes they
carry, can never leave them. *Titus Livius,* speaking of the French, saith,
Intolerantissima laboris corpora vix arma humeris gerebant (Liv. dec.
i. 10). *Their bodies most impatient of labour could hardly beare armour
on their backes.* Divers Nations, as they did in former times, so yet at
this day, are seene to goe to the warres, without any thing about them,
or if they had, it was of no defence; but were all naked and bare.

> *Tegmina queis capitum raptus de subere cortex.*
>
> Virg. *Æn.* vii. 742.

Whose caske to cover all their head,
Was made of barke from Corke-tree flea'd.

Alexander the most daring and hazardous Captain that ever was,
did very seldome arme himselfe: And those which amongst us neglect
them, doe not thereby much empaire their reputation. If any man
chance to be slaine for want of an armour, there are as many more
that miscary with the over-heavy burthen of their armes, and by them
are engaged, and by a counterbuffe are brused, or otherwise defeated.
For in truth to see the unweildy weight of our and their thicknesse, it
seemeth we but endevour to defend our selves, and we are rather
charged than covered by them. We have enough to doe, to endure the
burthen of them, and are so engyved and shackled in them, as if we
were to fight but with the shocke or brunt of our armes: And as if we
were as much bound to defend them, as they to shield us. *Cornelius
Tacitus* doth pleasantly quip and jest at the men of war of our ancient
Gaules, so armed, only to maintaine themselves, as they that have no
meane, either to offend or to be offended, or to raise themselves being
overthrowne. *Lucullus* seeing certaine Median men at armes, which
were in the front of *Tigranes* Army, heavily and unweildily armed, as
in an iron prison, apprehended thereby an opinion, that he might easily
defeat them, and began to charge them first, and got the victory. And
now that our Muskettiers, are in such credit, I thinke we shall have
some invention found to immure us up, that so we may be warranted
from them, and to traine us to the warres in Skonces and Bastions, as
those which our fathers caused to be carried by Elephants. A humour
farre different from that of *Scipio* the younger, who sharply reprooved
his souldiers, because they had scattered certaine Calthrops under the
water alongst a dike, by which those of the Towne that he besieged
might sally out upon him, saying; *that those which assailed, should*

resolve to enterprise and not to feare: And had some reason to feare, that this provision might secure and lull their vigilancy asleepe to guard themselves. Moreover he said to a young man, that shewed him a faire shield he had; Indeed good youth, it is a faire one, but a *Roman souldier ought to have more confidence in his right hand, than in his left.* It is onely custome that makes the burthen of our armies intolerable unto us.

> *L' usbergo in dosso haveano, e l' elmo in testa,*
> *Duo di quelli guerrier de i quali io canto.*
> *Ne notte o dì dopo ch' entraro in questa*
> *Stanza, gl' havean mai messi da canto;*
> *Che facile à portar come la vesta*
> *Era lor, perche in uso l' havean tanto.*

> ARIOSTO, *Orl.* can. xii. stan. 30.

> Cuirasse on backe did those two warriors beare,
> And caske on head, of whom I make report,
> Nor day, nor night, after they entred there,
> Had they them laid aside from their support:
> They could with ease them as a garment weare,
> For long time had they usde them in such sort.

The Emperour *Caracalla* in leading of his Army was ever wont to march afoot armed at all assaies. The Roman footmen caried not their morions, sword and target only, as for other armes (saith *Cicero*) they were so accustomed to weare them continually, that they hindered them no more than their limbs: *Arma enim, membra militis esse dicunt:* for they say armor and weapon, are a souldiers limbs. But therewithal such victuals as they should need for a fortnight and a certaine number of stakes, to make their rampards or palisadoes with; so much as weighed three score pound weight. And *Marius* his souldiers thus loden, marching in battal-array, were taught to march five leagues in five houres, yea six if need required. Their military discipline was much more laboursome than ours: So did it produce far different effects. *Scipio* the younger reforming his army in *Spaine,* appointed his souldiers to eat no meat but standing, and nothing sodden or rosted. It is worth the remembrance how a Lacedemonian souldier being in an expedition of warre, was much noted and blamed, because hee was once seene to seeke for shelter under a house: They were so hardened to endure all manner of labour and toyle, that it was counted a reprochfull infamy for a souldier to be seene under any other roofe than that of heavens-vault, in what weather soever: Were we to doe so, we should never lead our men far. *Marcellinus* a man well trained in the Roman wars, doth curiously observe the manner which the Parthians used to arme themselves, and noteth it so much the more, by how much it was far different from the Romans. They had (saith he) certaine armes so curiously enterwrought as they seemed to be made like feathers, which nothing hindered the stirring of their bodies, and yet so strong, that our darts hitting them, did rather rebound, or glance by, than hurt them (they be the scales our ancestors were so much wont to use). In another place, they had (saith he) their horses stiffe and strong, covered with thicke hides and themselves armed from head to foot, with massie iron plates so artificially contrived, that where the joynts are, there they furthered the motion, and helped the stirring. A man would have said, they had been men made of yron: For they had peeces so handsomely fitted and so lively representing the forme and parts of the face; that there was no way to wound them, but at certaine little holes before their eyes, which served to give them some light, and by certaine chinckes about their nostrils, by which they hardly drew breath.

> *Flexilis inductis hamatur lamina membris,*
> *Horribilis visu, credas simulacra moveri*
> *Ferrea, cognatoque viros spirare metallo.*
> *Par Vestitus equis, ferrata fronte minantur,*
> *Ferratosque movent securi vulneris armos.*
>
> CLAUD. *in Ruff.* ii. 358.

> The bending plate is hook't on limbes ore-spread,
> Fearefull to sight, steele images seem'd lead,
> And men to breathe in mettall with them bred,
> Like furniture for horse, with steeled head,
> They threat, and safe from wound,
> With barr'd limbs tread the ground.

Loe-heere a description, much resembling the equipage of a compleat French-man at armes, with all his bards. *Plutarke* reporteth that *Demetrius* caused two Armours to be made, each one weighing six score pounds, the one for himselfe, the other for *Alcinus*, the chiefe man of war, that was next to him, whereas all common Armours weighed but three score.

CHAPTER X

OF BOOKES

I MAKE no doubt but it shall often befall me to speake of things, which are better, and with more truth handled by such as are their crafts-masters. Here is simply an Essay of my naturall faculties, and no whit of those I have acquired. And he that shall tax me with ignorance, shall have no great victory at my hands; for hardly could I give others reason for my discourses, that give none unto my selfe, and am not well satisfied with them. He that shall make search after knowledge, let him seeke it where it is: there is nothing I professe lesse. These are but my fantasies, by which I endevour not to make things knowen, but my selfe. They may haply one day be knowen unto me, or have bin at other times, according as fortune hath brought me where they were declared or manifested. But I remember them no more. And if I be a man of some reading, yet I am a man of no remembring, I conceive no certainty, except it bee to give notice, how farre the knowledge I have of it, doth now reach. Let no man busie himselfe about the matters, but on the fashion I give them. Let that which I borrow be survaied, and then tell me whether I have made good choice of ornaments, to beautifie and set foorth the invention, which ever comes from mee. For, I make others to relate (not after mine owne fantasie, but as it best falleth out) what I cannot so well expresse, either through unskill of language, or want of judgement. I number not my borrowings, but I weigh them. And if I would have made their number to prevaile, I would have had twice as many. They are all, or almost all of so famous and ancient names, that me thinks they sufficiently name themselves without mee. If in reasons, comparisons and arguments, I transplant any into my soile, or confound them with mine owne, I purposely conceale the Author, thereby to bridle the rashnesse of these hastie censures, that are so head long cast upon all manner of compositions, namely young writings, of men yet living; and in vulgare, that admit all the world to talke of them, and which seemeth to convince the conception and publike designe alike. I will have them to give *Plutarke* a bob upon mine owne lips, and vex themselves, in wronging *Seneca* in mee. My weakenesse must be hidden under such great credits. I will love him that shall trace, or unfeather me; I meane through clearenesse of judgement, and by the onely distinction of the force and beautie of my Discourses. For my selfe, who for want of memorie, am ever to seeke, how to trie and refine them, by the knowledge of their country, knowe perfectly, by measuring mine owne strength, that my soyle is no way capable, of some over-pretious flowers, that therin I find set, and that all the fruits of my encrease could not make it amends. This am I bound to answer-for, if I hinder my selfe, if there be either vanitie, or fault in my Discourses, that I perceive not or am not able to discerne, if they be shewed me. For, many faults doe often escape our eyes; but the infirmitie of judgement consisteth in not being able to perceive them, when another discovereth them unto us. Knowledge and truth may be in us without judgement, and we may have judgement without them: Yea, the acknowledgement of ignorance, is one of the best and surest testimonies of judgement that I can finde. I have no other Sergeant of band to marshall my rapsodies, than fortune. And looke how my humours or conceites present them-selves, so I shuffle them up. Sometimes they prease out thicke and three-fold, and other times they come out languishing one by one. I will have my naturall and ordinarie pace seene as loose, and as shuffling as it is. As I am, so I goe on plodding. And besides, these are matters, that a man may not be ignorant of, and rashly and casually to speake of them. I would wish to have a more perfect understanding of things, but I will not purchase it so deare, as it cost. My intention is to passe the remainder of my life quietly, and not laboriously, in rest, and not in care. There is nothing I will trouble or vex my selve about, no not for Science it selfe, what esteeme soever it be-of. I doe not search and tosse over Bookes, but for an honester recreation to please, and pastime to delight my selfe: or if I studie, I onely endevour to find out the knowledge that teacheth or handleth the knowledge of my selfe, and which may instruct me how to die well, and how to live well.

> *Has meus ad metas sudet oportet equus.*
> PROPERT. iv. *El.* i. 70.

My horse must sweating runne,
That this goale may be wonne.

If in reading I fortune to meet with any difficult points, I fret not my selfe about them, but after I have given them a charge or two, I leave them as I found them. Should I earnestly plod upon them I should loose both time and my selfe; for I have a skipping wit. What I see not at the first view, I shall lesse see it, if I opinionate my selfe upon it. I doe nothing without blithnesse; and an over obstinate continuation and plodding contention, doth dazle, dul and weary the same: My sight is thereby confounded and diminished. I must therefore withdraw-it, and at fittes goe to it againe. Even as to judge well of the lustre of scarlet we are taught to cast our eyes over it, in running it over by divers glances, sodaine glimpses, and reiterated reprisings. If one booke seeme tedious unto me, I take another, which I follow not with any earnestnesse, except it be at such houres as I am idle, or that I am weary with doing nothing. I am not greatly affected to new books, because ancient Authors are in my judgement more full and pithy: nor am I much addicted to Greeke books, forasmuch as my understanding can [not] well rid his worke with a childish and apprentise intelligence. Amongst moderne bookes meerly pleasant, I esteeme *Bocace* his *Decameron, Rabelais,* and the kisses of *John* the second (if they may be placed under this title) worth the paines-taking to reade them. As for *Amadis* and such like trash of writings, they had never the credit so much as to allure my youth to delight in them. This I will say more, either boldly or rashly, that this old and heavie-pased minde of mine, will no more be pleased with *Aristotle,* or tickled with good *Ovid:* his facility, and quaint inventions, which heretofore have so ravished me, they can now a dayes scarcely entertaine me. I speake my minde freely of all things, yea of such as peradventure exceed my sufficiencie, and that no way I hold to be of my jurisdiction. What my conceit is of them, is also to manifest the proportion of my insight, and not the measure of things. If at any time I finde my selfe distasted of *Platoes Axiochus*, as of a forceles worke, due regard had to such an Author, my judgement doth nothing beleeve it selfe: It is not so fond-hardy, or selfe-conceited, as it durst dare to oppose it selfe against the authority of so many other famous ancient judgements, which he reputeth his regents and masters, and with whom he had rather erre. He chafeth with, and condemneth himselfe, either to rely on the super-ficiall sense, being unable to pierce into the centre, or to view the thing by some false lustre. He is pleased only to warrant himselfe from trouble and unrulinesse: As for weaknesse he acknowledgeth and in-geniously avoweth the same. He thinkes to give a just interpretation to the apparences which his conception presents unto him, but they are shallow and imperfect. Most of *Æsopes* fables have divers senses, and severall interpretations: Those which *Mythologize* them, chuse some kinde of colour well-suting with the fable; but for the most part, it is no other than the first and superficiall glosse: There are others more quicke, more sinnowie, more essentiall and more internall, into which they could never penetrate; and thus thinke I with them. But to follow my course; I have ever deemed that in Poesie, *Virgil, Lucretius, Catullus,* and *Horace,* doe doubtles by far hold the first ranke: and especially *Virgil* in his *Georgiks,* which I esteeme to be the most accomplished peece of worke of Poesie: In comparison of which one may easily dis-cerne, that there are some passages in the *Æneidos,* to which the Author (had he lived) would no doubt have given some review or correction: The fifth booke whereof is (in my mind) the most absolutely perfect. I also love *Lucan,* and willingly read him, not so much for his stile, as for his owne worth, and truth of his opinion and judgement. As for good *Terence,* I allow the quaintnesse and grace of his Latine tongue, and judge him wonderfull conceited and apt, lively to represent the motions and passions of the minde, and the condition of our manners: our actions make me often remember him. I can never reade him so often, but still I discover some new grace and beautie in him. Those that lived about *Virgils* time, complained that some would compare *Lucretius* unto him. I am of opinion, that verily it is an unequall com-parison; yet can I hardly assure my selfe in this opinion whensoever I finde my selfe entangled in some notable passage of *Lucretius*. If they were moved at this comparison, what would they say now of the fond, hardy and barbarous stupiditie of those which now adayes compare *Ariosto* unto him? Nay what would *Ariosto* say of it himselfe?

> *O sæclum insipiens et infacetum.*
> CATUL. *Epig.* xl. 8.

> O age that hath no wit,
> And small conceit in it.

I thinke our ancestors had also more reason to cry out against those that blushed not to equall *Plautus* unto *Terence* (who makes more shew to be a Gentleman) than *Lucretius* unto *Virgil*. This one thing doth greatly advantage the estimation and preferring of *Terence*, that the father of the Roman eloquence, of men of his quality doth so often make mention of him; and the censure, which the chiefe Judge of the Roman Poets giveth of his companion. It hath often come unto my minde, how such as in our dayes give themselves to composing of comedies (as the Italians who are very happy in them) employ three or foure arguments of *Terence* and *Plautus* to make up one of theirs. In one onely comedy they will huddle up five or six of *Bocaces* tales. That which makes them so to charge themselves with matter, is the distrust they have of their owne sufficiencie, and that they are not able to undergoe so heavie a burthen with their owne strength. They are forced to finde a body on which they may rely and leane themselves: and wanting matter of their owne wherewith to please us, they will have the story or tale to busie and ammuse us: where as in my [Author] it is cleane contrary: The elegancies, the perfections and ornaments of his manner of speech, make us neglect and lose the longing for his subject. His quaintnesse and grace doe still retaine us to him. He is every where pleasantly conceited,

> *Liquidus puroque simillimus amni.*
> HOR. ii. *Epist*. ii. 120.

So clearely-neate, so neately-cleare,
As he a fine-pure River were,

and doth so replenish our minde with his graces, that we forget those of the fable. The same consideration drawes me somewhat further. I perceive that good and ancient Poets have shunned the affectation and enquest, not only of fantasticall, new fangled, Spagniolized, and Petrarchisticall elevations, but also of more sweet and sparing inventions, which are the ornament of all the Poeticall workes of succeeding ages. Yet is there no competent Judge, that findeth them wanting in those Ancient ones, and that doth not much more admire that smoothly equall neatnesse, continued sweetnesse, and flourishing comeliness of *Catullus* his Epigrams, than all the sharpe quips, and witty girds, wherewith *Martiall* doth whet and embellish the conclusions of his. It is the same reason I spake of erewhile, as *Martiall* of himselfe. *Minus illi ingenio laborandum fuit, in cuius locum materia successerat* (MART. *præf*. viii.). *He needed the lesse worke with his wit, in place whereof matter came in supply;* The former without being moved or pricked cause themselves to be heard lowd enough: they have matter to laugh at every where, and need not tickle themselves; where as these must have foraine helpe: according as they have lesse spirit, they must have more body. They leape on horse-backe: because they are not sufficiently strong in their legs to march on foot. Even as in our dances, those base conditioned men that keepe dancing-schooles because they are unfit to represent the port and decencie of our nobilitie, endevour to get commendation by dangerous lofty trickes, and other strange tumbler-like friskes and motions. And some Ladies make a better shew of their countenances in those dances, wherein are divers changes, cuttings, turnings, and agitations of the body, than in some dances of state and gravity, where they need but simply to tread a naturall measure, represent an unaffected cariage, and their ordinary grace; And as I have also seene some excellent Lourdans, or Clownes attired in their ordinary worky-day clothes, and with a common homely countenance, affoord us all the pleasure that may be had from their art: Prentises and learners that are not of so high a forme, to besmeare their faces, to disguise themselves, and in motions to counterfeit strange visages, and antickes, to enduce us to laughter. This my conception is no where better discerned, than in the comparison betweene *Virgils Æneidos*, and *Orlando Furioso*. The first is seene to soare aloft with full-spread wings, and with so high and strong a pitch, ever following his point; the other faintly to hover and flutter from tale to tale, and as it were skipping from bough to bough, alwayes distrusting his owne wings, except it be for some short flight, and for feare his strength and breath should faile him, to sit downe at every fields-end.

> *Excursusque breves tentat.*
> VIRG. *Æn.* iv. 194.

> Out-lopes sometimes he doth assay,
> But very short, and as he may.

Loe here then, concerning this kinde of subjects, what Authors please me best: As for my other lesson, which somewhat more mixeth profit with pleasure, whereby I learne to range my opinions, and addresse my conditions; the Bookes that serve me thereunto, are *Plutarke* (since he spake French,) and *Seneca;* Both have this excellent commodity for my humour, that the knowledge I seeke in them, is there so scatteringly and loosely handled, that whosoever readeth them is not tied to plod long upon them, whereof I am uncapable. And so are *Plutarkes* little workes, and *Senecas* Epistles, which are the best and most profitable parts of their writings. It is no great matter to draw mee to them, and I leave them where I list. For, they succeed not, and depend not one of another. Both jumpe and suit together, in most true and profitable opinions: And fortune brought them both into the world in one age. Both were Tutors unto two Roman Emperours: Both were strangers, and came from farre Countries; both rich and mighty in their common-wealth, and in credit with their masters. Their instruction is the prime and creame of Philosophy, and presented with a plaine, unaffected, and pertinent fashion. *Plutarke* is more uniforme and constant; *Seneca* more waving and diverse. This doth labour, force, and extend himselfe, to arme and strengthen vertue against weaknesse, feare, and vitious desires; the other seem-eth nothing so much to feare their force or attempt, and in a manner scorneth to hasten or change his pace about them, and to put himselfe upon his guard. *Plutarkes* opinions are Platonicall, gentle and accom-modable unto civill societie: *Senecaes* Stoicall and Epicurian, further from common use, but in my conceit, more proper, particular, and more solid. It appeareth in *Seneca,* that he somewhat inclineth and yeeldeth to the tyrannie of the Emperors which were in his daies; for, I verily beleeve, it is with a forced judgement, he condemneth the cause of those noblie-minded murtherers of *Cæsar: Plutarke* is every where free and open-hearted; *Seneca,* full-fraught with points and sallies, *Plutarke* stuft with matters. The former doth move and enflame you more; the latter, content, please, and pay you better: This doth guide you, the other drive you on. As for *Cicero,* of all his works, those that treat of Philosophie (namely morall) are they which best serve my turne, and square with my intent. But boldly to confesse the trueth, (For, *Since the bars of impudencie were broken down, all curbing is taken away*) his manner of writing semeth verie tedious unto me, as doth all such-like stuffe. For, his prefaces, definitions, divisions, and Etymologies, consume the greatest part of his Works; whatsoever quick, wittie, and pithie conceit is in him, is surcharged, and confounded by those his long and far-fetcht preambles. If I bestow but one houre in reading him, which is much for me; and let me call to minde what substance, or juice I have drawne from him, for the most part, I find nothing but wind and ostentation in him: for he is not yet come to the arguments, which make for his purpose, and reasons that properly concerne the knot or pith I seek-after. These Logicall and Aristotelian ordinances are not availfull for me, who onely endevour to become more wise and sufficient, and not more wittie or eloquent. I would have one begin with the last point: I under-stand sufficiently what death and voluptuousnesse are: let not a man busie himselfe to anatomize them. At the first reading of a Booke, I seeke for good and solid reasons, that may instruct me how to sus-taine their assaults. It is neither grammaticall subtilties, nor logicall quiddities, nor the wittie contexture of choice words, or arguments, and syllogismes, that will serve my turne. I like those discourses that give the first charge to the strongest part of the doubt; his are but flourishes, and languish every where. They are good for Schooles, at the barre, or for Orators and Preachers, where we may slumber: and though we wake a quarter of an houre after, we may find and trace him soone enough. Such a manner of speech is fit for those Judges, that a man would corrupt by hooke or crooke, by right or wrong, or for children and the common people, unto whom a man must tell all, and see what the event will be. I would not have a man go about, and labour by circumlocutions, to induce and win me to attention, and that (as our Herolds or Criers do) they shall ring out their words.

Now heare me, now listen, or ho-yes. The Romanes in their Religion were wont to say, *Hoc age;* which in ours we say, *Sursum corda.* These are so many lost words for me. I come readie prepared from my house. I need no allurement nor sawce; my stomacke is good enough to digest raw meat: And whereas with these preparatives and flourishes, or preambles, they thinke to sharpen my taste, or stir my stomacke, they cloy and make it wallowish. Shall the priviledge of times excuse me from this sacrilegious boldnesse, to deeme *Platoes* Dialogismes to be as languishing, by over-filling and stuffing his matter? And to bewaile the time that a man, who had so many thousands of things to utter, spends about so many, so long, so vaine, and idle interloqutions, and preparatives? My ignorance shall better excuse me, in that I see nothing in the beautie of his language. I generally enquire after Bookes, that use sciences, and not after such as institute them. The two first, and *Plinie,* with others of their ranke, have no *Hoc age* in them, they will have to doe with men, that have forewarned themselves; or if they have, it is a materiall and substantiall *Hoc age,* and that hath his bodie apart. I likewise love to read the Epistles and *ad Atticum,* not onely because they containe a most ample instruction of the Historie, and affaires of his times, but much more because in them I descrie his private humours. For, (as I have said elsewhere) I am wonderfull curious, to discover and know, the minde, the soule, the genuine disposition, and naturall judgement of my Authors. A man ought to judge their sufficiencie, and not their customes, nor them by the shew of their writings, which they set forth on this worlds Theatre. I have sorrowed a thousand times, that ever we lost the booke, that *Brutus* writ of Vertue. *Oh it is a goodly thing to learne the Theorike of such as understand the practice well.* But forsomuch as the Sermon is one thing, and the Preacher an other: I love as much to see *Brutus* in *Plutarke,* as in himselfe: I would rather make choice to know certainly, what talke he had in his Tent with some of his familiar friends, the night foregoing the battel, than the speech he made the morrow after to his Armie: and what he did in his chamber or closet, than what in the Senate or market place. As for *Cicero,* I am of the common judgement, that besides learning, there was no exquisite excellencie in him: He was a good Citizen, of an honest-gentle nature, as are commonly fat and burly men; for so was he: But to speake truely of him, full of ambitious vanitie and remisse nicenesse. And I know not well how to excuse him, in that hee deemed his Poesie worthy to be published. It is no great imperfection to make bad verses, but it is an imperfection in him, that he never perceived how unworthy they were of the glorie of his name. Concerning his eloquence, it is beyond all comparison, and I verily beleeve, that none shall ever equall it. *Cicero* the younger, who resembled his father in nothing, but in name, commanding in *Asia,* chanced one day to have many strangers at his board, and amongst others, one *Cæstius* sitting at the lower end, as the manner is to thrust in at great mens tables: *Cicero* inquired of one of his men what he was, who told him his name, but he dreaming on other matters, and having forgotten what answere his man made him, asked him his name twice or thrice more: the servant, because he would not be troubled to tell him one thing so often, and by some circumstance make him to know him better, It is, said he, the same *Cæstius*, of whom some have told you, that in respect of his owne, maketh no accompt of your fathers eloquence: *Cicero* being suddainly mooved, commaunded the said poore *Cæstius* to be presently taken from the table, and well whipt in his presence: Lo-heere an uncivill and barbarous host. Even amongst those, which (all things considered) have deemed his eloquence matchlesse and incomparable others there have been, who have not spared to note some faults in it: As great *Brutus* said, that it was an eloquence, broken, halting, and disjoynted, *fractam et elumbem:* Incoherent and sinnowlesse. Those Orators that lived about his age, reproved also in him the curious care he had of a certaine long cadence, at the end of his clauses, and noted these words, *Esse videatur,* which he so often useth. As for me, I rather like a cadence that falleth shorter, cut like Iambikes: yet doth he sometimes confound his numbers; but it is seldome: I have especially observed this one place. *Ego vero me minus diu senem esse mallem, quam esse senem, antequam essem* (Cic. *De Senect.*). *But I had rather, not be an old man so long as I might be, than to be old before I should be.* Historians are my right hand; for they are pleasant and easie: and therewithall, the man with whom I desire generally to be acquainted, may more lively and perfectly be discovered in them, than in any other composition: the varietie and truth of his inward conditions, in grosse and by retale: the diversitie of the meanes of his collection and composing, and of the accidents that threaten him. Now, those that write of mens lives, forasmuch as they ammuse and busie themselves more about counsels than events, more about that which commeth from within, than that which appeareth outward; they are fittest for me: And that's the reason why *Plutarke* above all in that kind, doth best please me. Indeed I am not a little grieved that we have not a dozen of *Laertii,* or that he is not more knowne, or better understood: for, I am not lesse curious to know the fortunes and lives of these great masters of the world, than to understand the diversitie of their decrees and conceits. In this kind of studie of Historie, a man must, without distinction, tosse and turne over all sorts of Authors, both old and new, both French and others, if he will learne the things they so diversly treat-of. But me thinks that *Cæsar* above all doth singularly deserve to be studied, not onely for the understanding of the Historie, as of himselfe; so much perfection and excellencie is there in him more than in others, although *Salust* be reckoned one of the number. Verily I read that Author with a little

more reverence and respect, than commonly men reade profane and
humane Workes: sometimes considering him by his actions, and wonders of his greatnesse, and other times waighing the puritie and
inimitable polishing and elegancie of his tongue, which (as *Cicero*
saith) hath not onely exceeded all Historians, but haply *Cicero* himselfe: with such sinceritie in his judgement. Speaking of his enemies,
that except the false colours, wherewith he goeth about to cloake his
bad cause, and the corruption and filthinesse of his pestilent ambition, I am perswaded there is nothing in him to be found fault-with:
and that he hath been over-sparing to speak of himselfe: for, so many
notable and great things could never be executed by him, unlesse he
had put more of his owne unto them, than he setteth downe. I love
those Historians that are either verie simple, or most excellent. The
simple who have nothing of their owne to adde unto the storie, and
have but the care and diligence to collect whatsoever come unto their
knowledge, and sincerely and faithfully to register all things, without
choice or culling, by the naked truth leave our judgement more entire,
and better satisfied.

Such amongst others (for example sake) plaine and well-meaning
Froisard, who in his enterprize, hath marched with so free and genuine
a puritie, that having committed some over-sight, he is neither ashamed
to acknowledge, nor afraid to correct the same, wheresoever he hath
either notice or warning of it: and who representeth unto us the
diversitie of the newes then currant, and the different reports, that
were made unto him. The subject of an historie should be naked,
bare, and formelesse; each man according to his capacitie or understanding may reap commoditie out of it. The curious and most excellent have the sufficiencie to cull and chuse that, which is worthie to
be knowne, and may select of two relations, that which is most likely:
of the condition of Princes, and of their humours, therby they conclude
their counsels, and attribute convenient words unto them: they have
reason to assume authoritie unto them, to direct and shapen our
beliefe unto theirs. But truly that belongs not to many. Such as are
betweene both (which is the most common fashion) it is they that
spoile all; they will needs chew our meat for us, and take upon them
a law to judge, and by consequence to square and encline the storie
according to their fantasie; for, where the judgement bendeth one
way, a man cannot chuse but wrest and turne his narration that way.
They undertake to chuse things worthy to bee knowne, and now
and then conceal either a word or a secret action from us, which
would much better instruct us: omitting such things as they understand not, as incredible: and haply such matters, as they know not
how to declare, either in good Latin, or tolerable French. Let them
boldly enstall their eloquence, and discourse: Let them censure at
their pleasure, but let them also give us leave to judge after them:
And let them neither alter nor dispence by their abridgements and

choice, anything belonging to the substance of the matter; but let them rather send it pure and entire with all her dimensions unto us. Most commonly (as chiefly in our age) this charge of writing histories is committed unto base, ignorant, and mechanicall kind of people, only for this consideration that they can speak well; as if we sought to learne the Grammer of them; and they have some reason, being only hyred to that end, and publishing nothing but their tittle-tattle to aime at nothing else so much. Thus with store of choice and quaint words, and wyre-drawne phrases they huddle up, and make a hodge-pot of a laboured contexture of the reports, which they gather in the market-places, or such other assemblies. *The only good histories are those that are written by such as commanded, or were imploied themselves in weighty affaires, or that were partners in the conduct of them, or that at least have had the fortune to manage others of like qualitie.* Such in a manner are all the Græcians and Romans. For, many eye-witnesses having written of one same subject (as it hapned in those times, when Greatnesse and Knowledge did commonly meet) if any fault or oversight have past them, it must be deemed exceeding light, and upon some doubtfull accident. *What may a man expect at a Phisitians hand, that discourseth of warre, or of a bare Scholler, treating of Princes secret designes?* If we shall but note the religion, which the Romans had in that, we need no other example: *Asinius Polio* found some mistaking or oversight in *Cæsars* Commentaries, whereinto he was falne, only because he could not possiblie oversee all things with his owne eyes, that hapned in his Armie, but was faine to relie on the reports of particular men, who often related untruths unto him; or else because he had not been curiously advertised, and distinctly enformed by his Lieutenants and Captaines, of such matters as they in his absence had managed or effected. Whereby may be seen, that *nothing is so hard, or so uncertaine to be found-out, as the certaintie of a Truth,* sithence no man can put any assured confidence concerning the truth of a battel, neither in the knowledge of him, that was Generall, or commanded over it, nor in the souldiers that fought, of any thing, that hath hapned amongst them; except after the manner of a strict point of law, the severall witnesses are brought and examined face to face, and that all matters be nicely and thorowly sifted by the objects and trials of the successe of every accident. Verily the knowledge we have of our own affaires is much more barren and feeble. But this hath sufficiently been handled by *Bodine,* and agreeing with my conception. Somewhat to aid the weaknesse of my memorie, and to assist her great defects; for it hath often been my chance to light upon bookes, which I supposed to be new, and never to have read, which I had not understanding diligently read and run-over many yeares before, and all bescribled with my notes: I have a while since accustomed my selfe, to note at the end of my booke (I meane such as I purpose to read but once) the time I made an end to read it, and to set downe what censure or judgement I gave of it; that so, it may at least, at another time represent unto my mind, the aire and generall Idea, I had conceived of the Author in reading him. I will here set downe the Copie of some of mine annotations, and especially what I noted upon my *Guicciardine* about ten yeares since: (For what language soever my bookes speake unto me, I speake unto them in mine owne.) He is a diligent Historiographer, and from whom in my conceit, a man may as exactly learne the truth of such affaires as passed in his time, as of any other writer whatsoever: and the rather because himselfe hath been an Actor of most part of them, and in verie honourable place. There is no signe or apparance, that ever he disguised or coloured any matter, either through hatred, malice, favour, or vanitie; whereof the free and impartiall judgements he giveth of great men, and namely of those by whom he had been advanced or imployed in his important charges, as of Pope *Clement* the seaventh, beareth undoubted testimonie. Concerning the parts wherewith he most goeth about to prevaile which are his digressions and discourses, many of them are verie excellent, and enriched with faire ornaments, but he hath too much pleased himselfe in them: for, endevouring to omit nothing that might be spoken, having so full and large a subject, and almost infinite, he proveth somewhat languishing, and giveth a tast of a kind of scholasticall tedious babling. Moreover, I have noted this, that of so severall and divers armies, successes, and effects he judgeth of; of so many and variable motives, alterations, and coun-sels, that he relateth, he never referreth any one unto vertue, religion, or conscience: as if they were all extinguished and banished the world: and of all actions, how glorious soever in apparance they be of them-selves, he doth ever impute the cause of them, to some vicious and blame-worthie occasion, or to some commoditie and profit. It is im-possible to imagine, that amongst so infinite a number of actions, whereof he judgeth, some one have not been produced and compassed by way of reason. No corruption could ever possesse men so univer-sally, but that some one must of necessity escape the contagion; which makes me to feare, he hath had some distaste or blame in his passion, and it hath haply fortuned, that he hath judged or esteemed of others according to himselfe. In my *Philip de Comines*, there is this: In him you shall find a pleasing-sweet, and gently-gliding speech, fraught with a purely-sincere simplicitie, his narration pure and unaffected, and wherein the Authors unspotted-good meaning doth evidently appeare, void of all manner of vanitie or ostentation speaking of him-selfe, and free from all affection or envie speaking of others: his dis-courses and perswasions, accompanied more with a well-meaning zeale, and meere veritie, than with any laboured and exquisit sufficiencie, and all-through, with gravitie and authoritie, representing a man well-borne, and brought up in high negotiations. Upon the memories and historie of Monsieur du *Bellay:* It is ever a well-pleasing thing, to see matters written by those, that have assaid how, and in what manner they ought to be directed and managed: yet can it not be denied, but that in both these Lords, there will manifestly appeare a great declination from a free libertie of writing, which clearely shineth in ancient writers of their kind: as in the Lord of *Jonville,* familiar unto Saint *Lewis, Eginard,* Chancellor unto *Charlemaine;* and of more fresh memorie in *Philip de Comines.* This is rather a declamation or pleading for king *Francis* against the Emperour *Charles* the fifth, than an Historie. I will not beleeve, they have altered or changed any thing concerning the generalitie of matters, but rather to wrest and turne the judgement of the events, many times against reason, to our advantage, and to omit whatsoever they supposed, to be doubtfull or ticklish in their masters life: they have made profession of it: witnesse the recoylings of the Lords of *Momorancy* and *Byron,* which therein are forgotten; and which is more, you shall not so much as find the name of the Ladie of Estampes mentioned at all. A man may sometimes colour, and haply hide secret actions, but absolutely to conceal that which all the world knoweth, and especially such things as have drawne-on publike effects, and of such consequence, it is an inexcusable defect, or as I may say unpardonable oversight. To conclude, whosoever desireth to have perfect information and knowledge of King *Francis* the first, and of the things hapned in his time, let him addresse himselfe elsewhere, if he will give any credit unto me. The profit he may reap here, is by the particular [deduction] of the battels and exploits of warre, wherein these Gentlemen were present; some privie conferences, speechs, or secret actions of some Princes, that then lived, and the practices managed, or negotiations directed by the Lord of *Langeay,* in whom doubtlesse are verie many things, well-worthie to be knowne, and diverse discourses not vulgare.

CHAPTER XI

OF CRUELTIE

ME thinks vertue is another manner of thing, and much more noble than the inclinations unto goodnesse, which in us are ingendered. Mindes well borne, and directed by themselves, follow one same path, and in their actions represent the same visage, that the vertuous doe. But vertue importeth, and soundeth somewhat I wot not what greater and more active, than by an happy complexion, gently and peaceably, to suffer it selfe to be led or drawne, to follow reason. He that through a naturall facilitie, and genuine mildnesse, should neglect or contemne injuries received, should no doubt performe a rare action, and worthy commendation: But he who being toucht and stung to the quicke, with any wrong or offence received, should arme himselfe with reason against this furiously-blind desire of revenge, and in the end after a great conflict, yeeld himselfe master over-it, should doubtlesse doe much more. The first should doe well, the other vertuously: the one action might be termed goodnesse, the other vertue. For, *It seemeth, that the verie name of vertue presupposeth difficultie, and inferreth resistance, and cannot well exercise it selfe without an enemie.* It is peradventure the reason why we call God good, mightie, liberall, and just, but we terme him not vertuous. His workes are all voluntarie, unforced, and without compulsion. Of Philosophers, not onely Stoicks, but also Epicurians (which endearing I borrow of the common-received opinion, which is false whatsoever the nimble saying or wittie quipping of *Arcesilaus* implieth, who answered the man that upbraided him, how divers men went from his schoole to the Epicurian, but none came from thence to him: I easily beleeve-it (said he) for, *Of cocks are many capons made, but no man could ever yet make a cocke of a capon.* For truly, in constancie, and rigor of opinions, and strictnesse of precepts, the Epicurian Sect doth in no sort yeeld to the Stoicke. And a Stoicke acknowledging a better faith, than those disputers, who to contend with *Epicurus,* and make sport with him, make him to infer and say what he never meant, wresting and wyre-drawing his words to a contrarie sense, arguing and silogizing by the Grammarians privilege, another meaning, by the manner of his speech, and another opinion, than that they know he had, either in his minde, or manners, saith, that he left to be an Epicurian, for this one consideration amongst others, that he findeth their pitch to be over-high and inaccessible: *Et ii qui φιλήδονοι vocantur, sunt φιλόκαλοι et φιλοδίκαιοι omnésque virtutes et colunt et retinent* (SEN. *Epist.* xiii.). *And those that are called lovers of pleasure, are lovers of honestie and justice, and doe both reverence and retaine all sorts of vertue.*) Of Stoicke and Epicurian Philosophers, I say, there are divers, who have judged, that it was not sufficient to have the minde well placed, well ordered, and well disposed unto vertue; it was not enough to have our resolutions and discourse beyond all the affronts and checks of fortune; but that moreover, it was verie requisite, to seeke for occasions, whereby a man might come to the triall of it: They will diligently quest and seek out for paine, smart, necessitie, want, and contempt, that so they may combat them, and keep their minde in breath: *Multum sibi adjicit virtus lacessitæ. Vertue provoked addes much to it selfe.* It is one of the reasons why *Epaminondas* (who was of a third sect) by a verie lawfull way refuseth some riches, fortune had put into his hands, to the end (as he saith) he might have cause to strive and resist povertie, in which want and extremitie he ever continued after.

Socrates did in my minde more undantedly enure himselfe to this humour, maintaining for his exercise the peevish frowardnesse of his wife, than which no essay can be more vex-full, and is a continuall fighting at the sharpe. *Metellus* of all the Romane Senators (he onely having undertaken with the power of vertue, to endure the violence of *Saturninus Tribune* of the people in *Rome,* who by maine force went about to have a most unjust law passe in favor of the Communaltie: by which opposition, having incurred all the capital paines, that *Saturninus* had imposed on such as should refuse it) intertained those that led him to the place of execution, with such speeches: That *to doe evill was a thing verie easie, and too demissely base: and to doe well where was no danger, was a common thing; but to doe well, where was both perill and opposition, was the peculiar office of a man of vertue.* These words of *Metellus* doe clearely represent unto us, what I would have verified; which is, that *vertue rejecteth facilitie to be her companion:* And that an easefull, pleasant, and declining way, by which the regular steps of a good inclination of nature, are directed, is not the way of true vertue. She requireth a craggie, rough, and thornie way; She would either have strange difficulties to wrestle withall (as that of *Metellus*) by whose meanes fortune her selfe is pleased to breake the roughnesse of his course; or inward encombrances, as the disordinate appetites and imperfections of our condition bring unto her. Hitherto I have come at good ease; but at the end of this discourse, one thing commeth into my minde, which is, that the soule of *Socrates,* which is [absolutely] the perfectest that ever come to my knowledge, would, according to my accompt, prove a soule deserving but little commendation: For, I can perceive no manner of violence or vicious concupiscence in him: I can imagine no manner of difficultie or compulsion in the whole course of his vertue. I know his reason so powerfull, and so absolute mistresse over him, that she can never give him way to any vicious desire, and will not suffer it so much as to breed in him. To a vertue so exquisit, and so high-raised as his is, I can perswade nothing. Me thinkes I see it march with a victorious and triumphant pace, in pompe, and at ease, without let or disturbance. If vertue cannot shine but by resisting contrarie appetites, shall we then say, it cannot passe without the assistance of vice, and oweth him this, that by his meanes it attaineth to honour and credit? What should also betide of that glorious and generous Epicurian voluptuousnesse, that makes accompt, effeminately to pamper vertue in her lap, and there wantonly to entertaine it, allowing it for her recreation, shame, reproch, agues, povertie, death, and tortures? If I presuppose, that perfect vertue is knowne by combating sorrow, and patiently under-going paine, by tolerating the fits and agonies of the gout, without stirring out of his place; if for a necessarie object, I appoint her sharpnesse and difficultie; what shall become of that vertue, which hath attained so high a degree, as it doth not onely despise all manner of paine, but rather rejoyceth at-it, and when a strong fit of the collike shall assaile-it, to cause it selfe to be tickled; as that is which the Epicurians have established,

and whereof divers amongst them have by their actions left most
certaine proofes unto us? As also others have, whom in effect I finde
to have exceeded the verie rules of their discipline: witnesse *Cato*
the yonger; when I see him die, tearing and mangling his entrails; I
cannot simply content my selfe to beleeve, that at that time, he had
his soule wholy exempted from all trouble, or free from vexation:
I cannot imagine, he did onely maintaine himselfe in this march or
course, which the rules of the Stoike sect had ordained unto him,
setled, without some alteration or motion, and impassibilitie. There
was, in my conceit, in this mans vertue overmuch cheerefulnesse, and
youthfulnesse to stay there. I verily beleeve, he felt a kind of pleasure
and sensualitie in so noble an action, and that therein he more pleased
himselfe, than in any other, he ever performed in his life. *Sic abiit è
vita, ut causam moriendi nactum se esse gauderet* (Cic. *Tusc. Qu.* i.).
*So departed he his life, that he rejoyced to have found an occasion
of death.* I doe so constantly beleeve-it, that I make a doubt, whether
he would have had the occasion of so noble an exploit taken from
him. And if the goodnesse which induced him to embrace publike
commodities more than his owne, did not bridle me, I should easily
fall into this opinion, that he thought himselfe greatly beholding unto
fortune, to have put his vertue unto so noble a triall, and to have
favoured that robber, to tread the ancient libertie of his Countrie
under foot. In which action me thinks I read a kinde of unspeakable
joy in his minde, and a motion of extraordinarie pleasure, joyned to
a manlike voluptuousnesse, at which time it beheld the worthinesse,
and considered the generositie and haughtinesse of his enterprise,

> *Deliberata morte ferocior.*
> Hor. i. *Od.* xxxvii. 29. Cleopatra.

> Then most in fiercenesse did he passe
> When he of death resolved was.

not urged or set-on by any hope of glorie, as the popular and effeminate
judgements have judged: For, that consideration is over base, to touch
so generous, so haughtie, and so constant a heart; but for the beautie
of the thing it selfe in it selfe, which he, who managed all the springs,
and directed all the wards thereof, saw much more clearer, and in it's
perfection, than we can doe. Philosophie hath done me a pleasure
to judge, that so honorable an action, had been undecently placed
in any other life, than in *Catoes,* and that onely unto his it appertained to make such an end. Therefore did he with reason perswade
both his sonne, and the Senators that accompanied him, to provide
otherwise for themselves. *Catoni quum incredibilem natura tribuisset
gravitatem, eamque ipse perpetua constantia roboravisset, semperque
in proposito consilio permansisset: moriendum potius quam tyranni
vultus aspiciendus erat. Whereas nature had affoorded Cato an incredible gravitie, and he had strengthned it by continuall constancie,*

*and ever had stood firme in his purposed desseignes, rather to die
than behold the Tyrants face.* Each death should be such as the life
hath been. By dying we become no other than we were. I ever interpret a mans death by his life. And if a man shall tell me of any one
undanted in apparance, joyned unto a weake life; I imagine it to
proceed of some weake cause, and sutable to his life. The ease therefore of his death, and the facilitie he had acquired by the vigor of
his minde, shall we say, it ought to abate something of the lustre of
his vertue? And which of those, that have their spirits touched, be
it never so little, with the true tincture of Philosophie, can content
himselfe to imagine *Socrates,* onely, free from feare and passion, in
the accident of his imprisonment, of his fetters, and of his condemnation? And who doth not perceive in him, not onely constancie
and resolution (which were ever his ordinarie qualities) but also a
kinde of I wot not what new contentment, and carelesse rejoycing
in his last behaviour, and discourses? By the startling at the pleasure,
which he feeleth in clawing of his legges, after his fetters were taken-
off; doth he not manifestly declare an equall glee and joy in his soule,
for being rid of his former incommodities, and entring into the knowledge of things to come? *Cato* shall pardon me (if he please) his death
is more tragicall, and further extended, whereas this in a certaine
manner is more faire and glorious. *Aristippus* answered those, that
bewailed the same; when I die, I pray the Gods send me such a death.
A man shall plainly perceive in the minds of these two men, and of
such as imitate them (for I make a question whether ever they could
be matched) so perfect an habitude unto vertue, that it was even
converted into their complexion. It is no longer a painfull vertue,
nor by the ordinances of reason, for the maintaining of which, their
minde must be strengthned: It is the verie essence of their soule; it is
her naturall and ordinarie habit. They have made it such, by a long
exercise and observing the rules and precepts of Philosophie, having
lighted upon a faire and rich nature. Those vicious passions, which
breed in us, finde no entrance in them. The vigor and constancie of
their soules, doth suppresse and extinguish all manner of concupiscences, so soone as they but begin to move. Now that it be not more
glorious, by an undaunted and divine resolution, to hinder the growth
of temptations, and for a man to frame himselfe to vertue, so that the
verie seeds of vice be cleane rooted out; than by mayne force to hinder
their progresse; and having suffred himselfe to be surprised by the
first assaults of passions, to arme and bandie himselfe, to stay their
course and to suppresse them: And that this second effect be not also
much fairer, than to be simply stored with a facile and gentle nature,
and of it selfe distasted and in dislike with licentiousnesse and vice, I
am perswaded there is no doubt. For, this third and last manner,
seemeth in some sort, to make a man innocent, but not vertuous, free
from doing ill, but not sufficiently apt to doe well. Seeing this condition

is so neere unto imperfection and weaknesse, that I know not well how
to cleare their confines and distinctions. The verie names of Goodnesse
and innocencie, are for this respect in some sort names of contempt.
I see that many vertues, as chastitie, sobrietie, and temperance, may
come unto us by meanes of corporall defects and inbecilitie. Constancie
in dangers (if it may be termed constancie) contempt of death, patience in misfortunes, may happen, and are often seen in men, for want
of Good judgement in such accidents, and that they are not apprehended for such as they are indeed. *Lacke of apprehension and stupiditie, doe sometimes counterfeit vertuous effects.* As I have often seen
come to passe, that some men are commended, for things they rather
deserve to be blamed. An Italian gentleman did once hold this position
in my presence, to the prejudice and disadvantage of his nation; That
the subtiltie of the Italians, and the vivacitie of their conceptions was
so great, that they foresaw such dangers and accidents as might betide
them so far-off, that it was not to be deemed strange, if in times of
warre, they were often seene to provide for their safetie, yea, before
they had perceived the danger: That we and the Spaniards, who were
not so warie and subtill, went further; and that before we could be
frighted with any perill, we must be induced to see it with our eyes,
and feel it with our hands, and that even then we had no more hold:
But that the Germanes and Switzers, more shallow and leaden-headed,
had scarce the sense and wit to re-advise themselves, at what time they
were even overwhelmed with miserie, and the axe readie to fall on their
heads. It was peradventure but in jest, that he spake-it, yet is it most
true, that in the art of warrefare, new trained Souldiers, and such as
are but novices in the trade, doe often headlong, and hand over head
cast themselves into dangers, with more inconsideration, than afterward when they have seene and endured the first shocke, and are better
trained in the schoole of perils.

> —*haud ignarus, quantùm nova gloria in armis,*
> *Et prœdulce decus primo certamine possit.*

> Not ignorant, how much in armes new praise,
> And sweetest honour, in first conflict weighes.

Lo here the reason why when we judge of a particular action, we
must first consider many circumstances, and throughly observe the
man, that hath produced the same before we name and censure it. But
to speake a word of my selfe: I have sometimes noted my friends to
terme that wisdome in me, which was but meere fortune; and to deeme
that advantage of courage and patience, that was advantage of judgement and opinion: and to attribute one title for another unto me, sometimes to my profit, and now and then to my losse. As for the rest, I am
so far from attaining unto that chiefe and most perfect degree of
excellencie, where a habitude is made of vertue, that even of the second,

I have made no great triall. I have not greatly strived to bridle the desires, wherewith I have found my selfe urged and pressed. My vertue, is a vertue, or to say better innocencie, accidental and casuall. Had I been borne with a lesse regular complexion, I imagine my state had been verie pittifull, and it would have gon hard with me: for, I could never perceive any great constancie in my soule, to resist and undergoe passions, had they been anything violent. I cannot foster quarels, or endure co[n]tentions in my house. So am I not greatly beholding unto my selfe, in that I am exempted from many vices:

> —si vitiis mediocribus, et mea paucis
> Mendosa est natura, alioqui recta velut si
> Egregio inspersos reprehendas corpore nævos.
> Hor. i. Sat. vi. 65.

If in a few more fault's my nature faile,
Right otherwise: as if that you would raile
On prettie moles well placed,
On bodie seemely graced.

I am more endebted to my fortune, than to my reason for it: Shee hath made me to be borne of a race famous for integritie and honestie, and of a verie good father. I wot not well whether any part of his humours have descended into me, or whether the domestike examples, and good institution of my infancie have insensibly set their helping hand unto it; or whether I were otherwise so borne:

> Seu Libra, seu me Scorpius aspicit
> Formidolosus, pars violentior
> Natalis horæ, seu tyrannus
> Hesperiæ Capricornus undæ.—Hor. ii. Od. xvii. 17.

Whether the chiefe part of my birth-houre were
Ascendent Libra, or Scorpius full of feare,
Or in my Horoscope were Capricorne,
Whose tyrannie neere westerne Seas is borne.

But so it is, that naturally of my selfe, I abhorre and detest all manner of vices. The answer of Antisthenes to one, that demanded of him, which was the best thing to be learned: To unlearne evill, seemed to be fixed on this image, or to have any ayme at this. I abhorre them (I say) with so naturall, and so innated an opinion, that the very same instinct and impression, which I suckt from my nurse, I have so kept, that no occasions could ever make me alter the same: No, not mine owne discourses, which because they have been somewhat lavish in noting or taxing something of the common course, could easily induce me to some actions, which this my naturall inclination makes me to hate. I will tell you a wonder, I will tell it to you indeed: I thereby find in many things, more stay and order in my manners, than in my opinion:

and my concupiscence lesse debauched, than my reason. *Aristippus* established certaine opinions so bold, in favour of voluptuousnesse and riches, that he made all Philosophie to mutinie against him. But concerning his manners, *Dionysius* the tyrant, having presented him with three faire young Wenches, that he might chuse the fairest; he answered he would chuse them all three, and that *Paris* had verie ill successe, forsomuch as he had preferred one above her fellowes. But they being brought to his owne house, he sent them backe againe, without tasting them. His servant one day carrying store of money after him, and being so over-charged with the weight of it, that he complained, his Master commanded him, to cast so much therof away, as troubled him. And *Epicurus*, whose positions are irreligious and delicate, demeaned himselfe in his life verie laboriously, and devoutly. He wrote to a friend of his, that he lived but with browne bread and water, and entreated him to send him a piece of cheese, against the time he was to make a solemne feast. May it be true, that to be perfectly good, we must be so by an hidden, naturall, and universall proprietie, without law, reason, and example? The disorders and excesses, wherein I have found my selfe engaged, are not (God be thanked) of the worst. I have rejected and condemned them in my selfe, according to their worth; for, my judgement was never found to be infected by them. And on the other side, I accuse them more rigorously in my selfe, than in another. But that is all: as for the rest, I applie but little resistance unto them, and suffer my selfe over-easily to encline to the other side of the Ballance, except it be to order and empeach them from being commixt with others, which (if a man take not good heed unto himselfe) for the most part entertaine and enterchaine themselves the one with the other. As for mine, I have as much as it hath laine in my power, abridged them, and kept them as single, and as alone as I could:

> —*nec ultra*
> *Errorem foveo.*—JUVEN. *Sat.* viii. 164.

> Nor doe I cherish any more,
> The error which I bred before.

For, as touching the Stoikes opinion, who say, that when the wise man worketh, he worketh with all his vertues together; howbeit, according to the nature of the action, there be one more apparant than other (to which purpose the similitude of mans bodie might, in some sort, serve their turne; for, the action of choler cannot exercise it selfe, except all the humours set-to their helping-hand, although choler be prædominant) if thence they will draw alike consequence, that when the offender trespasseth, he doth it with all the vices together. I doe not so easily beleeve them, or else I understand them not; for, in effect, I feel the contrarie. They are sharpe-witte subtilties, and without substance, about which Philosophie doth often busie its selfe. Some vices I shun; but othersome I eschew as much as any Saint can doe. The

Peripatetikes doe also disavow this connexitie, and indissoluble knit·
ting together. And *Aristotle* is of opinion, *That a wise and just man may
be both intemperate and incontinent.* *Socrates* avowed unto them,
who in his Phisiognomie perceived some inclination unto vice, that
indeed it was his naturall propension, but that by discipline he had
corrected the same. And the familiar friends of the Philosopher *Stilpo*
were wont to say, that being borne subject unto wine and women, he
had, by studie, brought himselfe to abstaine from both. On the other-
side, what good I have, I have it by the lot of my birth: I have it neither
by law nor prescription, nor by any apprentiship. The innocencie that
is in me, is a kinde of simple-plaine innocencie, without vigor or art.
Amongst all other vices, there is none I hate more, than crueltie, both
by nature and judgement, as the extremest of all vices. But it is with
such an yearning and faint-heartednesse, that if I see but a chickins
necke puld off, or a pigge stickt, I cannot chuse but grieve, and I cannot well endure a seelie dew-bedabled hare to groane, when she is
seized upon by the houndes; although hunting be a violent sport. Those
that are to withstand voluptuousnesse, doe willingly use this argument, to shew, it is altogether vicious and unreasonable: That where
she is in her greatest prime and chiefe strength, she doth so over-sway
us, that reason can have no accesse unto us, and for a further triall,
alleage the experience wee feel and have of it, in our acquaintance or
copulation with women.

> —*cum iam præsagit gaudia corpus
> Atque in eo est Venus, ut muliebria conserat arva.*
>   LUCR. iv. 1097.

When now the bodie doth light-joyes fore-know,
And *Venus* set the womans fields to sow.

Where they thinke pleasure doth so far transport us beyond our
selves, that our Discourse, then altogether overwhelmed, and our reason
wholie ravished in the gulfe of sensualtie, cannot by any meanes discharge her function. I know it may be otherwise: And if a man but
please, he may sometimes, even upon the verie instant, cast his mind
on other conceits. But she must be strained to a higher key, and heedfully pursued: I know a man may gourmandize the earnest and
thought-confounding violence of that pleasure: for I may with some
experience speake of it; and I have not found *Venus* to be so imperious
a Goddesse, as many, and more reformed than my selfe witnesse her to
be, I thinke it not a wonder, as doth the Queene of *Navarre,* in one of
the Tales of her *Heptameron* (which respecting the subject it treateth-
of, is a verie prettie booke) nor doe I deeme it a matter of extreme
difficultie, for a man to weare-out a whole night, in all opportunitie and
libertie, in companie of a faire Mistresse, long time before sued-unto,
and by him desired; religiously keeping his word, if he have engaged

himselfe, to be contented with simple kisses and plaine touching. I am of opinion, that the example of the sport in hunting would more fit the same: wherein as there is lesse pleasure, so there is more distraction and surprising, whereby our reason being amazed, looseth the leasure to prepare her selfe against it: when as after a long questing and beating for some game, the beast doth suddainly start, or rowze up before us, and haply in such a place, where we least expected the same. That suddaine motion, and riding, and the earnestnesse of showting, jubeting and hallowing, still ringing in our eares, would make it verie hard for those, who love that kind of close or chamber-hunting, at that verie instant, to withdraw their thoughts else-where. And Poets make *Diana* victoriously to triumph both over the firebrand and arrowes of *Cupid*.

> *Quis non malarum quas amor curas habet*
> *Hæc inter obliviscitur?*—HOR. *Epod*. ii. 37.

> While this is doing, who doth not forget
> The wicked cares wherewith Loves heart doth fret?

But to returne to my former discourse, I have a verie feeling and tender compassion of other mens afflictions, and should more easily weep for companie sake, if possiblie for any occasion whatsoever, I could shed teares. There is nothing sooner moveth teares in me, than to see others weepe, not onely fainedly, but howsoever, whether truly or forcedly. I do not greatly waile for the dead, but rather envie them. Yet doe I much waile and moane the dying. The Canibales and savage people do not so much offend me with roasting and eating of dead bodies, as those which torment and persecute the living. Let any man be executed by law, how deservedly soever, I cannot endure to behold the execution with an unrelenting eye. Some one going about to witnesse the clemencie of *Julius Cæsar;* He was (saith he) tractable and milde in matters of revenge. Having compelled the Pirates to yeeld themselves unto him, who had before taken him prisoner, and put him to ransome, forasmuch as he had threatned to have them all crucified, he condemned them to that kind of death, but it was after he had caused them to be strangled. *Philomon* his secretarie, who would have poysoned him, had no sharper punishment of him, than an ordinarie death. Without mentioning the Latin Author, who for a testimonie of clemencie dareth to alleage, the onely killing of those, by whom a man hath been offended, it may easily be ghessed, that he is tainted with vile and horrible examples of crueltie, such as Romane Tyrants brought into fashion. As for me, even in matters of justice, *Whatsoever is beyond a simple death, I deeme it to be meere crueltie:* And especially amongst us, who ought to have a regardfull respect, that their soules should be sent to heaven, which cannot be, having first by intolerable tortures agitated, and as it were brought them to dispaire. A Souldier, not long since, being a prisoner, and perceiving from a loft a Tower, where he was kept, that store of people flocked together on a greene, and Carpenters were busie at worke to erect a skaffold, supposing the same to be for him, as one desperat, resolved to kill himselfe, and searching up and downe for some thing to make himselfe away, found nothing but an old rustie cart-naile, which fortune presented him with; he tooke it, and therewithall, with all the strength he had, strooke and wounded himselfe twice in the throat, but seeing it would not rid him of life, he then thrust it into his bellie up to the head, where he left it fast-sticking. Shortly after, one of his keepers coming-in unto him, and yet living, finding him in that miserable plight, but weltring in his goare-blood, and readie to gaspe his last, told the Magistrates of it, which, to prevent time before he should die, hastned to pronounce sentence against him: which when he heard, and that he was onely condemned to have his head cut-off, he seemed to take heart of grace againe, and to be sorie for what he had done, and tooke some comfortable drinks, which before he had refused, greatly thanking the Judges for his unhoped gentle condemnation: And told them, that for feare of a more sharply-cruell, and intolerable death by law, he had resolved to prevent it by some violent manner of death, having by the preparations he had seen the Carpenters make, and by gathering of people together, conceived an opinion, that they would torture him with some horrible torment, and seemed to be delivered from death onely by the change of it. Were I worthie to give counsell, I would have these examples of rigor, by which superior powers goe about to keep the common people in awe, to be onely exercised on the bodies of criminall malefactors: For, to see them deprived of Christian buriall, to see them haled, disbowelled, parboyled, and quartered, might haply touch the common sort as much, as the paines, they make the living to endure: howbeit in effect it be little or nothing, as saith God, *Qui corpus occidunt, et postea non habent quod faciant* (Luke xii. 4): *Those that kill the bodie, but have afterwards no more to doe.* And Poets make the horror of this picture greatly to prevaile, yea, and above death:

Heu reliquias semiassi Regis, denudatis ossibus,
Per terram sanie delibutas fœde divexarier.

Cic. *Tusc. Qu.* i.

O that the reliques of an halfe-burn't King, bones bared,
On earth besmear'd with filth, should be so fouly marred.

It was my fortune to be at *Rome*, upon a day that one *Catena*, a notorious high-way theefe, was executed: at his strangling no man of the companie seemed to be mooved to any ruth; but when he came to be quartered, the Executioner gave no blow that was not accompanied with a piteous voyce, and hartie exclamation, as if every man had had a feeling sympathie, or lent his senses to the poore mangled wretch. Such inhumane outrages and barbarous excesses should be exercised against the rinde, and not practised against the quicke. In a case somewhat like unto this, did *Artaxerxes* asswage and mitigate the sharpnesse of the ancient lawes of *Persia,* appointing that the Lords, which had trespassed in their estate, whereas they were wont to be whipped, they should be stripped naked, and their clothes whipped for them: and where they were accustomed to have their haire pulled-off, they should onely have their hat taken off. The Ægyptians so devout and religious, thought they did sufficiently satisfie divine Justice, in sacrificing painted and counterfeit hogges unto it: An over-hardy invention, to go about with pictures and shadowes to appease God, a substance so essentiall and divine. I live in an age, wherein we abound with incredible examples of this vice, through the licentiousnesse of our civill and intestine warres: And read all ancient stories, be they never so tragicall, you shall find none to equall those, we daily see practised. But that hath nothing made me acquainted with it. I could hardly be perswaded, before I had seene it, that the world could have afforded so marble-hearted and savage-minded men, that for the onely pleasure of murther would commit-it; then cut, mangle, and hacke other members in pieces: to rouze and sharpen their wits, to invent unused tortures and unheard-of torments; to devise new and unknowne deaths and that in cold blood, without any former enmitie or quarrell, or without any gaine or profit; and onely to this end, that they may enjoy the pleasing spectacle of the languishing gestures, pitifull motions, horror-moving yellings, deep fetcht groanes, and lamentable voyces of a dying and drooping man. For, that is the extremest point whereunto the crueltie of man may attaine. *Ut homo hominem, non iratus, non timens, tantum spectaturus occidat* (SEN. *Clem.* ii. c. 4). *That one man should kill another, neither being angrie, nor afeard, but onely to looke on.* As for me, I could never so much as endure, without remorse and griefe, to see a poore, sillie, and innocent beast pursued and killed, which is harmelesse and void of defence, and of whom we receive no offence at all. And as it commonly hapneth, that when the Stag begins to be embost, and finds his strength to faile-him, having no other remedie left him, doth yeeld and bequeath himselfe unto us that pursue him, with teares suing to us for mercie,

> *—questúque cruentus*
> *Atque imploranti similis:*—VIRG. *Æn.* vii. 521.

> With blood from throat, and teares from eyes,
> It seemes that he for pittie cryes.

was ever a grievous spectacle unto me. I seldom take any beast alive, but I give him his libertie. *Pythagoras* was wont to buy fishes of fishers, and birds of fowlers to set them free againe.

> *—primóque à cœde ferarum*
> *Incaluisse puto maculatum sanguine ferrum.*
> OVID. *Metam.* xv. 106.

And first our blades in blood embrude I deeme
With slaughter of poore beasts did reeking steeme.

Such as by nature shew themselves bloodie-minded towards harm-
lesse beasts, witnesse a naturall propension unto crueltie. After the
ancient Romanes had once enured themselves without horror to behold
the slaughter of wild beasts in their shewes, they came to the murther
of men and Gladiators. Nature (I feare me) hath of her owne selfe
added unto man a certaine instinct to humanitie. No man taketh delight to see wild beasts sport and wantonly to make much one of
another: Yet all are pleased to see them tugge, mangle, and enterteare
one an other. And lest any bodie should jeast at this simphathie, which
I have with them, Divinitie it selfe willeth us to shew them some
favour: And considering, that one selfe-same master (I meane that
incomprehensible worlds-framer) hath placed all creatures in this his
wondrous palace for his service, and that they, as well as we, are of his
houshold: I say, it hath some reason to injoyne us, to shew some
respect and affection towards them. *Pythagoras* borrowed *Metempsy-*
chosis of the Ægyptians, but since, it hath been received of divers
Nations, and especially of our *Druides:*

Morte carent animæ, sempérque priore relictâ
Sede, novis domibus vivunt, habitámque receptæ.—158.

Our death-lesse soules, their former seats refrained,
In harbors new live and lodge entertained.

The Religion of our ancient Gaules, inferred, that soules being eternall, ceased not to remove and change place, from one bodie to another:
to which fantasie was also entermixed some consideration of divine
justice. For, according to the soules behaviors, during the time she had
been with *Alexander,* they sayd, that God appointed it another bodie
to dwell-in, either more or lesse painfull, and sutable to her condition.

—muta ferarum
Cogit vincla pati, truculentos ingerit ursis,
Prædonésque lupis, fallaces vulpibus addit.
Atque ubi per varios annos per mille figuras
Egit letheo purgatos flumine tandem
Rursus ad humanæ revocat primordia formæ.
                                              CLAUD. *in Ruff.* i. 482, 491.

Dumbe bands of beasts he makes mens soules endure,
Blood-thirstie soules he doth to Beares enure,
Craftie to Foxes, to Woolves bent to rapes;
Thus when for many yeares, through many shapes,
He hath them driv'n in *Lethe* lake at last,
Them purg'd he turn's to mans forme whence they past.

If the soule had been valiant, they placed it in the bodie of a Lion;
if voluptuous, in a Swine; if faint-harted, in a Stagge, or a Hare; if

malicious in a Foxe, and so of the rest, until that being purified by
this punishment, it resumed and tooke the bodie of some other man
againe.

> *Ipse ego, nam memini, Troiani tempore belli*
> *Panthoides Euphorbus eram.*—OVID. *Metam.* xv. 160.

When *Troy* was won, I, as I call to mind,
Euphorbus was, and *Panthus* sonne by kind.

As touching that alliance betweene us and beasts, I make no great
accompt of it, nor do I greatly admit it; neither of that which divers
Nations, and namely of the most ancient and noble, who have not
onely received beasts into their societie and companie, but allowed
them a place farre above themselves; sometimes deeming them to be
familiars and favoured of their Gods, and holding them in a certaine
awfull respect and reverence more than humane, and others acknowledging no other God nor no other Divinity than they. *Beluæ à barbaris
propter beneficium consecratæ* (CIC. *Nat. Deor.* i.). *Beasts by the
Barbarians were made sacred for some benefit.*

> *—crocodilon adorat*
> *Pars hæc, illa pavet saturam serpentibus Ibin,*
> *Effigies sacri hic nitet aurea Cercopitheci.*
> JUVEN. *Sat.* xv. 2.

This Country doth the Crocodile adore,
That feares the Storke glutted with Serpents gore,
The sacred Babion here,
In gold shape doth appeare.

> *—his piscem fluminis, illic*
> *Oppida tota canem venerantur.*—7.

A fish here whole Townes reverence most,
A dog they honour in that coast.

And the very same interpretation that *Plutarke* giveth unto this
error, which is very well taken, is also honourable for them. For, he
saith, that (for example sake) it was neither the Cat nor the Oxe that
the Ægyptians adored, but that in those beasts, they worshipped some
image of divine faculties. In this patience and utility, and in that,
vivacity, or (as our neighbours the Borgonians with all *Germanie*)
the impatience to see themselves shut up: Whereby they represented
the liberty which they loved and adored beyond all other divine
faculty, and so of others. But when amongst the most moderate opinions, I meet with some discourses that goe about and labour to shew
the neere resemblance betweene us and beasts, and what share they
have in our greatest Privileges, and with how much likelyhood they
are compared unto us, truly I abate much of our presumption, and
am easily removed from that imaginary soveraigntie that some give

and ascribe unto us above all other creatures. If all that were to be contradicted, yet is there a kinde of respect, and a generall duty of humanity, which tieth us not only unto brute beasts that have life and sense, but even unto trees and plants. *Unto men we owe Justice, and to all other creatures that are capable of it, grace and benignity.* There is a kinde of enter-changeable commerce and mutuall bond betweene them and us. I am not ashamed nor afraid to declare the tendernesse of my childish Nature, which is such, that I cannot well reject my Dog, if he chance (although out of season) to fawne upon me, or beg of me to play with him. The Turkes have almes, and certaine Hospitals appointed for brute beasts. The Romans had a publike care to breed and nourish Geese, by whose vigilancy their Capitoll had beene saved. The Athenians did precizely ordaine that all manner of Mules which had served or beene imploied about the building of their Temple called *Hecatompedon* should bee free, and suffered to feed wheresoever they pleased, without any let or impeachment. The Agrigentines had an ordinary custome, seriously and solemnly to bury all such beasts as they had held deare; as horses of rare worth and merit, speciall dogs, choice or profitable birds, or such as had but served to make their children sport. And the sumptuous magnificence which in all other things was ordinary and peculiar unto them, appeared also almost notably in the stately sumptuousnesse and costly number of monuments erected to that end, which many ages after have endured and been maintained in pride and state. The Ægyptians were wont to bury their Wolves, their Dogs, their Cats, their Beares, and Crocodiles in holy places, embalming their carcasses, and at their deaths to weare mourning weeds for them. *Cymon* caused a stately honourable tombe to be erected for the Mares, wherewith he had three times gained the prize at running in the Olimpike games. Ancient *Xantippus* caused his Dog to be enterred upon a hill by the Sea shore, which ever since hath beene named by him. And *Plutarke* (as himselfe saith) made it a matter of conscience, in hope of a small gaine, to sell or send an Oxe to the shambles that had served him a long time.

CARLTON HOUSE